UNDERSTANDING THE FOUNDING

AMERICAN POLITICAL THOUGHT

Wilson Carey McWilliams and Lance Banning, Founding Editors

Understanding the Founding

The Crucial Questions

Second Edition, Revised and Expanded

ALAN GIBSON

 University Press of Kansas

Published by the University Press of Kansas (Lawrence, Kansas 66045), which was
organized by the Kansas Board of Regents and is operated and funded by Emporia State
University, Fort Hays State University, Kansas State University, Pittsburg State University,
the University of Kansas, and Wichita State University

Library of Congress Cataloging-in-Publication Data

Gibson, Alan Ray, 1961–
Understanding the founding : the crucial questions / Alan Gibson. — 2nd ed., rev. and
expanded.
      p. cm. — (American political thought)
Includes bibliographical references and index.
ISBN 978-0-7006-1751-7 (cloth : alk. paper)
ISBN 978-0-7006-1752-4 (pbk. : alk. paper)
1. Constitutional history—United States. 2. United States—Politics and government.
I. Title.
  KF4541.G534 2010
  342.7302'9—dc22

                                                  2010026291

British Library Cataloguing-in-Publication Data is available.

Printed in the United States of America

10 9 8 7 6 5 4 3 2 1

The paper used in this publication is recycled and contains 30 percent postconsumer
waste. It is acid free and meets the minimum requirements of the American National
Standard for Permanence of Paper for Printed Library Materials z39.48-1992.

Contents

Preface to the Second Edition

Fred Woodward and the editors of the University Press of Kansas have allowed me to use the occasion of the printing of the second edition of *Understanding the Founding: The Crucial Questions* to add a new chapter 5 and revise the introduction and what is now chapter 6. Even as I finished the original version of this book in 2007, I realized that I had neglected the most visible and one of the most important contemporary debates on the American Founding. That debate concerns questions about how the men who fought a revolution in the name of liberty and declared to the world that "all men are created equal" could have supported the institution of slavery and even owned slaves themselves, accepted the legal and social subordination of women, and been responsible for Indian removal and genocide against Native Americans. Efforts to criticize or defend the Founders on these issues of race, gender, and genocide have increasingly become a central feature of scholarship on the American Founding since the 1960s. They now constitute a sprawling and daunting body of scholarship addressing what David Brion Davis has called the "dilemmas of *slaveholding revolutionaries*" that raises some of the most vexing questions that Founding scholars face.[1] A new chapter 5 examines the three most prominent interpretive strategies that scholars have adopted for assessing the moral responsibility of the Founders, discusses the strengths and limitations of these approaches, and offers some suggestions about how we might move toward more mature and responsible evaluations of the Founders. The introduction and final chapter of this work have also been rewritten to accommodate the inclusion of this new chapter and to include my reflections on what debates about the moral responsibility of the Founders for slavery add to the study of the American Founding. I have also added some reflections on recent developments on the study of the intellectual foundations of the American republic to the final chapter.

In addition to the people and institutions thanked in the previous edition, I especially want to thank Richard Zinman of James Madison College of Michigan State University, Robert Tinkler, a colleague at CSU, Chico, Nic Wood at the University of Virginia, Brad Wilson at the James Madison Program at Princeton, Carson Holloway of the University of Nebraska, Omaha, Jim Read of the College of St. Benedict and St. John's University of Minnesota, Stephanie Bor, and the Earhart Foundation. Zinman has written a long review of *Interpreting the Founding* and *Understanding the Founding* that illustrates his deep understanding of the goals of these works and represents criticism in its highest, most constructive, and civil form.[2] The provocative and foundational questions and challenges that he has raised in this review and his correspondence with me have led me to think deeply about and reconsider both my substantive understanding of the American Founding and how it should be studied. Robert Tinkler has taught me a great deal about the development of slavery in the United States. Brad Wilson opened up the possibility for me to give a Constitution Day presentation at Princeton that became the basis of the new chapter for this edition. Nic Wood has generously shared his uniquely informed understanding of Jefferson's role in the abolition of the slave trade and thus improved the discussion in chapter 5. My friend Carson Holloway is a constant source of insight about the Founding and the history of political thought. Over the years, conversations with Jim Read have expanded my understanding of the Founding. I am also grateful for his willingness to let me use his catchy phrase "appropriate and inappropriate appropriations" as a subtitle in the last chapter. In addition, Henry Wiencek, Gordon Wood, Peter Onuf, Alan Megill, and Douglas Wilson—all eminent senior scholars—offered encouragement and insightful suggestions on how to improve the new chapter on slavery and moral responsibility. Stephanie Bor, a graduate assistant in the political science department, proved to be an excellent editor of the additions. Finally, the Earhart Foundation provided a generous grant that made it possible to complete revisions for a second edition of *Interpreting the Founding* and for this new edition of *Understanding the Founding*.

Alan Gibson
May 2010

UNDERSTANDING THE FOUNDING

Introduction to the Second Edition

The American Founding lies at the center of our historical and political consciousness. The Founding, we are often taught and told, was the crucible of our greatness and distinctiveness, the origin of the first principles of our political system, and thus is a wellspring of wisdom to which frequent recurrence should be made. Its cast of characters—"the Founding Fathers," or now "the Founders"—come into the minds of many Americans as magisterial and wise but distant figures from Gilbert Stuart paintings. They seem to have somehow reconciled contradictions. They were at once bold and prudent, visionary and sober, optimistic and hardheaded. They are celebrated as conservative revolutionaries for their immunity to the enthusiasm that later consumed Jacobins and Marxists and as revolutionary conservatives for casting aside the Articles of Confederation and instituting a republican government that stretched across an unprecedented geographic expanse. We marvel that these men—the most intelligent in their society—chose to serve in public office and scratch our heads at our inability to achieve a similar union of intelligence and office.

Perhaps most important, however, the reverence that Americans have for the Founders and their generation has conferred on them a degree of authority that is at once familiar, unique, and problematic. Political scientists often trace the virtues of the American political system to its original design and the origins of its problems to a movement away from its Edenic beginnings. Judges, politicians, and scholars alike often fight to establish that their rulings, interpretations, and prescriptions are consistent with the "intentions" of the Founders and the original meaning of the Constitution.

To be sure, the American Founding has its critics who have become increasingly numerous, vitriolic, and vocal at the beginning of the twenty-first century. To many of these scholars, the Founders are viewed as the unapologetic source of America's original sins, especially slavery, the subjugation of women, and the virtual extermination of the Native American population. The Founders, we are also told by their critics, created a clumsy, complex political system that blocked participatory democracy, prevented the development of meaningful community, and blunted the formation of a modern regulatory and welfare state. Nevertheless, even those scholars who criticize the Founders end up paradoxically conceding their significance by blaming them for contemporary political problems. Often praised and increasingly blamed, the American Founders are not easily ignored.

But if the importance of the Founders and their act of creation is almost universally recognized, contemporary scholarship on it provides considerable evidence that significance is seldom the parent of consensus. Throughout the twentieth century and now into the twenty-first, historians, American political theorists, and contemporary constitutional theorists have been sharply divided on a series of central questions. Were the Framers of the Constitution a cosmopolitan, consolidated economic group of creditors, mercantile capitalists, and large landholders? Was the constitution they proposed designed to protect and advance their own economic interests? Was it supported by members of creditor and capitalist interests and opposed by small farming and debtor interests? How democratic was the political system that they designed? How should we interpret the writings of the American Founders? Should we adopt a "deeply contextualist approach" to the study of the Founding, search for the linguistic conventions that were present, and try to understand the Founding entirely "as it was experienced by those who lived it," not as it anticipated the future?[1] Conversely, should we read and analyze the texts of the American Founders with the rigor often reserved for philosophical treatises and search for the "first principles" of the American regime and the enduring teachings of the Founders? Were the Founding Fathers the progenitors of modernity, liberalism, and capitalism, or were they the heirs of classical republicanism? Are the Founders morally responsible for slavery, the subordination of women in the early republic, and Indian removal? Finally, what were the legacies of the American Founding, and what are our obligations to the Founders? Did they construct a novel political theory that merits consideration alongside the great contributions to the history of political thought, or were they merely the clever architects of institutions that were grounded in principles of government that were conceived by greater minds? What effects did the original design of our political system have on the development of democracy, and what effects does it continue to exercise today on its contemporary character? Are we bound— for moral, legal, or even prudential reasons—to uphold their understanding of the Constitution and the original design of the American political system?

Understanding the Founding: The Crucial Questions addresses this constellation of questions and thereby the institutional and intellectual foundations of the American political system and the legacy and authority of the Founders. This is the second of two books that I have written about the modern—post-Beardian—study of the American Founding. The first, *Interpreting the Founding: Guide to the Enduring Debates over the Origins and Foundations of the American Republic,* provides a synoptic overview of the different frameworks of interpretation that have controlled modern scholarship on the American Founding, analyzes the weaknesses and enduring contributions of each, and speculates about the future direction of scholarship. In contrast, *Understanding the Founding* cuts through this same century of scholarship but examines it through the lens of the most prominent debates that it has generated, rather than the different frameworks or schools of interpretation that have been developed.

Both of these works reflect my continuing interest in the historiography of the American Founding. Contrary to the judgment of many scholars who find historiographical questions secondary and relatively unimportant, I have come to the conclusion that they often raise penetrating and intriguing issues. Scholars of the Founding, I have discovered, are unavoidably led to address (or assume the answers to) questions about the function of ideas and their influence on behavior, the proper definition of democracy and how it is most meaningfully institutionalized, the relationship between past ideas and current problems, and the character of liberalism and republicanism and their relationship to each other *before* they could address questions about the intellectual foundations of the American republic or the original design of the American political system. I have come to see, in other words, that these problems of interpretation—however consciously or unconsciously scholars address them—precede and inform interpretation and cannot themselves be said to be a product of historical investigation alone.

Understanding the Founding: The Crucial Questions examines these foundational issues in the historiography of the American Founding and the implications that the answers that we give to them have for contemporary political thought and our understanding of the American political system. It is also an effort to come to terms with questions about the proper role that the American Founding should play in our system of self-government today. Intellectually, it marks my maturation from a puerile, but remarkably typical, affection for the Founders to a deeper understanding of their place within the history of political thought and a more balanced assessment of their accomplishments and failures, especially the strengths and limitations of the political system that they founded.

Specifically, the successive chapters of this book revisit and address what I have come to believe are the five most important debates or "confrontations" around which modern scholarship on the American Founding has been framed. I borrow this phrase from an observation made by J. G. A. Pocock in one of his writings because I have become increasingly impressed with the truth of his contention that academic debates are often confrontations and rarely dialogues.[2] The confrontations examined in this book, I have come to see, were sparked and continue to be driven by the momentum created from the punch and counterpunch of academic exchanges. In each, a new interpretation was set forth and received by many as a challenge issued; it thus provoked a counterrevolution in favor of a more sophisticated and subtle version of the old interpretation. Debate then further intensified as adaptations (often unacknowledged or even disguised) were made by the participants. Eventually, the debate was dissolved, not resolved. Scholars either became bored or frustrated with the question, or they became convinced of their answer to it. They therefore identified a different set of problematics and then set out to examine a new question.

In particular, in the first chapter, I revisit the debate over the economic interpretation of the Constitution. This debate can be traced to the publication in 1913 of Charles Beard's *An Economic Interpretation of the Constitution*—one of the most provocative, persistently controversial, and influential academic books ever written.[3] Before this work, most studies of the American Founding had argued that the Framers of the Constitution were disinterested statesmen and that the Constitution embodied the sovereign will of the American people and represented the interests of all Americans. Charles Beard challenged such hagiographic portraits of the Founders and the "juristic" interpretation of the Constitution by arguing that the delegates to the Philadelphia convention were holders of a particular form of property that he called "personalty" (fluid capital held by mercantile interests) and opponents of the Constitution were holders of "realty" (land held by nonslaveholding farmers and debtors).[4] He also argued that the ratification struggle was a contest between holders of these two forms of property. Together, these two prongs of Beard's thesis—however much he resisted blunt formulations of them—amounted to saying that by writing and securing the ratification of the Constitution, the Framers had sought to protect and advance their immediate economic interests.

The story of the rise and fall of Beard's thesis is familiar to specialists in the American Founding. Several of the initial reviewers of *An Economic Interpretation of the Constitution* raised questions about the empirical validity of Beard's thesis.[5] Nevertheless, during the 1930s and 1940s, these criticisms had little impact, and Beard's thesis and the Progressive interpretation of the formation and ratification of the Constitution "became a new prevailing orthodoxy that almost no one was willing or able to challenge."[6] This changed rapidly during the 1950s, when scholars pointed to ambiguities and inconsistencies in Beard's thesis, exposed methodological errors in his work, and challenged his empirical findings.[7] These challenges broke the hegemony of Beard's interpretation and opened the door for the renewed interest in the intellectual origins of the American republic that has characterized Founding scholarship since the 1970s.

Contrary to common opinion, however, the studies challenging *An Economic Interpretation of the Constitution* did not discredit any economic interpretation. Instead, they profoundly and permanently complicated our understanding of the alignment of economic interests for and against the Constitution and prodded scholars to pursue broad, subtle, and empirically sound economic interpretations. Subsequent scholarship on the economic interpretation that has been done since the 1960s has been directed at this goal of establishing an economic interpretation that moves beyond Beard.

My modest goal in the first chapter is to chart the evolution of this debate as preliminary to the more ambitious goal of establishing what has and what has not been proven about the economic and social characteristics of the Federalists and anti-Federalists. To achieve these goals, I first set forth an interpretation of the character and foundation of Beard's thesis and identify and evaluate the most important criticisms that have been made of Beard's claims. My purpose in recounting and crystallizing these criticisms is not to subject Beard to another beating. It is instead to show how these specific criticisms have influenced the direction of subsequent research and the character of subsequent economic interpretations and raised points that, in some cases, have still not been resolved.

I then summarize the central tenets of two distinct groups of refurbished economic interpretations—one group set forth by Beard's postwar analysts and the other by rational and social choice theorists who resurrected this topic in the 1980s and continue to investigate it today. Finally, I end by addressing a series of questions raised in this debate with the goal of evaluating the strengths and weaknesses of economic interpretations of the formation and ratification of the Constitution and making suggestions about what kind of research would help resolve persistent questions. Examining

Beard's thesis, the criticisms lodged against it, and the several efforts to refurbish the economic interpretation allows me to highlight the evolving complexity and subtlety of economic interpretation as a prelude to assessing what we have learned and what we now need to do.

The second chapter explores an enduring question: how democratic was the political system created under the 1787 Constitution? This question is often linked with the economic interpretation because the Progressives treated them as inseparable. The Framers, according to the Progressives, crafted an antidemocratic document because they sought first to protect their immediate economic interests from the attacks of popular majorities and then to advance their interests using positive grants of power within the Constitution. Still, there is no *necessary* correlation between the Framers' economic holdings and the form of government that they tried to create. The debates over the economic interests of the Framers and the character of the Constitution thus pose conceptually distinct problems. Obviously, the Founders might have been members of an economic or social elite who held personalty but nevertheless drafted a democratic constitution, either because they did not believe that democracy was a threat to their interests or because protecting their interests was not their primary goal. Conversely, they might also have been holders of realty who nevertheless favored an aristocratic form of government. The first chapter therefore addresses the Progressives' contention that the Framers were members of the same economic groups or class, while the second critically evaluates scholars' understandings of the form of government that they created. Addressing these confrontations separately but sequentially allows me to evaluate each one independent of the baggage of the other before considering their relationship.

In particular, the question "how democratic was the original Constitution?" and the corollary question over whether the Constitution was a reaffirmation or repudiation of the principles of the American Revolution can be traced all the way back to 1788 and the original debate over the ratification of the Constitution. Here, the Framers responded to the anti-Federalists' charge that the Constitution created an aristocratic form of government by arguing that the Constitution was genuinely republican in character and thus consistent with the principles of the American Revolution and the genius of the American people. Nevertheless, once again, it was Beard and his Progressive colleagues who made this question central and gave it a modern flavor by linking it to efforts at constitutional reform. Establishing the antidemocratic character of the Constitution, the Progressives believed, would challenge its legitimacy and viability and pave the way for constitutional reform.

Beginning in the late 1950s, Martin Diamond presented the most popular and systematic response to the Progressives' interpretation of the original design. Diamond's response sprang not only from his genuine disagreement with the Progressives about the character of the Constitution, but also from his concern to defend the American political system against neo-Progressive and New Left critics during the cold war. Subsequently, debates over the legitimacy of the political system created by the Constitution have been fought, in large part, by examining its relationship to democracy. Following Diamond's scholarship, some scholars have characterized the original Constitution as democratic and argued against its reform; others have continued the Progressives' strategy of criticism with the implication that reform is necessary.

In chapter 2, I pursue a balanced assessment of the character of the Founders' Constitution. To this end, I first examine the evolving contours of the continuing conflict over this question. The most important way in which this debate has evolved, I argue, is that scholars have changed the criteria by which they evaluate whether the original Constitution was democratic. The Progressives were initially concerned with establishing that the Constitution was not responsive to popular majorities and that property qualifications within the states disenfranchised a "mass of men."[8] Many subsequent multicultural critics of the Constitution have maintained that the Constitution is undemocratic because, they allege, women and African Americans were excluded from voting and holding office under it. Yet a third group of scholars has also now emerged. This group points to equal representation of states in the Senate and the three-fifths clause as fundamental violations in the Constitution of the democratic principle of political equality.

In the preliminary section of this chapter, I also examine what scholars really disagree about in this debate and the reasons why debate on this question, unlike the other questions in this book, has remained polarized and intractable. My principal point here is that Diamond and his heirs and the Progressives and neo-Progressives do not disagree as much as we might think about the structure of the original design of the American political system. Instead, they disagree principally about how democracy should be defined in the first place. In other words, Diamond and his heirs and the Progressives and theirs present interpretations of the original design of the American political system that are similar in significant ways. Nevertheless, they have different standards about what constitutes democracy and are therefore led to different conclusions about whether the original design is democratic or undemocratic. I also observe that the normative character of the label "democratic" has meant that the answers that scholars give to this question are unavoidably politically charged. In this context, debates about "how democratic was the original Constitution?" have thus become part of a broader fight over the meaning of democracy and the legitimacy of the American political system. With stakes this high, it is not surprising that this debate has remained polemical and polarized.

Chapter 2 then evaluates the "Madisonian model" against the three dimensions of democracy that most scholars use to judge the character of the Framers' Constitution: inclusiveness in political participation, responsiveness to public preferences, and political equality. Discussions within each of these three sections are informed by a series of comparisons between the original design of the American political system and contemporaneous and contemporary systems, including the state governments at the time of the ratification of the Constitution, the Articles of Confederation, the British system at the time of the Founding, the French constitutions of 1791, 1793, and 1795, the conceptions of democracy developed by James Wilson and Thomas Jefferson, and the contemporary American Constitution with its twenty-seven amendments.

My strategy here is at least loosely Aristotelian. When faced with analyzing a concept about which there was widespread disagreement, Aristotle suggested examining common opinion and exploring what was common to and convincing within competing definitions. He also engaged in empirical analysis to compare and contrast the variety of existing political systems.[9] Similarly, my goal is to evaluate the Framers' Constitution against the dimensions of democracy identified by scholars as central and then to provide a multiplicity of comparisons. I am well aware that such a strategy will not depoliticize this debate or solve the intractable hermeneutic problems that confine it. I also do not claim to have grasped the essence of democracy and to have an incontestable standard from which to evaluate the character of the Framers' Constitution. Shortly after I began this chapter, I realized that the adoption of any standard of democracy would make me a partisan of some sort in this debate, but that adopting some standard was necessary to address the question. Engagement with this question has also long since dispossessed me of the hope of creating a consensus among scholars on whether the Constitution was democratic or not, or even of reconfiguring the debate. Democracy is the best example in political theory of an "essentially contestable concept" and the stakes of labeling the Framers' Constitution democratic or undemocratic are too great to expect scholars to agree.

Nevertheless, by considering how well the original Constitution measures up to core criteria of democracy, and by making multiple comparisons to other political systems, I hope to directly confront—even if we may never transcend—the intractable hermeneutic problems posed by this question and sharpen our focus and understanding of the character and original purposes of the American regime. An analysis based on a multiplicity of comparisons along three dimensions of democracy provides an alternative to studies—remarkably ubiquitous on this question—that judge the original design on the basis of a single dimension of democracy or an unarticulated definition of it. Considering the Framers' Constitution along several dimensions of democracy and comparing it to several models of democracy and actual political systems should also provide a concreteness lacking in such accounts by forthrightly addressing the question, "democratic compared to what?"

Finally, in addition to analyzing key constitutional provisions and the constitutional structure against core dimensions of democracy and informing this analysis with relevant comparisons, I also evaluate the interpretive judgments that scholars have made—including the evidence that they have relied on and the reasoning that they have used—in their assessments of the character of the original Constitution. My analysis in this chapter is, in other words, at once historical, empirical, and historiographical. I am as interested in understanding how other scholars have arrived at their interpretations of the fundamental question "how democratic is the Constitution?" and in evaluating their conclusions as I am in setting forth a distinctive interpretation of my own.

In the third chapter, I examine a methodological confrontation that has dominated modern study of the American Founding: the debate over whether we should study the American Founding using a profoundly historical and contextual approach or one that contends that the Founders addressed "perennial questions" in the history of political thought and examines the enduring guidance that they might provide in addressing these questions. The most recent recrudescence of this debate arose with the development of republican revisionism. Scholars who developed the "republican synthesis," "republican hypothesis," or "civic humanist" interpretation of the American Founding self-consciously set forth an approach to interpretation that attempted to justify the study of political ideas in the face of the Namieran, Marxist, and Progressive charge that ideas are merely projected rationalizations of underlying interests and rarely, if ever, motives for behavior.[10]

Many of these scholars also followed Quentin Skinner and J. G. A. Pocock in arguing that the political thought of historical actors (including the American Founders) should be studied by examining the linguistic conventions and political languages that these historical agents used to address the concrete political problems posed by their political life, not by attempting to establish their place among the authors of the "great books" of the Western political tradition or examining how they addressed perennial questions or set forth enduring concepts. Indeed, this group of scholars rejects outright the possibility that there are perennial questions in the history of political thought. The development of this approach naturally led to responses from more traditional scholars who hold a philosophical approach to the study of the history of political thought and the American Founding.

In chapter 3, I first summarize the dominant themes within linguistic contextualism by analyzing the methodological writings of Bernard Bailyn, Gordon Wood, Quentin Skinner, and J. G. A. Pocock. Specifically, I critically analyze their defense of the study of political ideas, their criticisms of the "great books" approach, their rebuke of the appropriation of past ideas for present purposes, their assumptions about the rationality and coherence of the individuals that they interpret, and their beliefs about what texts we should be interpreting. I then provide a series of suggestions about how the insights of the linguistic contextualists and the philosophical rationalists can be combined to create a historically sensitive but theoretically rich approach to the study of the American Founding.

In the fourth chapter, I revisit the now "notorious" and passé debate over whether the intellectual foundations of the American Republic are found in Lockean liberalism, republicanism, or some synthesis of these and other traditions of political thought.[11] This debate can be traced back to the late 1960s and early 1970s when historians began to argue that the American revolutionaries had accepted and evoked—to a degree that had heretofore been relatively neglected—a constellation of ideas that came to be labeled country party ideology, civic humanism, or, most frequently, classical republicanism. Set forth by seventeenth- and eighteenth-century radicals, this set of ideas included the belief that republics are fragile and easily degenerate, that power (understood here as the dominion of one man over another) is inherently expansive and antagonistic to liberty, that virtue (defined as the voluntary subordination of self-interest to the public good) is necessary to the preservation of republics, and that corruption (the pursuit of private gain at public expense by citizens and rulers) must be avoided. It also included the propositions that property and arms are necessary because they provide citizens with the independence to exercise civic virtue, that meaningful liberty included positive political acts of self-determination, and that the public good is the universal standard against which the acts of government should be measured.

At first, the recovery of republicanism was pursued by historians who viewed it as an advance in historical understanding and a challenge to the Hartz thesis. Before the articulation of the republican synthesis, scholars had almost uniformly followed Louis Hartz in contending that the United States was a liberal society and that political debate within American society was a dialogue between proponents of liberalism.[12] This interpretation had been the centerpiece of efforts to explain "American exceptionalism," the belief dominant during the cold war that America's natural abundance, coupled with the commitment of its citizenry to individualism and limited government, had inoculated Americans against totalitarianism and rendered us deaf to both Burkean conservatism and socialist ideologies. But with the discovery that "liberalism did not sprawl unimpeded across the flat intellectual landscape of American abundance," a number of historians began to rewrite the history of American political thought with a newfound sensitivity to the presence of alternative languages of political discourse throughout American history, the goal of finding when liberalism emerged as the dominant mode of American political thought, and in general with the goal of developing an alternative account of the trajectory and content of the American political tradition.[13]

Two developments, however, transformed these historical investigations into the character of eighteenth-century Anglo-American republicanism into one of the most visible and hotly contested academic debates of the 1980s and 1990s. First, whatever the original goals of the scholars of the republican synthesis, republicanism was taken up by political scientists, constitutional lawyers, and other scholars immediately interested in the relevance and application of this historical discovery.[14] Specifically, republicanism provided these scholars with an alternative political language from within the American political tradition that is rich with communitarian values.[15]

Second, many scholars, including historians and political theorists, began a Lockean or liberal counterrevolution against the republican synthesis. If earlier Hartz-inspired liberal interpretations of the American Founding had been simplistic and rooted in cold war debates, there was nevertheless, according to a new group of neo-Lockean scholars, a historically accurate and compelling liberal interpretation of the American Founding. The Founders, according to these scholars, held fast to the beliefs that individuals are naturally equal, self-interested, and passionate, that governments should be designed to control these passions and direct them to public purposes, and that governments should be based on the consent of the governed and function primarily to protect the rights of the people. The Founders, this interpretation further suggests, were proponents of an early form of commercial capitalism.[16]

The republicanism versus liberalism debate led to a voluminous body of literature and energized and ordered scholarship on the American Founding for over two decades. It also became part of a broader normative and empirical debate between communitarians and liberals about the character of American society, past and present. Within the last decade, however, both the debate about the contemporary political implications of republicanism and the debate about the potency and character of liberalism and republicanism in early America have come to seem arid even to those scholars who were initially its most enthusiastic participants. I began to survey this debate at the same time that many of these disgruntled scholars were leaving and disparaging it. I soon discovered, however, that although the republicanism-liberalism debate may indeed be dead, the broader debate over the intellectual origins and character of the American republic continues to be transformed as a result of it.

In particular, I discovered that the dialectic of the liberalism-republicanism debate has led most scholars of the American Founding to adopt a "multiple traditions" approach that allows them to show how the Founders' political thought is properly understood as an amalgam of liberalism, republicanism, and other traditions of political thought.[17] It has also led most scholars to the conclusion that liberalism and republicanism were, at least in several important ways, synergetic within the Founders' political thought. As Peter Onuf has observed, "Since the advent of the republican synthesis we have moved not in circles, but in a closing spiral, with liberal critics building on the revisionists achievements and revisionists recasting republicanism in ways that accommodate and explain the radical initiatives and innovations that constituted revolutionary change."[18]

Nevertheless, the "amicable historiographical consensus" that is now in place is hardly unproblematic.[19] Instead, it has led to the formation of a new set of questions and has opened new lines of argumentation. Specifically, scholars now have to consider whether the presence of multiple traditions in the Founders' political thought means that they were confused or were somehow able to combine sets of ideas that we believe are analytically distinct. Were they simply pragmatic historical actors unconcerned with theoretical consistency who drew on a multiplicity of political traditions to resolve concrete problems, or did they somehow coherently combine traditions of political thought that we normally consider conceptually distinct? Also, what sets of ideas constitute genuine intellectual traditions within the American Founding, and which ones do not rise to that level?

Over the past decade, scholars have set forth conflicting and increasingly sophisticated interpretations to explain the interactions between republicanism, liberalism, and other traditions in the political thought of the American Founders. More specifically, two distinct groups of scholars led by Michael Zuckert and Lance Banning, respectively, have, in different ways, sought to show how the Founders coherently combined liberalism and republicanism. In contrast, Rogers Smith has analyzed the relationship of the Founders' liberal republicanism to inegalitarian ascriptive ideologies—that is, sets of ideas that have functioned to exclude African Americans, women, Native Americans, and many immigrant groups from the political process, or, conversely put, to justify slavery, nativism, westward expansion, and the subordination of women. Whereas Zuckert, Banning, and others have sought to establish the capaciousness and coherence of the Founders' liberal republicanism, Smith has forthrightly suggested that the Founders' liberal republicanism was inconsistent with and even betrayed by inegalitarian, ascriptive ideologies.

In this chapter, I follow all of these scholars in arguing for the superiority of the multiple traditions approach. I then analyze these three alternative accounts of the interaction of multiple traditions in the political thought of the Founders, set forth a series of generalizations about what we should have learned from the republicanism-liberalism debate, and then make a series of suggestions about where the debate over the intellectual origins of the American republic should be headed. My broadest goal in this chapter is to analyze the permanent impact of the liberalism versus republicanism debate on our understanding of the intellectual origins of the American republic.

In addition to disputes raised in the first four chapters of this book, a fifth confrontation, which has created the most visible, inflammatory, and controversial debate in scholarship on the American Founding over the last half century, is addressed in a new chapter that is published in this revised edition. This question is often expressed as, "How could they have done that?" It concerns the excruciatingly complex and difficult issues surrounding the moral responsibility of the elite Founders for the legal and social subordination of women in the early republic, policies that led to the massive genocide of Native Americans, and especially slavery. Questions about whether slavery could be reconciled with the principles of the American Revolution and whether or not the Constitution was a pro-slavery document were fiercely debated in the early republic and in antebellum America. These debates, and more recent ones, form a long, unbroken discursive tradition with considerable historiographical baggage.[20]

The peculiar configuration and tenor of contemporary academic debates about slavery and the character of the Founders' Constitution and (even more) questions about the treatment of women and Native Americans, however, have a more recent origin. Beginning in the 1960s, neo-Progressive and multicultural historians revived the pro-slavery interpretation of the original Constitution, began to argue that slavery should be at the center of the study of American history, and began to explore the lives of slaves and ordinary men and women in the early republic and the legal and social sources of their subordination. These studies have placed a diverse group of historical actors onto the field for consideration and made their perspectives and their interactions with elites and with each other central topics. Furthermore, multiculturalism and diversity have gained popularity as frameworks for understanding American history, and accommodating diversity has become one of our nation's most important political goals. As the historical horizon in which judgments about the Founders are made has changed, scholars have increasingly come to blame the elite Founders for the legacies of racism and sexism. They have also blamed them for a nation-building effort that came at the expense of the lives, land, and labor of women, Native Americans, and African American slaves.[21] The creation of this liberation historiography and the proliferation of studies designed to counter traditional elite and celebratory narratives of the American Founding has in turn created a counterreaction from many traditional and conservative scholars who have flown to the defense of the Founders. Most broadly, this back and forth is one of the sources of a cycle of celebration and condemnation that has become a central feature of Founding scholarship.

Thomas Jefferson has become the most contested figure within this confrontation. Jefferson scholars have reconsidered questions about whether or not he sired Sally Hemings's children, the character and implications of the Hemings-Jefferson relationship, and most broadly and importantly, how the man who proclaimed that "all men are created equal" in the Declaration of Independence could have also owned slaves.[22] In addition, other Founders have also been reconsidered as the reputations of the leading Founders now rise and fall depending on their beliefs about race and slavery, whether or not they owned slaves, how they treated them, and their positions on and efforts in favor of or against emancipation.[23] Furthermore, interpretations of the Founders' beliefs about and policies concerning Native Americans and women in the early republic have become integral to broad questions about the accomplishments and failures of the Founding generation. They have also become integral to the more specific question about whether the American Revolution largely failed in its promise of equality for all or created a radical social transformation and thus can, at least indirectly, be considered the source of modern egalitarian ideas and reforms.[24] Today, these issues raise debates that resonate in classrooms and academic conferences across the country. Confrontations between the Founders' critics and defenders have also spilled over into the culture wars over such issues as how the elite Founders and slavery should be portrayed in national parks and taught in schools, and whether or not public schools and other public institutions should bear the names of former slaveholders.[25]

Remarkably enough, however, no one has stepped back and tried to make sense of this debate instead of simply staking out another position within it. With this goal in mind, I focus exclusively on the issue of slavery. This choice is governed by the importance of this topic and its paradigmatic quality as an issue for considering moral responsibility. I first identify and examine the structure of three interpretive strategies, which I call prosecuting, vindicating, and historicizing, that scholars have adopted to address issues of moral responsibility. I then expose the deepest sources of disagreement between proponents of these approaches, suggest their strengths and limitations, and make specific suggestions on a constellation of issues that Founding scholars must address when they consider these difficult issues of moral responsibility. The broadest goals of this new chapter are thus to explore the terms on which this debate is being conducted and the assumptions that scholars bring to their interpretations, to raise the consciousness of scholars about the issues that must be addressed in questions of moral responsibility, and to make specific suggestions about how we should proceed when we act as moral critics.

In the sixth and final chapter, I explore some of the broader implications of the relationship of these historiographical debates on the American Founding to issues in American political thought, American political development, and the proper place of the American Founders in American politics. Here, I hope to show that historiographical debates such as these are by no means simply debates of antiquarian interest. They are instead debates about how we are to understand the purposes and limitations of our political system, the content of our political tradition, and ultimately ourselves as a people. In particular, in this chapter, I address questions about which of the multiple traditions approaches that have been set forth in recent scholarship provides the best framework for interpreting the intellectual origins of the American republic. I also examine two recent efforts to redirect the study of the intellectual origins of the American Founding and American political thought. The first, by University of Virginia political scientist James

Ceaser, suggests that scholars should focus on foundational concepts in the study of American political thought. The other, set forth most prominently by Peter Onuf and David Hendrickson, argues that Founding scholars should focus first on the discourse of federalism and union that attended the American Revolution, the formation of the Constitution, and the party battles of the early republic.

Discussion of the development of the "unionist paradigm" and Ceaser's appeal for the study of foundational concepts provide an easy transition into a discussion of whether or not the political thought of the American Founding can really be said to be a contribution to the history of political thought and whether the original design of the American political system has facilitated or impeded the development of democracy in America and how it continues to shape its character. I also consider how we might differentiate between judicious and ill-conceived appropriations of the Founders' ideas and authority. Finally, I provide a defense of understanding the Founding, as opposed to prosecuting, vindicating, and historicizing; examine what this attitude and approach entails; consider some of the barriers that prevent us from breaking out of the cycle of celebration and condemnation that structures so much Founding scholarship; and weigh the prospects for the adoption of a historically sensitive, but also detached and philosophical, approach that is also defended in chapter 3. While I conclude that we are unlikely to soon develop a more balanced, mature, and responsible account of the Founders' moral responsibility for America's original sins, I also argue that this is the only defensible goal, although I acknowledge that this attitude and approach carries its own set of problems.

In general, the goal of this work is to understand modern historiography of the American Founding by critically examining five of the most important debates that it has generated, rather than, as is normally the case, by chronologically documenting the successive replacement of one paradigm of interpretation by another and considering how the central teachings of each school of interpretation reflect contemporaneous intellectual currents and the political aims of scholars. To this end, each of these chapters has been written to stand alone as commentary about and, I hope, a contribution to our understanding of an ongoing, conceptually distinct, and fundamental debate.

Nevertheless, these chapters are structured similarly and have common goals. Each includes substantial historiographical review, seeks to establish the terms on which debate has been framed, explores the underlying foundational disagreements between scholars who often proceed as if they disagree primarily about matters of historical facts, and identifies what stands in the way of further progress. Each addresses a series of questions: How did we get to where we are today? What have we learned? Where should we go from here? Answering these questions fosters a retrospective and prospective analysis of the debate. My goal, then, is not so much to take up each of these questions anew and provide a new interpretation (although I have not been able to resist setting forth my own interpretations and suggestions), but instead to examine how scholars have thought about each of these questions and the deepest sources of their disagreements.

These debates are analyzed in the order of their emergence in the modern study of the American Founding to provide the reader with an overview of the modern study of the American Founding and an appreciation for its trajectory. Briefly put, Beard and the Progressive historians contended that the Framers were motivated by economic self-interest and were members of a consolidated economic group, that they established an undemocratic political system, and that ideas should not be the focus of study. Scholars have reacted to these contentions first by challenging Beard's methodology and the validity of his empirical claims (chapter 1), then by challenging his claim that the Framers created an undemocratic political system (chapter 2), providing a new justification for the study of ideas (chapter 3), and setting forth new interpretations of the intellectual origins of the American republic (chapter 4). Debates about the moral responsibility of the elite Founders for slavery, patriarchy, and Indian removal and genocide (analyzed in chapter 5) have also emerged as multicultural scholars who are neo-Progressive in spirit, if not strictly in methodology, have issued sharp criticisms of the elite Founders and been countered by the Founders' defenders. Considering these confrontations in this order should provide the reader with an account of how and why these debates have unfolded as they have, as well as an analysis of their substance.

Finally, by directly revisiting and addressing five of the central confrontations that have given the post-Beardian study of the American Founding its significance and vitality, I hope to clarify the points of disagreement between scholars on these questions, explore what is at stake in these debates, and give contentious answers to them. Although I have no illusions that I have resolved or even fundamentally reoriented how we think about these debates, I hope that my struggle with them will be taken up by the reader, who of course need not agree with my conclusions in order to benefit from the pursuit. The residue of each of these confrontations is a rich body of scholarship—much of it glimpsing truth, all of it (as Heidegger suggests) masking as it simultaneously reveals, but some of it providing better answers to these questions than others. The broad background of understanding that I provide in this study will, I hope, help us to distinguish the better from the worse answers that scholars have given to these questions and help us move beyond current impasses. It is to that project that I now turn.

I

Still Hazy after All These Years
The Economic Interpretation and the Cloudy Legacy of Empirical Analysis

In American social studies we still live in the shadow of the Progressive era. Historians have openly assailed Beard, challenging economic motivations here and there and often transforming "radicals" into "conservatives." But after all is said and done Beard somehow stays alive, and the reason for this is that, as in the case of Marx, you merely demonstrate your subservience to a thinker when you spend your time attempting to disprove him.

Louis Hartz

The publication of Charles Beard's *An Economic Interpretation of the Constitution* in 1913 marks the origins of modern scholarship on the American Founding. To be sure, not every work that preceded his study can be dismissed as hagiography. Furthermore, several dimensions of Beard's thesis had been anticipated by previous scholars.[1] Nevertheless, it is no exaggeration to suggest that Beard's book is the most important work ever written on the American Founding, primarily because it liberated scholars to critically study the Founders rather than merely celebrate them. Only a few paths of modern scholarship on the American Founding return to Beard's thesis, but in a sense, all can be traced from it.

Despite its importance, the economic interpretation of the formation and ratification of the Constitution occupies an uncertain place in scholarship on the American Founding, and empirical analysis of the economic holdings of the Framers and ratifiers of the Constitution has left an ambiguous and cloudy legacy. On the one hand, scholars frequently conclude that the series of studies conducted by Forrest McDonald and Robert E. Brown (among others) during the middle decades of the twentieth century demolished Beard's thesis.[2] On the other hand, the significance of economic factors in the formation and ratification of the Constitution is almost universally accepted by scholars of the Founding. As James Hutson put it, since the postwar studies, it has been taken for granted that the "Constitution was an economic document, in the sense that economic forces helped to produce it." Nevertheless, "the exact nature, power, and configuration of those forces" has been "difficult to discern."[3]

There are several reasons why the contributions of nearly a century of empirical analysis are less than clear. Some of Beard's claims are ambiguous and have been given equally plausible but contradictory interpretations. This ambiguity has led to a burgeoning debate about what he claimed in the first place. Furthermore, when Brown, McDonald, and others set out to challenge Beard's economic interpretation, they exposed a daunting number and variety of logical, methodological, and empirical flaws in his thesis. Initially, however, these scholars followed Beard's mode of inquiry and produced a series of studies that are still very much economic interpretations, even though they show that the alignment of economic interests for and against the Constitution was exponentially more complex than Beard had suggested. E. James Ferguson, Staughton Lynd, Van Beck Hall, and Jackson Turner Main then further complicated the historiographical landscape during the 1960s and 1970s by setting forth economic interpretations that refurbish central aspects of the Progressive interpretation. More recently, social and rational choice theorists such as Calvin Jillson and Robert McGuire have applied the most sophisticated statistical methodologies to the data gathered by McDonald and others, resurrected the economic interpretation, and added to the array of economic interpretations that now exist.

Together, the original ambiguity of some of Beard's claims, the dizzying number and variety of criticisms of his interpretation, the responses of his defenders, and the articulation and persistence of alternative economic interpretations with varying degrees of sympathy for Beard's original thesis have led to considerable confusion about the role of economic interests in the formation and ratification of the Constitution. This chapter aims to remove some of that confusion and offers an assessment of the state of our understanding of the economic interpretation of the Constitution.[4] Toward this end, I provide an interpretation of Beard's thesis, characterize and categorize the most important criticisms of it, summarize the alternative economic interpretations of the Constitution that were developed in conjunction with these criticisms, attempt to establish what has and has not been proved in this debate, and suggest how to get beyond current impasses.

Beard's Thesis: An Interpretation

Like many classics, *An Economic Interpretation of the Constitution* has been the subject of voluminous, conflicting commentary.[5] One of the reasons for these disputes lies in the work itself. *An Economic Interpretation* is shot full of ambiguities, contradictions, and perhaps even deliberately duplicitous statements that are sure to cause consternation.[6] Furthermore, since its publication in 1913, *An Economic Interpretation of the Constitution* has been read as a condemnation of the motives of the Framers. Nevertheless, Beard defended his method of economic interpretation as "coldly neutral" and explicitly denied that he meant to sit in judgment of the Framers, leaving his readers to wonder whether he was being disingenuous or had been almost universally misunderstood.[7] Beard's position becomes even more confusing when it is pointed out that he profusely praised the intelligence, experience, and practicality of the Framers in several other works and even in *An Economic Interpretation.*[8]

Fortunately, even though *An Economic Interpretation* is cryptic, duplicitous, and surrounded by interpretive baggage, it is sustained by a consistent line of argumentation that provides a basis for identifying Beard's core claims. Beard begins his argument by posing a broad question. If, he writes, it could be shown that "substantially all of the merchants, money lenders, security holders, manufacturers, shippers, capitalists, and financiers and their professional associates are to be found on one side in support of the Constitution and that substantially all or the major portion of the opposition came from the non-slaveholding farmers and the debtors—would it not be pretty conclusively demonstrated that our fundamental law was not the product of an abstraction known as 'the whole people,' but of a group of economic interests which must have expected beneficial results from its adoption?"[9] *An Economic Interpretation of the Constitution* is formed around a series of interrelated propositions in support of this core thesis that the Constitution was created not by the whole people but rather by economic interests that expected to benefit from its passage.

The first of these propositions—derived from Beard's understanding of the economic interpretation of history—is that contending interests are present in every society, some of which seek to maintain the status quo and others of which seek change. These contending interests in eighteenth-century American society, Beard argues, were "personalty" and "realty," or "capital as opposed to land."[10] The realty interest, which favored the status quo, was made up of a coalition of three groups: a homogeneous group of small farmers that constituted a large debtor class, manorial lords of the Hudson valley region, and the slaveholding planters of the South. The personalty interest, according to Beard, was made up primarily of four groups: creditors, holders of public securities, manufacturers, and land speculators.

These personality groups, Beard argues, favored constitutional reform because the government under the Articles of Confederation was unable to guarantee the value of public securities and was ill equipped to protect American manufacturing interests, counter discrimination by foreign nations against American shipping, regulate foreign and interstate commerce, or repel foreign enemies from the frontier. Even more important, however, the legal system under the Articles of Confederation decentralized power and placed neither constitutional restrictions nor judicial control on the state legislatures. Within the states, realty interests controlled the legislatures and threatened the interests of the creditor class by printing inflationary paper money and enacting debtor relief legislation that, in the eyes of creditors, amounted to nothing less than the expropriation of their property.

Faced with these problems, members of the personalty group began a correspondence that forged unity in favor of constitutional reform. The economic interests of New England manufacturers, southern planters, land speculators, former continental soldiers, and creditors, Beard contends, were much closer to one another than to those of the small farmers, manorial lords, and debtors in their own regions. Thus, in Beard's eyes, constitutional revision was "the work of a consolidated group whose interests knew no state boundaries and were truly national in their scope," and personalty (especially in the form of public securities) was "the dynamic element in the movement for the new Constitution."[11]

At first, personalty interests attempted to secure constitutional reform through the political process. Failing this, they conducted a coup d'etat that eventually led to the calling of the Constitutional Convention. Perhaps most important, the convention, according to Beard, was composed of members who held the same economic interests that had been threatened by the state governments' assaults on personalty during the 1780s. To support this claim, Beard's long central chapter, which many scholars have designated the most important in the book, includes "economic biographies" of the property holdings of the members of the Constitutional Convention.[12] Such an analysis established that a majority of the Framers were lawyers; that most were from coastal regions or cities, where personalty was concentrated; that forty of them were holders of public securities; and that many others held personalty in the form of land for speculation, money loaned at interest, slaves, or interests in the mercantile, manufacturing, and shipping industries. These findings, in turn, led Beard to his famous conclusion that, far from being disinterested men whose actions were guided by abstract principles, the men who met in Philadelphia "were immediately, directly, and personally inter-ested in the outcome of their labors . . . and were to a greater or less extent economic beneficiaries from the adoption of the Constitution."[13]

Beard follows his survey of the economic holdings of the men who at-tended the Philadelphia convention with an equally influential interpreta-tion of the Constitution as an economic and antidemocratic document. In three ways, Beard concludes, the Constitution served to insulate and pro-mote the interests of the capitalist class that had been threatened by the debtor schemes of the 1780s. First, the system of staggered elections and indirect representation, the power and insulation given to the Senate, the ex-tended sphere of the republic, and especially the judiciary ("the keystone of the whole structure") served to break up the "attacking forces" of the pop-ular majorities among the public and to moderate them as they were re-flected in the political system. Second, the Constitution prohibited the state governments from issuing paper money or passing debtor relief laws. Third, unlike under the Articles of Confederation, the Constitution gave the new government the power to collect taxes, raise and support an army and a navy, regulate commerce, and dispose of western lands. The use of these powers, Beard maintains, ensured that "public creditors may be paid in full, domes-tic peace maintained, advantages obtained in dealing with foreign nations, manufactures protected, and the development of the territories go forward with full swing."[14]

Finally, Beard argues that the ratification struggle was a deep-seated con-flict between personalty and realty interests and that personalty (especially in the form of public securities) was the dynamic element. Personalty in-terests were able to push the proposed constitution through the ratification process hastily and with the support of only a small percentage of the Amer-ican people because, Beard argues, property qualifications imposed by the state constitutions disenfranchised a "mass of men" and, even more impor-tantly, the people were apathetic and indifferent. Together, these factors combined to ensure that only about 5 percent of the free persons in the United States at the time, or about 160,000 Americans, expressed an opinion for or against the Constitution. Of these, no more than 100,000 favored the adoption of the Constitution. These statistics meant that it was "highly prob-able that not more than one-fourth or one-fifth of the adult white males took part in the election of delegates to the state conventions" and that only about one in six favored the adoption of the Constitution.[15] According to Beard, these pieces of evidence, taken together, established that the Constitution had been ratified because large segments of the American public were in-different and because supporters of the Constitution had greater resources and better access to the press. It also succeeded because supporters of the Constitution were better organized, more immediately interested, more centrally located, and more aware of their common identity than were their opponents.

The Case against Beard's Economic Interpretation

Beard's interpretation met with considerable skepticism when it was first published in 1913. Indeed, initial reviewers foreshadowed many of the lines of criticism that would be pursued by later critics. Nevertheless, by the 1930s, Beard's thesis had become the dominant interpretation of the framing and ratification of the Constitution.[16] This hegemony was not shattered until the post–World War II studies of, among others, Robert E. Brown, Forrest McDonald, Lee Benson, Philip A. Crowl, William C. Pool, and Robert Thomas.[17]

For a substantial time *An Economic Interpretation of the Constitution* enraged many readers, but it ultimately convinced most of them; however, during the 1950s it proved vulnerable to a new generation of critics who were methodologically more sophisticated than Beard or his initial reviewers and had access to historical sources that were unavailable to previous scholars.[18] These critics combed Beard's text with a thoroughness expended on few works before or since, broke Beard's thesis into a multiplicity of discrete claims, and then developed a number of ways of systematically testing them. The criticisms that emerged from this scrutiny can be grouped into three broad categories: the claim that Beard's thesis is supported by sophistic argumentative techniques and contains numerous ambiguities and inconsistencies, the claim that it is plagued by methodological errors, and the claim that his empirical findings are incomplete and inaccurate.

Perhaps the most obvious sophistic argumentative technique is Beard's use of unproven propositions as the premises for his extended argument. Beard begins with the concession that his account is "frankly fragmentary" and "designed to suggest new lines of historical research rather than to treat the subject in an exhaustive fashion."[19] In almost every chapter he reminds readers that he has not done the research necessary to prove the particular proposition he has just asserted and then carefully outlines the additional research required to do so. As he moves forward in his argument, however, Beard's frankness about the status of his arguments does not prevent him from building on propositions that have never been proved.

In addition to this broad problem, at least three specific areas of Beard's thesis are ambiguous or confusing. First, Beard does not present a consistent or coherent understanding of what he means by an economic interpretation.

In particular, Beard uses the terms *economic determinism* and *economic interpretation* interchangeably, but they are actually significantly different concepts. His work, therefore, rests on an unresolved ambiguity that has been reflected in much subsequent scholarship on the economic interpretation. Was Beard claiming that the Framers were reflexively pursuing their *own* immediate economic gain (as some passages suggest, and as an economic determinist interpretation would demand), or was he making the much more limited, subtle, and plausible claim that the Framers acted as *representatives* of distinct economic groups or classes and that their ideas reflected their membership in those groups (as other passages suggest, and as an economic interpretation would support)?

In his introduction to the 1935 edition of *An Economic Interpretation of the Constitution*, Beard dismisses as "superficial critics" those scholars who interpret his work as suggesting that the Framers were profiteers and petty speculators and points to a quote from the original work. "The purpose of such an inquiry," he wrote in 1913, "is not, of course, to show that the Constitution was made for the personal benefit of the members of the Convention. Far from it. Neither is it of any moment to discover how many hundred thousand dollars accrued to them as a result of the foundation of the new government. The only point here considered is: *Did they represent distinct groups whose economic interests they understood and felt in concrete, definite form through their own personal experience with identical property rights,* or were they working merely under the guidance of abstract principles of political science?"[20] This admonition has led many scholars to reject as crass and unfair any reading of Beard's thesis that suggests that the Framers were motivated by the desire for personal gain.[21]

Nevertheless, if Beard was not making this suggestion, what did he mean when he wrote that the Framers were *"immediately* interested through their *personal possessions* in the outcome of their labors" or that their "direct impelling motive" was *"the economic advantages which the beneficiaries expected would accrue to themselves first?"*[22] Furthermore, why did he place such an emphasis on the Framers' securities holdings? Why did he say that the holders of public securities gained at least $40 million from the adoption of the Constitution and call public securities the "dynamic element" in the movement for a new national government if he did not mean to imply that the Framers hoped to increase the value of their securities and then redeem them for speculative profit?[23] The most sensible answer to these questions is provided by Richard Hofstadter. Although Beard may have wanted his text to be read one way, Hofstadter observes that it can plausibly be read as suggesting that Beard was either "casting a crude muckraker's imputation on their [the Framers'] motives" or implying that they were representatives of distinct interest groups and thus offering an "economic and sociological account of their ideas."[24]

Beard's interpretation of the characteristics of the groups for and against the Constitution represents the second area of confusion and ambiguity. Specifically, one of the central contributions of *An Economic Interpretation* is Beard's bold proposition that support for or opposition to the Constitution correlated with membership in certain economic groups. But what characteristics defined these different economic groups? At first glance, Beard's answer seems clear. He argues throughout that realty holders opposed the Constitution and personalty holders wrote and generally supported it. Nevertheless, Beard complicates this division by attaching other suggestive descriptors to these categories. In addition to being holders of realty, opponents of the Constitution were poor, debtors, and from the backcountry regions, whereas holders of personalty were usually wealthy, creditors, and from urban areas.[25]

Beard also makes numerous exceptions to these generalizations. At one point, he explicitly observes that manorial lords of the Hudson valley were *wealthy* realty holders yet anti-Federalists, and that many urban working-class men and small farmers favored ratification.[26] As Benson notes, Beard also observed that one significant group of realty holders (slaveholders) favored ratification of the Constitution.[27] Along these same lines, Clyde Barrow argues that Beard conceived of the personalty group as "a political coalition which was both geographically and socially widely diffused." Barrow notes that a careful reading of Beard's work shows that he recognized that some men of modest means held securities, some large property holders were heavily in debt, and some tidewater planters also engaged in significant commercial activities involving personalty; in addition, he recognized that some small farmers were engaged in trade and thus that their interests were interwoven with personalty interests.[28] So what was Beard suggesting? Was he suggesting that men supported or opposed the Constitution based on their wealth, the location of their residences, their indebtedness, or the nature of their primary property holdings (personalty or realty)?

Third, Beard presents contradictory interpretations of the extent to which property qualifications disenfranchised voters. At some points he asserts that "a large propertyless mass" was disenfranchised in 1787 and that property qualifications "operated to exclude a large portion of the adult males."[29] At other points he concludes that "while these [property] qualifications operated to exclude a large portion of the adult males from participating in elections, the wide distribution of real property created an extensive electorate and in most rural regions gave the legislatures a broad popular basis."[30]

At some point, Beard seems to conclude that the mass of men who were disenfranchised by property qualifications was not so massive after all, and he cites apathy as the primary reason that so few voted for delegates to the state ratifying conventions. Nevertheless, Beard's turn to apathy as an explanation for the success of personalty interests in securing ratification is hardly satisfactory. As Hofstadter observes, "to stress disfranchisement by property qualifications is to hint at an embattled class of underdogs clamoring for the opportunity to defend their interests by winning a part in politics." But "disfranchisement by apathy (if not by ignorance) suggests the possibility that great masses of common people were sufficiently content with the way that they were governed to leave the decision on the Constitution to others."[31] Furthermore, Beard states that the realty interest was extremely active in the enactment of debtor relief legislation during the mid-1780s; thus, Beard has to portray the majority of small farmers as a turbulent mass. But to explain why individuals with realty interests did not oppose ratification more strongly in many states, he has to portray them as a docile multitude.[32]

In addition to these logical inconsistencies, the methodology that Beard employs to test his hypothesis has been subjected to at least two decisive criticisms. First, *An Economic Interpretation of the Constitution* is based on a simple two-factor analysis, not multivariate analysis. Thus, contrary to Beard's claims, even if the evidence he presents for his thesis had been comprehensive, his study would not have proved that personalty was the dynamic element in the formation and ratification of the Constitution. Here, we must return to the question Beard poses at the beginning of his classic study. If, he writes, it could be shown that in 1788 merchants, creditors, security holders, and other capitalists were in favor of the Constitution and nonslaveholding farmers and debtors were opposed to it, could it not also be concluded that the Constitution was the product of the personalty interests that hoped to benefit from its adoption? As Cecelia Kenyon and Lee Benson have pointed out, the correct answer to this question is maybe, but not necessarily. An answer to Beard's question tells us nothing about the influence of factors other than economic self-interest on the adoption of the Constitution. "A simple statistical correlation between two factors," Kenyon observes succinctly, "does not necessarily establish a causal relationship between them in the presence of other possible causal factors."[33]

Second, compiling economic biographies of the 55 delegates to the Constitutional Convention or even the 1,648 delegates who cast votes at the state ratifying conventions (as McDonald did later) does not establish the division *within the electorate.*[34] Although this issue is explored more fully at the end of this chapter, it should be pointed out now that a methodologically sound study requires an analysis of the economic interests of at least a random sample of the approximately 160,000 individuals who participated in the ratification process by voting for delegates to the state conventions, and then an analysis of the economic interests of those individuals (along with other factors necessary to establish a multivariate analysis) compared to their positions on the Constitution. Put differently, we cannot assume that the *leadership* in the ratification struggle was a representative sample of all the participants.[35]

Criticisms of the conceptual veracity and methodological validity of Beard's study are important, but a final category of criticisms—those that challenge the validity of his empirical claims—is most telling in discrediting Beard's economic interpretation of the Constitution. This is true because Beard himself rests so much of his case on what he calls the "indubitable facts" that support his interpretation.[36] In particular, the empirical criticisms lodged against Beard's thesis can be divided into five areas.

First, besides the conceptual confusion created by Beard's categories of personalty and realty, they also prove to be empirically untenable. Beard can be read as suggesting that in American society in 1787 personalty interests were pitted against a large mass of debtor-farmers. Brown responds to this contention by observing that realty "was overwhelmingly the predominant economic interest in the country," constituting approximately 96 percent of the nation's economic interests.[37] Brown also argues that early America was an agrarian, middle-class, democratic society in which large numbers of white males held property. These economic characteristics, according to Brown, explain why almost all Americans favored the protection of property rights and why the Constitution was ratified by several agricultural states.[38] In general, commentators point out that eighteenth-century society was much less specialized and polarized than Beard sometimes suggests, that few eighteenth-century statesmen identified themselves as either personalty or realty holders, and that Beard's categories of analysis are unable to account for either the presence of a large middle class or the large number of individuals who held both forms of property.[39]

Second, Beard argues that the members of the Constitutional Convention were a "consolidated" economic group unrepresentative of American society in 1787.[40] The delegates to the convention, according to Beard, came largely from commercial coastal regions, were primarily lawyers and merchants, and were wealthy holders of personalty (especially in the form of public securities). In contrast, McDonald and Brown seek to establish the diversity and representativeness of the convention delegates. In particular, McDonald argues that the "delegations constituted an almost complete cross-section of the geographical areas and shades of political opinion existing in the United States in 1787." Specifically, after dividing the states into geographic regions and political factions, McDonald concludes that thirty-nine of fifty-five geographic areas and thirty-one of thirty-four political factions were represented at the convention. McDonald agrees with Beard that a majority of the delegates to the Philadelphia convention were lawyers (thirty-four), large commercial farmers (sixteen), or merchants or participants in the mercantile profession (fifteen).[41] But as these figures indicate, it is impossible to classify the fifty-five delegates into mutually exclusive groups. According to McDonald, several delegates were cross-pressured by their occupations, and twenty of the delegates "derived all or almost all of their income from the soil."[42]

Furthermore, Brown and McDonald contend that an examination of *all* the investments and property holdings of the convention delegates undermines Beard's generalization that the delegates were primarily holders of personalty. Based on Brown's findings, only six delegates had personalty in excess of realty, eighteen had realty in excess of personalty, and the economic holdings of thirty could not be ascertained.[43] McDonald presents a more complex picture, showing that "the value of the agricultural holdings of the delegates far outweighed their personalty," or, put differently, that farmland and slaves, not public securities, were the most valuable forms of property held by the convention delegates.[44] Still, he observes that "delegates having personalty interests outnumbered delegates having primarily realty interests thirty-one to twenty-four."[45]

Both Brown and McDonald sought to establish that the occupations and investments of most of the delegates to the convention were not so clear-cut; thus, it would have been difficult for them to offer knee-jerk support to the Constitution even if they had understood it as an instrument for the protection of personalty. Lawyers often represented clients with large realty interests; farmers held public securities; merchants or wealthy holders of realty were often debtors. Such cross-pressures, McDonald observes, makes it difficult to place delegates in "mutually exclusive categories."[46] In addition, as both McDonald and Brown imply, this overlap made delegates "immediately interested" in the protection and growth of *both* real and personal property.

Third, Beard argues that personalty was the "dynamic element" in the movement for the Constitution and that public securities constituted the largest proportion of personalty and thus "must have formed a very considerable dynamic element, if not the preponderating element, in bringing about the adoption of the new system." In support of this argument, Beard relies on records from the Treasury Department that established that no fewer than forty of the fifty-five delegates to the convention held securities and that twenty-four of these delegates were large security holders (which Beard defines as holding more than $5,000 worth of securities).[47] Beard's thesis also suggests that security holders could be expected to support the Constitution during the ratification process and that opponents of ratification would have few securities.

In one of the earliest reviews of *An Economic Interpretation of the Constitution,* Edward S. Corwin presents a short but devastating critique of Beard's argument about the influence of securities. Most of Beard's calculations about the Framers' security holdings at the time of the Constitutional Convention, Corwin observes, are speculative at best because the Treasury Department records he relies on did not establish *when* the holders bought their securities. Beard simply assumed that if a delegate to the convention appeared on Treasury records in the 1790s, he must have been a public creditor at the time of the convention. That assumption was, according to Corwin, "the most unmitigated rot."[48] There was a strong possibility that many of the public securities had been purchased after the Constitutional Convention as a speculative investment, when individuals expected their value to rise. Most important, if it could not be established that the Framers had owned securities before the convention, then increasing the value of those securities could not have been the motive behind the drafting of the Constitution. One of Beard's claims, then, was unproved and, at least based on the records Beard used, incapable of being proved.[49]

Corwin also points out that even if members of the convention had held securities in 1787 worth roughly $450,000, one-third of that probably would have been state certificates, and two-thirds of the remaining $300,000 worth of securities would have been held by five men who were not central actors at the convention. Conversely, five of the most fervent supporters of the Constitution—Alexander Hamilton, James Madison, Gouverneur Morris, James Wilson, and Charles Pinckney—held only $14,000 in securities.[50]

Finally, Corwin argues that Beard's thesis makes sense only if the delegates to the convention assumed that the Constitution mandated the funding of state debts (which constituted almost one-third of the total Revolutionary debt) and the redemption of continental securities at par for their current holders. Nevertheless, the language adopted—that "All Debts contracted and Engagements entered into, before the Adoption of this Constitution, shall be as valid against the United States under this Constitution as under the Confederation"—seems to have been understood to leave creditors in the same condition they had been in before ratification of the Constitution.[51] Conversely, it was not understood to guarantee redemption at par value to current holders of debt, to fund state debts, or to preclude discrimination between the original and present holders of continental securities.[52] The policies of full payment to current holders of debt and the assumption of state debts were adopted during the 1790s after bitterly fought political contests. The outcome and terms of these contests were hardly predictable in 1787. It was thus Hamilton's funding program, not the framing or adoption of the Constitution, that was principally responsible for the increase in the value of public securities.[53] In 1787, any Framer who hoped to increase the value of his securities by fighting for ratification was taking a substantial risk.[54]

Forty years after Corwin's review, McDonald conducted his prodigious research project that established the security holdings of the fifty-five delegates to the Philadelphia convention and most of the delegates to the state ratifying conventions. In some cases, McDonald was also able to establish when the Framers acquired their securities.[55] McDonald's findings are complex, and they are also amenable to different interpretations than he gave them. Nevertheless, he found that thirty of the fifty-five delegates held securities, but five of the men who walked out of the convention or refused to sign were among the largest security holders. In his analysis of the state ratifying conventions, McDonald found no direct relationship between the number of security holders and how quickly or easily the states ratified the Constitution. Instead, he found that in the three states that ratified the Constitution unanimously (Delaware, New Jersey, and Georgia), security holders were not numerous; in three other states where there were significant contests over ratification and substantial numbers of security holders (Rhode Island, Maryland, and Virginia), security holders were found in roughly the same percentages among anti-Federalists and Federalists; in three states (Pennsylvania, South Carolina, and New York), a larger percentage of *opponents* of the Constitution held securities than did supporters; and in only two states (Massachusetts and Connecticut) was the percentage of Federalists who held securities greater than the percentage of anti-Federalists who did so.[56]

McDonald also found that a large number of speculators had actually feared the appreciation of public securities. These speculators often bought public lands and agreed to pay for them with public securities. They expected the price of public securities to remain low or even decrease, meaning that they would actually pay less for the land than they had originally contracted to pay. For these individuals, a rise in the price of securities could lead to bankruptcy, because they would have to pay more for land than they expected. This, of course, was precisely what happened to several of them.[57] All this led McDonald to conclude that "contrary to Beard's assertion, they [security holders who opposed the Constitution] were as numerous as the security holders among the supporters of the Constitution."[58]

Fourth, although Beard does not test this proposition, his thesis suggests that voting alignments on central issues at the convention should conform to a division between holders of personalty, who supported nationalistic measures, and holders of realty, who opposed the formation of a strong national government. McDonald tested this proposition in several ways. Most important, he identified the individual votes of delegates (when they could be ascertained) on the sixteen key issues that concerned whether there would be a national government. This analysis, McDonald concludes, suggests that "no alignment of personalty interests versus realty interests existed in the Convention."[59]

McDonald also examined the correlation between delegates' economic holdings and their support of or opposition to provisions granting positive powers to the national government (including giving Congress the exclusive authority to regulate commerce and to fund the war debt) and imposing restrictions against the state governments (including prohibiting the states from issuing paper money or impairing the obligations of contracts). These features of the Constitution, McDonald observes, were ones that Beard argues were directly favored by holders of personalty as a means of advancing their immediate interests. Although McDonald identified four delegates who might have been voting explicitly to protect their security holdings, he also found considerable opposition to these provisions among holders of personalty.[60]

In yet another test, McDonald examined whether delegates to the convention who eventually supported the final version of the Constitution were primarily holders of personalty and those who opposed it were holders of realty, as Beard's thesis would predict. McDonald identified seven delegates who would have voted against the final version of the document if the Constitutional Convention had been a ratifying convention. Contrary to Beard's thesis, these delegates, according to McDonald, constituted an "all star team of personalty interests." Taken together, these analyses "conclusively demonstrated" that "there was virtually no correlation between economic interests and voting behavior in the Convention."[61]

Fifth, Beard argues that the economic interpretation of the Constitution would ultimately be upheld or refuted by the economic biographies of all the participants in the ratification process. Beard's limited research on the relationship between economic interests and the process of ratification led him to conclude that the ratification struggle was fundamentally a clash between individuals with personalty interests, on the one hand, and farmers and debtors with realty interests, on the other. After establishing the economic interests of most of the delegates to the state ratifying conventions, McDonald determined that Beard's conclusion is "entirely incompatible with the facts." In particular, McDonald emphasizes that the Constitution was ratified quickly and with the broad support of farmers and friends of paper money in three states (Delaware, New Jersey, Georgia). In two other states where ratification was contested (Virginia and North Carolina), a majority of the delegates were farmers. Even in the states where delegates with personalty interests were a majority (Massachusetts, Pennsylvania, New York, and Rhode Island) or a substantial minority (Connecticut, Maryland, South Carolina, and New Hampshire), Beard's thesis was "groundless" because farmers made up a substantial number of the supporters of the Constitution.[62]

Conversely, McDonald, Crowl, Pool, and Thomas all found that the anti-Federalists were neither debtor-farmers nor a homogeneous realty group, but that many held substantial personalty interests.[63] These scholars also uniformly conclude that the battle over the Constitution was a division within the aristocracy between holders of similar economic interests. Thomas, for example, found that in Virginia "the leaders of both the Federalist and Anti-Federalist parties came from the *same* class—slaveowners, large landowners, land speculators, army officers and professional people, in short, the gentry."[64] Meanwhile, McDonald found that opponents of the Constitution, especially in Pennsylvania, South Carolina, and New York, held substantial personalty in the form of public securities. In general, he concludes that the wealth and occupations of the Federalists and anti-Federalists were roughly the same in all the states that were divided on the Constitution.[65]

Recasting the Economic Interpretation

Pluralism versus Neo-Progressivism

Together, the numerous criticisms lodged against Beard's thesis by his initial reviewers and later critics are, as Hofstadter puts it, "bewildering in their variety, and in their totality quite formidable."[66] Most importantly, these studies destroy the idea that the division over the Constitution was between holders of realty and personalty. Nevertheless, it is far more accurate to claim that these criticisms refute specific dimensions of Beard's thesis and set the boundaries of subsequent economic interpretations than to suggest that they amount to a refutation of any economic interpretation. Indeed, the very studies that challenge Beard's economic interpretation either lay the groundwork for or are themselves broader, more refined, and more sophisticated economic interpretations.

In particular, two competing economic interpretations of the formation and ratification of the Constitution emerged from the post–World War II scrutiny of Beard's thesis. The debate between scholars espousing these competing approaches mirrored a broader debate in the academic community between "pluralist" and "power elite" interpretations of the American political system. The most sophisticated pluralist economic interpretation was set forth by Forrest McDonald. Characterizing even McDonald's early scholarship as an economic interpretation may seem inappropriate. After all, McDonald is considered by many to be Beard's most devastating critic, and he states flatly in the opening pages of *We the People* that an "economic interpretation of the Constitution does not work."[67] Nevertheless, perhaps no scholar of the American Founding has done more than McDonald to establish that the Framers were often "driven by base motives, especially greed," and, conversely, to support the contention that the "establishment of the Constitution was far from a philosophical matter."[68]

McDonald's first two books on the formation and ratification of the Constitution—*We the People* and *E Pluribus Unum*—employ this "realist" approach but also seek to replace Beard's account of the conflict between holders of personalty and realty with a complex, economic interpretation of the Constitution. In these studies, McDonald seldom portrays economic motives as singular, unambiguous, or disconnected from noneconomic considerations. Nor does he frequently refer to *class* interests. Instead, he examines how specific occupations, economic holdings, geographic locations, and other factors combined with ideology and experience to influence individuals' expectations about the proposed Constitution.[69] This "interplay of interests," McDonald argues, should be examined "within the framework of the thirteen state jurisdictions rather than in that of a single national arena."[70]

Most important for our purposes, McDonald's pluralistic approach leads to a subtle analysis of the sources of Federalism and anti-Federalism. McDonald maintains, for example, that the experience of elites during the Revolution was often a decisive factor in their position on the Constitution. Many leading Federalists, he concludes, supported the Constitution because they had served as officers in the Continental army or held national office and thus had experienced the frustration of administration by an impotent national government. More ordinary Americans might have supported it because their property had been confiscated or destroyed during the war or because they lived in a place that had been occupied by British troops. Some favored the Constitution because they lived in cities where they were exposed to commerce and ideas, and others who lived in "weak" states (such as Georgia) believed that a stronger union was imperative for survival.

Anti-Federalism, according to McDonald, sprang from equally complex patterns of ideology and interest mediated by experience. Some anti-Federalists were doctrinaire ideologues who feared an encroaching national government and the effects of an extended republic. In most states, opposition to the Constitution was dominant in the countryside, where commerce, diversity, and government were less likely to be encountered or desired. Others opposed the Constitution because they sought to preserve the offices they occupied at the state level or, even more directly, sought to secure their immediate economic interests. In New York, for example, George Clinton established a flagrantly partisan scheme for funding state securities and some national securities that resulted in a windfall for many prominent New Yorkers and entrenched Clinton in office.[71]

Even Beard's most sympathetic followers appreciate McDonald's emphasis on regional particularity and the diversity of the Framers' motives. What bothers Beard's heirs about McDonald's interpretation is that it is often cited as a decisive refutation of the Progressives' propositions that the movement for the Constitution was begun by wealthy members of a commercial class and that there were substantial economic and social differences between supporters and opponents of the Constitution. E. James Ferguson, Staughton Lynd, Jackson Turner Main, Gordon Wood, and Van Beck Hall have modified and reconstructed these claims.[72]

Ferguson's scholarship can be thought of as a refinement of Beard's claim that the Framers were a unified national elite responding to threats to their interests posed by a weak confederation government and overly democratic state governments.[73] During the course of the American Revolution, Ferguson observes, two central and inseparable questions emerged: How would the vast public debt that accrued from the American Revolution be funded? Would the power of taxation be lodged in the national government or remain in the states? As Ferguson notes, in the mid-1780s the obvious answer to these questions was to continue to withhold the power of taxation from the national government, allocate a portion of the debt to each of the states, and then allow the states to retire the debt using the traditional methods appropriate to the "currency" system of public finance. Under the currency system, state governments printed paper money and then used it to finance public expenditures and provide loans to farmers. With this system already in place, according to Ferguson, it was unnecessary for the central government to have a broad power of taxation. Furthermore, the currency system fit the decentralized, agrarian society of early America because it was democratic, inexpensive, and relatively neutral, and it discouraged the accumulation of large public debts.

Led by Robert Morris, however, a group of nationalists came up with the idea of using the Revolutionary War debt to help secure an alternative system of public finance, a strong national government, and a commercial capitalist state. This group of economic nationalists, Ferguson argues, was the driving force behind the formation of the Constitution and Hamilton's financial system of 1790. Based on the principles of high finance, sound money, free trade, the importance of government-backed banks, and the sanctity of contract, the Morris-Hamilton financial system depended on the national government's assumption of the Revolutionary War debt. Morris realized, according to Ferguson, that an undischarged federal debt would mean that Congress had to have the taxing power to at least discharge the interest on the debt. Lodging the taxing power in the national government, in turn, would make it a true sovereign. Morris therefore jealously guarded the debt as a prerogative of the national government. Although Morris's plan faltered in 1782, when he tried to force the states to accept an impost by ending interest payments on public securities, it was reborn immediately before the calling of the Constitutional Convention when "fear of social radicalism drove New England merchants and southern planters" to join middle-state delegates in the quest for political centralization.[74] The sound money finance system was then put in place with the enactment of Hamilton's fiscal program.

In addition to Ferguson's reconstruction, Lynd, Main, Hall, and Wood have modified and refurbished other dimensions of Beard's thesis. Main and Lynd respond to the charge that the formation and ratification of the Constitution must have been a "struggle between competing groups within the aristocracy" rather than a broader instance of class antagonism or social conflict.[75] As previously noted, Thomas and McDonald conclude that the ratification contest was a struggle between members of the aristocracy because many anti-Federalist leaders were from the same social class and had similar economic holdings as their Federalist counterparts. Main and Lynd both concede that anti-Federalist leaders were seldom ordinary yeoman. "Popular parties," Main observes, "typically derive their leadership from men of large property, and in nearly every state . . . the Antifederalists were led by men of means."[76] Nevertheless, as Main and Lynd point out, anti-Federalist leaders may have *represented* the genuine yeomanry of the interior without *typifying* those ordinary Americans.[77] The possibility that the constituency of anti-Federalist leaders comprised debtors and ordinary farmers opens the further possibility that there was "undeniable radicalism in much of the

Anti-Federalist electorate" and "profound social antagonism or class conflict surrounding the formation and ratification of the Constitution."[78]

Lynd and, even more visibly and influentially, Wood have tried to establish that even if both Federalist and anti-Federalist leaders were members of the gentry, they were different kinds of aristocrats.[79] The anti-Federalists, these scholars argue, were "new men on the make," "middling gentry," and "nouveau riche" politicians—ambitious, successful, and, in some cases, wealthy individuals, but also socially inferior men who lacked the cultivation, confidence, and ancestry of the older entrenched aristocracy and resented the latter's claims to superiority. Federalist leaders, in contrast, were much more likely to have coupled their wealth and superior ancestry with an elite social standing and a network of connections.[80]

Lynd, Main, and Hall argue that the formation and ratification of the Constitution are best understood as a series of contests over governance that started before 1776 and intensified in the following decade as Americans sought to settle the terms of their Revolution. Even before the advent of political parties, these scholars argue, Americans were divided into two stable factions—a popular faction that represented the interests of ordinary debtors and yeoman, and a conservative faction made up of elite leaders and their dependents. These parties fought within the states over such issues as whether and how to fund the Revolutionary debt; the confiscation and sale of loyalist lands; and the propriety of paper money, judicial enforcement of the sanctity of contracts, and laws suspending the debt. Most important, these scholars found that the economic groups and, "to a striking extent," the leaders that opposed the Constitution were the same ones who had earlier fought for paper money and debtor relief legislation and against the funding of the Revolutionary debt.[81]

Finally, Main and Hall provide substantial empirical support for the argument that state legislators who favored generous funding of the state and national debt, judicially enforced protection for creditors, and eventually the Constitution generally represented commercial coastal cities, while legislators who opposed these measures often came from the interior. Hall, for example, uses an elaborate system to place Massachusetts towns along a commercial-cosmopolitan continuum and divide them into three groups. Group A towns contained most of the commercial wealth, dominated the state's social and institutional activities, and included the greatest denominational diversity. These towns, according to Hall, were political and commercial centers with the most newspapers, lawyers, and courts. Group B towns had substantial agricultural development and some institutional and social connections with other communities. Group C towns were isolated and rural. Hall found that delegates who supported the Constitution were most likely to be representatives of group A towns or those group B towns that were interwoven with the interests of group A towns. He also concludes that "the split between the most and least commercial-cosmopolitan interest" was "the central feature of Massachusetts politics between 1780 and 1788."[82]

In general, the interpretations of Ferguson, Lynd, Main, Wood, and Hall have broad parallels to Beard's thesis and represent targeted responses to criticisms raised against class and social conflict interpretations. Each of these scholars, however, significantly modifies Beard's thesis, rejects any crude monolithic or deterministic interpretation of the Framers' motives, and follows Beard's critics in dropping or at least suggesting the limitations of Beard's personalty versus realty categories of analysis. Lynd, Main, and (implicitly at least) Hall also provide a modified class interpretation of the ratification of the Constitution even as they stress that "the overall significance of class is greatly reduced by the heavy majorities [in favor of the Constitution] in the towns, several states, and certain geographical areas."[83]

Rational Choice and the Rebirth of the Economic Interpretation

The interpretations of McDonald, Lynd, Main, Hall, and Ferguson mark the culmination of the postwar struggle with Beard's thesis. During these years, doubts were raised about the viability of Beard's thesis, the economic interpretation was refined into alternative perspectives, and the role of economic interests in the formation and ratification of the Constitution was left in a state of ambiguity that has plagued it ever since. As the postwar debate over Beard's thesis faded, however, a new approach to the study of politics—"rational choice" or "public choice" theory—was developed that has served as the foundation for the recrudescence of the economic interpretation.

At its core, rational choice or public choice theory involves the application of assumptions from classical economics to the behavior of political actors and institutions. The most important and controversial of these assumptions is that individuals strategically maximize their interests. Much as the private, market decisions of consumers and business owners are motivated by their desire to maximize their purchases and profits, the public choices of political actors—whether they are elected officials, bureaucrats, the framers of a constitution, or even ordinary citizens—are, according to rational choice theorists, also the result of strategic calculations that weigh costs and benefits. More broadly, the proponents of rational choice theory—a group that includes many political scientists, economists, and economic historians—are interested in explaining collective outcomes such as public policies, political practices, and constitutional frameworks as products of the actions of self-maximizing individuals. Rational choice theory has also been directed at understanding how different incentives and constraints affect the decision making of self-interested political actors.[84]

In particular, two major studies merit consideration in any assessment of the contributions and limitations of rational choice theorists to the economic interpretation of the Constitution. The first of these—Jillson's *Constitution Making: Conflict and Consensus in the Federal Convention of 1787*—examines the dynamics of the Constitutional Convention and addresses a perennial question: were delegates motivated by material interests, as Beard's thesis suggests, or by political principles, as other scholars have argued?[85] After analyzing all 569 recorded roll-call votes at the convention, Jillson identifies four coalition realignments (when one or more state delegations changed alliances) separating five periods of stable voting coalitions among the states.

Most important, according to Jillson, is that these patterns of stability and realignment empirically establish a distinction between "operational" levels of decision making, in which the delegates debated "distributional questions" and made direct reference to their political, economic, and social characteristics and the interests of their states and regions, and "higher-level" or constitutional questions. Jillson found that, when they were considering constitutional questions, delegates' decisions were based on their "general assumptions concerning the interplay among human nature, political institutions, and the good society," which in turn were heavily influenced by regionally based variations in the republican culture. Even on constitutional questions, however, the delegates did not adopt principles because they were able to transcend their own interests. In fact, delegates "were unlikely to see clearly what difference choices concerning such broad structural questions would make to them as individuals, or to their states and regions. Therefore, the constitution makers *had no alternative* but to base their decisions on impressions regarding the more diffuse and general interests of the community."[86]

If Jillson's account contains a submerged sympathy for Beard's understanding of motivation, it nevertheless has an ambiguous relationship with Beard's broader claims. The most fundamental difference is that Jillson analyzes the influence of interests and principles on the coalition patterns of *state* delegations, not the *personal* economic interests of the delegates. Furthermore, whereas Beard argues that economic forces are "primordial or fundamental," Jillson provides empirical verification that principles influenced voting patterns at the convention and argues that a "dynamic relationship of mutual interdependence existed—and, in fact, had to exist—between philosophical and material influences in the Convention."[87] Finally,

Jillson's work challenges the contention that the Constitution was an economic document in the sense that its purpose was to protect and promote only the economic interests of those who drafted it. Instead, Jillson portrays the Constitution as the product of a classic pluralist dynamic in which the delegates represented a wide range of economic interests—personal, social, state, and regional—and those interests formed the basis of conflicts and shifting coalitions. Thus, if the Constitution was intended as an economic document, it was an economic document that reflected not any one group's interests but rather the compromises among many.

Most recently, in his important work *To Form a More Perfect Union*, Robert McGuire has set forth a comprehensive new economic interpretation of the formation and ratification of the Constitution grounded in rational choice theory, including the propositions that individuals (here, the Framers and ratifiers) are self-interested, self-maximizing agents and thus should be the unit of study.[88] He then develops formal models to predict their behavior and applies advanced quantitative and statistical techniques—developed after the flourish of midcentury scholarship that toppled Beard—to the data collected primarily by McDonald. These advanced statistical techniques—especially logistical regression—allow McGuire to measure the relative impact of discrete economic interests on the Framers' and ratifiers' behavior while holding the influence of other interests constant. Previous studies asked how many Framers or ratifiers with a particular interest—slaves or public securities, for example—voted for the Constitution or for a provision at the Philadelphia convention that strengthened the powers of the national government. But, as McGuire notes, it is possible that a group of individuals favored the Constitution not because of the shared interest used to identify them but because of a constellation of other interests. Slaveholders as a group, for example, might have favored the Constitution, but owning slaves might actually have made delegates less likely to support nationalistic measures at the convention or to vote in favor of the Constitution.

McGuire's "new" economic interpretation offers several challenges to existing scholarship. As previously noted, in *We the People,* McDonald analyzes the delegates' votes on sixteen fundamental issues at the Constitutional Convention and concludes that "anyone wishing to rewrite the history of those proceedings largely or exclusively in terms of the economic interests represented there would find the facts to be insurmountable obstacles."[89] Analyzing these same sixteen issues, McGuire reaches a fundamentally different conclusion. "When specific issues arose at the Philadelphia convention that had a direct impact on important economic interests of the framers," he writes, "their economic interests even narrowly defined, significantly influenced the specific design of the Constitution, and the magnitudes of the influences were often quite large. The framers' choices of specific issues were influenced by the types of economic interests likely to account for a substantial portion of their overall wealth or represent their primary livelihood."[90]

This conclusion is supported in a number of ways. First, McGuire found several patterns of unanimous voting on specific issues at the convention. Merchants, he observes, voted unanimously against a provision that would have required a two-thirds vote by the national legislature to regulate commerce; the two noncommercial farmers at the convention voted unanimously against the proposal for an absolute veto of state laws; and delegates with private security holdings (men who owned bank stock or made loans) voted unanimously in favor of the prohibition against state paper money.[91]

Second, McGuire found statistically significant relationships between economic interests and voting on specific issues. For example, delegates who were creditors, including private and public security holders (especially those who owned portions of the Revolutionary War debt), were much more likely to vote to prohibit state paper money than were those who were not creditors. He also found that delegates representing states with heavy concentrations of slaves were more likely to vote for a provision requiring a two-thirds majority in the national legislature to enact any regulation of commerce between the United States and foreign nations or among the states. More decisively, he found that merchants and delegates representing commercial areas that were least distant from navigable water were much more likely than delegates from more isolated, interior regions to favor strengthening the powers of the national government at the expense of the states.[92]

McGuire's study advances even stronger conclusions about the impact of economic interests on the decision to vote for or against ratification. In this case he develops several sets of economic characteristics of the delegates to the state ratifying conventions and their constituents. One set includes the delegates to all the state ratifying conventions; another considers the votes among delegates within each ratifying convention separately; and still another considers the state conventions in the order that they ratified the Constitution to account for the momentum of the ratification process. There are significant differences in McGuire's findings when each state is considered separately, supporting McDonald's argument for the peculiarity of each contest for ratification. Nevertheless, unlike McDonald, McGuire found that support for the Constitution consistently came from merchants, delegates with private and public security holdings (especially those with security holdings over $1,000), delegates who owned western land for speculation, and (most decisively) delegates who represented coastal commercial regions.

Conversely, he found that delegates owning slaves (especially those with relatively large portions of their total assets in the form of slaves), those in debt, and those who represented isolated, frontier areas were much less likely to vote for ratification than were other delegates.[93]

In general, then, McGuire's economic interpretation challenges McDonald's critique of Beard's thesis, but rather than returning to Beard it reinforces Main's thesis that support for the Constitution came from delegates representing coastal commercial regions, and opposition to it came from the interior. Specifically, in contrast to Beard, McGuire concludes that the relationship between holding public securities and supporting the Constitution was not uniform and was rarely one of the strongest economic factors.[94] The most interesting of McGuire's empirical findings, however, and perhaps his most distinctive contribution to the existing literature concerns slavery and the effect of officeholding on support for or opposition to the Constitution. Beard and numerous other scholars postulated that slaveholders favored the Constitution because they wanted a national government that was strong enough to prevent slave uprisings and to secure their property in slaves. McGuire, however, found that "although a majority of slaveholders and a majority of the delegates from slave areas may have in fact voted for issues strengthening the central government or for ratification, the actual influence of slaveholding or of representing slave areas per se was to significantly decrease a delegate's likelihood of voting for strengthening the central government or for ratification." Similarly, almost all previous analysts had contended that being a state officeholder prior to the convention made it more likely that an individual would oppose the Constitution. McGuire, however, found no correlation between prior officeholding and support for or opposition to the Constitution.[95]

Conclusions and Inconclusiveness: What Empirical Analysis Has and Has Not Established

Where does this century of empirical analysis, claim and counterclaim, refutation and reformulation, leave us? In assessing whether the members of the Constitutional Convention were a consolidated economic group, it is first important to clarify what we mean. Beard claimed that the delegates at Philadelphia were a consolidated group of *personalty* holders, but his critics refuted this specific claim by establishing that the delegates had substantial holdings in both personalty and realty and that they represented diverse geographic areas and economic interests. Nevertheless, contrary to what Brown and McDonald suggest, the rejection of the claim that the Framers were a consolidated group of personalty holders does not refute the conclusion that they were, in other ways, members of a consolidated economic group. Instead, as Richard Brown puts it, these men "composed the uppermost layer of the Revolutionary leadership."[96] They were substantially better educated, more cosmopolitan, and wealthier than the average members of their society.[97] In addition, a disproportionate number were lawyers and professional politicians. Conversely, even though American society consisted largely of modest farmers, only two delegates could be so classified.[98] Thus, the Framers' unity—the sense in which they were members of a consolidated economic group—was based on their wealth in general and their elite occupations, education, and ancestry, not their personalty holdings.

More significantly, Beard's critics have been unable to establish that the delegates at Philadelphia represented each of the major interests in American society. McDonald tried to support this claim by identifying the different regions and political factions within each of the states and then contending that most of them were represented. Nevertheless, as both Benson and Main have shown, McDonald's conclusions are suspect because he subdivided the eastern, coastal areas of the states into many sections. This allowed him to conclude that most of the sections of a state were represented even though almost none of the delegates came from the interior. His analysis also included the nineteen delegates who were appointed to the Philadelphia convention but refused to serve, and he counted individuals as representatives of areas where they were born but no longer lived. Cumulatively, these interpretive maneuvers mask the fact that virtually all the delegates to the convention were from coastal regions and cities, that no radical leaders were present at Philadelphia, and thus that neither radical ideas nor debtor–small farmer interests were represented at the convention.[99]

If scholarship on the economic interpretation has shown that the convention delegates were members of a consolidated economic group in these narrow senses, it has provided only limited evidence that the delegates' voting patterns can be explained by their economic interests or that the Constitution they wrote reflected the economic interests they held or represented. To date, only the studies of Jillson, McDonald, and McGuire even begin to explore the delegates' voting patterns on the key clauses that affected their personal economic interests or those of the states and constituencies they represented.

Of these studies, Jillson's is both the most decisive and the most limited. Jillson provides decisive empirical verification that state interests shaped the voting alignments at Philadelphia, particularly the apportionment of representatives. He also establishes that the final stage of the convention was governed by a conflict between small northern states and large southern states over the election of the executive and the proper powers of the Senate in terms of foreign relations and appointments. This conflict, Jillson points out, was won by the small states and helped shape the moderate federal character of the Constitution. Jillson's study, however, does not measure the relationship between the personal economic interests of the delegates and the dynamic voting coalitions at the convention or the relationship between these interests and support for or opposition to specific clauses of the Constitution.[100]

In contrast, both McDonald and McGuire try to determine the votes of individual delegates on specific issues and thus test empirically the influence of delegates' personal economic interests on voting patterns at the convention and the ultimate character of the Constitution. In this endeavor, McGuire's analysis transcends and corrects McDonald's. Whereas McDonald argues that there was little discernible relationship between the delegates' economic interests and their votes at the convention, McGuire's analysis is based on logistical regression and establishes that at least one of the personal economic interests of the delegates was statistically significant for each of the sixteen votes tested.[101] Among the most illuminating of these findings, McGuire establishes that merchants voted unanimously against a clause requiring a two-thirds vote in the national legislature to enact laws regulating commerce and that private security holders voted unanimously to prohibit the states from issuing bills of credit and paper money.

McGuire's most important claim, however, is his proposition that slaveholding made a delegate much less likely to favor a universal negative on state laws and almost certain to favor prohibition of export tariffs by the national government.[102] This conclusion is plausible because most slaveholders could be expected to fear that the national government would use a universal negative of state laws to limit or even prohibit slavery, and because most slaveholders earned their living from exports of rice and tobacco and could be expected to oppose export taxes.[103] McGuire also provides strong evidence that the closer delegates lived to commercial, coastal regions, the more likely they were to favor measures strengthening the national government; the closer they lived to the interior, the more likely they were to oppose such measures.[104]

Although McGuire's results are suggestive, they are far from decisive. What is now needed is a comprehensive study of the relationship between the economic interests of the delegates and their votes at the convention. As previously mentioned, there were 569 recorded roll-call votes at the Constitutional Convention. By McGuire's own estimate, at least four or five dozen of these votes, in addition to the sixteen that he and McDonald analyzed, were important.[105] A study testing the effect of delegates' economic interests on their votes on these other important issues would be arduous to conduct, because the only way to determine the votes of specific delegates is through an indirect process of elimination. This requires examining the speeches and motions made at the convention, using Madison's notes to the few votes that he recorded, analyzing the personal correspondence and diaries of the Framers to estimate their positions on the issues, and then engaging in a process of elimination that compares the state delegation's vote to the positions of delegates whose votes can be confidently determined.[106]

Although the results of such a process would be imperfect, they would open the door for scholars to test the relationship between the delegates' economic interests and other characteristics and their votes on specific clauses that gave positive powers to the national government, restricted the states, and distanced the government from control by popular majorities—the three areas that Beard used to support his interpretation of the original Constitution as an economic document. A study that tested the relationship between the delegates' economic interests and their support for constitutional provisions giving the people control over public officials would be particularly important, because this dimension of the economic interpretation has never been subjected to empirical analysis and would test Beard's contentious proposition that the principal Framers of the Constitution were opponents of democracy.

When we turn from the Constitutional Convention to the ratification of the Constitution, we find even larger—and perhaps permanent—gaps in existing studies. The questions that can best be addressed, given the data that have been gathered so far, concern the economic and social characteristics of the leadership of the anti-Federalists and the Federalists. This research establishes the aristocratic character of the Federalist leadership. As Main has shown, compared with those who opposed the Constitution, Federalist delegates to the state ratifying conventions included more men who had attained the title of "Esquire," held high military rank, were college educated, held occupations with superior prestige (such as merchants, lawyers, judges, shipowners, and ship captains), held high political office, and were wealthy.[107]

Nevertheless, scholars in this debate have observed that some anti-Federalist leaders were also members of the gentry and among the wealthiest citizens in the young republic, and we still do not have an adequate study of the proposition that Federalist and anti-Federalist leaders were different kinds of aristocrats. Instead, the claims by Lynd and Wood—that the "real" anti-Federalists were ambitious, self-made men who resented their inferior social status and supported populist measures during the mid-1780s—rest on the analysis of only a limited number of individuals and are supported primarily by the rhetorical characterizations such leaders made of themselves and one another, not a systematic empirical study of economic interests or social status. At this point in this debate, then, we need a study that identifies and refines the distinctions among varieties of aristocrats in eighteenth-century American society, especially those related to economic holdings, family name, and social status; sets forth a kind of collective biography of Federalist and anti-Federalist leadership; and, in particular, attempts to explain the diversity within the anti-Federalist leadership.[108]

The most glaring hole in scholarship on the economic interpretation, however, concerns whether the ratification of the Constitution evinced a social or class struggle. Indeed, what Benson said almost half a century ago still holds true today: no study has been conducted that clearly illuminates the role of economic interests in the ratification of the Constitution and establishes whether the ratification struggle was a deep-seated conflict between opposing classes.[109] The best type of study would be based directly on individual data about the personal and economic characteristics of at least a random sample of the approximately 160,000 individuals who participated in the constitution-making process by voting for delegates to the ratification conventions.[110] To conduct such a study, however, we would need individual data about who voted in those elections, how they voted, and their personal and economic interests. Armed with such information, a scholar could use logistical regression to weigh the various factors that divided individuals who voted for Federalist candidates from those who voted for anti-Federalist candidates. Unfortunately, these voters were more obscure than even the most obscure delegates to the state conventions, and McDonald was unable to find information on a significant number of the delegates.[111] Furthermore, voting records for the election of delegates to the state ratifying conventions are sparse, they seldom exist for anything below county level, and they do not tell how particular individuals voted.

As the preceding literature review suggests, two different types of empirical studies of the ratification struggle have been conducted in the absence of such data. Both have significant limitations. Studies such as those by McDonald and McGuire attempt to provide an economic interpretation of the ratification of the Constitution by analyzing data about the personal and economic characteristics of the approximately 1,648 delegates to the state ratifying conventions. Proponents of these studies argue that data about individual voters are unnecessary to establish at least some version of an economic interpretation, because these delegates constituted a substantial portion of the decision makers in the early republic, few delegates were bound by instructions when they voted for or against the Constitution, and it was the delegates' votes (not those of their constituents) that gave the Constitution its sovereign authority.

At least three closely related problems, however, arise from studies that attempt to interpret the entire ratification process through an examination of only participants in the state ratifying conventions. First, as previously mentioned, the delegates to the state conventions were not a representative sample or microcosm of all the participants in the ratification struggle. We cannot assume that the leaders of the Federalists and the anti-Federalists typified those they represented. Second, the legitimacy of the Constitution rests on the belief that its ratification was a broad public act, not the act of only 1,648 men. Third, one of Beard's central and most disputed claims is that the ratification struggle was a deep-seated conflict between holders of different forms of property. Studies that analyze only the delegates to the ratifying conventions do little to illuminate the popular sources of Federalism and anti-Federalism or the interactions between elites and their constituents.

As we have seen, a second type of study—exemplified by the scholarship of Lynd, Main, and Hall—relies on indirect means and aggregate statistics to characterize the constituencies of Federalist and anti-Federalist leaders. These scholars examine the political rhetoric surrounding ratification, searching for signs of social antagonism and strain in the popular appeals made by the two factions' leaders. They also examine the alignments of different social groups on particularly disruptive political conflicts and issues— such as the confiscation of loyalists' lands and debtor relief legislation—that preceded the formation of the Constitution. They then try to establish the continuity between support for these popular measures and opposition to the Constitution. Finally, these scholars examine the aggregate economic characteristics of particular counties or regions and then suggest that the positions of ordinary Americans in these regions can be inferred from the voting patterns of the delegates they sent to the ratifying conventions. For example, if a region with a majority of small farmers elected a delegate who voted against the Constitution, the implication would be that small farmers from that region opposed the Constitution.

These studies by Lynd, Main, and Hall are based on prodigious research and display their authors' tactile knowledge of the economic interests and politics within the states. Nevertheless, scholars of the Founding should realize that these studies also rest on problematic methodologies and inferences. In particular, when neo-Progressive scholars and their sympathizers turn to political rhetoric as evidence, this introduces the same impressionistic interpretations that they had previously dismissed. This methodology also requires some means of distinguishing the moments of speech that expose genuine class and social tensions from those in which the participants are merely using rhetoric disingenuously. Nevertheless, no guidelines are set forth. Without begging the question, how can we justify the conclusion that an anti-Federalist leader who draws attention to class divisions is exposing a reality about the social structure, but a Federalist who says that he is speaking for the common good is rhetorically masking his own interests?[112]

Furthermore, efforts to prove continuity between support for radical fiscal policies during the mid-1780s and opposition to the Constitution are problematic because only the positions of particular leaders can be established. We cannot say that leaders reflected the views of their constituents based only on knowledge of the leaders' votes. What these studies really establish, then, is continuity among leaders, not their constituents or particular interest groups, in terms of support for these fiscal measures and opposition to the Constitution.[113]

This same problem arises in inferring the attitudes of different social groups and occupations based on the positions of the delegates. Although many of the delegates to the state ratifying conventions may have been elected because their positions on the Constitution faithfully reflected their constituents' views, others may have been elected because of their status as gentlemen, leaving them free to make up their own minds about the Constitution. Furthermore, even if it could be established that delegates' votes reflected the views of their constituents, it has not been established that the constituents' economic interests were the factors that led them to support either Federalist or anti-Federalist delegates. Their votes may have been affected by their age, religion, Revolutionary War experience, or some combination of these and other factors.

This discussion highlights the difficulty scholars face in attaining direct evidence and evaluating the limited evidence that is available, and therefore the difficulty of determining whether class or social conflict accompanied the ratification struggle. Let us return to basic facts: In 1788, approximately 160,000 men voted for delegates to attend state ratifying conventions to approve or reject the proposed constitution. There was no national referendum, and the vote for a particular delegate no doubt meant different things to different voters. It is likely that many voted for the candidate who was most closely aligned with their position on the Constitution. Others may have had no position at all on the Constitution. Still others may have been so dependent for their livelihoods that they could not differentiate their interests from their landlords'.

Most broadly, holes in existing research and the absence of historical data on the social divisions within the electorate make it difficult to choose between pluralist and Progressive accounts of the framing and ratification of the Constitution or to construct some better alternative. Certainly, McDonald's scholarship has established the inadequacies of Beard's personalty versus realty categories of analysis, highlighted the complexity of the Framers' and ratifiers' motives and experiences, and established the peculiarity of each state ratifying contest.[114] McDonald has also shown that whatever social or class conflicts existed in some states, these conflicts were suppressed by broader interests in security, commerce, and revenue that the Constitution promised.

Nevertheless, several important dimensions of a modified neo-Progressive interpretation remain strong in the face of limited historical data and a century of critical analysis. First, Beard's proposition that the movement for the Constitution was begun by an elite group of men who were disproportionately wealthy, urban, and commercial in their interests, and that they were responding to threats to their economic interests from within the states, is perhaps the strongest dimension of his thesis—especially as this contention has been reformulated by Ferguson and given empirical support by studies pointing out that the members of the convention were a consolidated group. Indeed, this part of Beard's interpretation has been so readily integrated within Founding scholarship that it is no longer a source of controversy.

Second, although studies of the voting patterns at the Constitutional Convention are limited, they suggest that the Constitution can be thought of as an economic document, at least in the sense that it was meant to abolish the currency system of finance that had been adopted by many states during the mid-1780s and to promote and protect commercial interests.

Third, empirical research supports the Progressive and neo-Progressive propositions that support for the Constitution came disproportionately from delegates who represented commercial coastal regions and that the opposition was led by delegates representing the interior. Indeed, there has been solid continuity over the past century for this geographic interpretation of ratification, which contains a modified class interpretation.[115]

Although other aspects of Beard's thesis have been demolished, these points (to borrow Hofstadter's famous metaphor about Beard's legacy) constitute the rooms within the "imposing ruin" of Beard's scholarly edifice that, with some modification, might still be "inhabitable."[116]

2

Democracy and the Founders' Constitution
Toward a Balanced Assessment

The Contours of the Continuing Confrontation

"When this plan [the Constitution] goes forth it will be attacked by the popular leaders. Aristocracy will be the watchword; the Shibboleth among its adversaries."[1] John Dickinson's oft-quoted words during the final stages of the Constitutional Convention have proved to be remarkably prescient. When the Constitution was presented for ratification in the fall of 1787, the shibboleth among its adversaries—the watchword marking the unity of the anti-Federalists—was that the Constitution would establish an aristocracy and was thus a repudiation of the principles of the American Revolution. The Federalists countered that the Constitution was "strictly republican" or "wholly popular" and a fulfillment of Revolutionary aims.[2] Thus began a debate that has taken many forms and resonated throughout American history, eventually becoming one of the most important scholarly confrontations in American historiography. Today, no serious student of the American Founding or American politics in general can avoid this debate.[3]

If the question "how democratic is the Constitution?" has been fundamental since the ratification debate, the terms on which it has been addressed have transformed subtly but substantially over the last half century as critics and defenders of the Framers and the Constitution have shifted among a variety of criteria for analyzing the Framers' Constitution. From the early twentieth century until the end of the cold war, scholars focused primarily on the relationship between the people and their representatives established in the Framers' Constitution and the extent to which property qualifications in the states disenfranchised white men. In this stage in the debate, Progressive, neo-Progressive, and New Left scholars charged that the Framers had "no faith in the wisdom or political capacity of the people" and feared violations of property rights by popular majorities.[4] The Framers, according to this account, led a movement to draft and secure the ratification of a new constitution that featured a cumbersome system of checks and balances to limit the power of popular majorities and distance the people from their government. Representation, the extended republic, the system of separation of powers, multiple branches of government, public officials elected from different constituencies and serving staggered terms, a difficult amendment process, and especially judicial review were, according to the Progressives, efforts to secure the "disintegration of positive action" by the citizenry.[5] Furthermore, these scholars observed that the Constitution's suffrage requirements for electors of members of the House of Representatives were the same as for electors to the state legislatures. The stiff property requirements in the states at the time thus resulted in the creation of a mass of disenfranchised men.[6]

Martin Diamond and his sympathizers countered these claims by arguing that the Framers of the Constitution established a "decent even though democratic" system based on the expectation that moderate and just public policies would emerge from heterogeneous and temporary coalitions among interest groups. Moreover, the system of checks and balances denounced by the Progressives actually established the Framers as wise partisans of democracy who recognized its dangers and limitations rather than foolish ones who believed that every impulse of the majority, no matter how ephemeral or irrational, should be immediately reflected in the political system.[7] These scholars also researched the extent of disenfranchisement in the states caused by property requirements and concluded that most white men were able to meet these qualifications, which were seldom enforced in the first place.[8]

In the mid-1980s, however, this debate entered a new phase in which scholars focused less on whether the constitutional system was immediately responsive to the will of the people or excluded substantial numbers of white men from political participation (although these have remained important questions) and more on the exclusion of women, African Americans, and Native Americans from the political process. This transformation occurred within the context of a broad turn in historical writing toward the social history of disinherited groups, renewed focus on the issues of slavery and women's rights, and scholars' tendency to judge historical actors against contemporary multicultural and egalitarian standards. Scholars writing from this perspective observed that the Constitution did not over-turn provisions in the state constitutions that denied women and African Americans the right to vote. They often characterized the Constitution as a pro-slavery (and thus necessarily undemocratic) document and maintained that it treated Native Americans as an ill-defined class whose members could be part of the American political community but were often denied the essential rights of citizenship.[9]

For their part, defenders of the Founders and exponents of the democratic interpretation of the Constitution responded to these charges by observing that the Constitution does not formally exclude women and African Americans from voting; rather, it leaves suffrage requirements to the states and speaks in universalistic language of the rights of persons, citizens, electors, or the people.[10] These scholars also emphasize that the principle of natural rights on which the Revolution and the Constitution were based "imparted into public life a tendency toward democratic inclusiveness." Thus, although the Founders themselves did not eradicate traditional racist and sexist institutions and practices, the principles they adopted "had a potency and expansibility, a developmental dimension that tended to broaden the base of government and extend the sphere of personal liberty and civil rights." The decision not to protect the political rights of women, blacks, and Native Americans, one scholar suggests, was based on "prudential" considerations. Nevertheless, "a good case can be made that the historic reforms of antislavery, the emancipation of women, and the democratization of political, social, and economic life reflected purposes and aspirations intrinsic to the framers' liberal constitutionalism."[11]

More recently, a small group of scholars has judged the Constitution against a third standard, perhaps catalyzing the debate into a third phase. Unlike Progressive or multicultural critics of the Constitution, these scholars do not stress the Constitution's famous series of filtering or restraining devices or the Framers' failure to guarantee participation for everyone regardless of property holdings, race, or gender.[12] Instead, these scholars argue that the Constitution was originally undemocratic because some of its most important features—especially equal representation of the states in the Senate and the three-fifths clause—fundamentally violate the principle of political equality.[13]

Equal representation in the Senate, these scholars observe, provides each state with an equal number of senators regardless of its population and then incorporates this "small state advantage" in the amendment process and in the selection of the president by the Electoral College.[14] Equal representation means that individuals living in states with small populations enjoy disproportionate weight or influence in the Senate and in presidential elections when judged against a population-based standard.[15] This greater political power bestowed on small states, these scholars contend, is unjustified on principles of equity and majority rule and gives small states the advantage in forming public policy and blocking legislation and constitutional reforms. Furthermore, it is virtually impossible to change the policy of equal representation in the Senate because constitutional amendments must be ratified by legislatures or conventions in three-fourths of the states, and it is unlikely that the necessary number of small states would agree to an amendment that diminished their influence in the Senate. Equal representation in the Senate is also unalterable because the Constitution stipulates that "no state, without its consent, shall be deprived of its equal suffrage in the Senate."[16] This last provision seemingly precludes even a constitutional amendment abolishing equal representation unless every state accepted it.

In addition to the "Senate bonus," several scholars have pointed to the "slave bonus" ensured by the three-fifths clause as a principal source of inequality in the original Constitution.[17] Before the Civil War amendments, this provision ensured that, for purposes of representation and taxation, slaves were counted as three-fifths of a person. The "federal ratio," in turn, resulted in slave states being allotted one-third more seats in the House of Representatives and an equal number of additional votes in the Electoral College than was warranted by their free populations.[18] This provision, these scholars argue, helped ensure that a disproportionate number of slaveholders or individuals sympathetic to slavery were elected to the presidency and appointed to the Supreme Court and held leadership posts in Congress. It also gave slaveholding states political leverage to block legislation and prevent the implementation of acts that would have halted the spread of slavery.[19]

Confronting the Hermeneutic Impasse

Together, the exchanges between defenders of the Constitution, on the one hand, and the Progressives, multiculturalists, and proponents of political equality, on the other hand, constitute one of the most polarized, inflammatory, and stagnant confrontations examined in this book. Indeed, as I establish in chapter 4, participants in the liberalism-republicanism debate have found considerable middle ground during the last decade, and the dialectics of the other confrontations have resulted in, or at least have the possibility of producing, a synthetic interpretation with broad appeal. In contrast, the scholars in this debate show little inclination toward consensus.

There are reasons why debates become polarized and debaters fall into familiar and stale patterns of argumentation. In this case, three closely related issues are prominent. The broadest and most important reason is also the most obvious: there is simply no common definition or standard of democracy against which the original design of the American political system can be measured. As I pointed out in the introduction, the contested character of democracy obscures the lines of disagreement between scholars in this debate. Actually, the Progressives and their heirs and Diamond and his do not interpret the original constitutional system as differently as we might expect. Although there are threads of disagreement (primarily over the purpose and effect of the separation of powers), there is also substantial agreement that the American political system was originally designed to constrain, temper, and refine popular majorities.[20] Instead, the primary source of disagreement between these two groups of scholars is that their judgments about the original design are informed by fundamentally different understandings of the meaning and purpose of democracy.[21]

Generally speaking, scholars who charge that the original Constitution was undemocratic hold "strong," "participatory," or "egalitarian" conceptions of democracy; echo the anti-Federalist critique of the Framers' Constitution; and judge the original design against either the state governments that existed at the time of ratification or some ideal or contemporary conception of democracy. To many of these scholars, any conception of democracy worth the name must readily translate public views into public policies, hold representatives strictly accountable, and involve the participation of all citizens in the formation of public policies. These scholars therefore reject the idea that the Federalists held a meaningful conception of popular sovereignty; they find numerous flaws with the original design and commonly advocate constitutional reform or even the adoption of a new constitutional system.[22]

In contrast, those who defend the Federalists' system of constitutionalism as democratic almost uniformly have minimal or "thin" conceptions of democracy; fall back on arguments used by the Framers to justify, for example, longer terms of office, a moderate number of representatives, and a less responsive political system; and defend the Framers conception of popular sovereignty.[23] They also usually resist judging the system against what they consider to be anachronistic, enthusiastic, or utopian standards of democracy, and they prefer to think of the development of democracy in the United States, as Richard Hofstadter once put it, as an "unfolding historical reality that must be understood at each point in its temporal context."[24] To these scholars, democracy is synonymous with popular sovereignty or the ultimate control of the people over their representatives, public policies, and the Constitution. These scholars often contend that a truly democratic political system must protect individual and minority rights and that at times it can do so only by restraining the wishes of the majority. Thus, they readily accept constitutional devices that discipline, transform, or even block majority rule as being consistent with democracy. They also suggest that such a system deserves profound respect, defend its cumbersome and complex features (including the amendment process and the Electoral College), and suggest that the Constitution should not be hastily reformed.

The second reason why this debate is so divisive also stems from the lack of a common definition or standard: because there is no agreement about what democracy is, there can be no agreement about what constitutional procedures or conceptions of representation are necessary to create a democratic political system.[25] Even scholars making good-faith efforts to determine whether the original constitutional design is democratic must make a series of judgments that necessarily yield contentious answers because they spring from different standards of democracy. How many representatives are necessary to create a democratic regime? What term of office for elected officials is consistent with democracy? Is an "agency" or a "trustee" conception of representation more democratic? Do term limitations (or what the Founders called "rotation in office") make a regime more democratic, because they ensure that a greater number of people will serve in public office, or do they make it less democratic, because they limit people's choices?[26] Is it democratic to bind representatives to the views of their local constituents, because this creates strong links of responsiveness and accountability, or does this merely create links between representatives and particular *segments* of society and prevent the kinds of deliberations necessary to create meaningful democracy? Does the Framers' willingness to draft a constitution with few barriers to voting for white men signal their partisanship for democracy? Conversely, were they willing to accept widespread white male suffrage only because they believed that expanded electoral districts would lead ordinary Americans to defer to and elect gentleman elites?[27] Do the original Constitution's protection of slavery and failure to guarantee women equal rights mean that we must reject outright any claim that it was democratic? What is the relationship between the desire to create a strong national government and democracy? In other words, is political centralization inseparably linked with opposition to democracy? None of these questions has a straightforward or indisputable answer, and once again, any answer depends heavily on the standards we adopt prior to our investigations.

A third reason for the divisiveness of this debate is that the term *democracy* has increasingly become the standard against which all forms of government are judged, and the label *democratic* has become increasingly normative and prescriptive. As Norman Barry puts it, over the last century, "the word 'democracy' has acquired remarkably strong emotive overtones. Its use is often as much designed to provoke a favourable attitude towards a political regime as it is to describe particular features of it."[28] What this means in the context of this debate is that there are obvious and important political implications when one contends that the original Constitution was either democratic or undemocratic. The most obvious implication is that those who label the system undemocratic are seen as its critics and reformers, and those who label it democratic are viewed as its defenders and preservers. Indeed, this debate raises the very legitimacy of the Constitution and the political system it created.

The Strategy and Limitations of This Analysis

What can be done at this point to provide a balanced assessment of the character of the original constitutional system? In this chapter, I pursue the following strategy: I divide my analysis into three sections that examine key provisions of the original Constitution and aspects of its design along the democratic dimensions of inclusiveness, responsiveness, and political equality.[29] Using these dimensions of democracy, I then compare the Framers' Constitution to several other constitutional designs and conceptions of democracy, including the Articles of Confederation; the state governments that existed at the time of the Constitutional Convention; the conceptions of democracy envisioned by Thomas Jefferson and James Wilson; the British political systems in 1787; the French constitutions of 1791, 1793, and 1795; and the U.S. Constitution today. I chose the criteria of inclusiveness, responsiveness, and political equality because they are accepted by virtually all participants in the debate as core dimensions of democracy and because they can be readily distinguished from other constitutional values that the Framers obviously hoped to promote, including federalism, impartiality in administration, stability, energy, and the protection of rights.

Such an interpretive strategy does not create a fundamentally different way of conceiving of the question of the Constitution's democratic nature; it does not bring scholars to a common definition or understanding of democracy or diminish the political import of any interpretation. Although any answer to the question unavoidably depends on the standard of democracy we use, this strategy pursues a complex judgment that is informed by a multidimensional understanding of democracy and a multiplicity of comparisons as a prophylactic against a narrow and simplistic evaluation based on an idiosyncratic, one-dimensional, or even unarticulated definition of democracy. It also provides us with a format for evaluating the many contentious judgments that scholars have made—including the evidence they relied on and the reasoning they used—in their assessments of the character of the original Constitution. Finally, this strategy provides conceptual tools that allow us to separate discussions about whether the original Constitution was democratic from discussions about whether it promotes "good" government.

Two final caveats are necessary. First, this chapter addresses to what extent the original Constitution was democratic; it does not address how democratic American society or political culture was in 1787. My focus is therefore on the constitutional provisions that governed political participation and the institutional or structural features that established the government's relationship to the governed and affected political equality. Conversely, I do not address questions about the development of a democratic political culture in the United States, even though much of what we now call democracy is a function of political culture and civil society, and much recent research on the Founding has highlighted extraconstitutional modes of political participation, such as public opinion as a form of political participation, political parties as agents of collective action and means of institutionalizing legitimate opposition, and the informal political power that women exercised in the early republic as mothers and participants in "parlor politics."[30] However important these topics are, they are not my concern here.

Second, although this chapter necessarily contains several specific comments about the original Constitution and slavery, I do not set forth a broad interpretation of whether the original Constitution was a pro-slavery document, as would no doubt be required to satisfy some neo-Progressive and multicultural critics of the Constitution. I am, however, sympathetic to their contention that the protection of slavery by the Framers' Constitution suggests that it was undemocratic. The most egregious violation of liberty in the United States in 1787 was the enslavement of hundreds of thousands of African Americans who were not merely excluded from political participation but also denied their most basic liberties. Nevertheless, addressing the question of whether the Constitution was pro- or antislavery in this context would only introduce one massive and complex issue in the context of another. Furthermore, if we do not at least temporarily bracket slavery, we will not get very far in understanding the role of the original Constitution in defining political participation and the complex relationship between the government and the governed envisioned and fostered by it.

The Question of Inclusiveness

Suffrage Requirements

The right to vote is often treated as the most important indicator of the inclusiveness of a political system, and rightly so. On this point, the Founders' Constitution stipulated only that "Electors in each state shall have the Qualifications requisite for Electors to the most numerous branch of the State Legislature."[31] This applied to voting for members of the House of Representatives, the only directly elected branch of the national government under the original Constitution. Moreover, the original Constitution granted rights to "persons," "citizens," "electors," or "the people" collectively. It thus did not *formally* restrict voting based on race, gender, or ethnicity. Some states extended the right of suffrage to women and free blacks without violating the Constitution.[32] Finally, the delegates to the Philadelphia convention rejected property-holding requirements for voting.

The Framers themselves and several contemporary scholars have seized on the broad language of the Constitution and the absence of formal requirements for voting as evidence of its liberality and inclusiveness.[33] In *Federalist* No. 57, James Madison defended the original Constitution against the charge that it would create an aristocracy by asking:

> Who are to be the electors of the Federal Representatives? Not the rich more than the poor; not the learned more than the ignorant; not the haughty heirs of distinguished names, more than the humble sons of obscure and unpropitious fortune. The electors are to be the great body of the people of the United States. They are to be the same who exercise the right in every State of electing the correspondent branch of the Legislature of the State.[34]

Several scholars, however, have argued that such claims are disingenuous and misleading. The Framers' decision to leave suffrage requirements to the states, they argue, reflected their acceptance of the status quo within a class-based, patriarchal, slaveholding society. Charles Beard, for example, argues that the absence of property-holding requirements for voters and candidates for federal office did not reflect the belief that such requirements were "inherently opposed to the genius of American government." Instead, the Framers' rejection of property requirements was premised on, among other factors, the belief that state restrictions then in force would provide protection against the democratic masses.[35] More recently, Rogers Smith has maintained that with regard to women and African Americans, the "salient fact" is that the Constitution "left intact the state constitutions that denied women [and blacks] the franchise and other legal and political privileges."[36]

The historical record of the Framers' intentions in leaving voting qualifications to the states is limited, providing little basis for adjudicating between these opposing positions.[37] The available evidence suggests that the Progressives' contention that the Framers believed that state property qualifications circumscribed the white male electorate is simply mistaken. Actually, most of the comments made at the convention point in the opposite direction—toward a consensus that suffrage in the states was "now exercised by every description of people" and that little could or should be done to reverse that trend.[38] Here, the Framers sensed what later historical investigations have confirmed—namely, that most white men could vote in the states in 1787.[39] Furthermore, it is important to remember that the Framers viewed the state legislatures as hotbeds of excessive democracy, where property rights had been continually violated, not as enclaves where property qualifications circumscribed the electorate and protected property. Indeed, as Jack Rakove has pointed out, it is remarkable that the Framers entrusted the same voters who elected popular leaders to the state legislatures to elect members of the House of Representatives.[40]

Nevertheless, contentions that the Framers purposely used race- and gender-neutral phrases such as "persons" rather than "men" or "white men" because they intended the Constitution to confer rights on individuals, that they limited the exercise of those rights to white men merely for "prudential" reasons, and that they can be credited with future expansions in the political community are equally strained.[41] Scholars who advocate this interpretation stress three related points. First, they read the inclusive—gender- and race-neutral—language of the Constitution as evidence of the Framers' broadest "aspirations" and "purposes." In other words, they read the Framers' intentions abstractly and claim that they purposefully included principles that promoted democratic inclusiveness.[42] Second, these scholars point out that documents such as the Northwest Ordinance and some state constitutions included specific gender and race qualifications for voting. The implication here is that since the Framers wrote specific exclusions into some of the documents they drafted, their decision not to write them into the Constitution must be viewed as a conscious and meaningful act.[43] Third, these scholars emphasize that owing to its race- and gender-neutral language, the Constitution was no obstacle to later efforts to create a more inclusive political community.[44]

This line of interpretation is misleading or false in at least three ways. First, this interpretation derives the Framers' intentions from the abstract language embedded in the Constitution and its silence on race and gender, but it ignores or misrepresents their specific writings and speeches about the political character of women and African Americans. As Jan Lewis has shown, the few clues provided in the debates at the Constitutional Convention establish that the Framers believed that women were members of civil society and should be counted for purposes of representation, but they would also be "non-voting citizens" who would be "virtually" represented through the votes of men. Founders such as James Wilson stressed the importance of civil society and believed that women would help constitute it and be productive members of it; they would have civil rights and important roles in cultivating culture and knowledge in the early republic. Still, these roles did not include voting or holding office.[45] Indeed, when we move beyond the convention debates and consider the more extensive—but still limited—writings of the Founders on the role of women, we find that many of them accepted the arguments from inegalitarian and ascriptive ideologies that were used to exclude women from full political membership in the states. These arguments were based on the Framers' perceptions of the nature and capabilities of women and were not merely prudential claims.[46]

Second, although it is true that the Framers based the conception of rights embedded in the Constitution and the Bill of Rights on the natural rights of mankind, there is no evidence that their commitment to natural rights principles led them to seriously consider guaranteeing voting rights to women and blacks or to believe that these principles would someday become the basis for progressive reforms that expanded the political community. Granting political rights to women was not discussed at the Constitutional Convention or during the ratification process; doing so would have been extraordinarily bold in the context of eighteenth-century America, and it would have been politically impossible to implement even if the Framers had been progressive enough to suggest it. A less shrewd but more historically accurate interpretation that attempts to ascertain the Framers' specific intentions rather than to vindicate them based on the broadest aspirations that can be associated with the language they used suggests that the Framers genuinely accepted the natural rights principles embedded in the Constitution and that the independent logic of these principles points toward inclusiveness. It also suggests, however, that the Founders simply did not accept the proposition that fidelity to these principles required granting full civil and political rights to all groups regardless of race, gender, or ethnicity.[47]

Third, this line of argumentation makes much of the point that women and blacks were not formally excluded from voting by the Constitution, but it dismisses the equally important points that women were formally excluded from voting in all the Revolutionary state governments except for New Jersey's, that the vast number of blacks were enslaved in the early republic and that many of those who were not slaves were formally excluded from voting by state laws, and that the Constitution made suffrage restrictions within the states applicable to federal elections. To be sure, the Framers' use of broad language and the decision to leave suffrage requirements to the states meant that "not one word of the Constitution had to be changed for women [or blacks] to obtain the vote."[48] Nevertheless, it is equally true that not one word in the Founders' Constitution had to be changed to allow the states to retain existing voting restrictions against blacks and women or pass additional ones. The Fifteenth and Nineteenth Amendments to the Constitution were necessary to prevent the states from restricting the suffrage rights of blacks and women.

In short, the position of the original Constitution with regard to voting rights can be grasped in two statements that are often opposed but are both true and should be held in tension. On the one hand, the original Constitution left in place state restrictions that disenfranchised women and free blacks and allowed the states to pass exclusionary policies. It thus failed to guarantee voting rights for a majority of the inhabitants of the United States.[49] On the other hand, the original Constitution set forth no additional formal voting requirements for federal offices. In 1787, those requirements were capable of being met by some free blacks, especially in the North; by single women in New Jersey; and, as the Framers suspected, by most white males. The Framers' Constitution was thus undemocratic by contemporary multicultural standards of inclusiveness, but it established a political class that "was of a proportion that had no precedent in a modern state, constituting for practical purposes the entire white male public."[50]

Qualifications for Office

In contrast to the ambiguity the Framers created by coupling broad constitutional language protecting the rights of persons with the stipulation that suffrage requirements be set by the state constitutions, the original Constitution was clear and—with one important exception—remarkably open and liberal with regard to qualifications for officeholders. In particular, the Constitution required only that representatives be twenty-five years old, citizens of the United States for seven years, and inhabitants of the state (not the district) they hoped to represent "when elected"; senators had to be thirty years old, U.S. citizens for nine years, and inhabitants of the state they hoped to represent "when elected"; and the president had to be thirty-five years old, "a natural born citizen," and a resident of the United States for fourteen years.[51] Remarkably, there were no race or gender qualifications for holding any federal office, and the Constitution set no formal requirements (including age or citizenship) for any federal judge, including Supreme Court justices.[52] These requirements have been interpreted to be exclusive. Neither Congress nor the states, the Supreme Court has determined, can add qualifications, the most likely of which in the eighteenth century would have been property qualifications.[53] Also, national officeholders were paid from the national treasury, thus further establishing their independence from state control and effectively extending the opportunity to hold elective office beyond the leisured class.[54]

Again, Madison and many later scholars have celebrated these provisions as evidence of the egalitarian and open character of the Constitution:

> Who are to be the objects of popular choice? Every citizen whose merit may recommend him to the esteem and confidence of his country. No qualification of wealth, of birth, of religious faith, or of civil profession, is permitted to fetter the judgment or disappoint the inclination of the people.[55]

With one important exception, this assessment is accurate. During the debates at the convention, delegates considered and rejected at least four distinct kinds of qualifications for officeholding in addition to the age and citizenship requirements that were eventually passed: the disqualification of public debtors or persons with unresolved accounts with the United States, residency requirements, and landed property qualifications.[56] They also rejected a provision that would have excluded federal legislators from holding any other federal office for one year after the expiration of their terms.[57] Finally, they did not require any religious tests for officeholders and, in fact, specifically forbade them.[58]

Ultimately, only three kinds of eligibility requirements for congressional and presidential candidates—age, residency requirements, and citizenship stipulations—were included in the original Constitution. Representatives and senators had to be inhabitants of the states from which they were elected at the time of the election, and presidential candidates were required to have resided in the United States for fourteen years prior to their election. These requirements have caused little controversy in the debate over the democratic character of the Constitution. Age stipulations engendered little debate at the Constitutional Convention and have not been a central point of contention among those who criticize the Constitution as undemocratic.[59]

Naturalization requirements for officeholders, however, were the source of a great deal more initial debate and have proved to be controversial.

During the debate at the convention, the Committee of Detail recommended three- and four-year citizenship requirements for representatives and senators, respectively, and mere citizenship as a requirement for becoming president. These short periods of naturalization were defended by Alexander Hamilton, James Wilson, Edmund Randolph, and James Madison, who argued that minimal eligibility requirements would welcome immigrants and allow the United States to utilize the talents of foreigners. This cosmopolitan defense of minimal eligibility requirements, however, was opposed by George Mason, Gouverneur Morris, Charles Pinckney, and Elbridge Gerry. These delegates argued that longer periods of naturalization were necessary for individuals to gain "local knowledge" of the circumstances, interests, and republican principles of their new country. They were also necessary to guard against foreign conspiracies and to ensure that public officials did not retain prejudices in favor of their native countries.[60]

Despite Madison's objections that such provisions introduced a "tincture of illiberality" into the Constitution, subsequent committees—seemingly acting on the sense of the debate in the convention—lengthened the terms of naturalization to seven years of citizenship for representatives and nine years for senators.[61] They also put in place the most severe qualification for office in the Constitution—the provision that the president must be a "natural born citizen."[62] Together, these provisions and the debates that precipitated them suggest, as Rogers Smith observes, that the Framers believed that "full political rights should be reserved to those whose loyalties could be trusted due to native birth or extensive domestic residence."[63]

More broadly, however, it is remarkable how few qualifications for office the Founders' Constitution contained. Except for age requirements (which are hardly strenuous and can perhaps be defended as making the political process more open) and the stiff requirement that the president be a natural-born citizen, the original Constitution was far more inclusive with respect to officeholders than were the state constitutions written between 1776 and 1786, which are frequently characterized as extremely democratic.[64] It was also more inclusive than the requirements for office established under British law in 1787 and compared favorably with the succession of French constitutions drafted during the French Revolution.

In particular, the group of state constitutions that Donald Lutz has termed the "first wave" and "second wave" of constitutions drafted after independence featured property qualifications, residency requirements, religious test oaths, and prohibitions against ministers holding office.[65] Property qualifications for candidates for the lower houses in most state constitutions were substantially higher than those set for voting; they were approximately twice as high for those seeking election to the upper house compared with the lower house and were higher still for governor. Two states—North Carolina and New York—even imposed greater property qualifications on voters for the upper house than for the lower house.[66] It seems unlikely that these state property qualifications (with the exception of the onerous qualifications for election to the senate or governorship of South Carolina) prevented many individuals from the wealthiest third of society from being elected to office.[67] Nevertheless, they are clearly less liberal than the federal Constitution, which included no property qualifications.

Unlike the Founders' Constitution, which required only that congressional candidates be residents "when elected," most state constitutions contained extensive residency requirements. Like property qualifications, residency requirements were progressively staggered, with stricter requirements for the upper house and governorship than for the lower house. These ranged from one to three years for members of the lower house (with one year being the most common), one- to seven-year residency requirements for the upper house (with two states requiring five years of residency and New Hampshire requiring seven years), and five- to ten-year residency requirements for governor.[68] Finally, all but two of the fourteen state constitutions adopted before 1787 required religious test oaths for office, and five of these constitutions had prohibitions against the clergy holding office.[69]

Similarly, the U.S. Constitution was more inclusive with regard to both voting and officeholding than were the political systems in countries that might arguably be labeled republican before 1800. In Great Britain, naturalized subjects were forbidden to serve in Parliament by the Settlement Act of 1701. Furthermore, in 1787, members of Parliament had to meet substantial property qualifications and take religious test oaths. Specifically, a county member of Parliament had to have land worth 600 pounds annually, and all military, ecclesiastical, and academic offices were limited to participating members of the Church of England, as established in the Second Test Act of 1678.[70]

Even among the French constitutions drafted in the 1790s, only the Jacobin Constitution of 1793 was substantially more liberal with regard to officeholding than the U.S. Constitution of 1787. In the short-lived constitutional monarchy established by the French Constitution of 1791, "active citizens" were allowed to hold office. This included Frenchmen who were at least twenty-five years old, met a residency requirement established by law, and paid a tax equal to the value of three days' labor.[71] The Jacobin Constitution of 1793 granted all French citizens the right to run for office and set up a remarkably easy naturalization process. Under these provisions, it was possible for a foreigner to become a French citizen and run for office within one year of arriving in France—or immediately if the legislature recognized him as having "deserved well of humanity."[72] The Constitution of Year III (1795) involved a substantial retreat from the radical constitution of 1793. This constitution created a bicameral legislature with a Council of Five Hundred and a Council of Ancients or Elders. Members of the Council of Five Hundred had to be at least thirty years old and had to have lived on French soil for the ten years immediately preceding the election. The 250 members of the Council of Ancients had to be at least forty years old, either married or a widower, and domiciled in the republic for fifteen years. Each of these French constitutions, it should be noted, excluded women from holding office, and the constitutions of 1791 and 1795 included substantial property requirements for the electors of national representatives, thus ensuring that the representatives would be members of the highest social ranks.

Expanded Electoral Districts, Informal Barriers to Office, and Class Bias

With the possible exception of naturalization requirements, the Framers set only nominal formal requirements for holding office, yet they have often been charged with creating a kind of informal exclusion by limiting the number of representatives elected to the national government in comparison to the state governments. According to this view, the Federalists' defense of elections from expanded districts was an effort to effectively eliminate the electoral chances of "local" candidates and those from poor and even middling ranks. Conversely, when Madison and other Federalists defended elections from large districts as a means of extracting the "purest and noblest characters" in society and promoting the choice of men with "the most attractive merit and the most diffusive and established characters," they were really using "code words" for a natural aristocracy and men with extensive property, education, refinement, and social status who were unlikely to favor paper money or low tax rates.[73] This charge, which has been made in slightly different formulations by Woody Holton, Jennifer Nedelsky, and Gordon Wood, echoes the contemporaneous charge made by numerous anti-Federalists.[74] In its subtler forms, this argument also implies that the Framers were willing to allow a broad electorate and nominal qualifications for office only because they had already slanted the electoral system in favor of wealthy, cosmopolitan elites.

In particular, the anti-Federalists identified inadequacy of representation as one of the principal objections to the proposed constitution and set forth a constellation of claims to support their charge that expanded electoral districts would advantage wealthy, cosmopolitan candidates. First, they argued, only wealthy, cosmopolitan candidates would have the extensive reputations necessary to get elected in districts of approximately forty thousand people, rather than the few thousand men who typically elected state legislators. The assumption behind elections from large districts, according to the anti-Federalists, was that only a few men would be known throughout the whole district, giving them a decisive advantage.

Second, the anti-Federalists contended that expanded electoral districts would diminish the importance of personal solicitations—of electioneering—and increase the importance of permanent popularity. Whereas the Federalists defended elections from large districts as a means of tempering the effects of demagoguery and crass electioneering, the anti-Federalists interpreted it as a means of preventing the election of local men who campaigned vigorously for office but had little property. Such men, the anti-Federalists argued, might win a majority of votes in circumscribed districts but would never be able to do so in large districts.

Third, the anti-Federalists argued that because of their resources and positions of influence, wealthy, cosmopolitan elites would find it easier to form associations and unite their interests. Whereas men of circumscribed reputations, lesser wealth, and fewer social connections would be divided in their electoral choices and unable to form associations, the wealthy would unite behind candidates of their own rank and have the resources necessary to consolidate support for their candidates.

Fourth, the anti-Federalists contended that only men of property and influence would have the confidence and social attributes necessary to attain office. Local men of lesser social standing would be dissuaded from even running because they might believe themselves to be unworthy of the post or that the effort to attain it would be futile.

Broadly, many anti-Federalists criticized expanded electoral districts as a means of preventing the representation of ordinary Americans by ordinary Americans. Melancton Smith, for example, argued famously at the New York ratifying convention that unless the number of representatives elected under the Constitution was expanded, men of middling wealth would be excluded altogether from the national councils. Smith did not deny that great men of property and extensive reputations should be elected. He argued instead that these elite men had to be counterbalanced by a group of men of middling property and fortune to express the interests of that class of society and to check the power of the aristocracy.[75]

For their part, the Federalists discounted as "altogether visionary" any attempt to secure representation by members of their own class or occupation and flatly denied that the "moderate" representation set forth in the original Constitution was intended to advantage wealthy candidates.[76] Hamilton, for example, argued that whether the voters elected a large or small number of representatives, their votes would "fall upon those in whom they have most confidence; whether these happened to be men of large fortunes or of moderate property or of no property at all."[77] But far from apologizing for favoring men with extensive reputations, the Federalists assumed that in free governments "merit and notoriety of character are rarely separated," and they explicitly defended elections from expanded electoral districts as a means of tempering the "vicious arts" of demagoguery and crass electioneering.[78] Federalists displayed considerable confidence that ordinary Americans would exercise virtue (understood here as containing a healthy dose of deference) in the selection of elite representatives if they were given a "free" choice between men of real virtue and character and demagogues or local parvenus.[79] Such an unimpeded choice based on merit alone, they argued, was best achieved in expanded electoral districts.

Deciding whether elections from expanded districts were part of a shrewd ploy by Federalists to secure and maintain power for men of their own social standing and class or a legitimate process of using competition to ensure the election of men of merit puts us at the crosshairs of the debate between anti-Federalists and Federalists over both the proper character and the aims of representation. Certainly, it cannot be denied that the number of representatives elected under the new Constitution was significantly less than the number of state legislators at the time. Only 65 representatives were elected to the First Congress, whereas there were approximately 1,500 state legislators in all the states combined.[80] Furthermore, fewer representative were elected to the First Congress than were elected to the British Parliament. In 1787 there were 558 members of Parliament to represent between 8 million and 9 million British citizens. This, Ahkil Reed Amar observes, was "more than eight times the size of America's new House, and with about three times as many lawmakers per free citizen."[81]

Nevertheless, the proposition that increasing the number of individuals who choose public officials *reduces* the likelihood of electing demagogues or men of middling rank is hardly unproblematic. The ability to secure that goal was dependent on a set of rich cultural assumptions that were already fading at the time of ratification of the Constitution and that the Federalists themselves were beginning to question. The problem with interpreting elections from expanded districts as a kind of sociological sieve, as Wood suggests, or as an electoral system imbued with class bias, as Nedelsky would have it, is that such an electoral device works only if "local parvenus," "new men," and "demagogues" either do not have or cannot develop the expansive reputations that enhance their prospects. It also works only if voters share the Federalists' belief that cosmopolitan and wealthy gentlemen are the most deserving representatives.

The most reflective Federalists understood this. Noah Webster favored the election of the most noble and virtuous representatives but asked, "how can a constitution ensure the choice of such men? A constitution that leaves the choice entirely with the people?"[82] Even as he advocated elections from expanded districts, Hamilton doubted that they would be as effective as Madison had suggested in a speech before the Constitutional Convention. "Demagogues are not always *inconsiderable* persons," Hamilton observed, and "an influential demagogue will give an impulse to the whole."[83] Indeed, as Hamilton, Madison, and other Federalists no doubt realized, reducing the number of national representatives and creating large electoral districts would not only require a greater number of qualified candidates to compete for fewer offices but also ensure that a greater number of unqualified candidates would compete.[84] Every district would always contain more ordinary men in the electorate than extraordinary ones. What prevented these ordinary men from identifying with one of their own, even in the face of a large number of cosmopolitan elites vying for office?

What is important here is that the Federalists chose not to restrict the electorate or impose extensive qualifications on candidates as means to institutionalize rule by a natural aristocracy. They opted instead to use expanded electoral districts as the means of promoting the election of elite representatives, ultimately leaving the kind of people who were elected up to the people. At that point, expanded electoral districts could result in the election of wealthy, cosmopolitan leaders only if *the people* identified these cosmopolitans as embodying the qualities they valued. Thus, Wood's famous suggestion that this electoral mechanism was meant to stem the tide of democracy and restore and prolong the rule of social elites in the early republic seems inverted.[85] Actually, the success of this electoral mechanism depended on the very qualities in the citizenry—deference among the many to the claims of the few to govern—that Wood argues it was meant to restore and prolong. In short, then, if elections from expanded districts were an effort to impose informal exclusions, they were not without considerable risk. In the end, there was no guarantee that the people would elect cosmopolitan elites rather than men like themselves.[86]

On balance, when the expanded electoral districts and qualifications for voting and holding office are considered together, it is apparent that the Framers' Constitution created few *formal* barriers to voting or officeholding and thus did not attempt to create an aristocratic republic through the use of constitutional requirements. Nor did they tie the right to vote or the eligibility to hold office directly to wealth or property holdings, family status, or education. The original Constitution empowered a white male electorate that was impressively broad for its day and created wide access to office, even as it extended state restrictions on voting by women and African Americans to federal elections, set relatively stiff naturalization requirements for federal office, and limited the number of representatives who would serve in the national councils in order to create strong competition in expansive electoral districts and thus eliminate local demagogues. Elections of representatives from large districts meant that the most significant barriers for ordinary men to gain elective office were informal ones, such as the ability to form extensive connections and to create the "diffusive and established characters" necessary to succeed in a wide electorate.[87]

Accountability and Responsiveness

The two other dimensions of democracy that have been central in scholars' judgments about the character of the original Constitution concern (1) the accountability of public officials and the responsiveness of the political system and (2) how well the Framers' Constitution achieved political equality. To constructively evaluate how well the original Constitution fares against these standards, we first need to consider the original design of the American political system and the Framers' defense of it. Then we can introduce comparisons, evaluate their appropriateness, evaluate the Federalists' defense of the original Constitution, and reconsider scholars' judgments.

A Madisonian Apologia for the Madisonian Model

The Framers characterized the Constitution's famous system of direct elections of representatives from expanded electoral districts, indirect and staggered elections and appointments for members of the other branches, and long terms of office (in comparison to those of state officials) as means of successively filtering public opinion and ensuring that the "*cool* and *deliberate* sense of the community*" rather than its irrational impulses would prevail.[88] Within this scheme, representatives were elected every two years directly by the people, and the number allocated to each state was based on total population, including all free citizens in the state plus three-fifths of its slaves. As noted earlier, the sixty-five representatives elected under the original Constitution were significantly fewer than those who served in most of the state governments, thus ensuring that representatives were elected by and served larger constituencies. The Framers defended this scheme not only (as previously mentioned) as a means of electing the most virtuous and enlightened leaders and tempering crass electioneering but also as a means of expanding the vision of representatives by making them responsible for a greater number of citizens and a greater variety of interests and striking a proper balance between sympathy for the people's views and responsibility to the broader ends of republican government.

The Federalists' defense of elections from large districts and "moderate" representation was, in turn, tied to a remarkable theory about the internal operations of legislative assemblies. Responding to the charge that representation under the proposed constitution would be inadequate, Madison argued that increasing representation beyond the number necessary to secure the public safety, provide information about local interests and views, and promote a diffusive sympathy with the whole society would have a profoundly and paradoxically *undemocratic* effect on the internal operation of the legislature. Unduly large legislative assemblies might appear to have a democratic demeanor, Madison argued in *Federalist* No. 58, but the decision-making process within such bodies inevitably became lodged in fewer hands, and its operations became more secret than those of a legislative body with a moderate number of representatives.[89] Contrary to the anti-Federalists' objections, then, the only way to ensure the democratic character of the House, Madison argued, was to carefully prescribe a mean number of representatives.

Madison and his colleagues conceded, however, that even if the number of representatives was kept to a moderate level, the House of Representatives might be overtaken by public passions because of its character as the most numerous and popular branch. They thus turned to the Senate to protect the long-term interests and reputation of the nation, which, almost all the delegates believed, would be best accomplished by long terms of office and staggered elections. The men who are often considered the principal Framers—including James Madison and James Wilson—also opposed the election of senators from the state legislatures and fought for proportional representation in the Senate. The election of senators from the state legislatures, they argued, would make the national government unduly dependent on the states for the execution of national measures and thus replicate the inadequacies of government under the Articles of Confederation. Proportional representation, Madison and Wilson argued, was the only means consistent with the principles of justice and equity. "As all authority was derived from the people," Wilson argued at the convention, "equal numbers of people ought to have an equal no. of representatives, and different numbers of people different numbers of representatives."[90]

Ultimately, however, Madison, Wilson, and Hamilton (among others) were unable to convince their fellow delegates that proportional representation and bypassing the state legislatures were essential to ensure the Senates' character as a deliberative body. In its final form, the Constitution provided for six-year terms for senators, staggered elections in which one-third of senators faced reelection every two years, election of senators by the state legislatures, and equal representation for each state regardless of population. The widely accepted vision of the Senate as a "great anchor" that enhanced the stability, reputation, and deliberative character of the political system was therefore combined in the Constitution with the goal of ensuring that states were represented as states within the national government.

The most indirect modes of appointment under the Framers' scheme and the "longest leashes" in the Madisonian model were given to federal judges and the president.[91] Judges were nominated by the president, confirmed by the Senate, and served terms of "good behavior" or life. Life tenure for judges was justified, most famously by Hamilton in *Federalist* No. 78, as an "indispensable ingredient" for securing judicial firmness and independence. Judicial independence, in turn, was justified as necessary to prevent legislative encroachments, protect private rights, limit the government's exercise of powers to those set forth in the Constitution, and promote "integrity and moderation" in the administration of the government.[92] The president was elected by the Electoral College system, under which each state was given a number of electoral votes equal to its number of representatives plus senators. To be elected president, a candidate had to win a majority of the electoral votes. If no candidate received a majority, the election would be thrown into the House of Representatives, where each state was given one vote.

Hamilton used classic Federalist reasoning to defend the Electoral College in *Federalist* No. 68. This method of presidential selection, he suggested, would consult the sense of the people, but then refine that sense because a group of capable men with greater "information" and "discernment" than the people would make a choice "under circumstances favourable to deliberation and to a judicious combination of all the reasons and inducements, which were proper to govern their choice."[93] Despite Hamilton's silence on these issues, the Electoral College was also adopted because of the concern that delegates from small states and slave states had to protect their interests.

The decision to adopt the Electoral College was made after the adoption of the three-fifths clause and equal representation in the Senate. In the wake of these compromises, delegates from small and slave states tied the number of presidential electors to representation in Congress. The inclusion of

House votes in the Electoral College strengthened the influence of the slave states because they were allowed to count three-fifths of their slave populations in the enumerations that determined their allotment of representatives (and thus electoral votes). The inclusion of two additional senatorial votes for each state in the Electoral College, regardless of population, significantly enhanced the power of the small states in the selection of president. Obviously, small states disproportionately benefited from the "senatorial bonus" in the Electoral College, because those states were given the same number of additional electors as large states. These provisions meant that small and slave states controlled a greater number of electoral votes than if those votes had been allotted based entirely on total free populations; it also meant that citizens in small and slave states cast weighted votes, because fewer citizens elected each presidential elector. Further, if no candidate won a majority of the electoral votes and the selection of the president was thrown into the House (as many Framers expected would often be the case), the small states would have even greater influence.[94]

The original Constitution contained four additional features that have engendered extensive commentary in the debate over democracy and the Constitution and bear on the question of how directly responsive to the people the political system created under the Constitution was meant to be. These four features are the prohibitions against Congress and the state legislatures established in Sections 9 and 10 of Article I, the amendment process, the extended republic, and the separation of powers. The prohibitions established in Article I, Sections 9 and 10, are relevant to this discussion because they placed certain substantive outcomes beyond the reach of elected officials who ostensibly reflect popular majorities. Under Section 9, Congress was prohibited from, among other things, suspending the writ of habeas corpus except in the case of rebellion or invasion, passing bills of attainder or ex post facto laws, and granting titles of nobility. Under Section 10, the states were prevented from, among other things, coining their own money; emitting bills of credit; making anything but gold and silver legal tender for the payment of debts; granting titles of nobility; and passing bills of attainder, ex post facto laws, and laws impairing the obligation of contracts. These prohibitions, in particular, arose from the Framers' experiences during the 1780s and their concern about the violation of property rights by democratic majorities in the states.

Like the Electoral College, the amendment process was based on the shared goals of enhancing deliberation and ensuring the states' influence as states in the national government. In particular, the Constitution provided four means of constitutional revision based on a combination of two methods for proposing amendments and two methods of ratifying amendments (amendments could be proposed by the concurrence of two-thirds of the members present in both houses of Congress or by a constitutional convention called at the request of two-thirds of the state legislatures, and amendments could be ratified by majority vote in three-fourths of the states or by vote in conventions in three-fourths of these states). As David E. Kyvig, the leading student of the amendment process, has written, this procedure synthesized two goals:

> The instrument [the Constitution] embodied their [the Framers'] concept of federalism. The national legislature could propose change, but any reform would have to be approved by the states; and if the national legislature declined to act when a substantial number of states wished it to do so, the latter could compel the calling of a convention to circumvent the former. Change binding on all required the assent of a preponderant majority of the states, though not their unanimous consent. The late eighteenth-century inclination toward representative government was likewise evident. Elected representatives, whether assembled in legislatures or conventions, were regarded as best equipped to draft proposed constitutional reforms. The final sanctioning of reforms in the name of the sovereign people could be carried out either by legislatures, where representatives were left to make their own judgments, or by conventions, where delegates chosen by voters to reflect particular principles would prevail.[95]

Furthermore, Kyvig notes, this process was intended to prevent "a tiny minority of states from obstructing widely desired reform while establishing an adequate requirement of consensus to avoid the constitutional instability inherent in simple majoritarianism."[96]

Contrary to what is often suggested, however, the amendment process is not a supramajoritarian procedure adopted by the Framers to prevent rash alterations in the Constitution. Indeed, it is not necessarily a majoritarian procedure at all. A minority of the people acting in a majority of the states can force Congress to propose amendments and ensure their ratification. Conversely, a minority of the people acting in a mere quarter of the states can prevent the ratification of amendments favored by a vast majority of Americans. The amendment procedure therefore was designed to require that a majority of the *states* assent to any constitutional amendments.

Finally, extent of territory and separation of powers were based on the principle of *divide et impera* to decrease the incidence of majority factionalism, create a proper balance between responsiveness to public demands and fidelity to the common interest, and create a deliberative republic. Extent of territory, Madison argued, would splinter majority factions across the republic and erect a number of barriers—including distance between citizens, distance between citizens and their representatives, a diversity of interests, and a large number of individuals—that would help break the concert of factious majorities.[97]

Likewise, the system of separation of powers was designed primarily to control popular majorities (not to prevent tyrannical acts by public officials independent of their constituents), in this case *after* they were reflected in the political system through the legislative branch. In part because of their experiences with state governments during the mid-1780s, and in part because of their accompanying understanding of the nature of republican governments, Madison and the Federalists viewed the House of Representatives as a passionate, powerful, ever-encroaching branch that necessarily "predominates" in republican governments.[98] Tyrannical majorities, they believed, would be most likely to capture this branch. Hence, the system of checks and balances espoused by the Federalists sought to increase the independence and the defensive power of the weaker and more indirectly selected branches. Separate constituencies, long terms of office, and specific checks on the House of Representatives—including the presidential veto and judicial review, but especially the senatorial check—would give the weaker branches sufficient means and motives to block unjust legislative majorities and defend themselves from constitutional encroachments. In the eyes of the Federalists, this system of separation of powers checked power where it was lodged—in the people and their representatives.[99]

Madison and his Federalist allies would have been incredulous about the frequently made charge that they hoped to either deadlock democracy or take power completely out of the hands of popular majorities. Separation of powers and extent of territory, as they explained and defended these provisions, were designed to prevent improper or unwise legislative decisions from being enacted into law and *unjust* popular majorities from forming. The Federalists assumed that the branches of government would work in unison to pass legislation that was constitutional and would advance the common interests. They also assumed that, just as diverse sentiments and interests would prevent unjust combinations of people, common sentiments and interests would help facilitate the formation of *good* majorities.[100] In general, like many later defenders of the Constitution, the Federalists argued that the constraints on the popular will embedded in the Constitution were necessary because they were certain that the system would be responsive, not because they sought to prevent it from being responsive.

More broadly, Madison and his peers defended the original design of the political system as "wholly popular" and "strictly republican."[101] This defense required particular and contentious conceptions of both popular sovereignty and republican government. In explaining their conceptions of popular sovereignty, Madison and his colleagues were frank in their evaluations of the capabilities of the people. The people, they asserted, "can never wil[l]fully betray their own interests." They are the public, and thus their understanding of the public interest is always earnest. Nevertheless, they may sometimes be "stimulated by some irregular passion" or "misled by the artful misrepresentations of interested men."[102]

The Federalists were also explicit in their rejection of "pure" democracies in which the people "assemble and administer the Government in person."[103] To Madison and the Federalists, popular sovereignty meant that the well-considered opinions of the people would *ultimately* prevail over the views of its rulers."[104] It also meant that the sovereign people could at any time alter or abolish and replace any government under which they lived. In their understanding of the system, the people therefore acted primarily during the making and unmaking of their government and during elections, when they could censure or approve of their representatives.[105] Nevertheless, representatives were meant to refine the public's views, not replace them with their own views, and they were certainly not supposed to pursue legislation that furthered their own interests at the expense of the broader public interest.

Meanwhile, Madison and his Federalist colleagues set forth a series of criteria that formed a novel and loose-jointed definition of a republican government. In particular, the criteria that gave the republican form of government its distinctiveness included representation, majority rule, legislative supremacy, nonhereditary public office, and the right of the people to alter and abolish their constitutions.[106] Madison's most elaborate definition of republicanism, which he seemingly developed to justify the institutional features of the Constitution, appeared in *Federalist* No. 39. A republic, Madison asserted, is

> a government which derives all its powers directly or indirectly from the great body of the people; and is administered by persons holding their offices during pleasure, for a limited period, or during good behaviour. It is essential to such a government, that it be derived from the great body of the society, not from an inconsiderable proportion, or a favored class of it; otherwise a handful of tyrannical

nobles, exercising their oppressions by a delegation of their powers, might aspire to the rank of republicans, and claim for their government the honorable title of republic. It is sufficient for such a government, that the persons administering it be appointed, either directly or indirectly, by the people; and that they hold their appointments by either of the tenures specified; otherwise every government in the United States, as well as every other popular government that has been or can be well organized or well executed, would be degraded from the republican character.[107]

Although this definition has received a substantial amount of commentary and has numerous implications, what is important here is that it encompassed even the most indirect modes of selection established in the Constitution and the longest terms of office, including life tenure, as being consistent with republicanism.[108]

Finally, Madison and the Framers defended their political system as an effort to reconcile foundational commitments to republicanism and popular sovereignty with a variety of characteristics of good government that were themselves in tension with one another. The Framers' experiences with the Articles of Confederation and the state governments created after 1776 had taught them that fidelity to popular sovereignty and republicanism did not necessarily translate into the multiple qualities that good government entailed. The essential goal for Madison—his "Great Desideratum"—was to reconcile the Revolutionary principles of popular sovereignty and majority rule with the impartial protection of rights and the disinterested promotion of the public good (the ends of government, which had been violated by both the national and state governments during the mid-1780s). This involved making the national government dependent enough on the people to prevent it from establishing "an interest adverse to that of the entire Society," yet independent enough that it could be sufficiently neutral with regard to the different interests in society.[109] Madison also explained the imperatives of constitutional design in terms of "mingling" in their "due proportions" an attention to republican liberty (which would best be promoted by deriving power directly from the people and having public officials serve short terms), stability (which was necessary to gain the respect of foreign nations and the confidence of Americans and was promoted by longer and indirect appointments), and energy (which was necessary for efficient administration and was promoted by both longer appointments and the lodging of power in the hands of a few individuals or a single person).[110]

A Comparative Perspective

The extended, deliberative, federal republic that was created in 1787 was, as Madison suggested, the product of "many heads and many hands."[111] It was also a result of compromises on a range of interests. Viewing the Constitution as the product of multiple variations of republicanism, compounded and complicated by compromises needed to accommodate multiple interests, does not necessarily reject the possibility that it contained an underlying theoretical rationale. It does, however, help explain why the Constitution embodied no single conception of political design or republicanism then in existence and was truly "a novelty in the political world."[112] In particular, the Framers explicitly rejected substantial aspects of the British constitutional monarchy as it was organized in 1787, ancient democracies, and the "short-leash" republicanism of the Articles of Confederation and the state governments formed after independence. In addition, the Framers' Constitution followed to only a limited degree the logic of one of the most important conceptions of democracy developed during the Founding era (Wilson's democratic nationalism), and it ran directly counter to the other most important one (Jefferson's ward republicanism). Together, these comparisons bring the uniqueness of the American constitutional design into sharp relief and clarify our understanding of the relationship between the government and the governed embodied within it.

In particular, the British constitutional monarchy that existed in 1787 and the mixed polity on which this system was based and justified contained hereditary and aristocratic features that were unacceptable to the genius of the American people and the fundamental principles of the American Revolution. Obviously, a monarchical head of state and an aristocratic and hereditary House of Lords were unacceptable to Americans. Even certain features of the House of Commons, including its system of rotten boroughs and indeterminate lengths of office, were anathema to republicanism as it had been defined and practiced in colonial and Revolutionary America.[113] It was plausible to think of the House of Commons as representing the people, the House of Lords as representing an aristocratic segment of British society, and the king as spokesman for the monarchical social order.

In contrast, as numerous scholars have pointed out, the Federalists realized that the American people could be better described as belonging to a single social order and divided among a multiplicity of factions or interest groups. It thus made no sense to design the government so that it incorporated distinct social orders, and Madison and the Framers divorced the separation of powers from the Polybian conception of mixed government. The

Federalists, in other words, did not conceive of the House of Representatives as the sole representative of the people; they did not structure the Senate to represent either property or the aristocratic element of the society; nor was the president equated with the British monarch. Instead, each branch was seen as an emanation from and spokesman for the interests of the whole people.[114]

As noted earlier, Madison also explicitly differentiated the system of representative republicanism espoused by the Framers from the classical conception of a "pure democracy . . . consisting of a small number of citizens, who assemble and administer the government in person." This form of government, which had been practiced in ancient Athens, in particular, offered no cure for the mischiefs of a majority faction. Thus, representation became the "pivot" of the new system.[115]

More directly and importantly, the 1787 Constitution represents a conscious rejection of the short-leash republicanism embodied in the Articles of Confederation and the state governments created between 1776 and 1787. The Articles of Confederation combined a series of short-leash and federative features. Delegates were elected annually in the manner prescribed by each state's legislature; they could be recalled at any time and were subject to rotation in office (no delegate could serve for more than three years in any six-year term).[116] The government created by the Articles of Confederation had only one branch (Congress) and thus no independent judiciary or executive and no scheme of separation of powers. A president was chosen by Congress to serve as presiding officer over the Committee of the States (a committee formed to do the business of Congress when it was not in full session). The president was also subject to rotation, being eligible to serve only one year in every three.

The federative qualities of the Articles of Confederation were exemplified in provisions that gave each state one vote in Congress, required extraordinary majorities to pass important measures (nine of the thirteen states were required to pass legislation on treaties, wars, and economic matters), and mandated unanimity to amend the constitution. The Articles also guaranteed that each state would retain its "sovereignty, freedom, and independence, and every power, jurisdiction, and right, which is not by this Constitution expressly delegated to the United States."[117] These provisions implied strict equality among the member states; suggested that unanimity or near unanimity was the proper standard for important measures, especially to change the terms of the original agreement; and established that the states were the real locus of authority.[118]

The case that the Articles of Confederation were more democratic than the Framers' Constitution—a case made by anti-Federalists and later by Progressive and neo-Progressive scholars—points to its short-leash features (annual elections, provision for the recall of delegates, and schemes of rotation in office) and especially its decentralized character. Neo-Progressive historian Merrill Jensen, for example, has argued that the Articles of Confederation were written and ratified by statesmen who sought to preserve the authority of local majorities within the states. Conversely, the nationalists who created the 1787 Constitution were elites who "saw in the creation of a national government a possible escape from the unpleasant fact of majority rule within the states."[119] Jensen's case for the Articles of Confederation as a democratic system, then, is best understood by thinking of the Confederation Congress as a tier in a system in which the state governments were the other, central tier. The state legislatures, which were structured to be highly responsive to popular majorities within the states, kept a short leash on delegates to a continental body that was expressly limited to powers that governed relations among the states and their collective relationship with foreign nations.

Federalists and later scholars who defended the democratic interpretation of the Constitution countered this case by stressing comparisons between the Confederation Congress and the national government created by the Framers' Constitution and by suggesting that the Constitution fell broadly in line with the institutional features and terms of office provided in the state governments.[120] These scholars observe that the Articles of Confederation, unlike the federal Constitution, were never ratified by the people, contained no directly elected branch of government, and required the unanimous consent of all states for amendment.[121] As I emphasize in the next section of this chapter, the Federalists often pointed out that provisions giving each state equal representation in the national assembly and requiring unanimity for amendments violated the principles of proportionality and majority rule and allowed a small minority to block legislation and constitutional changes that were favored by the many.

The problem with either defending or criticizing the Constitution by comparing it to the government created by the Articles of Confederation, however, is that the respective national governments were fundamentally different in character (if it can be said that the Articles created a national government at all). As Bernard Bailyn has said, the Articles established a "loose national confederation that was more a consultative body than a functioning government with the powers associated with national states."[122] Congress under the Articles, in other words, was primarily an executive and diplomatic body, not a national lawmaking assembly.[123] Furthermore, it was composed of delegates whose role was more like that of ambassadors from distinct sovereign nations rather than representatives of the people. They were, as Ahkil Reed Amar has suggested, the states' men, not statesmen. Collectively, the Confederation Congress was "the United States in Congress assembled."[124] In contrast, the Framers' Constitution established one entity at least—the House of Representatives—that was structured to recognize and respond to a majority of the nation's citizens conceived as a single political community. Congressmen in this new body voted as individual lawmakers, not as representatives of a state delegation. And the new Congress acted directly on the individuals within the states, not on the states in their corporate capacity.[125]

The most appropriate, straightforward, and revealing comparisons, then, can be made between the governments created by state constitutions from 1776 to 1787 and the government created by the Framers' Constitution. As G. Allan Tarr has noted, these comparisons establish that the Framers viewed the state constitutions as "models of avoidance rather than emulation."[126] The Framers' most explicit repudiation of the state constitutions was the replacement of direct ties of accountability and responsiveness with less direct modes of selection and longer terms of office. In comparison with the two-year terms for national representatives, twelve of the fourteen state constitutions adopted between 1776 and 1787 implemented annual elections for members of the lower house. Only the South Carolina Constitutions of 1776 and 1778 required two-year terms for members of the lower house. Similarly, whereas the federal Constitution called for six-year terms of office for the Senate, none of the Revolutionary state constitutions stipulated terms longer than five years for members of the upper house, and four states had annual elections.[127] Perhaps most dramatically, the federal Constitution gave the president a four-year term and made him perpetually reeligible for that office. In contrast, ten of the fourteen Revolutionary state constitutions had annual elections for the state's chief executive, two had two-year terms, and two had three-year terms.[128] The only area where federal terms of office closely matched state terms was in the judiciary. Nine of the twelve state constitutions that established state supreme courts stipulated "good behavior" as the proper tenure of office, two stipulated seven-year terms, and the Vermont Constitution of 1786 called for the annual appointment of state court judges.[129]

Furthermore, the state constitutions created political systems that featured far more directly elected offices than did the scheme of successive filtrations and indirect elections and appointments featured in the federal Constitution. The House of Representatives was the only branch directly elected under the Constitution. In contrast, the lower houses were directly elected under all fourteen state constitutions, and the upper houses were directly elected in eight.[130] The chief executive was directly elected by the people in five states and elected by the state legislature (which was directly elected and tied to the people through short terms of office) in the remaining nine states.[131] Finally, a variety of means were used to select the members of the judiciary under the state constitutions, but a majority of states either gave the power of appointment exclusively to the legislature or shared the power between the legislature and the governor. Only four states gave the governor the lion's share of the power in appointing judges.[132]

In addition to direct and frequent elections, the state constitutions featured a series of other constitutional requirements, institutional features, and plebiscitary devices designed to promote virtually unchecked legislative supremacy, keep public officials on a short leash, and promote the translation of popular majorities into legislative majorities in the states. Seven of the state constitutions featured schemes of rotation for the office of governor, three had schemes of rotation for the executive councils that advised the governor, and Pennsylvania provided for the rotation of assemblymen.[133] Furthermore, a majority of states guaranteed the people's right to instruct their representatives by writing it into their state Declarations of Rights.[134]

Both the federal Constitution and the state constitutions rested on the premise that the legislative branch would be predominant. Nevertheless, the Revolutionary state constitutions, unlike the federal Constitution, sought to restrain the executive and withheld from governors and state judges the powers given to the president and the federal judiciary. Furthermore, executives were guided and ostensibly restrained by advisory councils in several states; only the South Carolina Constitution of 1776 and the Massachusetts Constitution of 1780 gave the executive even a qualified veto over the acts of the assembly, and South Carolina took that power away in 1778.[135] Although there was general agreement among the Framers that the U.S. Supreme Court would exercise the power of judicial review, only three states allowed the judiciary to participate in reviewing legislation.[136] In contrast to the cumbersome system of congressional and state cooperation that was required to pass a federal constitutional amendment, the early state constitutions allowed amendments to be passed by the legislature or did not specify an amending procedure, supposing that the people had the right to amend the constitution if they chose.[137]

Finally, the state governments featured numerous representatives elected from small electoral districts confined to small geographic areas, compared with the vast, extended republic under the authority of the national government created in 1787. The large number of legislative seats increased the likelihood that state legislators would not be elite statesmen, and it channeled popular views into the legislature. Meanwhile, the relative proximity of the people to one another made collective action possible. Indeed, even the largest states in colonial and Revolutionary America regularly submitted legislation to the people for their consideration and based decisions on petitions that were submitted by ordinary citizens.[138] In short, in contrast to the large, extended republic splintered into a variety of factions that Madison envisioned, the state constitutions made possible a "relentless pursuit of direct consent by the majority."[139]

Another pair of illuminating contextual comparisons can be made between the original design set forth in the Framers' Constitution and Wilson's democratic nationalism and Jefferson's ward republicanism. Wilson is important because, had he had his way at the convention, the Constitution would have contained an original and consistent version of *national* democracy.[140] In general, Wilson envisioned the national government as a "federal pyramid" in which each of the branches except the judiciary would be directly elected by the people. Wilson also favored the least restrictive officeholding requirements of any delegate at the convention, proportional representation in both the House of Representatives and the Senate, and electoral districts of equal size within each state.[141]

Had they been enacted, Wilson's proposals would have institutionalized the logic of expanded electoral districts across the political system. Each of the branches except the judiciary would have been conceived as a direct spokesman for the people, and an increasingly widened electorate would have been expected to elect a candidate with a more diffusive reputation and great merit. This would have culminated in the election of a president who would be "the man of the people."[142] Although Wilson favored long terms of office for federal officials, and his system would have featured long leashes, it would have been much more consistently democratic than the final product of the convention was. It would not have introduced state agency into the national government (states would have been proportionally represented in the Senate, and senators would not have been elected by the state legislatures), and it would not have contained the schemes of indirect election (including the Electoral College) featured in the Framers' Constitution.[143] Eliminating the schemes of indirect election and equal representation in the Senate also would have eliminated the weighted votes and disproportionate political power exercised by small states. Wilson's system therefore would have more closely approximated the idea of "one man, one vote."

If the Framers' Constitution of 1787 can be thought of as imperfectly embodying Wilson's scheme of democratic nationalism, it deviates even further from Jefferson's system of decentralized democracy in ward republics. As Michael Zuckert has shown, the political system that Jefferson advocated late in his life was based on a series of gradations from wards to counties to states and finally to the national government. Powers were given to a higher level of government only when a lower one was incapable of performing that function. This placed the lion's share of governmental functions, including protecting civil rights, making laws, maintaining a police force, and administering other state concerns, outside the purview of the national government and reduced its role to defending the nation and conducting foreign and federal relations. Most important for our purposes, the ward republics, which were modeled after New England townships and would have been about one-fourth the size of an average Virginia county, represented Jefferson's effort to institutionalize his dramatically democratic conception of republicanism as "a government by its citizens in mass, acting directly and personally."[144]

The contrast between this system of ward republicanism and the sober republicanism envisioned in the Madisonian model is great. Jefferson invited localism as a means of achieving direct collective action by the citizenry. In contrast, Madison and the Framers were wedded to a conception of mass psychology that suggested that individuals were much more likely to act unjustly and irrationally when they acted in public and in groups.[145] Collective action by large segments of the population in the state governments during the mid-1780s led the Federalists to conclude that forms of direct democracy by the citizenry threatened both the public good and private rights. They therefore transferred the responsibility for making important decisions to the national government, greatly reduced the number of public officials who would be making those decisions, and restructured the national government to control the legislative branch.

Finally, if we move from the conceptions of republicanism present in the eighteenth century to the leading model of democracy in our day, the Framers' Constitution emerges once again as unique and less responsive than its alternative. Although they have long been characterized as the forerunners of pluralism because of a misreading of the argument of *Federalist* No. 10, the Federalists were not in any meaningful sense pluralists. They did not believe that representatives should represent the dominant interests in their constituencies or that just and moderate legislation would result from the compromising and bargaining of representatives. Unlike pluralists, they did not reject the concept of a public good. Instead, they hoped to ensure the election of elite representatives who would act as disinterested statesmen and consciously adopt policies that were for the public good.[146]

Political Equality and Apportionment

In addition to questions of inclusiveness and responsiveness, recent scholarship has introduced a third dimension of democracy—political equality—into this debate. This scholarship suggests that the Framers' Constitution adhered more strictly to the principle of political equality than did the British system in 1787 and, in a few select ways, than did the state governments in place at the time of the Constitutional Convention. In particular, the Constitution required that elections be conducted at fixed and regular intervals, mandated that a census be taken every ten years, and provided that congressional apportionment among the states be recalculated at this time. As Akhil Reed Amar has shown, the requirements of periodic elections at fixed intervals and proportional representation in the House of Representatives based on a census marked important democratic progress over British and American practices prior to the adoption of the Constitution. These provisions prevented any sitting legislature from lengthening its term of office, required Congress to track shifts in population and adjust representation among the states accordingly, and linked apportionment to population more directly than had been the case in Britain, where a large percentage of the members of Parliament were elected in rotten boroughs.[147]

The thrust of this recent scholarship, however, has suggested that the three-fifths clause and equal representation in the Senate violated the democratic principle of political equality by weaving into the constitutional fabric substantial privileges for slave states and small states. Furthermore, scholars have pointed out that the Framers' Constitution left the apportionment of representatives within the states up to each state government and did not require states to draw electoral districts with roughly equal numbers of people in them. In particular, under the Framers' Constitution, representatives were apportioned among the states based on calculations of the whole number of free persons—including women, children, and men with insufficient property to vote—and three-fifths of the slaves within each state. In adopting this provision, the convention rejected representation based on "quotas of contribution," wealth, or the total number of free inhabitants.[148] The decision to include women, children, and men without sufficient property to vote in the apportionment of representatives can be thought of as a substantial advance in democracy, because it meant that even those who could not vote were, in some sense, represented under the Constitution. No similar provisions were contained in the state constitutions.[149]

The three-fifths clause, however, introduced an abrupt anomaly into the constitutional text. This clause has been the subject of voluminous and increasingly contentious scholarship.[150] Fortunately, we do not have to get bogged down in the details of that debate to establish a basic point that is accepted by all participants: the three-fifths clause significantly enhanced the political power of slave states.[151] First, it gave slave states a number of what were, in effect "slave seats" in Congress. Leonard Richards has observed, "The slave states always had one-third more seats in Congress than their free populations warranted—forty-seven instead of thirty-three in 1793, seventy-six instead of fifty-nine in 1812, and ninety-eight instead of seventy-three in 1833."[152] Similarly, Amar has noted:

> The numbers from the 1790 census illustrate the practical effect of the three-fifths clause in its early years. New Hampshire's 140,000 free citizens entitled it to four seats in the expanded House, compared to six seats for South Carolina's 140,000 free citizens and 100,000 slaves. Connecticut boasted 20,000 more citizens than Maryland but won one less seat because Maryland got to count its 100,000 bondsmen. Although slave-less Massachusetts had a significantly larger free population than did Virginia, the Old Dominion got five more seats, thanks to her nearly 300,000 slaves.[153]

Second, as William Patterson and Gouverneur Morris observed at the Constitutional Convention, the three-fifths clause allowed the South the prospect of increasing its representation in Congress and its influence in presidential elections by obtaining more slaves. Indeed, when the three-fifths clause was combined with the 1808 slave trade provision that protected the importation of slaves for at least twenty years after the ratification of the Constitution, slaveholders were given a strong incentive and legal sanction to increase their slave populations as means of increasing their proportional power in Congress.[154]

Third, since the number of electoral votes for each state was calculated by adding its number of representatives and senators, these "slave seats" gave the South substantially greater power in the selection of the president than was warranted by their free populations.[155] Fourth, since the first stage in the most common method of amending the Constitution was passage by two-thirds of the members present in Congress, these extra seats in the House gave slave states extra political clout to either pass or block constitutional amendments.

In addition to the gross violation of the proportionality principle created by the three-fifths clause, the Constitution institutionalized political inequality through the states' equal representation in the Senate, regardless of their total populations. The inequalities in representation created by the

"Great Compromise" are easily illustrated with simple comparisons.[156] In 1790 the two senators from the largest state (Virginia) represented 747,550 citizens, or almost thirteen times the number represented by the two senators from the smallest state (Delaware), who represented 59,096 citizens. If slaves are removed from this calculation, Virginia's two senators represented roughly nine times as many free individuals as Delaware's did.[157] The total population of the four largest states in the nation in 1790—Virginia, Pennsylvania, North Carolina, and Massachusetts—was 1,954,772. The total population of the remaining nine states was 1,683,491. Thus, eight senators represented roughly 54 percent of the population, and the remaining eighteen senators represented about 46 percent.[158] If this calculation is changed to reflect only the free population, Massachusetts replaces North Carolina as the third largest state and New York becomes the fourth largest, but the percentage of total population represented by the eight senators from the four largest states remains essentially the same, at 53.5 percent.[159] Perhaps most remarkably, a majority in the Senate in 1790 (fourteen votes) could be gathered from senators representing seven states with about 28 percent of the total population of the United States.[160] Again, if only the free population is counted, the states in the list change, but the percentage represented by the seven least populous states remains essentially the same, at 28.6 percent.[161] And these 1790 figures represent some of the highest percentages of the total population ever needed to elect a majority of the Senate. As Frances E. Lee and Bruce I. Oppenheimer have observed, "at no point since 1810 has the theoretical minimum percentage of the nation's population necessary to elect a majority of senators been greater than 30 percent, and at no point since 1900 has it been greater than 20 percent."[162]

Like the inequality created by the three-fifths clause, this inequality in the Senate was also translated into the Electoral College and the amendment process. In the Electoral College, each state was given two additional electoral votes corresponding to its two senators. The proportional bonus given to each state in the Electoral College differed, however, depending on its population. For example, Rhode Island and Delaware had only one representative each (and thus one electoral vote), but their two additional senatorial electors meant that they each cast three electoral votes. Together, Rhode Island and Delaware cast six electoral votes in the first presidential election but had a combined population of less than 0.5 percent of the U.S. population. In contrast, Virginia, with roughly 20 percent of the population, cast twelve electoral votes in the first presidential election.

Finally, with regard to the amendment process, the requirement that two-thirds of both houses of Congress must pass any amendment before it can be submitted to the state legislatures or the special ratifying conventions meant that in 1790 the ten senators from the five smallest states, representing as little as 15 percent of the population, could block any constitutional amendment. Conversely, the eighteen senators from the nine smallest states, representing about 46 percent of the population, could ensure Senate passage of a constitutional amendment opposed by senators representing four states and 54 percent of the population. Furthermore, state legislatures from these same nine states could require the calling of a constitutional convention to consider constitutional amendments.[163]

A third dimension of inequality in the Framers' Constitution resulted from the convention's failure to require that congressional electoral districts have roughly the same number of citizens. The Constitution left the drawing of district lines to the states and set no standard for apportionment or reapportionment as populations increased or shifted within the states.[164] The absence of what Amar calls an "explicit intrastate equality norm in Article I" left open the possibility of electoral districts containing vastly different numbers of citizens having equal weight in the legislature. As Amar has noted, this situation makes it difficult to see how the legislature could claim to be a rough transcript of the society or an adequate substitute for the meeting of the people themselves.[165] Furthermore, since the state legislatures were given control over the time, place, and manner of conducting elections, the Constitution allowed the state legislatures to draw legislative districts that enhanced the election and reelection of favored representatives. Finally, the absence of an intrastate equality norm allowed state legislatures in the slave states to create congressional districts that favored slaveholding belts or regions. Thus, not only did slave holding states receive a greater number of representatives than they would have received if representation would have been allocated on the basis of the free population, but state legislators were free to (and often did) draw up Congressional district lines within each state that gave a relatively few number of citizens in slave belts greater Congressional representation than the relatively larger number of citizens laying outside of these belts.[166]

Such statistics and observations from recent scholarship leave little doubt that the Framers' Constitution included substantial deviations from the related principles of rule by numerical majorities and "one person, one vote." At this point, the question is whether it is proper to judge the Framers' Constitution on the basis of these standards. Or are such judgments anachronistic, severe, or otherwise improper? With regard to the three-fifths clause, it seems hard *not* to conclude that this provision was fundamentally undemocratic. It not only disproportionately increased the power of slave states in the national government but also effectively transferred that power to individuals who could not be said to represent slaves in any meaningful sense and who were, in fact, profoundly interested in their continued enslavement.

Equal representation in the Senate and the absence of a provision mandating legislative districts of roughly equal size are different cases and require more complex judgments. These questions cut to the heart of the character of representation and provide a vivid example of how interpreters in this debate disagree first and most fundamentally about standards of democracy and the essential requirements of a democratic system. Specifically, the charge that equal representation in the Senate violated norms of political equality and fundamental fairness is not anachronistic. The principles of political equality, proportionality, or fairness and majority rule were deeply embedded in the logic that some of the principal architects of the Constitution—including Madison and Wilson—used to oppose the Great Compromise. These delegates were vehemently opposed to equal representation in the Senate, which they saw as a barrier to majority rule and a violation of the principles of equity and justice. Nor were they persuaded by the argument that the antimajoritarian effects of equal representation in the Senate would be counterbalanced by the House of Representatives, which was based on the principle of majority rule. In his June 30 speech before the convention, Madison reduced much of his case against equal representation in the Senate to the leverage it would give to a *majority of the states* to block rule by a *majority of the citizens* of the United States. The majority of states, Madison suggested, could obstruct the wishes of the majority of the people, exhort measures from them, or even pass measures disfavored by them.[167]

Defenders of equal representation in the Senate did not respond directly to the charge of political inequality. Instead, the most sophisticated defenders seemingly conceded that it would create inequality even as they argued that it was necessary to ensure the states' agency in operations of the national government, protect the states in general from encroachments by the national government, and prevent the large states from capturing the national government and dominating the small states.[168] These defenses, however, implied that equal representation in the Senate was necessary for the preservation of democracy. This defense follows Jensen's defense of the government established under the Articles of Confederation as democratic. Equal representation in the Senate, according to this line of reasoning, was and is necessary to protect the autonomy of the states as independent political societies and to prevent the national government from absorbing powers meant to be exercised by the states. The states, in turn, were viewed as independent political societies in which democracy can be practiced within a small geographic sphere. Equal representation in the Senate, according to this argument, was necessary to preserve a system of decentralized democracy. Here, the principal point of disagreement between defenders and critics of equal representation in the Senate emerges. Whether scholars judge equal representation to be democratic or undemocratic depends on whether they envision a system of national democracy (in which case the Senate creates inequality and skews representation) or a system of decentralized democracy (in which case the Senate preserves democracy within the states).

Finally, whether the Framers' failure to mandate roughly equal-sized electoral districts makes the Constitution undemocratic obviously depends on one's standard of democracy and, even more fundamentally, on how one views the purposes of representation. In this case, the point of contention revolves around the related questions of whether population is the only possible object of representation, or whether representation of towns, interests, and other considerations is acceptable, and whether the standard of one person, one vote is vital to the very idea of democracy.

Once again, the Framers' Constitution cannot be insulated from criticism by the charge of anachronism. Certainly, the inequality or malapportionment created in the House of Representatives was not as great as that in eighteenth-century Britain, with its infamous rotten boroughs.[169] Still, seven of the state constitutions in place in 1787 had provisions that mandated increases in representation with increases in population, and two states—Pennsylvania and New York—had a reapportionment scheme that was designed to promote something roughly equivalent to the standard of one person, one vote.[170]

Nevertheless, as Felix Frankfurter said in his famous dissent in *Baker v. Carr,* the historical case that one person, one vote was understood as a requirement of representation in early America or that it constitutes an unquestionable principle of political representation is weak.[171] Even as early Americans grappled with the idea of proportionality and sought to avoid the British system of rotten boroughs and vast inequality, they did not conclude that population was the only proper basis of representation or that any deviation from one person, one vote was undemocratic. Towns, interests, and geographic areas— independent of population—were taken into consideration in the apportionment of representatives and the drawing of district lines throughout American history, until the reapportionment decisions of the 1960s.

In short, then, the strongest case that the original Constitution violated the principle of political equality has been made by studies that illustrate the profound inequality created by the three-fifths clause. Charges that inequality in the Senate and unequal electoral districts were fundamentally undemocratic rest on inherently disputable conceptions of democracy and representation. Those who observe that equal representation in the Senate created substantial inequality are correct, but their observations rest on an understanding of centralized democracy that had yet to develop fully, and they discount the possibility that equal representation in the Senate was necessary to protect a system of decentralized democracy. Those who observe that the Constitution failed to institutionalize the principle of one person, one vote are also correct, but it is contentious to claim that this principle is the only possible basis of representation consistent with democracy.

Thinking Clearly and Talking Intelligently about Democracy and Good Government

When the question "how democratic is the Framers' Constitution?" is based on concrete comparisons along several dimensions of democracy rather than diffusive or even unarticulated conceptions of it, the character of the Constitution is revealed as complex and ambiguous. Its most democratic dimension was its inclusiveness.[172] In this area, the Framers' Constitution established one of the most progressive political systems of its age. Consistent with its federal character, the Framers' Constitution stipulated only that those who elected U.S. representatives be the same as those who elected delegates to the most numerous branch of the state legislature. Although this provision created no clear mandate for future expansions of the electorate and left the voting rights of women and minorities vulnerable to white male majorities, it nevertheless recognized the most extensive electorate in the world at that time. Similarly, there were no property qualifications for holding federal office, and religious oaths for office were prohibited. Except for the anomalous provision that the president had to be a natural-born citizen, the minimal age and naturalization requirements for office in the Framers' Constitution were among the most liberal of any eighteenth-century constitution (including the Revolutionary state constitutions) and comport with modern standards of democracy.

The Framers' Constitution did not, however, explicitly recognize the right of all adults to vote and hold office regardless of gender or race. The constitutional recognition of such an electorate had to await the passage of the Fifteenth, Nineteenth, Twenty-third, and Twenty-sixth Amendments. Furthermore, the Framers' Constitution was far from fully democratic along the other two dimensions of democracy considered in this study. It embedded political inequality in the political system through the three-fifths clause and equal representation in the Senate, and it was decisively less responsive to popular majorities than were the Revolutionary state constitutions. In comparison to the state constitutions, it loosened the ties of direct accountability between the people and their representatives and made collective action by the people much more difficult.

What does this ambiguous and (I hope) balanced interpretation of the Framers' Constitution tell us about the deepest differences between the Progressive and democratic readings of the document, as well as their strengths and limitations? Most obviously, this interpretation of the Constitution as inclusive and, in important ways, historically progressive suggests a much more guarded evaluation than that provided in standard Progressive and multicultural critiques. It also suggests, however, that scholars who argue that the Framers' Constitution created a democratic republic are largely ignoring how it muted the direct expression of the people's will and was inconsistent with political equality.

At a deeper level, this interpretation exposes the different foundational assumptions, standards for judgment, and strategies of argumentation between the Progressive and democratic interpretations of the Constitution. The Progressives and their heirs argue that the Framers' Constitution was democratically deficient based on an analysis of three distinct types of provisions and claims. First, these scholars point to areas in which the Framers' Constitution was univocally undemocratic, such as its failure to recognize the full political rights of women and African Americans. In this dimension of democracy, they judge the Framers against standards of democracy that were extremely rare during their time. Second, the Progressives and their heirs point to features such as terms of office, numbers of representatives, and modes of selection—areas where the Framers explicitly sought to moderate and control the influence of popular majorities and to make public officials less directly accountable to the public. The assumption here is that more directly accountable modes of selection or terms of office are both more democratic and more desirable than long-leash features. Third, critics of the democratic interpretation of the Framers' Constitution point to violations of political equality created by equal representation in the Senate and the three-fifths clause. These scholars adopt a standard akin to one person, one vote in assessing these constitutional provisions.

For their part, proponents of the democratic interpretation of the Framers' Constitution argue that contemporary standards of inclusiveness are inappropriate because they are utopian or anachronistic. When they evaluate the long-leash features of the Framers' Constitution (and here I include Publius as the most sophisticated defender of its popular character), they pursue a complex strategy. At times, they argue that the practices of the states and Great Britain were varied and that the Framers' Constitution did not lie outside of those practices. At other times, they resist the standards of democracy and republicanism adopted by critics of the Constitution, suggesting, for example, that annual appointments were not essential attributes of republicanism. Yet another strategy is to deny the relevance of any comparisons by defending the distinctiveness of federal offices and powers. For example, Publius suggests that there could be fewer federal representatives than state delegates, and that they could safely serve longer terms, because the powers exercised by federal officials were more limited in scope. Longer terms of office, defenders of the Constitution have suggested, were justified because of the peculiar character of federal responsibilities. Besides having to travel great distances, federal officials, unlike state representatives, had to acquire knowledge of foreign affairs and of the laws and interests of all the states in order to exercise their powers over taxation and commercial regulation responsibly. Finally, they have suggested that features that might make the government more directly responsive to popular majorities, such as a greater number of representatives, would not make the system operate more democratically. A large legislative assembly, Madison argues, might appear to be more democratic, but decisions within it would be made by fewer individuals than in an assembly with only a moderate number of representatives.

More broadly, the most sophisticated proponents of the democratic interpretation have invited participants in the debate to consider a complex set of evaluations in which the question of the democratic nature of the Constitution is subsumed by a larger and even more complex debate about when it is legitimate and wise to restrict democracy and how to identify and balance constitutional values to achieve "good government." The Framers, they observe, did not believe that the Constitution should be judged solely on the basis of how democratic it was. Instead, they identified many attributes of good government and argued about whether the political system of 1787 would help secure an energetic, stable, and impartial system and one that properly balanced the powers of the national government and the states. The Framers, in other words, did not simply assume that democratic government was good government.

Finding an Archimedean point from which to arbitrate between these accounts is not easy, especially since their primary differences spring from fundamentally different standards of democracy. Still, a few substantive comments are suggested by this chapter. First, many proponents of the democratic interpretation argue that it is simply improper to judge historical actors against modern standards of inclusion or political equality, because these standards never occurred in the eighteenth century. They then suggest that historical standards provide an unproblematic alternative. This argument fails, however, because modern standards of democracy have roots that reach back to the Founding, and the historical standards of the time included anomalies. For instance, it occurred to men in the state of New Jersey to enfranchise single women, or at least not to interpret their state constitution in such a way as to exclude them. It occurred to James Otis that equality meant voting rights for women. It also occurred to constitutional designers in some states to periodically adjust the size of legislative districts to secure electoral districts with roughly the same number of individuals and thus approximate political equality. The scholar who admonishes the Framers for not guaranteeing women and African Americans full rights or criticizes them for not adopting policies that promote one person, one vote is therefore not being anachronistic. He or she is judging all the Framers against the most progressive standards of their day. In general, the inevitability that scholars will disagree about the meaning of democracy and thus what standards to use to judge the Framers' Constitution need not lead us to despair. It only means that these issues are inevitably linked to serious discussions about how democratic the Framers' Constitution was.

Second, the federal character of the Constitution poses a particular problem in interpretation that has not received enough attention or commentary. Many of the provisions cited by recent critics who argue that the Framers' Constitution violates principles of political equality reflect the federal character of the Constitution more than a desire to achieve or mute democracy. This is true even though these provisions were opposed as undemocratic at the time and have subsequently made the system deviate substantially from the principles of majority rule and political equality. In particular, as previously mentioned, whether we consider these provisions undemocratic or not depends on whether we are talking about a system of national democracy or a decentralized state-centered democracy. Furthermore, as witnessed by Wilson's conception of democratic nationalism and the decentralized conception of democracy envisioned by proponents of the Articles of Confederation, both visions had proponents. Some nationalists of the 1780s wanted to transfer decisions on matters such as currency, taxation, and commercial regulation to the national government to insulate them from popular majorities. But many of these same Framers favored proportional representation in both houses of the legislature and thus more strongly favored majority rule than did defenders of the continued sovereignty of the states, as long as the majority was drawn from the majority of the American people. In short, then, there is no straightforward or unambiguous relationship between nationalism and democracy.

Third, as proponents of the democratic interpretation suggest, we should not judge the Framers' Constitution without taking into account its multiple intended purposes. To do so imposes a single-factor analysis—how democratic was the Framers' Constitution?—onto a political system meant to achieve many goals. Conversely, we cannot simply accept the terms on which the Framers posed the questions. We must also consider whether we agree with the Framers about the proper attributes of "good" government and whether constitutional provisions defended as integral to good government really serve those purposes. For example, would shorter terms of office for senators have impeded the Senate's ability to check the House of Representatives and provide stability to the political system? Were life appointments necessary to ensure judicial independence and promote judges' capacity for impartial judgment? Was equal representation in the Senate really necessary as a defensive power for the small states or as a means of preventing the encroachment of federal power, or was it simply a sine qua non of the delegates from small states so that they could wield an unwarranted degree of power in the national government? More broadly, the fundamental assumption made by the Framers—and one that has controlled much subsequent reasoning about democracy in the United States—is that the more democratic a political system is, the more likely it is to violate rights. Nevertheless, it is certainly possible that greater commitment to political equality, political participation, and governmental responsiveness would engender greater respect for and acceptance of rights rather than endangering liberty.[173]

Finally, we must examine the Federalists' justifications and arguments. Was it adequate to say, as the Federalists did, that longer terms of office were justified because fit men would not otherwise undertake the burdens of travel that accompanied federal officeholding and because some of the responsibilities given to Congress and the president (especially the conduct of foreign affairs) required greater knowledge and experience and thus greater time to master? Does the decision-making process really become concentrated on fewer individuals in legislative assemblies with a large number of representatives? Only by addressing such questions can we hope to understand the character of the Constitution and surmount the tedious and repetitive exchanges between those scholars who want to raze and reform the Constitution and those who want to defend and preserve it.

3

How Should We Study the American Founding?
In Defense of Historically Sensitive
Political Philosophy

The debates over the economic interpretation of the Constitution and whether the political system created in 1787 was democratic or not illustrate the struggles of modern students with the legacy of Charles Beard and the Progressive historians. Scholars contributing to these debates unavoidably have to confront Beard's interpretations and take a stand either for or against them. The longest shadow cast by Beard, however, is over the study of the political ideas of the American Founding. Indeed, although the profoundness of its effect now seems remarkable, the charge by Beard and the Progressives that political ideas are mere reflections of underlying economic interests, and thus unworthy of study, stifled an examination of the intellectual origins of the American Republic for half a century.

For many scholars, the empirical studies of the 1950s and 1960s on the economic interests of the American Founders broke the hold of Beard's thesis. If it could not be proved that the Founders were members of a specific economic group intent on advancing their immediate economic interests, these scholars reasoned, then the study of the Founders' political ideas was defensible. For these scholars, however, the justification for the study of ideas rested on the thin reed of the inconclusiveness of the economic interpretation.

Most important for our purposes, however, an alternative approach to the study of political thought has subsequently been developed that seeks to justify the study of political ideas no matter what the eventual outcome of the empirical debate about the role of economic interests in the formation and ratification of the Constitution. What has been called the "new historicism" or the "ideological approach"—and what I call here "linguistic contextualism"—has become the theoretical foundation of much of the scholarship of the re-publican revisionists.[1] This approach also challenges the traditional, philo-sophical study of the history of political thought as a forum in which "peren-nial questions" are addressed through the interpretation of "great books."

The analysis that follows first characterizes the dominant themes within linguistic contextualism. In developing this characterization, I turned to the methodological writings of Bernard Bailyn, Gordon Wood, Quentin Skin-ner, and J. G. A. Pocock, the most theoretically self-conscious and sophisti-cated of the historians who have contributed to republican revisionism. These scholars have constructed a subtle and challenging approach to the interpre-tation of historical political texts by drawing diffusely on the doctrine of the social construction of reality, the concept of ideology as espoused by Clifford Geertz, the linguistic theories of Ludwig Wittgenstein and J. L. Austin, and the concept of language paradigms developed by Thomas Kuhn.[2]

Next, I provide a critique of the strengths and weaknesses of linguistic contextualism. This critique anticipates the specific suggestions about how scholarship on the American Founding should be conducted that I present later in the chapter. Here, I argue for an interpretive approach that seeks to discover impartially the Founders' self-understanding about their ideas and their project but, unlike linguistic contextualism, does *not* conclude that im-partial historical investigations inevitably lead only to the discovery of the irretrievability and differentness of the past or that the appropriation of past ideas for present purposes is always illegitimate. Instead, I argue that his-torical texts (including those surrounding the American Founding) make claims to truth that interpreters unavoidably confront. I also contend that there are indeed perennial questions or themes in the history of political thought (including American political thought) and that different political thinkers have espoused competing answers to these questions and themes. Contrary to the claims of the linguistic contextualists, such an approach is not simply possible but also immensely illuminating.

These conclusions and the approach defended here are hardly novel. Others have sought to steer between the Scylla of materialism and the Charybdis of historicism. Nevertheless, my goal in this chapter is not to pre-sent a novel approach to interpretation but rather to defend a sound one against the criticisms raised against it primarily by the linguistic contextual-ists. Unfortunately, in their efforts to liberate themselves from the Progres-sives' critique of idealism and defend the study of political language, the linguistic contextualists end up challenging the legitimacy and indeed the very possibility of the philosophical analysis of political texts. My goal, however, is emphatically *not* to reject the valid insights of linguistic contextualism or to deny the possibility or value of genuine historical knowledge. On the contrary, I agree with the linguistic contextualists that impartial historical understanding is possible and that political theorizing outside of it is not worth engaging in. Properly conceived, the study of the history of political thought, and of the American Founding in particular, can integrate what is sensible in linguistic contextualists' approach without falling into their erroneous conclusions. The question, then, is not whether historical understanding is imperative to the study of the American Founding but rather *how* it is important and whether a philosophical approach necessarily leads to many of the specific errors that Wood, Skinner, and Pocock associate with it.

Many scholars—especially historians—will doubtlessly disagree with these conclusions. However, I hope that even those readers will be able to use this chapter to reflect on four interrelated sets of questions that remain core problems in the interpretation of the history of political thought and the American Founding. First, can the study of political ideas be defended against the Progressive, Namieran, and Marxist criticism that ideas are nothing more than projected rationalizations of underlying interests? If so, what is the *best* defense against this charge? Second, how should the study of the history of political thought be conceived and justified? Is it properly conceived as a study of competing answers to perennial questions and an analysis of competing conceptions of enduring political concepts and themes, or as an exploration of an alien and irretrievable culture that teaches us that we are on our own to face our peculiar problems? Third, is the appropriation of past political ideas to address current political problems ever acceptable, or, conversely, is such an exercise only an attempt to evoke some great thinker in the service of a contemporary political agenda at the expense of impartial historical understanding? Fourth, which texts merit our attention and interpretation, and which ones do not? Should we choose texts because they are somehow extraordinary and thus can be designated as "great books," because they are "representative" of a past society and thus provide us with an accurate view of that society's political culture, or because they help us engage in contemporary political thinking?

Bailyn and Wood: Enveloping Behavioralism and Idealism

As it has been defended in the works of Bailyn, Wood, Pocock, and Skinner, linguistic contextualism is at once opposed to Beardian and Namieran criticisms of the study of ideas, to the Whig and neo-Whig contention that ideas can be studied as motives for behavior, and to the so-called great-books approach to the study of political thought. The opposition of these scholars to both the formalist defense of the study of ideas and the Progressive and behavioralist critique of it is best illustrated in the methodological writings of Bernard Bailyn and Gordon Wood.

Bailyn was one of the first scholars to realize the potential of Geertz's non-Marxist conception of ideology as a means of transcending and enveloping idealist (Whig) and behavioralist (Progressive) interpretations of the American Revolution.[3] Specifically, at the time that Bailyn and Wood began to develop their interpretations, the Progressive interpretation of the American Revolution, which rested on a behavioralist understanding of the function of ideas, was dominant. Nevertheless, this interpretation was being challenged by a resurgent Whig interpretation that sought to reestablish the centrality of ideas as a cause of the American Revolution.

For their part, the Progressives argued that the American Revolutionaries were irresponsible and self-interested, that their rhetoric was little more than conspiratorial and irrational propaganda, and that the American Revolution was unjustifiable because the colonists were freer and more prosperous than their English brethren. In contrast, neo-Whig historians sought to return to the contention—voiced by earlier Whig historians and the American Revolutionaries themselves—that the American Revolution was a conservative, principled response to the provocations of the English government and that the Revolutionaries were motivated by a consistent, resolute, and sincere commitment to constitutional liberties. Edmund Morgan, for example, contended that "the resolutions of the colonial and intercolonial assemblies in 1765 laid down the line on which Americans stood until they cut their connections with England." Far from leaping instrumentally through different arguments, as the Progressive historians contended, from 1765 to 1776 the colonists had, according to Morgan, consistently denied the authority of Parliament to tax them internally or externally, yet they simultaneously agreed to submit to laws that Parliament enacted for supervision of the entire British empire.[4]

When Bailyn pored over the pamphlets of the American Revolution in preparation for writing the studies that would culminate in *The Ideological Origins of the American Revolution,* he discovered and documented the profound influence of the "Commonwealth" or "opposition" ideology of seventeenth- and eighteenth-century English radicals on the American Revolution. But what made Bailyn's interpretation novel and important was not simply that he isolated the influence of ideas that had previously been considered relatively unimportant in explaining the American Revolution but also that he combined this insight with a broader explanation about the relationship of ideas to behavior. This served as the foundation for an interpretation of the American Revolution that transcends and absorbs important insights from both the Whig and Progressive, idealist and behavioralist, interpretations.

At its core, this explanation suggests that ideas become influential when they are crystallized into ideology. And ideology, Bailyn maintains (following the writings of cultural anthropologist Geertz), is capable of mediating social experience and crystallizing otherwise disparate strands of thought into patterns so powerful that they become influential. Numerous sets of ideas—including Enlightenment concepts, common-law precepts, and classical allusions—were evoked by the colonists. Opposition ideology, however, served as the "elaborate pattern of middle-level beliefs" that was responsible for "triggering" the insurrection. The ideas of English radicals were "compelling because they were a part of an elaborate map of social reality, part of a pattern that made life comprehensible" for the colonists.[5] "Formal discourse," Bailyn further contends,

> becomes politically powerful when it becomes ideology: when it articulates and fuses into effective formulations opinions and attitudes that are otherwise too scattered and vague to be acted upon; when it mobilizes a general mood, "a set of disconnected, unrealized private emotions," into "a public possession, a social fact"; when it crystallizes otherwise inchoate social and political discontent and thereby shapes what is otherwise instinctive and directs it to attainable goals; when it clarifies, symbolizes, and elevates to structured consciousness the mingled urges that stir within us. But its power is not autonomous. It can only formulate, reshape, and direct forward moods, attitudes, ideas, and aspirations that in some form, however crude or incomplete, already exist.[6]

To Bailyn, then, ideologies are properly thought of neither as motives for action nor as simply propaganda—a concept that, according to Bailyn, has little value to historians. Ideologies are embedded in society, where they structure consciousness and compel men to act in their image. Thus, Bailyn concludes, Tory and Progressive historians were wrong to dismiss the importance of the ideas of the American colonists in the American Revolution, just as patriot and Whig historians were wrong to consider them the pristine cause of it. The American colonists were marinated in radical opposition ideology and thus were led to see conspiratorial designs in the most trifling actions of British authorities and then to revolt, even though they were more prosperous and free than their British counterparts at home.

This "anthropological" interpretation of the American Revolution, according to Bailyn, is "neither whig nor tory, idealist or materialist, liberal nor conservative"; rather, it envelopes each and makes it possible to understand the peculiar importance of ideas in the American Revolution, the social disruptions and violence that accompanied it, and the social and political changes it created.[7] This interpretation also makes it possible to integrate the perspective of the losers (in this case, the Loyalists and the Crown) into a historical account and thereby reach the "ultimate stage of maturity in historical interpretation where partisanship is left behind."[8]

Bailyn worked out the broad outlines of this interpretation of the American Revolution and this explanation of the relationship between ideas and behavior. But it was Gordon Wood (Bailyn's student in the 1960s) who subsequently provided an even more elaborate version of this interpretation, extended the analysis of the centrality of ideology into the constitution-making period of the 1780s, and confronted the other group of important losers in early American history—the anti-Federalists.[9] Wood has also connected the relationship of ideas and behavior to a broader understanding of the character of the historical process and the relationship of past ideas to present political problems.

In particular, Wood (like Bailyn) urges scholars not to suppose that ideas are the *causes* of behavior. He also urges us not to address what he calls the "problem of motivation" by trying to establish that historical actors were motivated by sincerely held beliefs.[10] Such a proposition, according to Wood, could not be proved even if it were true (and Wood does not believe that it is). Moreover, such a tender-minded position leads scholars who interpret ideas to be dismissed by other scholars.

Nevertheless, even if ideas can never be shown to be the motives for or causes of behavior, this does not mean that they are merely the pageant behind which real motives, such as economic interests, are hidden. Like Bailyn and Geertz, Wood views ideas not as epiphenomenal abstractions but rather as much a part of the matrix of society as economic factors are. Considered collectively as social conventions or ideology, they serve as a kind of cognitive road map and bring together otherwise disparate strands of thought. Even more important, they "effect" actions by forcing justifications in their terms. "Human behavior," Wood writes (following Geertz), "is of a piece with the meanings or ideas we give to it," and "the meanings we give are public ones, and they are defined and delimited by the conventions and language of the culture of the time."[11] Individuals may well try to set forth ideas that are really nothing more than the projected rationalizations of their interests.

Nevertheless, we all live in a universe of discourse that we did not create and can never fully control. Moreover, we must define and justify our actions in reference to this public language. What is liberal or conservative, aristocratic or democratic, constitutional or unconstitutional, is determined by the matrix of social meanings. "The stakes are always high," Wood writes, "because what we cannot make meaningful—cannot conceive of, legitimate, or persuade other people to accept—in some sense we cannot do."[12] Thus, "if anyone in our intellectual struggles violates too radically the accepted or inherited meanings of the culture his ability to persuade others is lost."[13]

According to Wood, this matrix of public ideas and, indeed, some of our most cherished political concepts are the products of thousands of complex interactions and the unintended effects of these interactions. Therefore, scholars who study only the conscious designs and motives of historical agents and then suppose that historical events were the result of these designs miss much of the richness of the historical process. The historical process, as Wood sees it, is public, complex, and sloppy. Historical agents actually control very little of their destiny and are as much the victims of ideas as the manipulators of them. Ideas, Wood specifies, often take on "an elusive and unmanageable quality, a dynamic self-intensifying character" that transcends "the intentions and desires of any of the historical participants."[14] These ideas operate "over the heads of the participants, taking them in directions no one could have foreseen" and, as historian Perry Miller vividly illustrates with the example of the Puritans, creating a bewildering world that they can barely understand.[15]

Similarly, scholars who suppose that political concepts are the result of rational deliberation and "closet philosophizing" miss the true origin of these concepts. Political concepts such as separation of powers and federalism and even the Constitution itself, according to Wood, did not result from conscious design but instead were the products of "contentious political polemics" and of compromises and bargains between historical agents who were anxiously groping toward an uncertain future.[16] Most important, the fact that ideologies are both public and dynamic means that Beard and the Progressives were wrong. Men are the instruments of ideas just as often as ideas are the instruments of men.[17]

For Wood, several conclusions about the study of political thought follow directly from this understanding of the character and function of ideas and the historical process. First, he contends that historians of political thought should not be concerned with the truth of the arguments and ideas of the political thinkers they study. Such an approach would leave us "endlessly caught up in the polemics of the participants themselves."[18] Instead, according to Wood, they should try to identify impartially the sets of social conventions present in the society under study and show how political actors used these conventions to justify their actions and otherwise make sense of the world in which they lived.[19]

Like Bailyn, then, Wood does not believe that historians should try to determine whether the Whigs or the Tories had a more correct view of the causes of the American Revolution or whether the Federalists or the anti-Federalists had a more correct interpretation of the Constitution. Instead, they should strive to transcend and reconcile the opposing views of historical agents. This can best be done by explaining why each side adopted the meanings it did. Indeed, Wood asserts, there is no real or timeless meaning to a document like the Constitution or to the question of whether the American Revolutionaries were justified in rebelling. There are only the meanings and justifications that different historical agents give and, most importantly, the ones that society accepts. The belief that such questions have real answers may be a necessary myth for scholars in some disciplines, Wood maintains, but historians need not indulge that myth.

Second, scholars should not try to discover the answers to perennial questions in the texts of past political thinkers or try to appropriate past political ideas in the service of present political problems. For Wood, to impartially or objectively interpret eighteenth-century texts is to establish the radical "irretrievability" and "differentness" of the world in which they were written, the particularity of the problems they addressed, and the specificity of the authors' intentions.[20] Again applying the ideas of Geertz, Wood writes:

> Since idea- or symbol-making is itself a social process and is such a dynamic, effortful, instrumental, and problem-solving activity, ideas can only be considered in terms of the actors' intentions as historically specific and not as timeless. Although words and concepts may remain outwardly the same for centuries, their particular functions and meanings do not and could not remain static—not as long as individuals attempt to use them to explain new social circumstances and make meaningful new social behavior.[21]

Ideas, in short, are "important for what they do rather than for what they are" and thus should be studied for their function, not their content.[22] Moreover, their function changes. Thus, scholars who seek to apply the ideas derived from historical political texts to modern problems either do not understand how different the eighteenth century is from the present or are, in Wood's estimation, "ransacking" historical documents and setting forth interpretations that are "manipulations" of the meanings of the authors.[23]

For Wood, this view rests on his belief about the fundamentally different approaches and goals of the historian, on the one hand, and the political theorists or philosopher, on the other. The "agenda" of political theorists, he maintains, demands that they "see past ideas as merely the sources or seeds for present or future political thinking." They thus see the past as an anticipation of the future and incorrectly tend to hold the people of the past responsible for a future that they could not have imagined.[24] Furthermore, they often fail to see not only that the past is fundamentally different from the present but also that historical actors were trapped in "awful predicaments" and that their efforts to implement their ideas rarely resulted in what they intended. In contrast, historians ought to be concerned about how to "recover a past world as accurately as possible and try to show how that different world developed into our own." They should study the Founding, for example, to "see how it flows out of the previous events and into the subsequent events of American history."[25]

To achieve these goals, historians must ultimately remain attached to a fundamental article of faith that makes writing history possible: they must hold on to the positivist doctrine that there is a knowable past made up of facts and that this past—however elusive—can be grasped by the historian.[26] Historians should not get caught up in "ever more precious historiographical debates" or bother to muse abstractly about "the possibilities of actually representing past reality." They should instead go about the activity of representing that past reality, of writing history in such a way as to "actually advance our understanding of how we Americans came to be what we are."[27]

Together, Wood's justification for historical studies, his defense of the ultimate objectivity of historical research, his opposition to the appropriation of historical ideas, and his implicit (if largely undeveloped) opposition to the great-books approach to the study of political thought also inform his understanding of which texts should be studied. Interested primarily in establishing how historical actors used ideologies to solve their problems and make sense of their world, Wood contends that scholars should examine a wide variety of texts, including pamphlets, sermons, works of lesser-known political actors, and even "forms of expressive action." Indeed, according to Wood, since ideas and symbols are also "forms of expressive action and are more than what is embedded in literary texts, the mob's effigy may have been as meaningful as the learned pamphlet."[28]

Conversely, the "great thinkers," Wood asserts, are merely those individuals who see most clearly and "clarify . . . moments of transformation"; thus, their works should be thought of as "representative" of the age in which they were written.[29] In general, for Wood, the goal of the scholar

should be to understand fully the political beliefs of a past society—its political culture—not simply the ideas of a few thinkers who were subsequently designated as seminal. Only by understanding the broader sets of
conventions in past societies can we hope to understand how men "wrestle
with ideas and symbols in order to explain, justify, lay blame for, or otherwise make sense of what is happening, not just for themselves but for others."[30] For this reason, the historian of political thought is properly interested in examining the whole terrain of the social and political thought of
past societies, not simply the highest peaks.

Finally, interpreters should not presuppose that past political thinkers
such as the American Founders were necessarily rational, brilliant, or coherent. Philosophical distinctions—such as Garry Wills's interpretation of the
Declaration of Independence as a statement of the Scottish moral sentimentalism of Frances Hutcheson and a conscious rejection of the moral rational-
ism of John Locke—are, according to Wood, "too precious, too refined, too
academic for the dynamic culture of the eighteenth century. Jefferson was
scarcely capable of drawing such fine distinctions or of perceiving any antagonism or incompatibility between what Locke and Hutcheson had written."[31] These ideas had been blended and molded into a general Enlightenment consensus, and the scholar who seeks such refinements will miss the
complex marketlike configuration of the thought of previous societies.

Skinner: Challenging "Great Books" and "Perennial Questions"

Although scholarship on the American Founding has been directly informed by Bailyn's and Wood's writings, it has also been indirectly informed
by the methodological studies of Quentin Skinner.[32] Skinner has launched a
comprehensive attack on the prevailing notion that the history of political
thought should or even can be studied by examining the "timeless" questions
and answers set forth in "great books" in search of enduring political truths.[33]
He has also rejected the parallel possibility that the history of political
thought can be conceived as a means of exploring the different interpretations of the "fundamental concepts" that have been of "perennial interest."[34]

In its place, he hopes to establish a methodology that "might begin to
give us a history of political thought with a genuinely historical character."[35]
Toward this end, Skinner proposes that we adopt the axiom that "no agent
can eventually be said to have meant or done something which he could
never be brought to accept as a correct description of what he had meant or
done." An acceptable account of an agent's behavior, Skinner continues,
must "survive the demonstration that it was itself dependent on the use of

criteria of description and classification" available to the agent. The adoption of this methodology, Skinner promises, will not only enlarge our vision of the past but also enrich our understanding of the great books themselves and even "invest the history of ideas with its own philosophical point."[36]

In particular, in his seminal article "Meaning and Understanding in the History of Ideas," Skinner traces various forms of "historical absurdity" and "anachronistic mythologies" that, he contends, have "contaminated" the study of the history of political thought and resulted in "conceptual muddles" and "mistaken empirical claims." These historical errors, according to Skinner, are not merely coincidental with but rather endemic to two dominant modes of historical interpretation. The first approach makes the "text itself" the "self-sufficient object of inquiry and understanding" in search of answers to perennial questions. The second is based on the contention that a text should be understood in terms of its historical context. Both approaches, according to Skinner, fail for the same reason. Both ultimately "commit philosophical mistakes in the assumptions they make about the conditions necessary for the understanding of utterances."[37]

The bulk of Skinner's analysis is focused on outlining the mythologies that, he contends, unavoidably result from exegesis limited to the text alone. Such an approach is "logically tied" to a "great books approach" that searches for perennial questions in the history of political thought and universal propositions about political reality. This approach, Skinner continues, demands most of our attention because it is still the most pervasive, raises the most interesting philosophical questions, and gives "rise to the largest number of confusions." Furthermore, according to Skinner, proponents of this approach sharply distance themselves from the belief that historical context is important in interpretation, "for to suggest instead that a knowledge of the social context is a necessary condition for an understanding of the classic texts is equivalent to denying that they do contain any elements of timeless and perennial interest, and is thus equivalent to removing the whole point of studying what they said."[38]

Skinner's analysis here is quite complex, but he centers primarily on two historical mythologies: the "mythology of the doctrines" and the "mythology of coherence." The mythology of the doctrines results when an exegete believes that there is a set of doctrines or mandatory themes to which all great thinkers in the history of political thought must have contributed or, conversely, if they did not, should be criticized for not considering. Obviously, this approach makes a doctrine, an idea, or a given text itself (not the historical agent and his or her complex authorial intention within a particular linguistic context) the subject of inquiry and analysis. The dangers of this interpretive decision, according to Skinner, include the likelihood that an exegete will gather scattered remarks from a classic writer and construct them into the writer's understanding of a particular doctrine. In many cases, this leads an exegete to attribute to a historical agent an understanding of a particular doctrine or theme that he or she could not possibly have had because it did not exist at the time.

For example, the debate about whether Marsilius of Padua had a "real" conception of the separation of powers is both "brisk and wholly meaningless." Marsilius, according to Skinner, was drawing on Aristotle's discussion of the reasons for separating the executive from the legislative power and, unlike subsequent proponents of the separation of powers, was not concerned with the issue of political freedom. More important, the historical origins of the doctrine of separation of powers arose more than two centuries after Marsilius's death. Thus, Marsilius could not have meant to contribute to this debate because the terms of it were unknown to him, and the point of this debate would have been lost to him.[39]

Whereas the various forms of the mythology of the doctrines result from an exegete's efforts to interpret the thoughts of historical agents based on classifications set by a disciplinary paradigm, the mythology of coherence results, according to Skinner, from an exegete's assumption that a historical agent proposed a coherent, comprehensive, closed system of thought. This assumption, Skinner contends, is dangerous because it suggests that historical agents achieved a degree of coherence that they may not have actually achieved or to which they did not even aspire. An exegete who works from the assumption that coherence is present is forgetting Occam's razor (that an apparent inconsistency may indeed be an inconsistency) and will also feel authorized or even compelled to supply coherence where none is present. This decision to fill in where the historical actor has not spoken leads to a historical account of "thoughts which no one ever actually succeeded in thinking, at a level of coherence which no one ever actually attained."[40]

In general, interpreters who commit these and other methodological errors are guilty of forgetting some "commonplace, but amazingly elusive, facts about the activity of thinking." Historical actors, Skinner urges exegetes to remember, "may *consciously* adopt incompatible ideals and beliefs in different moods and at different times." Furthermore, thinking itself is not an effortless activity but rather "an often intolerable wrestle with words and their meanings" that causes us to "spill over the limits of our intelligence and get confused." "Our attempts to synthesize our views," Skinner concludes, "may in consequence reveal conceptual disorder at least as much as coherent doctrines."[41]

In contrast to his analysis of the problems of interpretation based on the text itself, Skinner's criticism of contextually based interpretation is brief and limited to the final pages of his long and complex essay. Here and in his other writings, he is far from dismissing the importance of the social and intellectual context in establishing a framework that allows the exegete to engage in legitimate historical analysis. Indeed, Skinner's seminal study, *The Foundations of Modern Political Thought,* is premised on the belief that scholars must have intimate knowledge of the "more general social and intellectual matrix" out of which texts were written and that "political life sets the main problems for the political theorist, causing a certain range of issues to appear problematic, and a corresponding range of questions to become the leading subjects of debate."[42] He even states at one point that "an understanding of any idea requires an understanding of all the occasions and activities in which a given agent might have used the relevant form of words."[43] A more demanding standard of contextual knowledge is hard to imagine.

What Skinner rejects is the proposition that the context of a text can be treated as a "determinant" of what is said.[44] Specifically, for Skinner, knowledge of historical context provides key information for grasping the *meaning* of a text, but it is not a sufficient condition and indeed may even be misleading in the exegete's efforts to *understand* the text. It is here that the full meaning of the title to Skinner's essay is clarified. It is also here that Skinner's affinity with J. L. Austin and Ludwig Wittgenstein's teaching that words are deeds comes into full view.

In particular, according to Skinner, context may help the interpreter grasp the antecedent conditions that caused an action (and he considers the expression of words in a text to be an action) and what the text was intended to mean (meaning). But context cannot illuminate what Skinner variously calls the historical agents' "intention in doing something" or "the point of the action for the agent who performed it" (understanding).[45] This is what Austin labels "intended illocutionary force." In understanding the force of an utterance or statement, contextual knowledge, according to Skinner, is not only insufficient but perhaps misleading, because the context itself can be read to be ambiguous. Skinner notes, for example, that context cannot help us understand whether Machiavelli's statement that "a prince must learn how not to be virtuous" was an endorsement of an accepted moral axiom or a revolutionary proposition. The context, according to Skinner, has been read to yield both possibilities and so cannot be used in favor of either. Thus, what we need in all interpretive endeavors is not simply to grasp what was said, or even its meaning, but rather to understand "*how* what was said was meant, and thus what *relations* there may have been between various different statements even within the same general context."[46]

As an alternative to the philosophical and empirical confusions rendered by existing approaches to interpretation, Skinner urges scholars to try to recover a complex intention of the author (including the author's intention in doing something) using knowledge of the linguistic context as a guide. As Michael Zuckert has observed, Skinner's principles of interpretation "turn us from the text itself to the context, or more accurately, to the kind of interaction between text and context in which illocutionary force is graspable."[47] Specifically, Skinner proposes that we must "delineate the whole range of communications which could have been conventionally performed on the given occasion by the utterance of the given utterance, and, next, to trace the relations between the given utterance and this wider *linguistic* context as a means of decoding the actual intention of the given writer." The exegete, then, should develop knowledge of the dense linguistic context in which utterances were made as a means of discovering what "in principle" the historical actor could have intended to communicate and do.[48]

Finally, Skinner concludes that if we adopt this approach we will invest the study of the history of political thought with its only legitimate philosophical purpose—namely, the recognition that there are no universal axioms or eternal verities to be discovered and therefore we must "learn to do our own thinking for ourselves." The classic texts, he asserts, reveal "not the essential sameness, but rather the essential variety of viable moral assumptions and political commitments" in the history of political thought. This approach to the study of political thought should also lead us to be on guard against "those features of our own arrangements which we may be disposed to accept as traditional or even 'timeless' truths," because they "may in fact be the merest contingencies of our peculiar history and social structure."[49] In short, the study of the history of political thought has two broad philosophical points: it teaches the lessons of moral relativism and false necessity.

Pocock: Studying Political Languages

A final scholar who has been central to the development of linguistic contextualism is J. G. A. Pocock.[50] Like Bailyn, Wood, and Skinner, Pocock is convinced that much of the scholarship in the history of political thought has taken a fundamentally ahistorical approach, and he is determined to rectify this problem. In particular, he traces the "confusion" that has characterized the study of the history of political thought to the way it has been conceived and conducted. Throughout much of the twentieth century, he observes, the history of political thought has been treated as the study of a traditional canon written by men who "could with fair plausibility be described as philosophers." Furthermore, this study has been "conducted by the methods of philosophic commentary on the intellectual contents of the tradition." The result, according to Pocock, is that "the coherence of a work or body of political writings, as political philosophy or as political theory, was mistakenly identified with its character as a historical phenomenon." In addition, it has been conducted by scholars who are not "concerned with what the author of a statement made in a remote past meant by it so much as with what he in his present can make it mean."[51]

Like Wood and Skinner, then, Pocock wants to shear the study of political thought from philosophical analysis and contemporary political life and transform it into a form of historical analysis. This can best be achieved, according to Pocock, not by supplying coherence to the thought of past political thinkers but rather by examining "on what levels of abstraction thought did take place."[52] Indeed, Pocock is even more confident than either Wood or Skinner in suggesting that a tactile knowledge of linguistic context will make it possible for historians to realize German historian Leopold Von Ranke's aspiration of writing history as it actually happened—of grasping, in Pocock's words, "what *eigentlich* happened" or what was "*eigentlich* meant."[53]

But whereas the methodological underpinnings of Bailyn's and Wood's approach are rooted centrally in Geertz's conception of ideology, and Skinner is heavily influenced by the speech act theory of Austin, Pocock's particular twist to linguistic contextualism comes from his use of the concept of language paradigms developed by Thomas Kuhn. Kuhn's monumentally influential study *The Structure of Scientific Revolutions* offers a fundamental reinterpretation of the character of scientific inquiry and the path of the history of science. Before Kuhn, the image of science that had been presented by the scientific community and was almost universally accepted by nonscientists suggested that scientific development was a process of the "accumulation of individual discoveries and inventions."[54] Pioneering scientists, the prevailing orthodoxy suggested, applied the techniques of the scientific method to overcome obstacles of error, myth, and superstition and add to the stockpile of scientific knowledge. In contrast, Kuhn suggests that scientific inquiry is governed as much by custom as by reason. He also denies that scientific discovery is either incremental or the result of individual efforts. Indeed, he raises questions about whether it is possible to assign specific scientific discoveries to any single individual and, even more remarkably, whether the history of science can be viewed as progressive at all.

More specifically, according to Kuhn, "normal science"—the day-to-day process of scientific inquiry—is rigidly governed by scientific paradigms. Paradigms, he later wrote, are used in two different senses in his famous book. In one sense, they stand for the "entire constellation of beliefs, values, techniques, and so on shared by the members of a given community." In another sense, paradigms are "the concrete puzzle-solutions which, employed as models or examples, can replace explicit rules as a basis for the solution" to scientific problems. For Kuhn, then, paradigms set the terms for what the scientific community accepts as an appropriate question and an acceptable answer. They even deflect inquiry from sets of facts that the prevailing paradigm cannot explain. Enforced by the rigorous and rigid training that scientists undergo, paradigms also serve as a basis from which authority is distributed within the scientific community.[55]

In contrast, "revolutionary science," according to Kuhn, takes place when "anomalies" appear that can no longer be plausibly denied. These sets of facts become apparent when, for example, a problem that scientists initially expected to be easily solved within the existing paradigm does not yield the anticipated result or when a research instrument reveals an anomaly. Anomalies, according to Kuhn, ignite investigations, which in turn result in the replacement of one paradigm by another—a process so revolutionary, according to Kuhn, that it amounts to nothing less than a change in worldview. A new paradigm, then, is "seldom or never just an increment to what is already known. Its assimilation requires the reconstruction of prior theory and the re-evaluation of prior fact, an intrinsically revolutionary process that is seldom completed by a single man."[56] Furthermore, transformations from one paradigm to another should not be thought of as providing progressively better understandings of the character of the universe. Paradigms, in Kuhn's estimation, are self-contained understandings of the universe. Each explains certain facts and is unable to explain others.

In retrospect, at least, it is easy to see how Kuhn's work influenced Pocock's approach to historical analysis even beyond what Pocock explicitly acknowledges. First, Kuhn does not look at past scientific paradigms for the contributions they make to the present or as competing paradigms of scientific explanation. Instead, he seeks "to display the historical integrity of that science in its own time," in the same way that Pocock insists on interpreting political texts exclusively for the particular, contextual political problems they address.[57] Second, Kuhn's portrait of the history of science draws attention away from the contributions of individual "great" scientists and focuses instead on communities of scientists who work out problems based on shared assumptions within a scientific paradigm. Translated into a study of political agents rather than scientists, such an approach can challenge the traditional method of studying the history of political thought and its examination of canonical thinkers and texts. Third, *The Structure of Scientific Revolutions* deliberately raises questions about whether there has been progress in the history of science. Similarly, in *The Machiavellian Moment* in particular, Pocock presents an explicitly anti-Whiggish account of the history of political thought that seeks to establish the continuity of civic humanism and, conversely, to challenge the shared assumption of Marxism and liberalism: the belief that the history of political thought is a progression toward liberalism.[58]

Most important, however, Pocock extrapolates Kuhn's idea of paradigms and combines it with new insights in linguistic theory to create an approach to the study of the history of political thought that centers on paradigms of political discourse or language and their histories and transformations. When Pocock speaks of languages of political thought, he means more properly "idioms, rhetorics, ways of talking about politics, distinguishable language games of which each may have its own vocabulary, rules, preconditions and implications, tone and style."[59] Concretely, such idioms include the language of the ancient constitution (the claim that the English legal system can be traced to antiquity and provides protection for ancient liberties), the language of apocalyptic prophecy (including the belief that England is an elect nation with a special place in God's plan), and the language of civic humanism.

By analyzing political languages, the history of political thought, Pocock reasons, can be reconceived as "a process both linguistic and political."[60] The history of political thought is a political process, Pocock maintains (following Kuhn), in the sense that language paradigms also distribute authority within a political community.

> That is to say, each [paradigm of political language] will present information selectively as relevant to the conduct and character of politics, and it will encourage the definition of political problems and values in certain ways and not in others. Each will therefore favor certain distributions of priority and consequently of authority; should a concept of authority itself be under discussion—as is likely to be the case in political discourse—it will present "authority" as arising in a certain way and possessing a certain character, and not otherwise.[61]

The history of political thought is a linguistic process, according to Pocock, because language paradigms order the "reality" of historical participants, form the framework of political thought and argument, and establish the boundaries of political imagination. Indeed, Pocock contends that thinking should be conceived not as an individual activity but rather as communication within a language paradigm. "Men think," Pocock writes in an oft-quoted phrase,

> by communicating language systems; these systems help constitute both their conceptual worlds and the authority-structures, or social worlds, related to these; the conceptual and social worlds may each be seen as a context to the other, so that the picture gains in concreteness. *The individual's thinking may now be viewed as a social event, an act of communication and of response with a paradigm-system*, and as a historical event, a moment in a process of transformation of that system and of the interacting worlds which both system and act help to constitute and are constituted by. We have gained what we lacked before; the complexity of context which the historian needs.[62]

In particular, political languages provide the exegete with a complex but determinate meaning context in which to understand specific statements by political thinkers. "The historian's first problem," Pocock asserts, is to "identify the 'language' or 'vocabulary' with and within which the author operated, to show how it functioned paradigmatically to prescribe what he might say and how he might say it."[63] Like Skinner, then, Pocock believes that the job of the historian of political thought is to locate the contemporaneous debates in which historical agents were engaged and the specific political languages they used to conduct these debates, and then to understand their texts as reflections of these debates, contributions to them, or perhaps even adaptations to and innovations in these political languages. Furthermore, although Pocock notes that some languages may successfully exclude others, any number of these idioms may be found within any political culture. Thus, political discourse is "typically polyglot," and the historian should be concerned with the "inconclusive contests for hegemony that go on, and the complex dialectics to which they give rise, between languages which compete, and argue, with one another."[64]

The Contributions of the Linguistic Contextualists

As a group, Bailyn, Wood, Skinner, and Pocock share several points about the proper method for studying political thought that justify treating them collectively.[65] Foundationally, they believe that historical study is properly conceived as an impartial investigation into a historical agent's self-understanding of his or her writings and actions. They also see the past as a foreign world and seek "to understand that world not as it anticipated the future but as it was experienced by those who lived in it."[66] Their peculiar twist to these otherwise standard interpretive axioms is that they believe that the agent's self-understanding can best be retrieved by studying the ideologies or political language paradigms present in the historical agent's society and understanding the historical agent's discourse as a communication within that paradigm. For scholars who adopt this approach, interpretation is, as John Gunnell has succinctly observed, a "matter of locating the writer's discourse in the context of a normative language system that was available to the author and then relating it to particular historical events."[67] Interpreting political texts by locating and "closing" the linguistic context in which they were produced promises to give the study of the history of political thought a genuinely historical character, tie it closely to political life, and thereby establish its relevance—indeed, indispensability—for the analysis of political behavior.[68]

As we have seen, establishing a link between ideas and political life is central to justifying the study of political thought against the criticisms of Progressives, Namierans, and behavioralists of all stripes. This defense takes place on several levels. On one level, each of these scholars views the formation and transformation of ideologies as a historical event in itself that is as deserving as any other for study. Furthermore, each of these scholars believes that "reality" is socially constructed because it is mediated by ideology or languages. Ideology and languages stand between historical agents and the world they inhabit, structuring their consciousness, limiting the political imagination of individuals and societies, and providing the context in which political argumentation must be conducted and behavior justified (or judged to be illegitimate).

The contention that political languages and ideologies constrain what thinkers can say and do provides the linguistic contextualists with a basis for arguing that language and behavior are inseparable. Since the linguistic context affects behavior, they maintain, ideas must be considered even by the staunchest Namieran or Progressive. As Daniel Rodgers has noted, scholars who adopt this methodology seek to "invest ideas with social power so unmistakeable that even the behavioralists in the profession would have to pay attention."[69] Furthermore, these scholars—especially Skinner—search not merely for what a text says or means but also for what its author intended to do by writing it. Approached in this manner, statements become forms of behavior. Words, as Wittgenstein said, become deeds.

Finally, the methodological writings of Wood, Skinner, and Pocock are also a direct and forceful challenge to a philosophical approach to interpreting political texts. Indeed, their writings may be thought of as an indictment of the historical integrity of much of the political theory scholarship that has taken a philosophical approach, as a challenge to the practice of appropriating past political ideas for current political purposes, and as a renouncement of the very act of political theorizing in general—at least as this has traditionally been conceived.

This does not, however, mean that these scholars believe that historical analysis is without its share of contemporary lessons. These lessons, however, are about the historical process itself, not lessons learned directly from the historical participants or from the past. For Wood, studying the historical process teaches prudence and guards against self-righteousness. If we study history carefully, he suggests, we will see that the actions of historical agents are severely circumscribed by their historical circumstances and that few end up achieving what they set out to achieve. More often, they end up bitter and estranged, prisoners of the world they created by the unintended effects of their actions and their words. For Skinner, the purpose of the study of political thought is to illustrate the variety of moral assumptions and cultures, to remind us that we are on our own in solving the peculiar problems presented to our peculiar culture, and to expose the contingency of our institutions.

There is much that is worthy in this methodology and even more in the spirit that animates it. Certainly, most scholars of the American Founding (if not the broader academic profession) are at least willing to recognize both the possibility and the value of impartial historical interpretation and the importance of establishing the social and intellectual matrix out of which a text emerged in order to understand the author's meaning and purpose. Conversely, scholarship on the American Founding has not been influenced by the Gadamerian belief that interpretation is unavoidably an act of "production" rather than reconstruction and that, far from being an obstacle to be overcome, the distance between the past and present provides the scholar with a prejudgment that is an opening to an understanding of the text. Moreover, a "new critic" who suggests that the text in itself is a "self-sufficient object of inquiry and understanding" would be as out of place among scholars of the American Founding as the Chicago Cubs in the World Series.[70]

In addition to this foundational point, interpreters of the American Founding would do well to study carefully the interpretive errors that Skinner documents and that Wood and Pocock complain about. Indeed, the central contribution of Skinner's methodological studies is that they exhort us to develop the tactile knowledge necessary to understand the context in which a particular work was written, and they point the way to possible errors that can arise from not fully understanding that context. As Nathan Tarcov has observed, Skinner "provides useful warnings against rashly assuming past writers to have had doctrines on what we consider the requisite subjects, to have met our standards of coherence, to have intended later results, or otherwise to correspond to what is familiar to us. These warnings are an articulation of good historical method: we should not impose our themes or notions on the thinkers of the past but strive to understand their thought as they understood it themselves."[71]

Furthermore, the linguistic contextualists remind us of the problem of "ransacking" and "plundering" historical records for facts to inform contemporary arguments and of the practice of evoking the names of past political actors in the service of current political problems merely as a means of attempting to "fix one's own prejudices on to the most charismatic names."[72] Pocock, Wood, and Skinner are correct that politically motivated studies parading under the name of scholarship constitute a cottage industry. In scholarship on the American Founding, such studies follow understandably—if not justifiably—from the reverence held for the Founders in the American public consciousness and the political currency that flows from it.

Perhaps most important, Skinner and Wood are correct to suggest that we can indeed learn valuable lessons from an understanding of the historical process itself, independent of the lessons we might learn directly from historical agents. In particular, scholars would do well to keep in mind that the world of the Founders was radically different from our own, that the historical process is complex, and that unintended effects are often central in the outcome of events and the development of political concepts. We would also do well to keep in mind Wood's point that the historical participants themselves are often tragically limited in how they can act. Historical investigation pursued on these humanistic terms can inculcate a capacity for empathic understanding, jar us out of our parochialism, and serve as a kind of prophylactic against hasty moralistic judgments about the beliefs and decisions of past political actors.

The Inadequacies of Linguistic Contextualism

But despite the prudent warnings and undoubted truths conveyed in their approach to the study of the history of political thought, the linguistic contextualists are simply wrong on a number of specific methodological points and, most importantly, in their general contention that the history of political thought cannot be legitimately conceived as a search for enduring answers to perennial questions and studied as a means of enhancing contemporary political thinking. Let us consider four specific areas in which this approach to the study of political thought is problematic: methodological errors, the limitations of Bailyn's and Wood's defense of the study of political ideas against the criticisms of the behavioralists, the failure of Skinner's case against perennial questions, and the failure of the linguistic contextualists' case against appropriation.[73]

Methodological Errors

First, as numerous scholars have pointed out, the claim that ideologies or political languages structure consciousness becomes highly problematic when it is expanded into the assertion that these ideologies become closed and imprison or determine the political thinking of historical agents. At minimum, it is certainly an act of extreme hubris for a modern interpreter to say that a historical agent could not think a particular thought because the conventions necessary to conceive that thought were not present in that society. Such a claim not only supposes a degree of knowledge about the linguistic context of a past society that we cannot reasonably hope to have but also supposes that linguistic context determines what can and cannot be thought.[74] Joyce Appleby, in particular, has repeatedly and rightly urged scholars of the American Founding to appreciate the mutability and complexity of the political languages of eighteenth-century America and not to remove individual agency and rationality from the study of the political thought of the Founders. As Appleby has observed, eighteenth-century America was an open, dynamic, and pluralistic community, and the Founders were innovators of political languages as well as inheritors of them.[75] Furthermore, such an assumption is not necessary to gain the insights provided by a close analysis of the linguistic context in which the Founders wrote and acted. Again, as Appleby has noted, "it is possible to explore with an anthropologist's sensitivity the riches of symbolic systems without subscribing to the view that these systems possess a power to inhibit the creation of new symbols."[76] Appleby might have gone even further to point out that language may be as much a resource for the invention of ideas and concepts as a barrier to the development of new ones.

Such observations have led Pocock and Terence Ball to investigate and propose explanations for "conceptual change" and innovation in political thought.[77] Pocock has also observed that he never suggested that a single ideology dominated political societies, including Revolutionary America; rather, he has always been concerned with the interaction among the multiplicity of languages present in any political society.[78] These modifications are part of the dialectic of this debate and have led the linguistic contextualists into more moderate and defensible positions, but they also raise an unaddressed tension within the linguistic contextualists' account. On the one hand, these scholars insist that language paradigms have "conditioning" and even "imprisoning" effects and act as "highly authoritative linguistic formulations."[79] This claim has served as the foundation for their claim that opposition ideology triggered the American Revolution and, in general, for their contention—against behavioralists and Namierans—that ideas affect behavior. On the other hand, they stress that political languages perform a variety of functions; embrace "statements, propositions, and incantations of virtually every kind"; and are ambiguous and cryptic because they must "say many things to many men at once."[80] But if the political languages in a community are indeed numerous, ambiguous, and malleable, then how can they really be said to have the power to structure consciousness and to limit what can be said and done? In short, when the linguistic contextualists defend their approach against the charge of linguistic determinism by suggesting that political languages are not monolithic, highly structured, or authoritative, their claim that political languages have the power to condition perception and affect behavior loses much of its force.

Moreover, some of the suppositions that underlie the methodology of the linguistic contextualists are as flawed as the ones it seeks to redress. For example, Skinner, Pocock, and Wood criticize those committed to a great-books approach for "filling in" where a philosophical statesman appears to be incoherent and for presupposing the coherence of the thinkers they interpret. Still, their interpretive presuppositions almost certainly have the opposite effect of underestimating the capabilities of the historical actors they interpret.[81] This is particularly evident in Wood's suggestion that Jefferson was "scarcely capable" of drawing refined philosophical distinctions between, for example, Hutcheson's moral sense philosophy and Locke's ethical egotism.[82] Garry Wills made this distinction, and if contemporary scholars are able to do so, it seems reasonable to assume that Jefferson—who was among the most cerebral of the Founders—could do so as well. Moreover, even if, as Wood claims, the philosophies of Locke and Hutcheson had been blended into a diffuse, enlightened consensus by the time Jefferson wrote the Declaration of Independence, this hardly means that Jefferson was incapable of making refined distinctions among aspects of that consensus.[83] In general, this supposition leaves no room for the possibility that modern exegetes are simply not intelligent enough to grasp a deeper coherence achieved by a historical agent.[84]

An Inadequate Response to the Behavioralists

In addition to these specific methodological problems, the justification used by the linguistic contextualists to defend the study of ideas against the criticisms of the behavioralists ultimately comes at a considerable price.[85] It is doubtlessly true, as Bailyn, Wood, and Skinner have noted, that public ideologies form conventions in any society that limit what historical actors can publicly say, justify, and do. It is thus also true that this observation provides an argument against the behavioralists' claim that ideas can be endlessly manipulated and are nothing more than the pageant behind which individuals hide their underlying interests.

Nevertheless, contrary to Wood's assertions, there is no reason to adopt a defense of the study of political ideas that concludes that ideas are only "important for what they do rather than for what they are" or that focuses exclusively on "what ideas did in a particular situation and why the historical participants used the particular ideas in the way they did."[86] Indeed, Wood lets the Progressive historians, Namierans, and Marxists set the terms on which he addresses this question. In particular, Wood gets entangled in the "problem of motivation" because he concedes to these groups that "professed beliefs" and principles are never the springs of behavior—or at least we can never "prove" that they are—and because he rejects the possibility of analyzing the content or validity of ideas.[87] Nevertheless, scholars who study ideas for their substance or content, or what Tarcov has called the "text's claim to truth," need never become entangled in the "problem of motivation" in the first place.[88]

Stated succinctly, a political theorist or political philosopher who is concerned with the content of ideas and not simply with their function can immediately distinguish between the motives that generated an idea and that idea's claim to truth.[89] Consider Wood's example of the debate between the Federalists and the anti-Federalists. Contrary to Wood's assertion, we do not have to "prove" that the Federalists acted out of their professed motives or show that they were limited in what they said by the linguistic conventions of the time to justify taking their ideas seriously. Even if we concede that Beard and the Progressives were correct and that the Federalists acted only out of their basest and narrowest economic self-interest, an analysis of their motives says nothing at all about the value of their account of the Constitution or the relative merits of the ideas of the Federalists and anti-Federalists. Certainly, as Wood suggests, any good-faith effort to interpret the formation of the Constitution must also engage in a sympathetic analysis of the ideas of the anti-Federalists in order to understand their arguments. But a good-faith effort does not have to concede that the accounts of the Federalists and anti-Federalists are equally valid in order to establish its comprehensiveness or impartiality.

Wood rejects any such search for the truth because, he contends, there is no true interpretation of the Constitution, and he believes that a scholar who supports one side or the other gives up any claim to impartiality. Nevertheless, it is unclear whether such an interpretive strategy is even possible.[90] The impartiality of Wood's famous interpretation of the "Federalist persuasion" in *The Creation of the American Republic* can certainly be questioned. The Constitution, according to Wood, was an "aristocratic" document that repudiated the utopian and egalitarian aspirations of the American Revolution.[91] This analysis moves far beyond an interpretation of the function of these ideas within their historical context. The Federalists certainly would not have accepted this interpretation as an accurate assessment of their goals, and it is not clear how it reconciles and transcends the perspectives of the historical participants. Actually, it is an anti-Federalist interpretation of the Framers' Constitution. Wood, in other words, has sharply criticized other scholars for adopting the Federalist arguments and supplying a Federalist brief for the Constitution.[92] But he relies on the "professed beliefs" of the anti-Federalists to critique the Federalists and provides precisely the kind of judgments he says historians should avoid. Indirectly but no less decisively, Wood evaluates the validity of the Federalists' and anti-Federalists' interpretations of the 1787 Constitution and makes a choice between them.[93]

Perhaps equally important, even if it is possible to sympathetically account for the varying positions of different historical agents without judging their claims to truth, is such an approach always appropriate? It might be appropriate when judging the conflict between the Federalists and the anti-Federalists and between the British and the American Revolutionaries, but what about the conflict between the North and the South in the Civil War, the Allies and the Axis powers in World War II, or the United States and Iraq in the Gulf Wars? Does each of these parties deserve equal consideration? Should a history of racism (or homophobia, anti-Semitism, or misogyny) be written with the goal of transcending and reconciling the positions of racists and nonracists and discovering (without judging who was right or wrong) why racists expressed their ideas the way they did and why—given their historical understanding of the world in which they lived—there was no other explanation available for them to use?

The primary point here is that Wood's understanding of the role of the historian comes at a considerable price. If universally adopted, such an interpretive strategy would preclude historians from addressing what are ultimately some of the most engaging and meaningful questions. It would thus prevent the intellectual community from benefiting from the peculiar insights provided by the historical mode of inquiry. Wood and scholars of his temperament defend historical interpretation because, they argue, it can provide an empathetic understanding of the views of people radically different from ourselves and serve as a prophylactic against self-righteous judgments. But the choice between empathetic understanding and self-righteous judgment is a false one. We need the empathetic understanding that historical knowledge provides to make judicious judgments, not to avoid making them at all.

The Failure of Skinner's Case against Perennial Questions

In addition to their reductionistic defense of the study of ideas, Pocock, Wood, and Skinner challenge two closely related propositions in the traditional study of the history of political thought. First, they challenge the belief that the study of the history of political thought can be meaningfully conceived as a transhistorical dialogue between historical agents who are addressing essentially the same question. Second, they challenge the legitimacy of the appropriation of past ideas for present political purposes. The first of these challenges rejects the very possibility of learning about our problems from historical agents; the second challenges the legitimacy of any answers we might get from such an inquiry.

Skinner in particular provides the most forthright rejection of the belief that the history of political thought can be conceived as a comparative analysis of competing answers to perennial questions or central political concepts. Remember, the conclusion of his seminal methodological article is that the real "philosophical point" of studying the history of political thought is the realization that "we are on our own," or, conversely, that we cannot consult the works of past great thinkers to address our problems. Skinner writes:

> On the one hand, it has I think become clear that any attempt to justify the study of the subject [the history of ideas] in terms of the "perennial problems" and "universal truths" to be learned from the classical texts must amount to the purchase of justification at the expense of making the subject itself foolishly and needlessly naive. Any statement, as I have sought to show, is inescapably the embodiment of a particular intention, on a particular occasion, addressed to the solution of a particular problem, and thus specific

to its situation in a way that it can only be naive to try to transcend. The vital implication here is not merely that the classic texts cannot be concerned with our questions and answers, but only with their own. There is also the further implication that—to revive Collingwood's way of putting it—there simply are no perennial problems in philosophy; there are only individual answers to individual questions. There is in consequence simply no hope of seeking the point of studying the history of ideas in the attempt to learn directly from the classic authors by focusing on their attempted answers to supposedly timeless questions.[94]

Skinner's point, then, is not that we must get our history right before we do our political thinking. It is rather that when we get our history correct, we will realize that past historical agents offer nothing that can improve our theorizing.

A foundational problem with this contention is that Skinner's methodology is rooted in an impoverished conception of intentionality. Skinner contends that we should separate statements made by historical actors into discrete units—"utterances"—and understand them as *"inescapably* the embodiment of a *particular* intention, on a *particular* occasion, addressed to the solution of a *particular* problem."[95] He then contends that we should interpret a text by analyzing what the historical agent could "in principle" have meant to say and do. Not surprisingly, the interpretations that result from the application of these interpretive axioms are characterized by an exclusive attention to the immediate contextual political debates and contemporaneous issues in which a historical actor engaged. Indeed, for Skinner and Pocock, at least, this is the fundamental value of this approach.

Contrary to Skinner's bald assertions, however, the works of at least some of the philosophical statesmen in the history of political thought are not simply the embodiments of "particular" intentions, nor are they (at least in the eyes of their authors) addressing novel questions. When some philosophical statesmen are presented with problems arising from their political lives, they seek answers by engaging in a transhistorical conversation with others who (they believe) have addressed essentially the same problems. For example, Rousseau's desire to address the question of political legitimacy, or what he calls the "principles of political right," may have been pressed on him by the particular circumstances of his political life (rather than by an abstract concern with this question). Nevertheless, he addressed it by taking issue with the answers given by Filmer, Hobbes, and Grotius to the same question a century earlier.[96] Gandhi believed that he learned about civil disobedience from Thoreau, even though Thoreau wrote more than half a century earlier and addressed a radically different culture.[97]

A modern exegete can choose to analyze political texts only as responses to particular, historically contextual debates and issues and can conclude that any political thinker who believes that he or she is addressing perennial questions or addressing posterity is mistaken. But to do so ignores (at least sometimes) what many of the authors themselves hoped to achieve and how they hoped to be understood. Indeed, at this point, Skinner's own interpretive axioms clash, and he presents an interpretation that is ahistorical and that the agent himself "could never be brought to accept as a correct description of what he had meant or done."[98]

A still stronger claim can be made that historical actors contribute to the particular contextual debates and issues of their age while simultaneously and *unavoidably* contributing to more far-reaching debates. At its core, the methodology of Skinner, Pocock, and Wood is premised on the contention that we cannot maintain historical legitimacy while bringing the thoughts of historical agents into a conversation that involves issues they did not personally confront and persons with whom they did not actually converse. But this depends on the level of abstraction we use to pose the problem and the way we conceive of intentions. Intentions, as the linguistic contextualists must be aware, are neither monolithic nor necessarily particular. By addressing a specific contextual problem arising out of his contemporary political life, a philosophical statesman unavoidably has broader—more abstract—intentions as well. Thus, for example, when Plato set forth a particular conception of justice in *The Republic,* he was no doubt both reflecting and challenging the Greek assumptions about and conceptions of justice outlined in the initial stages of the dialogue. But when we consider what Ronald Dworkin calls "abstract" intentions, it becomes clear that Plato was also unavoidably making claims about the character of justice in and of itself and contributing to a debate about justice.[99]

Along these same lines, philosophical statesmen sometimes unknowingly and unintentionally contribute to "doctrines" and debates whose terms are not yet fully developed, thus bringing into question a complete reliance on intentions. Recall Skinner's analysis of the claim that Marsilius of Padua could not "in principle" have had a doctrine of separation of powers or contributed to the formulation of the debate about this doctrine because this debate did not exist yet. Foundationally, whether Marsilius did or did not have a doctrine of separation of powers or contribute to the development of this concept must be based on an analysis of Marsilius's writings, not on the assertion that the debate began two centuries after his death. Skinner baldly begs the question here. When the debate began and whether Marsilius had such a doctrine are precisely the issues under consideration. If it can be demonstrated that Marsilius's writings contain an analysis of this doctrine, then it is Skinner's assertion that the doctrine began two hundred years later that is wrong, not a scholar's suggestion that Marsilius may have contributed to this debate.

But even if Skinner is correct about when the modern conception of separation of powers was formulated, Marsilius may have contributed to this debate without knowing about the debate or intending to contribute to it. Skinner may be quite correct to conclude that Marsilius did not conceive of separation of powers in the same way that the American Founders did, or that he espoused this same political concept for very different reasons (for example, to contrast the executive role of a ruler with the legislative role of a sovereign people, rather than considering how separation of powers might promote political liberty). Nevertheless, this does not mean that later thinkers cannot learn from Marsilius's understanding and fuse it with their own. The central political concepts and doctrines studied in the history of political thought have taken numerous forms and have been contested over long periods. Historical agents in different historical contexts draw on threads of previous understandings and then combine these old conceptions with new thoughts about how a concept should be conceived and what purposes it should serve. For example, a previous conception of separation of powers may be taken and reformulated by historical actors who have different purposes for it. The previous conception becomes retrospectively important in the development of the new one. Tracing such a development under the rubric of the analysis of a single political concept is thus hardly illegitimate.[100]

In general, Tarcov provides a concise summary of the problems that arise from Skinner's assumptions. He writes:

> There is a danger, moreover, that his [Skinner's] strictures and proposals may lead to the opposite mythologies: to assumptions that philosophic writers of the past could not in principle have had coherent doctrines, addressed posterity, intended ambitious results that have come to pass, or surpassed the confused intelligences or limited imaginations of twentieth-century scholars and thereby have something to teach us. Attention to their social and linguistic contexts and especially to their indications of how they themselves saw those contexts, need not result in a view of them as confused and merely timely. It may help us to distinguish their accommodations

to those contexts and prevent those accommodations from obscuring our vision of the coherence and importance of their thought.[101]

The failure of Skinner's case against perennial questions becomes even more evident when the precise character of his remarkable claim is highlighted by the examples he uses. It is wrong, Skinner asserts, to suppose that when Lenin says that "every cook ought to be a politician and Plato [says] that men ought to restrict themselves to the exercise of their special function in the state" that they are concerned with the same problem. There is, Skinner concedes, "some semantic sameness" between the problems raised by these political thinkers. Nevertheless, those who take a philosophical approach to the study of political thought claim that "the problem is the same in the sense that we may hope directly to learn from a study of the *solution* that Plato offers to it." But "it is not enough," Skinner concludes, "that the discussion should seem, at a very abstract level, to pose a question relevant to us. It is also essential that the answer Plato gave should seem relevant and indeed applicable (if he is 'right') to our own culture and period." However, when we turn to Plato's arguments, we find out that he believed that the "cook should not participate because he is a slave."[102]

First, note that Skinner's conclusion at the end of his essay is quite different from the broad assertion he has been pursuing throughout. Earlier, Skinner asserts that there are no perennial questions, but now he concludes that if we choose to phrase questions in an abstract manner to achieve a broad "semantic sameness" (so that the question becomes, in effect, a perennial one), we will find that the answers are inapplicable to our culture. Skinner's example concedes what his argument has heretofore denied—namely, that it is possible to phrase questions and examine political concepts in such a manner that political actors from radically different times and cultures are aligned around a common problem and that their answers can be viewed as competing answers to the same problem.

If we use Skinner's example, we find that the perennial or (better still) common questions being addressed here are: Who gets to participate in politics? What justifications are made for excluding some and including others? Furthermore, contrary to Skinner's assertion, we can learn from the answers of Plato and Lenin—particularly from their justifications for why some are included and some excluded—even if the solutions they provide are inapplicable to our culture. We might, for example, explore the criteria that Plato and Lenin used for considering who should be included and excluded from political participation. Suppose that Plato believed that citizenship and rationality were prerequisites to political participation and that slaves were excluded from participation because they were not citizens or did not partake adequately of the rational faculty. Suppose that Lenin either had different criteria for addressing the question of participation or came to different conclusions when he applied similar criteria. Even though we might find Plato's or Lenin's answers to this problem inadequate, inapplicable, or even immoral, we might find the criteria they used to address it altogether relevant. We could be led to ask why they believed that rationality and citizenship were prerequisites for political participation. The answers we derived from this process could then be applied to our own situation. Should we exclude children from voting? If so, why? Should we continue to take voting privileges away from convicted felons? Again, if so, why?

Obviously, neither Plato nor Lenin addressed these questions about our political culture, so neither provides *direct* answers to these questions. But this is hardly the same as saying that they and numerous other political thinkers throughout history have nothing to offer us. In only the strictest sense, then, is Skinner right. We will ultimately be doing our thinking on our own, but we will not be doing it in a vacuum or without guidance from the past. We will be addressing our problems while being informed by conversations with others who have addressed the same problems. Indeed, the only alternative is to remain ignorant about previous answers.[103]

In general, if we adopt this attitude and approach, then the study of the history of political thought can be conceived and conducted as a form of comparative analysis of the competing answers to perennial questions and the competing interpretations of broad political concepts. The history of political thought can thus be conceived as a forum for competing answers to questions about the good life, human nature, the origin and legitimate power of the state, and obligation to the law, for example. It need not be thought of as a series of sequential, unrelated answers to essentially different questions.

Contrary to Skinner's assertion, such an approach does not mean that an exploration of a statement's historical context is unimportant. Those who concede that an understanding of social context is necessary for an understanding of the classic texts, Skinner maintains, must also deny that these texts contain any elements of timeless and perennial interest. If there were any such elements in these texts, he maintains, they would be evident without knowledge of context. This statement, however, is a bald non sequitur. Knowledge of social context may be important for determining what ideas were expressed in the first place, and a text may contain both timeless and timely elements.[104]

Finally, a search for enduring answers to enduring questions need not lead us to conceive of the history of political thought as a univocal conversation, to the belief that every political thinker has something to offer on every question or doctrine, or to the belief that the answers we gain from this study are necessarily applicable to our culture. We will doubtlessly find that not every thinker addressed all the major questions and that the answers given by Plato, Lenin, Madison, or whoever are often unacceptable, irrelevant, inapplicable, or all of the above. But that determination will always be a *prudential* judgment, a judgment about whether we can apply the teachings of past thinkers to our political culture. Such applications cannot be ruled out a priori.

The Failure of Wood's and Skinner's Case against Appropriation

Although Wood's and Skinner's strictures against the appropriation of old ideas for present purposes is certainly understandable, given the avalanche of scholarship that attempts to evoke the ideas of "great thinkers" (including the Founders) in support of contemporary political programs, they should be heeded only to a limited degree. All scholars should of course oppose those who try to advance present-day political agendas by evoking the Founders in support of propositions with which they have only the most tenuous relationship.

Nevertheless, we need not be driven to the conclusion that it is always improper to appropriate the Founders' ideas for our political purposes. American political thought has been conducted around a fairly stable set of fundamental political concepts, and the Founders' political thought represents perhaps the most profound reasoning in American history. Even Bailyn observes that "the writings of this early period (the American Revolution) drew together the basic ideas which flow through all subsequent stages of American political thought, and provide the permanent foundation of the nation's political beliefs."[105] Failing to learn from this body of thought or ignoring the relevance of these ideas to our political life is as wrongheaded as evoking the Founders in the service of political programs that their ideas cannot support.

Most important, not all scholarship that attempts to understand how the ideas of past political thinkers can inform our understanding of contemporary problems is necessarily manipulative or exploitative. Here, Wood and Skinner present a false choice between two forms of inquiry—one designed to discover impartially genuine historical meaning, and another that ransacks and manipulates in order to evoke great thinkers for present political purposes. For these scholars, the test of whether historical scholarship is objective is apparently its irrelevance to our problems and its ability to establish the "differentness" of the past and the present.[106] What is ignored or explicitly rejected here, however, is the possibility of learning about a present political problem by reading past political texts, good-faith efforts to appropriate past political ideas to address current political problems, and the value of thinking through a current political problem as a historical agent might have.

Both Wood and Skinner deny these possibilities because they mischaracterize what scholars who study past political ideas for their present value do. They believe that ideas derive their meaning wholly from the historical context in which they were set forth and can never be considered in relationship to ideas from other contexts. They also seem to believe that historical concepts are constellations of ideas and that parts of this constellation can never be disconnected without radically changing their meaning.

At the center of this misjudgment is the belief that scholars concerned with the political implications of past ideas unavoidably have an agenda when they study a text and pull from it what they want. Contrary to this assertion, however, a historically sensitive scholar who is engaged in a good-faith effort to grasp an author's self-understanding of his words and actions, but who also believes that those words and actions may have value in the present, has the possibility of finding something he or she did not expect (that is, learning from the text rather than simply ransacking it). This scholar need not be any less alert than a historian to the variety of moral assumptions of past thinkers and cultures or any less sensitive to how foreign they are to our own. Indeed, it is often the radical difference of the author's perspective and moral assumptions that most interest this scholar.

The essential difference between the historically sensitive political theorist or philosopher and the historian who follows Wood's advice is that the political philosopher also seeks to explore which of these different moral assumptions, ideas, and forms of political organization is best and how they can inform and possibly improve the world. The answers to these questions will necessarily be at least partially elusive, and they should be contingent, but it is not illegitimate to ask them. Indeed, a scholar who is engaged in a good-faith effort to learn from the past should realize that there is a kind of built-in punishment for the shortsighted activity of manipulation and ransacking. Scholars who take political agendas to the texts of historical agents and misrepresent their ideas actually give up the possibility of learning from the texts. For these scholars, short-term political currency is achieved only at the expense of lasting knowledge.

Finally, the linguistic contextualists' case against appropriation faces the same problem as their case against perennial questions: it imposes on historical actors assumptions about historical inquiry that they did not share and thus violates the claim that their approach is based on an account that historical actors would have accepted. This is especially true of the study of the American Founders, who not only understood history as providing direct lessons about political truth that could be used in the present but also (as I point out in the next chapter) selectively appropriated past ideas, creatively synthesized them, and applied them in novel contexts to address contemporary political problems. Indeed, the American Founders engaged in precisely the kind of "ransacking" that Wood and Skinner now reject as illegitimate.

As an example, James Madison engaged in a sweeping study of the history of ancient confederacies in the mid-1780s to discover their animating principles and shed light on the reasons for the failure of the government under the Articles of Confederation. Madison's study was intended to discover the very character or nature of confederacies, was premised on the belief that historical analysis has direct lessons to teach those who engage in it, and was designed to convey those lessons not only to his contemporaries but also to posterity. Can an account that suggests that it is illegitimate to search in the past for illumination about the present really be said to be informed by Madison's self-understanding of his project?

None of this is meant to suggest that great thinkers provide solutions or political programs that can be mechanically transferred to solve our problems. One need not believe that there are eternal verities that can be plucked like pearls of wisdom from the past and applied in the present to believe that the Founders speak to our problems. Nevertheless, the proper solution for an improper appropriation of or an improper appeal to the authority of a past historical agent is to point out how and why the solution is unfaithful to the ideas of the historical agent who generated them, not to abandon these constructive activities. As Michael Zuckert has said, "when sensibly done," appropriating and thinking with a historical actor from the past about a present problem is "an eminently sensible thing to do."[107]

Interpreting the American Founding: Historical Integrity and the Paradox of Relevance

The analysis in this chapter has focused primarily on reinforcing the importance of historical integrity while blunting many of the criticisms of the linguistic contextualists about studying the history of political thought as a means of illuminating contemporary political life. It has also foreshadowed much of what I believe about the proper relationship between historical and philosophical modes of analysis in the study of the history of political thought. I want to conclude this chapter, however, by making some suggestions about how the interpretation of the American Founding should proceed. These suggestions fall far short of being a comprehensive analysis; rather, they are reflections on how we might address some common errors in the interpretation of the American Founding, integrate what is sensible from the approach of the linguistic contextualists, and promote both historical integrity and philosophical reflection in the study of the American Founding.

The most sensible interpretive axiom set forth by the linguistic contextualists is that we should strive to grasp historical actors' self-understanding of their ideas, presuppose that the world of the past is radically different from our own, and remain keenly alert to its distinctiveness. It follows from these foundational propositions that we should use every tool available to develop a tactile knowledge of the context of the American Founding, and we should understand "context" capaciously. In particular, this involves a sensitivity to the peculiarities of eighteenth-century language. Familiar words, as most scholars of this period realize, often have substantially different meanings from their present ones. For instance, *reputation* often meant what we now call *character*; *democracy* often referred to a specific form of government with good and bad properties and had not yet taken on its current normative dimension;[108] *discover* often meant *reveal*, not *find*;[109] and *disinterested* meant *impartial*, not *indifferent*.[110] Thus, for an interpreter of the American Founding, the *Oxford English Dictionary* should never be out of reach. In a broader sense, as the linguistic contextualists have also suggested, the interpreter should come to terms with the political languages and idioms that were dominant at the time the Founders wrote, including the languages of common law, country party ideology, natural rights republicanism, and the numerous illiberal ideologies that were used to justify inequality and exclusion. Analyses of political languages that the Founders used can help establish the public character of ideologies and thus document the matrix of ideas against which individuals had to justify their ideas and actions. The development of a genuinely historical approach also involves a mastery of the forms of communication used in eighteenth-century America, including newspaper editorials, state papers, public speeches, and private correspondence. In particular, scholars must remain alert to the peculiarly public character of private correspondence in eighteenth-century America.

In addition to mastering the forms and languages of eighteenth-century Anglo-American culture, scholars must pay attention to the multiple levels of discourse in the early republic. We must, in other words, determine (as Pocock put it) "on what levels of abstraction thought did take place," examining the thoughts of both great and lesser lights and giving each its due.[111] This often leads the exegete to interpret many of the participants in the debate surrounding the American Revolution and the formation and ratification of the Constitution by focusing primarily on the contextually specific problems they addressed and how the ideas in wide circulation in their society influenced what they could say and do. As Bailyn has observed, many of the "spokesmen of the Revolution" were "active politicians, merchants, lawyers, plantation owners, and preachers." These reflective statesmen were not philosophers or a "detached intelligentsia," and they were not "attempting to align their thought with that of major figures in the history of political philosophy who modern scholars would declare to have been seminal."[112]

Nevertheless, other members of the Revolutionary generation were both active statesmen and "thinking Revolutionaries."[113] We should not homogenize the thoughts of these individuals, suppose that their ideas simply reflect common opinion, rule out the possibility that they formed their ideas in conversation with great minds from their own and earlier eras, or assume that surface contradictions in their writings are necessarily real ones. Instead, we should treat the works of these individuals—Thomas Jefferson, John Adams, James Wilson, James Madison, and the most articulate of the anti-Federalists, for example—with extreme care. This involves considering the possibility that surface contradictions mask a deeper coherence that surpasses our limited understanding. It also involves paying close attention to the author's understanding of his context and treating the text itself as a dimension of that context, searching for the structure of the argument and relating parts of the author's argument to the whole, just as we would with the works of the most complex political philosopher.[114] Finally, with these individuals, we should strive to understand how they sought not only to reflect popular political culture but also to mold it, and how they often had a clear and profound understanding of what they were doing.

All this—including treating the works of great minds as if they were produced by great minds—is simply sound historical methodology. Nevertheless, contrary to what the linguistic contextualists have suggested, the philosophical point of making every effort to establish the self-understanding of historical agents need not be limited to the indirect lessons we can learn about prudence, the contingency of our institutions, the peculiarity of our ideas, or the prophylactic effect of historical studies against acontextual judgments—as important as these insights are.

Actually, historically sound interpretations of the American Founding can establish the direct contemporary relevance of some of the Founders' ideas and enrich our contemporary political life in at least three ways. First,

the political ideas of the Founders may present us with competing interpretations of some of the foundational concepts in American politics. The
Founders' conceptions may, in turn, inform our own political thinking and
vocabulary. This is true even if these conceptions are radically different from
our own, because (contrary to Wood's assertions) establishing their differentness does not necessarily establish their irretrievability. Instead, it may
paradoxically be the very reason they are useful to us.[115] The Founders' political thought may, in other words, provide us with provocative conceptions
of, for example, the meaning of equality, liberty, power, majority rule, and
individual rights. We may then reflect on the meaning of these concepts,
piercing conventional ways of considering them and in general thinking
about them with a degree of intensity that is not otherwise possible. This
process may also lead us to see that our ideas are not necessarily better than
theirs and to consider the possibility that our political thought may, in some
ways, be a devolution rather than an evolution. We might, for example, see
that the Founders understood liberty in a way that transcended and reconciled "negative" liberty with "positive" liberty.

We can also reason with the Founders about some of our most enduring problems. As Lance Banning has written:

> Nevertheless, for all the differences between their time and ours, we
> still employ ideas and live with institutions that the founding gen-
> eration shaped. We still define ourselves, in part, by reference to the
> values of their Revolution. . . . We might do well to realize that
> many of the founding generation, fallible and mortal though they
> were, did think about the fundamentals with a clarity and depth that
> few today have matched. Sometimes this was true when they con-
> fronted issues not dissimilar to those that trouble us today: the use-
> fulness and limitations of a bill of rights; a swollen public debt; dis-
> parities of wealth in a republic; the necessity of public spirit; or the
> nature of a sound relationship among those citizens and democratic
> statesmen. When this was so, it may be worth our while to listen in
> on their discussions and to notice how they thought. Not infre-
> quently, this can encourage us to see familiar problems from a dif-
> ferent angle and in terms that seem as fresh, when they are resur-
> rected, as they were when they were first employed.[116]

In addition to the problems that Banning mentions, the Founders thought
profoundly about a range of other issues—from the exquisitely narrow to
the broad—with which we continue to struggle. They dealt, for example,
with the proper extent of the power of the president, the proper approach

to constitutional interpretation, the problem of reconciling majority rule to minority rights, the tension between liberty and equality, the relationship of private and public power, the character and nature of representation, and the proper relationship of church and state. In addressing these issues, we should indeed look to the architects of the plan for illumination. The debates between the anti-Federalists and Federalists over whether people should be represented by members of their own class and occupation or by those who are best qualified and most enlightened have rough parallels with and can help inform our current debates about the propriety or impropriety of racial gerrymandering. The debates between Pacificus and Helvitius can help us frame and address debates over the nature and character of executive power. The discourse in the early American Republic over the relationship of church and state can inform our understanding of the debate between those who advocate state neutrality toward religion and those who favor direct accommodation of religion by government. Indeed, not considering how the Founders dealt with these issues would be as foolish as simply accepting their answers as authoritative.

Finally, the thought of the Founders may provide opportunities to appropriate their ideas for present political purposes. Here, historical investigations into the Founders' ideas and critical appraisals of them can be combined with creative reconstructions of aspects of their political thought that are deemed worthy of reconsideration and capable of being translated into terms that can be applied in our culture. To be sure, this process of appropriation cannot be a literal or mechanical replication of every element of a concept from one context to another. Appropriation must always be selective (it unavoidably extrapolates only parts of a concept), and it puts an idea into a radically different historical context. Nevertheless, none of this means that appropriation is the same as manipulation or ransacking.

In the broadest possible sense, historical integrity and contemporary relevance are synergetic in both the negative ways that the linguistic contextualists identified and more positive ways as well. A good-faith effort to apply some of the Founders' ideas to today's society often leads to the conclusion that these ideas are unjust, improper, or simply irrelevant. Similarly, a good-faith effort to locate in the Founders the origins of particular strengths and weaknesses of the American political system and American society may lead to the discovery that "they are only distantly and partially responsible for what we like or hate about America today."[117]

When the ideas of the Founders are indeed irretrievable, we should attempt to understand the differences between us and them, establish a complex account of institutional change and political development, and develop broad categories of contemporary American politics for which the Founders are neither the cause nor the cure. More positively, however, those who engage in the arduous task of trying to understand the Founders as they understood themselves may find them relevant precisely because their views are not framed by our scholarly conventions and political concerns. Such an activity may expose paths not taken and ideas now forgotten but applicable, when translated, to our own political culture. On these occasions, thinking with the Founders about fundamental concepts and problems and judiciously appropriating their ideas for present purposes may enrich our political discourse. At this point, the historian's invitation into the alien world of the Founding may legitimately feed the imagination of the theorist.

4

Ancients, Moderns, and Americans
The Republicanism-Liberalism Debate Revisited

Transcending Republicanism versus Liberalism

The debate between proponents of philosophical and historical approaches to the political thought of the American Founders and to the history of political thought in general has, at times, been vitriolic. What is most important about that debate, however, is the shared assumption of both sides. Both sides agree that ideas matter in a variety of ways and that political thought must be taken seriously. The Progressives' charge that ideas are mere projections of underlying economic interests no longer serves as a barrier to the serious study of political ideas. Indeed, this argument has now reached the apex of unimportance: it is no longer subjected to elaborate refutations but is instead ignored and treated with indifference.

During the 1980s and 1990s, the consequence of this agreement about the importance of ideas was renewed attention to the study of the political thought of the American Founding. At first, this took the form of a highly visible and lively debate over whether the political thought of the Founders is best characterized as a species of classical republicanism or Lockean liberalism. This debate has now faded from center stage in the academy. Many scholars—including a number of American historians who were central in pioneering the debate in the 1970s and then fueled it throughout the 1980s and into the 1990s—now find it sterile, unproductive, and even nauseating.[1]

Nevertheless, scholars continue to explore the intellectual origins of the American Founding and to build on lessons learned in the republicanism-liberalism debate. In particular, scholars have formed an "amiable historiographical consensus"[2] around the conciliatory and catholic but also diffuse claim that the Founders' political thought is best understood as an amalgam of liberalism, republicanism, and perhaps other traditions of political thought.[3] These scholars have, in Michael Zuckert's apt phrase, moved the debate over the intellectual character of the American Republic out of an "either/or" stage and into a "both/and" mode of analysis.[4] Indeed, the most salient goal in recent scholarship has been to show how liberalism, republicanism, and other traditions of political thought interpenetrated and interacted within the Founders' political thought.

There are several reasons why this agreement and the concomitant shift in scholarship mark an important step forward in our understanding of the intellectual origins of the American Republic. First and most fundamentally, efforts to interpret the political thought of the Founders as a reflection of a single tradition or language of political thought run headlong into a body of evidence amassed in the last thirty years. What James Kloppenberg wrote in 1987 is even truer in 2006: "partisans of both the republican and the liberal interpretations have identified strands of American political culture whose presence can no longer be convincingly denied." Scholars who dismiss the influence of either republicanism or liberalism, Kloppenberg continues, "ignore an increasingly impressive body of scholarship not merely suggesting, but showing, evidence of contrast and diversity."[5]

Second, interpretations that ask whether the Founders' political thought was a species of liberalism or republicanism impose analytic distinctions on eighteenth-century political actors that those actors would not have recognized and did not accept. As Gordon Wood has suggested, interpretations that judge the relative influence of republicanism and liberalism on the Founders assume "a sharp dichotomy between two clearly identifiable traditions that eighteenth century reality will not support."[6] Statements such as Wood's, which are common in this literature, make two interrelated points.[7] They recognize that liberalism and republicanism are at worst labels and at best analytical constructs that contemporary scholars have fashioned to help simplify complex patterns of thought. They also suggest that liberalism and republicanism were intertwined in the political thought of the Founders in ways that an either-or formulation cannot explain.[8]

Third, only an analysis that rejects the reductionism inherent in an either-or formulation really takes seriously the possibility that the Founders were reflective and creative agents who not only adopted but also reformulated political ideas. Scholars who adopt either a liberalism or a republicanism formulation are inevitably and unavoidably led back to the belief that the political thought of the Founders is derivative. It may be derivative of the "new science of politics" of Hobbes, Locke, and Hume or of classical re-publicanism, but it is nonetheless derivative. In contrast, scholars who begin with the understanding that a multiplicity of intellectual traditions was available to the Founders can show that they were active agents who drew selectively from these traditions, reshaping them to construct novel conceptions of political thought in the face of eighteenth-century American experience.

These and similar arguments have led many scholars of the American Founding to conclude that we must now trace out the synthetic quality of the political thought of the Founders.[9] But even if this approach is superior to an either-or formulation, it raises as many questions as it answers. Does the presence of several traditions or languages of political thought in the writings of the Founders mean that they indiscriminately drew on a multiplicity of political traditions without concern for theoretical consistency or coherence? Did this profusion of tongues, as one scholar put it, necessarily signal a confusion of tongues?[10] Conversely, does the synthetic quality of the Founders' political thought mean that they were able to combine liberalism and republicanism in ways that challenge the analytical distinctions we have used to classify their political thought? Did the Founders (to borrow Lance Banning's formulation of the problem) achieve a coherent if not altogether consistent conception of political thought?[11] Most important, if the Founders coherently combined republicanism, liberalism, and other traditions of political thought, on what terms was this synthesis effected? In other words, how did all these traditions entwine and interact in the political thought of the Founders?

The Multiple Traditions Approach: Alternative Interpretations of Interaction

Since the 1980s, scholars have increasingly confronted these questions and presented several strategies for explaining the interactions of republicanism, liberalism, and other traditions in the Founders' political thought. This chapter analyzes these alternative conceptions of the "multiple traditions approach" in an effort to better understand the terms on which the debate over the intellectual foundations of the American Republic is now being conducted.[12] Toward this end, I first identify and explicate three such strategies that I call the neo-Lockean synthesis, liberal republicanism, and illiberal liberalism. Next, I make five broad points about the intellectual character of the Founders' political thought that we should have learned from the studies setting forth these strategies of interaction and from the dialectic of the republicanism-liberalism debate in general. Here, I argue that, collectively, these five points amount to much more than simply the diffuse claim that a multiplicity of traditions of political thought influenced the American Founding. Instead, they can serve as a framework for an interpretation that allows us to understand the Founders' political thought on its own terms. Finally, I make several suggestions about how the debate over the intellectual origins of the American Republic should proceed.

The Neo-Lockean Synthesis: Liberal Ends, Republican Means

During the last twenty years, a number of scholars have argued that the political concepts identified as republicanism were present in the political thought of the Founders but do not constitute an alternative to liberalism.[13] J. David Greenstone, in particular, has emphasized the presence of both republicanism and liberalism within the political thought of the Founders, but he has also argued that this diversity can be embraced within a broader consensus of liberalism. Put differently, these scholars have argued that rather than considering Anglo-American republicanism as an alternative to liberalism, it must be treated as a species or variation of liberalism. Specifically, Greenstone has stated that "Anglo-American republicanism did not prescribe a comprehensive vision of human well-being, nor did it assign the function of prescribing such a vision to any official body or collectivity such as church, tribe, or polis."[14] It was instead a set of political concerns (such as the fear of corruption among public officials, the danger of political power and the corollary belief in limited government, the necessity of virtue in leaders and citizens, and the importance of an independent, vigilant citizenry) that begot specific institutional arrangements (especially a system of institutional checks and balances designed to ensure an independent legislature). As such, American republicanism mirrored liberal aspirations and even reinforced liberal goals. Republican governments were valued by the Founders, Greenstone writes,

> because they imposed severe limits on the power of the state and its officials, leaving broader questions of individual and social good to the citizens themselves. Colonial republicanism was so much a theory of limited government that both Thomas Jefferson and John Adams linked it to a Lockean belief in individual rights with no sense of contradiction. Second, republican public spiritedness helped solve the characteristically liberal problem of coordinating autonomous, even warring individuals. Such coordination often depends on mutual reliance and widely trusted political institutions.

By proscribing selfish behavior among either ruled or rulers and strictly limiting the government's power, republicanism offered just this prospect.[15]

Most important, according to Greenstone, almost all currents of American political thought—from the Founding to today—have accepted the ideals of limited government and separation of powers, the importance of citizen virtue, and the suspicion of official corruption. "Here, indeed," Greenstone declares, "is the real American liberal consensus."[16]

Two brilliant studies by Zuckert reinforce this understanding of Lockean liberalism as the core of the Founders' political thought while simultaneously showing that other species of political thought were assimilated into it. In *Natural Rights and the New Republicanism,* Zuckert provides both an analysis of the ascendancy of Lockean political philosophy within the Whig political tradition and a prequel to his other recently completed study of the American Founding. For our purposes, two aspects of this study are important: Zuckert's critique of the scholarship of Gordon Wood, J. G. A. Pocock, and (to a lesser extent) Bernard Bailyn, and his framework of analysis for showing that the political thought of *Cato's Letters* and the American Founders was a synthetic and coherent mixture of republicanism and liberalism.

Specifically, Zuckert argues that Wood and Pocock have erroneously attributed classical republican understandings of liberty, property, virtue, and the public good to seventeenth- and eighteenth-century Whigs and the American Founders. Textual evidence, Zuckert contends, does not support Wood's and Pocock's claims that Cato, the neo-Harringtonians, and the American Revolutionaries conceived of society as an organic whole, understood the public good as distinct from and more important than the individual, believed that individuals had to exercise a self-sacrificing form of virtue if the republic was to survive, or understood republicanism principally in terms of active and independent participation by equals sharing in the exercise of political power.

For Pocock, Zuckert maintains, such misreadings result because he first identifies a series of "republican" precepts, including arms, property, fear of standing armies, ministerial corruption, executive encroachment, autonomy, virtue, and citizenship. These precepts then serve as "markers, rather like radioisotopes, whereby he [Pocock] could trace the presence and permutations of civic humanism." The fundamental error that Pocock commits, however, is that when "he espies one or another of the elements of this chain . . . he infers the entire chain even when the other elements are not explicitly present."[17] But according to Zuckert, the fear of corruption, standing armies, and executive encroachment did not signal a commitment to classical republican understandings of virtue or positive liberty for seventeenth- and eighteenth-century Whigs.

Even more important, according to Zuckert, scholars of the republican synthesis have not distinguished the levels of political discourse that take place on the plane of political science from those that take place on the plane of political philosophy. Once this distinction is made, he contends, it can be shown that seventeenth- and eighteenth-century English Whigs fused a republican political science to a Lockean political philosophy and that this synthesis "became authoritative for the Americans preceding and immediately following 1776."[18] Here, Zuckert provides an analysis of the political thought of *Cato's Letters* by John Trenchard and Thomas Gordon as an example of how a "genuine and immensely powerful synthesis" between Lockean political philosophy and some of the themes of Whig republican political science could be achieved.[19]

Lockean political philosophy, Zuckert maintains, is the source of Cato's understanding of "the issues of political philosophy." Cato is thus a "thoroughgoing individualist, methodological and ontological," who accepts the Lockean principles later embedded in the American Declaration of Independence.[20] Nevertheless, according to Zuckert, republicanism is also present in Cato's political thought, but this does not take the form, as Pocock and scholars of the republican synthesis have contended, of a commitment to republican conceptions of the public good, public liberty, and virtue that require self-abnegation and autonomous political participation rooted in freehold property. Instead, Cato's republicanism includes specific components of the oppositional ideology of the radical Whigs, such as a resistance to standing armies, concerns about executive influence and ministerial corruption, and commitment to a mixed and balanced constitution. Far from serving as an alternative to Lockean fundamentals, this Whig science of politics supplements and reinforces Lockean fundamentals.

In *The Natural Rights Republic: Studies in the Foundation of the American Political Tradition*, Zuckert focuses his analysis exclusively on the American Founding and defends the "old and traditional view" that "the natural rights philosophy as articulated in the Declaration was indeed the understanding of political right on which the founding was conducted and which has served as the cornerstone of the American political tradition." To this end, Zuckert first defends an "essentially Lockean teaching" of the Declaration of Independence against numerous alternative interpretations. Specifically, Zuckert argues that when Jefferson declares that "all men are created equal," he is referring to the condition of men in the state of nature before the institution of civil society. Like Locke, Jefferson understands natural equality as the belief that all individuals are independent and equal before the formation of civil society because no one is by nature subject to the authority of others. Furthermore, according to Zuckert, the Declaration also rests on the natural rights–Lockean understanding of government as an artifice created by the consent of the governed and that the right of revolution follows directly from the belief that government is made by the people and thus can be unmade by them. Above all, however, the Declaration stresses the centrality of inalienable rights and the liberal proposition that "government exists for the sake of securing rights, and only for that."[21]

But in addition to this Lincolnian reading of the Declaration of Independence as "the foundation statement of the American political order," Zuckert stresses the importance of other traditions of political thought in the American Founding. Indeed, he argues that the outstanding aspect of the Declaration's natural rights philosophy has been its ability to assimilate and reshape "a variety of what are often thought to be competing traditions of political thought"—including British constitutionalism or the Whig tradition of positive rights of Englishmen, Protestant Christianity, and classical republicanism—"into a more or less coherent whole." Here, Zuckert pursues a complex argument in which he shows not only how the natural rights tradition differs from these alternative traditions and has remained the "senior partner" in the American amalgam but also how it is capable of assimilating important aspects of them. Zuckert, in other words, argues for the importance of other traditions while still maintaining that "the natural rights philosophy remains America's deepest and so far most abiding commitment, and the others could enter the amalgam only so far as they were compatible, or could be made so, with natural rights."[22]

In general, both Zuckert and Greenstone see themselves as combating caricatures and criticisms of the nature and effects of liberalism and the content and influence of the political thought of John Locke, and they argue that the diversity of political traditions in the American Founding can be drawn together under the rubric of a capacious conception of liberalism.[23] Here, these scholars draw diffusely on and contribute to a broader defense of liberalism that has been developed since the mid-1990s.[24] Responding to communitarian critics of liberalism, Nathan Tarcov in particular has argued that rather than rejecting liberalism or the belief that the American Founding was rooted in liberalism based on the portrait of it painted by its critics, scholars should reconsider the historical foundations of liberalism in Locke. Communitarian critics of liberalism, Tarcov contends, have too readily portrayed Lockean liberalism as a defense of atomism, greed, and selfishness. But according to Tarcov:

> Locke's political teaching is *not* one of self-interest but one of *rights*. Argument from interest rather than rights represents a degradation of Lockean politics and of the political theory of our nation's founding. Lockean politics include a conception of the common good and a conception of civil society as more than an aggregate of atomistic individuals. His understanding of human nature exhibits a profound appreciation of human sociability, and families and churches play crucial roles in Lockean civil society. Locke teaches not a narrowly calculating selfishness but a set of decent moral virtues. Nor is his fundamental concern with property the justification of money-grubbing.[25]

An interpretation rooted in this understanding of Locke's political thought, according to Tarcov, puts scholars in a position to provide a more accurate and defensible view of the Founding than if they interpret the Founders as classical republicans. Zuckert in particular has accepted Tarcov's invitation to first reconsider Locke's political thought before abandoning the idea of a Lockean Founding. The result is at once a sympathetic and complex interpretation of liberalism and a defense of the American Founding grounded in this "broader, deeper, and loftier liberalism."[26]

Liberal Republicanism: A Premodern Synthesis

A second and distinct interpretation of how the Founders integrated liberalism and republicanism can be culled from the scholarship of Ralph Ketcham, Drew McCoy, Garrett Ward Sheldon, and especially Lance Banning. Banning was one of the pioneers of the "republican synthesis"— or, as he would prefer, the "republican hypothesis"—during the 1970s and 1980s and has grappled with the relationship of liberalism and republicanism as seriously and perceptively as any scholar of the American Founding. In general, Banning sees the American Founding as a period of transition in which distinguishable—though not rival—idioms of political thought converged. Liberalism, he has argued, was certainly present in the American Founding; the masterworks of the republican interpretation were not intended to suggest otherwise, but only to establish the neglected but "vital role of neoclassical or civic humanist ideas" in the early republic. Now that it is recognized that liberalism and republicanism were both present and important in the American Founding, Banning asserts, scholars should show how the

American Revolutionaries and Framers of the Constitution managed "so coherently to blend traditions which seem incompatible to us."[27]

Banning's efforts to establish both the complexity and the coherence of the political thought of the American Founders have led him to urge scholars to examine the duality of the seventeenth- and eighteenth-century British opposition ideology from which the political thought of the Revolutionary generation was built. English opposition ideology, Banning asserts, combined contractual and liberal understandings of the origins and limitations of government with understandings of virtue, civic participation, and commercialization that were influenced by civic humanism. Thus, liberalism and republicanism "came into the English-speaking world together—and as allies, for the most part, rather than as foes."[28] Equally important, this rich and complex intellectual heritage was reflected and Americanized in the early republic. For Banning, then, the task is to show how republicanism and liberalism were "linked and blended in the minds of early modern individuals whose thinking changed as they attempted to assimilate and manage new phenomena and new events, but who were neither truly classical nor fully modern."[29]

Even though he acknowledges that liberalism became increasingly influential in the early nineteenth century, Banning is hesitant to suggest that republicanism ever faded away. Contrary to the teachings of Louis Hartz and the consensus historians, an enveloping liberalism may never have achieved uncontested hegemony in the American Republic. Indeed, Banning asserts, there was no simple transition from republicanism to liberalism in the early republic. Complexity, duality, and tension characterized the political thought the American Founders drew on, the political thought they produced, and the legacy they left. The movement in Revolutionary ideology should therefore be understood as a transition in which liberalism became increasingly important over time, but republicanism remained as a distinguishable political language.[30]

Beyond the broad outlines provided by Banning's analysis of change, he, Ketcham, and McCoy have used a number of strategies, either alone or in combination, to trace out the synthetic quality of the Founders' political thought.[31] First, they have argued that key concepts such as "liberty" and "virtue" took on meanings during the American Founding that straddled and transcended classical and liberal definitions of these terms. Ketcham, for example, has argued that the conception of liberty accepted by most of the Founders synthesized "personal liberty" with "political freedom." The Framers sought to promote personal liberty—or, what scholars following Isaiah Berlin have come to call "negative liberty"— by imposing restrictions on governmental power, such as those found in the Bill of Rights and in Article I, Section 9 (which prohibits the national government from suspending the writ of habeas corpus, passing bills of attainder or ex post facto laws, or issuing titles of nobility). This understanding of liberty sprang from the tradition of opposition to kings and tyrants that had been present in England since the Magna Carta and blossomed in Revolutionary America during the eighteenth century. But alongside this tradition of "freedom from" government, Ketcham maintains, was the concept of "positive liberty," or "freedom to" participate in political affairs. This tradition of liberty is implicit in Article I, Section 8, of the Constitution, which gives the national government numerous powers to act for the public good. Most important, according to Ketcham, the Constitution partakes of both traditions of liberty. It is predicated on a belief in active citizenship and positive government meant to achieve the public good, but it also places certain freedoms outside the province of government. Thus, "the center of the philosophy of the Constitution"—indeed, its "very aspiration and genius"—"is to repudiate the dichotomy and even the tension" between these forms of liberty so that each might be fostered.[32]

Second, Banning, McCoy, Ketcham, and numerous other historians have focused on how republican concepts were Americanized and synthesized with liberalism as the Founding generation confronted concrete daily problems and practices. Eighteenth-century society, these scholars maintain, was highly dynamic, and the Founders and ordinary Americans were often caught between their republican beliefs and the practices of an increasingly modern, liberal society.[33] In this light, consider McCoy's analysis of the political economy of the Jeffersonians, who began with classical republican assumptions. They idealized the independence and virtue of the farmer and designed a plan of political economy that would help ensure a "republican distribution of citizens" against the pressures of increasing population growth and development. Nevertheless, the Jeffersonians realized that American farmers would necessarily be commercial farmers; they would often produce surplus crops and would want to market those surpluses. The Jeffersonians were therefore among the eighteenth century's most enthusiastic advocates of the free trade and commercial liberalism of Adam Smith. Free markets meant that American surpluses could be traded for European manufacturing items, which would not have to be produced in the United States. Most important, McCoy's interpretation illustrates that Jeffersonian political economy was neither a romantic and nostalgic ideal rooted in classical republicanism nor an unqualified forerunner of modern liberalism and capitalism. The Jeffersonians were neither and both. They fought for free trade and commerce but against industrialization, urbanization, wage labor, greater division of labor, broad inequalities of wealth resulting from increased development, and efforts to facilitate the growth of capital and centralize it in the national government. In short, according to McCoy, Madison and the other Jeffersonians were "caught between conflicting claims of classical republicanism and modern commercial society"; they struggled "to define and implement a viable synthesis that was relevant to the American experience."[34]

A third strategy used to explore the synthetic quality of the Framers' political thought is to show how the Founders individually or collectively combined a multiplicity of traditions.[35] In *The Political Philosophy of Thomas Jefferson,* for example, Garrett Ward Sheldon argues that Jefferson's political thought was a "coherent blending of liberalism, classicism, moral sense psychology, and Christian ethics." Jefferson, according to Sheldon, combined appeals to the "ancient constitution" and the seventeenth-century tradition of Saxon liberties with the precepts of Lockean liberalism to justify rebellion against Great Britain and to combat the centralizing threats of the Federalist Party. But Jefferson turned to classical republicanism and moral sense psychology in the development of his famous conception of participatory democracy in ward republics. Most important, according to Sheldon, Jefferson used liberalism to critique and combat distant, corrupt governments, but he used classical republicanism and moral sense psychology to defend local legislative politics. Jefferson could argue for both the protection of natural rights and participatory republicanism, Sheldon argues, because he believed that the greatest threat to natural rights came from distant, centralized governments and that participatory democracy would protect, not threaten, individual rights.[36]

In general, the interpretations of Banning, Ketcham, McCoy, and Sheldon can be grouped together and differentiated from those of Greenstone and Zuckert. Unlike scholars of the neoliberal synthesis, Banning and his colleagues resist efforts to understand the Founders' political thought as a tight synthesis constructed from the fusion of Lockean ends and republican means and to interpret republicanism primarily as a form of government. Eighteenth-century Americans, these scholars contend, still understood republicanism as a set of beliefs about the importance of public liberty, virtue, and the public good. These concepts, they emphasize, had great longevity. And even if the Founders' interpretation of these concepts was not strictly classical, they nevertheless retained aspects of their original classical meaning. In short, because this group includes many of the scholars who formerly espoused the republican synthesis, they tend to stress the persistence of classical republicanism in the face of modernity and, in Ketcham's words, to view "the Revolution, and perhaps even more the Constitution, as shaped, uniquely and creatively, by the tension between a still-vigorous classical republican outlook and the new, modern, democratic liberalism."[37]

Illiberal Liberalism: Inegalitarian and Ascriptive Ideologies

In contrast to both scholars who argue that a diversity of conceptions of American political thought can fit within a broad, capacious understanding of liberalism and those who argue for the synthesis of distinct idioms of political thought, University of Pennsylvania professor Rogers Smith has recently tried to dethrone the liberal interpretation and expose the incoherence of much American political thought.[38] Almost all students of American political culture and development, Smith observes in *Civic Ideals: Conflicting Visions of Citizenship in U.S. History,* have relied on a framework of analysis derived extensively from Tocqueville and Hartz. This framework suggests that American society was founded as a liberal, democratic society and has been dominated by a pervasive liberal, egalitarian ideology that has shaped American political institutions and served as the logic of American political development.

Smith concedes that such accounts contain "real if partial truths."[39] He observes, for example, that there has never been a European-style aristocracy in the United States; material conditions (especially the abundance of land) have mitigated against gross inequalities among white males, and an emphasis on the protection of individual rights has operated against repressive structures and supported the rule of law, tolerance, and the market system. Nevertheless, Smith charges that the Tocquevillian-Hartzian framework is narrow and misleading, primarily because it suggests that the absence of one form of ascriptive hierarchy (hereditary monarchy and nobility) signals the absence of all forms of ascriptive hierarchy. But in America, according to Smith, "the comparative moral, material, and political egalitarianism that prevailed at the Founding among moderately propertied white men was surrounded by an array of other fixed, ascriptive systems of unequal status."[40] "America's civic laws," Smith states flatly, "have often been starkly illiberal, riddled with racial, sexual, ideological, ethnic, and xenophobic discriminations."[41] These discriminations, in turn, have been justified by appeals to inegalitarian ascriptive ideologies.

Defined briefly, inegalitarian ascriptive ideologies are sets of ideas that attempt to justify inequality based on characteristics that are believed to be natural or ascribed, such as race, ethnicity, and gender. Smith's challenge to

Tocqueville and Hartz, then, is built around his documentation of the variety, potency, and persistence of these ideologies and his explanation of their strategic importance. In documenting the potency and persistence of these ideologies, Smith's prodigious study chronicles various forms of nativism; biblical, scientific, and racial justifications for slavery and the displacement of Native Americans; and "coverture," "republican motherhood," and "domestic sphere" ideology as justifications for the depoliticization of women.[42] In explaining their potency and strategic importance, Smith notes that inegalitarian ascriptive ideologies have been continually evoked by political elites (out of both conviction and a desire for electoral success) and have served as the foundation for the political identities of many Americans—even some who have ultimately been oppressed by such ideologies. Indeed, Smith notes that inegalitarian ideologies can do what liberalism cannot because they do not suffer from its "great political liability."[43] Whereas liberalism is universalistic and demanding (suggesting that everyone must be recognized as equal and included in the political community), inegalitarian ideologies have recurring power in American history because they address people's desire to believe that they are unique and part of a special political community ordained by God. For these reasons, inegalitarian ascriptive ideologies have been "deeply constitutive of American national identity" and, however perverse and wrongheaded they now seem, must be recognized as "genuine" or even "prestigious intellectual *traditions,*" not ephemeral prejudices.[44]

All this leads Smith to abandon the belief that there is a core set of principles in American political thought or a progressive logic to its development. Instead, he emphasizes the degree to which American laws, institutions, and constitutions have "emerged as none too coherent compromises among the distinct mixes of civic conceptions."[45] He also seeks to explain the complex relationship among liberalism, republicanism, and inegalitarian ascriptive ideologies and to assign praise and blame to each. In particular, unlike the other scholars analyzed in this chapter, Smith spends little time addressing the relationship of liberalism and republicanism. Instead, he simply observes that "even proponents of republican historiography now concede that Americans have more often blended liberalism and republicanism than opposed them and that at some point in US history liberalism became predominant."[46]

In contrast, the relationship of inegalitarian ascriptive ideologies to liberal republicanism figures centrally. Here, Smith treats these two ideologies as discrete, "*rival* civic ideologies" and as "intertwined but relatively autonomous systems of ideas" that "many Americans have inconsistently endorsed."[47] This position has led to considerable criticism from scholars on the Left, who maintain that "liberalism and exclusion betray an underlying consistency" and that inegalitarian ideologies and a patriarchal and racist structure are endemic to liberal republicanism and an essential part of it.[48] Smith, however, contends that liberalism and inegalitarian ideologies have "social psychological and political" linkages, not logical or essential ones.[49] Separating out these civic ideologies leads Smith to praise liberalism as the inspiration and engine behind many of the most egalitarian and progressive reforms in American history. Nevertheless, contrary to what his critics suggest, Smith does not exonerate liberalism from its share of the blame in the construction of civic exclusions. As noted earlier, he traces the popularity of inegalitarian ascriptive ideologies to a core weakness of liberalism and notes that these sets of ideas flourish in periods of backlash against egalitarian reforms.

Most important for the purposes of this study, when Smith's multiple traditions approach is applied to the history of the early American Republic, it yields a substantial challenge to the Hartz thesis and several revisionary interpretations. Two are central here. First, Smith places citizenship issues at the center of the party conflicts of the 1790s between the Jeffersonians and the Federalists, and he contends that their policy differences sprang from contrasting blends of liberal republicanism and ascriptive notions of American identity. The Federalists, he observes, advanced classical liberal policies that favored financial and commercial elites. Initially, at least, they sponsored relatively passive policies toward unconquered western tribes and were opponents of slavery. Nevertheless, "a predilection toward nativism" and the continued subordination of women were also deeply embedded in the political thought of the Federalist Party. The Jeffersonians, in contrast, were the party of westward expansion, state power, and agrarian republicanism, but also, "in a bitter irony, [they were] the defenders both of citizenship based on mutual consent [for white males] and of aggressive civic racism."[50]

Second, Smith's study challenges the view of republicanism presented in many studies of the republican synthesis of the 1970s and 1980s and the parallel works of communitarian political theorists. In at least some of these studies, Smith notes, republicanism is portrayed as a historic alternative to liberalism that was "eventually eclipsed" but now demands reconsideration. Republicanism, these scholars suggest, led men to conceive of the public as an organic whole, to encourage citizens to make virtuous sacrifices in favor of the public good, and to value extensive political participation among the citizenry. Smith's analysis of the historic impact of republicanism, however, provides scholars with little to romanticize. Indeed, he traces "an alliance [throughout American history] between republican concerns for homogeneity and ascriptive Americanism."[51] In particular, Smith notes that the concept of federalism retained the belief that the republican form of government could exist only in a small geographic area with a homogeneous and martial citizenry. These requirements, Smith observes, have consistently been used to justify state control of citizenship issues and the passage of state laws excluding immigrants, Native Americans, and African Americans from political participation. Furthermore, the republican requirement that citizens have economic independence and display "manly" (martial) virtue has perennially been used to bar women (who were precluded by law and custom from expressing these qualities) from the public realm. Finally, Smith notes that the republican emphasis on a homogeneous citizenry has been used to promote restrictive naturalization policies by those who want to prevent the wrong sorts of people from becoming Americans.

Retrospect: What We Should Have Learned

Considered collectively, the works of these three groups show that, far from burning out, as many have suggested, the debate over the intellectual character of the American Republic has progressed and intensified since the 1990s. The result is a body of scholarship that provides a more vivid and complex portrait of the American Founding than we had previously. Most important, however, these works provide the occasion to take a step back and make some broad points about what we should have learned from this debate.[52]

The Significance of the Natural Rights–Social Contract Tradition

The contention that the Founders were deeply committed to the natural rights–social contract tradition is readily accepted by most scholars of the American Founding.[53] The studies of Zuckert, in particular, remind us that the Founders almost universally accepted the constellation of concepts embedded in the Declaration of Independence. They began their reasoning about the origins and legitimate ends of government with the belief that men are created equal. By this, they meant that no individual is by nature a slave or a king, and thus all legitimate governments derive their just power from the consent of the governed. They also believed that men possess inalienable or natural rights given by God. These rights cannot be transferred to the government, even if an individual wanted to, so they can never be justly violated by the government. Finally, the Founders understood government as a human artifact (not as a natural, organic whole necessary to complete the human personality) that men make with their consent and can legitimately overthrow if it violates their inalienable rights.

Beyond these precepts, the Founders also held fast to other political concepts that are rightly considered aspects of a liberal political philosophy. They began their reasoning about politics and institutional design with the assumption that men often pursue self-interest at the expense of the public interest; they feared concentrated power, whether it was lodged in an interested majority or an interested prince, and thus advocated a system of checks and balances that gave a defensive power to both the governing and the governed. They also advocated the privatization of many concerns—such as religious belief—that ancient and medieval thinkers had contended should be deliberately promoted by the government. Put conversely, few of the Founders believed that the formation of belief and opinion or the development of a common character among the citizenry was the province of the government. To borrow a phrase from Madison, in the American political system, the censorial power would be in the people over the government, not in the government over the people.[54]

Together with the cardinal principles of the Declaration of Independence, this understanding of human nature and the character and purposes of government formed a profoundly important dimension of the political thought of the Founders, though by no means was Locke the exclusive source. These liberal precepts were, to borrow language from Tocqueville, "fundamental facts" of the American Founding.

The Distance of the Founders' Political Thought from Classical Republicanism

The corollary of the Founders' commitment to the natural rights–social contract tradition is the distance of their political thought from classical republicanism, rigorously defined.[55] A broad outline of these differences might be constructed by comparing an Aristotelian understanding of classical republicanism and the political thought of the Founders on three central and interrelated points: the nature of man, the character of government, and the purposes of government. Here, Paul Rahe's analysis of ancient republics is invaluable for understanding not only the content of classical republican political thought but also how classical republicanism took form in ancient republics.

Specifically, as Rahe has shown, the "primacy of politics" in ancient republics, as well as the importance of political liberty, reflects the belief that man is a political animal. When the ancients made this assertion, they meant that man becomes fully human only if he exercises his unique capacity for the use of language to determine and to persuade others about the advantageous, the just, and the good. Aristotle sets up the following argument: Nature makes nothing in vain. Man is peculiar in that he has the faculty of language and the ability to engage in deliberation to determine what is advantageous, just, and good. Man is thus by nature a political animal or an animal with an "immanent impulse" to political association. Furthermore, the polis is prior to the individual, not because the polis forms before the individual in time (it does not) but because man reaches his true nature only inside it. The polis is the natural whole (the most complete human association) that brings man's nature to completion. Outside of the polis, man is either a beast (incapable of political association and the use of his capacity for language) or a god (who has, by definition, achieved self-sufficiency and is not in need of political association to develop fully).[56]

The importance of political liberty in ancient republics followed from this view of human nature and was, in turn, reflected in the conception, organization, and ends of the polis. The polis was conceived as "a moral community of men permanently united as a people by a common way of life."[57] It was central to the completion of the human personality because it opened up a "middle ground"—a public forum—in which citizens could use their unique capacity for logos and was thus organized to allow for political deliberation. Indeed, many ancient republics were, in Madison's words, societies "consisting of a small number of citizens, who assemble and administer the government in person."[58] Within these societies, government was not a detached entity that administered to the citizenry, nor was the economy conceived as a sphere independent of the government. Instead, as Rahe points out, the citizenry meeting collectively was the state or government, and the economy and civil society were embedded in the polity.[59]

As Rahe has shown, this peculiar form of social organization and high-toned conception of political liberty came at an immense price. The quest for political liberty often led to war with other republics and produced factions within the polis. The principal ends of the political association were therefore to suppress factions and to prepare for war to defend the common way of life that political liberty identified. Within classical republican societies, factions were suppressed by the adoption of *paidea*—comprehensive sets of laws that were the instruments of moral education. These laws touched almost every aspect of a citizen's life. In other words, there was almost no private sphere in classical republics, except for a small degree of privacy accorded to the household to promote procreation. Women were essentially instruments for procreation, and slaves were instruments for labor, which provided leisure for citizens to engage in politics. In sum, as Rahe observes, ancient republics were at once participatory democracies and closed societies. Citizens had no rights against the government, and "the civic community's claim was, in principle, total."[60] Nevertheless, those privileged to be recognized as citizens exercised a form of political participation more meaningful than we can comprehend today.[61]

When this understanding of classical republicanism is compared with the constellation of concepts, anxieties, and aspirations from the writings of seventeenth- and eighteenth-century English radicals (which scholars of the republican synthesis labeled classical republican ideology), it is easy to understand why many scholars (especially political theorists deeply read in classical texts) first winced at the appellation *classical republicanism* to refer to English opposition ideology and the political thought of the American Founders, and why they then began a counterrevolution against republican revisionism.[62] In its conception of the nature of man and its understanding of the character and purposes of government, the political thought of the American Founders is fundamentally different from classical republicanism as it was understood and practiced by the ancients themselves. Unlike the ancients, the American Founders did not conceive of man as a "political animal" or believe that the human personality could fully develop only by political participation. Rather, they began their political reasoning with the belief that men are naturally equal, possessed of inalienable rights, self-interested, and often contentious, especially in groups.[63] This set of beliefs, in turn, was part of the reason that the Framers of the Constitution severely criticized "pure (classical) Democracies," advocated an extended republic, defended representation as "the pivot" of the new political system, and understood "political liberty" primarily as popular control rather than as direct citizen participation.[64]

Similarly, the Founders did not understand government as a natural moral community designed to promote a common way of life, but rather as an artificial entity established by the consent of the governed. They therefore did not view the purpose of government as the promotion of *homonoia* (political oneness) through the use of comprehensive sets of laws to repress faction and to develop a common character among the citizenry. Instead, they believed that the government should protect the individual rights of the citizenry and promote the interests they shared in common, while leaving to individuals the right to define the good life for themselves.[65] In short, whereas classical republican political thought emphasized the ontological priority of the society (conceived as an organic whole) over the individual and contended that the central purpose of politics was to foster a common understanding of the good life, the political thought of the Founders is best thought of as squarely within the tradition of deontological liberalism.

Here, a statement I quoted earlier bears repeating: "Anglo-American republicanism," Greenstone keenly observes, "did not prescribe a comprehensive vision of human well-being, nor did it assign the function of prescribing such a vision to any official body or collectivity such as church, tribe, or polis."[66]

The Importance of English Opposition Ideology

In addition to establishing the significance of the natural rights–social contract tradition and the distance of the Founders' political thought from classical republicanism rightly understood, the republicanism-liberalism debate has reinforced the importance of English opposition ideology. Such a claim may seem contradictory to the two previous points. After all, English opposition ideology is usually characterized as a reflection of classical republicanism or at least linked with the beliefs that man is a political animal and that self-denying virtue is necessary for the maintenance of a republic. It has then been set in opposition to the natural rights–social contract tradition.

Zuckert's contribution, however, has been to qualify the interpretations of the republican revisionists, refuting exaggerated claims, modifying others, and, most important, disconnecting English opposition ideology from classical republicanism and linking it to the natural rights–social contract tradition. These interpretive maneuvers, in turn, have paved the way for understanding how liberalism and Anglo-American or eighteenth-century republicanism were combined in the minds of the Founders. Specifically, Zuckert has shown that Pocock and Wood made exaggerated claims when they contended that the Founders conceived of man as a *zoon politikon* or insisted that the Founders believed that the citizenry had to act virtuously and surrender their interests to an abstracted public good if the republic was to survive. As he points out, the Founders were precluded from such beliefs by their acceptance of the cardinal principles of the natural rights–social contract tradition. The Founders could not have believed both that men are naturally equal, independent, and endowed with rights and that man's nature is completed only inside a political community in which he is at once ruler and ruled.[67]

Furthermore, Zuckert has established that republican revisionists erred when they characterized English opposition ideology as a species of classical republican ideology or as a marker of the presence of classical republican concepts. Clearly, the Founders feared "corruption," opposed standing armies and public debts, were convinced that men craved power and that liberty was fragile, and had firm commitments to a mixed and balanced form of government, rotation in office, and a variety of other constitutional mechanisms. Nevertheless, this did not make them *classical* republicans or signal their commitment to genuinely classical percepts. Finally, these scholars might have pointed out that English opposition ideology called for a libertarian view of the purposes of governments, which stressed the importance of a limited government and a broad private sphere. But again, the opposite view prevailed in ancient republics. There, the community's claim on the individual was virtually complete, and the private sphere was limited to the goals of procreation and household management.

Nevertheless, when it is disconnected from exaggerated claims about its character and pedigree and is understood in conjunction with the natural rights–social contract tradition, English opposition ideology—this same constellation of anxieties, hopes, and constitutional mechanics—is immensely important in understanding the American Founding. Scholars have repeatedly reaffirmed the importance of English opposition ideology in the American Revolution, often echoing Bailyn's statements that it was "devoured by the colonists" and provided "not merely the vocabulary but the grammar" of American Revolutionary thought.[68] Indeed, in the forty years since the publication of *The Ideological Origins of the American Revolution,* scholars have become even more convinced of the profound influence of *Cato's Letters* (the quintessential statement of English opposition ideology) in forming and synthesizing the grievances of the American Revolutionaries.[69] Bailyn's permanent contribution to scholarship on the American Founding has been to show that Americans' reaction to the reimposition of British rule in the colonies after 1763 cannot be grasped without an understanding of the roots of their fears and anxieties in English opposition ideology.

English opposition ideology is also important for understanding both anti-Federalism and the political thought of the Framers of the Constitution. Here again, Bailyn is helpful. Most recently, he has argued that the anti-Federalists' fear of standing armies, unlimited taxation, corrupt representation, encroachment by the national government on the states' powers, and violation of the natural rights of the people sprang directly from their passionate commitment to English opposition ideology. Furthermore, he has shown that the political thought behind the Constitution, which so many scholars have characterized as a decisive break with English opposition ideology, was really only an effort to rephrase these ideas and to show that many of the fears raised in the English libertarian tradition were irrelevant in the American experience. The Framers of the Constitution, for example, did not reject the belief that standing armies are a threat to liberty. Instead, they argued that the permanent army created by the U.S. Constitution would be under the control of popularly elected officials.[70]

But perhaps most important, English opposition ideology is an invaluable interpretive construct for understanding the party battles between the Federalists and the Jeffersonians. As the works of Lance Banning, John Murrin, Drew McCoy, and, most recently and comprehensively, Stanley Elkins and Eric McKitrick have shown, Hamilton's financial program of a funded national debt, a national bank, and government support for public manufacturing was a bold attempt to re-create in America the system of political economy that had fueled the financial revolution of the late seventeenth and early eighteenth centuries in England.[71] Equally important, Hamilton's presentation of this "court party" model of state-sponsored capitalism was condemned by the Jeffersonians, in characteristic fashion, as "an unholy alliance of commerce, manufacturing, money, and public credit, fostered by an intrusive and interfering government."[72]

Virtue, Liberty, and the Public Good: Multiple Conceptions and Modified Meanings

A fourth broad point that should have been established by now is that the key political concepts of the American Founding—virtue, liberty, and the public good—were given multiple and modified definitions in the early republic, yet these various definitions had a common core of meaning or could at least be rephrased in ways that made them compatible. When this common core is examined, it becomes clear that few of the Founders ever held fully classical understandings of these concepts or abandoned a belief in their importance in favor of liberal axioms. Here, the suggestion—implicit in the works of Banning, Ketcham, and other scholars—that the Founders developed unique understandings of these concepts that straddled and transcended classical and liberal conceptions is particularly helpful.

For example, recent scholarship on the concept of virtue has suggested that few of the Founders believed that Americans would consistently exercise a sublime or self-abnegating form of virtue that required them to ignore their own interests. But it has also shown that they remained attached to the belief that virtue is the foundation of republican government and that no system of separation of powers can substitute for it.[73] Richard Vetterli and Gary Bryner provide an excellent synopsis of this position. The American Founders, they write,

> had come to the conclusion that classical philosophy had relied too
> heavily on the expectation of the consistency of stringent virtuous
> behavior, devoid of any self-interest. Their understanding of the

nature of man reflected a profound awareness of his selfishness and aggressiveness. Nevertheless, they believed that man had certain redeeming qualities, that he had the potential for self-government. The Founders believed that the "auxiliary precautions" they had devised, *combined* with, rather than replacing, individual virtue, might just make it all possible. They also believed that no structure of government in a republic would long survive the absence of virtue in the people.[74]

The apparent paradox in the Founders' expectation that men would often act selfishly and their belief that the American people had enough virtue to maintain a republic can be resolved only if we understand that the Founders significantly modified the classical understanding of virtue. Indeed, if we hope to grasp the complexity of the Founders' understanding of the relationship between virtue and interest, we must give up the belief that they saw virtue and interest as wholly independent or that they attempted to substitute a politics of interest for a politics of virtue. We must accept that they had a subtle and ambiguous understanding of human nature that included both its unfortunate tendencies and its possibilities, that this understanding was rooted in an appreciation of the multiple dimensions of human motivation, and that they believed that constitutional structures and constraints had a profound effect on whether men acted on their best or worst inclinations.

Similarly, the Founders' ideas about the meaning of this concept and its cognates the "common good" and the "common interest" are not easily categorized as liberal or republican. Specifically, the Founders did not conceive of the United States as an organic moral community bound by a common conception of justice and good; nor did they believe that the purpose of the government they founded in 1787 was to promote a single conception of the good life. Thus, they were not strictly classical in their understanding of the public good or the government's role in promoting it. Nevertheless, unlike many modern proponents of interest-group liberalism, they did not simply dismiss the concept of the public good or the common interest as an incomprehensible abstraction or as the residue of the conflict of interests.[75] Nor did they understand it merely as the aggregation of individual interests, the maintenance of public institutions, or the protection of individual rights, although the protection of rights and the maintenance of institutions were essential elements of the public good. Instead, most of the Founders seem to have understood the public good or the common interest as the collective articulation of self-interest properly understood. Much as an individual citizen is supposed to control his immediate passions and make small sacrifices with the understanding that doing so will serve his long-term interests, the government is expected to obey the reason, not the passions, of the public; blunt particular and short-term interests; and promote the long-term interests of the nation.[76]

The Inadequacies of the Possessive-Individualist and Liberal-Pluralist Interpretations

Finally, this debate should have moved away from interpretations of the Founders as possessive individualists or interest-group liberals. The Founders, according to these interpretations, began with the realistic, Calvinistic, or Hobbesian view that humans are equal, self-interested or even rapacious, and naturally diverse in their desires. Such individuals, the Founders reasoned, would and should not trust one another or any rulers they might elect. They therefore constructed a government that rested on the consent of the governed, that institutionalized the policy of counter-vailing powers as a solution to the "defect of better motives" among the rulers and the ruled, and that was designed exclusively to protect the individual rights—especially property rights—of the citizenry. Inequalities in wealth naturally emerged from the protection of property rights and were legitimated by liberal ideology and protected by the government.[77]

Meanwhile, according to these interpretations, American political institutions were designed to reflect and channel interests and to promote the accommodation and aggregation of interests. More concretely, as interests formed in the pluralistic society, they would penetrate the political system through representatives acting as spokesmen for particular interests. As these representatives bargained and compromised, ephemeral majorities would form and re-form. A substratum of temporary agreement would emerge as a residue of clashing interests. When a new issue arose, the process would begin again. Interests would fight and engage in give-and-take, and a new consensus would emerge. In general, the political system was designed to act as a neutral receptacle for all interests. Conversely, it was not designed to ensure the selection and training of elite statesmen, to promote the redistribution of wealth, or to make choices between interests based on shared values or on a substantive conception of the common interest.

At a broader level, according to this interpretation, the branches of the government were also set in constructive competition with one another. Fearing power, the Founders distributed it among the executive, the legislature, and the judiciary. Action by this complex government required concert among its dissimilar parts. Inefficiency was risked to prevent tyranny.

Overall, the Framers sought to form a "machine that would go of itself,"[78] "a harmonious system of mutual frustration"[79] rooted in the "unique virtues of proceduralism and purposeless consensus,"[80] a system in which the public good was understood as the aggregate of results of the free pursuit of private interests," a system designed to "channel and manipulate self-interestedness into a social equilibrium."[81]

Furthermore, according to many versions of these interpretations, the system of government established by the Framers was designed to serve as the institutional framework for commercial capitalism. The goals of classical polities had been to promote virtue and a common character among the citizenry and to identify and develop the elite who were designated by nature to rule. Medieval political philosophers had argued that the government should promote the salvation of the souls of the citizenry. In contrast, the Founders lowered the ends of government to the solid and attainable goals of the protection of individual rights, especially property rights. The protection of property rights, the Framers believed, would catalyze acquisitiveness and transform explosive ideological and religious conflicts to more moderate conflicts between interest groups. The central goals of government would now be to ensure the safety of the citizenry and the stability of the republic and to promote economic growth and the conditions under which commodious living was possible.[82]

Aspects of this possessive-individualist, liberal-pluralist, or commercial-republican interpretation of the American Founding have been reaffirmed in recent scholarship. Again, the Founders almost uniformly began their reasoning about politics with a number of beliefs consistent with liberalism. They believed that individuals often pursue their self-interests, that legitimate governments rest on the consent of the governed, that the protection of individual rights is one of the chief ends of a political system, and that commerce is essential to the prosperity of the United States. In general, the strength of this interpretation is that it highlights the distance between the Founders' essentially deontological understanding of the purposes of government and the perfectionistic goals of ancient regimes and the high-toned means enacted to achieve them.

Nevertheless, twenty years of scholarship from both sides of this debate should have taught us that the possessive-individualist and liberal-pluralist interpretation synthesizes a series of half-truths into a fundamental misreading of the Founding's intellectual character and the American political system's original design. Specifically, these interpretations commit four errors. First, they suggest that the Founders abandoned their belief in the importance of public or political liberty, virtue, and the public good and adopted the view that vice or interest compounded would somehow result in realization of the public good if the government was properly constructed. As I pointed out earlier, however, it is far more accurate to say that the Founders remained attached to these concepts even as they rephrased and modified them in novel ways.

Second, the liberal-pluralist interpretation misrepresents the relationship the Founders hoped to create between interest groups and the government. The Founders were not interest-group liberals who believed that the central purpose of the American political system was to integrate and accommodate interests. Instead, most of the Framers of the Constitution were fastened to a republican conception of impartial representation, believed that the government should advance the common interest within the sphere of its limited power, and thought that this could be achieved only by deliberate acts of the government made through its representatives (not through the mysterious workings of a self-regulating political system). As I have explained elsewhere, "impartial" representation meant that representatives could not use their office to advance their personal interests or advance the interests of their constituents at the expense of the public good.[83] What is most important here is that this conception of representation became the means by which the interests and views of the whole nation could be brought together and the common interest determined and advanced. Representation also made it possible for the wisest and most virtuous men in the republic to deliberate about the ends and goals of public policy. Representation thus institutionalized for a few elite leaders the "middle ground" that classical republics had given to all citizens.[84]

Third, far from trying to create a deadlocked, inefficient, or automatic system of government, as the liberal-pluralist interpretation suggests, the Founders believed that they had designed a political system that would discern national goals and serve them efficiently and with dispatch. Separation of powers was intended to promote deliberation about public policies and "good government" in general, as well as to deflect unwise or unjust policies.[85] Thus, although the American political system was originally designed to rely on countervailing powers to prevent arbitrary independent actions by the government, this was only a precondition to the exercise of power. In short, then, the American political system was initially structured not only to ensure a limited government that would protect individual rights but also to promote constructive action by the government within its limited sphere of activity.

Fourth, the relationship of the American Founding to the development of capitalism is much more problematic than these interpretations suggest. Although some of the Founders were "commercial republicans" and can fairly be characterized as at least the forerunners of capitalists (Hamilton and John Marshall were among this group), the tradition of agrarian republicanism was deeply embedded in the political thought of others (especially the Jeffersonians). As McCoy has shown, the Jeffersonians were land-expansion agrarians who hoped to use commercial discrimination to expand America's commercial agricultural products and land expansion to delay the advent of large-scale public manufacturing. They were both advocates of free trade and opponents of the improper acceleration of economic development. They favored commercial and landed expansion because they believed that the nation would remain largely an agrarian society and that independent freeholders were the best basis of public liberty.[86]

This constellation of beliefs and concrete policies, however, has been consistently misinterpreted. On the one hand, some scholars have maintained that the Jeffersonians' commitment to commerce and free trade was evidence that they advocated a modern, capitalistic, growth-oriented economy.[87] On the other hand, it is possible to read this conception of political economy as the direct descendant of classical republicanism. Nevertheless, both these interpretations focus on one dimension of this complex and ambiguous universe of ideas. Jeffersonian agrarianism was not strictly classical. The Jeffersonians were firmly committed to commerce and scientific farming.[88] Further, the Jeffersonians' idealization of the independent farmer was not the equivalent of the classical republican desire to define and foster a single conception of the "good life." Indeed, the Jeffersonians disclaimed any desire to secure a "republican distribution of the citizens" by "violence on the will or property of individuals."[89] Jeffersonian agrarianism was therefore consistent with the view that government should not prescribe a comprehensive vision of human well-being.

Nevertheless, the Jeffersonians were not proto-capitalists or engaged in an effort to subordinate politics to economics. Once again, they opposed industrialization, urbanization, a high division of labor, broad inequalities of wealth resulting from commercialization, and efforts to facilitate the growth of capital and centralize it in the national government. Although they certainly did not oppose economic growth, this was simply not the Jeffersonians' central goal. Jeffersonian agrarianism was still very much a conception of *political* economy; it was a conception of the economy that had political goals—namely, the preservation of a republican citizenry.[90] Finally, as Banning notes, this constellation of beliefs expressed the Jeffersonians' "reservations about the eager, unrestrained pursuit of economic opportunity" and their "even stronger reservations about the use of government to speed the process of change."[91]

Prospect: The Agenda for Scholars

If the dialectic of the republicanism-liberalism debate has given rise to these generalizations, it has also exposed weaknesses in previous scholarship, suggested new avenues for research, and opened new areas of confrontation. The question now becomes, how can we apply what we have learned, and in what direction is the multiple traditions approach taking us?

First, the central contribution of this approach may be that it gives scholars the tools they need to produce studies that better characterize the complex nature of eighteenth-century political discourse. By understanding the American Founding as a period of transition in which myriad idioms of political thought were available, rather than interpreting it as a reflection of a central tradition, scholars can explore the range of intellectual traditions the Founders drew on and the relationship among these traditions, the concrete problems the Founders faced, and the way they selectively adopted, creatively integrated, and substantially reconstructed these traditions of political thought to address these problems.

Reconsidering Civil Society

Beyond this basic point, there are four specific areas that scholars should now turn their attention to, based on what we have learned. First, the dialectic of the republicanism-liberalism debate has made it necessary to reconsider and examine more intensely the Founders' conception of civil society and the institutions they believed would support it. Scholars of the republican interpretation have emphasized the degree to which the republican concepts of liberty, virtue, and the public good remained important to the Founders. Attention to these concepts, according to republican revisionists, was demanded by the Founders' repeated statements about the necessity of virtue—understood as requiring self-sacrifice for the public good—to the preservation of the republic. Although the republican revisionists misunderstood the Founders' conception of virtue and made exaggerated claims about its place in the Founders' political thought, it should not be doubted that such statements and a deep commitment to "public spirit" were very much a part of the discourse of the early republic.[92]

What scholars should now realize, however, is that such statements were not about the role or proper function of the national government; rather, they expressed the Founders' beliefs about the necessary character or content of civil society if republicanism was to survive in America. In other words, as my previous analysis suggests, the Founders did not believe that it was the function of government to promote virtue among the citizenry or to foster a particular conception of the good life. They constructed essentially a deontological political system. Nevertheless, they did not believe that the government they had constructed could exist in the absence of virtue.

At this point, the question becomes, what did the Founders believe would promote such virtue? How did they believe that public spirit would be fostered and maintained? The most obvious answer is that they looked to education, religion, and social and economic arrangements to foster and maintain a republican citizenry. Yet surprisingly little scholarship has focused on the various ways the Founders believed that virtue could be fostered indirectly by voluntary associations and the institutions of civil society.[93] Such studies, however, are necessary to show why the Founders designed a government that would achieve essentially liberal goals, such as protecting rights and ensuring national security and economic prosperity, yet persistently maintained that virtue among the citizenry was necessary for the preservation of the American Republic.

Appreciating the Founding's Distinctiveness

Second, and most fundamentally, recent scholarship on the American Founding challenges scholars to explore how the Founders' political thought differed from both ancient and modern political thought and to more fully appreciate its peculiarity. Specifically, in the past, we analyzed the Founders' political thought by asking whether they believed that rulers and citizens would be self-interested or virtuous, whether they believed that virtue was necessary or could be replaced by constitutional mechanics, whether they understood liberty as a right to political participation or a right to be protected from governmental interference, and whether they believed that the principal purpose of government was to protect individual rights or to promote the public good.

But the framework of analysis suggested by the studies examined in this chapter suggests that the Founders' political thought will always remain elusive if we pose problems in this crude manner. It also suggests that the Founders made a unique contribution to the history of political thought by developing a novel conception that synthesized previous traditions into an amalgam that is unlike any of them.

This novel conception of political thought—whether we call it natural rights republicanism, liberal republicanism, or republican liberalism—acknowledges the influence of English opposition ideology in the Founders' political thought; links this constellation of concepts, aspirations, and anxieties to the understanding of the origins and ends of government that is now associated with liberalism; but shows that despite the Founders' construction of an essentially deontological political system, not all of them were proto-capitalists and none believed that institutional arrangements alone could replace public vigilance and statesmanship. It also compels us to understand the Founders' political thought in its historical ambiguity and recognize its distinctiveness not only from ancient political thought but also from our contemporary pluralistic politics of bargaining, compromising, and logrolling.

At a deeper level, an appreciation of the Founders' political thought as distinct from both classical and modern political thought should lead us to reconsider the general interpretation that underlies our polar portraits of the American Founding. More specifically, for all their points of disagreement, both classical republican and liberal interpretations of the American Founding are rooted in the belief that the history of political thought represents a battle between the ancients and the moderns, or at least a transition from ancient to modern political thought. Scholars have disagreed about whether the Founders were allies of the ancients or the moderns and about which side of the pivot between ancient and modern political thought the American Founding lies. Both sides, however, contend that the Founders accepted this great antithesis of ancients and moderns and thus believed that they had to make this choice.[94]

The Straussians and the scholars of the republican interpretation, however, have assumed rather than convincingly shown that this was indeed the Founders' understanding of the history of political thought and their place in it. Until such a case is convincingly made, such interpretations are problematic because they contradict the foundational assumption held by both groups—namely, that past political thinkers should be interpreted from a genuinely historical perspective that attempts to understand how they understood themselves. But what if the Founders did not view themselves as having to choose a side in a grand struggle between the ancients and the moderns? What if the ancients-versus-moderns framework of analysis is yet another—indeed, the grandest—analytic construct through which the political thought of the American Founders has been strained?

Although a full answer to this question would require a comprehensive analysis of the Founders' view of the history of political thought and their beliefs about their place in it, it seems plausible to say that the current framework of ancients versus moderns is problematic and that it masks as much as it illuminates. At the very least, such interpretations attempt to map the political thought of the Founders onto a framework of analysis that no scholar has proved they held.[95] In addition, it is clear that an alternative understanding of the Founders' view of their project is not only possible but also necessary if we are to transcend caricatured portraits of their political thought, understand the Founders on their own terms, and grasp the peculiarity and thus the significance of their project.

Consider the broad outlines of such an interpretation. In general, instead of viewing the Founders either as proponents of Lockean liberalism who refuted classical republicanism or as embattled opponents of modernity who clung to classical concepts in the face of increasing pressure to abandon them, we should begin with the particular set of problems they identified and addressed. These include the failures of ancient republics and confederacies and the problems they encountered in the American experience. But it also includes their desire to distance themselves from the problems faced by many European governments and societies. A multiple traditions approach would allow us to see how they drew on numerous intellectual traditions to address these concrete problems.

Such an analysis would best begin, I suggest, by concentrating on a fundamental point that many scholars have lost sight of: the fact that the Founders were first and perhaps most fundamentally opponents of "monarchical absolutism," of corrupt hereditary monarchies with unlimited power such as those prevalent in early modern Europe. The Founders' opposition to monarchical absolutism, the rule of men rather than the rule of law, and British corruption was at once the progenitor and the product of the American Revolution. Most important, coupled with their belief that the "genius" or character of the American people was republican, this vehement opposition to monarchical absolutism convinced the Founders that a republic was the only form of government suitable for the United States.

But if the American Revolution and the view of European history that accompanied it made the Founders into republicans, the American experience following the Revolution made them into cautious and, they hoped, wise and innovative republicans. Specifically, for the Framers of the Constitution, the initial experience in self-government from the Revolution to the creation of the Constitution gave rise to and reinforced a particular view of the problems of classical republics. Classical democracies and ancient confederacies, the Framers maintained, had been poorly organized and deserved much of the criticism they received. Classical democracies, they repeatedly emphasized, had been "spectacles of turbulence and contention," "incompatible with personal security or the rights of property," and "as short in their lives as they have been violent in their deaths."[96] Meanwhile, loose-jointed confederacies tended toward "anarchy among the members," not "tyranny in the head."[97] Such a means of organizing government was "subversive of the order and ends of civil polity" and unavoidably led to violence as a means of control rather than the salutary sanction of law.[98] Here, as the Framers read history, the American experience paralleled the histories of ancient republics. The government formed under the Articles of Confederation had failed because it was subject to the same tendencies as all previous confederacies; likewise, in the minds of the Framers, the turbulence and injustices in the state governments during the mid-1780s were roughly analogous to the problems besetting classical democracies.[99]

Perhaps most important, their acknowledgment of these two sets of problems led the Framers of the Constitution to strengthen the national government and turn to the inventions of modern political science. Fortifying the national government would control the centrifugal tendencies of the state governments, and the inventions of modern political science—representation, bicameralism, extent of territory, separation of powers, and lifetime tenure for judges—would mitigate the effects of majority factions yet still guard against the tyranny of rulers.[100] Together, these reforms would improve the republican form so that it could be justly applauded as a viable alternative to monarchical absolutism.

Finally, in trying to understand the Founders' "map to the great political and moral campaign of history," we should not forget that some of them (particularly the Jeffersonians) looked to recent (for them) European history and identified a set of problems they hoped to avoid, including urbanization and overcrowding. This criticism of European society was built from observations and stories (many of them idiosyncratic), but it also rested on an almost universally accepted understanding of the patterned evolution of human civilizations.

As numerous scholars have now pointed out, most of the Founders approached questions of political economy with the belief that societies naturally and unavoidably evolved in stages from hunter-gather societies to subsistence agrarian societies to commercial agrarian societies and finally to manufacturing societies.[101] Each stage was believed to be characterized by a different set of human relationships and by a different pattern of behavior. Furthermore, the manufacturing stage was thought to be created when the population became dense and tillable land was no longer available; this stage was thought to be characterized by a high division of labor and by the desire for conveniences and luxuries. The Founders held a spectrum of beliefs about whether governments should try to advance society through these stages, delay their arrival, or reach a particular stage and then attempt to prevent development beyond it. Most important, the Jeffersonians identified the advanced stage of social development with the corrupt and decaying societies of Europe. They thus sought to combine commerce, agriculture, and landed expansion in a way that distanced America from the problems that seemed unavoidable in Europe.

The Founders, then, did not see themselves as moderns bent on repudiating classical political philosophy or as nostalgic republicans hoping to delay the advent of modernity. Rather, they saw themselves as opponents of early modern absolutism, of the organizational scheme of classical republics, and (for those who would later become Jeffersonians, at least) of the decay at work in the most advanced European societies. Furthermore, when they sought to address these problems—during the American Revolution, the 1780s, and into the 1790s, when they formed the world's first organized political parties—the Founders drew from the full range of their intellectual inheritance, including liberalism, republicanism, and a host of other traditions of political thought. Natural rights philosophy and the liberal conception of the origin and limitations of government served as the bedrock of their political thought, but it expressed their repudiation of monarchical absolutism, not their repudiation of classical republicanism. Opposition ideology reinforced this repudiation and indeed acted synergetically with natural rights philosophy. Opposition ideology rested on the natural rights–social contract philosophy and called attention to the problems of public debt, standing armies, executive influence, and ministerial corruption and, more broadly, to the insatiable nature of power and the fragility of liberty.[102] Furthermore, these Lockean fundamentals were buttressed, and Whig anxieties were addressed, by a universe of republican concepts—virtue, political participation or public liberty, and (for some of the Founders) an agrarian political economy—that the Founders believed would help preserve the liberal republic they had created.

Identifying Inegalitarian Ideologies and Ascriptive Hierarchies

Third, scholars need to meet the challenges raised by the scholarship of Rogers Smith. They need to identify the inegalitarian ideologies that were present in the Founders' political thought, show what purposes they served, and then make suggestions about their relationship to the Founders' synthesis of liberalism and republicanism. In particular, Smith has documented that American citizenship laws were riddled with exclusions that were, in turn, justified by inegalitarian ascriptive ideologies. Smith examined citizenship laws in part because he believed that they would provide a "rough but useful empirical indicator" of the strength of various sets of ideas in

American political culture.[103] This type of study—examining not only political writings but also constitutions, statutes, and judicial rulings for the instantiation of ideologies—can be extended to numerous other areas of the law, including property law and laws governing questions of freedom of speech. Here, as in Smith's study, it would serve as an empirical indicator of the relative strength of ideologies.

Such a suggestion will certainly be resisted by scholars of the American Founding as an effort at "politically correct" scholarship. And clearly, such scholarship should not be motivated by the impulse to lay blame on the Founders for present injustices. Nevertheless, Smith's essential point cannot be denied. The sets of ideologies that justified the exclusion of women, Native Americans, and African Americans from citizenship were undeniably a part of the intellectual origins of the American Republic. Thus, illiberal ideologies cannot be treated as prejudices or simply dismissed or ignored. Nor should they be treated in an independent wing of scholarship that analyzes the "dilemmas" of the Founding but fails to relate them back to liberal and republican beliefs. Instead, we need dispassionate scholarship that addresses the whole universe of the Founders' political thought and attempts to understand it by carefully considering the parts and their relationship to one another.

At its deepest level, such scholarship would raise the question whether there was in fact a core to the Founders' political thought around which other parts were fused. In other words, we would have to consider whether Zuckert is correct when he interprets the American Founding as an amalgam in which the "cornerstone" was natural rights philosophy and other traditions of political thought were assimilated to the degree they were compatible with this philosophy, or whether it is better conceived (as Smith would have it) as an unsteady polyglot composed of conflicting traditions.[104] We would also have to consider (as Smith's critics from the Left contend) whether liberalism paradoxically generates the illiberal ideologies that compromise it and "liberalism and exclusion betray an underlying consistency," or whether the linkages between liberalism and illiberal ideologies are more tenuous, psychological, and political.[105]

*Identifying Tensions in the Amalgam and Considering Their
Present Implications*

Fourth, scholars need to explore more fully how the structure of American political institutions, the path of American political development, and even contemporary discourse in American politics have been and continue to be structured by the interactions of multiple traditions of political thought. Several of the scholars analyzed in this chapter have already made observations to this effect. Zuckert, for example, notes that the current configuration of the American political system is a result of the grafting of a Jeffersonian "expressive" conception of republicanism onto a more elitist Madisonian framework of government. The Madisonian constitutional system, Zuckert observes, was designed to protect individual and minority rights and to restrain public passions so that government could be energetic, competent, and prudent. Nevertheless, the Jeffersonian tradition of expressive republicanism, Zuckert suggests, has provided a broad rationale for institutions and reforms directly linking citizens to their government, such as political parties, the mass media, the direct election of senators, and the expansion of suffrage. In short, Zuckert concludes, the "less strenuously republican Madisonian constitutional system has set the fundamental frame for American politics, but it has been infused with a more Jeffersonian spirit." Most important, the peculiar hybrid political system that Americans live under today is the product of this infusion of popular spirit into the Madisonian constitutional system. And, Zuckert implies, if we are to understand why it operates as it does, we must understand the tensions and ambiguities caused by the synthesis of the two distinct variations of republicanism that went into its creation.[106]

Smith has observed that illiberal ideologies have a continuing role in America—as justifications for policies such as English-only laws, anti-immigrant policies, and periodic calls for racial segregation.[107] As I noted earlier, Smith has also suggested that there is a logic to American political development based on the interaction of illiberal and liberal-republican ideologies. Illiberal ideologies inevitably become popular, Smith contends, following periods of reform because they serve as counterrevolutionary doctrines for those seeking to rebuild structures of privilege.[108]

Finally, numerous scholars have observed that the rivalry between the traditions of American political thought is a central source of persistent and intractable conflicts. Most obviously, one of the central conflicts in American politics—the conflict between private rights and the public good, or the cognate conflict between majority rule and individual rights—can be seen as a tension between republican and liberal strains of political thought. This tension continues to resonate in the way issues are framed for debate in the United States. For example, affirmative action is either justified as an advancement of the broad social goal of enhancing diversity or decried as a fundamental violation of the right to be treated equally as an individual. Gun control is either seen as a necessary means of protecting the public safety or opposed as a violation of the rights of gun owners. Libertarians argue that majoritarian religious groups have no legitimate power to use government as an engine to promote religious belief and plead for their rights of conscience, but many religious groups see efforts to deny them use of the public space as contributing to a naked public square in which morality is undermined. In each example, a broad public purpose is set against individual rights. Since each kind of claim is recognized as legitimate and deeply embedded in the history of American political discourse, it is no wonder that participants in such debates quickly reach a point of incommensurability.

As these observations suggest, the final promise of a multiple traditions understanding of the American Founding and American political thought in general may be that it provides us with an approach for understanding the sources of this incommensurability, finding creative ways of addressing the United States' most persistent and intractable conflicts, and developing an appreciation for the submerged complexity, elusiveness, limitations, and strengths of American political thought.

5

How Could They Have Done That?
Slavery and the Question of Moral Responsibility

The Founders on Trial: The Academic Debate beneath the Culture Wars

In March 2003, Marguerite Talley-Hughes, an African American kindergarten teacher at Thomas Jefferson Elementary School in Berkeley, California, spearheaded an effort to change the name of the school where she taught. Talley-Hughes, according to the petition she and two other teachers submitted to the local school board, had become "increasingly uncomfortable to work at a site whose name honors a slaveholder."[1] Jefferson's wealth, political power, and prominence in American history were secured, Talley-Hughes argued, "because he owned slaves, not in spite of that fact." Jefferson used the "threat of physical violence" to elicit forced labor from slaves. He also advertised rewards for the capture of his runaway slaves, ordered slaves flogged, and sold them away from their families. Furthermore, Jefferson could not be exonerated as "a man of his time." Many men and women of Jefferson's generation opposed slavery, and some took extraordinary efforts to end the practice. "With that information," Talley-Hughes concluded, "we do not need to rely on contemporary ethics and morality to find Jefferson lacking in the integrity and courage which generally define a hero."[2]

The teachers' petition set off a divisive debate in the school and the local community that gained national attention and swept through the conservative blogosphere. In the Berkeley community, opponents of the name change charged their opponents with creating conflict in the once peaceful and unified school district and protested that they were being labeled racists for supporting Jefferson.[3] For

[169]

their part, proponents of the name change told of threatening e-mails and broken friendships.[4]

In the blogosphere, several conservatives offered serious reasons for retaining Jefferson's name. Jefferson's public record on slavery, one commentator insisted, established his credentials as an opponent of slavery. Several other opponents of the name change argued that a complex and multifaceted man like Jefferson should not be judged by the singular fact that he was a slaveholder. Still others pointed out that Bishop George Berkeley had bought slaves to work his Rhode Island plantation during his short stay in America.[5] Although these bloggers failed to connect the dots, the implication was clear: if being named after a slaveowner was now the standard for change, the citizens of Berkeley had better be prepared to rename the city and its most prominent university.

Still other conservative bloggers simply could not contain their contempt. The alternative name changes suggested by bloggers included "George Jefferson Elementary School" (after the character played by Sherman Hemsley on the 1970s and '80s situation comedy *The Jeffersons*) and "Tupac Elementary," which the blogger suggested should be affiliated with "C-Murder Middle School" and "50-Cent High School." Two other bloggers suggested that the school be named after Alexander Hamilton. "Hamilton was, in fact, born in the West Indies," the first suggested sarcastically. "So, he's, like, totally multicultural and stuff. . . ." "Heck," a second added, "he was even born a bastard, so that should be another point in his favor." "Jefferson was your typical French-loving slave-owning rich politician who claimed to be a man of the people," another blogger quipped. "Very much like our modern Democrats like Corzine, Kerry, Soros, etc." One conservative blogger spoke for most of the others when he said, "Given that it is a school in Berkeley. I'd bet Jefferson wouldn't mind [having his name removed]."[6]

Back in Berkeley, the teachers' petition set in motion a procedure that took over two years to complete. Under policies established by the local school board, 20 percent of the students, parents, faculty, and staff of the school first had to request a name change. If this was achieved, then a list would be drawn up and a vote would be taken to select a name that would challenge Jefferson in a runoff election. If the challenger won, the school board then had to vote on whether or not to approve the name change.[7]

A petition signed by 20 percent of the students, parents, and teachers was easily secured. A list of proposed alternative names based on suggestions by parents and one student was then drawn up. This list included, among others, Ralph Bunche (the United Nations diplomat and first black to win the Nobel Peace Prize), Sojourner Truth (the former slave who became a leading abolitionist and woman's rights advocate), Cesar Chavez (the Hispanic founder of the National Farm Workers Association), Rose (the name of the street where the school was located), Ohlone (the original native American tribe who had first settled the land surrounding Berkeley), and Sequoia (after three prominent sequoia trees on school grounds). Following district policy, a vote was then taken in which Jefferson school parents, staff members, and students (some as young as five years old) chose sequoia as the most worthy name to be pitted against Jefferson in a runoff election.[8]

In the runoff election, these same groups opted 239 to 177 to rename Thomas Jefferson elementary after the three sequoia trees. This victory, however, was short-lived: only a week later, the Berkeley school board voted 3 to 2 to keep Jefferson as the school's name. This decision was announced in an emotional meeting in which students wept; the school board member who cast the deciding vote for Jefferson apologized for disappointing many; and several proponents of the change cried foul play at the board's administrative decision to overturn the majority vote of the students, parents, staff, and teachers. Most dramatically, immediately after hearing the decision, advocates of the name change stood and sang the civil rights song "We Shall Overcome," only to be told by at least one opponent of the name change to "get over it."[9] No one thought of pointing to the irony that Jefferson—America's apostle of democracy—had been saved against majority sentiment by an administrative decision.

Although dismissed as frivolous and treated comically by many distant from the dispute, the debate over removing Jefferson's name from the Berkeley elementary school was deeply serious to its participants. Moreover, it parroted efforts to change the names of schools named after slaveholders across the country over the last decade and raised many of the same issues and arguments raised in a variety of other disputes that have often brought the American Founders into the center of the culture wars.[10] Similar disputes have been waged over, for example, whether Thomas Jefferson sired Sally Hemings's children and how their relationship should be presented to the public at Monticello, claims for the influence of Native American ideas in the formation of the American Constitution, and the debates over school curriculum surrounding the National History Standards Project. Most recently, disputes have broken out over whether slave quarters at the excavation site of Robert Morris House in Philadelphia (where George Washington resided at times during his presidency) should be identified and how slavery should be displayed at Independence National Historical Park. These disputes raise specific questions about when and how we should evaluate and possibly change our civic symbols and more general ones about the politics of historical memory.

Most important for purposes of this chapter, however, public debates between critics and defenders of the Founders reflect and are informed and structured by equally inflammatory and controversial academic debates over the moral responsibility of the American Founders for the subjection of women, Native American genocide, and especially slavery. Since the 1960s, scholars of the Founding, like the citizens of Berkeley, have been increasingly pressed to consider how the men who declared independence on the proposition that "all men are created equal" could also have owned slaves. More broadly, we have been asked to explain how a generation that fought a revolution in the name of liberty and equality could have denied equal liberty to blacks, women, and Native Americans, perpetuated legal and social structures of inequality, and even created new ones. Answers to these questions, in turn, now form the basis of a complex and dense literature that has come to occupy a greater and greater proportion of the scholarship devoted to the American Founding.

This chapter confronts that body of literature and identifies and evaluates the interpretive and argumentative strategies that scholars have used to formulate judgments about the Founders' moral responsibility. I focus on two issues that have been flash points: the enduring debate over whether or not the original Constitution was a pro-slavery document and scholars' radically different judgments about the moral responsibility of the Founders (especially Thomas Jefferson) for slavery. My goal is not to present novel interpretations of either of these issues, but rather to use them to illuminate the anatomy of scholars' moral evaluations of the Founders and to identify the foundational differences between the accounts of critics and defenders of the Founders. The other primary goal of this chapter is to consider how we might move toward more fair and responsible moral judgments about the Founders.

I begin by culling three interpretive frameworks, which I call "prosecuting," "vindicating," and "historicizing," from some of the most important and controversial works that address the Founders and the question of moral responsibility.[11] Prosecutors such as Paul Finkelman and Conor Cruise O'Brien view their role as that of iconoclastic debunkers of Founding myths and patriotic histories and interpret the Founders as the unapologetic source of America's original sins, especially slavery. Prosecutors often wield accusations and ad hominem arguments, including denouncing Jefferson and other Founders as slaveholding racists and hypocrites. The most sophisticated and persuasive, however, combine such condemnations with complex and intricate arguments about why Jefferson and other Founders fail the test of moral greatness largely on the basis of the conclusion that the Founders could have done much more, in particular, in preventing the spread of slavery and expediting abolition.[12] For many prosecutors, such criticisms are integral to a broader multicultural critique of racism and patriarchal authority in American society that has revolutionized the study of American history since the 1960s. Such criticisms are also integral to the contention, which is also a frequent conclusion of prosecutors, that the Founders offer little guidance for contemporary multicultural societies.

Vindicators include such scholars as Don Fehrenbacher, Tom West, and Dumas Malone. In contrast to prosecutors these scholars defend the Founders' reputation.[13] Defending the Founders, these scholars often suggest, requires getting our historical facts straight and establishing the proper standards for judgment. It also requires grasping the prudential considerations that governed the Founders' decisions that, in turn, requires understanding what reforms were possible and which were utopian, as well as determining the consequences that would have followed from more immediate and comprehensive reforms. Once we do our historical homework, understand the limited range of possibilities available to the Founders, and adopt the proper standards for judgment, we will realize, vindicators suggest, that the Founders were progressive and that they were quite successful in their efforts against slavery. Conversely, we will also be in position to understand that many criticisms of the Founders emanate from the excesses of effete, politically correct multiculturalism. If prosecutors believe that it is necessary to criticize the Founders in order to pave the way for the realization of a more egalitarian and just society, vindicators are commonly proponents of what might be called restoration politics and thus seek to reestablish or affirm the importance of values that, they argue, constitute America's founding principles. Defending the Founders against charges of injustice, racism, sexism, and genocide, in turn, is often an essential precondition for calling for a return to Founding principles.

For their part, historicists adopt an approach and cultivate a sensibility that leads them to resist putting the Founders on trial—an endeavor, historicists believe, that distorts the Founding.[14] The goal of historical research, scholars such as Gordon Wood, Bernard Bailyn, Doug Wilson, Henry Wiencek, and Peter Onuf insist, is first to recreate the foreign world of the Founding, including the moral horizon in which the Founders made decisions. "Jefferson made sense to himself," Onuf observes, "and he can make more sense to us now if we engage him on his own terms and in his own cultural and moral contexts."[15] To be sure, historicists' concern with reconstructing the moral universe of the Founders does not prevent them from criticizing the Founders or (more frequently) commenting on their complex legacies. Instead, most historicists view deeply contextual historical analysis as a prophylactic against unduly confident assertions about the Founders' intentions, facile appropriations of their ideas, crude efforts to extrapolate "lessons" from their writings and experiences, and more generally both simple-minded defenses and flippant, presentist criticisms of the Founders. Historicists thus seek to distance themselves from both the teleological assumptions about the superiority of contemporary moral values that often inform the judgments of prosecutors and from the restoration politics often underlying the analysis of vindicators.

After characterizing these three interpretive strategies through an analysis of the key works that employ them, I then identify the different assumptions, standards for judgment, and argumentative strategies that scholars rely on, but seldom subject to concentrated reflection, as they sift through historical evidence. Extrapolating these foundational points of disagreement in turn sets the stage for considering the problems that accompany efforts to put the Founders on trial, whether by prosecuting or vindicating, and for establishing the strengths and limitations of historicizing. In the final section of this chapter, I then provide several specific recommendations about how we might move beyond the cycle of celebration and condemnation that sets the terms on which so much contemporary Founding scholarship is conducted and towards more responsible moral judgments about the Founding.

Prosecutors: The Neo-Garrisonian Constitution and the Myth of the Anti-Slavery Jefferson

In a series of essays crystallized in his important study, *Slavery and the Founders: Race and Liberty in the Age of Jefferson,* Paul Finkelman provides a quintessential prosecution of the Founders. In particular, Finkelman's analysis combines a neo-Garrisonian interpretation of the Founders' Constitution as a pro-slavery document with a relentless and unforgiving attack on Thomas Jefferson for his racism, failures to act aggressively enough against slavery, and in general for the "giant chasm between his words and his deeds on the question of race and liberty."[16]

Finkelman's neo-Garrisonian interpretation rests on an analysis of the constitutional text and a revised account of the dynamics of the Constitutional Convention. Several scholars have stressed the absence of the words *slave* and *slavery* in the Constitution of 1787 and suggested that this omission meant that the Framers were unwilling to afford legitimacy to slavery or give it full legal sanction.[17] In contrast, Finkelman argues that the omission of the word *slavery* was largely meaningless. Prior acts of the Confederation Congress, Finkelman observes, had also not explicitly used the word *slavery* but rather had substituted a description of it. The use of circumlocutions was a matter of delicacy to make the document more palatable to Northern delegates. "As long as they were assured of protection for their institution," Finkelman concludes, "the southerners at the Convention were willing to do without the word 'slave.'"[18]

Furthermore, many scholars have limited their analysis of slavery in the Founders' Constitution to three provisions: the three-fifths clause, which provided that three-fifths of the slaves of each state would be counted for purposes of apportioning representatives and lodging direct taxes; the 1808 slave trade provision, which prohibited Congress from banning the slave trade until 1808; and the fugitive slave clause, which required the return of runaway slaves to their owners and thus prohibited states from serving as a safe haven for them. Finkelman points to two additional clauses that dealt directly with slavery: Article I, Section 9, Paragraph 4, which stipulated that any "capitation" or direct tax had to be apportioned on the basis of the three-fifths clause, and Article V, which prohibited any amendment of the slave importation or capitation clauses before 1808. He also points to numerous other provisions in the original Constitution that supplemented these five and yet another group of constitutional provisions that did not inherently favor slavery but were interpreted by the courts and implemented by Congress to protect it.[19] Finally, he suggests that the structure of the entire document and limited powers given to the national government supported slavery. Granting sovereignty to each state over the question of slavery within its boundaries, Finkelman suggests, was itself a pro-slavery decision.

In particular, Finkelman argues that the explicit clauses that dealt with slavery in the Constitution "gave the South a strong claim to 'special treatment' for its peculiar institution."[20] The three-fifths clause gave Southern slaves "extra political muscle" in the House of Representatives and the Electoral College.[21] The fugitive slave clause joined Northern states with Southern ones in the capture and return of slaves to their owners. The capitation clause ensured that if a head tax was levied, slaves would be taxed at three-fifths the rate of whites. Scholars who have opposed the pro-slavery interpretation of the Constitution have contended that even the delayed grant of authority to prohibit the slave trade in 1808 must be considered anti-slavery because the Articles of Confederation granted no such federal power at all.

Finkelman counters that the slave trade clause was a remarkable exception to the plenary power of Congress to regulate commerce (not a flat prohibition of the slave trade after 1808), that the convention never considered such a flat prohibition, and thus that even when the protection for the slave trade ended in 1808, Congress had to muster the political will to prohibit the slave trade.

How did the South win concessions at the convention for these clauses and provisions? Standard accounts of the dynamics of the convention debates emphasize divisions between large and small states. They also suggest that slavery provisions in the Constitution were a sine qua non demanded by Southern states to join the union. Finkelman, however, emphasizes the increasing importance during the course of the convention and the ultimate centrality of *sectional* conflicts between slaveholding and nonslaveholding states. The three-fifths clause, Finkelman argues, did not result from a compromise over representation and taxation with Northern delegates willing to accept disproportionate representation by slave states in exchange for the willingness of those states to assume a proportion of taxation that included three-fifths of their slaves being counted. Instead, the three-fifths clause was established early in the convention and resulted from a debate between "those who wanted to count slaves fully for purposes of representation and those who did not want to count slaves at all."[22] Few of the delegates believed that direct taxes would constitute a substantial portion of federal revenue. Thus, even though the three-fifths clause gave "the South enormous political leverage," it "was accepted without any real *quid pro quo* from the North."[23]

The 1808 slave trade provision, according to Finkelman, became a part of the Constitution as the result of a "dirty compromise" between the three New England states and the deep Southern states. This compromise emerged over the course of debates and involved the willingness of Northern states to support a prohibition on export taxes and an explicit protection of the slave trade if they were given the power to regulate commerce by simple majority rule. In tracing the outlines of this "alliance for profit," Finkelman argues that although many New Englanders repeatedly voiced moral objections to slavery and the slave trade, they were willing to protect the slave trade because increases in slaves meant the production of more commodities to be carried by Northern shippers.[24] Conversely, opposition to protection of the slave trade came primarily from delegates from the upper South who, like the New Englanders, often couched their opposition to the slave trade in moral terms. Many of these delegates, however, were really opposed to the slave trade because their states already had an excess number of slaves, and discontinuation of the slave trade would increase their market value. The convention thus featured remarkable exchanges in which New Englanders defended the rights of Carolinians and Georgians to engage in the slave trade against objections by Virginians.

In general, Finkelman finds only limited evidence for the contentions of scholars who suggest that the slavery provisions in the Constitution were forced onto the majority of the delegates by Southern delegates. The compromise that led to the three-fifths clause, Finkelman has conceded, "probably had to be made."[25] Nevertheless, Finkelman doubts that the South Carolinians and Georgians meant what they said when they suggested that they were unwilling to support the union if the slave trade was not temporarily protected. These states, according to Finkelman, were not actively importing slaves from Africa in 1787 anyway, and such a restriction would not have fundamentally damaged their economies. Scholars who make this claim are suggesting that the "states of the Deep South would have rejected the Constitution over the right to import slaves *in the future* when they in fact were not currently importing them."[26] Furthermore, the fugitive slave clause, Finkelman observes, was debated late in the convention. By this time, Northern delegates had secured congressional power to regulate commerce by majority vote and were tired, complacent, and governed by the spirit of amity that characterized the late stages of the convention. The fugitive slave clause thus passed unanimously and without any real debate about its meaning or implications. This, Finkelman suggests, is hardly the stuff of necessity.

In addition to arguing that slaveowners "got substantially what they wanted" in the Constitution of 1787, Finkelman also excoriates Thomas Jefferson.[27] Several scholars, Finkelman observes, have set forth the "myth of the antislavery Jefferson."[28] These scholars have pointed to numerous condemnations that Jefferson made against the institutions of slavery and the slave trade and several proposals that he offered to abolish or confine it. These include: (1) Jefferson's support during his earliest service in the Virginia legislature for a bill to allow slaveholders to voluntarily free their slaves; (2) his attempt as a young lawyer to win the freedom of a man of mixed blood who was held in bondage; (3) his admonitions against King George III—edited out of the Declaration of Independence by the Continental Congress—for waging "cruel war against human nature itself" and "violating its most sacred rights of life and liberty" by perpetuating the African slave trade and preventing any attempt by the Virginia legislature to prohibit or restrain it; (4) his call for manumission and the plan of emancipation that he set forth in *Notes on the State of Virginia;* (5) his draft constitution for the state of Virginia, where he included a provision that banned the importation of slaves and contained a provision for the emancipation of slaves born after December 31, 1800; (6) his proposal in the Territorial Governance Act of 1784 to prevent slavery from being introduced into new states formed out of lands ceded to Congress under the Articles of Confederation; and (7) the bill that he proposed, supported, and signed into law in 1808 while he was president outlawing the African slave trade.

Despite this extensive record, Finkelman concludes that "there is little substance to the antislavery Jefferson."[29] Conversely, Jefferson, according to Finkelman, does not measure up to the intellectual, political, and cultural leaders of *his* age. And this standard, according to Finkelman, is the only proper one to judge Jefferson against because he is an American icon emblazoned on our coins, stamps, and monuments, not an ordinary man to be judged by ordinary standards.[30] Jefferson's treatment of his slaves, his writings on race, and his moral leadership—or rather lack of moral leadership—in effecting a scheme of emancipation implicate Jefferson deeply in the institution of slavery. As a slaveowner, Finkelman observes, Jefferson used his slaves as "forms of capital" when he needed money to satisfy his insatiable appetite for fine things, "which to judge from his lifelong behavior, was far more important than the natural rights of his slaves."[31] He also hunted slaves down when they escaped, had "no qualms" about separating families, increased the number of slaves that he owned over his lifetime, and worked steadily to increase the productivity of their labor and their value as property.[32] Blind to the denial of their liberty, he displayed instead a "self-deluding inability to see slaves as human beings."[33]

This obtuseness, according to Finkelman, was starkly illustrated in Jefferson's treatment of Sally Hemings and her (and perhaps his) children. Scholars, Finkelman observes, have been obsessed with whether or not Jefferson had an illicit sexual relationship with one of his slaves. But whatever the verdict on the paternity of Hemings's children, Sally Hemings was the half-sister of Jefferson's deceased wife and thus Jefferson's half-sister-in-law.[34] In assessing Jefferson's morality and character, Finkelman provocatively asks, "Does it matter much whether Jefferson held his nieces and nephews and brothers- and sisters-in-law in slavery or whether he held his own children in slavery?"[35] More broadly, "Jefferson's negrophobia was profound."[36] He desperately feared miscegenation and race warfare, and he invented pseudoscientific explanations to explain black inferiority even when confronted with examples of black imagination, excellence, and intelligence. His scientifically baseless views of blacks "undermined the concept of human equality in the early republic."[37] Furthermore, Jefferson simply never believed that blacks should exercise political rights and never envisioned free blacks living equally alongside whites in a republican society.

As a public leader, Finkelman continues, the author of the Declaration of Independence was far less progressive than many of his contemporaries. He advocated "harsh, almost barbaric, criminal punishments for slaves or free blacks," proposed legislation to make emancipated blacks outlaws in Virginia, and proposed other legislation that would have expelled from the commonwealth white women who had interracial children and their off-spring.[38] John and Herny Laurens, Robert Carter, John and Jonathan Pleas-ants, Joseph Mayo, John Randolph of Roanoke, Edward Coles, and George Washington freed their slaves. Jefferson, in contrast, freed only eight of his slaves during his lifetime and failed to free almost two hundred others at this death. These eight slaves, Finkelman calculates, were less than 2 percent of the total number that he owned in his lifetime.[39] All were his relatives, and only one was female. Indeed, far from making the sacrifices necessary to re-lease his own slaves or advancing a workable plan of national emancipation, Jefferson advised his peers against releasing their slaves and consistently dodged the question of slavery after 1790. The time was never ripe for Jef-ferson to address the problem of slavery, according to Finkelman. For Jef-ferson, slavery was always someone else's responsibility.

What does Finkelman make of the string of condemnations that Jef-ferson made against slavery and the slave trade and his efforts to abolish or confine both? Jefferson's pronouncements against slavery and the slave trade do not interest or impress Finkelman. Jefferson's admonitions against the king for foisting the slave trade on the colonies, he suggests, were largely polemical and without credibility. In general, when Jefferson could be prod-ded to address the issue of slavery, he was duplicitous. To opponents of slav-ery, he could sound like an abolitionist; but to slaveowners, he offered ad-vice and succor. Whatever the reasons for his ambiguity, Finkelman argues, he was ultimately unwilling to make the sacrifices—including curbing his desires—necessary to free his own slaves. He was also unwilling to take any political risks to make good on his calls for emancipation.

When he turns to Jefferson's specific efforts against slavery, Finkelman is equally unforgiving. Jefferson's efforts, Finkelman argues, were either fab-ricated by Jefferson, undertaken for selfish motives, inconsequential, or not really anti-slavery at all. For example, Jefferson's support as a young legisla-tor for a bill allowing slaveholders to voluntarily free their slaves was, ac-cording to Finkelman, not really an anti-slavery measure and would not have freed a single slave. It was instead an effort to protect slaveowners' prop-erty rights by allowing them to dispose freely of their property in slaves. Jefferson's support during his presidency for ending the African slave trade on the date in which that became constitutional was also not important. "It is likely that the trade would have been ended in 1808," Finkelman speculates, "if almost any of the early national leaders had been president."[40] Besides, opposition to the slave trade did not necessarily signify opposition to slavery. Many slaveowners, Finkelman observes, supported the ban on the African slave trade to preserve the market value of their slaves by limiting their number. Jefferson also favored the ban on the slave trade, Finkelman speculates, because he simply did not want the black population in the United States to increase. Finally, Finkelman concludes that Jefferson's proposal to prevent slavery from being introduced into the states created out of the Southwest Territory could not have been successful. Jefferson's plan, Finkelman observes, allowed slaves to be brought into that territory—already heavily populated with slaves—for sixteen additional years before it placed a ban on slavery. Slavery would have then been too deeply entrenched to eradicate.

If Finkelman seeks to discredit Jefferson's opposition to slavery and sharply criticizes his racism, Conor Cruise O'Brien extends these criticisms still further and draws out their implications for Jefferson's place in American civil religion.[41] Concisely put, O'Brien offers two broad charges against Jefferson. First, he argues that Founders such as Washington, Adams, Hamilton, and Madison were "spiritually Burkeans" in the sense that they believed that liberty should be combined with the power of government and tempered with concerns for, among other considerations, order, protection of property, and morality and religion. In contrast, Jefferson was a fanatical enthusiast for "wild liberty, absolute, untrammeled, universal," which he sought to emancipate from any limits. For Jefferson, O'Brien continues, liberty was "a powerfully emotive concept" that remained "unanalyzed and without intellectual content" and was the source of his repulsion to governmental authority.[42] Second, O'Brien focuses on Jefferson's racism and concludes that it renders him unfit to be included in the pantheon of heroes that make up the American civil religion.

Jefferson's zealous commitment to wild liberty, according to O'Brien, was vividly illustrated in his famous defense of Shays's Rebellion and in his "manic enthusiasm for the French Revolution," which he sought to couple with the American Revolution in a single glorious cause for liberty, long after the mobbing and violence of the reign of terror had become known in America.[43] Jefferson, O'Brien observes, defended Shays's Rebellion on the basis of his famous contention that "the tree of liberty must be refreshed from time to time with the blood of patriots and tyrants. It is its natural manure."[44] Furthermore, in the course of the French Revolution, Jefferson set forth his now equally famous "Adam and Eve" letter. "My own affections have been deeply wounded by some of the martyrs of this cause," Jefferson admitted to one of his friends, "but rather than it should have failed, I would have seen half the earth desolated. Were there but an Adam and Eve, left in every country, and left free, it would be better than it now is."[45] This "apology for genocide," according to O'Brien, was not "an isolated flash of hyperbole," but rather faithfully illustrated Jefferson's unwillingness to flinch at the atrocities committed in the French Revolution.[46] Together with his defense of what came to be called "permanent rebellion," it illustrates that Jefferson set virtually no limits—geographical or moral, or in terms of bloodshed—on what should be done in the "holy cause of freedom."[47] Thus, however unsettling it may seem to "pious Jeffersonians" today, Jefferson's vacuous and abstracted conception of liberty and his belief that anything could be done to further the sacred cause of liberty would leave him without any means of condemning acts of violence—including the 1995 bombing of the federal building in Oklahoma City by Timothy McVeigh—that the perpetrators of those acts sincerely believed were done to further the cause of liberty. Indeed, according to O'Brien, "it is difficult to resist the conclusion that the twentieth-century statesman whom the Thomas Jefferson of January 1793 would have admired most is Pol Pot." Pol Pot, like Jefferson, did not see any reason to place limits on the amount of bloodshed that was necessary to further his holy cause.[48]

Second, O'Brien argues that although it has been scrupulously and strategically avoided in celebratory accounts of Jefferson, Jefferson was "demonstrably a racist, and a particularly aggressive and vindictive one at that" who saw no place in America for free blacks.[49] Like Finkelman, O'Brien calls attention to Jefferson's support within his famous revision of the laws of Virginia for a law that would have prevented blacks from entering the state on their own accord or staying for more than one year after they were emancipated, and another that would have required any white woman who had a child by a black man to leave the state within one year or be placed "beyond the protection of the law." This legal status, O'Brien concludes, would have been "a license for lynching: for the physical destruction of mother and child by any Virginian who might care to do the job. Volunteers would not be lacking."[50] To be sure, Jefferson believed that blacks were destined to be free and wanted to end slavery. But once free, O'Brien observes, Jefferson wanted blacks to be colonized to another country—in other words, "sent packing."[51]

Taken together, Jefferson's enthusiastic and unbounded conception of liberty, his concomitant revulsion to federal authority, and his racism render the predominant, genteel liberal Jefferson school of thought incoherent and make Jefferson "a most unsuitable and embarrassing figure in the pantheon of the modern American civil religion."[52] Liberal Jeffersonianism, O'Brien contends, is no more coherent than liberal racism.[53] Furthermore, the American civil religion has traditionally sought divine sanction for the use of power and in support of civil authority and today must be unequivocally multiracial if it is to serve as a bonding force. Yet Jefferson was an extreme libertarian who championed localism and states' rights and held a vision of the future of America that was "lily-white."[54] These realities about Jefferson and his beliefs, O'Brien predicts, will lead to a schism within the American civil religion. Advocates of a multiracial society will discover Jefferson's racism and drop him, but he will be picked up by right-wing extremists such as the Ku Klux Klan (who are "ideologically descended from Thomas Jefferson"), Southern states' rights reactionaries, and members of various militias who will propose a dangerous, alternative civil religion with Jefferson as its apostle.[55] These groups can find in the corpus of Jefferson's writings justification for extreme libertarianism and nullification, the quest to create a white America, and the doctrine of permanent revolution. Thus, "the spellbinding and anarchic racist prophet" will be reborn again as the "patron of the fanatical racist far right in America."[56]

Vindicators: The Lincolnian Constitution, the Founders' Accomplishments, and the Case for the Anti-Slavery Jefferson

In their characterization of the Founders' Constitution as pro-slavery, prosecutors draw much of their inspiration from and expand on arguments originally set forth by William Lloyd Garrison, Wendell Phillips, and the Garrison wing of the abolitionist movement. The neo-Garrisonians suggest that slavery was either directly or indirectly implicated in many clauses of the Constitution, that these clauses provided substantial support for slavery, and that they readily lent themselves to pro-slavery interpretations. They also argue that some of the compromises that led to passage of these provisions were not necessary to preserve the union, but rather were concessions made to Southern states or even agreements that allied Northern and Southern states in defense of slavery.

In contrast, vindicators draw inspiration from and build on Abraham Lincoln's interpretation of the Founding project as an effort to put the institution of slavery on a path toward extinction. Don Fehrenbacher has provided the pioneering and foundational version of this neo-Lincolnian defense of the original Constitution.[57] Fehrenbacher's account rests on several points. First, he observes that we must distinguish the Constitution as it was originally understood from the interpretations, pro-slavery laws, and practices by the federal government that transformed it in the years before the Civil War into a pro-slavery instrument. Second, he repeatedly emphasizes that the Framers saw slavery as an institution of the state governments. Thus, none of the delegates at Philadelphia "conceived of slavery as a problem waiting to be addressed by national authority" or themselves as "having been empowered and charged to settle the destiny of the institution."[58] It followed that the Constitution that emerged from debate was "carefully phrased to treat slavery as an entity owing its legal existence solely to state law."[59]

Third, he observes that even as slavery emerged naturally in the course of discussions at the Constitutional Convention about a new federal design and was eventually afforded "a measure of protection" in the Constitution, the Framers "never once called the institution by name."[60] The circumlocutions that were used in the Constitution to refer to slaves and the "stylistic tone of repugnance" toward slavery in the document, according to Fehrenbacher, indicated only a "shamefaced recognition" of slavery in a document that otherwise "lent no explicit reinforcement to the idea of human property."[61] This was important because law, Fehrenbacher argues, gains its meaning primarily from the language of the text, not the purposes of the drafters, and "the sharp contrast here between text and purpose has its own significant effect, whether intended or not."[62]

When he turns to the three most explicit slavery clauses in the Constitution—the three-fifths clause, the 1808 slave trade provision, and the fugitive slave clause—Fehrenbacher argues that they became a part of the Constitution naturally, as "side effects of progress toward a new constitutional design."[63] The three-fifths clause resulted from the transformation from equal representation of all states under the Articles of Confederation to proportional representation in the House of Representatives in the new constitution; the 1808 slave trade provision emerged as an exception to the plenary power to regulate commerce granted to Congress; the fugitive slave clause emerged as an extension of the provision for interstate rendition of fugitives.

Contrary to the mischaracterizations and distortions of the Garrisonians and neo-Garrisonians, these clauses were not, according to Fehrenbacher, pro-slavery. The standard Garrisonian interpretation of the three-fifths clause as a "political bonus for slave holders," Fehrenbacher argues, assumes that free population was the only appropriate basis for allocating legislative power among the states. Yet, as a matter of political theory, it made just as much sense in 1787 to base such an allocation on the whole population, including slaves, women, children and other elements of society that were not part of the body politic. Thus characterizations of the three-fifths clause as a *bonus* for slaveholders, resting as it does on mere assumption, is not intrinsically sounder than the view (held by Frederick Douglass, for instance) that it was a *penalty* on slave-holding. One side sees a bottle three-fifths full and the other, a bottle two-fifths empty.[64]

Furthermore, Fehrenbacher argues that the 1808 slave trade provision pointed toward "restriction [of the slave trade] and ultimate extinction [of the institution of slavery]," and "the Constitution, viewed as a whole, represented a major step forward in the crusade against further importation of slaves."[65] The slave trade clause, Fehrenbacher emphasizes, was placed in Article I, Section 9, of the Constitution among the enumerated limitations on the power of Congress because it was a "temporary restriction on a broad power over foreign commerce."[66] This temporary suspension of the possibility of banning the foreign slave trade "plainly acknowledged" that the federal government had the power to outlaw the foreign slave trade after the suspension passed.[67] Indeed, according to Fehrenbacher, this provision even extended the power to abolish the *domestic* slave trade. The commerce clause, Fehrenbacher observes, not only empowered Congress to regulate trade with foreign nations, but also "among the several states." Thus, if commerce included slave traffic when referring to foreign commerce, it must also have "recognized congressional power to regulate or even abolish the interstate slave trade at any time after 1807."[68]

The temporary suspension for banning the foreign slave trade, Fehrenbacher continues, applied only to the original thirteen states (states coming into the union could be banned from the beginning from participating in the foreign slave trade), and it "suspended only federal power over the *importation* of slaves, not federal power over all aspects of the African slave trade." Thus, Congress in 1794 legally prohibited the *exportation* of slaves from the United States to other nations.[69] Finally, the slave trade provision, according to Fehrenbacher, was the classic example of how a constitutional provision can have an effect different from that envisioned by its authors. The slave trade provision did not mandate the end of the foreign slave trade in 1808. It only made it constitutional for Congress to do so. Nevertheless, this clause had the effect of creating what came to be seen as a "target date for federal prohibition of the traffic."[70]

The only "unambiguously proslavery provision" of the Constitution, Fehrenbacher concludes, was the fugitive slave clause.[71] "It is a striking fact," Fehrenbacher observes, "that the fugitive slave clause became a part of the Constitution with virtually no discussion of its exact meaning or potential."[72] Even this clause, however, was placed in the Constitution to suggest its narrow purpose and was written in "vague and passive terms" that diluted its reach.[73] First, it was placed in Article IV, Section 2, a section that deals with interstate comity, not in Article I, among the positive powers of Congress. Second, it required that a fugitive slave be "delivered up" to the party legitimately requiring his or her service, but the passive construction of the clause left the question "delivered up by whom?" unanswered.[74] Thus, while it guaranteed slaveholders a right to reclaim fugitive slaves across state lines without interference from the state government, this clause did not extend federal power or responsibility to include an obligation to oversee the return of fugitive slaves. It "imposed a restriction on state authority, though without specifying the means of enforcing that restriction" and let the scope of federal responsibility rest on the "vague imperative" in the Constitution.[75]

Together, these three provisions in the Constitution, according to Fehrenbacher, acknowledged the "legitimate presence of slavery in American life while attaching a cluster of limitations to the acknowledgement."[76] Such limitations were placed in the Constitution, according to Fehrenbacher, because "a good many of the delegates, including some of the slaveholders, seem to have believed or hoped that somehow in the flow of time, slavery would disappear. The imprint of that expectation is visible in the document that they finally approved."[77] Thus, the Framers of the Constitution "viewed slavery bi-focally—that is, plainly visible at their feet, but disappearing when they lifted their eyes."[78]

In addition to Fehrenbacher's subtle neo-Lincolnian account of the Constitution, University of Dallas professor Thomas West presents a signature vindication of the Founders that makes the strategies and standards within this interpretation readily visible.[79] In particular, West seeks to vindicate Jefferson and the Founders by challenging misperceptions that are contained within three common charges against the Founders by arguing that the original Constitution was not a pro-slavery document, and by defending the Founders' decision not to immediately abolish slavery and bestow the full rights of citizenship on blacks. The three common charges that West challenges are that the Founders did not really believe that "all men are created equal," or, put differently, that they excluded blacks and women from that proposition and claimed that slavery was right in principle. The second is that they truly believed in human equality but did not understand the implications of this doctrine. The third is that although they believed in human equality and understood its true meaning, they openly betrayed their own principles when they failed to abolish slavery.

In challenging the first of these charges, West first provides several quotes that, he argues, establish that the Founding generation believed that all individuals—including blacks and women—were born free and possessed of inalienable rights and thus that slavery was wrong. To be sure, West acknowledges, blacks and women were denied basic civil liberties and privileges, but this does not mean that the Founders denied that they had the same natural right to human liberty as white men. This charge confuses inalienable rights that the Founders believed are possessed by everyone regardless of the law with legal rights that are bestowed on those favored by the law.

Furthermore, contrary to the second charge, the Founders, according to West, came to more fully understand by the end of the American Revolution that their principles were incompatible with the institution of slavery. As Americans came to base their arguments on the natural rights of all men rather than simply the British constitution and the rights of Englishmen and set forth arguments that anyone who was taxed without his consent was a slave, West argues, they concluded that slavery was unjust. After all, "slavery by definition 'takes the property of another without his consent.'"[80] Indeed, according to West, the American Revolution produced protests that were "the first in history to condemn slavery as an inherently unjust institution on the ground that all human beings are born free."[81] Thus, far from being unaware of the full implications of their beliefs in natural equality and inalienable rights, the Founders understood that the logic of the Revolution was incompatible with slavery, "condemned it in the strongest terms," and "refused to flinch before the stark contradiction between slavery and the principles of their country."[82] Indeed, according to West, "the whole Revolution was an antislavery movement—for the colonists."[83]

In addressing the third charge—that the Founders betrayed their own principles because they failed to abolish slavery—West first points to several often neglected accomplishments that the Founding generation made toward abolishing slavery. The Founders, he observes, "limited and eventually outlawed the importation of slaves from abroad; they abolished slavery in a majority of the original states; they forbade the expansion of slavery into areas where it had not been previously permitted; they made laws regulating slavery more humane; individual owners in most states freed slaves in large numbers."[84] These accomplishments, and more broadly, the success of the Founders in condemning, confining, and setting in motion the forces that would eventually extinguish slavery, West suggests, are what was remarkable within the context of the eighteenth century about the Founders and slavery, not the Founders' ultimate failure to secure emancipation.

But if the Founders recognized blacks as fully human and possessed of inalienable rights, fully understood that slavery was incompatible with their deepest principles of political morality, and made numerous advances to place slavery on the road to extinction, then why did they not go the full distance and immediately and completely extinguish slavery? Shouldn't they be admonished for this failure? West argues that such judgments follow from a failure to appreciate the wisdom inherent in the Founders' decision to balance their principled commitments to equality and liberty against a series of prudential considerations and their realization that the "immoderate pursuit of moral perfection" often recoils in misery and terror.[85] "The American Founders," West continues, "understood political morality not in terms of right intentions but rather in terms of just results. For them, moral principles give us the goal or end, but prudence (sensible judgment) must determine the means."[86]

Slavery, West emphasizes, was a "terrible injustice."[87] The Founders were too often motivated by greed and also were naive in their belief in the inevitability of human progress. Still, they understood better than their subsequent critics that slavery could not be immediately ended without threatening the union and the republican experiment in a government by consent.[88] Had the Founders attempted to abolish slavery, the South, West proclaims, would have seceded. Southern succession, in turn, would have isolated slavery in the South and prevented the North from having an ameliorating influence over its course. Emancipation might also, West speculates, have led to a race war—the threat of which was immediately evident to Americans in the Haitian revolution of 1791 to 1804 in which over one hundred thousand blacks and whites were killed. Yet another consideration, West maintains, was that African Americans were not yet qualified to exercise the rights of full citizenship, or at least were not believed to be so qualified. Like their fears of race war, the Founders' contentions that slavery had rendered blacks unfit to exercise full citizenship were not unwarranted or based on prejudice. These conclusions, West insists, were instead based on "*observed* differences in conduct" between whites and blacks that were "widely acknowledged" by everyone, including blacks.[89] The Founders, according to West, believed that the abolishment of slavery would eventually come with the inevitable progress of liberty. Believing that union would be lost and that progress was on the horizon, the Founders asked, "Why press it, especially when *real* victories for liberty—for example, the Constitution and the union that it established—might otherwise be endangered?"[90]

These prudential considerations, West observes, led many of the Founders to propose the colonization of former slaves as the only appropriate means of emancipation. Colonization, West asserts, did not violate the principles of the Declaration of Independence. The principle of human equality in the Declaration of Independence establishes that "all human beings have a right to liberty. But a right to liberty does not include a right to live in the country of one's choice, without the consent of those already citizens in that place."[91] Furthermore, colonization was neither impractical nor necessarily unjust—at least not when contrasted with the cost and cruelty of the Civil War.

When he turns to defending the Constitution against the charge that it was a pro-slavery document, West also evokes the proposition that "there was little that opponents of slavery could have done about slavery at the Convention unless they were willing to risk breaking up the union."[92] Preserving the union required compromises with some delegates at the Constitutional Convention who "demanded major concessions to slavery" and to "some extent" got them in the form of the three-fifths clause, the 1808 slave trade provision, and the fugitive slave clause.[93]

Nevertheless, these provisions, West hastens to add, were "by no means as proslavery as they have often been said to be."[94] The three-fifths clause gave greater representation to Southern slaveholding interests, but it did not mean that the Framers thought of blacks as three-fifths of a person. The 1808 slave trade provision protected the slave trade for twenty years after the ratification of the Constitution, but was a "grudging temporary concession," and after 1808, Congress was free to abolish the slave trade.[95] Furthermore, because in 1787 many of the Founders did not realize that the indigenous slave population would rapidly increase even without the addition of imported slaves, many of them believed that this provision would put slavery on the road to extinction. Finally, although the fugitive slave clause "might seem unambiguously proslavery," it deliberately avoids the use of the word *slavery* and was "meant to show no approval of slavery."[96]

Dumas Malone's heralded biography, *Thomas Jefferson and His Time*, provides a final example of the arguments and strategies of vindicators.[97] Written over the span of four decades, Malone's six-volume comprehensive biography was begun in a more innocent age of historiography, but finished just as the proliferation of studies criticizing Jefferson had begun to gather steam. Unlike Finkelman and O'Brien, Malone judges Jefferson, as Gordon Wood has said, "not by his lapses but by the general tenor of his life."[98] When Jefferson's positions on slavery and treatment of his slaves are considered, Jefferson emerges, Malone suggests, as a humane, progressive eighteenth-century liberal who "does not deserve the censure he has received from some modern historians of the antislavery movement."[99]

More specifically, Malone's discussion of Jefferson and slavery focuses primarily on his early political career and his retirement years. At an early point in his studies, Jefferson, Malone emphasizes, came to believe that slavery was a fundamental violation of natural law and a moral evil—a position that he never deviated from throughout the rest of his life. The belief that slavery was fundamentally immoral was underneath Jefferson's commitment to ending the foreign slave trade (which culminated in the bill that Jefferson signed into law as president in 1807), his opposition to the spread of slavery (especially in the Territorial Governance Act of 1784), and his articulation of an emancipation plan along the lines first set forth in Notes on the State of Virginia. The Territorial Governance Act of 1784, Malone argues, "applied to the territory ceded and to be ceded—that is, to the region south as well as north of the Ohio." Thus, Jefferson's ordinance "was designed to prevent the spread of slavery as a legal institution outside of the original states, and it would have made secession impracticable if not impossible. Only in the light of tragic history can the wisdom of his preventative measure be fully appreciated."[100] Similarly, Malone praises Jefferson as "one of the first Americans to propose a specific plan of emancipation."[101] Jefferson's plan, he concludes, was "humane," and "he regarded it as realistic."[102]

In striking contrast to numerous critics of Jefferson, Malone also argues that Jefferson was a "notably just and humane master" who "made the best of an institution which he deplored."[103] Jefferson, according to Malone, insisted on humane overseers for his slaves, resented their designation as property, and treated his slaves as dependents and members of his extended family. Moreover, he sold primarily the slaves that he had inherited from his father-in-law, John Wayles; and he sold slaves to unite families, and only "under circumstances of necessity."[104] "He was sure that, with rare exceptions, they [his slaves] were wholly unprepared for self-government, and he liked to think that for the present they were safe and relatively comfortable."[105] What else, Malone implicitly asks, would his critics have liked Jefferson to have done? "To have emancipated the whole body of his slaves, depriving himself thereby of his entire labor force and a large part of his property while turning them loose in an inhospitable world, would have been neither practicable nor kind."[106]

But what about Jefferson's opposition to a multiracial nation, his infamous comments about Negro inferiority, and his equally infamous reticence late in life to publically support abolition? In explaining each of these, Malone places Jefferson in his best light. Malone acknowledges that "for reasons which to him seemed sufficient"— especially his fear of race war—Jefferson never believed that former slaves could be incorporated alongside whites in the young republic.[107] Jefferson's infamous comments about Negro inferiority, Malone suggests, represent "the tentative judgment of a kindly and scientifically minded man who deplored the absence of sufficient data and adequate criteria."[108] Finally, Malone concedes that by the time of his presidency, Jefferson had "reached an impasse" about the institution of slavery, and that his interest in abolition was largely "theoretical" throughout the rest of his life because support for this cause was so feeble.[109] "He was certainly in grave doubt," Malone remarks, "as to the means of effecting emancipation and may be said to have both desired and feared it."[110] Malone, however, follows Jefferson in suggesting that Jefferson's intervention on this volatile issue may have backfired, that Jefferson had the right to a private life in retirement after his long career of public service, and that the responsibility for abolishing slavery had now passed to the next generation. If Jefferson's contemporaries were, as Jefferson said, "unwilling as yet to do anything to solve this problem," then nothing could be done.[111] Jefferson, Malone concludes, was correct to devote himself to the "business at hand": the "completion and preservation of American independence, along with the maintenance of true republicanism."[112]

Historicists: The Founders' Moral Universe

Unlike prosecutors and vindicators, historicists are distinguished by their claim that the principal task of scholars should not be to put the Founders on trial, but rather to understand their decisions within the intellectual and moral universe they inhabited. Historicists' commitment to explaining the past "on its own terms" and establishing its distinctiveness and irretrievability often leads these scholars to be more critical of presentist judgments against the Founders than of the Founders themselves. It also often leads them to suggest that the Founders can offer no direct meaningful guidance for our problems because they did not experience them.[113] The historicist approach to questions of moral responsibility is thus best thought of as the defense of historical sensibility and the cosmopolitanism that understanding past civilizations on their own terms engenders.

Five of the most accomplished Founding scholars who employ the historicist sensibility in addressing questions about the Founders, slavery, and moral responsibility are Bernard Bailyn, Gordon Wood, Douglas Wilson, Henry Wiencek, and Peter Onuf. Throughout their illustrious careers, both Bailyn and Wood have examined the question of slavery and moral responsibility within the context of a long and tragic view of the historical process.[114] Like West, these scholars conclude that the most salient fact about the Founders' position on slavery is not their inability to eradicate it, but rather their willingness to challenge it. Slavery, Wood observes, "had been taken for granted for thousands of years prior to the mid-eighteenth century."[115] It was of course a brutal and degrading institution, but it was also a piece with the "comprehensive oppression" that was woven into the fabric of eighteenth-century life and also affected white servants and the poor in general.[116] The American Revolution, however, had the effect of liberating ordinary people and creating a new moral consciousness that placed slavery on the defensive. Interpreted through the prism of this historical context, Bailyn argues,

> to note only that certain leaders of the Revolution continued to enjoy the profits of so savage an institution and in their reforms failed to obliterate it inverts the proportions of the story. What is significant in the historical context of the time is not that the liberty-loving Revolutionaries allowed slavery to survive, but that they—even those who profited directly from the institution—went so far in condemning it, confining it, and setting in motion the forces that would ultimately destroy it.[117]

To be sure, the Founders were limited in their quest to abolish slavery by their respect for slaveholders' property in their slaves, by their inability to envision a multiracial nation that integrated freed slaves in the community, and by their desire to maintain the union and republican institutions that they had created. Nevertheless, union was not desired merely as a good in itself, but rather as the means of furthering liberty. "A successful and liberty-loving republic," Bailyn asserts, "might someday destroy the slavery that it had been obliged to tolerate at the start; a weak and fragmented nation would never be able to do so." Most importantly, at the time of the Founders' births, slavery had been "assumed and securely established." Upon their death, it had been "challenged, confined, and transformed into an inescapable moral problem."[118] Wood extends this argument even further. The American Revolution, he states flatly, is the source of "all our current egalitarian thinking." Thus, if the Founders and the American Revolution did not secure freedom for slaves and convey equal rights on women, they nevertheless made later movements for abolition and woman's rights possible.[119]

More broadly, Wood argues that proponents of assigning praise or blame to the Founders fail to grasp the tragedy of history. They fail to see that past historical actors—including even profoundly intelligent men like the Founders—operate from radically incomplete knowledge about the future and within a very limited range of possibilities. Wood notes, "The drama, indeed the tragedy, of history comes from our understanding of the tension that existed between the conscious wills and intentions of the participants in the past and the underlying conditions that constrained their actions and shaped their future."[120] This understanding of history, Wood argues, should lead scholars to resist making blithe moral judgments and depicting the past in terms of heroes and villains. It should also provide a broader picture of history that gives historians an appreciation that historical actors are under only limited control of their destinies and disconnects historians from attachment to any set of historical actors.[121]

In addition to this general defense of the Founders presented by Wood and Bailyn, Douglas Wilson has provided an eloquent and widely read historicist's defense of Jefferson's views and practices on race and slavery.[122] Wilson confronts the problem of establishing a fair standard against which to judge Jefferson and directly addresses the abiding question, "how could Jefferson have proclaimed that all men are created equal and yet owned slaves?" This question, Wilson observes, suggests that because Jefferson held slaves, he must also have defended the institution and thus been a hypocrite. But Jefferson, Wilson argues, did not consider slavery morally acceptable. Furthermore, both the question and the assumption that underlies it, according to Wilson, are stunning examples of "presentism," or the application of "contemporary or otherwise inappropriate standards to the past" and "the widespread inability to make appropriate allowances for prevailing historical conditions."[123] Understood in its proper historical context, Wilson argues, the question should be "how did a man who was born into a slave holding society, whose family and admired friends owned slaves, who inherited a fortune that was dependent on slaves and slave labor, decide at an early age that slavery was morally wrong and forcefully declare it ought to be abolished?"[124]

Those who still insist that Jefferson was a hypocrite and a racist because of his failure to free his own slaves and because of his writings on race, Wilson continues, are equally disconnected from Jefferson's world. The eighteenth-century Virginia slaveholder who sought to free his slaves faced numerous obstacles, including not only a myriad of legal restrictions, but also the problem of finding a place for their former slaves to live, as well as finding them a viable means of making a living. Such considerations meant that even the most compassionate slaveowner might not choose to release his slaves. Furthermore, Wilson writes, "Jefferson can hardly be counted bigoted or backward for seriously doubting that a racially integrated society of white Europeans and black Africans was truly feasible."[125] Imagining a multiracial nation, Wilson observes, required a profound leap. Like Malone and West, Wilson also argues that criticism of Jefferson because of his views on race must be tempered by a consideration of the uncertainty and tenuousness with which he set them forth and his admission that social conditions and opportunities for education might explain the disparity between the races. Yet another consideration is that Jefferson never came to the conclusion—common among his slaveholding brethren—that blacks were only fit for slavery. Instead, he concluded that the depredations of slavery that white Americans had imposed on slaves created the obligation to educate and train them and provide them with temporary support as they were relocated.

Finally, Wilson suggests that the author of the Declaration of Independence must be given considerable credit for the force that the ideal of equality has had in American history. "One way of looking at American history from Jefferson's day down to our own is as the series of changes and adjustments in our laws and institutions necessitated by the ideals implicit in Jefferson's Declaration."[126] Our own social and legal equality, Wilson implies, would not have been possible without Jefferson's original framing and Lincoln's reframing of it. The natural rights philosophy of the Declaration, he argues, has often provided a standard from which inegalitarian and racist doctrines have been condemned. Considered from the perspective of the sweep of American history, it is difficult to deny the progressive quality of the natural rights philosophy or Jefferson's importance to that philosophy.

In the hands of Bailyn, Wood, and Wilson, the historicist sensibility becomes a means of tempering criticisms of the Founders and of criticizing scholars who rush to judgments about them. Other historicists, including Eric Foner, Gary Nash, and Henry Wiencek, however, characterize the historical context of the Founding differently and end up with fundamentally different judgments about the Founders. Foner, Nash, and Wiencek argue that there is nothing anachronistic or "presentist" about criticizing many of the Founders for their failure to act more aggressively against slavery. The Founding generation, these scholars observe, was not trapped in an impervious historical consciousness that suggested that slavery was morally acceptable. African Americans and many of the leading Founders insisted that slavery was immoral. "Those who owned slaves," Foner states flatly, "made a conscious choice, which posterity has a right to judge."[127]

The ability of particular Founders to grasp the fundamental immorality of slavery, to take decisive actions, and thus to serve as a standard against which other Founders might be judged is most vividly brought out in Wiencek's justly celebrated study, *An Imperfect God: George Washington, His Slaves, and the Creation of America*.[128] At its core, *An Imperfect God* is the story of Washington's moral evolution from a slave master who was deeply enmeshed in the slave system and committed many of the atrocities characteristic of his peers into the only member of the Founding pantheon who set terms for the emancipation of his slaves in his will. Washington's initial position on slavery and his treatment of his slaves, Wiencek observes, was conditioned by innumerable cultural cues, the psychology of mastery, and the economic importance that slavery played in the construction of Washington's plantation empire.

In many ways, the young Washington was a typical slaveholder. He gave permission for his slaves to be whipped. He frightened the most unruly ones into obedience by threatening to sell them into bondage in the sugar plantations of the West Indies, where disease and crippling labor would ensure that the rest of their lives were short and agonizing. As a young planter, Washington shipped off at least three slaves to the West Indies. In one of these sales, he even directed a selling agent to barter his slave for an assortment of sweets and liquor.[129] As Washington surrounded himself with the luxuries commensurate with his position as a plantation master, he nevertheless searched for ways to strain more labor from his slaves and provided them with only the barest necessities. By Washington's own accounts and those of visitors, his slaves were "miserably clothed" and provided with shabby and flimsy housing. Each mother was provided with one blanket for each newborn, but most slaves had to wait years for a blanket to be replaced. Moreover, Washington required them to use these blankets to haul leaves to be used as lining for beds for his livestock.[130] Most dramatically and unfortunately, Washington, Wiencek discovered, was one of the directors of a lottery that raffled off black children and "wenches" so that he might recover debts owed to his wife by a man who had gone bankrupt.[131]

What led Washington to change his position, to view slavery as a great moral evil, and to plan—against the wishes of his extended family—the release of his slaves? What eventually gave him an insight into the humanity of African Americans that so few of his peers were able to achieve? Unlike previous scholars, Wiencek suggests that Washington's moral transformation was not a deathbed conversion, but rather a long and gradual process that resulted from numerous experiences and many incremental steps. The first cracks in Washington's conscience, according to Wiencek, were evident in his decision in 1775 to abandon the practice of splitting up slave families.[132] During the Revolutionary War, Washington also witnessed many acts of uncommon bravery by African Americans who composed from 6 to 13 percent of his troops by the middle of the Revolution, and perhaps even more at the end.[133] Although Washington was reticent to accept plans for the emancipation of slaves to bolster troop numbers, he eventually supported the recruitment of free blacks.[134] Other experiences that Wiencek suggests were pivotal included Washington's meetings with Northern blacks such as the black poet Phillis Wheatley, who wrote a poem honoring Washington and who eventually met with the general, and Washington's friendship with the French Marquis de Lafayette, who detested slavery and once remarked that the French had not allied themselves with the Americans in order to promote the extension of slavery. Such experiences, Wiencek argues, led Washington to believe more strongly than Jefferson that servitude stunted the development of blacks and that they were the intellectual equals of whites.[135]

Washington's moral evolution, Wiencek establishes, continued in the late 1780s and 1790s as Washington began secretly to plan the emancipation of his own slaves. At this point, Washington, according to Wiencek, had to work in secret because he knew that his family—especially Martha and her family—did not share his antipathy for slavery. The culmination of Washington's moral evolution was his remarkable will. This document not only set terms in uncompromising language for the emancipation of every slave whom he legally controlled (he did not control the "dower slaves" whom he had inherited as a result of his marriage to Martha), it also provided for funds for Washington's slaves to live, for the education of the young slaves so that they might become self-sustaining free blacks, and for the care of the elderly and the infirm until their deaths.[136]

Perhaps most importantly, Wiencek's analysis of Washington's moral evolution leads him to confront the possibility of an alternative history of the end of slavery in the United States and to argue that Washington was a "game changer" who should be seen as a standard against which the other elites of his generation are judged and found wanting.[137] If Washington evolved from a typical slaveholder to an opponent of slavery, Wiencek asks unapologetically, what prevented his peers from making the same evolution?

The obvious objection to many modern inquiries into the morality of slaveholding is that they apply modern standards of ethics to the people of the past in a way that is manifestly unfair, illogical, and futile. To conduct a just inquiry, we would need an advocate of moral law from that time. In fact we have one. As we have done so many times in the past, we need only look to George Washington. He pronounced his judgment on this era, and upon himself, when he freed his slaves and declared slavery to be repugnant. Of all the great Virginia patriots, only Washington ultimately had the moral courage and the farsightedness to free his slaves.[138]

Later, Wiencek continues this same line of reasoning:

Slavery wrecks the simple heroic narrative of the Founding. This narrative worked so long as slavery was depicted as part of the refinement and gentility of the eighteenth century. When the harsher aspects of slavery began to be presented we entered the era of the paradox, in which somehow slavery and the campaign for liberty coexisted. Because the founders were considered, a priori, good people, incapable of doing anything manifestly evil, it was surmised that they were blind to slavery's evil. It was deemed inappropriate to impose modern standards on them. But avoiding judgments requires a very careful selection of subject matter, in order to create a narrative that can make sense and that never collides with a moral puzzle. The yearning for pure narrative conquers any wish for an examination of difficult and vexing historical issues. Once we go beyond the state of paradox, which has often become a perpetual suspension of judgment, we enter a dangerous and, some would say, "unhealthful" realm of questioning. Could the Founders have ended slavery then and there? Washington freed his slaves. He did not think emancipation was impossible. Why did the others not follow? Why not judge Washington's peers by Washington's standards?[139]

For Wiencek, then, Washington "destroys the presentist defense and casts the other slaveholders of the era in a very harsh light."[140] Indeed, Wiencek's research on Washington has led him to conclude that the real purpose of the "presentism defense" of the Founders and slavery is not to ensure historical integrity, but to shield Americans from the injustices of our national creation. "The true beneficiary of the presentism defense," according to Wiencek, "is not the past but the present— it guards and preserves our fervent wish to have sprung from innocent origins."[141]

Wiencek's study of Washington and slavery illustrates that historicists summon historical context in ways that criticize as well as defend the Founders. The scholarship of Peter Onuf, however, raises the possibility that it might allow scholars to break free altogether from the "vicious circle of celebration and condemnation" that has often characterized Founding scholarship, especially studies of Thomas Jefferson.[142] Both the mythic Jefferson as a champion of democracy and human rights and the image of him as a hypocrite and a profligate, self-indulgent aristocrat, according to Onuf, "pay fealty to Jeffersonian principles, and so follow Jefferson's own script even while reaching radically different conclusions about the man himself."[143] Whether he is defended or condemned, Jefferson is judged against his own natural rights philosophy and the democratic vision that Americans attribute to him. Many of these studies also employ Jefferson's strategy of unmasking opponents, even if they turn it against Jefferson. In contrast, "historicizing Jefferson" opens the possibility of bridging "the gap between private and public, practice and profession, that Jefferson himself took such pains to cultivate."[144] Locating Jefferson in his own moral universe also opens up the possibility of understanding Jefferson in ways that are not dictated by him—ways that do not equate Jefferson with all that is right or wrong about America, and that do not load our anxieties and aspirations onto him.

Nevertheless, unlike other historicists, Onuf does not resign Jefferson to the past. "No amount of scholarly distance or detachment," Onuf maintains, "can reduce Jefferson to a mere historical figure."[145] He will be with us as long as America exists and as long as Americans seek to explore who they are, because Jefferson has been "the touchstone" and "deepest source" for Americans' conception of their nationhood.[146] Instead, "the historian's challenge is to sustain the tension between past and present, to restore our subjects to their own uncertain world while reconnecting it to ours by fresh translations from the increasingly foreign language of a distant time and place."[147] Extricating Jefferson's intentions from the subsequent history of what our nation became and scraping away the accumulated residue of facile appropriations, celebratory narratives, and flippant criticisms—most either parroted from Jefferson or reflexively spun in reaction to his self-serving accounts—can make Jefferson "more vital to us by restoring him more fully and more perfectly to his own time and place."[148]

This paradoxical approach—recovering the historic Jefferson to promote fresh translations of his meaning in American culture and to "reinvigorate our cross-generational conversation" about the meaning of American nationhood—leads Onuf to reject the strategies for interpreting and judging Jefferson employed by most contemporary scholars and to turn much Jeffersonian scholarship on its head.[149] Leading Jefferson scholars have concluded that Jefferson is "impenetrable" and contradictory, a "sphinx" whose "psychological agility, his capacity to play hide-and-seek within himself, was a protective device he developed to prevent his truly radical and highly romantic personal vision from colliding with reality."[150] A related strategy—encouraged by Jefferson's own writings and the secrecy with which he guarded his private life—has been to make a sharp distinction between Jefferson's public and private lives that in turn has encouraged analyses contrasting his words with his deeds. Such approaches have often led to the conclusion that Jefferson was a hypocrite (the slaveholding apostle of equality and the self-righteous moralist against miscegenation who fathered children with Sally Hemings), an unprincipled man who was unwilling and incapable of living up to his ideas (the opponent of slavery who lived lavishly off the fruits of the institution), or a deeply tortured soul engaged in the employment of strategies of denial. Still other scholars have backed away from Jefferson's private life and from psychological explanations of the "inner Jefferson" altogether, suggesting that such probing and speculations are tawdry, self-righteous, and unscholarly. Whatever their approach, most scholars have asked whether or not Jefferson deserves to remain in the pantheon of American Founders and concluded that this question requires an assessment of Jefferson's character.

In contrast, Onuf argues that the very idea of an impenetrable inner self is a product of *our* psychologized view of the world and is as time bound as the sentimentalism of Jefferson's day. Furthermore, Jefferson's "impenetrability is as much a function of their [scholars'] unwillingness to probe as of their subject's unwillingness to be probed."[151] "Jefferson's contradictions," Onuf argues, "should be an opening to understanding," not an excuse to disengage from him.[152] The materials that Jefferson used in the highly conscious construction of his self-understanding, Onuf continues, are readily available in the literary forms of his day. We will understand Jefferson—the "real" historic Jefferson as well as the "inner Jefferson"—when we follow the most insightful recent scholarship by engaging these materials and by viewing Jefferson in the concrete contexts that he inhabited in both his public and private life—as, for example, a man of letters and the patriarch of Monticello, where he ruled over his family and slaves. Still, the goal of understanding Jefferson's private life, Onuf insists, should not be to find him either deserving or wanting as an American icon. Rather, it should proceed from the premise that "Jefferson's life and thought are inextricably linked," and thus that his private life can be a window into understanding the relationship between his principles and practices.[153]

Onuf also resists the efforts to characterize Jefferson either as a hypocrite or a "guilt-ridden schizophrenic" torn apart by the contradictions between his egalitarian beliefs and the reality of his slaveholding world.[154] Such characterizations are either misleading or ultimately unsatisfying. Jefferson, according to Onuf, was "no hypocrite in the conventional sense; as an exponent of 'natural speech' and 'self-evident' truths, he did not deploy glittering phrases with a cynical, instrumental disregard for what he took to be their meanings. The disjunction of speech and act, so apparent to us, does not necessarily reveal a flawed character."[155] Moreover, Jefferson "was not gripped by guilt over slavery or torn by its contradictions. If he had been, he could not have found refuge at Monticello from the 'torrents' of political life, for he would have been constantly, inescapably tormented by his personal failure to take any effective action against this most barbarous and unjust institution." He was instead an "enlightened slaveholder, evidently satisfied with the self he so arduously fashioned."[156]

The subtleties of Onuf's efforts to move beyond character analysis and psychological probing are further evident when Onuf turns to specific questions about why Jefferson never acted as a moral crusader against slavery and why he was fastened to the obviously unworkable idea of colonization as a solution to the problem of slavery. Jefferson, Onuf observes, never believed that slavery was morally justified, never sentimentalized its effects, and never underestimated the threat that it posed to the future of the republic. Slavery, Jefferson acknowledged, had been introduced into America by an original breach of natural law by the colonists' forefathers. Its effect was to degrade slaveholders and slaves alike, creating a school of despotism for white slaveholders and their children and reducing slaves to dependent children and robbing them of any amor patriae. Furthermore, Jefferson was convinced that slaves would eventually be free and that if they revolted, slaveholders would have no moral claim to victory against them. For this reason, slavery constituted the chief threat to the otherwise glorious future of the young republic.

The answer to why Jefferson did not call for an immediate government-administered plan of abolition, why he did not free his own slaves and discouraged voluntary manumissions, why he never envisioned a multiracial nation, and why he eventually thrust the problem off to the next generation, Onuf suggests, lies in numerous suppositions that Jefferson made about the threats of race war and miscegenation, the character of moral progress, the relationship of rights to civic communities, and most generally and importantly, American nationhood. Specifically, beginning with the *Summary View of the Rights of British America*, Jefferson conceived of whites and blacks as independent "races" or "nations" (the terms were synonymous to Jefferson) and believed that the natural state of relations between slaves and their owners was a state of war. Slaves were thus not a part of the civic community, but rather a "captive nation, only kept from unleashing vengeance on its oppressors by the institution of slavery."[157]

Jefferson's equally profound lifelong fear was miscegenation or race mixing. This threat was even "more insidious" to Jefferson, according to Onuf, because it "threatened to complicate and subvert the natural racial order," make it increasingly difficult to distinguish the races, and thus "make the stain of blackness ineradicable."[158] By Jefferson's account of the natural order of the beauty of the races, white slaveholders should not have been tempted to have sex with their black slaves. But reality, Jefferson realized, was quite different. Given prerogatives over the bodies of their female slaves by the institution of slavery, slaveholders had proven unable to control their unnatural, "boisterous" passions for sex with their slaves. Moreover, as whites continued to exploit their female slaves, Jefferson realized that it would become increasingly evident that slaveholders held their own children in bondage. It would also become evident that "increasingly arbitrary and violent destruction of evermore complex ties in mixed race families" would be required to separate the races.[159] In short, slavery resulted in race mixing that, in turn, produced shadow families that blurred the lines between slave and free persons. It thus threatened Jefferson's vision of the nation as a family of families bound by ties of affection and by consensual unions.

If, however, the threats of slavery were concrete and imminent to Jefferson and perhaps pointed to prompt action, his beliefs about the relationship of rights to civic communities and his philosophical understanding of the character of moral progress suggested caution. Jefferson, according to Onuf, did not believe that slaves were entitled to the recognition of rights, or even that their rights were being violated, at least in any jurisprudential sense, by slavery. To be sure, Jefferson believed that everyone was endowed by their creator with inalienable rights. Nevertheless, Onuf argues, Jefferson believed that "only by uniting under some government and determining their own destiny as a people, could a group of individuals claim rights and become proper historical subjects."[160]

Furthermore, following the Scottish moral philosopher Henry Home (Lord Kames), Jefferson, according to Onuf, rarely thought of moral problems outside a particular civic community, believed that morality was learned by constant practice within the unfolding of history, and thus believed that slavery could be eliminated only when the majority of Americans had come to see its evils. Such moral progress would take place over time but could not be rushed by a few moral crusaders who sought to speak for the sentiments of the community. It also could not be eliminated by the premature use of a governmentally administered program, or even by seemingly heroic but actually self-indulgent acts of individual manumissions by slaveholders. Virginians, Jefferson believed, had to come to understand that slavery was wrong and then collectively extricate themselves from the problem. They could then reverse "the process of historical development that had deprived Africans of their freedom," but do so "in a way that would not jeopardize the free institutions that were themselves the products of history."[161] From Jefferson's viewpoint, individual manumission was an indulgence, and one that threatened the fruits of victory won during the Revolution.

Together, Jefferson's fears of miscegenation and race war, his beliefs about the degrading effect of slavery on white Americans, his understanding of the incremental character of moral progress, his beliefs that Americans had to act collectively to eradicate the institution, and his belief that slaves could only effectively exercise rights when they were formed into a people go a long way toward explaining Jefferson's infamous reticence about acting against slavery, his insensitivity to the impact of slavery on its human victims, and his lifelong conviction that colonization was the only appropriate remedy. Jefferson, Onuf observes, understood that forced colonization would cause intense suffering among black families by separating sons and daughters from their parents. Still, he also believed that these parents would be willing to endure this suffering in order to ensure that their children were free. Educated and then consolidated as a people in a new land, former slaves could then demand recognition of their natural rights, begin a process of progressive development, and enter into the international community as an independent nation. Most important, however, colonization would serve the interests of eighteenth-century Americans whose birthright as the revolutionary generation was to a union based on consent, affection, and interest rather than coercion. Colonization, Jefferson's "great panacea," would first act as a kind of peace pact, averting an otherwise inevitable race war. It would also ease the temptations of race mixing by ensuring that future generations of female slaves were not at the disposal of their masters, prevent white Americans from raising their children in a school of despotism, and preserve Jefferson's vision of the nation as a family of families. In these ways, "Jefferson's commitment to racial separation was fundamental, not provisional; it was inextricably linked to his conception of American nationhood."[162]

Despite his image as an antigovernment libertarian, Jefferson, according to Onuf, understood that nation building came first and democracy later. Jefferson is thus best thought of as the apostle of self-determination, not democracy. If we understand that Jefferson envisioned the United States as a homogeneous, white republic, then the link between colonization and nation building come together. The United States would be the strongest nation on the earth because its citizens would be progressively bound in tighter and tighter bonds of affection. With the enemies of republicanism vanquished, Old World churches banished, and blacks colonized, religious sects would compete for the allegiance of an increasingly rational public, and the bonds of affection between Americans would be strengthened.

Onuf's interpretation constitutes the most sophisticated and powerful reconstruction in print of Jefferson's moral universe and the reasoning he employed within it. Unlike Wood, Bailyn, and Wilson, however, Onuf's efforts to understand Jefferson within his moral universe do not prevent him from also criticizing Jefferson. Even as he admonishes scholars for acontextual, simple-minded juxtapositions of Jefferson's words and deeds, he also observes that Jefferson "never aimed to weaken the legal institutional basis of slavery itself."[163] This failure was particularly pointed, Onuf observes, given Jefferson's understanding that slavery represented a major obstacle to the success of republicanism. Unlike West, Onuf concludes that Jefferson believed that blacks were inferior by nature and that this, in addition to the threat of race war, prevented Jefferson from imagining a union of both blacks and whites on the North American continent. Furthermore, even in his most vehement anti-slavery moments, Jefferson, Onuf states flatly, was not first concerned with the freedom of slaves and expressed almost no concern throughout his life with the well-being of individual slaves. Instead, Jefferson's goals in promoting education and colonization were not to free black people or advance their civilization, but rather to redeem the American republic from its most imminent threat and to "free white people from the moral evil of being slaveholders."[164] Most broadly, Onuf's most attentive readers leave his scholarship with an understanding of how Jefferson's views on race, slavery, nationhood, and intergenerational sovereignty were inextricably linked and with an appreciation of how having chosen one constellation of values (union, security, and national unity) and pursing a particular vision of nationhood, other values and visions (especially our current goal of accommodating diversity in a multiracial society) never entered Jefferson's world of possibilities.

Central Issues and Foundational Differences

What do these scholars really disagree about? If the interpretations above are compared and further explicated, it becomes clear that debates over the moral responsibility of the Founders for slavery, such as debates about "how democratic is the Constitution?" and whether the Founders' political thought is best characterized as a species of liberalism or republicanism, are hardly exclusively disagreements about historical facts. Most obviously, scholars within these interpretive frameworks differ over how they view their role. Prosecutors and vindicators more readily enter into the fray of the trial of the Founders and defend or criticize the Founders, but historicists see their primary role as contextualizing and complicating such judgments. This difference has profound implications. It leads prosecutors and vindicators to craft indictments and apologias, to summon historical facts that aid their case, to ignore or explain away those that do not, and to introduce aggravating and mitigating circumstances. Historicists, however, develop thick descriptions of the moral universe of the Founders and generally provide more oblique defenses and guarded criticisms of the Founders.

A second foundational disagreement among these scholars is evident in the different standards that precede and unavoidably inform the moral judgments that they make. In particular, the perennial debate over whether or not the original Constitution was pro-slavery is first an argument about what level of support to slavery earns the appellation "pro-slavery." In characterizing the original Constitution as pro-slavery, Finkelman includes not only the provisions that directly aided slavery, but also those that indirectly aided it and even those that could be interpreted to aid it. He thus admonishes scholars for suggesting that only three clauses in the original Constitution concerned slavery, and instead names no fewer than thirteen different provisions that aided slavery directly or indirectly, or could be interpreted in that direction. In contrast, Fehrenbacher chides neo-Garrisonians who include provisions that aided slavery in only the most indirect manner. This line of reasoning, Fehrenbacher argues, constitutes a reductio ad absurdum because any of the powers granted in the Constitution or institutions created by it including the creation of the presidency and a Supreme Court could have been used for pro-slavery (or anti-slavery) purposes.[165] In place of what they believe is the loose-jointed standard evoked by the neo-Garrisonians, Fehrenbacher and other vindicators suggest that the original Constitution was compatible with the hope that slavery would pass away and thus cannot legitimately be labeled pro-slavery. Only a constitution that named slavery explicitly and treated slaves unambiguously as property, they suggest, would earn the label "pro-slavery."[166]

More broadly, prosecutors, vindicators, and historicists disagree about how best to characterize the historical context of the Founding and thus what standard is appropriate for judging the Founders' moral responsibility for slavery. Almost all scholars of the American Founding, even the most uncompromising prosecutors, have now concluded that judging the Founders on the basis of contemporary standards of race and gender equality is unfair and inappropriate.[167] Still, this diffuse consensus in favor of judging the Founders against strictly historical standards has only led scholars to formulate different interpretations of the historical context of the American Founding. These different interpretations, in turn, have led to different judgments about the Founders. In particular, prosecutors such as Finkelman observe that the context of the Founding included several remarkable men who transcended the conventions of their time, released their slaves, and even developed plans for emancipation on the American continent. As previously mentioned, Finkelman concludes that because Jefferson was an American icon, he must be judged against the beliefs and actions of these progressive Founders, not against the ordinary men of his time. In contrast, vindicators such as West and many of the historicists such as Bailyn, Wood, and Wilson who condemn "presentist" judgments argue that the pervasiveness of slavery and inequality in the eighteenth century should be our starting point for judging Jefferson and the Founders' beliefs and actions. According to these scholars, within the eighteenth-century world of comprehensive oppression that they inhabited, the ability of many of the Founders to recognize and their commitment to begin to address the injustices of slavery is itself a remarkable accomplishment.

In addition, scholars of the American Founding also disagree about the range of possibilities open to the Founders and thus whether they acted out of necessity or choice. These scholars unavoidably propose different counterfactual histories about what would have happened if the Founders had acted more aggressively against slavery. For their part, vindicators argue that the Founders were constrained from acting against slavery at the convention by the opposition of the delegates from South Carolina and Georgia, the necessity of achieving consensus on the design of the federal republic, the understanding that whatever was passed would have to be ratified by the people, and most broadly by the exigencies of creating and preserving union. Vindicators thus criticize prosecutors for suggesting that the Framers were "free to do whatever they liked about slavery and that the choices they made were rigid in their effect, severely restricting the freedom of later public leaders to deal with the issue."[168] Twenty-first-century scholars, vindicators further imply, are in no position to second-guess the Founders on the range of possibilities open to them.

In contrast, prosecutors are far less likely to accept the Founders' accounts of their historical context and motives and are thus much more skeptical of the proposition that the Founders had to choose between union and the protections given to slavery in the Constitution. "So much more," Finkelman concludes, "could have been done."[169] In particular, Finkelman concedes that the three-fifths clause was probably necessary to prevent the dissolution of the convention and the union, but discounts the idea that either the 1808 slave trade provision or the fugitive slave clause was the product of necessity. The 1808 slave trade provision, he contends, became a part of the Constitution as a result of political compromise that benefited economic interests in the North and the South, while the fugitive slave clause emerged late in the convention as a concession to slaveholders. More generally, whereas vindicators judge the Founders by comparing what they inherited with what they bequeathed, prosecutors compare what the Founders bequeathed with what they as contemporary scholars believe was possible. A much more stubborn resistance to pro-slavery demands for special treatment, they argue, was possible in 1787. Indeed, according to several prosecutors, slavery was uniquely vulnerable during the Founding, although this window of opportunity to eradicate it would soon pass when slavery became entwined with cotton production.[170]

Finally, whereas vindicators emphasize what the Founders accomplished, prosecutors emphasize what was left undone. Thus, vindicators emphasize the importance of private manumissions, the Founders' accomplishments in abolishing slavery in the North, and their abilities to limit its spread. Prosecutors, in contrast, emphasize the inability of the Founders to envision a biracial nation, their unwillingness to make the financial and physical sacrifices necessary to release their slaves, and their ultimate failure to abolish slavery.

The Case against Prosecuting and Vindicating

Despite their importance, these foundational differences mask a still broader point of agreement between prosecutors and vindicators. Both groups view themselves as participants in an adversarial process in which the Founders are put on trial. This decision in turn leads to the polarization of the debate, to the creation of a cycle of celebration and condemnation of the Founders, and to many of the interpretive errors and excesses—especially selectivity and lack of balance—that are evident in some of these works. This dynamic is vividly illustrated by focusing on the most strident and virulent examples of each interpretive framework: Finkelman's prosecution of Jefferson and the Founders, and West's vindication of them. For his part, Finkelman provides a strong case for the centrality of the sectional dynamics of the Constitutional Convention and an equally strong case that these dynamics played into the hands of pro-slavery forces. He also establishes the pro-slavery effects of many of the clauses of the original Constitution and sets forth several original, bold, and telling criticisms of Jefferson.

Nevertheless, Finkelman's interpretation is infected with exaggerated claims, shifting standards of evaluation, unsound analysis, and unfair judgments.[171] Two of Finkelman's most glaring exaggerations are evident in the opening pages of *Slavery and the Founders*, while a third appears in his chapter on Jefferson. In the opening pages, Finkelman states that Jefferson "did not in fact believe that blacks were entitled to the same rights as other Americans" and that DNA testing "prove[d] that Jefferson did in fact father children with his slave Sally Hemings."[172] In his chapter on Jefferson, Finkelman states that after a proposal that Jefferson sponsored to allow for the private manumission of slaves failed in 1769, he "never again worked for amelioration or reform of slavery."[173]

If Jefferson's beliefs are found in his words, then Finkelman's claim that Jefferson denied that blacks possessed natural rights is simply false. Although Jefferson sometimes strongly suggested that blacks were intellectually inferior by nature to whites, he also famously argued that "whatever be their degree of talent it is no measure of their rights. Because Sir Isaac Newton was superior to others in understanding, he was not therefore lord of the person or property of others."[174] Moreover, Finkelman misstates the case when he says that DNA testing proved that Jefferson was the father of Hemings's children. These tests establish that someone with the male Jefferson Y chromosome fathered Eston Hemings, Sally Hemings's youngest child. The DNA evidence does not implicate Jefferson exclusively, and it provides no evidence whatsoever about Hemings's other children. It is possible that one of the other twenty-five individuals with this DNA living in Virginia at this time could have fathered Jefferson's children.[175] When considered alongside studies of Jefferson's proximity to Sally Hemings at the likely times that she conceived and the black oral tradition of the Hemings family, the DNA evidence establishes only a high degree of probability, not a certainty, that Thomas Jefferson fathered Hemings's children.[176]

Finkelman's statement that after 1769 Jefferson "never again worked for amelioration or reform" of slavery and "never [again] stuck out his neck on slavery while holding office" is the most egregious of all of these statements.[177] As Finkelman's own account establishes, Jefferson proposed an emancipation scheme in *Notes on the State of Virginia*. This book, written in 1781 and published in 1785, contained some of Jefferson's most famous and frequently quoted statements about the injustices and effects of slavery and made his proposal for emancipation widely known among his contemporaries. Moreover, as noted earlier, as a congressman in 1784, Jefferson introduced legislation to prevent the spread of slavery into western territories; as president in 1806, he called for legislation to end the participation of the United States in the international slave trade and signed that bill into law in 1807. In each of these efforts, Jefferson worked against slavery and stuck his neck out.

Even more important than these misstatements of fact, Finkelman's effort to dismantle the "myth of the antislavery Jefferson" leads him to a series of excessively critical judgments of Jefferson that are based on a blanket of contradictory arguments.[178] One of the most vivid examples of this comes in his treatment of Jefferson's support for the 1769 law allowing private manumission. In correspondence late in his life and in his autobiography, Jefferson maintained that he brought the subject of manumission to the attention of Colonel Theoderick Bland, a respected elder statesman in the Virginia assembly. Bland then spoke for the measure in debate but was "denounced as an enemy of his country & treated with the grossest indecorum." Jefferson, according to his own account, was spared equal censure because he was the younger delegate.[179]

Finkelman first suggests that this 1769 proposal was not really progressive because it did not directly free slaves. It was instead, he argues, about giving slaveholders greater control of their property. Shortly thereafter, he switches course to suggest that the bill "would have been a meaningful step toward freedom" because it made manumission possible, but that Jefferson "exaggerated his role" in "the Bland proposal."[180] First, there is no evidence one way or another to judge whether Jefferson exaggerated his role in this measure. As Finkelman observes, no records have survived other than Jefferson's account that would shed light on the history of this proposal. More important, Finkelman's claim that the measure was not anti-slavery contradicts his suggestion that Jefferson had little role in the passage of anti-slavery legislation. Actually, there is no reason to characterize this bill as either an effort to encourage private manumissions or an effort to allow slaveholders to dispose of their property in slaves as they saw fit. It did both at once. Most importantly, as Finkelman concedes, it allowed for private manumissions in Virginia where none had been previously possible, and thus was good for slaves and bad for slavery. Would it have been better, one might ask Finkelman, if Jefferson had opposed this bill rather than sponsored it?

Another example of Finkelman's excessive attack on Jefferson occurs in his treatment of the 1807 act of Congress that abolished the slave trade in the United States. As previously noted, Jefferson called for the end of the slave trade in his 1806 annual message to Congress. He then eventually signed this bill into law on March 3, 1807, and it took effect on January 1, 1808—the first day that it was constitutional for Congress to ban the slave trade. Finkelman dismisses the possibility that Jefferson was exercising leadership in a humanitarian cause with the observation that "it is likely that the trade would have ended in 1808 if almost any of the early national leaders had been president" and by maintaining that public opinion was strongly in favor of abolishing the slave trade.[181] He also speculates that Jefferson's motives included self-interest and racism. Many slaveholders like Jefferson, Finkelman observes, sought to end the slave trade because they wanted to maintain the market value of their slaves by limiting their number. Jefferson, Finkelman further observes, wanted the United States to be a white nation.

Assessing Jefferson's motives and the degree of credit that he deserves for the passage of 1807 legislation that led to the abolition of the slave trade in the United States is complicated. According to Nic Wood, an authority on the legislation that abolished the slave trade in the United States, Congress took the lead in calling for the ban after South Carolina reopened the slave trade in 1803. By that date, everyone expected the ban to be enacted as soon as it was constitutional. The only question at this point was whether legislation banning the slave trade could be constitutionally passed in 1806 and then implemented in 1808, or whether Congress had to wait until 1808 to even pass the bill. Jefferson's main role was to press for the passage of the bill in 1806 rather than wait until 1808. He was motivated, Wood argues, primarily by the desire to pass this ban before George III passed a similar law for Britain.[182] Jefferson's motives, then, seem to have included a strange mix of self-interest, racism, humanitarian considerations to stop the slave trade, political ambition, and a regard for his long-term reputation.[183] Nevertheless, if we conclude that Jefferson was motivated, even in part, by the humanitarian effects that the law was sure to have and by the desire to beat George III to the punch in passage of humanitarian legislation, Jefferson emerges in a different light than Finkelman suggests. Indeed, in a sense that Finkelman is unwilling to concede, the 1807 legislation then is best conceived as part of Jefferson's extended indictment of George III that began in "A Summary View of the Rights of British America" and the Declaration of Independence for foisting the slave trade on the colonies and preventing them from ending it.

Whatever Jefferson's motives, he should, at minimum, be credited with the fact that this remarkable and important legislation was passed while he was president and with his support.[184] Abolishment of the slave trade in 1808, William Freehling has observed, was "the jewel of the Founding Fathers' antislavery effort." "The federal closure's impact," according to Freehling, "reached as far as Africa. Brazil and Cuba imported over 1.5 million Africans between 1815 and 1860, largely to stock sugar and coffee plantations. Slaveholders in the United States could have productively paid the then prevailing price for at least that many black imports to stock southwestern sugar and cotton plantations."[185] Another illuminating statistic is that when South Carolina reopened the slave trade from 1803 to 1808, some 40,000 additional slaves were brought into North America. Freehling observes that assuming standard percentages of natural increase, these slaves probably multiplied to about 150,000, or 4 percent of the nation's slave population, by 1860.[186] In short, there is no doubt that there would have been far more slaves in the United States at the eve of the Civil War without the 1808 slave trade provision and that slavery would thus have been an even more difficult institution to eradicate if the 1808 bill had not passed.

Finally, Finkelman gives Jefferson no credit at all for the enduring impact of his early public statements against slavery and for articulating the proposition that "all men are created equal." This famous statement in the Declaration of Independence is perhaps the most influential moral proposition in American and world history and highlighted the illegitimacy of slavery.[187] Jefferson's role as the author of the Declaration, his calls for emancipation in *Notes on the State of Virginia,* and his depiction of the despotic character of plantation life in the same place established his reputation among many of his contemporaries and later generations of Southerners as an opponent of slavery.[188] Stated flatly, more than any of the Founders, Jefferson ensured the circulation of this principle of political right that helped educate his fellow Americans in the immorality and illegitimacy of slavery.

This observation suggests that even though Finkelman is correct that Jefferson was generally unwilling to take political risks to oppose slavery after 1790, Jefferson's words in the Declaration and his memorable statements about the injustices of the institution had widespread impact, whatever his intentions. Failure to acknowledge this impact, in turn, ignores, as Sean Wilentz has observed, the ways in which Jefferson may have had a *more* positive influence than his predecessors who freed their slaves, including even George Washington. Unlike Washington, Jefferson took several important public anti-slavery stances early in his political career and "propounded throughout his life an egalitarian politics that Washington eschewed."[189] In taking this position, Jefferson thus served as an inspiration to generations of abolitionists and proponents of racial and gender equality, including Fredrick Douglass, Abraham Lincoln, Elizabeth Cady Stanton, and Martin Luther King Jr. These men and women cited Jefferson's democratic creed to contrast America's ideas with its realities. "Who," Wilentz asks provocatively,

> finally is more admirable: a political leader (like Jefferson) who was against slavery early in his career, consistently expressed egalitarian ideas, but then fell short of those ideals by trimming his sails over the issue in politics and failing to free his slaves; or a political leader who never professed egalitarian ideals, kept his new anti-slavery opinions confined to his private correspondence, and then finally, but only at his death, arranged to free his slaves?[190]

To be sure, Wilentz hastens to add, slaves at Mount Vernon and Monticello would have favored Washington's plan for private emancipation to Jefferson's hypocrisy. As Wilentz suggests, however, the answer is not obvious if we consider the broader nation and its future. "Sometimes the public hypocrite can have a far more auspicious influence on history than a private convert."[191]

Most importantly, throughout his indictment of Jefferson, Finkelman does not balance Jefferson's anti-slavery efforts and accomplishments against his racism, failures to act, and unfortunate silence. He also does not attempt to identify and explain the range of motives that sparked Jefferson's actions. If Jefferson supports legislation that is prima facie anti-slavery, Finkelman looks for an alternative characterization. When Jefferson supports a measure that is so clearly anti-slavery that it cannot be characterized otherwise, Finkelman suggests that Jefferson deserves little or no credit for it, observes that it was never passed, or suggests that it was impractical and would not have worked even if it had been passed. If Finkelman cannot convincingly deny either Jefferson's support for or the humanitarian effect of a proposal, he pauses to consider why Jefferson did not do more. Throughout his analysis, Jefferson is never credited with anything but the basest motives. Finkelman's moral compass only points in one direction: whatever Jefferson does is wrong.

Like Finkelman's prosecution of the Founders, West's vindication of them has several strengths. West clearly establishes that the elite Founders that are most studied—Washington, Madison, Jefferson, Hamilton, Adams, and Franklin—believed that blacks were endowed with a natural right to liberty. He is also correct to emphasize that, unlike later Southern apologists, none of the leading Founders provided explicit justifications for slavery.[192] Instead, they viewed it as an indefensible but entrenched institution that could not be easily or immediately eradicated. Like other scholars who defend the Founders' record on slavery, he also identifies several accomplishments of the Founding generation in abolishing slavery in the North and providing restrictions on its spread. Finally, he lays waste to several inaccurate propositions that are commonly circulated such as the belief that the three-fifths clause meant that the Founders believed that blacks were three-fifths of a human being.

Still, West's strained efforts to vindicate the Founders lead him to skewed interpretations and wholesale selectivity. One of the best examples of the skewed and selective character of West's account is evident in his effort to defend Thomas Jefferson and the Founders generally against the charge of racism. Jefferson set forth what Rogers Smith has called "the cornerstone statement of American scientific racism."[193] Nevertheless, West devotes only a single paragraph to Jefferson's racism under the heading "Were the Founders Prejudiced against Blacks?":

> More important, in his *Notes on the State of Virginia* Jefferson makes clear that the inferiority question is irrelevant to natural rights. Based on his observations of slaves, he argues, "as a suspicion only," that blacks "are inferior in the faculties of reason and imagination." He admits that this opinion "must be hazarded with great diffidence," for Jefferson knows that "the conditions of life," not their nature, is at least partly responsible for their lesser accomplishments. In spite of his "suspicion," Jefferson was able to write on the subject of slavery, later in the same book, "I tremble for my country when I reflect that God is just: that his justice cannot sleep forever."[194]

Anyone who has read Jefferson's infamous speculations on the differences between whites and blacks in *Notes on the State of Virginia* can immediately spot the skewed and scant character of this interpretation. First, despite West's suggestions, Jefferson's firm assertions that blacks have equal natural rights with whites and his statements about the injustices of slavery do nothing to excuse or even mitigate the edge of his observations on black inferiority. Many racists—at the Founding and since—have been opponents of slavery and believed that blacks had the same natural rights as whites. Second, it is true that Jefferson recognized the provisional character of his "scientific" case for black inferiority and even wished that science would eventually establish the equality of the races.[195] Nevertheless, this observation, which is offered also by Malone and Wilson in defense of Jefferson, has the effect of masking Jefferson's reliance on nature as an explanation for black inferiority.[196] One of the central purposes of Jefferson's infamous discussion of blacks' abilities in Query XIV of *Notes on the State of Virginia* was to establish the "gradations" in the races of man that "nature" has established. In the course of unfolding his speculations about these gradations, Jefferson speaks of the "real distinctions which nature has made" between whites and blacks. He also contends that when the races are mixed, blacks improve in both body and mind. This, Jefferson argues, "proves that their [black's] inferiority is not the effect merely of their condition of life." Finally, he observes that white slaves in antiquity—though subjected to more deplorable conditions than black slaves in America—did not suffer from the deficiencies in imagination and reason that he detects in blacks. This is further evidence, in Jefferson's estimation, that it is "nature which has produced the distinction."[197]

Jefferson's unwillingness to conclude flatly that scientific evidence had already established the natural inferiority of blacks resulted not from any ambiguity he found in his observations about blacks (he was relentlessly ungracious throughout his life in acknowledging black intellectual talents or attributing blacks' inequality to the condition of slavery), but rather the character of the scientific process. The scientific process, Jefferson observed, was a longer and more uncertain process when applied to human faculties than physical substances because humans, unlike physical substances, could not be "submitted to the anatomical knife, to optical glasses, to analysis by fire, or by solvents."[198] Tellingly, throughout his life, Jefferson did not begin with the presumption that blacks and whites had equal intelligence and powers of reason and then suggest that science had to prove otherwise. He began with the presumption of black inferiority and placed the burden on science to prove otherwise.

Third, unfortunately, the differences that Jefferson identified between blacks and whites did not stop, as West suggests, at his suggestion that blacks are inferior in the faculties of reason and imagination, but rather extended into the most degrading of stereotypes. Blacks, Jefferson maintained, are more gifted in music than whites, but less beautiful, less able to display emotion, and subject to a "very strong and disagreeable odor." They are at least as brave as whites, but this courage proceeds from a want of forethought, which prevents them from seeing danger until it is present. Once presented with danger, however, they do not have the "coolness" and "steadiness" of whites. Blacks' understanding of love, Jefferson further speculates, is more akin to lust than a "tender delicate mixture of sentiment and sensation."[199]

Was Thomas Jefferson prejudiced against blacks? How can anyone reasonably argue that he was not? Were the elite Founders in general prejudiced, and was their society profoundly prejudiced? Certainly, each of the elite Founders should be judged on the basis of his particular writings and not the supposition that he simply reflected the conventions of his time. But quotes from Alexander Hamilton and Benjamin Franklin expressing positive sentiments about the capabilities of blacks—and this is all West provides—do not overturn the documentation that scholars have amassed about the prejudices that were used to justify slavery.[200]

Like his account of Jefferson's views on blacks and the question of racial prejudice at the Founding, West's account of the accomplishments of the Founders with regard to abolishing slavery is selective and skewed. Consider how each of the accomplishments that West lists should be qualified, amended, or corrected—and most importantly, consider what is *not* said.[201]

The Slave Trade

West: West contends that the growth of slavery was *"quickly limited* by reducing or abolishing the slave trade." By 1789, he observes, every state had outlawed slavery, but South Carolina renewed the slave trade from 1803 until 1808. In 1808, the twenty-year moratorium set up in the Constitution against interference with the slave trade ran out, and Congress outlawed it.[202]

Corrective: Abolishing the slave trade constitutes perhaps the greatest accomplishment of the Founding generation in weakening slavery. Nevertheless, the Founders' actions against the slave trade can hardly be said to have quickly limited the growth of slavery. Instead, the slave trade initially flourished, in large part as a result of the twenty-year protection provided by the Constitution, and this moratorium had a profound effect on the growth of slavery in the United States. As Peter Kolchin reports, "During this period, labor-hungry planters in the lower South imported tens of thousands of Africans; indeed, more slaves entered the United States between 1787 and 1807 than during any other two decades in history."[203]

The Abolishment of Slavery in a Majority of the Original States

West: West observes that total abolition of slavery took place quickly in three New England states after the Revolution where the populations of slaves were limited (New Hampshire, Vermont, and Massachusetts had only a few hundred slaves in them), but abolition "came harder" in other Northern states with higher slave populations that enacted "gradual emancipation" laws.[204]

Corrective: More accurately, the southernmost New England states (Connecticut and Rhode Island) and the Middle Atlantic seaboard states (Pennsylvania, New Jersey, and New York) in which the slave population was between 1 and 5 percent of the state's total population enacted "post nati" abolition statutes. These statutes freed only *future-born* slaves, not slaves then in bondage, and often released even those future-born slaves only after they were well into adulthood—that is, after their most productive years of labor. In New York and New Jersey, as a deadline neared, many slaveowners sold slaves scheduled to be released into perpetual slavery to slaveholders in Southern states (where no post nati laws existed). Abolition of slavery was achieved in the North, it should be emphasized, over a period lasting longer than half a century.[205]

The Founders and the Expansion of Slavery

West: West strengthens his case for the anti-slavery credentials of the Founders and the effects of their actions in weakening the institution by stressing their containment of slavery.[206] The Founders, he contends, "forbade the expansion of slavery into areas where it had not been previously permitted." As West points out, slavery was forbidden in the Northwest Territories in the Northwest Ordinance passed by Congress in 1787. This ordinance had far-reaching implications: it banned slavery in areas that would become the states of Illinois, Indiana, Michigan, Wisconsin, and Ohio. West also notes that Congress permitted slavery in the Southwest Territory, which included the future states of Kentucky, Tennessee, Alabama, and Mississippi. These areas, according to West, had been "ceded to the national government with the expectation that slavery would continue." North Carolina had ceded this territory only on the condition that Congress would not emancipate slaves in the region. Thus, "this was generally regarded not as an endorsement of slavery expansion but an acceptance of it where it already existed."[207]

Corrective: First, although slaves were banned from the Northwest Territory, Congress made no provision to free slaves already there, and slavery (disguised as indentured servitude) existed in the Northwest Territory until pro-slavery forces were defeated in Illinois in the 1820s.[208] Second, the vote on Jefferson's 1784 proposal in the Continental Congress to ban slavery in all of the territories ceded by the states under the Articles of Confederation illustrates that there was no uniform expectation that the territory south of the Ohio River would necessarily contain slaves. Jefferson's proposal failed by only a single vote, and according to Jefferson, it would have passed if a New Jersey congressman had not been at home ill. What this vote means is that effectively half of Congress did not accept as binding the statements that slavery should not be interfered with in this territory that had been issued by the seaboard states when they ceded these lands. Furthermore, most of these Congressmen knew that the effect of not passing this ordinance was the expansion of slavery and that their failure was a portentous act. "The fate of millions unborn," Jefferson said famously, was "hanging on the tongue of one man, and heaven was silent in that awful moment."[209]

Third, the most glaring omission here is that West does not mention the expansion of slavery into territories acquired by Jefferson in the Louisiana Purchase and by James Monroe's 1819 treaty with Spain that secured the areas of Florida, southern Alabama, and southern Mississippi. Although expanding slavery does not seem to have been the motive of securing these territories, they already contained slaves, and their acquisition eventually led to the addition of four new slave states and parts of two others. These purchases, and the failure to forbid slavery in them, greatly increased the economic and political power of slaveholding interests. Thus, although strictly speaking, it is true, as West suggests, that the Founders "forbade the expansion of slavery into areas where it had not been previously permitted," slavery was secured in the South under their watch and spread into *acquired* territories, strengthening slaveholding forces in Congress.[210]

Humanizing Laws Regarding Slavery and Voluntary Manumissions

West: West argues that the Founders "made laws regulating slavery more humane" and that "individual owners in most states freed slaves in large numbers."[211] The more humane laws that West refers to here are the laws in several states making it easier for owners to emancipate their slaves, proposals granting freedom to slaves who fought in the Revolution, and laws that recognized the rights and humanity of blacks, such as those that made it murder to kill a slave.

Corrective: There is considerable evidence that the Revolution helped to somewhat humanize treatment of slaves. Nor, as West suggests, should we "disparage" private manumissions, if that means failing to acknowledge the moral courage and self sacrifice of such acts.[212] Nevertheless, West's account of the effects of the Revolution ignores the stubborn persistence of legal inequalities, the backlashes against the anti-slavery sentiments and policies that attended the Revolution, and the places and ways in which slavery became even more entrenched after the Revolution than it had been before. Furthermore, voluntary manumission was never a practical solution to the problem of slavery. Private manumissions—especially those of George Washington and Edward Coles—have become among the most celebrated acts of the Founders and one of the principal means in which individual Founders are defended from the charge that they neither recognized the injustice of slavery nor acted against it. Nevertheless, the exceptional acts of moral courage were precisely that: exceptional. They were much rarer and had a much more limited impact on the total number of free blacks than West suggests, especially in the South. In the two border states in which voluntary manumission schemes were the sole means of eradicating slavery, Delaware and Maryland, slave populations persisted. Delaware had 9,000 slaves in 1790 and 1,800 seventy years later; Maryland had 103,000 slaves in 1790 and 84,000 slaves in 1860. In Southern states, according to the estimates of William Freehling, less than 10 percent of slaves were released voluntarily by their owners. Thus, the percentages of blacks who remained slaves in the South was particularly high, and it stayed that way. By 1830, only 2 percent of South Carolina or Georgia blacks and only 8.5 percent of Virginia blacks were free.[213]

None of these points alone is decisive, but cumulatively, they point to a much different narrative of the accomplishments and failures of the Founders and their generation with regard to slavery. Far from the whole Revolution being, as West suggests, an anti-slavery movement, it was from the beginning, especially in the South, in many ways an effort to contain the implications of the principles of the American Revolution and *preserve* slavery.[214] For example, when in 1774 Lord Dunmore announced his famous proclamation offering freedom to slaves with rebel masters, Virginians did not counter Dunmore's proclamation with a similar offer to free slaves who fought with the Patriot cause.[215] Instead, they issued a counter-proclamation observing that Dunmore's offer extended only to the male slaves owned by revolutionaries (not female slaves or the slaves of loyalists). This counter-proclamation also reminded slaves that they would have to make a decision between staying with their families and joining the British, and that the penalty for insurrection was death.[216] The limitations of any anti-slavery impulse in the South are also evident in the stubborn resistance throughout the South to troop recruitment schemes that offered blacks emancipation.[217] West points to discussions of such schemes as evidence of the liberating influence of the Revolution, but in the South, only Maryland ever authorized the enlistment of slaves into the army. In contrast, four states—Georgia, South Carolina, North Carolina, and Virginia—enticed troops to join the American cause with bounties that included land and slaves for their service.[218] More broadly, although there was considerable variation of the impact of the American Revolution on slavery even in the South, it is at least arguable that the Revolution really had little impact in weakening slavery in the region. The historian Richard S. Dunn writes, "In those Chesapeake districts where most blacks lived, slavery was more deeply rooted when Jefferson stepped down from the presidency [1809] than when he composed the Declaration of Independence [1776]."[219] Finally, when the Revolution ended, American officials illustrated the limitations of the reforms that they were willing to accept as a result of the Revolution in the Treaty of Paris ending the war. This treaty stipulated that British troops were to withdraw from the United States "without carrying away any Negroes or other property of the American inhabitants." This phrase, as even Fehrenbacher notes, unambiguously characterizes slaves as property.[220]

At this point, West would probably argue that emphasizing the Founders' concessions to slavery, the limitations of their accomplishments, and the length of time that these accomplishments took is to fail to recognize what was possible and to ignore the consequences of going further. Such judgments, in West's estimation, follow from flippantly opposing morality and expediency rather than judiciously balancing principle and prudence. In the case of slavery in America, West reasons, prudence dictated that if this "terrible injustice" was not temporarily accepted, the union would have dissolved. Dissolution of the union, in turn, would have meant that "the North would have lost all influence over the South," "the South would have been free to develop slavery without restraint, and the eventual abolition of slavery might never have occurred."[221] Thus, abolitionists such as William Lloyd Garrison were not zealous defenders of liberty, but rather "impatient and shrill" cranks who "promoted Southern intransigence and Northern disgust with antislavery opinion."[222] Contemporary scholars who excoriate the Founders for not abolishing slavery, West implies, are even further from eighteenth-century realities.

What does West make of the charge that the Founders could have done more? West blunts this line of reasoning by suggesting that the Founders were simply correct—that is, that the reasons they gave for not immediately abolishing slavery and giving blacks full civil and political rights are decisive. Some of the Founders suggested that a race war might follow from emancipation, that slaves were not yet ready to exercise the rights of citizenship, and most importantly that immediate abolition would also lead to the end of the union. These fears and concerns, West concludes, were based on observations and experiences and were thus sound. West even follows some of the Founders into accepting colonization as a just and workable solution to slavery.

There are several problems with West's analysis here, even if we accept that devotion to principle necessarily carries it with prudential considerations about how best to further those principles, that the uncompromising pursuit of even the most just goal can have disastrous consequences, that sometimes it is necessary to accept a lesser evil to avoid a greater one, and that slavery could not have been immediately abolished during the Founding without risking the whole American experiment in republican liberty. First, West's analysis suggests that the Founders were of one mind about the boundaries of what constituted prudent practical action, when in fact questions about the proper timeline for emancipation and the best means of achieving it were, among other issues, quite divisive. Edward Coles and George Washington voluntarily emancipated their slaves and obviously believed that this was appropriate. Jefferson advised Coles not to release his slaves and considered private manumission a dangerous indulgence and an act of betrayal against Virginia.[223] Madison agreed with Jefferson that colonization was part of the proper solution to slavery, but John Adams thought it was cruel and unworkable.[224] After 1790, Jefferson became largely silent on the issue of slavery and how it might best be ended. At about that same time, in his final days, Franklin sponsored a petition to Congress calling for the immediate end of the slave trade (despite its protection by the Constitution) and publicly lampooned the arguments used to defend the slave trade and to oppose abolition.[225] West's apologia for the Founders, then, is not a consensus view of the Founders' understanding of the only prudent course of action. Many of the Founders also believed that more was possible. It is instead a defense of what was achieved and an argument that more was not possible based on selected quotes from selected Founders. West's account thus does not so much take the Founders' arguments seriously as it uncritically parrots the ones that fit his goal of vindicating the Founding project.[226]

Second, even if the Founders had been uniform in their understandings of the boundaries of practical action against slavery, their judgments alone cannot be decisive. To be sure, the Founders' understanding of what was possible and what was out of bounds must certainly be given great weight. Still, we also have to at least consider the possibility that the Founders, as William Freehling suggests, "exaggerated all the problems in freeing blacks, and that exaggeration paralyzed them, turned them into procrastinators, led to infrequent stabs at limited reforms."[227]

Third, West's case that the Founders were correct when they said that concessions to slavery were necessary to prevent still greater evils is based almost entirely on historical counterfactuals given by the Founders themselves about the consequences of actions *not* taken. The place of historical counterfactuals in judgments about the Founders' moral responsibility will be discussed later. For now, it is sufficient to observe that if historical truth about what happened is not easily discovered, historical truth about what might have happened is more elusive. West's confidence that the Founders were simply correct in their assessments of the disastrous consequences that some of them said would follow from alternative policies is thus misplaced. Each counterfactual question—would emancipation have resulted in race warfare? was colonization a workable solution to slavery? would pressing for more immediate abolition have resulted in the breakup of the union?—has to be taken by itself. To be sure, the Founders' perceptions, statements about their own motives, and arguments about the consequences of alternative actions should be accorded great weight. Still, these judgments have to be considered alongside other evidence before we can even begin to consider what was possible and thus whether to accept or reject the Founders' claims. None of this means that we need to excoriate the Founders for not immediately abolishing slavery. But it also means that criticisms of the Founders cannot simply be dismissed as a failure to realize the limitations the Founders faced.

The Contributions and Limitations of Historicism

The point of all of this is not just that neither Finkelman nor West provides fair moral judgments or approaches a comprehensive interpretation, but rather that neither is in a position to achieve these goals. Both act as attorneys, creating the narrative most beneficial to their clients. Finkelman is compelled to ignore important accomplishments by the Founders, emphasize what they left undone, and thus establish their guilt for slavery and its subsequent consequences. For equally partisan reasons, West ignores the darkest dimensions of the Founders and apotheosizes, apologizes, and praises to preserve. Furthermore, Finkelman's excoriation of Jefferson is driven by arrogant assumptions about the moral superiority of the present and contemporary delusions that the problems of the Founding era had easy solutions. Conversely, West sanitizes the American Founding, telling much of the story of subsequent developments as a fall from grace and suggesting that his interpretation is the only one respectful of the Founders and the nation.

Much of the work of the historicists is more judicious, complex, and comprehensive, in no small part because the best scholarship of these scholars works from a framework that better allows them to integrate both the Founders' accomplishments and failures. The historical record is evidence to be marshaled in one direction or another for both prosecutors and vindicators. It is something to be approached on its own terms for historicists. Nevertheless, the historicists' approach lacks theoretical clarity about the proper role of the scholar, and contrary to the suggestion of its proponents, it has not and perhaps cannot generate agreement about the proper standards for making moral judgments about the Founders, let alone meaningfully structure discussions about the Founders' moral responsibility for slavery. It thus also cannot lead us out of the cycle of celebration and condemnation that characterizes so much Founding scholarship.

In particular, it is not at all clear that historicists, who are represented in this chapter almost exclusively by practicing historians, provide a coherent account of "presentism" and what is required to avoid it, and thus of the interpreter's proper role. Two distinct and contradictory claims have been set forth under the admonition against presentism. Broadly speaking, historicists contend that their role should be to approach the past on its own terms. Acting like anthropologists, they should be sensitive to the radically different culture and assumptions of the people who lived in the past. They should then recreate that foreign world, establishing its distinctiveness and irretrievability, but simultaneously translating the foreign language and culture of the past into one that is understandable to the present. Some historicists connect this general proposition to the sweeping claim that it is improper for historians to make moral judgments. The historians' craft is an empirical and analytical process designed to faithfully represent the past to the present. Historians should strive for truth about the past, not judgment of its participants. Professional historians, proponents of this line of reasoning may add, are not trained or equipped to engage in moral judgments. Implicit here is at least the possibility that moral philosophers and scholars from other disciplines are qualified to make moral judgments, but not historians. Other historicists, however, do not read the historians' commitment to pursuing the past on its own terms as an injunction against making moral judgments per se, but rather as an injunction against making them on the basis of standards other than the moral categories present in the Founders' world. For these historicists, the historians' professional code, then, is "never to judge the past by present standards."[228]

The inability of a strictly historical approach to short-circuit moral judgments altogether is illustrated by the numerous moral judgments—implicit and explicit—made by the historians analyzed in this chapter alone. Some historians may say that the professional historian should never make moral judgments, but many historians obviously do not accept this characterization of their craft, and fewer still really adhere to it, if indeed that is even possible. More decisively, in practice, historians make moral judgments in the very act of depicting historical context as they choose which features of any particular historical context to emphasize. The context of the Founding, like any historical moment, is a complex, ambiguous, and contested historical fact that can be portrayed in a number of ways. As noted earlier, Bailyn and Wood characterize the Founders' world as a time of ubiquitous inequality in which the expectation that some would live off the labor of others was widely accepted. Wood believes that this world of comprehensive oppression and inequality "must be the starting point in any assessment of its [slavery's] influence on early American politics and nationhood."[229] Other historians such as Nash, Wiencek, and Foner characterize the Founding as a time in which moral revulsion against slavery opened a window of opportunity for its eradication and point to extraordinary acts that some of the Founders made to free their own slaves and to eradicate slavery.[230]

Each of these depictions of the historical context of slavery and the American Founding is rooted in historical fact. Historicists therefore strain credibility when they suggest that their depiction of the historical context is uniquely the fact of the matter and thus the only proper standard for moral judgments. If they were more truthful about or conscious of the character of their scholarship, they would admit that their interpretations of historical context are based on a selective account of historical facts summoned at least in part to condition and influence judgments about the Founders. Certainly, when Bailyn and Wood say that the comprehensive inequality of the eighteenth century must be the starting point for assessments of slavery, they are emphasizing one dimension of the historical context of the Founding over others in order to temper judgments about the Founders and make a moral point—namely, that it is the emergence of a moral consciousness against slavery during the Founding and the Founders' willingness to act against it that should be emphasized, not their failures to eliminate slavery. When Nash, Wiencek, and Foner point to the array of Founders who knew that slavery was wrong and acted to eliminate it, they are marshaling a different set of historical facts to establish a different understanding of the historical context and to set the stage for a different assessment of the Founders.

But even if the line of reasoning I am pursuing is wrong and it could be shown that historians can somehow avoid making moral judgments by relying on specific historical knowledge and the standards within their profession, the question only transforms. The question now becomes, why *should* historians refrain from making moral judgments? Far from being unqualified to make moral judgments, historians become peculiarly situated to make and inform moral judgments about the Founders as a result of the tactile historical knowledge that they acquire during their researches. Historians who refuse to engage the debate over moral responsibility are declining to enter into a conversation that they are eminently, and in some ways peculiarly, qualified to inform.

Historians who make the second of these claims—that historians should only make moral judgments from within the moral categories supplied by the historical participants themselves—are suggesting that there are only time-bound standards for making moral judgments, and/or that it is fundamentally unfair to judge the Founders against our (morally better) understandings of race and gender. In chapter 2, I quoted Richard Hofstadter's conclusion that the development of democracy in America should be conceived as an "unfolding historical reality that must be understood at each point in its temporal context."[231] Historicists who argue that judgments about the Founders should be made only after making "appropriate allowances for prevailing historical conditions" are in effect saying that issues of slavery, race, and gender must also be conceived as an unfolding historical reality in which each temporal context creates a different standard for judgment.[232] They are also implicitly suggesting that the adoption of strictly historical standards for judgments will provide a common set of standards by which historical actors are judged and thereby serve as a prophylactic against hasty and moralistic condemnations of the Founders.

There are, however, at least two problems with this claim that moral judgments outside of the moral universe of the historical participants are improper. First, the argument that every age supplies the moral standards by which its historical actors are judged makes historical actors judges in their own cause, rests on a global moral skepticism or ethical relativism, and eliminates the possibility of impartial judgments that are based on independent moral standards. Second, the claim that it is unfair to judge historical participants by contemporary standards rests on the same teleological assumptions about the superiority of present values that many historicists hope to transcend. It can only be unfair to judge past actors by present standards if contemporary standards are judged a priori to be superior.

More broadly, historicists fool themselves when they suggest that adoption of this axiom will break the cycle of celebration and condemnation, create a consensus about the proper standards for judging the Founders, or ensure mature and responsible judgments about the Founders. As the discussion of the divisions within the historicists has, I hope, already established, the assertion that the Founders should only be judged against the historical standards of their day has not established a common standard, but rather created a debate over which of the several historical standards of the Founders' day are relevant in addressing questions of moral responsibility. It has also led historians to charge other historians with the politicization of history.

Finally, if historicism has not provided a common standard for moral judgments, it has in practice led more to the proliferation of strictures against presentism and the glorification of a state of the perpetual suspension of moral judgments than to the development of mature and responsible ones. To be sure, historicists are correct to protest against flippant judgments and facile appropriations of Founders' names and ideas. They are equally correct to suggest that we need a deeply contextualist approach to the Founders before we address the constellation of questions that this topic poses. Still, at some point, questions of moral responsibility cannot be addressed simply by admonishing contemporary scholars for their hasty or acontextual judgments. We need to move beyond such admonitions, if for no other reason than because they are now hoary and deflect attention from the most substantive issues. The question of moral responsibility cannot be addressed by ever more complex assessments of the Founders' moral universe and how they reasoned within it, or by ever more subtle explanations of how they came to believe what they believed. These otherwise valuable endeavors become obstacles when they become means to delay and frustrate moral judgments rather than discipline them. The best interpretations of the Founders and moral responsibility are not necessarily the most oblique. The glorification of complexity can become a glorification of duplicity and an excuse to avoid the question of moral responsibility. To say that we do not need to prosecute or vindicate the Founders is not to say that we do not ultimately need to provide responsible moral judgments.

Toward More Responsible Moral Judgments

If prosecuting and vindicating lead scholars to selective and unbalanced interpretations and the historicist approach provides important but ultimately limited guidance, then is there an alternative approach, and what would it look like? Furthermore, can we ever hope to break the cycle of celebration and condemnation that informs so much Founding scholarship and move toward more responsible moral judgments? If so, then how? In chapter 6, I provide an explication and defense of *understanding* the Founding as an alternative—both in attitude and approach—to prosecuting, vindicating, and historicizing. At this point, however, I want to limit my analysis to specific observations about how we might proceed toward more responsible moral judgments.

As the analysis above has already established, the articulation of moral judgments by Founding scholars is no simple task. It involves addressing a dizzying number and variety of vexing but interrelated issues that scholars have seldom identified or isolated for consideration. These include foundational questions about the proper role of the scholar and the proper standards that should be used in judging the Founders. They also include a constellation of issues that arise as scholars assess the Founders' moral responsibility for slavery. There is of course no guidebook for addressing these questions, and they are not the kind of interpretive questions that can be reduced to strict rules anyway. Still, the analysis in this chapter points to the following suggestions.

Perhaps most fundamentally, scholars cannot avoid the articulation of moral judgments about the Founders. The point is not that scholars invariably slip up and make judgments that are based on unacknowledged biases. The point, rather, is that making moral judgments is endemic to this question, which is unavoidably a question about moral responsibility. Thus, even the most sophisticated attempt to suggest that scholars can and should avoid acting as moral judges—Gordon Wood's tragic view of history—fails. Wood, it will be remembered from the discussions in this chapter and from chapter 3, argues that historical actors are often caught up in circumstances that they have only the most limited ability to control and do not fully comprehend. Such an understanding of the historical process and the horizon of historical actors, Wood further argues, should render historians much less likely to make blithe moral judgments and to think in terms of good and bad guys. It should also provide a calm, distant perch in which the contemporary historian can show how, for example, Tory and Whig perspectives of the American Revolution and Federalist and anti-Federalist perspectives on the Constitution are equally worthy, and then explain how historical actors came to think and act as they did.

This understanding of the historical process contains a wealth of prudential insight, reflects and inculcates qualities of humility and historical wisdom, and conversely militates against hubris and self-righteousness. Still, the tragic view of history provides only limited guidance for analyzing questions of evil and moral responsibility. It is possible to see how in a long, tragic view of history, Federalist and anti-Federalist views on the Constitution and even Whig and Tory perspectives of the American Revolution are equally worthy, or at least that both sides present plausible arguments. It is also easy to understand why historians would want to develop interpretations that somehow envelop the different perspectives of the historical actors and stand outside of the arguments of any of them. With regard to slavery, the tragic view of history may point to the limitations of what could be done to abolish slavery and may steer us away from hasty judgments about the proper means for eradicating slavery (whether, for example, immediate private manumission was best, or whether the Founders had to wait until collective, administrative manumission was possible).

Still, the fundamental immorality of slavery cannot be denied. On this issue, there are no equally plausible sides for scholars to envelop and transcend, no neutral perch on which they can stand above the historical actors they analyze. The perspective of those Founders who instructed their fellow citizens in the immorality of slavery and acted on their best understanding of the most effective means of expediting its eradication cannot be integrated with the perspective of those who did not. Furthermore, taken to its logical conclusion, the tragic view of history denies, or at least severely diminishes, human agency and individual responsibility. But in analyzing slavery, scholars must do more than show how the Founders did not fully comprehend their options or fully control events. They will ineluctably praise and blame.

The reality that scholars must engage in moral judgments in this debate points us to the second foundational question: What standard should we use in our assessments of moral responsibility? The common interpretive axiom that the Founders should seldom be judged by contemporary moral standards provides a judicious starting point. The reason that the Founders should seldom be judged outside of the moral standards of their time is not, however, that no transhistorical standards exist or that we adopt the proposition that every age sets the standards of judgment for the historical actors who lived at that time. Instead, the reason that we should not judge the Founders by contemporary moral standards in the areas of race and gender is because such judgments are both unfair and unilluminating. They are unfair because we have made substantial moral progress since the Founding—at least on issues of race and gender. Even more, such judgments are now jejune. Little purpose is served by condemning the Founders for not reaching our moral standards on these issues.

With this said, the discussion above has already established that the adoption of the axiom that we should seldom judge the Founders by standards outside of their own time only begins this debate. Recent debates, I have argued, have established the complexity of the Founders' moral universe and put on the table a number of standards, each historically grounded, by which the Founders might be judged. This realization should encourage scholars to have a multiplicity of standards in mind as we consider these issues. In other words, here, as in the case of determining whether or not the Constitution is democratic, there is no reason that we have to confine ourselves to any single standard within the Founding in addressing questions about the Founders and moral responsibility. If, as Gordon Wood maintains, the "fact that slavery had been taken for granted for thousands of years prior to the mid-eighteenth century must be the starting point in any assessment of its influence on early American politics and nationhood," there is no reason that this fact must also be the ending point.[233] Scholars can readily move from the understanding that the revolutions of the eighteenth century created a novel emergence of moral consciousness against slavery that is itself an accomplishment to the realization that some of the Founders were far more willing than others to trace out the full implications of that growing consciousness and to engage in more aggressive acts to eradicate slavery. Individual judgments about individual Founders will necessarily enhance the reputations of some (such as Gouverneur Morris) but lower those of others (including Thomas Jefferson). This process is ongoing and can be constructive if it further enhances our understanding of the range of ways that slavery was abided and opposed.

Questions concerning whether scholars should act as moral critics and questions about the proper standards for judgment are difficult and lend themselves to controversial answers, but they are nevertheless straightforward and specific. In contrast, the process of actually setting forth moral judgments about particular Founders or about the Founders collectively requires the articulation of a general theory of moral responsibility, or at least assumptions about the proper answers to the numerous issues that underlie such a theory. Here much work needs to be done. If scholars have debated the questions "how democratic is the Constitution?" and "is the Founders' political thought best understood as a species of liberalism or republicanism?" with little attention to and self-consciousness about the protean character of democracy, republicanism, and liberalism, then their efforts to judge the Founders for slavery have been positively bereft of efforts to articulate and defend a general theory of blameworthiness. Instead, we have relied on our basic moral intuitions but failed to examine the broader framework that underlies and informs those intuitions.

At minimum, a theory of moral responsibility and blameworthiness needs to address a series of questions. Has the historical agent performed a wrong act? Did he or she know that this act was wrong? Was the act generated by bad motives? Was it done voluntarily? What other options were open to the historical agent? What actions constitute supererogatory acts? How should inaction be judged?[234] Fortunately, the first two of these questions can be readily settled. A few scholars continue to try to exonerate the Founders by arguing that slavery was ubiquitous and morally accepted during their lifetimes. Unfortunately for these scholars, the more salient fact is that none of the elite Founders believed that slavery was morally acceptable, and each explicitly acknowledged its evil character. The acceptance of this generalization by scholars, in turn, has meant that debates over moral responsibility have revolved around questions about the Founders' motives, the range of choices open to them, and whether we should emphasize what they achieved or what was left undone. To a lesser but still significant degree, these debates have also revolved around how the Founders treated their slaves and how this question bears on the Founders' moral character.

On these issues, the discussion above points to the following recommendations. First, at this point in this debate, crude and reductionistic statements about the motives of the Founders are no longer convincing. Founding scholars must move beyond simplistic statements such as "the Founders did not eradicate slavery because they wanted to live lavish lifestyles" or, conversely, that they maintained slavery because "union was in the balance." Scholars have now established that the Founders' motives were rarely singular, unmixed, or even necessarily coherent and rational. Fortunately, we now have exemplary studies such as Peter Onuf's complex analysis of Jefferson's *agon* with slavery and Henry Wiencek's story of Washington's evolution from typical slaveholder to emancipator that begin to balance and explain the kaleidoscope of motives and cross pressures that governed the Founders' evolving positions and actions on slavery.

Second, scholars need to explicitly address the equally ticklish question of the relative importance of the Founders' intentions versus the effects of their ideas and actions. Too often, scholars have bounced back and forth between analyses of the Founders' intentions and the effects of their laws and policies, depending on which factor serves the purpose of either prosecuting or vindicating the Founders. Even Don Fehrenbacher, who is otherwise consistently logical, falls into this error. In the course of his argument that the original Constitution was not pro-slavery, for example, he makes much of the effect of the 1808 slave trade provision in creating a target date for the abolishment of the slave trade, even though there is no evidence that this was intended by the Framers or even discussed at the Constitutional Convention. In his treatment of the fugitive slave clause, however, he forcefully argues that later enactments by Congress that gave the national government supervisory power over the capture of fugitive slaves were not intended by the Founders or explicitly authorized by the original understanding of the Constitution. The Founders, he thus concludes, cannot be held accountable for this development. In short, then, Fehrenbacher dismisses the unintended effects of constitutional provisions and their subsequent course when they support a pro-slavery interpretation, but emphasizes them when they point to the opposite conclusion.[235] Conversely, as emphasized above, Finkelman excoriates Jefferson when his intentions are pro-slavery, but then examines the futility of his proposals if his intentions were clearly anti-slavery. In each case, his goal is to blame Jefferson. Most importantly, scholars should be held accountable for explicitly explaining how they judge intentions and effects and for exploring and establishing their understanding of the contours of foreseeability.

Third, discussions of the options open to the Founders in eradicating slavery or limiting its spread bear directly on the question of whether the Founders acted on the basis of necessity or coercion, and thus on the question of moral responsibility. Vindicators have most often insisted that had the Framers not accepted the concessions to slavery demanded at the convention, especially by South Carolinians, that the union would have dissolved. Prosecutors have countered that more could have been done to expedite the elimination of slavery, limit its spread, and diminish the power of slaveholders without substantially risking union.[236] One problem with the effort to suggest that the Framers acted out of necessity is that some of the concessions made at the Constitutional Convention, especially the enactment of the fugitive slave clause and perhaps even the 1808 slave trade provision, were not conditions of continuing the debate. Conversely, proponents of the proposition that the Founders' options were much wider than often suggested have boldly challenged the observations of the historical participants themselves who found their options quite limited.

At this point, we need a much more careful consideration of the proper use of historical counterfactuals. To be sure, historical counterfactuals are necessary and useful tools for scholars, especially as heuristic devices. But few efforts have been made to distinguish the conditions under which they are responsibly made and illuminating from those in which they are merely argument-stopping fictions. One of the few historians to discuss explicitly the proper contours of historical counterfactuals is University of Virginia historian Allan Megill. Megill makes an important distinction between two types of counterfactual history, "restrained" and "exuberant," that should be introduced into this debate. Restrained counterfactual history, according to Megill, "involves an explicit canvassing of alternative possibilities that existed in a real past." The proponent of this kind of historical counterfactual offers speculations but is "pinned down by what actually did happen in the end." This historian searches in the past for actual historical alternatives that were planned or being executed and asks how things might have turned out differently than they did. In contrast, exuberant counterfactual history "deals in past historical outcomes that never in fact came to be true." Like scholars engaged in restrained historical counterfactualism, scholars using exuberant historical counterfactuals also begin at a real, pivotal historical moment. They, however, speculate into the future about an imaginary event that never took place. In short, proponents of restrained counterfactual history move back in time from an event that took place, ask how some other outcome might have happened, and do so on the basis of concrete historical evidence. Proponents of exuberant counterfactual history move forward in time guided by speculation.[237] What is important here is that the proponents in the debate on moral responsibility and slavery have engaged in exuberant historical counterfactuals. Prosecutors speculate that proponents of slavery would have backed down in such a battle of chicken; vindicators suppose that the union would have broken apart. Both groups project from the convention into the future and confidently assert that they know what would have happened if opponents of slavery had taken a stand. Neither group, however, can know any such thing.

Fourth, in addition to more carefully considering the use of historical counterfactuals, scholars also need to assess the numerous studies of the slave system that have been written since the 1960s, not only with an eye toward how they illuminate the choices open to the Founders, but also to consider how the existence of this system should affect our moral judgments. Is it true, as Garry Wills has charged, that no large-scale political career was open to Southerners who refused to defend the slave system?[238] Equally important, if this is indeed true should it mitigate our judgments of political leaders who defended the system? Conversely, should we conclude that they should have opted out of the system altogether? What do multiple stories of private emancipation tell us about the obstacles that slaveholders had to the release of their slaves? What do we know about the subsequent histories of released slaves? Did released slaves in fact face situations in which they were unable to care for themselves? Most broadly, how do we treat the Founders' own efforts to blame the slave system?[239]

Fifth, this debate needs to be informed by much more explicit conversations about supererogatory acts and how inaction, especially by men in positions of power, should be addressed. Henry Wiencek has forcefully argued that George Washington's decision to free his slaves set a new standard by which all of the Founders should be judged. Wiencek's claim, however, is hardly self-evident, especially if private manumissions are considered supererogatory acts. At any rate, multiple stories should establish a range of responses among the Founders to slavery, from the most heroic to the most despicable, and thus help scholars think about what actions were morally extraordinary. An independent justification will then be necessary to establish which of these actions provide the proper standard for judging the other Founders. On the other end of the spectrum, scholars need to address a host of equally difficult questions about the conditions under which inaction should be morally culpable. These questions are perhaps most evident in the judgments that have been given of Thomas Jefferson's infamous silence after 1790 on the issue of slavery.

Addressing these specific points and constructing a more general theory of slavery and moral responsibility should raise scholars' consciousness as they engage what Wiencek has called "the moral maze of slavery."[240] Most broadly, it should also put us in a better position to weigh and perhaps even reconcile the accounts of prosecutors who have suggested that the Founders did too little to address the injustices of slavery and inequality against the accounts of vindicators who suggest that they did quite a lot. Situating the Founders in their own time and bringing both their accomplishments and failures into view at once opens the possibility for recognizing that some of them did quite a lot to counter the injustices of their time (more, indeed, than the immediate generation that followed them), but that those efforts of course did not prove to be enough to abolish slavery.

Together, the specific points above suggest that we will develop more responsible moral judgments of the Founders when either historians immerse themselves in moral philosophy or when moral philosophers develop a tactile knowledge of slavery in eighteenth-century America and teach us how to think through these issues. Such a convergence is unlikely, but nothing less will do.

6

Taking Historiography Seriously

Running men out of town on a rail is at least as much an American
tradition as declaring inalienable rights.

Garry Wills

Is American historiography incurably foundationalist, a search for the
true principles on which the republic was founded, so that any attempt
to see the foundation as inherently debatable is inevitably presented as a
new (and false) foundationalism?

J. G. A. Pocock

In the early 1990s I submitted a proposal to form a panel on
the political thought of the American Founding at the Midwest Political Science Association's annual meeting. The proposal, which
was generically entitled "The History and Historiography of the
American Founding," suggested a panel based upon three essays.
Two of them analyzed recent trends in the historiography of the
American Founding; the other examined the political thought of
Alexander Hamilton. Several months later the chair of the political
theory section—a major scholar in the field—called to tell me the results. There was no space on the program, he explained, for the two
historiographical essays, but the paper on the political thought of
Alexander Hamilton had been accepted and placed on a separate
panel. The "merely" historiographical essays were not as important
as the analysis of a political thinker. The essay on Hamilton, he continued, was political theory. Historiographical essays were second-
order analysis. When I pressed him on the soundness of this distinction and his judgment about its implications, the conversation
ended with a bald assertion. "Look," he barked. "I have to have some
basis on which to make distinctions, and this is a common one."

Although this was hardly my first experience with prejudices about the secondary status of historiography, it was the most blunt. Historiography, I have learned, is the Rodney Dangerfield of academic analysis: it gets no respect. So why engage in it? Why should we examine the study of the Founding when we can directly interpret the writings of the Founders? Why analyze confrontations among contemporary scholars when academic reputations are made by interpreting the political thinkers themselves—or even better, by constructing grand theory? In particular, of what significance are the historiographical debates and revisions examined in this book, and of what relevance are they to contemporary debates in American politics and political theory?

Part of the answer to these questions, as I suggested in the introduction, lies in the desire to remain as conscious as possible about the assumptions underlying our interpretations of the Founders' writings and some of the key concepts in our political vocabulary. After graduate school, few scholars go back to challenge the methodological assumptions and intellectual frameworks underlying the approach that they have adopted. Furthermore, whatever they claim, even fewer scholars operate outside the contours of the conventional intellectual frameworks that are both the product and progenitor of scholarship.

One of the broadest purposes of this book has been to make the assumptions underlying conflicting schools of interpretation and approaches evident. Such an exercise challenges us to reconsider whether we have made the right methodological choices. It also challenges us to look at the intellectual frameworks that inform our interpretations in and of themselves. It thus should also force us to reflect deeply about and perhaps challenge the assumptions on which our interpretations of the writings of the American Founders rest. Similarly, when done properly, historiography should lead us into a fruitful exploration of the variety of meanings of key concepts such as liberalism, republicanism, democracy, and interest. Much of this book has been spent trying to uncover the assumptions that scholars have about the meanings of these terms and to decide not simply which of these meanings is more faithful to the Founders, but also which of them is the best understanding of the characteristics of that concept. For these reasons, when historiography is pursued seriously, it can be *more* fundamental than direct interpretation of historical thinkers because it can lead us to examine the assumptions on which we *begin* interpretation of those writings.

If we move from the defense of the study of historiography in general to questions about why the particular confrontations in this book are worth reconsidering, answers are also easily supplied. First, these confrontations have been among the most important debates in the academy in the twentieth and now the twenty-first centuries and are reflected in and affect still broader debates. For example, the debate between Beard and the heirs to the Progressive tradition with their critics over the economic interests of the Founders, the character of the American political system, and the value of studying the ideas of the Founders is also part of a broader debate over the continuing viability and legitimacy of the Constitution and the political system that it created. This debate also raises fundamental questions about how we ascertain motives, what role an analysis of motives should play in our scholarship, and the possibilities and limitations of empirical analysis. In its most sophisticated formulation, the debate over whether the political thought of the Founders was best characterized as a species of liberalism or republicanism is a debate about the Founders' conception of human nature (about whether they conceived of man as a political animal and believed that virtue was necessary for the sustenance of the republic), what they understood the proper ends of government to be, and ultimately the defining characteristics of the American character. Finally, the debate between the linguistic contextualists and their "great books" opponents is nothing less than a debate about the relationship of philosophy and history.

Broadly speaking, then, the positions that we take on these confrontations and even how we choose to answer them has and continues to have profound implications on other debates over American political development, American exceptionalism and identity, constitutional law and theory, and American politics. These historiographical debates continue to reflect and shape how we identify ourselves as a people, how we understand the nature and limitations of our political system, and whether we seek to defend, criticize, or reform it. Despite what many historians expect or would like, debates such as the liberalism-republicanism debate will never be simply historiographical or even historical debates.[1] They are, as Jean Bethke Elshtain has noted, "best understood as a contestation over the appropriation of tradition itself."[2]

Most important, however, analyzing the confrontations in this book should serve as a catalyst for thinking freshly and rigorously about some of the central topics in the study of the American Founding and the American political system. These include questions about the character of the Founders' political thought, its ultimate significance, the original design of the American political system and its effects on the development and practice of democracy in America, and the proper use of the Founders' ideas and their place in the American political system. I close with some additional observations about these four topics.

Searching for the Essence of the American Amalgam:
Which Traditions? Whose Multiple Traditions Approach?

The now solidified consensus that the Founders' political thought was a combination of liberalism, republicanism, and other traditions raises an important question: what kind of multiple traditions approach provides the best framework for interpreting the American Founding and for understanding the course of American political development? Should we adopt a multiple traditions approach that suggests that liberalism was pervasive, provided the organizing logic upon which other sets of ideas were integrated, and was thus the empirical center of American political thought, or should we adopt a multiple traditions approach that suggests that no single political tradition—even liberalism—has organized and ordered the others?

In addressing this question, the confrontation that I posed at the end of chapter 4 between Michael Zuckert and Rogers Smith is central.[3] As the debate over the intellectual origins of the American republic and the viability of Hartz's interpretation has spun out, Zuckert and Smith have set forth the two most sophisticated and challenging frameworks of interpretation. Their accounts should therefore be given a second and deeper examination and explicitly compared to determine the points where choices have to be made between them and where their insights might be constructively combined.

Zuckert, it will be remembered, has argued that the political thought of the American Founding and American political thought in general is best understood as an amalgam of Lockean natural rights philosophy, the common-law tradition of the rights of Englishmen, Protestant Christianity, and classical republicanism. Within this amalgam, according to Zuckert, natural rights philosophy has so far set the terms on which other ideologies can enter. This amalgam or partial synthesis interpretation, Zuckert further suggests, should be contrasted with a synthetic interpretation (such as St. Thomas Aquinas's integration of Aristotelian philosophy and Augustinian Christianity into a new and unique whole) and a jumble interpretation (where the ideas lie beside each other in their original form).[4] At the expense of mixing metaphors, in Zuckert's understanding of the American political tradition, liberalism is a large central piece to a complex puzzle, and the contours of this central piece determine the shape that the other pieces of the puzzle must assume in order to fit. The contours of both the central piece and the others remain visible to those who view it with a trained eye. Nevertheless, a "more or less coherent whole" is formed by their fusion.[5]

Zuckert tells multiple stories to illuminate the character of the American amalgam and to illustrate how the peripheral ideologies of common law, Protestant Christianity, and classical republicanism were reshaped by Lockean natural rights philosophy as they were brought into the American amalgam. For example, Zuckert examines how American Protestantism was transformed from original Puritan statements such as the Mayflower Compact and John Winthrop's classic sermon "A Modell of Christian Charity" to statements by eighteenth-century American clerics. The original settlement of colonial America during the seventeenth century by the Pilgrims and Puritans, according to Zuckert, was dedicated to the beliefs that God ordained men to be unequal and to inhabit different stations in life, to a search for the one true Protestant politics, to an effort to enforce a unity of religious belief, and in general to an explicit union of politics and religion.

By the eighteenth century, however, American clerics had given up the effort to establish a theocracy and were delivering sermons that illustrated a "Lockean conquest, or at least assimilation of Puritan political thought" by the natural rights philosophy. At this point, Locke became for eighteenth-century American clerics an oracle for the proper organization and function of the "earthly kingdom." Eighteenth-century American clerics, Zuckert maintains, integrated Lockean conceptions of toleration, equality, and natural theology; the origin, extent, and ends of government; and the right of resistance to authority. These same sermons, Zuckert observes, also appealed to scripture, announced the consequences of divine judgment, and discussed the role of religion in promoting sound politics and civic virtues. Eighteenth-century American clerics, however, did not Christianize Lockean political thought, but rather reinforced the normative positions of Lockean political philosophy with religious doctrine and rhetoric.[6]

Analysis such as this provides Zuckert with a basis for numerous insights into the course of American political development. In part, he finds the construction of the amalgam itself revealing of later developments. Zuckert observes, for example, that eighteenth-century American clerics who Lockeanized Protestantism, but who nevertheless did so in religious tones, paved the way for the adoption of a peculiar and enduring relationship between church and state. Here, governmental functions are secularized and religious belief for all is protected, but the secular sphere remains respectful of religious belief and recognizes its function in upholding civic order. Most important, however, Zuckert contends that the history of American political development can be explained by perceiving the tensions that occur when various elements within the American amalgam pull away from each other. Zuckert argues, for example, that the perennial conflict in American political life between the rights of individuals and minorities and the importance of democratic self-governance is an instance of the pulling away of elements within the American amalgam from each other.[7]

In contrast to Zuckert's analysis of American political thought as a liberal amalgam, Rogers Smith provides a multiple traditions interpretation that analyzes the interactions of three major traditions—republicanism, liberalism, and inegalitarian and ascriptive ideologies—while suggesting that none of these sets of ideas served as the framework on which others were organized. Smith's effort to establish the conceptual identity and independence of ascriptive and inegalitarian ideologies that includes sexist, racist, and nativist beliefs marks the most novel and controversial dimension of his interpretation and his most important difference with Zuckert. As observed in chapter 4, before Smith's work, most scholars had characterized these beliefs as mere prejudices or ephemeral ideologies held by estranged and backward people. Smith, however, argues that they must be considered as traditions of political thought alongside the liberal and republican beliefs that scholars often place at the center of the American creed.

The configuration of American political thought at any given moment, Smith further suggests, is the result of concrete and often immediate political imperatives. Political elites fashion together disparate and often contradictory ideas, according to Smith, to build broad and potent political coalitions. Illiberal and inegalitarian ideologies play a central role in this process of coalition building because they have attractions that the universalistic principles of liberalism do not. They allow politicians to appeal to the need that many individuals have to believe that they are a superior people chosen by God with special capabilities and commitments that ostensibly qualify them to rule on earth and achieve salvation upon death. Meanwhile, liberalism often provides a kind of inspirational ideology and aspirational rhetoric that reformers evoke.

Once we grasp the function that Smith attributes to illiberal and inegalitarian ideologies and his contention that they have deeply penetrated and persistently compromised American political thought, it becomes clear why it is impossible for him to think of liberalism as the central piece of a broader puzzle or to conceive of American political thought as a more or less coherent amalgam. It also becomes clear why he does not accept Whiggish narratives of the trajectory of American political thought, such as those suggested by Louis Hartz and his followers, or even aspects of Zuckert's sophisticated account of the path of American political development. To Smith, American political thought is not an amalgam but rather an unsteady symbiotic alliance of liberalism and rival ideologies. It is also centerless, amorphous, kaleidoscopic, and often self-contradictory and incoherent.

Smith certainly agrees with Zuckert that American political thought is riddled with tensions and that American political development can largely be explained by examining the conflicts that have arisen out of these tensions. Nevertheless, Smith does not believe that it will do to concentrate on the perennial conflict between the Jeffersonian commitment to expressive democracy and the Madisonian commitment to protecting individual rights and refining the public will, or even what has happened when the elements within the amalgam have pulled away from each other. Instead, Smith would have us examine the irreconcilable and contradictory commitments that Americans have made between the values of liberalism and the inegalitarian and illiberal ideologies that have subordinated and excluded many.

When American history is interpreted through the lens of this version of the multiple traditions approach, the American experience displays a "serpentine" path.[8] Civic reforms and victories for liberalism and equality, according to Smith's account, have come at great expense, and far from being inevitable or automatic, they have instead been most likely to occur when hegemonic groups (typically white Protestant men) have been politically vulnerable, such as during political crises and war. Moreover, Smith observes, proponents of civic exclusions have not always lost, and even when reforms have taken place, they have often been followed by periods of reaction and the articulation of inegalitarian ideologies designed principally to restore the previous hegemony.

There are significant areas of agreement in the interpretations of Smith and Zuckert. Most important, both defend liberalism and see it as the moral core of American political thought—or at least as a set of aspirations to which Americans should strive.[9] But there are also significant differences. Zuckert argues that liberalism has been the "cornerstone" or "senior partner" in American political thought and has provided the organizing logic around which other sets of ideas were assimilated into American political thought.[10] Smith, however, does not believe that American political thought can be said to have an empirical center or one set of ideas that was dominant and that shaped the terms on which others have been assimilated. Zuckert and Smith also disagree about which traditions of political thought should be included among the multiple traditions and in how these traditions relate to each other. These differences in turn lead to distinct—although not necessarily contradictory—understandings of the trajectory of American political development and different assessments of the strengths and weaknesses of the American Founding.

In assessing these differences, a threshold question emerges: should we accord conceptual identity to inegalitarian and ascriptive ideologies? If we agree with Smith that these sets of ideas comprise one or perhaps even several distinct traditions of American political thought, then we cannot say with Zuckert or any of the neoconsensualist scholars that liberalism (however intricately it is conceived) has been the cornerstone of American political thought or provided the organizing logic for incorporating other traditions of political thought. We will also unavoidably be led to examine the conflicts in American history between inegalitarian and ascriptive ideologies and America's liberal values and to account for the times when progressive-liberal reforms have been defeated.

There are at least three compelling reasons why we should follow Smith in according conceptual identity to inegalitarian and ascriptive ideologies. First, Smith has set forth plausible criteria for establishing what constitutes a tradition and ample evidence that racism, sexism, and nativism meet these criteria. Sets of ideas become traditions, Smith suggests, if they have widespread popularity and longevity; if they affect public policy; and if they are defended by leading intellectuals. The massive evidence presented in *Civic Ideals* establishes not only that inegalitarian and ascriptive ideologies meet these criteria, but also that these ideologies have existed throughout American history as a self-conscious or "explicit" tradition.[11]

Second, the identification of illiberal and inegalitarian ideologies provides an indispensable tool for understanding many of the intellectual positions of the Founders and the texts of the American Founding. To provide only a few famous examples, how are we to understand Jefferson's account in *Notes on the State of Virginia* of African American men as naturally passionate, foul smelling, and inferior in reason and imagination to whites but as a species of scientific racism? How also are we to understand James Wilson's tortured defense in his *Lectures on Law* of the exclusion of women from politics—even in the face of his declaration that women were neither less honest, virtuous, or wise than men—but as a "textbook account of the 'domestic sphere' of 'republican motherhood'?"[12]

Furthermore, as Smith has observed, even texts that are read as classic expressions of Lockean liberalism contain the use of illiberal ideologies to create broad and politically potent appeals. Tom Paine's *Common Sense*, for example, not only contains a classic denunciation of monarchy based on the principles of Lockean liberalism, but also attempts to spur Americans to revolution by suggesting that the ancient people of Israel, not the British, were the revolutionaries' forebears and that Americans, like the ancient Israelites, were God's chosen people.[13] Similarly, the Declaration of Independence not only contains the quintessential statement of the Lockean understanding of the origins and ends of government, but also grievances against the king for limiting Americans abilities to subordinate and exclude Native Americans.[14]

Third, Smith has established that inegalitarian and ascriptive ideologies were central in the construction of identities for many Americans, including women, African Americans, and Native Americans. In many cases, Smith observes, inegalitarian ideologies were foisted onto these groups to subordinate them and render them politically powerless. But it was also the case that many members of these groups adopted these same ascriptive ideas in their own self-identification. Many nineteenth- and even twentieth-century women, for example, defended the tenets of domestic sphere ideology and explained their lives on the basis of the propositions within it. In either case, for much of American history, individuals within these groups did not and really could not plausibly have explained their lives or constructed their identities on the basis of values of equality, individualism, democracy, and capitalism. There is thus no way that we can deny the existence of illiberal ideas or dismiss them as merely ephemeral prejudices (as opposed to recurring, highly structured, and sophisticated, if repulsive, modes of thought) without also diminishing the gravity of the injustices that they have been used to perpetuate, minimizing the difficulties that reformers have faced in fighting them, and diminishing the difficulties that minorities and women have faced in thrusting these sets of ideas off and reconstructing political identities that established their equality.

To suggest that we should acknowledge the importance of inegalitarian and ascriptive ideologies is not, however, to dismiss the considerable empirical strengths of Zuckert's multiple traditions approach or his insights into the course of American political development. As Zuckert has pointed out, unlike Smith, his approach more fully accounts for the positive influence of the common-law tradition in the establishment of respect for rights in the United States and the sweeping influence of religion in American political thought. The Whig tradition, Zuckert observes, "includes many of the commitments that remain central to American political life to this day," and religion was profoundly important at the Founding and continues to play "a deep and pervasive role" in America today.[15] Furthermore, Zuckert's suggestion that different traditions of political thought are transformed as they enter into combination with each other, his observations about the roots of contemporary church-state relations in America, and his contention that much political conflict in the United States has resulted from the tensions between Madisonian and Jeffersonian conceptions of democracy provide keen insight into the course of American political development and the character of American politics.

Most important, when liberalism, republicanism, the common-law tradition of the rights of Englishmen, Protestantism, and inegalitarian and ascriptive ideologies are included, a multiple traditions framework emerges that provides a powerful interpretive tool for identifying the variety of traditions that have been brought together within American political thought, for understanding the trajectory of American political development, and for analyzing the character of our political conflict. Indeed, a multiple traditions interpretation that integrates the empirical insights of Zuckert and Smith can also acknowledge the contributions of consensus history and the literature on American exceptionalism even as it envelops and moves beyond them.

In particular, a multiple traditions approach that includes the identification of racist, sexist, and nativist ideologies does nothing to diminish the power of Hartz's insight into how the hegemony of liberalism resulted from the absence of feudalism and precluded the development of socialist and Burkean traditions of political thought in the United States. Nor does such a recognition force us to abandon the very real insights that consensual frameworks have given us into the conservative character of the American Revolution, America's early and lasting embrace of capitalism, and the remarkable stability (with the exception of the Civil War) of American politics and society.[16] Finally, such an approach allows us to emphasize the dynamic, constructive, and aspirational quality of America's liberal principles, especially the role that our fundamental commitment to equality played in, for example, the woman's and civil rights movements while also acknowledging that victories for progressive causes have been tenuous and have often been followed by conservative counterrevolutions.[17]

Foundational Concepts and the Unionist Paradigm: The Continued Search for New Interpretive Categories

In addition to these continuing debates about the proper character of the multiple traditions approach, two new approaches to the study of the American Founding and American political thought in general have gained prominence since the publication of the first edition of this book that merit our consideration. These include James Ceaser's appeal for an analysis of foundational concepts and what has been called the federal interpretation or unionist paradigm. Ceaser's appeal for the study of foundational concepts represents a significant methodological challenge to approaching the study of American political thought through the use of traditions. Traditions, according to Ceaser, are "package[s] of ideas" or "prefabricated essences, such as liberalism, republicanism, or Anglo-Protestantism, that analysts have imported from the outside in order to organize and make sense of the disparate ideas of American political life." These traditions are said to define the polity and set "the boundaries within which political discourse takes place."[18] As the language in his description suggests, Ceaser worries that the interpretation of texts through the prism of scholarly constructs—often organized around the present concerns and presuppositions of contemporary interpreters—ignores the concepts that historical actors themselves used, may misunderstand the connections between ideas within their political thought, and cannot serve as a meaningful scheme of classification, in part because proponents cannot adequately account for changes within traditions. The liberal tradition, Ceaser observes, has been used to refer to both the Founders' natural rights liberalism and the liberalism of nonfoundationalist thinkers such as Richard Rorty, even though elements of these two systems of political thought fundamentally contradict each other. Furthermore, traditions are hardly static. "If the parts of the tradition change," he asks, "at what point does it cease to be the same thing?"[19]

Instead of interpreting political thought by imposing traditions onto the political discourse of historical actors, Ceaser proposes that scholars turn their focus to the study of foundational concepts and adopt an approach that involves only the "gentlest intervention of the researcher" and allows "links among the different levels of ideas to emerge as a result of the inquiry itself, rather than to be designated beforehand as an intrinsic property of a tradition."[20] A foundational concept, Ceaser argues, is an idea "offered in political discourse as a first cause or ultimate justification for a general political position or orientation. It is usually presented as requiring no further argument, since it is thought to contain within itself its first premise. It supplies the answer to the question 'Why,' beyond which any further response is thought unnecessary."[21] Foundational concepts, then, are claims about a proper standard of right and wrong. Still, they are not simply the province of philosophers or important only as claims about political truth. Instead, they are "encountered as tangible political phenomena that are in play in the practical political world" and are important collectively because they establish authoritative standards for the whole community and serve as means of mobilizing citizens to action.[22]

Foundational concepts, Ceaser continues, commonly take three forms: appeals to nature, appeals to history, or appeals to religion or faith. Appeals to nature as the standard of political right provide a "justification by reference to something in the structure of reality as it can be accessed by reason."[23] Various forms of appeals to nature from Darwinists and sociobiologists have been made in the course of American history, Ceaser observes, but the understanding of nature "as referring to something unchanging or permanent" provided in the Declaration of Independence has had a "privileged status" in political discourse.[24] By a foundation in history, Ceaser does not mean those instances in which political actors find or ground political first principles in ordinary narrative or analytic history. Rather, he means that historical foundations that are appeals either to something that is held to be sacred because it conforms to a deeply held tradition, or appeals to a principle because it conforms to the direction of history. Finally, appeals to religion or faith as a standard of right refer, for example, to deductions from biblical texts that establish a principle (such as "democratic government is verified by faith") or that attempt to establish that certain principles are consistent with God's plan or Providence. This classification of foundational statements, Ceaser hastens to add, is not mutually exclusive. Foundational appeals frequently do not fit neatly into one of these three categories, but rather are confused or deliberately mixed by political actors for a variety of purposes.

Concretely, Ceaser's approach would require scholars to consider the public intellectuals who "import them [foundational concepts] into political discussion and the theorists and philosophers, perhaps far removed from ordinary politics, who are their originators."[25] Scholars would also examine the different iterations of foundational concepts adopted by specific statesmen, political parties, and political movements, the different groundings that these actors gave to foundational concepts, and the consequences of the adoption of particular foundational concepts. Most broadly, scholars adopting this approach would set the various answers to these questions given by historical actors into a broader conversation with others to create a Platonic dialogue about foundations itself.

Ceaser contends that this would be a more substantive, useful, engaging, and historically accurate approach to the study of American political thought than the imposition of traditions. First, it might prove useful in establishing causal connections between foundational concepts and major events and subsequent thought. Scholars might be able to show direct connections between foundational concepts (the concept of nature in the Declaration of Independence) and major events (the American Revolution). They might also be able to show less direct and immediate but perhaps even more profound effects of foundational concepts (a concept of nature held by the Revolutionaries did not cause the Revolution, but "the strength of the concept grew in the wake of the Revolution and in turn altered much of American politics and the history of the West").[26] Second, the study of foundations might supply political actors who formulate ideas to try to influence political life with a "framework to help guide their reflections" about the selection of foundational concepts and the likely consequences of their adoption. This would replace the "haphazard mix of musings" that currently characterizes efforts by intellectuals to construct a public philosophy.[27] Third, the comparative study of the meaning, grounding, and consequences of foundational ideas could serve as a means of furthering our understanding of the foundational concepts in and of themselves and ultimately for better understanding nature, history, and religion. The debate between advocates of foundational concepts and antifoundational thinkers, Ceaser argues, is the most important debate in politics today. Studying the role and performance of foundational concepts in political discourse promises to provide us with a rich basis for addressing this question.

Proponents of the study of political thought through the use of languages and traditions may protest that they adopted this approach in the first place in search of genuinely historical methodology. Certainly, Pocock, Quentin Skinner, and the Cambridge school of linguistic contextualists have written painstakingly about the importance of studying political languages as a prophylactic against attributing to past political actors thoughts that they could not have held.[28] To be sure, however, Ceaser is correct: many political theorists continue to lose touch with the ideas of the historical actors that they interpret because they approach them through the analysis of preconceived interpretive constructs and mine the political discourse of the past in search of intellectual ammunition in what Rogers Smith has aptly called the battle of "warring isms."[29]

Will the study of foundational concepts provide a more historically sound methodology? What effect would it have on Founding studies? With regard to the first question, there is certainly no guarantee that scholars will transcend present prejudices by pursuing foundational concepts. There is no reason to believe that scholars reconstructing debates about fundamental concepts are more impartial than those using other methods, or that they are any less susceptible to interpreting those debates in terms of our contemporary concerns. The accurate reconstruction of the political thought of historical actors depends on adherence to sound historical methods, including good-faith efforts to first reconstruct the thought of political actors on its own terms, and only then to criticize and appropriate it. Whether we search in the political discourse of the past for traditions or foundational concepts, we need to move in a process—akin to John Rawls's reflective equilibrium—in which we move back and forth between the analytic labels that we give to broad systems of political thought and the specific idioms that compose those schemes until we have a tight fit between our analytic constructs and the idioms that we identify with them. Furthermore, it is hard to see how an analysis centered on foundational concepts will create an impartial forum for a debate about the merits and problems of foundationalism versus antifoundationalism. Instead, it seems more likely that a study of foundations would be conducted by scholars who, like Ceaser, are sympathetic to foundational thinking. It also seems likely that moving the study of foundational concepts to the center would create a prejudice in their favor.

With this said, Ceaser is correct to say that "observation and common sense already indicates that foundational ideas are of sufficient importance to merit attention and analysis."[30] Certainly, the American Founding is unusually rich in foundational concepts and statements, and the study of such statements in the early republic—although hardly neglected in previous studies—should nevertheless be illuminating. Comparing the foundational concepts of the American Founders and their grounding and consequences with those adopted by later thinkers holds out the promise of further establishing the distinctiveness and significance of the Founding as a historical moment. It might also lead us to mature reflections about whether foundational concepts from the Founding such as Jefferson's statements in the Declaration of Independence merit the privileged status that Ceaser rightly suggests that they have.[31]

Experimentation with the study of foundational concepts has at least the possibility of creating genuine independence from studies that examine different traditions of American political thought and kick-starting debates over the intellectual origins and character of the American political tradition. Scholars would no longer be searching for an alternative tradition to liberalism—a quest that has paradoxically reinforced liberalism as the default tradition of American political thought. Instead, we would have a new fundamental category to analyze political discourse. Admittedly elitist, it would focus on great thinkers thinking about central issues. Although it is hard to see how this category could integrate the insights of the Progressives, the exploration of the meaning, grounding, and consequences of foundational concepts would also certainly provide a different perspective to the relative importance of liberal, republican, Christian, and ascriptive ideas in American political discourse and would further illuminate their roles and interactions.

A second promising approach to the study of the American Founding that merits extensive consideration has been called the unionist paradigm or the federal interpretation.[32] Articulated by, among other scholars, John Phillip Reid, Jack P. Greene, David Armitage, Max Edling, and Lance Banning, this interpretation has been most comprehensively advanced by David Hendrickson and Peter Onuf, who have forcefully argued for it as an alternative historiographical tradition in the American Founding. The methodology underlying much of the work in this interpretive paradigm is best described as critical conceptual history. Proponents of critical conceptual history map the origins and transformations of political concepts—in this case, concepts such as *nation, empire, sovereignty,* but especially *union*—within the context of the events and conflicts in which they figured.[33]

The broadest and most important conclusion resulting from this research is that "the central problem in American political discourse from the imperial crisis through the Civil War was the definition of the federal union."[34] In their debates about the proper character of their union with Great Britain and then their successive efforts to create a more perfect union among the diverse American states after independence, American colonists, revolutionaries, constitution makers, and state builders, according to proponents of the unionist interpretation, dealt with essentially the same set of issues of sovereignty, burden sharing, and representation. They also engaged in conversations about and historical investigations into why particular political associations had held together or broken apart, considered whether these associations threatened or preserved important values in the law of nations, and debated whether the American states needed to be firmly associated or would be naturally peaceable because of their commercial and democratic character. The unionist paradigm is the "stream of speculation" that Americans drew on and produced as they addressed these questions and attempted to define, create, and sustain a federal union.[35]

Attention to the Founders' discourse on federalism and concrete efforts to achieve union has given structure to a novel, comprehensive narrative of the American Founding that features bold reinterpretations of the American Revolution and the Declaration of Independence, the original purpose and character of the Constitution, and the various visions of empire and nationhood developed by leading Founders. In its portrayal of the American Revolution, this narrative subtly restates the idea of salutary neglect and stresses the importance of debates over constitutional principles in the American Revolution. Jack Greene in particular has argued that the British government lacked the resources and will to impose tight controls on American colonists, and thus that British authority in the colonies was never unified or complete. When British authorities attempted to rationalize administrative procedures in the colonies and imposed restrictions, colonists rebelled because such policies disrupted the colonists' expectations of self-governance, insulted their sense of identity as British citizens, and ran in the face of their previously negotiated relationships with Parliament and the Crown.[36] According to John Phillip Reid, the colonists, angered by these policies, evoked their traditional rights as British citizens and became fastened to a thoroughly traditional interpretation of the British constitution. Within this interpretation, American colonists eventually claimed the right to legislate for themselves, independent of the control of Parliament. Still, they did not declare independence until it became clear that the Crown would never recognize this understanding of union.[37]

The American Declaration of Independence that secured separation from Great Britain, according to David Armitage, is best understood as a statement performed in the language of *jus gentium* (the law of nations) rather than *jus civile* (civil law).[38] Scholars who have interpreted the Declaration of Independence as a timeless and universal statement about human rights or a statement of fundamental political right meant to inform domestic policies, Armitage argues, have anachronistically neglected its diplomatic, strategic, and international purpose as a speech act, communicating the fact of the colonies' independence to the world as it simultaneously performed that act. The Declaration's primary audience, Armitage maintains, was other nations, and its original purposes were to announce the arrival of this new actor on the world stage and to establish that the United States had the right to exercise the powers possessed by all independent states, including levying war, concluding peace, regulating commerce, and forming alliances.

When proponents of the unionist paradigm move forward from the Revolution, they emphasize the myriad of local, regional, and sectional loyalties that diminished the prospects for union; they thus resist imposing a national framework onto studies of the formation of the early republic. They also emphasize Americans' fears that a European state system with standing armies, perpetual debts, and unending conflicts would be established in North America, and the numerous security problems that these threats and foreign intervention in North America posed. Yet another point these scholars have stressed is the continuity of debates between the Revolution and the formation of the Constitution over sovereignty, the fair distribution of benefits and burdens among the member states, the proper foundation and conception of representation, and most broadly the proper relationship of the center of the union to its peripheries.

Attention to these concerns of interstate relations, national security, and state building rather than problems within the state governments before the formation of the Constitution has led proponents of the unionist paradigm to offer a novel reading of the goals of constitutional reform in the 1780s and of the original purposes of the American Constitution. After the Revolution, Americans, according to proponents of the unionist paradigm, naturally chose a loose-jointed union that gave power to the peripheries in order not to recreate the tyranny of the center that had led to the Revolution. Soon, however, centripetal forces—especially sectional conflicts over the future of western lands, debt, finance, trade, and frontier disorders—led Americans to reconsider the proper character of the union that they had created. Fearing civil war, foreign intervention, and the establishment of a European state system with monarchs and standing armies in North America, Americans had to face the realities of the international system that they sought to join and the imperatives of state building. These realities led the Framers of the Constitution to draft and secure the ratification for a new constitution that established a powerful national government that had unlimited power to tax its citizens and raise a standing army. Ratification of this military-fiscal state, however, was a particularly ticklish problem because of the intense current of antistatism in the American political tradition. Champions of the Constitution solved this problem through the use of creative statesmanship—especially federalism and the use of indirect sources of revenue raising—that made this powerful government nevertheless function invisibly among the citizenry. Even more broadly, the significance of the original Constitution was not so much that it marked a transition from a politics of virtue to one of interest, or even that it reconciled majority rule with the protection of individual rights through the creation of a republic of unprecedented length. Considered from a broad geopolitical perspective and a long historical one, the 1787 Constitution represented nothing less, David Hendrickson has argued, than a peace pact between the states akin to the great peace settlements in European history.[39]

Finally, proponents of the unionist paradigm have identified the various visions of empire and union held by leading Founders and explored how sectional conflicts from the Founding era were projected into antebellum America and culminated in the Civil War. Scholars of the unionist paradigm have explored Jefferson's vision of an expanding empire of liberty made up of a federal union of self-governing republics tied together through cords of harmonious interests, common principles, and love of republican principles, Hamilton's vision of a commercial-manufacturing republic able to command respect at home and abroad because it was anchored in an energetic government and protected by a strong army and navy, and Madison's vision of a true federal union in which the national government was supreme within its sphere but states retained their sovereignty.[40] Proponents of this approach have also established that sectional conflicts were always on the front burner in American politics, and that disunion was an omnipresent possibility. Indeed, considered from this perspective, proponents of the unionist paradigm find it more remarkable that the American union stayed together for as long as it did rather than that it eventually split apart.

Scholarship produced by proponents of the unionist paradigm has already made significant contributions to the study of the American Founding and seems on its way, as one reviewer put it, to becoming "the next big thing."[41] Most importantly, these scholars have identified a new paradigm of political thought based on political writings from the Founding era and a new set of problematics that have previously been slighted. The languages of common law and international law, proponents of the unionist paradigm have established, provided a diverse and rich fund of ideas for Americans to address problems of interstate relations and national security. By placing the dialogues of the American Founding in a geopolitical context and focusing on the security issues that the Founding generation faced, proponents of this interpretation have also turned scholars away from abstract concerns about whether liberalism, republicanism, or some mixture of these and other ideologies were central in the American Founding and back to the concrete and pressing problems faced by that generation, including the proper character of their union with Great Britain, how to achieve peace between the states, how to protect the United States from external threats, and how to raise money and arms for these purposes. Paradoxically, in doing so, they may well have also provided a key to understanding the terms on which the Founders brought together multiple traditions of political thought. Concisely put, the unionist paradigm makes it possible to understand how solving the various problems of union led the Founders to draw on and put to work a multiplicity of intellectual traditions.

In addition to possibly providing a new framework for the multiple traditions approach, the unionist paradigm also represents an important alternative to standard progressive, liberal, and republican interpretations of the American Founding. Proponents of the progressive and neo-Progressive interpretations of the Founding have stressed the importance of economic interests as a cause of the American Revolution and contended that the revolution over home rule was paralleled by an equally important social revolution among the colonists about who should rule at home. For their part, proponents of American exceptionalism and the liberal interpretation of the American Founding have often suggested that the United States was initially insulated from foreign intervention by the Atlantic, that American political culture was naturally immunized by the terms of its settlement from monarchs and standing armies, and that the American state was still-born and limited, providing only a framework for the protection of rights and the accommodation of interests. Meanwhile, proponents of republican interpretations, led by Bernard Bailyn, have suggested that the American colonists reacted to the imposition of British authority in the colonies after 1763 with a frenzied, paranoid, and implausible response that could only be explained by examining the influence of English opposition ideology on the colonists' thinking.

In contrast to both the Progressive and republican interpretations of the Revolution, proponents of the unionist paradigm have presented the provocative interpretations that constitutional principles mattered gravely in the Revolution, that the colonists' case based on these principles was conservative and entirely plausible, and that if we hope to understand the Revolution, we need to focus first on its transatlantic and geopolitical character, not the internal disputes that accompanied it. In contrast to American exceptionalism and the liberal interpretation, scholars of the federal interpretation have established that Americans were not provincials, but rather squarely in the middle and capable of holding their own in continental dialogues within the peace plan tradition and transatlantic debates about the rights of Englishmen. The unionist paradigm further challenges American exceptionalism by historicizing it and thereby suggesting both its limitations and insights. Americans, as Max Edling in particular has established, were not able to avoid the implications of European state building. The imperatives of national security—defense of the American state from enemies abroad and the threat of civil war from within—meant that the Americans, like their European counterparts, had to create a national government that included the unlimited power to tax and raise an army. In another sense, however, the federal interpretation subtly reinforces American exceptionalism by suggesting that the American Founders—especially the architects and defenders of the American Constitution—were acutely aware of the insularity and exceptional status of American society and the conditional character of that status. Union, defenders of the Constitution came to realize, was the necessary condition for Americans' immunity to the introduction of expanding monarchies and the European state system within North America.

On the Founders' Contribution to the History of Political Thought

In addition to questions about the intellectual origins of the American republic, a second set of questions that emerge from this study concerns the significance of the political thought of the American Founding. What are the strengths and weaknesses of the Founders' political thought? Did the

Founders set forth a novel conception of human flourishing or make any enduring contributions to the history of political thought?

Here, recent scholarship has established the importance and enduring appeal of one quality of the Founders' political thought (its complexity and multiple goals), reenforced another (its resiliency and realism), and pointed toward three additional ones (the Founders' insights into the relationship between power and liberty, the sophisticated relationship between interest and virtue embedded in the institutional design of the American political system, and the Founders' contribution to international relations theory). Together, these qualities suggest that the Founders' political thought merits the most serious consideration of all students of the history of political thought.[42]

The first of these qualities—the complexity and diverse goals of the Founders—is in some ways the corollary of the observation that their political thought was capacious and synthetic. The Founders drew from many intellectual traditions because they sought to balance many commitments, address many problems, and achieve many goals. Most prominently, the Founders sought to balance power with liberty and local and partial interests with the common interest. They also sought to reconcile majority rule with the protection of individual rights, prevent excessive centralization in the national government yet simultaneously control the centrifugal tendencies of the states, and explain how self-interested individuals could be brought to have allegiance to the national government in a nation of unprecedented size. Furthermore, the political system that they formulated was concerned not simply with preserving liberty, but also with promoting stability, energy, and impartial administration.

To achieve these goals, specific sets of ideas were employed to serve specific purposes, creating a tension-ridden configuration of political thought. Liberalism justified the Founders' commitments to natural equality, natural rights, and governments based on the consent of the governed. English opposition ideology expressed the Founders' profound and lingering distrust of undue governmental power. Many of the Founders explained how self-interested individuals would be led to support the newly formed national government by turning to the idea—drawn from Scottish moral sense philosophy—that a sentiment of allegiance had to be fostered. This could be achieved, Federalists in particular argued, if the national government was soundly administered.[43] In general, the republican commitment to the promotion of the common interest was balanced against the liberal goal of protecting individual rights.

Second, the conception of political thought and the political system that was produced by this synthesis has proven to be resilient and realistic. Typically, the resiliency and realism of the American Founding is established by contrasting it with the excesses of the French Revolution. The American Revolution is said to be "a revolution of sober expectations," in contrast to the French Revolution, which is said to have been premised on a misguided effort to create mass fraternity and to transform the human condition.[44] Peter Onuf has recently made this point succinctly. "The American founders," Onuf observes, "are celebrated for their gritty realism, for their immunity to the utopian aspirations that corrupted and destroyed the French Revolution. The Americans' revolutionary optimism was predicated, not on the exercise, but on the restraint of power."[45]

This insight can also be extended to include the claim that the Founders' political thought stands as a testament against the errors and evils of utopianism and totalitarianism, ancient and modern. In general, the Founders found "impracticable" and unacceptable the goal of trying to give to "every citizen the same opinions, the same passions, and the same interests" and expanded toleration (especially religious toleration) to dimensions that had not previously been achieved.[46] Furthermore, unlike classical republicanism, the Founders' political thought did not rest on what Jean Bethke Elshtain has called "armed civic virtue"—the dangerous proposition that the city-state should have complete control of human bodies for the purposes of labor, procreation, and war.[47] Unlike Marxism, the Founders' natural rights republicanism was not rooted in the belief in a socially constituted self or in the natural progression of history and society toward an Eden of unlimited abundance or human perfectibility. The Founders seemed to have almost universally believed that partiality and selfishness and thus faction were "sown in the nature of man," and that conflicts between individuals and nations were an enduring feature of the human condition.[48] Furthermore, although some of the Founders began to absorb the principles of libertarianism into their conceptions of political economy, few of them accepted the equally utopian proposition that spontaneous harmony emerges from the magical workings of an invisible hand if self-interest is simply given room for fair play.

Third, the American Revolution and their subsequent experience with government under the Articles of Confederation and within the states led the Founders to develop a unique and profound understanding of the proper relationship of power and liberty. Put briefly, as the historians of the republican synthesis have established, Americans began their revolution with the assumption that governmental power was aggressive, expansive, and inherently antagonistic to liberty. As they took up the process of self-government, and in particular as they experienced government under the impotent Articles of Confederation and within the states during the mid-1780s, the Framers of the Constitution in particular came to realize that during the Revolution, they had focused inordinately on the threat to liberty that was posed by excessive governmental power, and they had not paid enough attention to the threats posed by inadequate governmental power, poor institutional design, and majority tyranny. In 1788, James Madison wrote,

> It has been remarked that there is a tendency in all Governments to an augmentation of power at the expense of liberty. But the remark, as usually understood, does not appear to me well founded. Power, when it has attained a certain degree of energy and independence, goes on generally to further degrees. But when below that degree, the direct tendency is to further degrees of relaxation, until the abuses of liberty beget a sudden transition to an undue degree of power. With this explanation the remark may be true; and in the latter sense only is it, in my opinion, applicable to the existing Governments in America. It is a melancholy reflection that liberty should be equally exposed to danger whether the Government have too much or too little power, and that this line which divides these extremes should be so inaccurately defined by experience.

"Wherever the real power in a Government lies," Madison also contended, "there is the danger of oppression." In republican governments, the real power lies in the majority, and thus acts of oppression are most likely to spring from "acts in which the Government is the mere instrument of the major number of the Constituents," not from "acts of Government contrary to the sense of its constituents."[49] Once this realization was made, the Framers' goal became to strike the proper balance between power and liberty and to find the proper institutional design and divisions of power that were necessary to secure that balance of power and liberty. That search resulted in numerous variations on the theme of power and liberty that deserve consideration as conceptual contributions to the history of political thought.[50]

Finally, many scholars have argued that the Founders accepted liberal understandings of the ends and purposes of government and did not set forth a new or unique conception of human flourishing. They thus cannot be said to have been engaged in writing political theory in the grand sense, and their contributions to the history of political thought were little more than an exploration of the proper institutional implications of liberalism.

This interpretation, however, ignores their contributions to the development of federalism as a political concept, and more broadly the possibility that the originality and sophistication of the institutional design of the constitutional system of 1787 should be seen in and of itself as conceptual and theoretical accomplishments worthy of consideration as a contribution to the history of political thought. In general, the argument here is that the Founders established a novel conception of federalism, provided a resoundingly loud and clear voice in the history of political thought in favor of the proposition that institutions matter, and established institutions that rested on an astute and sophisticated understanding of the relationship of interest and virtue.

More specifically, the original institutional design of the American political system rests on a conception of revolutionary federalism that is itself a contribution to the history of political thought.[51] Within this system, the states retained no power to nullify acts made by the national government, but the powers of the national government were nevertheless also limited.[52] Second, this division of powers between the national government and the states has allowed for continuous interplay and contests between the desire of local communities to engage in self-determination and the protection to individual autonomy afforded by the national government.

To the Founders, the proposition that institutions matter was simply the common sense of the matter and suggested that institutional design is one of the most important determinants of the context in which politics is conducted. Institutions, the Founders held, were important in shaping political conflict and influencing how it was addressed and perhaps resolved, in affecting whether and how citizens responded to government, and most broadly in forming the political culture within a society. Having learned from Montesquieu that effective and enduring governments must reflect the spirit of their people, they also came to realize that governments could, to some degree, affect the political culture or spirit of the society.

Furthermore, the original design of the American political system rested on an astute differentiation and analysis of the capabilities of the electorate and representatives and the different motives that govern their behavior, on a novel and perhaps even compelling understanding of the relationship of context, interest, virtue, and constitutional design to behavior, and on an equally compelling understanding of the possibilities of leadership and of systems of checks and balances necessary to control leaders. In particular, the authors of *The Federalist* believed that the motives of enlightened statesmen would often be quite different from those of ordinary citizens, and also that rulers were capable of recognizing and pursuing the public good to a degree that ordinary citizens were not. Nevertheless, by no means did they or the other Framers design the constitutional system on the confidence that rulers would uniformly engage in virtuous behavior. Instead, they displayed a keen appreciation of the multiple dimensions of human motivation and coupled this with an equally strong belief that the situation in which citizens and public officials alike were placed would profoundly affect their behavior. They then designed the constitutional system around a series of carrots and sticks that would tap into an array of motives and thereby elicit virtuous behavior in representatives and provide barriers against self-interested actions.

In particular, one of the carrots established by the Constitution was the honor of office. As many authors have noted, the Founders expected the elite rulers who would be cast into positions of power in the republic to be motivated by the cultivation of their reputations and the thirst for lasting fame, not mere notoriety.[53] Public offices would be scarce rewards, and thus symbols of distinction for those statesmen who "possess the most attractive merit and the most diffusive and established characters."[54] Once in office, these statesmen, Madison argued in *Federalist* No. 57, could be expected to be motivated by duty, gratitude, interest, and ambition to perform actions that were consistent with the long-term interests of the people and that would enhance the nation's reputation. They would also be constrained by the realizations that they had to be reelected if they were to continue in office, and that they could make no laws that would not also operate on themselves.[55] Finally, Madison's famous passages from *Federalist* No. 51 indicate that he believed that the interest and ambition that public officials would have in the sphere of constitutional power that they were authorized to exercise would act as a motive for them to resist encroachments by the other branches and help to maintain the proper distribution of constitutional powers.[56]

In addition to this famous system of checks and balances, James Madison and his colleagues also understood that for bad inclinations or motives to issue in improper behavior, individuals had to be given the opportunity to act on these inclinations. They thus thought of the large geographic area over which the nation would spread, properly designed political institutions, and indeed even ordinary public policies as means to "remove the pretext" for improper actions by separating the interested or unjust motive from the opportunity to act inappropriately on it.[57] An extended republic would diffuse factious sentiments and motives, making it less likely that individuals with common unjust motives would be able to realize that they shared these motives. This in turn would make it less likely that they would be drawn by the passions of the many into improper actions and thereby remove the pretext for bad actions. Sound economic policy that created and spread economic prosperity, the Framers believed, would diminish discontent among the citizenry and thus remove the pretext for events like Shays's Rebellion. Finally, a strong union supporting a respectable nation would make it less likely that foreign nations would believe that they could successfully intimidate or coerce the United States, thus removing the context for such invasions.

This interpretation of the relationship of virtue, interest, context, and constitutional structure stands in contrast on the one hand to the scholarship that suggests that the Founders had a "truly noble vision of virtuous impartial leaders," and on the other hand to interpretations that they expected rulers to act on calculations of interest and power with the understanding that institutional organization would nevertheless produce virtuous results.[58] Instead, it shows that the Federalists understood the force of interest and ambition as well as virtue as motives in human behavior, even as they continued to disdain self-interested behavior.[59] This bears emphasizing because it is ignored in most analyses of this question. The Founders, especially the Framers of the Constitution, knew that citizens and public officials would too infrequently be motivated by a sublime, self-abnegating, or disinterested pursuit of virtue. But they nevertheless believed that the fear of being rebuked, ambition, self-interest, and the desire for fame could be spurs to virtuous actions by these same imperfect humans. By eliciting virtue from those most likely to exercise it, channeling ambition and interest in the service of the public good, and arranging institutions to block the worst tendencies of human nature, they hoped to prevent a defect of better motives from translating into a deficiency of good behavior among public officials.

Certainly, this interpretation of the Founders' expectations about human nature suggests that they have rightly earned the appellation of hard-headed realists. Indeed, by recognizing important dimensions of human goodness and impartiality and the ultimate necessity of some degree of trust in public officials, while nevertheless remaining profoundly aware of the self-interested tendencies of human nature, the Founders were far more realistic than either their cynical or utopian critics. Although we have traveled a long way since Gordon Wood published *The Creation of the American Republic* over forty years ago, the conclusions that Wood reached about this conception of political thought and institutional design still bear repeating. The Founders' political thought, Wood wrote in the last sentence of his magisterial work, "was not political theory in the grand manner, but it was political theory worthy of a prominent place in the history of Western thought."[60]

A final dimension of the Founders' political thought suggests a still broader contribution than even Wood suggests. In both *Peace Pact,* his foundational study of the unionist paradigm, and his most recent book, *Union, Nation, and Empire,* David Hendrickson has argued that the Founders' adaptations of the axioms of representative government, the rule of law, bicameralism, and independent judiciaries to the popular governments that they founded did not require or spark a "fundamental reorientation in the basics of constitutional thought," but rather involved a "fairly straightforward task" of the application of familiar concepts.[61] Conversely, however, the Founders' speculations within the unionist paradigm about creating stable systems of cooperation among diverse, autonomous communities constitute a "far richer examination of the possibilities and limits of international cooperation and peace than anything written by Immanuel Kant, usually considered the formative influence on contemporary internationalism."[62]

In particular, according to Hendrickson, the Founders produced a body of international relations theory that was neither realist in the Machiavellian tradition nor idealist in the Kantian one. The Founders held two competing fears (the anarchy of states and the despotism of consolidated empire) and sought to secure two interdependent values (independence and union). The Founders' accomplishment and contribution, Hendrickson argues, was to chart a middle ground between despotism and anarchy and consequently to affirm the values of independence and union. This was achieved with a body of thought about the relationship of independent sovereigns that was at once internationalist and Grotian. It was internationalist in its opposition to mercantilism, its vision of the United States as a liberal trading regime, and its goal of ending British maritime domination and replacing it with an international system based on balance of power. But it was Grotian in its commitment to the law of nature and nations.

Americans, then, did not happen onto internationalist modes of thought in the second half of the twentieth century. Instead, a peculiarly American species of internationalism emanates from the Founding that, Hendrickson persuasively argues, is significant because it served as the foundation for consensual axioms that guided American foreign policy until at least the second half of the twentieth century. These include the belief that the United States should avoid permanent entangling alliances, the belief that the use of force was dangerous to the free institutions of the republic, and the contention that other nations would do well to adopt the American form of government and American ideals, but that these should be propagated by example, not force. Most important, the Founders' consensual beliefs about foreign policy and speculations within the unionist paradigm speak to timeless and timely questions and merit our continued respect and perhaps even our allegiance. "It is striking," Hendrickson writes,

> that the founders' discourse on federalism anticipates in crucial respects our own discourse on nationalism, internationalism, and imperialism, with the structure of the argument continuing to revolve around similar theories, predicaments, and aspirations. Like the cluster of ideas associated with liberalism and republicanism, the values and theorems embraced in the unionist paradigm continue to find expression in the contemporary world, and it appears not simply likely but inevitable that this should continue to be the case.[63]

From Intention to Consequence: The Framers' Constitution and the Development and Character of American Democracy

In addition to leading us to reconsider questions about the center and significance of the Founders' political thought, the confrontations addressed in this book should also lead us to reconsider the effects of the Framers' Constitution on the course of American political development, the character of American democracy today, and whether we want to reform our constitutional system, and if so, how. The topics here are related to, but conceptually distinct from, the question addressed in chapter 2. We are not examining how democratic or undemocratic the Framers' Constitution was intended to be or originally was, but rather perhaps even more vexing and intricate issues of how the Framers' Constitution has shaped the development of democracy in America and the continuing effects on the character of American democracy of living under essentially the same constitutional framework.

This topic is perhaps best explored in the context of two excellent works: Jennifer Nedelsky's *Private Property and the Limits of American Constitutionalism: The Madisonian Framework and Its Legacy*, and Robert Dahl's *How Democratic Is the American Constitution?* These works are exemplary not only because they directly address the question of democracy, but also because they provide unusually sophisticated interpretations of the Founders' ideas and institutional design, because they challenge some of the core assumptions that governed the Founders' thoughts about democracy, and because they are written by two scholars who, although critical of the Founders, have tremendous respect for and knowledge about them.

For her part, Nedelsky argues that the Framers of the Constitution, especially James Madison, were preoccupied with the problem of protecting property rights against invasion from propertyless popular majorities.[64] Although this is a familiar observation, Nedelsky does not provide a restatement of the Progressive interpretation. Unlike the Progressives, she does not argue that the Framers were concerned with protecting their specific economic interests. Rather, she is concerned with how the "idea of property" shaped their political thought and the original institutional design of the American political system.[65] Furthermore, she does not suggest that the protection of property was the only value held by Madison and his colleagues or the only value explicitly institutionalized in the Constitution. Instead, she argues that Madison was a moderate who sought to balance civil rights (the rights of persons and property) with political rights.

Nevertheless, according to Nedelsky, Madison's preoccupation with the threat to property rights from democratic majorities led him to favor a system that tilted that balance in the favor of the protection of property rights—or as she puts it, institutionalized "the hierarchy of civil over political rights."[66] This system, Nedelsky continues, although ultimately resting on the consent of the governed, relied on geographical scope, separation of powers, indirect elections that distanced the people from public officials, and eventually judicial review as means of containing and limiting the rule of the people. In her analysis, Nedelsky repeatedly emphasizes the Federalists' scheme for electing representatives from expanded electoral districts as evidence that Madison and the defenders of the Constitution hoped to ensure the election of an economic elite who shared similar backgrounds and economic interests. Madison's desire to secure the election of an economic elite and his willingness to trust them to rule, Nedelsky further argues, points to a fundamental contradiction in his reasoning. Although Madison preached against leaving the interests of any group to the disinterestedness of another, his preoccupation with the threat of the propertyless poor led him to inadvertently design a constitutional system that left the interests of the poor at the mercy of the wealthy and thus is best thought of as indirectly and subtly but nevertheless decisively class-based.

Most important for our purposes here, Nedelsky advances three closely related propositions about the legacies of the Founders' commitment to the idea of property and to institutions designed to protect it. First, she argues that the Framers "treated the ability to govern as essentially fixed (rather than as a capacity that could be developed) and as class-based. Thus they were not concerned with expanding or enhancing the peoples' competence and involvement in public affairs." "For the Federalists," she continues, "the challenge was to make republican government compatible with the security of rights, not to design institutions that would foster men's ability to govern themselves. The democratic values that prevailed in 1787 were shallow values, and, in the subsequent tradition of American political thought, they have remained so."[67]

Second, she argues that the Framers conceived of property as a basic right enmeshed with notions of freedom and autonomy rather than as a social construct. They therefore considered the redistribution of property beyond the scope of legitimate governmental activity. Especially since the New Deal, Americans have nevertheless engaged in redistribution as a means of remedying social ills. We thus have a redistributive state without an underlying justification for redistribution or a conception of property to support it. "The status of property as boundary lingers," Nedelsky observes, "despite its disintegration as a constitutional concept."[68]

Third, according to Nedelsky, the Framers did not adequately account for or address the relationship between economic and political power. Obsessed with protecting the property of the few from a propertyless majority, they developed a political system that insulated the people from their government. Effective insulation, in turn, "required wealth based inequality of access to political power." In short, Nedelsky argues that "the Framers' preoccupation with property generated a shallow conception of democracy and a system of institutions that allocates political power unequally and fails to foster political participation." Moreover, these problems are "best understood not as anomalous failures, but as integral parts of the coherent system of ideas and institutions."[69]

In *How Democratic Is the American Constitution?* Robert Dahl provides a similarly sweeping critique of the character and effects of the original design on the course of American democracy and its contemporary conduct.[70] But whereas Nedelsky criticizes the Framers for creating a class-based system, Dahl focuses on what he believes are structural deficiencies of the Constitution, arguing that equal representation of all states in the Senate and selection of the president by the Electoral College in particular make the Constitution into an undemocratic, anomalous relic. Representation in the Senate, Dahl argues, unjustifiably weights the votes and privileges the interests of citizens from small states and provides them with a veto over desirable legislation and necessary reforms to the system. In the most extreme case, Wyoming has one-seventieth of the population of California but nevertheless has an equal number of senators. The interests and rights of citizens in small states, Dahl observes, are already protected equally with those of citizens of large states. The burden for those who seek to defend this "profound violation of the democratic idea of political equality," then, is to provide a principle of general applicability that establishes that geographical location entitles citizens or groups with special rights and interests in addition to existing protections available to all.[71]

Meanwhile, the Electoral College is the "most telling example of their [the Founders'] failure to provide a constitutional system that would be appropriate for a democratic republic."[72] As it has operated, this system amounts to "nothing more than a rather peculiar and ritualized way of allocating the votes of the states for president and vice president."[73] It mirrors the injustices of unequal representation in the Senate by providing citizens in small states with disproportionately weighed votes. It also regularly ensures that the leader of the world's most powerful nation is elected by a minority of the citizenry, and sometimes that that individual did not even receive the greatest number of votes for the office.

In addition to fundamentally violating the democratic principle of political equality, the Constitution, Dahl argues, created a political system that is "something less than impressive" when compared to twenty-two other democratic nations in areas such as securing representation for women and minorities, enhancing voter participation, insuring adequate social expenditures, promoting energy efficiency, and increasing foreign aid.[74] Conversely, American achievements are hardly heartening. The United States, Dahl observes, has the highest rate of incarceration in the world and the greatest disparity of income between its richest and poorest citizens.

In general, Dahl blames the Framers of the Constitution and the original design for many of these problems without suggesting that the Framers were either unintelligent or dishonest. Indeed, according to Dahl, the Framers, especially James Madison, were the wisest and most committed public servants in our history. Their problem is that they wrote before the wave of democratization that began in the nineteenth century and continues today, and thus they were unavoidably ignorant about what we have learned about democracy over the past two centuries. Furthermore, they were also crucially limited in the kind of government that they could propose. They could not have abolished slavery or proposed a unitary system that did away with the state governments. Furthermore, unlike Nedelsky, Dahl does not seem to believe that the current problems with the American political system are the result of an unresponsive government or that the solution to these problems lies in making the constitutional system more responsive. Instead, the thrust of his case against the American constitutional system is rather that it is structurally deficient because, like a plane built by the Wright brothers, its design is based on antiquated knowledge. These structural deficiencies, Dahl suggests, could be corrected by abolishing equal representation of all states in the Senate, directly electing the president, and replacing the current winner-take-all electoral system with a multiparty parliamentary system that is based on proportional party representation.

Together, Nedelsky and Dahl's works point to some persistent—and in some cases decisive—criticisms of the contemporary effects of the original design on the character of American democracy. It is true, as Nedelsky suggests, that most of the Framers treated the ability to govern as essentially fixed, rather than as a quality to be developed by education or actual political participation and feared popular participation as a threat to individual rights, rather than as a possibility for informing the people and transforming their character. It is also true that, at least before the 1790s, the Framers neglected the problem of fostering political participation among ordinary citizens. That neglect followed from their assumption—impressed on the Founders by their experiences with the state governments during the 1780s— that the political system would be too responsive.[75]

In addition, the criticism that equal representation in the Senate creates arbitrary privileges in the Senate, the Electoral College, and the amending process for citizens who live in small states is decisive and points to examples of a contemporary injustice that can be directly traced to the original design.[76] Indeed, Frances E. Lee and Bruce Oppenheimer have made this case even more forcefully and decisively than Dahl.[77] Far from protecting the rights and interests of any identifiable minorities, Lee and Oppenheimer point out, equal representation in the Senate advantages white Americans because larger percentages of Hispanics and African Americans live in urban areas within states with large populations and thus end up being underrepresented in the Senate. Equal representation also leads to less competitive senatorial races in small states, small-state senators who are more likely than senators from large states to pursue particularized benefits for their states, and a system of allocation that sends disproportionate amounts of federal funds to small states. Furthermore, Lee and Oppenheimer point out, these problems will, if anything, increase because states with the largest populations are also those that are increasing the most in population.[78]

But if these studies point to several important criticisms of the effects of the original design on the future of democracy in America, they also misunderstand aspects of the character of the original design and misrepresent and exaggerate its effects on the operation of the system today. Most broadly and importantly, these studies point to the problems inherent in the virtually universal practice of attempting to explain the character of contemporary American democracy by examining the original design and the Framers' ideas.

Specifically, Nedelsky's characterization of the original design as a class-based system is problematic on several points, some of which explicitly emerge in her own analysis. According to Nedelsky, the Federalists' scheme for the election of representatives from expanded electoral districts was a centerpiece of their constitutional design and betrays the class bias of the system because the Framers expected that this electoral arrangement would help ensure the election of representatives from their own economic and social class. Nevertheless, as the analysis in chapter 2 established, the Constitution contained few formal barriers for either voting or holding office, and certainly none that explicitly restricted voting or holding office on the basis of wealth. The right of suffrage, it will be remembered, was governed by the state legislatures, with the stipulation that requirements for election to the House of Representatives had to be the same as the requirements for election to the most numerous branch of the state legislatures. Individuals seeking office had only to meet citizenship requirements and minimal age requirements.

Nedelsky is of course aware of the liberality of these qualifications, but she nevertheless concludes that the Framers relied on expanded electoral districts rather than formal restrictions to secure a class-based system because they believed that "the people could be relied upon to discriminate on the basis of property holding more effectively than any stated qualification."[79] It is doubtlessly true that the Framers associated being in the elite social class with the capability of governing—although they also believed that merit could elevate one from the lower and middle classes to the elite classes that were qualified to govern. As mentioned earlier, the Federalists believed that elections from large electoral districts would help to secure the election of men with these unequal abilities because they believed that virtue and a broad reputation were linked, and that the diffusive reputations of gentlemen would counteract electioneering in large districts. They also had faith that the people had both the intelligence to recognize those capable of governing and the virtue (conceived here with a healthy dose of deference) to elect them.

Nedelsky's remarkably frank observation that the Federalists trusted the people to do the discriminating, however, undermines much of her argument that the Constitution relied on wealth-based inequalities because it concedes that the only way that the wealthy will be put into office under the Framers' Constitution is if the people put them there. Expanded electoral districts promote the election of individuals who best exemplify the broadest values of the electorate—that is, individuals who have the broadest reputations. As mentioned in chapter 2, the only way that wealthy individuals or those of an elite social status can attain office under the Framers' Constitution is if the people identify wealth or social status as a characteristic of electoral merit and elect them on this basis. Put differently, for expanded electoral districts to promote the election of members of Madison's social class, the people must agree with the elites that only members of that social class are capable of governing and continue to have the deference to elect them. But then the election of men of this social class can only be said to have resulted from democratic choice and to reflect the values of the rich and the poor, not the class-based character of the Constitution. Contrary to Nedelsky's assertion, nothing in the Framers' Constitution "required [or promoted] wealth based inequality of access to political power."[80]

This is not to say that Nedelsky (or Gordon Wood or Woody Holton) is wrong to detect elitism in the original design of the American Constitution or to challenge her charges about the inadequacies of how the system works today. The point, rather, is that Nedelsky mistakes the character of the original design as a prelude to mistaking—both by misunderstanding and exaggerating—its effect on the future of American politics. In particular, Nedelsky conflates every form of elitism and thus confuses the accountable-elite model of republicanism present in the original design with a class-based system. She then holds the Founders and their constitutional system directly responsible for the contemporary oligarchic character of American politics, when it in fact seems to be only incidental to those tendencies. To make her case, Nedelsky would have to establish either that the original design of the American political system, with its schemes of indirect elections and elections from expanded electoral districts, and the Framers' understanding of property are somehow more to blame for the contemporary oligarchic character of the political system than contemporary laws, rulings, and policies, or she would have to suggest that these laws and policies necessarily follow directly from the original design and the Founders' ideas. But is the contemporary oligarchic character of our system more the result of the original design and the Founders' ideas, or, to consider but three possibilities, is it the result of Supreme Court rulings in such cases as *Santa Clara County v. Southern Pacific Railroad, Buckley v. Valeo,* and now *Citizens United v. Federal Election Commission,* legal entitlements given to corporations, and specific taxation and distribution policies? In short, Nedelsky adopts virtually a structuralist interpretation of the Constitution that suggests that it guarantees the dominance of the wealthy, rather than adopting an interpretation that suggests that the Constitution is, in large part, what it is because of how it has been interpreted, the laws passed in pursuance of it, and how those laws have been administered.

This same tendency—to hold the Framers' ideas and the original constitutional system responsible for our problems rather than to look to ourselves, recent rulings and policies, and broader historical forces—is present in Dahl's claims about the performance of the American political system relative to other nations and Nedelsky's suggestion that the original constitutional design has stood and continues to stand in the way of the development of democracy in the United States. Specifically, as Dahl acknowledges, "questions about the relative performance of different constitutional systems are easy to pose but extraordinarily difficult to answer responsibly," and it is "not easy to determine the extent to which a country's constitutional arrangements influence the country's performance on such matters" as crime, income disparity, voter participation, and energy efficiency.[81] Indeed, it seems implausible that the constitutional system is the primary cause or even a major contributing factor to several of the problems that Dahl raises. Is the incarceration rate in America, for example, really a failure of the constitutional system or any arbitrary inequalities embedded in it? Actually, this problem seems to be the direct result of the war on drugs, which has extensive support among ordinary Americans. Similarly, it seems hard to believe that our constitutional system is as nearly responsible for the vast inequality in income and wealth in the United States as is the sweeping technological revolution that has brought about globalization, unduly rewarded technical knowledge in the labor market at the expense of service industry labor, and placed American labor in competition with impoverished laborers from other nations.

Nedelsky's claim that the original design has been overtly hostile to the development of democracy in America is similarly unproven and suspect. Specifically, her claim seems to have two prongs, the first of which is a critique of the original design and the second of which is a critique of the Founders' ideas. First, she claims that the Founders created a constitutional system that so distanced the people from their government that it rendered "not just public office, but public affairs relatively inaccessible to them."[82] Second, she argues that the Founders were the source of an impoverished democratic tradition that did not take into account the possibility that ordinary citizens could gain competence in public affairs and grow and develop through meaningful political participation. Conversely, an adequate constitutional system for Nedelsky would not only promote widespread political participation, but would also be rooted in the possibility that citizens could grow in their capabilities to practice politics and would treat political participation as an end in itself.

One of the major problems with the first of these assertions—the proposition that the original constitutional design prevented the development of meaningful democracy in the United States—is that American culture and politics democratized dramatically after the Framers' Constitution was put in place and before passage of the numerous amendments (especially the Fifteenth, Seventeenth, Nineteenth, Twenty-third, Twenty-fourth, and Twenty-sixth Amendments) that democratized the constitutional system. How, then, can the original design be said to have prevented the development of democracy? As Jack Rakove has pointed out in response to a similar criticism of the American political system by Richard Matthews,

> The Constitution was not itself a political mandate whose adoption necessitated the erosion of state and communal frameworks of governance and political competition. By all accounts, American politics became far more participatory and democratized in the nineteenth century than it had been in 1787, and it did so because the Constitution gave new impetus to political mobilization while it preserved the decentralized patchwork of jurisdictions that has always left the American state relatively weak and often vulnerable (as today) to centrifugal forces. This patchwork of jurisdictions may not have functioned as Jefferson meant his ward republics to do, but it hardly makes sense to argue that the adoption of the Constitution foreclosed the creation of a more participatory politics than Madison the liberal prince deemed prudent.[83]

During the 1790s, Rakove might have added, national politics were also decisively democratized in the United States as the Founders—particularly the Jeffersonians—addressed the problems of collective action that arose as a result of the creation of the first extended republic. The formation of the first political parties, the development of a free press, and the corresponding development of a conception of government by public opinion furthered American democracy both by changing its character and by increasing the number of ordinary citizens who participated in it. Furthermore, Madison was a central actor in developing these modes of participation, and they were, in some ways at least, advanced by the original Madisonian framework.[84]

What these observations suggest is that we need to consider the possibility that we should treat the influence of the Framers' Constitution and the original constitutional design as one variable in the context in which the particular form of democracy that we have today took shape, rather than as overly hostile to democracy. Although a full exploration of this point is beyond my purpose here, a few observations will help illuminate some of its implications. First, if, as the discussion above suggests, it is dubious to suggest either that expanded electoral districts were the centerpiece of a class-based Constitution or that they helped to prolong the influence of elites in the American political system, then what effect did they have? Again, the Founders' relative liberality over suffrage and their effort to secure the election of elites to office through this procedure meant only that the electorate revealed its broadest values in the kind of candidates that it selected. When those values changed, so did the kind of individuals who were elected to office. When, in other words, deference broke down in American culture, then the very procedures that had once contributed to the election of a social elite now contributed to the election of much more ordinary Americans. In both cases, Americans got the kind of leaders that they wanted and deserved.

Second, the decision to leave suffrage requirements to the states with the stipulation that they correspond to the requirements for voting for the most numerous branch of the state legislature had an ambiguous and complex effect on American democracy. On the one hand, the decision to leave suffrage requirements—especially property qualifications—to the states proved valuable to the development of democracy in the United States. As the American political culture democratized, state property qualifications fell in a kind of cascading effect that led to virtually universal white male suffrage. Furthermore, leaving suffrage requirements to the states opened up important—though often short-lived—windows of opportunity in which women in particular voted even before the passage of the Nineteenth Amendment. Women voted in New Jersey—despite being disenfranchised across the country—from 1776 until 1807. Women also voted in school elections in Kentucky as early as 1838, a practice that spread to twenty-six different states by 1920, and increasingly in municipal elections throughout the nineteenth century. Finally, women had gained full suffrage rights in four Western states by 1896, and another nine Western states granted full women's suffrage between 1910 and 1918. This gave momentum to the passage of the Nineteenth Amendment.[85]

On the other hand, the failure of the Founders to establish a single conception of citizenship with voting as an integral element within it left women and ethnic groups vulnerable to the exclusionary policies that were set forth by the states. A document that could have been a progressive force for democratic inclusion provided no barriers to exclusionary policies. As Alexander Keyssar has noted, the legacy of the decision to leave suffrage requirements to the states was "long and sometimes problematic." The Constitution adopted in 1787, Keyssar writes, left the federal government without any clear power or mechanism, other than through constitutional amendment, to institute a national conception of voting rights, to express a national vision of democracy. Although the Constitution was promulgated in the name of "We, the people of the United States," the individual states retained the power to define just who "the people" were. Stated somewhat differently, citizenship in the new nation—controlled by the federal government—was divorced from the right to vote, a fact that was to have significant repercussions for almost two centuries.[86]

The most important point here is not simply that we need to tell a much more complex story of American political development—although that is certainly an important point. Instead, two points are central. First, even particularly subtle studies of the effects of the original design and the Founders' ideas on contemporary problems such as Nedelsky's and Dahl's fail to show any real appreciation of how, to borrow a phrase from Lance Banning, "distantly and very partially responsible" the Founders are for what America is today.[87] Nedelsky and, to a lesser extent, Dahl proceed from the proposition that the current system—including its achievements and its weaknesses—is the product of the Framers' intentions. In some cases, such as the privileges that citizens from small states enjoy as a result of their undue influence in elections for senators and the president, that proposition is doubtlessly true. In general, however, this assumption has more strategic value than veracity. It provides both critics and defenders of the American political system with a finite, identifiable set of actors—the American Founders—and an identifiable structure—the Madisonian model—that can either be glorified or condemned for the way the system operates today. It also provides a straightforward account of the path of American political development, suggesting that our history and institutions have followed a trajectory set by the Founders. Nevertheless, and this is the second point, straightforward explanations of the relationship of current problems to the original design may be dangerous because they lead us to misunderstand the cause of our problems and thus the proper remedy. It makes a very real difference whether the weaknesses of our institutions can be traced to the initial design of the political system, to later changes in institutional structures and practices, to transformations in the beliefs and expectations of the electorate, or still yet to relatively recent laws, rulings, and policies. Dahl makes a decisive case that structural irregularities in the Constitution perpetuate some current injustices and have arbitrarily provided privileged positions of power, and in turn have resulted in misguided policies. Thus, we should take his case for constitutional reform in certain areas quite seriously. In contrast, the ability of constitutional reform to effect economic and cultural change is much more tenuous and should be greeted with considerable skepticism. In general, telling the longer, sloppier story of American political development, identifying the areas where the Founders are partially and distantly the cause of our problems as well as the areas where they had really nothing, positively or negatively, to do with them, finding later developments that have caused these problems, and accepting the blame when we are responsible is at once more difficult, less satisfying, and more opaque in its implications than blaming the Founders and the original design. But it is also the only prudent way to locate responsibility and approach reform.

Appropriate and Inappropriate Appropriations

A fourth set of questions raised by the confrontations in this book concerns the legitimate boundaries of appropriation for the Founders' ideas. When is it proper and legitimate to draw on the Founders' ideas to address our current problems? Should we think of the ideas of the Founders and the principles underlying the original design of the American political system as "first" or "true" principles from which we should not deviate lest we form a different type of regime, or should we conclude that founding principles have no more authority than subsequent ideas and practices? Are we legally or morally bound to accept their ideas? If not, would it still be prudent to consider them? In short, what authority do the Founders have over us, and what is the foundation of that authority?

In chapter 3, I sought to establish in the face of the claims of Skinner and Wood that appropriation of the Founders' ideas is sometimes legitimate. But that only raises the question, how can legitimate appropriation be differentiated from manipulation and ransacking? What are appropriate and inappropriate appropriations? There is no handbook for making such distinctions. Furthermore, although this does not differentiate it from any other hermeneutic activity, judgments about legitimate and illegitimate appropriation will unavoidably rest on complex criteria, create disagreements, and require elaborate accounts. Thus, when the ideas of a historical agent are set forth as the proper solution to a contemporary problem, a dialogue should (and of course often does) follow—not only about whether the solution is proper, but also whether it is faithful to the ideas of the historical agent being evoked. Two criteria, it seems to me, are fundamental and should have a central place in that dialogue, and thus ultimately a place in our judgments about whether a scholar is legitimately trying to bring one of the Founders into a conversation about how to address a contemporary problem or is engaging in an illegitimate appropriation of the Founders to promote an idea of his or her own. First, scholars engaged in appropriation should be explicitly clear to their readers about which aspects of their ideas come directly from the Founders and which ones are extrapolations necessary to make the Founders' ideas work today. Second, scholars should not invoke the name of the Founders in the service of proposals they explicitly opposed.

The way in which these criteria may be helpful starting points in separating legitimate appropriations from what David Hackett Fischer has called "rhetorical raids" can again perhaps best be illuminated with examples.[88] One of the best recent examples of the legitimate appropriation of the Founders' ideas can be found in Cass Sunstein's use of republicanism in general and his appropriation of James Madison's idea of deliberative democracy in particular. Sunstein, a contemporary constitutional law scholar rather than a historian, begins his analysis by readily and fully acknowledging that his task is not simply one of excavation, that republicanism in its original formulation carried with it many dimensions (such as strategies of exclusion) that are unacceptable, and that he is calling for the selective adoption of the Founders' ideas.

Sunstein then establishes that Madison's approach to interest groups has been profoundly misunderstood. Madison, according to Sunstein, was not an interest group liberal but rather a proponent of deliberative democracy. Taking Madison's conception of representation seriously, Sunstein argues, would transform our understanding of a variety of issues in constitutional and administrative law. It would, for example, lead judges to engage in close scrutiny of congressional acts to see whether they were rationally related to some discernible public interest and were the product of "deliberative responsibility" and "reasoned analysis." Finally, and most contentiously, Sunstein argues that republicanism would lead to proposals for the public financing of political campaigns, proportional representation of minority groups, and rulings that would enhance federalism in order to promote local self-determination. Most important, with the exception of his call for proportional representation of minority groups, Sunstein maintains a Madisonian spirit throughout his discussion.[89]

A much less careful and more tenuous use of Madison's ideas is found in Lani Guinier's important study, *The Tyranny of the Majority*. In the introduction to this study, Guinier correctly points out that Madison's greatest fear during the mid-1780s was majority tyranny and that he had hoped to resolve this problem by breaking majority factions apart, thus preventing the formation of a permanent majority and promoting the formation of shifting coalitions that would form majorities. Guinier then suggests, however, that this solution to the problem of majority factions is analogous to her call for the sharing of power or the alternating of decision making between minority groups on the one hand and the majority on the other through measures such as cumulative voting and racially conscious districting that would give minority groups a turn in the decision-making process.

The problem here is that what Guinier promotes under Madison's name is positively anti-Madisonian. First, Madison did hope to break apart majority factions, but he hoped to do so through geographic size (by extending the sphere of the republic), not through cumulative voting schemes. Indeed, Madison was fundamentally committed to the principle of majority rule; he simply believed that gathering that majority from a larger geographical area with a greater diversity of interests would have beneficial effects on the quality of administration and also serve to help protect private and minority rights. But Madison never sought to give the minority a turn. He sought to have minorities form coalitions until they became a majority, and he believed that that process would help promote the formation of majorities that were based on principles of "justice and general good."[90]

Second, Madison was committed to the principle of geographic representation and shared Hamilton's view that actual representation of economic groups by members of that group (and by extension to the actual representation of racial groups by members of that race) was "visionary." The purpose of expanded electoral districts was to promote the election of the most virtuous and meritorious men as representatives on the premise that these individuals could best represent everyone. The belief that virtue and merit should be the proper criteria for selecting representatives is an assumption of Guinier's opponents, and her intellectual kinship is actually much closer to the anti-Federalists, or even John C. Calhoun.[91]

Understanding the Founding

A final set of issues raised by this book concerns what a mature understanding of the Founding would entail, and whether we can break out of the cycle of celebration and condemnation that characterizes so much Founding scholarship. In the original edition of this book, I defined and defended understanding the Founding by differentiating it most strongly from what I have now labeled prosecuting and vindicating. Understanding the Founding, I wrote in language that I still accept, involves the adoption of a historically sensitive, complex, and detached view of the Founders that allows us to confront them in their moral ambiguity, independent of either romanticism and puerile worship on the one hand and self-righteous, acontextualized condemnation on the other.

Such an approach, I argued, would lead us to interpret the American Founding neither as virgin birth nor original sin, neither as a repository of true or first principles nor as a source of shame and guilt. Rather, it would provide the materials for an intelligent and necessarily perpetual conversation about what our foundations are and what role they should play in the present. It would also allow us to confront the Founders in all of their glorious and inglorious ambiguity, as erudite statesmen who were remarkably— but sometimes superficially—eclectic, as slaveholders who pronounced universal equality, as patriarchs who (as Gordon Wood has taught us) exploited revolutionary rhetoric to stir the many to rebellion, but then ended up as irascible old men in a democratic culture they had loosed. Yet another implication of adopting this attitude about the Founders and this approach to the study of their beliefs and legacies, I argued, is that it would mean that the Founders have authority over our ideas, actions, and institutions only so far as reason abides. Instead of blind veneration or flippant criticism, we would need to learn to follow their advice when they were right and because they were right, not because they were Founders. This, I wrote and still believe, is the most we owe the Founders and the least we owe ourselves.

Both this edition of this book and the previous one have also featured a sustained, conflicted engagement with a historicist's approach to the study of the Founding. The historicists' approach, I have observed, views the Founding as a radically foreign culture that can only be understood after it is reconstructed on its own terms. In its most uncompromising form, this approach suggests that any effort to appropriate ideas or practices from the Founding is illegitimate; the Founders did not ask the same questions we do, and thus they cannot be consulted for guidance about the problems that we face. In dealing with questions about the Founders' moral responsibility for slavery and America's other original sins, historicists have insisted on judging the Founders only on the basis of the moral assumptions of their age. Conversely, they have argued that judging the Founders on the basis of contemporary moral precepts about slavery, race, and gender is unfair and inappropriate.

I hope that the reader who has been with me throughout this work realizes that I have a deep respect and appreciation for the work of the practicing historians who study the Founding and considerable sympathies for concerns, temperament, and sensibilities of historicists. In particular, I share with many of these historians the belief that scholars should strive for objectivity and impartiality, and that these goals can be approximated, if never fully achieved. I also share with many of them the belief that recapturing the moral universe of the Founders is central to these goals, and that the interpretive propositions that historical actors should be understood as they understood themselves and should not be judged outside of the context of their own moral universe are sound.

Nevertheless, historicists, I have also argued, commit a series of logical and methodological errors in their misconceived case against philosophical approaches to the study of the American Founding and their contention that we can never learn directly from the Founders. They also overstate the case when they suggest that any appropriation of the Founders' ideas is inappropriate. Finally, the historicists' approach is limited in its ability to help us break out of the cycle of celebration and condemnation that characterizes so much Founding scholarship, and in general in its ability to address the vexing questions of moral responsibility. Specifically, many historicists have been so concerned with admonishing scholars who engage in presentism and so concerned with complicating moral judgments about the Founders that they have glorified a perpetual state of delay in making judgments, and paraded this process of delay as a substitute for balanced and responsible judgments. Furthermore, despite the claim of many historicists, contextualizing the Founding does not lead to the adoption of a common standard for assessing questions of moral responsibility, let alone common judgments. Instead, debates about the Founders' moral responsibility reemerge as historians offer different versions of the historical context and set forth different interpretations of the moral universe of the Founding.

In contrast, the approach that I am defending suggests that moral judgments about the Founders are unavoidable, that such judgments cannot be made sound merely by the adoption of the historians' axiom that historical actors should not be judged outside the context of their own moral universe, and that the task of assessing the moral responsibility of the Founders cannot be satisfied by ever more complex treatments of the context or ever more complex interpretations of how they came to believe or act as they did. It also suggests that we can learn directly from the Founders about something more than our distance and differentness from them. The Founders made claims to truth about politics and the human condition, and we have to at least consider that they may have been right. Their unique combination of realism and idealism and their understandings of institutional arrangements in particular should be a source of sustained reflection and may be a source for creative appropriation.

At this point, even readers who have weighed the strengths and weaknesses of my arguments and who generally agree may well conclude that this is all fine and well, but it is not likely to happen. Americans, they might point out, are unlikely to adopt the detached, philosophical, and complex view of the American Founders that I have pressed on my readers. I agree. Frankly, the more that I understand the place that the Founders serve in the American civil religion and the construction of American identity, and the better that I understand the strengths and limitations of American political discourse, the more skeptical I have become of the prospect that Founding scholars, let alone statesmen or ordinary citizens, will ever achieve such a conflicted and ambiguous view of the Founders and their legacy, or come to understand the authority of the Founders as based solely on whether we can rationally affirm their ideas. The reasons that few citizens, statesmen, or scholars are likely to break out of the cycle of celebration and condemnation and achieve a complex view of the Founders are woven into the very (important) purposes that they serve in our civil religion and political culture and the moral and (for many) legal authority that they have in our political system. Put bluntly, we have such difficulty achieving complex understandings and responsible judgments of the Founders because we have called on them to serve important political functions (such as promoting cultural unity), placed them at the center of our civil religion and political culture, and thus unavoidably introduced them into the culture wars. The Founders, placed in the center of the American civil religion and set forth as icons, become targets for iconoclastic critics and for those who hope to reform or raze the American civil religion.[92] Furthermore, as long as we ask the Founders to serve these purposes, we will tend to view them as either heroes or villains. Not even the most subtle contextualization of their ideas and actions will get us out of the cycle of celebration and condemnation.

A mongrel nation needs a founding moment.[93] Unlike the citizens of other nations, the identity of Americans does not flow from common origins or a shared ethnicity. It flows from holding certain fundamental beliefs, especially those set forth in the preamble to the Declaration of Independence. Furthermore, as Rutgers historian Jan Lewis has noted, unlike other nations that have experienced major revolutions—particularly Russia, Britain, and France—the identity of the people in these nations was already substantially formed before their revolutions and was not fundamentally altered by them. In contrast, the United States was, in Lewis's words, "created, literally, by the Revolution, and that era is the touchstone for American identity."[94] Most important, a nation that gains so much of its identity from ideas generated by a particular group of individuals and particular historical events (especially the American Revolution and the Constitutional Convention) must also be held together by these ideas, individuals, and events.

The Founders' place in our political culture and their role in the construction of our political identity profoundly complicate the study of the American Founding. Scholars like me who bemoan facile appropriations of the Founders' ideas and tiring exchanges between those who venerate and those who flippantly criticize the Founders must nevertheless acknowledge that the political purposes served by the Founders are hardly insignificant. Moreover, scholars and statesmen are unlikely to give up the authority that the Founders' name evokes. We must also acknowledge that the development of such a more mature, detached, and impartial attitude and approach toward them raises a series of additional questions. Would we be better off if we had a complex and conflicted view of the Founding? Is the myth of a pristine Founding America's noble lie, necessary to create cultural unity, American identity, and common purpose? Can we really do without heroes and villains, and what blameless or better icons do we have to replace the Founders if we criticize them too severely?

These are important questions that merit serious, extended answers, but it is doubtful that they will soon become relevant. What seems far more likely is that in the minds of many, the Founders will remain magisterial, wise, and distant figures from Gilbert Stuart paintings, and in the minds of others, they will remain the perpetrators of America's original sins. What seems almost certain is that we will continue to fight about the proper place of the American Founders in our political culture.

Notes

Preface to the Second Edition

1. David Brion Davis, *The Problem of Slavery in the Age of Revolution, 1770–1823* (New York: Oxford University Press, 1999), 12. Emphasis is Davis's.

2. Richard Zinman, "Thinking about the Founding," *Interpretation: A Journal of Political Philosophy* 36 (Winter 2009): 103–144; Alan Gibson, "Beyond Ancients, Moderns, Heroes, and Villains: Thinking about the Founding with Richard Zinman," *Interpretation: A Journal of Political Philosophy* 36 (Summer 2009): 273–303.

Introduction to the Second Edition

1. Bernard Bailyn, *The Ideological Origins of the American Revolution*, enlarged ed. (Cambridge, Mass.: Belknap Press of Harvard University Press, 1992), v.

2. J. G. A. Pocock, "Languages and Their Implications: The Transformation of the Study of Political Thought," in *Politics, Language, and Time: Essays on Political Thought and History* (New York: Atheneum Press, 1971), 4.

3. Gordon Wood has called *An Economic Interpretation of the Constitution* "the most influential history book ever written in America," while Cushing Strout refers to it as "one of the most controversial and influential pieces of historical writing ever to disturb the American mind." Similarly, Forrest McDonald has written that "no historian who followed [Beard] in studying the making of the Constitution has been free from Beard's view of it." Wood, "The Greatest Generation," *New York Review of Politics*, March 29, 2001, 17–22; Cushing Strout, *The Pragmatic Revolt in American History: Carl Becker and Charles Beard* (New Haven, Conn.: Yale University Press, 1958), 92; Forrest McDonald, *We the People: The Economic Origins of the Constitution* (Chicago: University of Chicago Press, 1958), v.

4. Charles A. Beard, *An Economic Interpretation of the Constitution of the United States*, with a new introduction by Forrest McDonald (1913; reprint, New York: Free Press, 1986), 10, 31.

5. See especially Edward Corwin, "Review of an Economic Interpretation of the Constitution of the United States," *History Teachers Magazine* 5 (February 1914): 65–66; John H. Latane, "Review of an Economic Interpretation of the Constitution of the

United States," *American Political Science Review* 7 (November 1913): 697–700, especially 699; Orin G. Libby, "Review of an Economic Interpretation of the Constitution of the United States," *Mississippi Valley Historical Review* 1 (June 1914): 113–117; William K. Boyd, "Review of an Economic Interpretation of the Constitution of the United States," *South Atlantic Quarterly* 12 (July 1913): 269–273. See also Orin G. Libby, "Review of Economic Origins of Jeffersonian Democracy," *Mississippi Valley Historical Review* 3 (June 1916): 99–102. See Ellen Nore, *Charles A. Beard: An Intellectual Biography* (Carbondale: Southern Illinois University Press, 1983), 63–66, for a short but excellent analysis of Beard's initial critics.

6. Forrest McDonald, "A New Introduction" to *An Economic Interpretation*, xxii.

7. Lee Benson, *Turner and Beard: American Historical Writing Reconsidered* (Glencoe, Ill.: Free Press, 1960); Philip A. Crowl, "Anti-Federalism in Maryland, 1787–1788," *William and Mary Quarterly* 4 (October 1947), 446–469; Cecelia Kenyon, "'An Economic Interpretation of the Constitution' after Fifty Years," *Centennial Review of Arts and Science* 7 (1963): 327–352; William C. Pool, "An Economic Interpretation of the Ratification of the Federal Constitution in North Carolina," *North Carolina Historical Review* 27 (April–July–October 1950), 119–141, 289–313, 437–461; Robert Thomas, "The Virginia Convention of 1788: A Criticism of Charles Beard's *An Economic Interpretation of the Constitution*," *Journal of Southern History* 19 (February 1953): 63–72; Robert E. Brown, *Charles Beard and the Constitution: A Critical Analysis of "An Economic Interpretation of the Constitution"* (Princeton, N.J.: Princeton University Press, 1956); McDonald, *We the People*; McDonald, "The Anti-Federalists," *Wisconsin Magazine of History* 46 (Spring 1963): 206–214. Critical reviews of the impact of this scholarship on Beard's economic interpretation of the Constitution include: Richard Hofstadter, *The Progressive Historians: Turner, Beard, Parrington* (New York: Alfred A. Knopf, 1968), especially 218–224; James H. Hutson, "The Constitution: An Economic Document?" in *The Framing and Ratification of the Constitution*, ed. Leonard Levy and Dennis Mahoney (New York: Macmillan, 1987), 259–270.

8. Beard, *An Economic Interpretation*, 24.

9. See *Aristotle's Posterior Analytics*, translation with commentaries and glossary by Hippocrates G. Apostle (Grinnell, Iowa: Peripatetic Press, 1981), 97b, 14–26, 66; *Nicomachean Ethics*, trans. (with introduction and notes) Martin Ostwald (Indianapolis: Bobbs-Merrill, 1962), 1098b, 18–19.

10. Robert Shalhope coined the term "republican synthesis" and gave conceptual identity to the republican interpretation in two important historiographical essays. See Shalhope, "Toward a Republican Synthesis: The Emergence of an Understanding of Republicanism in American Historiography," *William and Mary Quarterly* 29 (1972): 49–80; Shalhope, "Republicanism and Early American Historiography," *William and Mary Quarterly* 39 (1982): 334–356; see also Daniel Rodgers, "Republicanism: The Career of a Concept," *Journal of American History* 79 (June 1992): 11–38, for an excellent overview of the rise and fall of the republican interpretation, the variety of forms that it took, and its methodological foundations.

11. Quote is from Lance Banning, "The Republican Interpretation: Retrospect and Prospect," in *The Republican Synthesis Revisited: Essays in Honor of George Athan Billias*, ed. Milton M. Klein, Richard D. Brown, and John B. Hench (Worcester, Mass.: American Antiquarian Society, 1992), 92.

12. Louis Hartz, *The Liberal Tradition in America: An Interpretation of American Political Thought since the Revolution* (San Diego: Harcourt Brace Jovanovich, 1955).

13. Quote is from Joyce Appleby, "Republicanism in Old and New Contexts," *William and Mary Quarterly* 43 (January 1986): 26.

14. See Gordon Wood's comments in the preface to the 1998 edition of *Creation of the American Republic, 1776–1787* (1969; reprint, Chapel Hill: University of North Carolina Press, 1998), v–xiii.

15. See Laura Kalman, *The Strange Career of Legal Liberalism* (New Haven, Conn.: Yale University Press, 1996).

16. See John Patrick Diggins, *The Lost Soul of American Politics: Virtue, Self-Interest, and the Foundations of Liberalism* (New York: Basic Books, 1985); Issac Kramnick, "Republicanism Revisionism Revisited," *American Historical Review* 97 (June 1982), 629–664; Joyce Appleby, *Capitalism and the New Social Order: The Republican Vision of the 1790s* (New York: New York University Press, 1984); *Liberalism and Republicanism in the Historical Imagination* (Cambridge, Mass.: Harvard University Press, 1992); Thomas Pangle, *The Spirit of Modern Republicanism: The Moral Vision of the American Founders and the Philosophy of Locke* (Chicago: University of Chicago Press, 1988).

17. The term "multiple traditions approach" was coined by Rogers Smith. I adopt and apply it here. See Smith, "Beyond Tocqueville, Myrdal, and Hartz: The Multiple Traditions in America," *American Political Science Review* 87 (September 1993): 549–566.

18. Peter S. Onuf, "The Scholars' Jefferson," *William and Mary Quarterly* 50 (October 1993): 680.

19. Rogan Kersh, "The Founding: Liberalism Redux," review of *The Foundations of American Citizenship: Liberalism, the Constitution, and Civic Virtue,* by Richard C. Sinopoli, *Review of Politics* 55 (Fall 1993): 729. In general, see Alan Gibson, "Ancients, Moderns, and Americans: The Republicanism-Liberalism Debate Revisited," *History of Political Thought* 21 (Summer 2000): 261–307. See also my exchange with Paul Carrese: Paul Carrese, "The Complexity, and Principles, of the American Founding: A Response to Alan Gibson," *History of Political Thought* 21 (Winter 2000): 711–717; Alan Gibson, "Searching for the Soul of the American Amalgam: A Reply to Paul Carrese," *History of Political Thought* 22 (Spring 2001): 166–173.

20. David Brion Davis's magisterial scholarship on slavery has established that during the late eighteenth century, after centuries of indifference to the institution of slavery, numerous statesmen and philosophers began to find slavery an unacceptable form of human exploitation. Davis provides decisive evidence for the high degree of self-consciousness among the Founders and their generation about contradictions between their cries for liberty and the institution of slavery. See David Brion Davis, *The Problem of Slavery in Western Culture* (Ithaca, N.Y.: Cornell University Press, 1966); *The Problem of Slavery in the Age of Revolution, 1770–1823* (New York: Oxford University Press, 1999), especially 39–83; David Brion Davis, "Slavery and the American Revolution," in *Slavery and Freedom in the Age of the American Revolution* (Charlottesville: University Press of Virginia, 1983), 262–280; David Brion Davis, *Inhuman Bondage: The Rise and Fall of Slavery in the New World* (New York: Oxford University Press, 2006), especially 141–156.

Later classic expressions of the contradictions between the principles of the American Revolution and slavery include the writings and speeches of William Lloyd Garrison, Frederick Douglass, Wendell Phillips, and Samuel P. Chase. For a sampling of Garrison's views on the Declaration and the Constitution and the hypocrisy of fighting a revolution in the name of liberty but practicing slavery, see *The Liberator,* December 29, 1832, and July 1, 1842, in *William Lloyd Garrison and the Fight against Slavery: Selections from "The Liberator,"* ed. William E. Cain (Boston: Bedford Books, 1995), 87–89, 109; *The Liberator,* December 8, 1837, in *Classics of American Political and Constitutional Thought,* ed. Scott J. Hammond, Kevin R. Hardwick, and Howard L. Lubert, 2 vols. (Indianapolis: Hackett, 2007), 1:979–980; for Douglass, see "What to the Slave Is the Fourth of July?" in *Classics of American Political and Constitutional Thought,* 1:1012–1021, and "The Constitution and Slavery," in *The United States Constitution: 200 Years of Anti-Federalist, Abolitionist, Feminist, Muckraking, Progressive, and Especially Social Criticism,* ed. Bertell Ollman and Jonathan Brinbaum (New York: New York University Press, 1990), 91–95; for Wendell Phillips, see *The Constitution: A Pro-Slavery Compact. Selections from "The Madison Papers," &c* (1844; reprint, New York: Negro Universities Press, 1969), 3–7; for Salmon P. Chase, see *Reclamation of Fugitives from Services: An Argument for the Defendant, Submitted to the Supreme Court of the United States, at the December Term, 1846, in the Case of Wharton Jones vs. John Vangandt* (Cincinnati: R. P. Donogh, 1847).

Unlike Garrison, Phillips, and Chase, John C. Calhoun presented the argument for the pro-slavery Constitution as part of a defense of the institution of slavery. He also rejected the doctrine of the Declaration of Independence that "all men are created equal." See especially his "Southern Address," http://sciway3.net/2001/john-c-calhoun/SAddress.htm, and the "Oregon Bill Speech," http://www.teachingamericanhistory.org/library/index.asp?document=944.

The most important and informative secondary scholarship on these antebellum debates includes William Lee Miller, *Arguing about Slavery: The Great Battle in the United States Congress* (New York: Alfred A. Knopf, 1996); David F. Ericson, *The Shaping of American Liberalism: The Debates over Ratification, Nullification, and Slavery* (Chicago: University of Chicago Press, 1993); David F. Ericson, *The Debate over Slavery: Antislavery and Proslavery Liberalism in Antebellum America* (New York: New York University Press, 2000). Some of the best and most frequently cited contemporary assessments of the Founders, slavery, and the original Constitution include: Akhil Reed Amar, *The Constitution: A Biography* (New York: Random House, 2005), especially 20–21, 87–98, 120–121, 150–151, 156–159, 256–264; William W. Freehling, "The Founding Fathers and Slavery," *American Historical Review* 77 (February 1972): 81–93; Freehling, "The Founding Fathers, Conditional Anti-slavery, and the Nonradicalism of the American Revolution," in *The Reintegration of American History: Slavery and the Civil War* (New York: Oxford University Press, 1994), 12–33; Don E. Fehrenbacher with Ward M. McAfee, *The Slaveholding Republic: An Account of the United States Government's Relations to Slavery* (New York: Oxford University Press, 2001), especially 1–47; Herbert Storing, "Slavery and the Moral Foundations of the American Republic," in *The Moral Foundations of the American Republic,* ed. Robert H. Horwitz (Charlottesville: University of Virginia Press, 1979), 313–332; William M. Wiecek, "The Witch at the Christening: Slavery and the Constitution's Origins," in *The Framing and Ratification of the Constitution* (New York: Macmillan, 1987), 167–184.

21. For an overview of this historiographical school, see Alan Gibson, *Interpreting*

the *Founding: Guide to the Enduring Debates over the Origins and Foundations of the American Republic*, 2nd ed. (Lawrence: University Press of Kansas, 2010), 64–85.

22. For the transformation of Jefferson's reputation and the controversy surrounding him, see Garry Wills, "Storm over Jefferson," *New York Review of Books* 47, March 9, 2000, http://www.nybooks.com/articles/197, and Gordon S. Wood, "The Disappointments of Jefferson," *New York Review of Books* 28, August 13, 1981, http://www.nybooks.com/articles/6931. For the conclusion that Jefferson was the likely father of Hemings's children and the discussion of the implications of this relationship, see Annette Gordon-Reed, *Thomas Jefferson and Sally Hemings: An American Controversy* (1997; reprint, Charlottesville: University Press of Virginia, 1999); Jan Ellen Lewis and Peter Onuf, eds., *Sally Hemings and Thomas Jefferson: History, Memory, and Civic Culture* (Charlottesville: University Press of Virginia, 1999); "Forum: Thomas Jefferson and Sally Hemings Redux," *William and Mary Quarterly* 57 (January 2000): 121–210. This forum contains essays by Jan Lewis, Joseph Ellis, Lucia Stanton, Peter Onuf, Annette Gordon-Reed, and Fraser Neiman: "Report of the Research Committee on Thomas Jefferson and Sally Hemings," Thomas Jefferson Memorial Foundation, January 2000, http://www.monticello.org/plantation/hemingscontro/hemings_report.html. For criticism of the conclusion that Jefferson fathered the Hemings's children, see White McKenzie (Ken) Wallenborn, "Thomas Jefferson Foundation DNA Study Committee Minority Report," April 12, 1999, http://www.monticello.org/plantation/hemingscontro/minority_report.html; "The Scholars Commission Report," http://www.tjheritage.org/scholars.html; Eyler Robert Coates, ed., *The Jefferson–Hemings Myth: An American Travesty* (Charlottesville: Jefferson Editions, 2001); Robert F. Turner, "The Truth about Jefferson," *Wall Street Journal*, July 3, 2001.

23. Jefferson has been the great loser in these reassessments. As Joseph Ellis has observed, as race and slavery have become more central to our understanding of American history, Jefferson's "stock was fated to fall in the scholarly world." Joseph Ellis, *American Sphinx: The Character of Thomas Jefferson* (New York: Alfred A. Knopf, 1997), 16. Conversely, the reputation of Gouverneur Morris has risen as a result of his criticisms of slavery, especially those presented at the Constitutional Convention. Not coincidentally, Morris has recently been the subject of three laudatory biographies. See William Howard Adams, *Gouverneur Morris: An Independent Life* (New Haven, Conn.: Yale University Press, 2003); Richard Brookhiser, *Gentleman Revolutionary: Gouverneur Morris, the Rake Who Wrote the Constitution* (New York: Free Press, 2003); James J. Kirschke, *Gouverneur Morris: Author, Statesman, and Man of the World* (New York: Thomas Dunne Books, 2005). The issue of slavery has also become important in reassessments of George Washington. See Kenneth Morgan, "George Washington and the Problem of Slavery," *Journal of American Studies* 34 (2000): 279–301; Joseph Ellis, *His Excellency George Washington* (New York: Alfred A. Knopf, 2004), 161–167, 201–203, 244, 257–264; and especially Henry Wiencek, *An Imperfect God: George Washington, His Slaves, and the Creation of America* (New York: Farrar, Straus, and Giroux, 2003).

24. For the question of whether the American Revolution was revolutionary in its effects, including its effects on women, see Michael McGiffert, ed., "Forum: How Revolutionary Was the Revolution? A Discussion of Gordon S. Wood's *The Radicalism of the*

American Revolution," *William and Mary Quarterly* 41 (1992): 677–716. This exchange contains essays by Joyce Appleby, Barbara Clark Smith, Michael Zuckerman, and Gordon Wood.

25. See my presentation at the James Madison Program entitled "The American Founders and the Culture Wars," which may be found at http://web.princeton.edu/sites/jmadison/calendar/fall07.html.

Chapter 1: Still Hazy after All These Years

Epigraph: Louis Hartz, *The Liberal Tradition in America: An Interpretation of American Political Thought since the Revolution* (San Diego: Harcourt Brace Jovanovich, 1955), 27–28.

1. The most famous predecessor of Beard's is Orin Grant Libby, *The Geographical Distribution of the Vote of the Thirteen States on the Federal Constitution* (Madison: University of Wisconsin, 1894).

2. Forrest McDonald, *We the People: The Economic Origins of the Constitution* (Chicago: University of Chicago Press, 1958); Robert E. Brown, *Charles Beard and the Constitution: A Critical Analysis of "An Economic Interpretation of the Constitution"* (Princeton, N.J.: Princeton University Press, 1956).

3. James Hutson, "The Constitution: An Economic Document?" in *The Framing and Ratification of the Constitution,* ed. Leonard Levy and Dennis Mahoney (New York: Macmillan, 1987), 267.

4. Three essays, now dated, had a similar goal. See D. W. Brogan, "The Quarrel over Charles Austin Beard and the American Constitution," *Economic History Review* 18 (August 1965): 199–223; Cecelia Kenyon, "'An Economic Interpretation of the Constitution' after Fifty Years," *Centennial Review of Arts and Science* 7 (1963): 327–352; Hutson, "The Constitution: An Economic Document?" 259–270.

5. Scholars have offered an array of interpretations about Beard's understanding of the Framers and the Constitution, his contemporary political goals, and the relationship between his political goals and his scholarship. Indeed, Beard has been read as a Progressive, neo-Jeffersonian, Marxist, and democratic socialist and as everything from a muckraker of the Framers to a celebrant of them. Richard Hofstadter's interpretation of Beard as a Progressive historian, as well as a Progressive reformer, is perhaps standard. See Richard Hofstadter, *The Progressive Historians: Turner, Beard, Parrington* (New York: Alfred A. Knopf, 1968), 167–317. Beard has also been given numerous other readings that, although not necessarily rejecting him as a Progressive, suggest that he had substantial differences with the Progressives or that he viewed other concerns as more central. Max Lerner and Staughton Lynd read Beard as a neo-Jeffersonian who celebrated the small farmer and opposed commercial oligarches. See Max Lerner, "The Political Theory of Charles A. Beard," *American Quarterly* 2 (Winter 1950): 303–321 and Staughton Lynd, *Class Conflict, Slavery, and the United States Constitution* (Indianapolis: Bobbs-Merrill, 1967), 11–12, 247–269. Shlomo Slonim reads Beard as a Marxist. Shlomo Slonim, "Beard's Historiography and the Constitutional Convention," *Perspectives in American History* 3 (1986): 204–206. Morton White and Cushing Strout read Beard as a pragmatist and an opponent of legal formalism who was sympathetic to, but also had significant disagreements with,

Marx. See Morton White, *Social Thought in America: The Revolt against Formalism* (London: Oxford University Press, 1976), 107–127; Cushing Strout, *The Pragmatic Revolt in American History: Carl Becker and Charles Beard* (New Haven, Conn.: Yale University Press, 1958).

The most revisionary interpretations of Beard's views on the Framers and the Constitution and his contemporary political position have been offered by Pope McCorkle and Clyde Barrow. McCorkle argues that Beard defended—indeed, even celebrated—the Framers and the Constitution but simultaneously favored the Progressive reform movement. This paradoxical fusion of historical Federalism and contemporary Progressivism, according to McCorkle, is made consistent when we see that Beard was one of only a few Progressives who favored a form of Hamiltonian "new nationalism." See Pope McCorkle, "The Historian as Intellectual: Charles Beard and the Constitution Reconsidered," *American Journal of Legal History* 28 (1984): 314–363. Barrow recently argued, against the thrust of most of the interpretations already mentioned, that Beard was not a Progressive reformer but rather a non-Marxist democratic socialist and that his political agenda and his interpretation of the formation and ratification of the Constitution were much different from the Progressives'. See Clyde Barrow, *More Than a Historian: The Political and Economic Thought of Charles A. Beard* (New Brunswick, N.J.: Transaction, 2000). See also John Patrick Diggins, "Power and Authority in American History: The Case of Charles A. Beard and His Critics," *American Historical Review* 86 (October 1981): 701–730, especially note 9.

6. Forrest McDonald has suggested that Beard deliberately slanted data, ignored important facts, and set forth misrepresentations to promote his broader goal of jarring the historical profession out of its sterile and unrealistic view of the Founders. Charles A. Beard, *An Economic Interpretation of the Constitution of the United States* (1913; reprint, New York: Free Press, 1986), xvi–xviii. All subsequent citations to *An Economic Interpretation* are to this edition; citations to "New Introduction" and "Introduction to the 1935 Edition" refer to McDonald's 1986 introduction and Beard's 1935 introduction, respectively, and are also from this volume.

7. Beard, "Introduction to the 1935 Edition," xlv–xlvi.

8. See Charles A. Beard, *The Supreme Court and the Constitution* (New York: Macmillan, 1926), especially 86–89; see 87 for an example of Beard's praise of the Constitution. See also Beard's *An Economic Interpretation*, 100–114, 125–126, 133–136, for his praise of Hamilton, Madison, and Robert Morris. For a discussion of Beard's ambiguity about the Founders, see Strout, *Pragmatic Revolt*, 93–99.

9. Beard, *An Economic Interpretation*, 17.

10. Ibid., 63.

11. Ibid., 61, 325, 51.

12. For comments about the centrality of this chapter in Beard's argument, see McDonald, *We the People*, 8; Hofstadter, *The Progressive Historians*, 211; Brown, *Charles Beard and the Constitution*, 73.

13. Beard, *An Economic Interpretation*, 149–151; the quote is on 149.

14. Ibid., 161–162, 176.

15. Ibid., 24, 251, 250.

16. McDonald, "New Introduction," xxii.

17. See Brown, *Charles Beard and the Constitution*; McDonald, *We the People*; Forrest

McDonald, "The Anti-Federalists," *Wisconsin Magazine of History* 46 (Spring 1963): 206–214; Lee Benson, *Turner and Beard: American Historical Writing Reconsidered* (Glencoe, Ill.: Free Press, 1960); Philip A. Crowl, "Anti-Federalism in Maryland, 1787–1788," *William and Mary Quarterly* 4 (October 1947): 446–469; Kenyon, "'An Economic Interpretation of the Constitution,'" 327–352; William C. Pool, "An Economic Interpretation of the Ratification of the Federal Constitution in North Carolina," *North Carolina Historical Review* 27 (April, July, October 1950): 119–141, 289–313, 437–461; Robert Thomas, "The Virginia Convention of 1788: A Criticism of Charles Beard's *An Economic Interpretation of the Constitution*," *Journal of Southern History* 19 (February 1953): 63–72. Critical reviews of the impact of this scholarship on Beard's economic interpretation of the Constitution include Hofstadter, *The Progressive Historians*, especially 218–224, and Hutson, "The Constitution: An Economic Document?" 259–270.

18. McDonald attributes much of the impetus for the challenge to Beard to "a veritable explosion of readily available primary resource materials." McDonald, "New Introduction," xxv.

19. Beard, *An Economic Interpretation*, v.

20. Beard, "Introduction to the 1935 Edition," lii. The original quote is from *An Economic Interpretation*, 73 (emphasis added).

21. See, for example, Barrow, *More Than a Historian*, 125–126; McCorkle, "The Historian as Intellectual," 314–363.

22. Beard, *An Economic Interpretation*, 324, 17–18 (emphasis added).

23. Ibid., 35, 51.

24. Hofstadter, *The Progressive Historians*, 213–218; the quotes are on 231–214. See also Benson, *Turner and Beard*, 107–109.

25. Beard, *An Economic Interpretation*, 61, 252, 291.

26. Ibid., 28–29.

27. Benson, *Turner and Beard*, 143.

28. Barrow, *More Than a Historian*, 122–123; the quote is on 123.

29. Beard, *An Economic Interpretation*, 324, 71, 24. Beard's claims about disenfranchisement have been challenged by Brown, *Charles Beard and the Constitution*, 61–72, 158–165, 197. For a challenge to Brown's conclusions, see Benson, *Turner and Beard*, 176–194.

30. Beard, *An Economic Interpretation*, 71, 242.

31. Hofstadter, *The Progressive Historians*, 280.

32. Brown, *Charles Beard and the Constitution*, 61–62.

33. Kenyon, "'An Economic Interpretation of the Constitution,'" 329–330, 334; the quote is on 334; Benson, *Turner and Beard*, 152–160.

34. David Siemers has calculated that there were 1,648 delegates to the state ratifying conventions, not including delegates to the second ratifying convention held in North Carolina. See David Siemers, *Ratifying the Republic: Antifederalists and Federalists in Constitutional Time* (Stanford, Calif.: Stanford University Press, 2002), 274 n. 2, appendix B.

35. On this point, see Benson, *Turner and Beard*, 166.

36. Beard, "Introduction to the 1935 Edition," xlv, l.

37. Brown, *Charles Beard and the Constitution*, 20–21, 49–54, 94; the quote is on 50.

38. Robert E. Brown, *Reinterpretation of the Formation of the American Constitution*

(Boston: Boston University Press, 1963), 1–20; Brown, *Charles Beard and the Constitution,* 20–21, 34–45, 48–51, 94.

39. See Benson, *Turner and Beard,* 119–121.

40. Beard, *An Economic Interpretation,* 325.

41. McDonald, *We the People,* 21–37; the quote is on 37. See also Clinton Rossiter, *1787: The Grand Convention* (New York: Macmillan, 1966), 139–140.

42. McDonald, *We the People,* 86–88; the quote is on 87.

43. Brown, *Charles Beard and the Constitution,* 73–91, especially 89.

44. Forrest McDonald, "Charles A. Beard and the Constitution: Forrest McDonald's Rebuttal," *William and Mary Quarterly* 17 (January 1960): 106; McDonald, *We the People,* 38–92, especially 86–92.

45. McDonald, "McDonald's Rebuttal," 106; McDonald, *We the People,* 95.

46. McDonald, *We the People,* 93.

47. Beard, *An Economic Interpretation,* 51, 290, 20–22, 74–75 n. 3, 149–150.

48. Edward Corwin, "Review of *An Economic Interpretation of the Constitution,*" *History Teachers Magazine* 5 (February 1914): 65–66.

49. When Beard addressed this criticism, he argued—with considerable temerity—that it was wrong to suggest that the Framers had purchased their securities after 1787 as a speculative investment rather than prior to 1787, when the fortunes of the government were at considerable risk. "Respect for the framers," Beard argued, "should impel us" to accept the idea that they risked their money when the government was at a low ebb. Charles A. Beard, *Economic Origins of Jeffersonian Democracy* (New York: Macmillan, 1915), 106 n. 1; Beard, *An Economic Interpretation,* 75 n. 3.

50. Corwin, "Review of *An Economic Interpretation of the Constitution,*" 65–66.

51. United States Constitution, Article 6, Clause 1.

52. A provision that stated that "the legislature *shall* discharge the debts & fulfill the engagements of the U[nited] States" was rejected in favor of the clause that eventually passed. This provision seemingly would have bound the government to fund the debt at full face value rather than allowing greater flexibility. See Phillip B. Kurland and Ralph Lerner, eds., *The Founders' Constitution,* 5 vols. (Indianapolis: Liberty Fund Press, 1987), 5:585–587.

53. Van Beck Hall has found, for example, that "the market value of state and national securities held by Massachusetts investors skyrocketed from $1.5 million in 1788 to over $5.5 milliion in later 1791, giving the commonwealth and its speculators a tidy profit of over $4.0 million." Van Beck Hall, *Politics without Parties: Massachusetts, 1780–1781* (Pittsburgh: University of Pittsburgh Press, 1972), 42.

54. Corwin, "Review of *An Economic Interpretation of the Constitution,*" 65–66. See also the discussion of this same point in Brown, *Charles Beard and the Constitution,* 51–52.

55. In a letter to the author dated August 23, 2003, McDonald takes issue with Ferguson's comment that, "For want of complete data on security holdings before 1790, it will probably never be possible to verify the financial stakes held by most of the leading actors in the drama" (E. James Ferguson, *The Power of the Purse: A History of American Public Finance, 1776–1790* [Chapel Hill: University of North Carolina Press, 1961], 253). "It is entirely possible (in many instances, though not always)," McDonald writes, "to know

when the Framers acquired the securities they held." In *We the People,* he points out, he often comments on when the Framers acquired their securities. This is true, for example, for Rufus King, Roger Sherman, Elbridge Gerry, Oliver Ellsworth, Alexander Hamilton, and Jonathan Dayton (see McDonald, *We the People,* 42, 48, 49, 52).

56. McDonald, *We the People,* 89–91, 355–357.

57. See Forrest McDonald, *E Pluribus Unum: The Formation of the American Republic, 1776–1790* (Boston: Houghton Mifflin, 1965), 329–330; McDonald, "New Introduction," viii–ix.

58. McDonald, *We the People,* 357. McDonald's analysis of security holders in the state ratifying conventions rested on a determination of the percentage of opponents versus supporters of the Constitution who owned any securities at all. McDonald did not make generalizations about the dollar value of the securities owned by anti-Federalists and Federalists. This issue was later taken up by Robert Schuyler, who observed that if McDonald had focused on the amount of the holdings rather than simply the number, he would have found that of the 200 "large" security holders (those with more than $1,000 in securities) he identified, 139 voted for ratification and only 61 voted against. See Robert Livingston Schuyler, "Forrest McDonald's Critique of the Beard Thesis," *Journal of Southern History* 27 (1961): 76–78.

59. McDonald, *We the People,* 100–101.

60. Ibid., 101–108.

61. Ibid., 109; McDonald, "McDonald's Rebuttal," 106.

62. McDonald, *We the People,* 350–355; the quote is on 354.

63. McDonald, "The Anti-Federalists," 206–214; McDonald, *We the People,* especially 356–357; Crowl, "Anti-Federalism in Maryland," 446–469; Pool, "An Economic Interpretation of Ratification in North Carolina," 119–141, 289–313, 437–461; Thomas, "The Virginia Convention of 1788," 63–72.

64. Thomas, "The Virginia Convention of 1788," 64–65.

65. McDonald, *We the People,* 89–91, 356–357, 253.

66. Hofstadter, *The Progressive Historians,* 224.

67. McDonald, *We the People,* vii.

68. Ibid., 358; McDonald, *E Pluribus Unum,* 15, 40, 129, 310.

69. McDonald, "The Anti-Federalists," 206–214; MacDonald, *E Pluribus Unum,* especially 317–330.

70. McDonald, "New Introduction," xxxii.

71. McDonald, "The Anti-Federalists," especially 208–211.

72. Staughton Lynd, *Anti-Federalism in Dutchess County, New York: A Study of Democracy and Class Conflict in the Revolutionary Era* (Chicago: Loyola University Press, 1962); Lynd, *Class Conflict, Slavery, and the United States Constitution.* For Main's central works, see *The Social Structure of Revolutionary America* (Princeton, N.J.: Princeton University Press, 1965); "Government by the People: The American Revolution and Democratization of the Legislatures," *William and Mary Quarterly* 17 (July 1966): 391–407; *The Upper House in Revolutionary America, 1763–1788* (Madison: University of Wisconsin Press, 1967); *Political Parties before the Constitution* (Chapel Hill: University of North Carolina Press, 1973); and *The Antifederalists: Critics of the Constitution, 1781–1788* (New York: W. W. Norton, 1974). For Wood, see note 79. For Hall, see *Politics without Parties.*

73. See in particular Ferguson, *The Power of the Purse;* E. James Ferguson, "Currency Finance: An Interpretation of Colonial Monetary Practices," *William and Mary Quarterly* 10 (April 1953): 153–180; Ferguson, "Political Economy, Public Liberty, and the Formation of the Constitution," *William and Mary Quarterly* 40 (April 1983): 389–412; Ferguson, "The Nationalists of 1781–1783 and the Economic Interpretation of the Constitution," *William and Mary Quarterly* 56 (September 1969): 241–261; Stuart Bruchey, "The Forces behind the Constitution: A Critical Review of the Framework of E. James Ferguson's *The Power of the Purse,*" *William and Mary Quarterly* 19 (July 1962): 429–434; Ferguson, "E. James Ferguson's Rebuttal," *William and Mary Quarterly* 19 (July 1962): 434–438.

74. Ferguson, *The Power of the Purse,* 250.

75. Thomas, "The Virginia Convention of 1788," 72.

76. Jackson Turner Main, "Charles A. Beard and the Constitution: A Critical Review of Forrest McDonald's *We the People,*" *William and Mary Quarterly* 17 (January 1960): 94.

77. Lynd, *Anti-Federalism in Dutchess County,* 5–7.

78. Ibid., 7.

79. See especially Wood, *Creation of the American Republic,* 485–488; Wood, "Interests and Disinterestedness in the Making of the Constitution," in *Beyond Confederation: Origins of the Constitution and American National Identity,* ed. Richard Beeman, Stephen Botein, and Edward C. Carter II (Chapel Hill: University of North Carolina Press, 1987), 93–100.

80. Lynd, *Anti-Federalism in Dutchess County,* 7, 4.

81. Ibid., 4.

82. Hall, *Politics without Parties,* 62.

83. Jackson Turner Main, "An Agenda for Research on the Origins and Nature of the Constitution of 1787–1788," *William and Mary Quarterly* 44 (July 1987): 594; see also Main, *The Antifederalists,* 261–274.

84. For summaries of the central assumptions and common criticisms of rational choice theory, see David Laman, Joe Oppenheimer, and Piotr Swistak, "Formal Rational Choice Theory: A Cumulative Science of Politics," in *Political Science: The State of the Discipline II,* ed. Ada W. Finifter (Washington, D.C.: American Political Science Association, 1993), 77–104; Donald P. Green and Ian Shapiro, *Pathologies of Rational Choice Theory: A Critique of Applications in Political Science* (New Haven, Conn.: Yale University Press, 1994); Jon Elster, ed., *Rational Choice* (Washington Square, N.Y.: New York University Press, 1986), 1–33; Kristen Renwick Monroe, "The Theory of Rational Action: What Is It? How Useful Is It for Political Science?" in *Political Science: Looking to the Future,* vol. 1 (Evanston, Ill.: Northwestern University Press, 1991), 77–98.

85. Calvin Jillson, *Constitution Making: Conflict and Consensus in the Federal Convention of 1787* (New York: Agathon Press, 1988). For studies that emphasize the importance of debate over philosophical principles and the importance of shared political principles at the convention, see Herbert Storing, "The Constitutional Convention: Toward a More Perfect Union," in *American Political Thought: The Philosophic Dimension of American Statesmanship,* ed. Morton J. Frisch and Richard G. Stevens (New York: Scribner, 1971), 51–68; Lance Banning, *The Sacred Fire of Liberty: James Madison and the Founding of the Federal Republic* (Ithaca, N.Y.: Cornell University Press, 1995), 111–191, especially 111–112; Martin Diamond, *The Founding of the Democratic Republic* (Itasca, Ill.: F. E. Peacock, 1981), 15–60, especially 29–30.

86. Jillson, *Constitution Making*, 17, 16 (emphasis added).

87. Beard, "Introduction to the 1935 Edition," xlviii; Jillson, *Constitution Making*, xi.

88. Robert McGuire, *To Form a More Perfect Union: A New Economic Interpretation of the United States Constitution* (New York: Oxford University Press, 2003). This work is the culmination of a number of studies that also illuminate the economic interpretation of McGuire and his coauthor for a number of works, Robert Ohsfeldt. See Robert McGuire and Robert Ohsfeldt, "Economic Interests and the American Constitution: A Quantitative Rehabilitation of Charles A. Beard," *Journal of Economic History* 44 (1984): 509–519; McGuire and Ohsfeldt, "An Economic Model of Voting Behavior over Specific Issues at the Constitutional Convention of 1787," *Journal of Economic History* 46 (1986): 79–111; McGuire, "Constitution Making: A Rational Choice Model of the Federal Convention of 1787," *American Journal of Political Science* 32 (1988): 483–522; McGuire and Ohsfeldt, "Public Choice Analysis and the Ratification of the Constitution," in *The Federalist Papers and the New Institutionalism*, ed. Bernard Grofman and Donald Wittman (New York: Agathon Press, 1989), 175–204; McGuire and Ohsfeldt, "Self-Interest, Agency Theory, and Political Voting Behavior: The Ratification of the United States Constitution," *American Economic Review* 79 (1989): 219–234; McGuire, "Economic Interests and the Adoption of the United States Constitution," *EH.Net Encyclopedia*, ed. Robert Whaples, http://www.eh.net/encyclopedia/article/mcguire.constitution.us.economic.interests (accessed August 15, 2001).

89. McDonald, *We the People*, 110.

90. McGuire, *To Form a More Perfect Union*, 5.

91. Ibid., 66.

92. Ibid., 70–73, 65.

93. Ibid., 131–206.

94. For McGuire's ambiguous findings about the role of public securities, see *To Form a More Perfect Union*, 68, 72, 83–85, 102–103. McGuire's study suggests that public securities were statistically significant on only a few of the sixteen issues studied. Paradoxically, he also found that delegates whose public securities appreciated in value were *less* likely to support a universal veto on all state laws, even though this was an important nationalistic provision that certainly would have benefited the creditor class. Finally, he suggests that a hypothetical delegate to the Constitutional Convention with "average" values for all economic interests and characteristics did not vote significantly different from an "average" security holder.

95. McGuire, *To Form a More Perfect Union*, 6, 107, 179, 182, 206. McGuire gathered data on whether an individual was a local, state, or national officeholder prior to the convention to test the proposition—stated most succinctly by Hamilton in *Federalist* No. 1— that many state officeholders would oppose the Constitution because they had an "obvious interest" in resisting "all changes which may hazard a diminution of the power, emolument, and consequences of the offices they hold under the State establishments." Alexander Hamilton, James Madison, and John Jay, *The Federalist Papers*, ed. Jacob E. Cooke (1961; reprint, Middletown, Conn.: Wesleyan University Press, 1989), 4.

Political experience after ratification of the Constitution was also used as an indicator of a delegate's ambitions at the time of ratification. McGuire found that a delegate's political experience either before of after the convention had virtually no significance in terms of his likelihood of supporting or opposing the Constitution. This, in my estimation, is the least persuasive of McGuire's findings. Even discounting the problem with using experience after ratification as an indicator of ambitions before ratification, it is hard to see how local or state officeholding before ratification of the Constitution can serve as an indicator of the kind of person Hamilton sought to identify. Until ratification of the Constitution, state offices were the most prestigious ones. Furthermore, service in the Confederation Congress was limited by the Articles of Confederation to three years in every six. Thus, even the most fervent nationalists and supporters of constitutional reform likely would have had significant political experience in state office. Indeed, it would be remarkable if they lacked such experience. For Hamilton's proposition to be tested, scholars must devise some way of separating these nationalists who held state office from other politicians who held state office and opposed the formation of the national government because they feared the loss of their local power.

96. Richard D. Brown, "The Founding Fathers of 1776 and 1787: A Collective View," *William and Mary Quarterly* 33 (1976): 465–480.

97. Even McDonald, who emphasizes the diversity of the interests of the delegates at Philadelphia, does not suggest that they were men of modest means. Responding to Main's complaint that he had "made men of means appear to be the opposite," McDonald noted that he had actually found that many of the members of the convention had more property than Beard had suggested. See Main, "Critical Review of *We the People*," 89–91; McDonald, "McDonald's Rebuttal," 104–106.

98. See Brown, "The Founding Fathers of 1776 and 1787," 465–480; Rossiter and McGuire list Jacob Broom of Delaware and William Few of Georgia as the only farmers of modest means at the convention. Rossiter, *The Grand Convention*, 144; McGuire, *To Form a More Perfect Union*, 51–53, 93.

99. Main, "Critical Review of *We the People*," 87–89; Benson, *Turner and Beard*, 229–231. Even Rossiter, who shares McDonald's belief that most of the factions in the states were represented at the convention, concedes a "dearth of men who lived in the back country." Rossiter, *The Grand Convention*, 130. For an interesting argument that anti-Federalism was virtually unrepresented at the Constitutional Convention, see William Riker, "The Lessons of 1787," *Public Choice* 55 (1987), 9–21.

100. Jillson limits his analysis primarily to the delegates' representation of their state interests because he is skeptical of attempts to ascertain their individual positions on specific clauses and thus measure the effect of their personal economic interests on voting at the convention. Scholars who engage in this type of analysis, Jillson observes, "end up relating data on the delegates to a couple of dozen votes and then stretching an interpretation across the entire Convention, its operation, and meaning." E-mail from Calvin Jillson, September 9, 2003.

101. McGuire, *To Form a More Perfect Union*, 65–66, 68.

102. Ibid., 66–67, 72.

103. Ibid., 68, 72–73. McGuire's results for the convention should not be overstated. Before he stresses the impact of several particular interests on the delegates' voting at Philadelphia, he observes that "the influence of a delegate's personal interests on voting might not appear especially strong as there are few statistically significant results overall" (ibid., 65–66).

104. Ibid., 65.

105. Ibid., 58–59.

106. McDonald, *We the People*, 97–100.

107. Main, *The Antifederalists*, 263–265. See also Main, "Critical Review of *We the People*," 89–100, and *Political Parties before the Constitution*, 357–358.

108. The most recent and sophisticated contemporary scholarship acknowledges social and economic diversity within the anti-Federalist leadership without providing a systematic or comprehensive empirical foundation for these differences. Saul Cornell differentiates between "elite" and "popular" anti-Federalist thought, while David Siemers separates anti-Federalism of the "Middling Class" and "Elite Anti-federalism." Saul Cornell, *The Other Founders: Anti-Federalism and the Dissenting Tradition in America, 1788–1828* (Chapel Hill: University of North Carolina Press, 1999), 51–119; David Siemers, *The Antifederalists: Men of Great Faith and Forbearance* (Lanham, Md.: Rowman and Littlefield, 2003), 115–147, 183–221.

109. Benson, *Turner and Beard*, 175.

110. In *An Economic Interpretation of the Constitution*, Beard estimates that 160,000 men participated in the ratification process by voting for delegates to the state ratifying conventions. McDonald praises Beard's estimate of these figures, saying that they were "remarkably accurate" and based on a series of "ingenious calculations." No one has subsequently challenged them. McDonald, *We the People*, 14, n. 11.

111. McDonald, *We the People*, 195, 199. See also Benson, *Turner and Beard*, 231–232. Benson notes that obscure delegates whose occupations could not be ascertained by McDonald were disproportionately anti-Federalists and speculates that they held low-status occupations.

112. See John P. Kaminski and Richard Leffler, eds., *Federalists and Antifederalists: The Debate over the Ratification of the Constitution* (1989; reprint, Lanham, Md.: Madison House, 1998), 178–219, for rhetorical evidence of the class tensions underlying the debate between the Federalists and anti-Federalists.

113. Lynd pinpoints the areas where anti-Federalist leaders lived as well as the areas where the tenant riots of 1766 took place and hypothesizes that the latter were also areas of anti-Federalist support among the rank and file. He concedes, however, that because voting records do not exist at the precinct level, this correlation cannot be verified. See Lynd, *Anti-Federalism in Dutchess County*, 20–54, especially 21–22, 26, 32–33.

114. McDonald's advice about the importance of understanding the peculiarity of each state in terms of ratification has recently been emphasized in an excellent study of ratification in Connecticut. See Christopher Collier, *All Politics Is Local: Family, Friends, and Provincial Interests in the Creation of the Constitution* (Hanover, N.H.: University Press of New England, 2003).

115. An important exception to this conclusion is provided by Owen S. Ireland, who concludes that support for the Constitution in Philadelphia was virtually unanimous but that backcountry voters—with the exception of a stubborn minority—also supported it. Ireland argues that ethnic, religious, and long-standing political differences are much more important in explaining the division of the vote in Pennsylvania than are class or ideological differences. Owen S. Ireland, *Religion, Ethnicity, and Politics: Ratifying the Constitution in Pennsylvania* (University Park: Pennsylvania State University Press, 1995).

See also Donald Lutz, *Popular Consent and Popular Control: Whig Political Theory in the Early State Constitutions* (Baton Rouge: Louisiana State University Press, 1980), 171–212. Lutz offers qualified support to Main's sectional-economic interpretation of the Constitution but notes that ratification was possible only because 30 percent of the small towns in the western regions of the states voted for it. Lutz also explains Federalism and anti-Federalism broadly in terms of two contrasting political cultures—one (Whig) rooted in localism, tradition, and assumptions about the homogeneity of the people's interests; the other (Federalist) rooted in a defense of individualism, self-interest, and a belief in the natural heterogeneity of the people's interests.

116. Hofstadter, *The Progressive Historians*, 344.

Chapter 2: Democracy and the Founders' Constitution

1. John Dickinson, speech of August 13, in *Notes of Debates in the Federal Convention of 1787 Reported by James Madison*, ed. Adrienne Koch (New York: W. W. Norton, 1987), 448.

2. Quotes are from *Federalist* No. 14, 84; No. 39, 250, in Alexander Hamilton, James Madison, and John Jay, *The Federalist Papers*, ed. Jacob E. Cooke (1961; reprint, Middletown, Conn.: Wesleyan University Press, 1989). All subsequent citations are to this volume.

3. Martin Diamond (*The Founding of the Democratic Republic* [Itasca, Ill.: F. E. Peacock, 1981], 62) believes that the question "how democratic is the Consitution?" is the most important and disputed issue concerning the American Founding because it "speaks to the fundamental nature of a regime" and "profoundly influences both practical politics and the way politics is studied." Similarly, Gordon Wood ("Democracy and the Constitution," in *How Democratic Is the Constitution?* ed. Robert A. Goldwin and William A. Schambra [Washington, D.C.: American Enterprise Institute, 1980], 1) notes that this was "the central question asked at the time the Constitution was framed, and it is a question that Americans have raised ever since."

4. J. Allen Smith, *The Spirit of American Government* (1907; reprint, Cambridge, Mass.: Harvard University Press, 1965), 27–185; the quote is on 32.

5. Charles Beard, *An Economic Interpretation of the Constitution of the United States* (1913; reprint, New York: Free Press, 1986), 159–168; the quote is on 161.

6. The most famous version of this argument is found in Beard, *An Economic Interpretation*, 64–72.

7. Diamond, *Founding of the Democratic Republic*, 3–12, 61–110 (the quote is on 9); Martin Diamond, "Democracy and *The Federalist*," *American Political Science Review* 53 (March 1959): 52–68. For a defense of the Constitution against the charges brought by New Left scholars along the lines suggested by Diamond, see George Carey, *In Defense of the Constitution* (Indianapolis: Liberty Fund, 1995). Cecelia Kenyon's scholarship has also served as an important counterweight to the Progressive interpretation. In contrast to Progressive and neo-Progressive scholars who suggest that the anti-Federalists were champions of democracy, Kenyon argues that they were ideologically conservative "men of little faith." She also maintains that the anti-Federalists favored a more extensive system of checks and balances than the Federalists and were not majoritarians with respect

to the national government. Cecelia Kenyon, "Men of Little Faith: The Anti-Federalists on the Nature of Representative Government," *William and Mary Quarterly* 12 (January 1955): 3–43.

8. See in particular Robert E. Brown, *Charles Beard and the Constitution: A Critical Analysis of "An Economic Interpretation of the Constitution"* (Princeton, N.J.: Princeton University Press, 1956), 61–72, 158–165, 197; Brown, *Reinterpretation of the Formation of the Constitution* (Boston: Boston University Press, 1963), 45–49; Brown, *Virginia, 1705–1786: Democracy or Aristocracy?* (East Lansing: Michigan State University Press, 1964), 125–150; Brown, *Middle-Class Democracy and the Revolution in Massachusetts, 1691–1780* (Ithaca, N.Y.: Cornell University Press, 1955), 21–60.

9. These themes resonate through Thurgood Marshall's famous speech "A Bicentennial View from the Supreme Court," reprinted in *The United States Constitution: 200 Years of Anti-Federalist, Abolitionist, Feminist, Muckraking, Progressive, and Especially Socialist Criticism*, ed. Bertell Ollman and Jonathan Birnbaum (New York: New York University Press, 1990), 300–305. The most sophisticated analyses of the exclusionary character of the Constitution include Rogers M. Smith, *Civic Ideals: Conflicting Visions of Citizenship in U.S. History* (New Haven, Conn.: Yale University Press, 1997), 130–134; Joan Hoff, *Law, Gender, and Injustice: A Legal History of U.S. Women* (New York: New York University Press, 1991), especially 21–118; Jan Lewis, "'Of Every Age Sex and Condition': Representation of Women in the Constitution," in *What Did the Constitution Mean to Early Americans*, ed. Edward Countryman (New York: Bedford/St. Martin's Press, 1999), 115–140. The most forceful recent statement of the Constitution as a pro-slavery document can be found in Paul Finkelman, "Slavery and the Constitutional Convention: Making a Covenant with Death," in *Beyond Confederation: Origins of the Constitution and National Identity*, ed. Richard Beeman, Stephen Botein, and Edward C. Carter II (Chapel Hill: University of North Carolina Press, 1987), 188–225; Finkelman, *Slavery and the Founders: Race and Liberty in the Age of Jefferson*, 2nd ed. (Armonk, N.Y.: M. E. Sharpe, 2001), 3–36.

10. Representative versions of this argument include Herman Belz, "Liberty and Equality for Whom? How to Think Inclusively about the Constitution and the Bill of Rights," *History Teacher* 25 (May 1992): 263–277; Robert A. Goldwin, *Why Blacks, Women, and Jews Are Not Mentioned in the Constitution, and Other Unorthodox Views* (Washington, D.C.: American Enterprise Press, 1990), especially 9–20; Thomas West, *Vindicating the Founders: Race, Sex, Class, and Justice in the Origins of America* (Lanham, Md.: Rowman and Littlefield, 1997).

11. Belz, "Liberty and Equality for Whom," 263–277; the quotes are on 273, 270, and 273, respectively.

12. The Progressives made the Senate a central part of their case that the original Constitution was undemocratic. Specifically, they emphasized the powers of the Senate, the indirect election of senators from the state legislatures, and the length of senatorial terms. The Progressives did not, however, develop arguments about the inequity or effects of equal representation regardless of population. Indeed, the only mention I am aware of occurs in Smith, *The Spirit of American Government*, 339. One explanation for this neglect is that this critique does not jibe with other parts of the Progressives' interpretation. According to the Progressives, Madison, Hamilton, Wilson, and the other "nationalists" were the principal opponents of democracy among the Framers; neverthe-

less, they favored proportional representation in the Senate based on principles of equity and majority rule. Accounting for this contradiction would have caused the Progressives considerable difficulty.

13. Robert Dahl, *How Democratic Is the American Constitution?* (New Haven, Conn.: Yale University Press, 2001), especially 17–18, 46–50; Richard N. Rosenfeld, "What Democracy? The Case for Abolishing the United States Senate," *Harpers Magazine*, May 2004, 35–44; Frances E. Lee and Bruce I. Oppenheimer, *Sizing Up the Senate: The Unequal Consequences of Equal Representation* (Chicago: University of Chicago Press, 1999), especially 1–5, 16–43; William N. Eskridge Jr., "The One Senator, One Vote Clauses," and Suzanna Sherry, "Our Unconstitutional Senate," in *Constitutional Stupidities, Constitutional Tragedies*, ed. William N. Eskridge Jr. and Sanford Levinson (New York: New York University Press, 1998), 35–39, 95–97; Daniel Lazare, *The Frozen Republic: How the Constitution Is Paralyzing Democracy* (New York: Harcourt Brace, 1996), 285–295.

14. Under Article V of the Constitution, an amendment can be proposed for ratification only if two-thirds of the members present in both houses of Congress agree to it. This provision gives senators from small states the ability to block amendments. Furthermore, any amendment must be ratified either by three-fourths of the state legislatures or by ratifying conventions in three-fourths of the states. This gives the small states an effective veto over any amendment during the ratification stage. The senatorial advantage for small states in the selection of the president results from each state's receipt of two electoral votes in addition to the electoral votes equal to its number of representatives. This means that fewer individuals select the electors in small states than in large states; in other words, the votes of individuals in small states are disproportionately weighted in comparison to the votes of individuals in large states.

15. In the initial Congress, 30 percent of the population could elect a majority of the Senate; since 1970, that percentage has never been greater than 20 percent. Also, in 1790 a majority of the population lived in four states; thus, this majority elected eight senators, and the nine other states where a minority of the population lived elected eighteen senators. Lee and Oppenheimer, *Sizing Up the Senate*, 10–11, 35.

16. Article V, U.S. Constitution.

17. Finkelman, *Slavery and the Founders*, 10–21; Don E. Fehrenbacher, *The Slaveholding Republic: An Account of the United States Government's Relations to Slavery*, completed and edited by Ward M. McAfee (New York: Oxford University Press, 2001); Leonard L. Richards, *The Slave Power: The Free North and Southern Domination, 1780–1800* (Baton Rouge: Louisiana State University Press, 2000); Garry Wills, *"Negro President": Jefferson and the Slave Power* (Boston: Houghton Mifflin, 2003), 1–13; Akhil Reed Amar, *America's Constitution: A Biography* (New York: Random House, 2005), 87–98, 156–159.

18. Richards, *The Slave Power*, 56–57.

19. Wills, *"Negro President,"* 5–9.

20. This point is exemplified in Martin Diamond's critique of the Progressive literature. Although he writes in polemical tones to suggest extreme disagreement with the Progressives, Diamond never disagrees with their contention that the Framers hoped to check mass democracy. Instead, he maintains that "the Founding Fathers did in fact seek to prejudice the outcome of democracy; they sought to alter, by certain restraints, the likelihood that the majority would decide certain political issues in bad ways. These re-

straints the Founders justified as mitigating the natural defects of democracy." Diamond, "Democracy and *The Federalist*," 57.

21. The problems of definition that plague contemporary commentaries can be traced to the Founding. The Founders themselves at least initially accepted a specific definition of democracy embedded in Aristotle's classification of regimes, but the word *democracy* was already being contested and was undergoing considerable change during their lifetimes. Within Aristotle's classification scheme, democracy was one of the three pure forms of government. It referred to rule by the poor in their own interests and was classified as a corrupt form of government. Such a government could be expected to consistently pursue the interests of the people, and because those interests were the common interests, there was little danger of the people betraying their own interests. Nevertheless, the people were also considered incapable of recognizing and pursuing their real interests.

At some point—probably in the early nineteenth century—these assumptions and the understanding of democracy that accompanied them were replaced by a definition of democracy more akin to our contemporary diffusive and normative understanding of the term—that is, as a form of government that encourages widespread political participation among the citizenry, is based on political equality, and idealizes a government that is responsive to the will of the public but also protects individual rights. To make matters even more confusing, during the late eighteenth and early nineteenth centuries, the terms *democracy* and *republic* were increasingly conflated and confused, and republics were seen as taking both "aristocratic" and "democratic" forms.

For the assumptions about democracy initially accepted by the Founders, see Douglass Adair, *Fame and the Founding Fathers: Essays by Douglass Adair*, ed. Trevor Colbourn (New York: W. W. Norton, 1974), 121–123; Willi Paul Adams, *The First American Constitutions: Republican Ideology and the Making of the State Constitutions in the Revolutionary Era*, trans. Rita Kimber and Robert Kimber (Chapel Hill: University of North Carolina Press, 1980), 99–117; Wood, "Democracy and the Constitution," 7–8; Jack Scott, ed., *An Annotated Edition of Lectures on Moral Philosophy by John Witherspoon* (Newark: University of Delaware Press, 1982), 142–144. This Aristotelian definition was also included in the standard dictionary of the eighteenth century—Samuel Johnson's *A Dictionary of the English Language*, first published in 1755. See Jack Lynch, ed., *Samuel Johnson's Dictionary: Selections from the 1755 Work that Defined the English Language* (Delray Beach, Fla.: Levenger Press, 2002), 133.

See also J. R. Pole, "Historians and the Problem of Early American Democracy," *American Historical Review* 67 (April 1962): 626–646; Robert R. Palmer, *The Age of the Democratic Revolution: A Political History of Europe and America, 1760–1800*, 2 vols. (Princeton, N.J.: Princeton University Press, 1959, 1964), 1:13–20; and Palmer, "Notes on the Use of the Word 'Democracy' 1789–1799," *Political Science Quarterly* 68 (June 1953): 203–226, for a discussion of eighteenth-century uses of the word *democracy*.

The best studies of the invention of the egalitarian, normative conception of democracy that we hold today are Gordon Wood, *The Radicalism of the American Revolution: How a Revolution Transformed a Monarchical Society into a Democratic One Unlike Any that Had Ever Existed* (New York: Vintage Books, 1991), and Robert Shalhope, *The Roots of Democracy: American Thought and Culture, 1760–1800* (Boston: Twayne, 1990). The division of republics into aristocratic and democratic ones was best known through the works of Baron Charles Secondat Montesquieu, such as *On the Spirit of the Laws* [1748], ed. and trans. Anne M. Cohler, Basia Carolyn Miller, and Harold Samuel Stone (Cambridge: Cambridge University Press, 1989), 10–17.

22. These tendencies among proponents of the antidemocratic interpretation of the Constitution are illustrated in the works of Charles Beard, James Allen Smith, Michael Parenti, Joshua Miller, Robert Dahl, and Richard Rosenfeld. See Smith, *The Spirit of American Government,* 27–185, especially 40 and 126–128; Michael Parenti, "The Constitution as an Elitist Document," in Goldwin and Schambra, *How Democratic Is the Constitution?* 39–58; Joshua Miller, "The Ghostly Body Politic: *The Federalist Papers* and Popular Sovereignty," *Political Theory* 16 (February 1988): 99–119; Dahl, *How Democratic Is the American Constitution?* especially 15–20; and Rosenfeld, "What Democracy?" 35–44. See also Ollman and Birnhaum, *The United States Constitution: 200 Years of Criticism;* Richard Matthews, *If Men Were Angels: James Madison and the Heartless Empire of Reason* (Lawrence: University Press of Kansas, 1995); and Richard Hofstadter, *The American Political Tradition and the Men Who Made It* (1948; reprint, New York: Vintage Books, 1974), 3–21; but then compare the different conclusions Hofstadter reached twenty years later in *The Progressive Historians: Turner, Beard, and Parrington* (New York: Alfred A. Knopf, 1968), 252–263.

There are exceptions to the generalization that proponents of the antidemocratic Constitution want to reform it. Gordon Wood sees the Constitution of 1787 as an aristocratic document but nevertheless recently argued against constitutional reform. See Wood, *The Creation of the American Republic, 1776–1787* (1969; reprint, Chapel Hill: University of North Carolina Press, 1998), 91–124, 483–499, 519–532; Wood, "Democracy and the Constitution," 1–17. For his opposition to constitutional reform, see Wood, "Rambunctious American Democracy," *New York Review of Books,* May 9, 2002, 20–21. For a similar interpretation of the Federalists' intentions, see Alfred Young, "Conservatives, the Constitution, and the 'Spirit of Accommodation,'" in Goldwin and Schambra, *How Democratic Is the Constitution?* 117–147. Another interesting twist of the antidemocratic interpretation is offered by the conservative scholar Walter Berns, who argues that the Constitution's democratic or undemocratic nature was not the fundamental question in the ratification struggle and is not the primary point today. According to Berns, both the ordinary people who ratified the Constitution and the elites (Federalists and anti-Federalists alike) understood that the fundamental point of the original design was to protect rights, not to foster democracy. Thus, the Constitution contained significant antidemocratic elements, but these were advocated by those who ratified the Constitution and were justified. See Walter Berns, "Does the Constitution 'Secure These Rights?'" in Goldwin and Schambra, *How Democratic Is the Constitution?* 59–78.

23. Martin Diamond characterized the different standards adopted by scholars as reflecting the difference between those who believed in "the self-doubting, self-restraining American constitutional democracy" and those who believed in the "democracy of enthusiastic egalitarianism." Diamond, "The American Idea of Equality: The View from the Founding," *Review of Politics* 37 (July 1976): 328.

In his classic essay "Democracy and *The Federalist,*" Diamond conflated democracy with republicanism by tracing both to the common genus of "popular government." He also maintained that the Federalists were committed to formal equality, popular sovereignty, and a pluralist understanding of representation (52–68). This essay and its framework of analysis have been profoundly influential, especially among Straussians and their sympathizers. See, for example, Ann Stuart Diamond, "Decent, Even Though Democratic," in Goldwin and Schambra, *How Democratic Is the Constitution?* 18–38; Jeane Kirkpatrick, "Martin Diamond and the American Idea of Democracy," *Publius* 8 (Summer 1978): 7–31.

Although he has considerable differences with other aspects of Diamond's interpretation of Madison, Lance Banning has provided a similarly enthusiastic defense of Madison as a genuine democrat. See Banning, *The Sacred Fire of Liberty: James Madison and the Founding of the Federal Republic* (Ithaca, N.Y.: Cornell University Press, 1995), especially 9–10, 371–372. Other scholars who suggest that Madison and the Framers were advocates of "deliberative" democracy include Joseph Bessette, "Deliberative Democracy: The Majority Principle in Republican Government," in Goldwin and Schambra, *How Democratic Is the Constitution?* 102–116; Ralph Ketcham, "Publius: Sustaining the Republican Principle," *William and Mary Quarterly* 54 (July 1987): 576–582. See also the classic article by John P. Roche, "The Founding Fathers: A Reform Caucus in Action," *American Political Science Review* 55 (December 1961): 799–816.

24. Hofstadter, *The Progressive Historians,* 248. In a similar vein, Gordon Wood has recently written that "those who indict the framers for not creating a more democratic and egalitarian constitution—one more like the one we have today—are committing the grossest kind of anachronism." Wood, "How Democratic Is the Constitution," *New York Review of Books,* February 23, 2006, http://www.nybooks.com/articles/18717. The most comprehensive and accomplished interpretation of the Framers' Constitution as a thoroughly democratic document by eighteenth-century standards is Amar's *America's Constitution,* 57–98, 131–166, 218–225, 285–298; see especially 64–66, 151, 466, 469, and 471–473 for statements that either summarize Amar's case or provide explicit statements about his preference for historical standards.

25. This point is made with particular clarity and force in Ronald Dworkin, *Freedom's Law: The Moral Reading of the American Constitution* (Cambridge, Mass.: Harvard University Press, 1996), 15.

26. For contrasting views on this question, see George Will, *Restoration: Congress, Term Limits and the Recovery of Deliberative Democracy* (New York: Free Press, 1992); Garry Wills, "Undemocratic Vistas," *New York Review of Books,* November 19, 1992, 28–34, available at http://www.nybooks.com/articles/2756.

27. The charge that the Federalists sought to use expanded electoral districts to secure the election of social elites and thereby stem the rising tide of local democracy is the thesis of Gordon Wood's highly influential scholarship. See Wood, "Democracy and the Constitution," 12–17; Wood, *Creation of the American Republic,* especially 471–518.

28. Norman Barry, *An Introduction to Modern Political Theory* (New York: St. Martin's Press, 1989), 257.

29. Obviously, other criteria could have been adopted. The analysis in this chapter neglects at least three other criteria that modern democratic theorists consider central: the presence of political parties as vehicles of competitive elections; the protection of democratic rights, such as the freedom of speech and the press; and the openness or transparency of the political process and the publicity given to its proceedings. Since the

Framers wrote before the development of modern political parties, the first of these criteria is irrelevant. Establishing the protection of rights as a criterion of democracy suggests the paradox that, in the name of democracy, certain outcomes should be placed beyond the reach of popular majorities. The problem with adopting such a substantive understanding of democracy is that it requires a determination of what rights could be upheld in the name of democracy and what rights would have to be protected in the name of some other value. This task is essentially philosophical and problematic, and it is a bog in which I choose not to become mired. Besides, the importance of protecting individual rights has not been a source of conflict between proponents of the democratic and antidemocratic interpretations of the Constitution. As for openness and visibility, the Framers' Constitution was clearly part of a progression in the recognition of the importance of these values. Nevertheless, these concerns have received less attention by scholars than the criteria I adopt and were not as central to the Framers. For a discusssion of how the Framers' Constitution lagged behind some state constitutions but was nevertheless broadly in line with a movement for disclosure of public proceedings, see Amar, *America's Constitution*, 82–83.

30. See Catherine Allgor, *Parlor Politics: In Which the Ladies of Washington Help Build a City and a Government* (Charlottesville: University of Virginia Press, 2000); Stanley Elkins and Eric McKitrick, *The Age of Federalism: The Early American Republic, 1788–1800* (New York: Oxford University Press, 1993); Todd Estes, "Shaping the Politics of Public Opinion: Federalists and the Jay Treaty Debate," *Journal of the Early Republic* 20 (Fall 2000): 393–422; Estes, *The Jay Treaty Debate, Public Opinion, and the Evolution of Early American Political Culture* (Amherst and Boston: University of Massachusetts Press, 2006); Alan Gibson, "Veneration and Vigilance: James Madison and Public Opinion, 1785–1800," *Review of Politics* 67 (Winter 2005): 5–35; Richard Hofstadter, *The Idea of a Party System: The Rise of Legitimate Opposition in the United States, 1780–1840* (Berkeley: University of California Press, 1969); Linda Kerber, "The Republican Mother; Women and the Enlightenment—an American Perspective," *American Quarterly* 28 (Summer 1976): 187–205; Colleen Sheehan, "Madison v. Hamilton: The Battle over Republicanism and the Role of Public Opinion," *American Political Science Review* 98 (August 2004): 405–424.

31. U.S. Constitution, Article I, Section 2. These same qualifications for the electorate were adopted in 1913 when the Seventeenth Amendment was passed and senators were popularly elected.

32. Slaves were considered property and excluded from political society, but free blacks and women voted in a number of areas in colonial and Revolutionary America. In the early eighteenth century, only Virginia, South Carolina, and North Carolina prohibited free blacks from voting by law. In 1737 North Carolina reenfranchised them, but in 1761 Georgia excluded free blacks from the polls. Colonial practices with regard to suffrage for blacks were carried forth into the late eighteenth and early nineteenth centuries before the adoption of universal white male suffrage led paradoxically to the disenfranchisement of free blacks. Leon Litwack has shown that during the first half of the nineteenth century, free blacks were disenfranchised in New Jersey, Pennsylvania, and Connecticut, and by 1840, "some 93 per cent of the northern free Negro population lived in states which completely or practically excluded them from the right to vote." Furthermore, no state admitted into the Union from 1819 until the end of the Civil War per-

mitted free blacks to vote. For this story, see Leon Litwack, *North of Slavery: The Negro in the Free States, 1790–1860* (Chicago: University of Chicago Press, 1961), 75–94; the quote is on 75. See also Alexander Keyssar, *The Right to Vote: The Contested History of Democracy in the United States* (New York: Basic Books, 2000), 54–59.

Women with significant standing in the community were occasionally allowed to vote in several colonies before the American Revolution. Most dramatically, single women with property voted in New Jersey from 1776 to 1807. In 1807, however, a political scandal took place, leading to a reversal of the interpretation of the state constitution that had established female suffrage and the passage of a statute disenfranchising women. Women were given the right to vote in school board elections and municipal elections in several states during the middle of the nineteenth century. Eventually, western states entering the Union in the late nineteenth century extended full suffrage rights to women. Acceptance of women's suffrage in western states led to pressure for its adoption in eastern ones. Eventually, the Nineteenth Amendment was passed on the basis of the critical leverage gained from the adoption of women's suffrage, in some form, in twenty-nine states by 1919. See Judith Apter Klinghoffer and Lois Elkins, "'The Petticoat Electors': Women's Suffrage in New Jersey, 1776–1807," *Journal of the Early Republic* 12 (Summer 1992): 159–193; Robert J. Dinkin, *Before Equal Suffrage: Women in Partisan Politics from Colonial Times to 1920* (Westport, Conn.: Greenwood Press, 1995), 12–13, 19–20, 101–121; Amar, *America's Constitution*, 419–428; Keyssar, *The Right to Vote*, 172–221.

Native Americans were initially considered members of foreign nations and were denied the right to vote. Native Americans were not granted full citizenship until the enactment of the Indian Citizenship Act of 1924 (*U.S. Statutes at Large* 43 [1924]: 223, 253). But even then they were denied their right to vote with devices similar to those imposed on blacks. See Jeanette Wolfley, "Jim Crow, Indian Style: The Disenfranchisement of Native Americans," *American Indian Law Review* 16 (1991): 167–202.

33. Belz, "Liberty and Equality for Whom?" 263–277; Goldwin, *Why Blacks, Women, and Jews Are Not Mentioned*, 9–20; West, *Vindicating the Founders*, 71–83, 111–130.

34. *Federalist* No. 57, 385.

35. Beard, *An Economic Interpretation*, 167, 164–168.

36. Smith, *Civic Ideals*, 131.

37. The debates at Philadelphia and during the ratification struggle over the qualifications of electors for the House focused on two issues. First, the Federalists defended the decision to leave suffrage requirements to the states as a principled and prudent middle ground between two alternatives, one improper, the other impractical. The right of suffrage, Madison argued, was so fundamental that it was improper to leave it to the discretion and regulation of either Congress or the states. In addition, leaving the right of suffrage to the states would have made the House, which should have been dependent only on the people, unduly dependent on the states. Nevertheless, it was also impractical to establish national standards for voting rights in the Constitution in the face of such diverse state qualifications (*Federalist* No. 52, 354).

Second, the historical record provides insight into why the Framers rejected a freehold requirement for voting in House elections. Such a requirement had the support of some of the leading members of the Constitutional Convention, including James Madison, John Dickinson, and Gouverneur Morris. It was based on a long-standing tradition that the holding of landed property was necessary to ensure that voters had an "independent" will and a stake in their society and thus would be, in Madison's words, the "safest depositories of Republican liberty" (Koch, *Notes of Debates*, 403). Under present conditions, they contended, a freehold requirement would not create animosity among the people because a majority of them held land. In the future, however, those without landed property would outnumber freeholders, and property rights would be endangered.

This familiar set of arguments was rejected at the Philadelphia convention as impractical, unpopular, unjust, and inconsistent with the principle of federalism. Restricting the right to vote to holders of landed property, several delegates argued, was impractical because state laws varied, making it difficult to create a uniform rule for property qualifications. A freehold requirement would be unpopular because it would create different privileges for different citizens and thus create resentment among the people. It would also be unpopular, several delegates suggested, because in some states it would disenfranchise individuals who now voted, and it would create a situation in which individuals could vote for state but not federal offices. Furthermore, a freehold requirement was unjust, some Framers argued, because manufacturers and merchants exercised the franchise in several places and had proved themselves to be just as capable as freeholders of doing so, indicating that landed property was not the only appropriate measure of a permanent attachment to society. After all, merchants and manufacturers also paid taxes. As Jack Rakove (*Original Meanings: Politics and Ideas in the Making of the Constitution* [New York: Alfred A. Knopf, 1996], 225) has said, "it seems evident that many delegates opposed the pleas for a republic of freeholders on the principled grounds that landed property could no longer be treated as the preeminent source of political rights." Finally, several delegates opposed a uniform rule of suffrage in the Constitution because it would be a federal imposition into an area where the states were best qualified. "The States," Oliver Ellsworth asserted, "are the best Judges of the circumstances and temper of their own people" (Koch, *Notes of Debates*, 401). This debate was conducted on August 7 at the convention. See Koch *Notes of Debates*, 401–405. On the case for and against property qualifications, see also Adams, *The First American Constitutions*, 207–217.

38. Koch, *Notes of Debates*, 403.

39. Although estimates vary, most historians now believe that about two-thirds of the adult white males in the early republic were able to meet the suffrage requirements set by the states. Most scholars also suggest that even these minimal qualifications were often not enforced. This reversal in historians' perceptions about the extent to which property-holding requirements for suffrage disenfranchised ordinary white men in Revolutionary America began with the scholarship of Robert E. Brown and seemingly has little opposition today, even among scholars who favor other aspects of the Progressive interpretation. See Brown, *Charles Beard and the Constitution*, 62–72, 157–170, 196–199; Adams, *The First American Constitutions*, 196–207, 293–311. Adams observes that studies to date indicate that "by and large the property clauses prohibited at least a quarter—and in some states possibly as many as half—of the white male adults from voting for representatives to their state legislatures" (199). Donald Lutz surveyed the estimates of a number of scholars (including neo-Progressive historian Jackson Turner Main) and concluded that 65 to 75 percent of adult white males were qualified to vote in the states dur-

ing the 1780s. Lutz, "Political Participation in Eighteenth-Century America," *Albany Law Review* 53 (Winter 1989): 331, 333–335; Lutz, "The First State Constitutions," in *The Framing and Ratification of the Constitution,* ed. Leonard Levy and Dennis J. Mahoney (New York: Macmillan, 1987), 73. See also Lutz, "The Theory of Consent in the Early State Constitutions," *Publius* 9 (Spring 1979): 22–26. Gordon Wood ("The Significance of the Early Republic," *Journal of the Early Republic* 8 [1988]: 7) contends that "sixty to eighty percent of adult white males could legally vote in the colonial period." Alexander Keyssar (*The Right to Vote,* 7) argues that the rate of property ownership in colonial America was falling at the time of the American Revolution and that the proportion of adult white males who could vote was far greater than in England but was probably less than 60 percent. Thomas West (*Vindicating the Founders,* 111–117) sets forth the highest estimate with his conclusion that "the American electorate grew from about 65 percent in colonial days to about 85 to 90 percent in the 1790s" (114).

40. Jack Rakove, "The Structure of Politics at the Accession of George Washington," in *Beyond Confederation: Origins of the Constitution and American National Identity,* ed. Richard Beeman, Stephen Botein, and Edward C. Carter II (Chapel Hill: University of North Carolina Press, 1987), 267. As I pointed out in the first chapter, Beard's discussion of the effect of state property qualifications on the size of the electorate is confusing and ambiguous. At times, he suggests that property qualifications provided safeguards against democracy by restricting the electorate. At other times, he suggests that the electorate in Revolutionary America was quite wide. Beard, *An Economic Interpretation,* 71, 242.

41. Belz, "Liberty and Equality for Whom?" 270, 273.

42. Ibid., 273.

43. Ibid., 267, n. 18; Goldwin, *Why Blacks, Women, and Jews Are Not Mentioned,* 16; West, *Vindicating the Founders,* 75.

44. West, *Vindicating the Founders,* 75; Goldwin, *Why Blacks, Women, and Jews Are Not Mentioned,* 14, 18.

45. See Lewis, "'Of Every Age Sex and Condition,'"113–140. Lewis notes that women were not counted for purposes of representation in any of the state constitutions enacted during the Revolution and that this enumeration was itself "a significant extension of democratic trends that were reshaping representation in the states" (118).

46. Belz does not explain what he means by "prudential" considerations. It could mean that the Founders believed in principle that women and blacks should be full members of the political community but that it was imprudent to include them at the time. Belz, however, seemingly rejects this interpretation when he notes that the Founders created a form of government based on principles of natural rights that "in a formal sense" included everyone, but they also "recognized that because individuals differ in ability and aptitude, to have rights is not necessarily the same thing as to exercise rights." This observation seems to trace the Founders' unwillingness to make women and blacks full members of the political community to ascriptive beliefs. Belz, "Liberty and Equality for Whom?" 273.

Two related justifications, with widespread but not universal acceptance, were given for the disenfranchisement of women in eighteenth-century America. Both were grounded in arguments about the natural (and thus fixed) characteristics and capabilities of women. Neither can properly be characterized as a prudential consideration.

First, women were characterized as delicate, lacking discretion, and suited by nature for the domestic sphere. Second, the common-law doctrine of coverture established the man as the legal representative of his wife and her property in public. This doctrine left married women without sufficient independent property to meet voting qualifications and was premised on the belief that wives lacked sufficient will independent from their husbands to justify their participation in politics.

The most famous of the few explicit statements by the American Founders on the proper role of women are provided in James Wilson's public lectures on law and John Adams's correspondence. See Robert G. McCloskey, ed., *The Works of James Wilson*, 2 vols. (Cambridge, Mass.: Belknap Press of Harvard University Press, 1967), 85–88; John Adams to Abigail Adams, April 14, 1776, in *Adams Family Correspondence*, ed. L. H. Butterfield et al. (Cambridge, Mass.: Belknap Press of Harvard University Press, 1963), 1:382; John Adams to James Sullivan, May 26, 1776, in *Papers of John Adams*, ed. Robert Taylor et al. (Cambridge, Mass.: Belknap Press of Harvard University Press, 1979), 4:211–212. Abigail Adams to John Adams, March 31, 1776, and May 7, 1776, are reprinted, along with an excellent analysis of Abigail Adams's progressive beliefs about the role of women and John Adams's less than progressive replies, in Elaine Forman Crane, "Political Dialogue and the Spring of Abigail's Discontent," *William and Mary Quarterly* 56 (October 1999): 745–774.

See also Kerber, "The Republican Mother," 187–205; Linda Kerber, *Women of the Republic: Intellect and Ideology in Revolutionary America* (Chapel Hill: University of North Carolina Press, 1980), 11–12, 269–288; Smith, *Civic Ideals*, 110–114, 146–149. Kerber has shown that the American Revolution expanded and politicized women's unique and natural function as guardians of the domestic sphere by suggesting that women should serve as "republican mothers" who were responsible for raising virtuous sons to sustain the republic.

47. West and Belz shift among a variety of arguments to insulate the Founders from this conclusion. Both scholars suggest that any interpretation that maintains that the Founders did not accept the full implications of the natural rights principles they advocated denigrates the Framers because it suggests that they were hypocrites; were not knowledgeable about, serious about, or attached to the principles they espoused; or were "slaves to the ruling prejudices of their age." The idea that the Founders accepted the conventional assumptions of their age, West contends, is rooted in historicism—the belief that thinkers of any given age cannot think outside of leading linguistic and social conventions. Unlike West, Belz is more worried about self-righteousness and utopianism than historicism and admonishes scholars who judge the Founders based on contemporary standards of diversity and inclusiveness. Belz, "Liberty and Equality for Whom?" 268, 273–275; West, *Vindicating the Founders*, 72.

There is no reason to doubt the Framers' sincerity or their commitment to natural rights. Their specific writings, however, provide little evidence that many of them escaped the conventional understandings of their age in applying these principles to African Americans and women. Contrary to West's assertion, this conclusion does not necessarily spring from historicism. The point is not that the Founders *could not* have escaped the conventions of their time but rather that—on this specific issue—most of them *did not* escape those conventions. West and Belz concede as much in their own analyses. West acknowledges that the Founders "rejected the inference that equal natural rights requires equal voting rights" (*Vindicating the Founders*, 79). Belz concedes that the Framers "permitted traditional racial and sexual institutions to exist in the states; therefore, because of the dependence of federal citizenship upon state citizenship, not all persons were included in the limited political community of the nation" ("Liberty and Equality for Whom?" 270). Finally, I share Belz's concerns about self-righteous judgments of the Founders based on contemporary standards—in this instance, of inclusiveness. Hence, throughout this chapter, I have attempted to provide a multiplicity of perspectives—historical and contemporary—on which to judge the character of the Founders' Constitution. Ultimately, however, judgments based on standards outside the perspectives of historical actors are appropriate to avoid precisely the historicism that these scholars oppose.

48. West, *Vindicating the Founders*, 75.

49. The original Constitution also contains another arbitrary exclusion—the disenfranchisement of the residents of Washington, D.C.—that apparently was not discussed extensively at the convention or during the ratification process. In *Federalist* No. 43, Madison defends congressional authority over the nation's capital and maintains that the rights of the citizens in this area will be secured in a compact between the state ceding the land to the national government and the citizens of the ceded region and by the creation of a municipal legislature that such citizens will elect. Madison does not indicate whether he believes that their right to vote in federal elections will be among the rights secured in this compact (*Federalist* No. 43, 289). In the New York ratifying convention, Thomas Tredwell criticized the Framers for "subjecting the inhabitants of that district [the capital] to the exclusive legislation of Congress, in whose appointment they have no share or vote." Phillip Kurland and Ralph Lerner, eds., *The Founders' Constitution*, 5 vols. (Indianapolis: Liberty Fund Press, 1987), 3:225.

50. Elkins and McKitrick, *The Age of Federalism*, 717. For similar comments, see Lutz, "The First State Constitutions," 76, and Amar, *America's Constitution*, 64–66. The two eighteenth-century political systems that provide the most reasonable grounds for comparison in the area of suffrage rights are Great Britain's and France's. In Great Britain, suffrage requirements were controlled by law, and after 1430, the right to vote in counties was confined to "40 shilling freeholders," whereas suffrage requirements in boroughs varied greatly. Donald Lutz estimates that those who earned forty shillings in rent or income from their land must have owned between forty and sixty acres, which amounted to around 6 percent of the population ("Political Participation in Eighteenth-Century America," 335 n. 41). Other scholars have suggested that up to one-third of free adult males were eligible to vote in seventeenth- and eighteenth-century Britain. Obviously, even the highest estimates are significantly exceeded by eligibility levels in colonial and Revolutionary America. See Chilton Williamson, *American Suffrage: From Property to Democracy, 1760–1860* (Princeton, N.J.: Princeton University Press, 1960), 5, 7–8; Edmund Morgan, *Inventing the People: The Rise of Popular Sovereignty in England and America* (New York: W. W. Norton, 1988), 175.

Beliefs about who should be included for purposes of political participation in late-eighteenth-century France are best viewed through the successive constitutions drafted in 1791, 1793, and 1795. In the French Constitution of 1791, only active citizens were allowed to vote for electors, who in turn elected deputies to the national assembly. To be an active citizen, a person had to be a born or naturalized French citizen, be at least twenty-five years old, be a resident in a city or canton for a length of time to be determined by law, and pay a tax equal to the value of at least three days' labor. The electors—those active citizens who directly selected the national deputies—were required to pay a tax equal to ten days' wages. In his classic study *The Age of the Democratic Revolution,* Robert R. Palmer estimates that three-quarters of the active citizens, amounting to some three-sevenths of all Frenchmen over age twenty-one, were qualified to be electors under these property requirements. Again, however, this figure falls far below suffrage estimates in the United States. Later, property qualifications were changed by the Constituent Assembly to require that an elector be a proprietor or usufructuary of a property assessed on the tax rolls at a value equal to 100 to 400 days' labor, depending on whether the citizen lived in a rural or urban area and the size of the city where he lived. This requirement, however, never took effect because the Constitution of 1791 did not take effect. See Frank Maloy Anderson, ed., *The Constitutions and Other Select Documents Illustrative of the History of France, 1789–1907,* 2nd ed. (New York: Russell and Russell, 1908), 66–68; Palmer, *Age of the Democratic Revolution,* 1:522–528, especially 524–525.

The Jacobin French Constitution of 1793, which was ratified in a national referendum but was never implemented because of civil war and foreign threats, established direct election of national representatives or deputies and set forth a stunningly capacious conception of citizenship and voting. Every man born and living in France older than twenty-one years was a citizen and eligible to vote. Foreigners who had resided in France for at least a year and lived by their own labor, had acquired property, had adopted a child, supported an elderly person, or were recognized by the legislature as "worthy of being treated humanely" could gain citizenship and be allowed to vote. See Anderson, *Constitutions,* 175.

The 1795 constitution reestablished a system of indirect elections in which primary assemblies chose electors, who elected deputies; it also set up a bicameral legislature. Citizens included any male older than twenty-one who had lived a year on French soil and paid a direct land or personal property tax, although soldiers were exempt from the tax requirement. Naturalized citizens included those who had declared an intention to settle in France, had resided in the republic for seven consecutive years, paid a direct tax and possessed real estate or an agricultural or commercial establishment, or married a French woman. The constitution also provided for a literacy test. To vote in the primary assembly, a Frenchman also had to have been a resident for at least a year in the canton where he sought to vote. Electors who chose the members of both houses of the legislative branch had to be at least twenty-five years old and proprietors or usufructuaries of property valued at between one hundred and two hundred days of labor, depending on whether they lived in rural or urban areas and the size of the communes where they lived. See Anderson, *Constitutions,* 215–220.

51. U.S. Constitution, Article I, Section 2, Clause 2; Article I, Section 3, Clause 3; Article II, Section 1, Clause 5.

52. The U.S. Constitution uses male pronouns thirty times in discussions of federal officeholders, but its preferred nouns are gender neutral, including *members, persons,* or *parties.* The gender-specific pronouns *he* and *his* were never interpreted by the federal courts to restrict officeholding to men, in part because male pronouns were also used in Article IV, Section 2, which required the extradition of fugitives charged with treason,

felonies, or other crimes and was clearly intended to apply to women as well as men. See Smith, *Civic Ideals*, 131, 534, n. 35.

Obviously, the absence of gender requirements for officeholding in the original Constitution was not an invitation for women to run for office, any more than foreigners would have been welcome to serve as Supreme Court justices, despite the absence of any restriction against them doing so. In fact, the lack of formal restrictions made little difference in the patriarchal context of eighteenth-century America, where women were subordinated by intricate structures of laws and social norms. As far as I can determine, no woman in the early republic ever exploited the agnostic quality of the Constitution's officeholding requirements and tried to run for federal office. If she had, it might have forced an interesting confrontation.

Although the original Constitution did not formally exclude women from holding office, it did not guarantee them that right either—even after passage of the Nineteenth Amendment. Federal statutes guaranteed this right to women. Despite the Nineteenth Amendment, in Iowa a separate struggle was required for women to gain the right to hold federal and state offices. See Linda Kerber, "The Meanings of Citizenship," *Journal of American History* 84 (December 1997): 840. See also Amar, *America's Constitution*, 427, for the suggestion that the right to vote should be interpreted to imply the right to be voted for.

53. Amar has argued that the Constitution "barred both Congress and states from adding statutory property qualifications—or any other qualifications, for that matter—to Article I's short list of age, residency, and citizenship requirements." Amar points out that the Articles of Confederation allowed states to impose additional qualifications on their congressional delegations and that two states, New Hampshire and Maryland, imposed additional property qualifications. Amar also notes that *Powell v. McCormack*, 395 U.S. 496 (1969), and *U.S. Term Limits v. Thornton*, 512 U.S. 1286 (1994), maintain that the requirements for federal officeholding set forth in the Constitution are exclusive. See Amar, *America's Constitution*, 66, 529 n. 22. These rulings may settle for our purposes the exclusivity of the Constitution's requirements for office, but it is not clear that this was originally accepted. What would have been the status of a state law excluding women from holding federal office? Would such a law have been considered unconstitutional because it added to the list of requirements for office? Furthermore, Edward S. Corwin has argued that Congress can enlarge or modify the eligibility requirements for president to exclude persons convicted of a serious crime. See Corwin, *The President, Offices and Powers: History and Analysis of Practice and Opinion* (New York: New York University Press, 1941), 33–34.

54. Amar, *America's Constitution*, 72–74.

55. *Federalist* No. 57, 385. See also *Federalist* No. 52, 355.

56. Provisions disqualifying public debtors and those with public accounts from holding office were supported by only a few members who sought to prevent individuals from seeking office for the purpose of passing legislation that diminished their debts or advanced their interests. Nevertheless, most of the speakers suggested that such a measure was too blunt and would have excluded many patriotic citizens who had performed services for the United States. In addition, delegates argued, it would disproportionately burden members of the commercial and manufacturing classes, who reg-

ularly ran accounts with the government. Finally, it might be used by the government to target and disqualify individuals by delaying the settlement of their accounts.

The convention also rejected landed property qualifications for officeholders and refused to allow Congress to establish such requirements. As in the case of suffrage, such qualifications were dismissed as unjust, impractical, and impolitic; they would exclude members of the monied interest, were not necessarily evidence of real wealth, and would weave veneration for wealth into a republican constitution. Furthermore, if they were set too low, they would provide no security for the protection of property; if they were set too high, they would exclude representatives of the commercial and manufacturing classes.

Finally, the delegates also rejected one- and three-year residency requirements for congressional candidates as excessive and even spurned the use of the word *resident*, preferring to require only that candidates be "inhabitants" of the state (not the district) where they were running "when elected." This left open the possibility of candidates moving into a state immediately before an election. Residency requirements were defended by several delegates, who argued that candidates needed time to gain local knowledge and familiarity with their constituents, and they cited such requirements as means of preventing rich out-of-state men from using corrupt methods to gain office. These arguments, however, were unconvincing to a majority of delegates, who trusted the electorate to guard against candidates with a lack of local knowledge or improper designs. Delegates also feared that such a provision, like the one excluding debtors, would be selectively enforced to bar individuals who were disliked. See Koch, *Notes of Debates,* 372–378, 406–408, 437–442.

57. For the debate on this proposal and modifications of it, see Kurland and Lerner, *The Founders' Constitution,* 2:346–352.

58. U.S. Constitution, Article VI, Clause 3: "No religious Test shall ever be required as a Qualification to any Office or public Trust under the United States." This provision was passed with only North Carolina opposing and Maryland and Connecticut divided. See Koch, *Notes of Debates,* 561. For commentary on the purposes of this clause, see Daniel L. Dreisbach, "The Constitution's Forgotten Religion Clause: Reflections on the Article VI Religious Test Ban," *Journal of Church and State* 38 (1996): 261–295; the division among the states on the religious test oath is on 271.

59. George Mason asked his fellow delegates to consider the "deficiency of young politicians" by examining the quality of their own political opinions when they were young. Only James Wilson spoke against the age requirement for representatives, citing examples of men who had engaged in exemplary public service before age twenty-five. Koch, *Notes of Debates,* 174. The only contemporary constitutional commentator that I am aware of who suggests that any of the age requirements in the Constitution are inappropriately exclusionary is Matthew D. Michael. He argues that the age requirement for president disadvantages the young in terms of gaining a fair hearing on a host of intergenerational public policies, such as Social Security, that will end up transferring trillions of dollars of future liabilities onto the young. See Michael, "The Presidential Age Requirement and Public Policy," in Eskridge and Levinson, *Constitutional Stupidities,* 67–70.

In contrast, relying exclusively on arguments from the Founding, Amar makes a strong argument that age qualifications for both members of Congress and the president had the intention and effect of "dampen[ing] intergenerational aristocracy" (*America's Constitution,* 71). If age requirements for the House and Senate had been lower, wealthy individuals from established families would have been able to use their resources and reputations to secure office for their young male relatives, counting on voters' and legislatures' desire to send the state's favorite sons into federal service. This service, Amar maintains, would have given the rich, well born, and well known a head start in contests for higher federal offices. A lower age requirement for the president would have allowed these favorite sons to use their names rather than their accomplishments to win elections. Conversely, the thirty-five-year age requirement "created a clean and easily enforceable rule leveling the playing field somewhat, obliging favorite sons to bide their time and show off their stuff and giving other men a chance to show theirs," and it "gave low birth men a chance to outshine famous favorite sons" (ibid., 163). See *America's Constitution,* 70–72, for Amar's analysis of congressional age requirements as a barrier to the election of favorite sons and 159–164 for a similar analysis of the presidential age requirement.

60. Koch, *Notes of Debates,* 418–422 ; Smith, *Civic Ideals,* 128–129.

61. Koch, *Notes of Debates,* 419.

62. The constitutional provision requiring that the president be natural born emerged from revisions provided by a Committee of Eleven (one delegate was appointed from each state represented at the convention) and was not debated. For the journal record on this requirement, see Kurland and Lerner, *The Founders' Constitution,* 3:563. See Randall Kennedy, "A Natural Aristocracy?" in Eskridge and Levinson, *Constitutional Stupidities,* 54–56, for a strong condemnation of this requirement.

Rogers Smith contends that this provision was even stricter than it seems in the text of the Constitution. There were, Smith observes, two possible understandings of the requirement: that the president be born to parents who were U.S. citizens (jus sanguinis), or that the president be born on American soil (jus soli). The "nativistic tone of the debate," Smith argues, suggests that the Framers had jus soli in mind when they passed this clause, seemingly ruling out a person born abroad to parents who were American citizens (*Civic Ideals,* 130). Smith's conclusions, however, are directly challenged in Charles Gordon, "Who Can Be President of the United States: The Unresolved Enigma," *Maryland Law Review* 28 (1968): 1–32. Gordon argues that the meaning of "natural born" in British common-law doctrine prior to 1787 suggested that children born abroad to British subjects were full citizens. He also suggests that, although the historical record is thin, the Framers meant to exclude only naturalized citizens from the presidency. Amar argues that the natural-born requirement was meant to "lay rest to public anxieties about foreign monarchs" and prevent European noblemen from aspiring to or conspiring for office in America. It was not, according to Amar, motivated by a general nativistic suspicion of foreign-born persons (*America's Constitution,* 164–165). Finally, Jill A. Pryor argues that the debate about who the Framers considered "natural born" is largely indeterminate, but the Framers intended to allow Congress to use its Article I power to create uniform rules of naturalization to modify the natural-born requirement for the president in Article II. Under Pryor's approach, the Constitution requires that an individual be a citizen at birth (no one who acquires citizenship later can be president), but it provides that Congress has the power to determine by statute or treaty what classes of individuals meet that requirement. For this innovative argument, see Pryor, "The Natural-Born Citizen Clause and Presidential Eligibility: An Approach for Resolving Two Hundred Years of Uncertainty," *Yale Law Journal* 97 (1998): 881–899.

63. Smith, *Civic Ideals*, 130.

64. See note 59 for Amar's argument that longer age requirements were a democratic feature of the original Constitution. British law required members of Parliament to be only twenty-one years old, making it slightly more inclusive than the U.S. requirements for representatives and senators under the Constitution. See St. George Tucker, *View of the Constitution of the United States with Selected Writings*, foreword by Clyde N. Wilson (Indianapolis: Liberty Fund, 1999), 159.The state constitutions enacted between 1776 and 1786 did not systematically stipulate age requirements, but those that did so did not differ significantly from the consitutional requirements. The constitutions of North Carolina (1776) and New Hampshire (1784) set the age requirement for governor at thirty years, while Maryland's (1776) established twenty-five years as the minimum age for governor. Age requirements were most frequently imposed on members of the upper house. Maryland (1776), Virginia (1776), and Delaware (1776) required that members of the upper house be at least twenty-five years old, while South Carolina (1778) and New Hampshire (1784) required them to be thirty. Maryland (1776) required that members of its House of Delegates be at least twenty-one years old, and Georgia (1776) required that members of its unicameral legislature be twenty-one.

65. The first wave of constitutions came at independence. By the end of 1776, eight new state constitutions had been written: New Hampshire, South Carolina, Virginia, New Jersey, Delaware, Pennsylvania, Maryland, and North Carolina. In the same year, Rhode Island and Connecticut, which had essentially republican charters, eliminated all references to royal authority in these documents. The second wave of constitutions was drafted from 1777 to 1780. In 1777 New York, Georgia, and Vermont drafted new constitutions. Finally, in 1780 Massachusetts adopted its famous constitution.

The generalizations throughout this chapter are based on comparisons with the following fourteen first- and second-wave constitutions: Delaware (1776), Georgia (1777), Maryland (1776), Massachusetts (1780), New Hampshire (1784), New Jersey (1776), New York (1777), North Carolina (1776), Pennsylvania (1776), South Carolina (1776 and 1778), Virginia (1776), and Vermont (1777 and 1786). In examining these constitutions, I am considering the state constitutions adopted from 1776 to 1786—the period from the Declaration of Independence to the drafting of the Constitution, which is the core constitutional moment in the American Founding. I have omitted the state constitutions adopted in 1776 by Connecticut, Rhode Island, and New Hampshire because these states either simply readopted their colonial charters or, in the case of New Hampshire, provided a constitution that sketched only the barest features of institutional design. The third-wave constitutions adopted from 1789 to 1798 are not considered because they fall outside this moment and were influenced by the enactment of the U.S. Constitution. Twelve of these state constitutions are conveniently located at http://yale.edu/lawweb/avalon/18th.htm in the Avalon Project at Yale Law School. The New Hampshire Constitution of 1784 is available in William F. Swindler, ed., *Sources and Documents of United States Constitutions* (Dobbs Ferry, N.Y.: Oceana Publications, 1976), 4:344–357; the Massachusetts Constitution of 1780 can be found at http://www.nhinet.org/ccs/docs/ma-1780.htm. See Lutz, "The First State Constitutions," 72–73, and Donald Lutz, *Popular Consent and Popular Control: Whig Political Theory in the Early State Constitutions* (Baton Rouge: Louisiana State University Press, 1980), 44–45, for his classification of the state constitutions of the Founding era.

66. See Adams, *The First American Constitutions*, 293–307, and Lutz, *Popular Consent and Popular Control*, 90, for helpful appendixes and tables that list state property qualifications for office.

67. Lutz estimates that in colonial America only 30 percent of white males owned property worth 500 pounds or more. If this is true, then members of this segment of society would have been eligible to run in every state for both the lower house and the upper house (with the exception of nonresidents running for the senate in South Carolina under that state's constitution of 1776 or 1778; they also would have been excluded from running for governor in South Carolina). See Lutz, "The Theory of Consent," 28, table 5, 29, table 6 n. c. See also the generalizations by Jackson Turner Main, *The Upper House in Revolutionary America, 1763–1788* (Madison: University of Wisconsin Press, 1967), 189, about the minimal effects of property qualifications in excluding men with relatively little property from the state senates from 1763 to 1788.

68. The constitutions of New York (1776), Delaware (1776), and South Carolina (1776) had no residency requirements for any public office. One-year residency requirements were stipulated for members of the lower house in Maryland (1776), Massachusetts (1780), New Jersey (1776), and North Carolina (1776). Georgia's constitution required one year of state residency but only three months in the county of election, while Vermont's constitutions of 1777 and 1786 required one year of residency for citizens running for the lower house and two years for foreigners who settled to become citizens. Finally, the New Hampshire Constitution of 1784 stipulated a two-year period of residency, the Pennsylvania Constitution of 1776 required two years of residency for citizens and foreigners, and the South Carolina Constitution of 1778 required three years of residency to run for the lower house.

One-year residency requirements were stipulated for members of the upper house in North Carolina (1776) and New Jersey (1776), Maryland (1776) required three years of residency, Massachusetts (1780) and South Carolina (1778) required five years, and New Hampshire required seven years. Residency requirements for governors or presidents of the states were five years in Maryland (1776) and North Carolina (1776), seven years in Massachusetts (1780) and New Hampshire (1784), and ten years in South Carolina (1778).

69. The constitutions of Virginia (1776), Delaware (1776), Maryland (1776), North Carolina (1776), and New York (1777) excluded clergy from officeholding. Marc W. Kruman suggests that such prohibitions sprang from the fear that "Catholics as rulers might destroy the Protestant character of American society" and that Catholic and Jewish clergy would be tyrannical leaders. Kruman, *Between Authority and Liberty: State Constitution Making in Revolutionary America* (Chapel Hill: University of North Carolina Press, 1997), 96–97. Phillip Hamburger argues that "Americans barred clergymen from civil office for many reasons, including an odd combination of Calvinism, anti-Catholicism, theories of taxation and representation, solicitude for the clergy, and suspicion of the clergy." Hamburger, *Separation of Church and State* (Cambridge, Mass.: Harvard University Press, 2002), 79–88; the quote is on 83.

70. Amar, *America's Constitution,* 69–70; the Second Test Act is reprinted in Carl

Stephenson and Frederick George Marcham, eds. and trans., *Sources of English History: A Selection of Documents from A.D. 600 to the Present* (New York: Harper and Brothers, 1937), 556–557.

71. French Constitution of 1791, Sections 2 and 3, in Anderson, *Constitutions*, 63.

72. "Constitution of the Year I," in ibid., 171–184.

73. "Vices of the Political System," in *The Papers of James Madison*, 17 vols., ed. William T. Hutchinson et al. (Chicago: University of Chicago Press; Charlottesville: University of Virginia Press, 1962–), 9:357; hereafter cited as *PJM*. The phrase "code words" is from Wood, "Democracy and the Constitution," 13.

74. Woody Holton has argued that expanded electoral districts were linked to both personnel and policies, especially those involving taxation and paper money. Proponents of elections from small electoral districts, according to Holton, almost uniformly favored low taxation rates and were the friends of paper money. Holton, "'Divide et Impera': *Federalist 10* in a Wider Sphere," *William and Mary Quarterly* 62 (April 2005): 175–212. As I discuss in the final chapter, Jennifer Nedelsky argues that expanded electoral districts were the central feature in a constitution that "required wealth based inequality of access to political power." Nedelsky, *Private Property and the Limits of American Constitutionalism: The Madisonian Framework and Its Legacy* (Chicago: University of Chicago Press, 1990), 2. Gordon Wood has argued that expanded electoral districts were part of the Federalists' efforts to stem the rising tide of democracy, especially as this was expressed in the election of "new men" who did not have the social attributes of the gentlemen elite. Wood, *Creation of the American Republic*, 469–518; Wood, "Democracy and the Constitution," 10–17. The interpretations of Holton, Nedelsky, and Wood most closely resemble the claims of anti-Federalist Melancton Smith. See "Speeches by Melancton Smith in New York's State Convention," in David J. Siemers, *The Antifederalists: Men of Great Faith and Forbearance* (Lanham, Md.: Rowman and Littlefield, 2003), 137–147.

75. These arguments are set forth in "Speeches by Melancton Smith," 137–147; Holton, 'Divide et Impera,' 175–212; Wood, *Creation of the American Republic*, 506–518.

76. *Federalist* No. 35, 219.

77. Ibid., 220.

78. "Observations on Jefferson's Draft of a Constitution for Virginia," in *PJM*, 11:268; *Federalist* No. 10, 63.

79. Madison's faith in the electorate was powerfully illustrated in his oft-quoted statement from the Virginia ratifying convention: "But I go on this great republican principle, that the people will have the virtue and intelligence to select men of virtue and wisdom. Is there no virtue among us? If there be not, we are in a wretched situation. No theoretical checks no form of government can render us secure. To suppose that any form of government will secure liberty or happiness without any virtue in the people, is a chimerical idea. *If there be sufficient virtue and intelligence in the community, it will be exercised in the selection of these men; so that we do not depend on their virtue, or put confidence in our rulers, but in the people who are to choose them.*" "Speech of June 20, 1788," in *PJM*, 11:163 (emphasis added).

80. Merrill Peterson et al., eds., *The Documentary History of the Ratification of the Constitution*, 19 vols. to date (Madison: State Historical Society of Wisconsin, 1976–), 3: 392 n. 8.

81. Amar, *America's Constitution*, 77, 81, 83–84. Although he somewhat acknowledges the force of the anti-Federalists' objection about inadequate representation, Amar provides additional comparisons and judgments (that mostly parrot arguments from *The Federalist Papers*) that mitigate against too harsh a judgment of the original Constitution. First, Amar observes that if each state had sent the full number of delegates (seven) allowed under the Articles of Confederation to the Confederation Congress, the total number of delegates for all thirteen states would have been ninety-one—exactly equal to the number of representatives (sixty-five) and senators (twenty-six) chosen to serve in the First Congress. Second, Amar points out that Parliament had both local and national responsibilities, but the House and Senate would have purely national responsibilities and therefore did not need as many members. Third, he observes that roughly half the members of Parliament were chosen in "rotten" or "pocket" boroughs, and thus only half could be said to represent a substantial number of actual voters. Fourth, Amar observes that the Federalists promised to increase the number of representatives soon after ratification.

Ultimately, these observations do not provide a strong defense against the charge of inadequate representation. As Amar himself notes, few states sent full delegations to the Confederation Congress, and there were rarely more than a few members present at any session. Furthermore, Amar's observation about the relationship between powers and responsibilities and the numbers necessary to achieve adequate representation can be turned against him in comparisons of the Articles and the original Constitution. Delegates to the Confederation Congress were essentially ambassadors from independent nations; unlike congressmen, they did not directly represent voters, and the scope of their powers and responsibilities was considerably more restricted, suggesting that significantly fewer of them were needed. In addition, the promise of greater representation after ratification of the Constitution was just that—a promise, not a constitutionally mandated requirement.

More broadly, the inadequacy of representation in the original Constitution was one of the most persistent concerns even while the convention was still in session, and several attempts were made or supported by leaders at the convention, including Madison, Hamilton, and Washington, to address this problem. On one occasion, Madison called for doubling the number of representatives—from 65 to 130—and on another occasion, he seconded a motion for increasing the number of representatives. One of the last acts of the convention, and the only one that Washington urged on his fellow delegates, was to change the maximum number of representatives from one for every 40,000 people to one for every 30,000, thus allowing a greater number of representatives at the first census and reapportionment of representatives in 1790. Amar acknowledges that the concern about greater representation was strong even among the Federalists, and he includes these motions in his account, but they do not change the ultimate thrust of his analysis, which is to moderate the criticism that the original Constitution provided for too few representatives. See Amar, *America's Constitution*, 79–80; see Koch, *Notes of Debates*, 263, 608, 634–635, 655, for each of these motions at the convention.

82. Noah Webster, "Review of 'Thoughts upon the Political Situation of the United States of America, etc.,'" *American Magazine*, October 1788, 804.

83. Hamilton's reservations about expanded electoral districts were expressed in

notes that he took during Madison's June 6 speech at the Constitutional Convention and are provided in *PJM*, 10:34 n. 2.

84. Charles Kesler, *"Federalist* 10 and American Republicanism," in *Saving the Revolution: The Federalist Papers and the American Founding* (New York: Free Press, 1987), 37.

85. Wood, *Creation of the American Republic,* 513.

86. This discussion expands on an insight developed by Jack Rakove. Rakove has argued that—given the absence of formal eligibility requirements—the Federalists' scheme for electing cosmopolitan representatives from large districts rested on an "act of faith" and constituted a prediction rather than a guarantee. Rakove does not discuss the informal advantages of resources and reputation that, according to Holton and Wood, underlay the Federalists' "faith" in the electoral prospects of cosmopolitan elites in expanded districts. My point here is that these informal advantages would help secure the election of elite statesmen only if the people identified members of the gentleman elite as having qualities they admired. See Rakove, "Structure of Politics," 261–294; the quote is on 264.

The question of whether elections alone—absent restrictions on the electorate, formal eligibility restrictions, and incentives of office—would result in finding the best leaders was also raised during the Founding by Noah Webster, William Beers, and Jonathan Jackson. See Webster, "Review of 'Thoughts upon the Political Situation,'" 804–807; William Beers, *An Address to Legislature and People of the State of Connecticut, on the Subject of Dividing the State into Districts for the Election of Representatives in Congress* (New Haven, Conn.: Printed by T & S Green, 1791); Jonathan Jackson, *Thoughts upon the Political Situation of the United States of America . . .* (Worcester, Mass.: Printed by Isaiah Thomas, 1788).

Contemporary scholars who have addressed this question include Thomas Pangle, *The Spirit of Modern Republicanism: The Moral Vision of the American Founders* (Chicago: University of Chicago Press, 1988), 104–111. Pangle criticizes the Federalists for not making adequate provision for the recruitment, cultivation, and selection of elite leaders. Kesler, *"Federalist* 10 and American Republicanism," 36–37, observes that Publius's "obvious considerations," which indicate the advantages of large electoral districts in securing elite representatives, are far from obvious.

87. *Federalist* No. 10, 63.

88. *Federalist* No. 63, 425 (emphasis added).

89. On Madison's beliefs about the irrationality of large assemblies and the paradox of centralized power in large ones, see *Federalist* No. 58, 395–396. See also *Federalist* No. 55, 374.

90. Koch, *Notes of Debates,* 97.

91. I borrow the concept of "long-leash" republicanism from Michael Zuckert. Following Zuckert's lead, I compare the "short-leash republicanism" embodied in the Articles of Confederation and the state governments created in the 1780s with Madison's "long-leash" republicanism that rejected these models of government. See Michael Zuckert, "The Political Science of James Madison," in *History of American Political Thought,* ed. Bryan-Paul Frost and Jeffrey Sikkenga (Lanham, Md.: Lexington Books, 2003), 149–166, especially 155–165.

92. *Federalist* No. 78, 524, 528.

93. *Federalist* No. 68, 457–462, 458.

94. Another way to explain the purposes of the Electoral College is to examine the problems with the two other methods of presidential election considered at the convention. Although Madison considered the people to be "the fittest" group for choosing the president, and popular election was eloquently defended by Wilson, popular election of the president was rejected at the convention. Some delegates thought that it would lead to the election of candidates from large states exclusively, others believed that the people were incapable of selecting effective statesmen, and still others (including Madison) noticed that it would prevent slave states from gaining political leverage from their nonvoting slaves. Legislative election—the only other option seriously considered at the convention, and the method used to elect governors in nine states in 1787—was opposed by delegates who feared that the president would be unduly dependent on the legislators who had elected him. In short, the Electoral College afforded the prospect that an informed group of individuals would select a president after due deliberation, and it would protect the interests of small states and slave states.

For the Framers' intentions regarding the Electoral College, see Kurland and Lerner, *The Founders' Constitution,* 3:534–561; Donald Lutz, Philip Abbott, Barbara Allen, and Russell Hanson, "The Electoral College in Historical and Philosophical Perspective," in *Choosing a President: The Electoral College and Beyond,* ed. Paul D. Schumaker and Burdett A. Loomis (New York: Chatman House, 2002), 31–52, especially 31–35; Finkelman, *Slavery and the Founders,* 21–22; Paul Finkelman, "The Proslavery Origins of the Electoral College," *Cardozo Law Review* 23 (2001–2002): 1145–1157. Finkelman has convincingly argued that the Electoral College was not conceived primarily because the Framers doubted the people's ability to select a president or even because small states sought to protect their interests and enhance their influence. The primary reason for the adoption of the Electoral College, according to Finkelman, was that southerners sought to ensure the election of a pro-slavery president, particularly a Virginian. Direct presidential elections were unacceptable to delegates from slave states (including Madison), Finkelman argues, because these states had fewer eligible voters. By using the number of representatives as the primary means of determining the number of electoral votes, the Electoral College included the slave population, thus enhancing the power of the slave states.

95. David E. Kyvig, *Explicit and Authentic Acts: Amending the U.S. Constitution, 1776–1995* (Lawrence: University Press of Kansas, 1996), 43.

96. Ibid., 60–61.

97. See George Carey, *The Federalist: Design for a Constitutional Republic* (Urbana and Chicago: University of Illinois Press, 1989), 28–30, 38–44; Alan Gibson, "Impartial Representation and the Extended Republic: Towards a Comprehensive and Balanced Reading of the Tenth *Federalist,*" *History of Political Thought* 12 (Summer 1991): 282–295.

98. *Federalist* No. 51, 350. See also the even stronger comments in *Federalist* No. 48, 332–338.

99. This interpretation of the separation of powers and the system of checks and balances suggests that the Constitution placed immediate restraints on Congress through the senatorial check, the presidential veto, and judicial review as means of controlling the popular majorities reflected in the House of Representatives. Nevertheless, the Constitution ultimately rested on the principle of legislative supremacy because it

lodged the powers of finance, impeachment, and the declaration of war in Congress. For this view of the separation of powers as a means of controlling the powerful and passionate legislative branch, see Wood, *Creation of the American Republic*, 446–463; Diamond, *Founding of the Democratic Republic*, 85–98; Ann Stuart Diamond, "The Zenith of Separation of Powers Theory: The Federal Convention of 1787," *Publius* 8 (Summer 1978): 45–70; Judith A. Best, "Legislative Tyranny and the Liberation of the Executive: A View from the Founding," *Presidential Studies Quarterly* 17 (Fall 1987): 697–709; Louis Fisher, "The Efficiency Side of Separated Powers," *Journal of American Studies* 5 (August 1971): 113–131; William Kristol, "The Problem of Separation of Powers: Federalist 47–51," in *Saving the Revolution: The Federalist Papers and the American Founding* (New York: Free Press, 1987), 100–130; Keith Whittington, "The Separation of Powers at the Founding," in *The Separation of Powers: Documents and Commentary,* ed. Katy J. Harriger (Washington, D.C.: Congressional Quarterly Press, 2003), 1–14.

This reading explicitly rejects George Carey's contention that the Founders (especially Madison) conceived of the separation of powers primarily as a means of preventing governmental tyranny, not checking tyrannical majorities. Madison's writings, such as the famous *Federalist No. 51*, according to Carey, differentiate sharply between governmental tyranny and majority tyranny, and it was the former that Madison sought to control. In contrast, I argue that the Federalists devolved power to the people and then sought to channel and control the popular will as it was projected into the system of government. The governmental tyranny that Madison feared in 1787 would be created as popular majorities captured the House of Representatives, making it a mere instrument of a majority of the citizenry. Most important, the Federalists' system of separation of powers enhanced the independence and power of the least responsive branches of the national government (the Senate, president, and judiciary) in order to check popular majorities as they were reflected in the House of Representatives. It thus risked tyranny created by independent acts of public officials in order to control tyranny created by the influence of popular majorities. For Madison's belief about which tyranny was more likely, see his famous bill of rights letter: Madison to Jefferson, October 17, 1788, in *PJM*, 11:298–299. Compare my analysis to George Carey, "Separation of Powers and the Madisonian Model: A Reply to the Critics," *American Political Science Review* 22 (March 1978): 151–164. See also Samuel Kernell, "'The True Principles of Republican Government': Reassessing James Madison's Political Science," in *James Madison: The Theory and Practice of Republican Government* (Stanford, Calif.: Stanford University Press, 2005), 92–125.

100. See Gibson, "Impartial Representation," 282–295; Gibson, "Veneration and Vigilance," 16–23.

101. *Federalist No. 14*, 84; No. 39, 250.

102. *Federalist No. 63*, 424–427; the quotes are on 426 and 425. See also *Federalist No. 71*, 482–483.

103. *Federalist No. 10*, 61. See also Madison's famous comment in *Federalist No. 63* (428) that the "true distinction" between ancient constitutions and American ones "lies in the total exclusion of the people in their collective capacity" from governing in American constitutional systems. In this sense, Wood's argument that the Federalists disingenuously "appropriated and exploited" the language of popular sovereignty that "more rightfully belonged to their [anti-Federalist] opponents" seems misguided. Indeed, the

Federalists may well be the last American politicians to speak frankly to the public about the dangers of direct democracy. See Wood, *Creation of the American Republic*, 562–564.

104. *Federalist* No. 63, 425.

105. Perhaps the clearest version of the Federalists' conception of popular sovereignty was in an amendment proposed by Madison in the initial version of the Bill of Rights but later rejected. It read: "That all power is originally vested in, and consequently derived from the people. That government is instituted, and ought to be exercised for the benefit of the people; which consists in the enjoyment of life and liberty, with the right of acquiring and using property, and generally of pursuing and obtaining happiness and safety. *That the people have an indubitable, unalienable, and indefeasible right to reform or change their government, whenever it be found adverse or inadequate to the purposes of its institution*" ("Amendments to the Constitution," June 8, 1789, in *PJM*, 12:200). For the Federalists' conception of popular sovereignty, see also James Wilson, *An Introductory Lecture to a Course of Law Lectures* (Philadelphia: Press of T. Dobson, 1791), 31–36, and Garry Wills, "James Wilson's New Meaning for Sovereignty," in *Conceptual Change and the Constitution*, ed. Terence Ball and J. G. A. Pocock (Lawrence: University Press of Kansas, 1988), 99–106.

106. For representation as a distinguishing characteristic of republican government, see *Federalist* Nos. 10 and 63, 62, 427; for majority rule, see *Federalist* No. 22, 139; for legislative predominance, see *Federalist* Nos. 48 and 51, 333–334, 350; for the absence of hereditary offices, see *Federalist* No. 39, 251; for the right of the people to alter and abolish their constitutions, see *Federalist* No. 78, 527.

107. *Federalist* No. 39, 251.

108. Michael Zuckert's excellent commentary on this passage suggests that Madison's definition was more democratic than most contemporaneous definitions, but less democratic and strenuous than Jefferson's conception. According to Zuckert, most definitions—including Montesquieu's—allowed for hereditary features in a government called republican. Madison, however, rejected any hereditary offices; he required that the people select rulers either directly or indirectly and that those rulers serve for fixed terms or be removable for bad behavior. Madison's definition, Zuckert also notes, suggests that "political authority is thoroughly public in character—no one has any private or personal claim of any sort to it." Nevertheless, unlike Jefferson, Madison did not require that the people be involved directly, immediately, and continuously in public affairs for the government to earn the appellation republican. Zuckert, "The Political Science of James Madison," 151, 156–157. See also Zuckert, *The Natural Rights Republic: Studies in the Foundation of the American Political Tradition* (Notre Dame, Ind.: University of Notre Dame Press, 1996), 232–243, comparing Madisonian and Jeffersonian republicanism.

109. James Madison to Thomas Jefferson, October 24, 1787, in *PJM*, 10:214.

110. *Federalist* No. 37, 233–234.

111. James Madison to William Cogswell, March 10, 1834, in *The Records of the Federal Convention of 1787*, ed. Max Farrand (1911; revised, New Haven, Conn.: Yale University Press, 1937), 3:533.

112. *Federalist* No. 14, 88. In a preface written for the publication of his convention notes, Madison describes the Constitution as forming "a system without a[n] example ancient or modern, a system founded on popular rights, and so combining, a federal

form with the forms of individual Republics, as may enable each to supply the defects of the other and obtain the advantages of both." Koch, "A Sketch Never Finished nor Applied," in *Notes of Debates*, 3.

113. Parliament pledged in 1694 to hold elections every three years, but in 1716 it reneged on that promise, voted to give its members four additional years on each term, and promised to hold septennial elections thereafter. Amar, *America's Constitution*, 74–75. See Madison's account of this in *Federalist* Nos. 52 and 53, 355–356, 361.

114. Wood, *Creation of the American Republic*, especially 606–615.

115. *Federalist* No. 10, 61; No. 63, 427–428.

116. The state legislatures elected delegates in all the states except Rhode Island, where the people directly elected them, and Connecticut, where the people nominated seven candidates and the legislature chose two to four to represent the state. Amar, *America's Constitution*, 64 n. 16, 528.

117. Articles of Confederation, Article II.

118. Excellent analyses of the character and purposes of the Articles can be found in Peter Onuf, "The First Federal Constitution: The Articles of Confederation," in *The Framing and Ratification of the Constitution*, ed. Leonard Levy and Dennis J. Mahoney (New York: Macmillan, 1987), 82–97; Wood, *Creation of the American Republic*, 354–363; Martin Diamond, "What the Framers Meant by Federalism," in *As Far as Republican Principles Will Admit: Essays by Martin Diamond*, ed. William A. Schambra (Washington, D.C.: AEI Press, 1992), 96–98; Michael Zuckert, "Federalism and the Founding: Toward a Reinterpretation of the Constitutional Convention," *Review of Politics* 48 (Spring 1986): 167–172; Jack Rakove, *The Beginnings of National Politics: An Interpretive History of the Continental Congress* (New York: Alfred A. Knopf, 1979).

119. Merrill Jensen, *The Articles of Confederation: An Interpretation of the Social-Constitutional History of the American Revolution, 1774–1781* (1940; reprint, Madison: University of Wisconsin Press, 1948), especially 109–110, 237–245; the quote is on 28.

120. As Publius, Madison and Hamilton engage in an ingenious set of arguments in which the differences between the state constitutions and the federal Constitution are first minimized and then made to justify ratification. In *Federalist* Nos. 52 and 53 (353–366), for example, Madison makes a case for two-year terms of office for House members by suggesting that in the states, the term lengths for lower house members vary greatly and that this variation does not result in a better government for one state than another. This line of argumentation obscures the fact that every state but South Carolina stipulated annual elections for the lower house and that the reconstituted charters of Rhode Island and Connecticut called for half-year elections. Madison then argues that two-year terms are safe because congressmen will exercise only limited power and are justified by the distinctiveness of federal office. Federal representatives, he argues, must be given time to acquire knowledge about different state laws and foreign affairs in order to govern effectively. He also argues that if annual elections were adopted, it would be hard to recruit fit men to serve because they would be unwilling to travel such a great distance for only one-year terms.

Similarly, in his discussion of the number of representatives who will serve in Congress (*Federalist* Nos. 55 and 56, 372–383), Madison first suggests that the states themselves are hardly uniform (obscuring the fact that the number of representatives in proportion to constituents is much greater in the states than will be the case in the federal Constitution); he argues that the number will be augmented within three years after the first census, and that it will grow to at least 200 (from 65) within twenty-five years (seemingly conceding that there will be too few representatives at the inception of the government). He then argues, once again, that the limited number of representatives at the inception of the Constitution will not endanger the public safety because representatives will exercise limited powers and be controlled by the collateral legislatures; further, increasing the number of representatives in a legislature does not make it operate more democratically, but rather throws power into the hands of a few representatives. Neither Hamilton nor Madison ventures systematic comparisons of the terms of office for U.S. senators versus those for delegates to the states' upper houses; the four-year term and perpetual reeligibility of the president versus the tenure of governors, who were elected annually and subject to rotation in office in most states; and in general the number of directly elected branches in the states versus the number in the political system created by the Constitution. In *Federalist* No. 69 (463), Hamilton compares the four-year term of the president to the three-year term of the governor of New York but ignores the annual election of governors in most states.

121. See, for example, Amar, *America's Constitution*, 9, 64–65, 285–287.

122. Bernard Bailyn, *To Begin the World Anew: The Genius and Ambiguities of the American Founders* (New York: Alfred A. Knopf, 2003), 108.

123. See Jerrilyn Greene Marston, *King and Congress: The Transfer of Political Legitimacy, 1774–1776* (Princeton, N.J.: Princeton University Press, 1987) for the largely executive and diplomatic functions exercised by the Continental Congress from 1774 to 1776 and for an analysis that establishes why Congress before 1787 was unable to function as a national lawmaking body.

124. Amar, *America's Constitution*, 58; Articles of Confederation, Article XIII.

125. Amar, *America's Constitution*, 58, 142.

126. G. Allan Tarr, *Understanding State Constitutions* (Princeton, N.J.: Princeton University Press, 1998), 64. In contrast, Shlomo Slonim has suggested that the federal Constitution "represented a composite of various practices instituted in the states for securing representative republican government." Slonim, "Beard's Historiography and the Constitutional Convention," *Perspectives in American History* 3 (1986): 173–206; the quote is on 201. It is true, as Slonim suggests, that almost all the institutional features of the federal Constitution could be found in at least one of the state constitutions. The state constitutions and the federal Constitution also contained broad similarities, including systems of separation of powers based on a tripartite division of the government and featuring (in all but four of the fourteen state constitutions) bicameralism. Like the federal Constitution, most of the state constitutions also featured life tenures for judges and stipulated longer terms of office for the senate, executive, and judiciary than for the lower house of the legislature.

Slonim's observation, however, ignores the specific differences in terms of office, modes of selection, and relative powers given to the legislative versus the other branches of government. The thrust of scholarship on the state constitutions, which is reflected in the conclusions reached above, establishes the short-leash features of the state constitutions and the distinctiveness of the federal Constitution. See Allan Nevins, *The American States during and after the Revolution, 1775–1789* (New York: Macmillan, 1924), 117–205; Adams, *The First American Constitutions;* Wood, *Creation of the American Republic,* 127–255, 430–463; Kruman, *Between Authority and Liberty;* Tarr, *Understanding State Constitutions,* 60–93; Lutz, *Popular Consent and Popular Control;* Lutz, "The First State Constitutions," 69–81; Lutz, "The Theory of Consent," 11–42; Peter S. Onuf, "The Origins and Early Development of State Legislatures," in *American Legislative System: Studies of the Principal Structures, Processes, and Policies of Congress and the State Legislatures since the Colonial Era,* 3 vols., ed. Joel H. Silbey (New York: Charles Scribner's Sons, 1994), 1:175–194; Bernard Bailyn, "Notes on State Constitutions, 1776–1790," in *The Debate on the Constitution,* 2 vols., ed. Bernard Bailyn (New York: Library of America, 1993), 1:1117–1112.

127. Pennsylvania, Georgia, and Vermont (constitutions of 1777 and 1784) stipulated unicameral legislatures. The other ten state constitutions created upper houses. New Jersey, New Hampshire, North Carolina, and Massachusetts had upper houses with annual elections; South Carolina (constitutions of 1776 and 1778) required two-year terms for members of the upper house; Delaware's senators served three years; members of the upper house in New York and Virginia had four-year terms; and only Maryland had a five-year term. These comparisons and those appearing later were facilitated by an appendix in Slonim, "Beard's Historiography," 204–206.

128. States used the term *governor* or *president* to describe their chief executives. The constitutions of New Jersey, North Carolina, Pennsylvania, Virginia, Georgia, Maryland, New Hampshire, Massachusetts, and Vermont (1777 and 1786) established annual elections for governor. Both South Carolina constitutions had two-year terms, and New York and Delaware elected their governors every three years.

129. The nine state constitutions that stipulated that judges could serve for "good behavior" were Virginia, New Hampshire, Massachusetts, Maryland, New York, Delaware, North Carolina, and South Carolina (twice). New York required judges to retire at age sixty, and the Massachusetts, New Hampshire, and both South Carolina constitutions provided for the removal of judges. New Jersey and Pennsylvania had seven-year terms for judges. The Vermont Constitution of 1776 and the Georgia Constitution of 1777 did not establish state supreme courts.

130. The eight states where the upper house was popularly elected were South Carolina, North Carolina, Delaware, New York, Massachusetts, New Jersey, New Hampshire, and Virginia. The upper house in South Carolina (called a legislative council) was chosen by the lower house, and in Maryland it was chosen by an electoral college.

131. Under seven state constitutions (New Jersey, North Carolina, South Carolina [1776 and 1778], Virginia, Delaware, and Maryland), governors were elected by a joint ballot of both houses of the state legislature. In Pennsylvania, the chief executive of the state was the president of an executive council of twelve and was elected by a joint ballot of the (unicameral) legislature and the executive council. In Georgia, which also had a unicameral legislature, the governor was elected exclusively by that branch. The remaining five state constitutions—New York, Massachusetts, New Hampshire, and Vermont (1777 and 1786)—had popular elections for governor. The governor of New York was apparently the person who got the most votes. The other three states, however, re-

quired legislative election of the governor—either by joint ballot or by the senate (with two nominations supplied by the house)—if no candidate received a majority of the votes in the initial election.

132. Judges were appointed exclusively by the legislatures in four states (New Jersey, North Carolina, Virginia, and South Carolina [1776 and 1778]), where a joint ballot of both houses was used. The power of appointment was shared between the governor and the legislature in New York, where a council of the legislature made judicial appointments, with the governor presiding; in Delaware; and in Vermont (1786 Constitution), where there was joint election by the legislature and an executive council. Appointment of the judiciary was an exclusive function of the executive branch in Pennsylvania, Maryland, Massachusetts, and New Hampshire. In these states, the governor made the appointment with the advice of an executive council.

133. Schemes of rotation for governor were provided in seven state constitutions: Delaware, Maryland, North Carolina, Pennsylvania, Virginia, Georgia, and South Carolina (1778). Members of the executive councils in Delaware, Pennsylvania, and South Carolina (1778) were also rotated. In Pennsylvania, assemblymen were allowed to serve only four years out of every seven. Two states—Maryland and North Carolina—had rotation schemes for their delegates to Continental Congress, in addition to the requirements laid out in the Articles of Confederation. Several states had staggered elections, along the lines of the U.S. Senate, with members of the upper house being reelected at different intervals. Finally, six states stipulated rotation in office for sheriffs and coroners. See Wills, "Undemocratic Vistas." An appendix documenting state schemes of rotation in office is also provided in Adams, *The First American Constitutions,* 308–311.

134. Lutz, "The Theory of Consent," 30–33.

135. Article VII of the South Carolina Constitution of 1776 gave the president of the state the power to reject bills passed by the general assembly and the legislative council and made no provision for a legislative override. The Massachusetts Constitution of 1780 (Article II, Section 1) stipulates that the governor's veto can be overridden by two-thirds of the members present in both houses. Lutz notes that "during the first wave of constitution-making the state executives were almost completely stripped of their power" ("The Theory of Consent," 17).

136. New York provided for review of legislation through a Council of Revision composed of the executive and the judiciary, but this council could be overridden by a two-thirds vote of the legislature. New Hampshire and Massachusetts allowed the courts to provide advisory opinions on the constitutionality of legislation, but these opinions were not binding. Tarr, *Understanding State Constitutions,* 72.

137. By 1800, most states had provisions for the calling of special constitutional conventions to amend their constitutions. Tarr, *Understanding State Constitutions,* 73–75; Lutz, "The Theory of Consent," 35–36; Lutz, "The First State Constitutions," 74.

138. The Pennsylvania Constitution of 1776 (Section 15) provided that except in cases of "sudden necessity," all bills had to be printed for public consideration before they were read in the general assembly for the last time, to allow debate and amendment; they could be passed only in the next sessions of the assembly. This provision, in effect, required the assembly to pass any bill twice—before and after it had been considered by the public. One of the most famous examples of the importance of collective action

among the people and the influence of public petitions on the action of state legislatures in Revolutionary America was the struggle over disestablishment and the passage of Jefferson's "Bill for Establishing Religious Freedom" in Virginia in 1786. See Thomas E. Buckley, *Church and State in Revolutionary Virginia, 1776–1787* (Charlottesville: University of Virginia Press, 1977).

139. Lutz, "The Theory of Consent," 13.

140. See Mark David Hall, *The Political and Legal Philosophy of James Wilson, 1742–1798* (Columbia: University of Missouri Press, 1997), 90–147, for Wilson's democratic vision. Hall makes the important point, however, that Wilson also favored long terms of office for public officials and strong schemes of separation of powers (including an absolute veto for the president) designed to restrain the most popular branches of government.

141. Wilson wrote that "all elections ought to be equal. Elections are equal when a given number of citizens, in one part of the state, choose as many representatives as are chosen by the same number of citizens in any other part of the state. In this manner, the proportion of representatives and of the constituents will remain invariably the same." Malapportioned districts, he concluded, are a violation of the fundamental principle of majority rule, and the "majority of people wherever found ought in all questions to government the minority." Quoted in Hall, *Political and Legal Philosophy of James Wilson*, 115.

142. Quoted in ibid., 116.

143. Wilson was central to the development of the Electoral College as a means of electing the president; however, he supported the Electoral College only because direct election of the president was rejected.

144. Zuckert, *The Natural Rights Republic*, 232–239; the Jefferson quote is on 232.

145. See, for example, *Federalist* No. 15, 96; "Vices of the Political System of the United States," in *PJM*, 11:356.

146. Gibson, "Impartial Representation and the Extended Republic," 263–304.

147. Amar, *America's Constitution*, 84–85.

148. The convention engaged in a long and torturous struggle to devise a proper standard for apportioning representatives among the states. The Virginia Plan originally linked the apportionment of representatives to "the quotas of contribution, or to the number of *free* inhabitants, as the one or the other rule may seem best in different cases." The provision to apportion representatives based on "free" inhabitants was favored by Hamilton and doubtlessly several other northern delegates, but it was opposed at the earliest stages of the convention by Madison and had no chance of adoption after the provision that became the three-fifths clause was introduced on June 11. "Quotas of contribution" was left undefined. Some delegates apparently considered it a rough indicator of wealth, and others took it to mean a state's capacity to contribute to the treasury based on its size and resources. This provision did not refer to "actual" contributions to the treasury—a standard that was explicitly rejected. On July 9, a committee report set the allocation of representatives among the states and then set the standards for changes in representation based on wealth and number of inhabitants. This idea of apportioning representatives based on a state's wealth was dropped on July 14. Ultimately, this standard was rejected because delegates expressed concern that wealth could not be accu-

rately measured, and many believed that population provided a rough surrogate for wealth and productive capacity anyway. See Koch, *Notes of Debates*, 30, 97, 99, 103, 245–248, 257, 259–260, 270–288.

Amar observes that the Framers might have considered a provision linking the number of representatives given to each state to the number of *eligible* voters, as New York had linked the apportionment of representatives and voters. Such a provision, Amar argues, would have been consistent with the Framers' desire to create a legislative body that was a transcript of the society and thus serve as a substitute for the meeting of voters in person. This would not, however, have solved the problem of malapportionment *within* the states. A provision linking representatives and eligible voters also would have given states an incentive to expand their suffrage in order to expand their representation in Congress. This was not discussed at the Constitutional Convention, in large part because the Framers did not necessarily see the expansion of suffrage as desirable and certainly did not believe that it was the national government's role to create such an incentive. See Amar, *America's Constitution*, 88.

149. As Amar has observed, the decision to count women, children, and men who did not own sufficient property to meet state voting requirements for purposes of apportioning representatives among the states established a kind of virtual representation for these three groups in the Constitution. This did not extend to slaves, however, who were owned by masters and whose interests were not a concern of public officials. See Amar, *America's Constitution*, 92.

150. Recent scholarship has uniformly refuted the older view of the three-fifths clause as the product of a straightforward sectional compromise meant to burden the South with additional taxation while granting it disproportionate representation. Nevertheless, scholars have been sharply divided over a host of issues concerning the three-fifths clause and whether its passage actually represented a victory for southern states. See Amar, *America's Constitution*, 87–98, 156–159; Finkelman, *Slavery and the Founders*, 12–22; Fehrenbacher, *The Slaveholding Republic*, 21–25, 28–33, 40–41, 44; Jan Lewis, "The Three-fifths Clause and the Origins of Sectionalism," in *The National Capital in a Nation Divided*, ed. Paul Finkelman (Athens: Ohio University Press, forthcoming); Earl M. Maltz, "The Idea of the Proslavery Constitution," *Journal of the Early Republic* 17 (Spring 1997): 37–59; Howard A. Ohline, "Republicanism and Slavery: Origins of the Three-fifths Clause in the United States Constitution," *William and Mary Quarterly* 28 (October 1971): 563–584; Richards, *Slave Power*, 7–9, 32–51, 56–58, 60–62, 68–70, 80–82, 103; Donald Robinson, *Slavery in the Structure of American Politics, 1765–1820* (New York: W. W. Norton, 1979), 168–206; Wills, *"Negro President,"* especially 50–61.

151. Whether the additional political power given to the slave states as a result of the three-fifths clause was decisive in the election of any particular presidential candidate or the election or appointment of any other federal official, and whether it explains the hegemony of southerners in general in the early national government or the passage or obstruction of any particular law or amendment, is much more difficult to assess. This would involve weighing a number of different factors that might have influenced the outcome. In short, then, although scholars uniformly concede that slave states received a bonus as a result of the three-fifths clause, they do not agree about whether this increase was particularly important in the course of American history. Those who

oppose the idea that the three-fifths clause was the independent variable in ensuring pro-slavery personnel and policies in the early republic and into the antebellum period observe that slave states never had an outright majority in the House of Representatives. They also point out that since each state was equally represented in the Senate, and since there were initially only five states that were generally regarded as slave states—Maryland, Virginia, North Carolina, South Carolina, and Georgia—the Senate was controlled by northern, non-slave-state senators. These scholars also point out that, remarkably, the Senate turned out to be the body that more consistently supported a pro-slavery agenda in the early republic.

For critiques of the "slave power" thesis with regard to the three-fifth clause, see Lance Banning, "Three-fifths Historian: A Review of *"Negro President": Jefferson and the Slave Power* by Garry Wills, Claremont Institute for the Study of Statesmanship and Political Philosophy, http://www.claremont.org/writings/crb/fall2004/banning.html; Maltz, "The Idea of the Proslavery Constitution," 41–50; Sean Wilentz, "American Historians versus American Founders: The Details of Greatness," *New Republic,* March 29, 2004, 27–35; Joyce Appleby, "Having It All; Two New Books Reckon with a President's Complicated Legacy: Review of *"Negro President": Jefferson and the Slave Power* by Garry Wills and *Jefferson's Demons: Portrait of a Restless Mind* by Michael Knox Beran," *Washington Post,* November 16, 2003; Gordon Wood, "Slaves in the Family," *New York Times Book Review,* December 14, 2003, 10.

152. Richards, *The Slave Power,* 56–57. See also Amar, *America's Constitution,* 94.

153. Amar, *America's Constitution,* 91.

154. See the speeches of Patterson on July 9 and Morris on July 11 and August 8 in Koch, *Notes of Debates,* 259, 276, 411–412. Amar has noted that the three-fifths clause "gave a state extra credit for each new unit of slave property it could breed, buy, or steal." Amar, *America's Constitution,* 93.

155. Amar, *America's Constitution,* 97–98, 156–159.

156. These calculations were conducted using census data from the Geospatial Statistical Data Center, University of Virginia Library, available at http://fisher.lib.virginia.edu/. I have not included the populations of the territories with any of their parent states.

157. Delaware's free population was 50,209, and Virginia's free population was 454,923.

158. See Lee and Oppenheimer, *Sizing Up the Senate,* 35.

159. The total free population of Virginia, Pennsylvania, Massachusetts, and New York was 1,582,431, or 53.5 percent of the total free population (2,956,436) of the original thirteen states.

160. The total populations of the seven smallest states—Delaware, Rhode Island, Georgia, New Hampshire, New Jersey, Connecticut, and South Carolina—was 1,023,522, or 28.1 percent of the total population of 3,638,213.

161. The seven states with the smallest free populations—Delaware, Georgia, Rhode Island, New Hampshire, South Carolina, New Jersey, and Maryland—had a total of 844,776 free citizens, or 28.6 percent of the total free population of 2,956,436.

162. Lee and Oppenheimer, *Sizing Up the Senate,* 10–11; see the graph on 11, charting the decreasing percentage of the U.S. population necessary to elect a majority of senators.

163. These figures merely reaffirm that the amendment process is not a majoritarian procedure; rather, amendments require assent from a majority of states to be passed.

164. The Constitution did not stipulate that electoral districts had to contain equivalent numbers of individuals or that representatives had to be elected from single-member, geographically defined districts (which also might have had a bearing on the question of political equality). Over the course of American history, states have experimented with four methods of electing representatives: multimember, geographically defined districts; single-member, geographically defined districts; statewide elections of the entire delegation of representatives; or some combination in which some representatives were elected in single-member districts and some in at-large districts. See Kenneth C. Martis, *The Historical Atlas of United States Congressional Districts, 1789–1983* (New York: Free Press, 1982), 2.

165. Amar, *America's Constitution,* 97. Amar suggests that many Federalists were sympathetic to the idea of congressional districts of roughly equal populations and believed that the constitutional provision under Article I, Section 4, that gave Congress the right to override state election laws concerning the time, place, and manner of holding elections for U.S. representatives and senators would be used to prevent malapportioned electoral districts. Amar speculates, however, that the Federalists refused to include an explicit formula for intrastate congressional apportionment because that would have required the delegates to determine how slaves would be counted for purposes of apportionment *within* each state. Such a consideration would have led to the adoption of a three-fifths rule within the states (any other standard would have been considered hypocritical) and would have given special credit to slave belts within each state—a privilege that even reform-minded southerners might not have wanted to grant. See ibid., 87–89, 537 n. 94.

166. Ibid., 97–98.

167. Koch, *Notes of Debates,* 224.

168. For an analysis of the most sophisticated defense of equal representation in the Senate, see Zuckert's discussion of Dickinson Federalism in "Federalism and the Founding," 190–207.

169. Amar, *America's Constitution,* 86.

170. See Adams, *The First American Constitutions,* 236–243; Tarr, *Understanding State Constitutions,* 83–84.

171. *Baker v. Carr,* 369 U.S. 186 (1962).

172. This chapter has concentrated on the operation of the Framers' Constitution. Another important democratic dimension of the Constitution, however, was its popular ratification, which provided a democratic source for its legitimate authority. See Morgan, *Inventing the People,* for the invention of the "fiction" of popular sovereignty as a foundation for legitimacy.

173. Dahl, *How Democratic Is the American Constitution?* 132–139.

Chapter 3: How Should We Study the American Founding?

1. I first heard the term *new historicism* from Professor Fred Dallymar while I was a graduate student at the University of Notre Dame. I have subsequently seen it used by

John Gunnell to describe the approach of Pocock, Skinner, and John Dunn. Joyce Appleby has labeled Pocock and the other republican revisionists "ideological historians" and speaks of the "ideological approach." In contrast, I follow Mark Bevir in using the term *linguistic contextualists* because it provides the richest description of their method and because the phrase *new historicism* seems somewhat derisive and has been resisted by Pocock. For the use of these labels, see Joyce Appleby, "Republicanism in Old and New Contexts," *William and Mary Quarterly* 43 (January 1986): 29; Mark Bevir, "Mind and Method in the History of Ideas," *History and Theory* 36 (May 1997): 167–189; John Gunnell, "Method, Methodology, and the Search for Traditions in the History of Political Theory: A Reply to Pocock's Salute," *Annals of Scholarship* 1 (1980): 31. For Pocock's opposition to this label see J. G. A. Pocock, "Intention, Tradition, and Methods: Some Sounds on a Fog-horn," *Annals of Scholarship* 1 (1980): 57–62.

This is not to say that these scholars do not share much in common with historicists. They share at least the belief that human thought and behavior are determined by historical situation; that there are no fundamental questions or issues that all humans across time have addressed or that the truth about these issues is unknowable, because our minds are prejudiced by the age in which we live; and that the history of political thought should be seen as a series of sequential, irretrievable events and ideologies, none of which can be judged to be better or worse ways of thinking and living. Wood, Pocock, and Skinner, however, disagree with historicists on one important dimension. They believe that a contemporary historian can understand the past "as it really was" independent of their current historical situation. Most historicists, however, would contend that this is impossible because the perspective of the historian would also be governed by the horizon of his or her historical circumstances. As far as I can tell, these scholars believe that they can achieve a critical distance from the present even though past historical agents could not distance themselves from their present. On this difference between the Cambridge historians and traditional historicists, see Michael Zuckert, "Appropriation and Understanding in the History of Political Philosophy: On Quentin Skinner's Method," *Interpretation* 13 (1985): 403–404.

2. The primary works drawn on by the linguistic contextualists include Peter L. Berger and Thomas Luckmann, *The Social Construction of Reality: A Treatise in the Sociology of Knowledge* (Garden City, N.Y.: Doubleday, 1967); Thomas S. Kuhn, *The Structure of Scientific Revolutions,* 2nd ed. (Chicago: University of Chicago Press, 1970); Clifford Geertz, *The Interpretation of Cultures* (New York: Basic Books, 1973); Ludwig Wittgenstein, *Philosophical Investigations* (Oxford: Basil Blackwell, 1984); J. L. Austin, *How to Do Things with Words* (New York: Oxford University Press, 1965).

Several works illuminate the influence of broader intellectual currents on the linguistic contextualists and provide excellent summaries of the interpretive principles of this approach. See in particular Joyce Appleby, "Republicanism and Ideology," *American Quarterly* 37 (Fall 1985): 461–473; John G. Gunnell, *Political Theory: Tradition and Interpretation* (Cambridge, Mass.: Winthrop, 1979), especially 96–102; David Hollinger, "T. S. Kuhn's Theory of Science and Its Implications for History," *American Historical Review* 78 (April 1973): 370–393; Daniel T. Rodgers, "Republicanism: The Career of a Concept," *Journal of American History* 79 (June 1992): 11–39; Ronald G. Walters, "Signs of the Times: Clifford Geertz and Historians," *Social Research* 47 (1980): 537–556.

3. See in particular Bernard Bailyn, "The Central Themes of the American Revolution: An Interpretation," in *Essays on the American Revolution*, ed. Stephen G. Kurtz and James H. Hutson (Chapel Hill: University of North Carolina Press, 1973), 3–31. See also Bailyn, *The Ideological Origins of the American Revolution* (1967; new edition, Cambridge, Mass.: Belknap Press of Harvard University Press, 1992); Bailyn, "Political Experience and Enlightenment Ideas in Eighteenth-Century America," *American Historical Review* 67 (1961–1962): 339–351.

4. Edmund S. Morgan and Helen M. Morgan, *The Stamp Act Crisis: Prologue to Revolution* (Chapel Hill: University of North Carolina Press, 1953), 295.

5. Bailyn, "Central Themes," 7.

6. Ibid., 11.

7. Ibid., 23, 14–15.

8. Ibid., 15–16; the quote is on 15.

9. Wood's two magisterial studies are *The Creation of the American Republic, 1776–1787* (1969; reprint, Chapel Hill: University of North Carolina Press, 1998), and *The Radicalism of the American Revolution: How a Revolution Transformed a Monarchical Society into a Democratic One Unlike Any that Had Ever Existed* (New York: Vintage Books, 1991). Wood's most explicit methodological writings include "Rhetoric and Reality in the American Revolution," *William and Mary Quarterly* 23 (October 1966): 3–32; "Intellectual History and the Social Sciences," in *New Directions in Intellectual History*, ed. Paul Conkin and John Higham (Baltimore: Johns Hopkins University Press, 1979), 27–41; and "Ideology and the Origins of Liberal America," *William and Mary Quarterly* 44 (July 1987): 628–634. Wood's effort to resurrect the reputation of the anti-Federalists and to integrate their understanding of the Founding into an impartial analysis can be found in "Interests and Disinterestedness in the Making of the Constitution," in *Beyond Confederation: Origins of the Constitution and American National Identity*, ed. Richard Beeman, Stephen Botein, and Edward C. Carter II (Chapel Hill: University of North Carolina Press, 1987), 69–109.

10. Wood, "Rhetoric and Reality," 16.

11. Wood, "Ideology and the Origins of Liberal America," 631.

12. Ibid.

13. Wood, "The Fundamentalists and the Constitution," *New York Review of Books*, February 18, 1988, 40.

14. Wood, "Rhetoric and Reality," 22.

15. Ibid., 23. Wood's idea of "declension" is heavily influenced by Perry Miller's analysis of the Puritans. See especially Perry Miller, *The New England Mind: The Seventeenth Century* (New York: Macmillan, 1939); Miller, *Errand into the Wilderness* (Cambridge, Mass.: Belknap Press of Harvard University Press, 1956).

16. Wood, "Fundamentalists and the Constitution," 39.

17. This argument is also set forth by Skinner and Pocock. See Quentin Skinner, *The Foundations of Modern Political Thought*, 2 vols. (Cambridge: Cambridge University Press, 1978), 1:xi–xiii; J. G. A. Pocock, "The History of Political Thought: A Methodological Enquiry," in *Philosophy, Politics, and Society*, ed. Peter Laslett and W. G. Runciman (Oxford: Basil Blackwell, 1962), especially 191–194.

18. Wood, "Rhetoric and Reality," 16.

19. For an excellent concrete example of the application of this interpretive principle, see Gordon Wood, "Conspiracy and the Paranoid Style: Causality and Deceit in the Eighteenth Century," *William and Mary Quarterly* 39 (July 1982): 401–441. Here, Wood illustrates how the conspiratorial language that Bailyn identified as characteristic of eighteenth-century Americans was deeply embedded in "the general presuppositions and conventions—in the underlying metaphysics—of eighteenth-century culture" (407).

20. Wood, *Creation of the American Republic,* xvi.

21. Wood, "Intellectual History and the Social Sciences," 34. In a later essay, however, Wood backs away from the position that intentions must be understood as historically specific. In defending himself and other historians against the charge of historicism, he writes: "For historians ideas do not always remain ideology, do not remain rooted in the specific circumstances of time and place. Ideas can, and often do, become political philosophy, do transcend the particular intentions of their creators and become part of the public culture, become something larger and grander than their sources." Wood, "Fundamentalists and the Constitution," 38.

22. Wood, "Intellectual History and the Social Sciences," 34.

23. Gordon Wood, "An Exchange on James Madison," *New York Review of Books,* May 23, 1996, 53.

24. Ibid.

25. Wood, "Fundamentalists and the Constitution," 38, 36.

26. Gordon Wood, "Writing History: An Exchange," *New York Review of Books,* December 16, 1982, 59.

27. Gordon Wood, "Afterword," in *The Republican Synthesis Revisited: Essays in Honor of George Athan Billias,* ed. Milton M. Klein, Richard D. Brown, and John B. Hench (Worcester, Mass.: American Antiquarian Society, 1992), 151, 143.

28. Wood, "Intellectual History and the Social Sciences," 34.

29. Ibid., 38.

30. Ibid., 35.

31. Gordon Wood, "Heroics: Review of Garry Wills' *Explaining America: The Federalist,"* *New York Review of Books,* April 2, 1981, 16.

32. The summary that follows is based primarily on Skinner's seminal article "Meaning and Understanding in the History of Ideas" in *Meaning and Context: Quentin Skinner and His Critics,* ed. James Tully (Princeton, N.J.: Princeton University Press, 1988), 29–67, 291–304, and the preface to his important study *The Foundations of Modern Political Thought,* 1:ix–xv. Other works by Skinner include "Motives, Intentions, and the Interpretation of Texts," *New Literary History* 3 (1972): 393–408; "Some Problems in the Analysis of Political Thought and Action," *Political Theory* 2 (August 1974): 277–303; "Conventions and the Understanding of Speech Acts," *Philosophical Quarterly* 20 (1970): 118–138; "Hermeneutics and the Role of History," *New Literary History* 7 (1975–1976): 209–232. For a sympathetic reading of Skinner's method, see Gordon Schochet, "Quentin Skinner's Method," *Political Theory* 2 (August 1974): 261–276.

33. Significantly, the initial draft of Skinner's "Meaning and Understanding in the History of Ideas" was entitled "The Unimportance of the Great Books in the History of Political Thought." See Margaret Leslie, "In Defense of Anachronism," *Political Studies* 18 (1970): 433 n. 1.

34. Skinner, "Meaning and Understanding," 30. In this proposition, Skinner's arguments resemble the earlier historicism of R. G. Collingwood. Collingwood wrote: "the history of political theory is not the history of different answers given to one and the same question, but the history of a problem more or less constantly changing, whose solution was changing with it" (quoted in Gunnell, *Political Theory*, 131).

35. Skinner, *Foundations of Modern Political Thought*, xi.

36. Skinner, "Meaning and Understanding," 48, 30.

37. Ibid., 32, 57, 29, 30, 29.

38. Ibid., 30.

39. Ibid., 33.

40. Ibid., 40.

41. Ibid., 49.

42. Skinner, *Foundations of Modern Political Thought*, x.

43. Skinner, "Meaning and Understanding," 57, 63–64.

44. Ibid., 64.

45. Ibid., 59, 63.

46. Ibid., 61–62. Without challenging his broader point—that it is central to understand the "intended illocutionary force" of a text, or what a historical agent is doing in setting forth an argument—the validity of this particular example is suspect. Skinner argues that context cannot help us determine whether Machiavelli's statement is revolutionary or merely commonplace. But the problem here is not that context is inadequate but rather that historians have an inadequate understanding of the character of that context and thus disagree about it. Whether statements such as "a prince must learn how not to be virtuous" is an endorsement of an accepted moral axiom or a repudiation of prevailing moral conventions is an empirical question about the historical context in which Machiavelli lived. Because historians disagree about the character of that context does not mean that they provide equally plausible accounts. Most important, if we settled the empirical question about the historical context, we would know whether Machiavelli's statement is revolutionary or commonplace.

47. Zuckert, "Appropriation and Understanding," 414.

48. Skinner, "Meaning and Understanding," 63–64.

49. Ibid., 67.

50. Pocock's methodological articles are numerous. See in particular "The History of Political Thought," 183–202; "Languages and Their Implications: The Transformation of the Study of Political Thought," in *Politics, Language, and Time: Essays on Political Thought and History* (New York: Atheneum, 1971), 3–41; "Virtue and Commerce in the Eighteenth Century," *Journal of Interdisciplinary History* 3 (Summer 1972): 119–134; "Political Theory, History, and Myth: A Salute to John Gunnell," *Annals of Scholarship* 1 (1980): 3–25; "Intentions, Traditions and Methods," 57–62; *The Machiavellian Moment* Revisited: A Study in History and Ideology," *Journal of Modern History* 53 (March 1981): 49–72, especially 50–53; "Virtues, Rights, and Manners: A Model for Historians of Political Thought," *Political Theory* 9 (August 1981): 353–368; "Introduction: The State of the Art" in *Virtue, Commerce, and History: Essays on Political Thought and History, Chiefly in the Eighteenth Century* (Cambridge: Cambridge University Press, 1985), 1–34; "The Concept of a Language and the *Metier d' historien*: Some Considerations on Practice," in *The*

Languages of Political Theory in Early-Modern Europe, ed. Anthony Pagden (Cambridge: Cambridge University Press, 1987), 19–38; "Communications," *William and Mary Quarterly* 45 (October 1988): 817.

51. Pocock, "Languages and Their Implications," 5–6.

52. Pocock, "The History of Political Thought," 186.

53. Pocock, "Languages and Their Implications," 7.

54. Kuhn, *The Structure of Scientific Revolutions,* 2.

55. Ibid., 175, 46.

56. Ibid., 7.

57. Ibid., 3.

58. Joyce Appleby has made this observation and eloquently analyzes its importance. She writes: "Shrewdly aware that both Marxists and liberals drew their intellectual hubris from a common assumption that they understood progress, Pocock removed the place for progress from the Anglo-American world view. Taken as a whole, his work can be seen as a formidable indictment of the reductionism in liberal and Marxist historiography" (Appleby, "Republicanism and Ideology," 466).

59. Pocock, "The Concept of a Language," 21.

60. Pocock, "Languages and Their Implications," 13, 14.

61. Pocock, "Introduction: The State of the Art," 8.

62. Pocock, "Languages and Their Implications," 15 (emphasis added).

63. Ibid., 25.

64. Pocock, "The Concept of a Language," 21; Pocock, "Communications," 817.

65. The only important difference among the interpretations of any of these scholars seems to be the importance that Skinner places on intentions, especially intended illocutionary force, in contrast to Pocock's emphasis on reading texts as reflections of the political languages and idioms present in society. This contrast is brought out in Bevir, "Mind and Method," especially 169–176.

66. Bailyn, *Ideological Origins,* v.

67. Gunnell, *Political Theory,* 100–101.

68. The phrase "closing" the context is borrowed from Charles D. Tarlton, "Historicity, Meaning, and Revisionism in the Study of Political Thought," *History and Theory* 12 (1973): 308. Joyce Appleby has made this point concisely: "The republican revisionists have self-consciously reached out for social scientific models to free intellectual history from its distortingly rationalistic assumptions about the life of the mind. In the sympathetic analysis of belief systems done by anthropologists they found the means for studying the thought as a social phenomenon. What anthropologists also offered was a concept of ideology which concentrated upon the means rather than the causes or consequences of specific beliefs." Appleby, "Republicanism and Ideology," 467.

69. Rodgers, "Republicanism: The Career of a Concept," 21.

70. Skinner, "Meaning and Understanding," 30.

71. Nathan Tarcov, "Quentin Skinner's Method and Machiavelli's *Prince,*" in Tully, *Meaning and Context,* 203.

72. Skinner, "Meaning and Understanding," 37.

73. The critique that follows is an attempt to bring together and order many of the criticisms of the methodology of linguistic contextualism over the past thirty years. The

best critical appraisals of linguistic contextualism include Appleby, "Republicanism in Old and New Contexts," 20–34, especially 26–31; Appleby, "Republicanism and Ideology," 461–473; Bevir, "Mind and Method," 167–189; John Patrick Diggins, "The Oyster and the Pearl: The Problem of Contextualism in Intellectual History," *History and Theory: Studies in the Philosophy of History* 23 (May 1984): 151–169; Ralph Lerner, "The Constitution of the Thinking Revolutionary," in Beeman, Botein, and Carter, *Beyond Confederation*, 38–68; Leslie, "In Defence of Anachronism," 433–447; Bhikhu Parekh and R. N. Berki, "The History of Political Ideas: A Critique of Quentin Skinner's Methodology," *Journal of the History of Ideas* 34 (1973): 163–184; Tarlton, "Historicity, Meaning, and Revisionism," 307–328; Tarcov, "Skinner's Method and Machiavelli's *Prince*," 194–203; Zuckert, "Appropriation and Understanding," 403–424.

74. I particularly like Paul Rahe's characterization of this problem. "Circumstance and the climate of opinion," Rahe writes, "no doubt limited in certain respects what could be accomplished by philosophical statesmen in ages gone by, and they certainly circumscribed what such men could openly and publicly *say*. But there is no compelling reason to suppose that these meaningfully restricted what the greatest of our early modern predecessors could *think*." Rahe, *Republics: Ancient and Modern: Classical Republicanism and the American Revolution* (Chapel Hill: University of North Carolina Press, 1992), 12 (emphasis added).

75. Appleby, "Republicanism in Old and New Contexts," 26–31; Appleby, "Republicanism and Ideology," 468–469.

76. Appleby, "Republicanism in Old and New Contexts," 29.

77. Terence Ball and J. G. A. Pocock, eds., *Conceptual Change and the Constitution* (Lawrence: University Press of Kansas, 1988); Terence Ball, *Transforming Political Discourse: Political Theory and Critical Conceptual History* (Oxford: Basil Blackwell, 1988).

78. See in particular Pocock, "Communications," 817.

79. Pocock, "Virtue and Commerce," 121; Pocock, "Languages and Their Implications," 18.

80. Pocock, "Languages and Their Implications," 17, 19.

81. On this point in general, see Lerner, "Constitution of the Thinking Revolutionary," 38–68.

82. Wood, "Heroics," 16.

83. None of this means that Jefferson made the distinction between Hutcheson and Locke that Wills attributed to him. There is strong evidence that Jefferson did not see Hutcheson and Locke as expressing rival ideas and perceived his own role as expressing the "harmonizing sentiments of the day." Thus, he may have been consciously trying to reflect a general liberal Enlightenment consensus. This does not change the point that Jefferson was certainly *capable* of making such refined distinctions. We will run into problems if we suppose that our perceptions and capabilities are more acute than those we interpret. Jefferson quote is in Wood, "Heroics," 16. On Wills's interpretation, see Ronald Hamowy, "Jefferson and the Scottish Enlightenment: A Critique of Garry Wills's *Inventing America: Jefferson's Declaration of Independence*," *William and Mary Quarterly* 36 (October 1979): 503–523.

84. On how this problem also arises in Skinner's work as a result of his "fallacy of coherence," see Zuckert, "Appropriation and Understanding," 410–413. As Zuckert has

noted, Skinner's interpretive axioms might lead scholars to suppose that every *appearance* of incoherence is in fact incoherence.

85. Skinner and Pocock have set forth similar understandings of the relationship of ideology to political behavior and also use this as a defense against the criticisms of behavioralists. See Skinner, *Foundations of Modern Political Thought*, xii–xiii; Pocock, "The History of Political Thought," 191–194. For an unorthodox critique of this defense of ideology that argues that the Founders' beliefs about the relationship of ideas to behavior were similar to those set forth by Charles Beard, see John Patrick Diggins, *The Lost Soul of American Politics: Virtue, Self-Interest, and the Foundations of Liberalism* (New York: Basic Books, 1984), 347–365.

86. Wood, "Intellectual History and the Social Sciences," 34. The Progressives' assertion that ideas are mere reflections of underlying interests can also be easily deflected in other ways. For example, instead of examining rhetoric or the language of historical agents, one can examine laws and constitutions to determine what ideologies they manifest. Contrary to what the Progressives suggested, laws and constitutions often serve as "rough but useful empirical indicators" of ideologies and betray (rather than mask) the motives of those who enacted them. Rogers Smith, *Civic Ideals: Conflicting Visions of Citizenship in U.S. History* (New Haven, Conn.: Yale University Press, 1997), 2.

87. Although I agree with Wood that the study of political thought can be defended even if we accept the axiom that professed beliefs are never the motives of behavior, I disagree with his proposition that individuals never act on their professed beliefs. Wood asserts that "anyone who knows how people really behave" will not be convinced that someone was motivated by professed beliefs and principles. He further asserts that "all that we have learned about the psychology and sociology of human behavior suggests that the realists are right and that such a simple-minded notion that people's professed beliefs . . . are the motives for their behavior will never be persuasive." Wood, "Intellectual History and the Social Sciences," 33; "Ideology and the Origins of Liberal America," 630.

These propositions, however, are logically untenable and empirically false. First, few people are willing to concede that their own actions are never motivated by their professed beliefs and principles. It would therefore be extremely self-righteous for us to believe that we are capable of acting on principled motives while others are not. Second, it has become increasingly hard to claim that professed beliefs, at least in some form, are never motives for action. In light of recent historical experience, it is hard to deny that the *ideas* of radical Islamists or Christian fundamentalists are masks for economic interests and are not at least part of the motivation for their actions. Third, Wood is also wrong to suggest that modern psychological and sociological studies prove that individuals are never motivated by principles and professed beliefs. As the collection of essays in Jane Mansbridge's important work *Beyond Self-Interest* (Chicago: University of Chicago Press, 1990) illustrate, recent sociological and psychological studies have in fact established a firm empirical basis for the proposition that individuals act on motives that include "commitment to moral principles, concern for others, 'we-feeling,' and readiness to cooperate when cooperation does not serve self-interest narrowly conceived" (ix). For all its self-proclaimed realism, then, the declaration that principles, ideas, or professed beliefs are always the stepchild of interests is not very realistic.

Fourth, Wood does not prove that ideas can never be motives for actions: he simply declares such a line of analysis out of bounds for serious-minded scholars or at least those who want to be taken seriously. Apparently, if we encounter evidence that individuals are motivated by ideas, we should simply dismiss this possibility because we know that it can never really happen. Nevertheless, if an interpreter conducts a multivariate study of two groups who voted differently on whether to ratify the Constitution and finds that the only difference between them was their ideas, he or she would be warranted in attributing their votes for or against the Constitution to ideas; likewise, if an interpreter finds that the only difference between the anti-Federalists and the Federalists was their different economic interests, he or she would be justified in attributing their votes to economic interests.

Finally, the claim that self-interest alone motivates human behavior runs into the problems of vagueness and circularity. If this proposition is meant to suggest that individuals are always motivated by narrow *economic* self-interests, then it is easily refuted by noting the power of noneconomic sources of motivation, including not only admirable motives such as commitment to principle and concern for others but also love of power, lust, and fame. But if all these motives are included under the rubric of self-interest, the claim becomes circular and vague. Self-interest is transformed from a specific and testable concept to one that embraces all that humans do. The person making this claim begs the question because he first says that humans are motivated only by self-interest and then redefines self-interest to include all that humans do. As Mansbridge has observed, "the claim that self-interest alone motivates political behavior must be either vacuous, if self-interest can encompass any motive, or false, if self-interest means behavior that consciously intends only self as the beneficiary" (*Beyond Self-Interest,* 20).

88. Nathan Tarcov, "On a Certain Critique of 'Straussian,'" *Review of Politics* 53 (Winter 1991): 15.

89. Examples that illustrate this distinction can easily be multiplied. During the recent Gulf Wars, the government of Iraq accused the United States of becoming involved in the Middle East only because of concern over the region's oil interests. Pronouncements by George W. Bush, George H. W. Bush, and others about the tyrannical tendencies of Saddam Hussein, Iraq argued, were merely rhetorical flourish designed to mask the United States' true motives. The problem with the Iraqi position, however, should be obvious. Arguments about whether the United States became involved to secure its oil interests, to end Hussein's aggression, or, most likely, for both these reasons do not address whether Hussein acted inappropriately or whether the United States was justified in opposing him. Even if U.S. motives were entirely self-interested, U.S. actions might have been justified because of their effect (such as providing the conditions for peace in the region). If we adopt Wood's approach, we would have to conclude that historians who analyze this conflict should not judge the relative merits of these claims, but rather produce an interpretation of the conflict that examines the functions of ideas within the context of the situation and sympathetically accounts for the positions of both Iraq and the United States. Any other explanation would seemingly get us "endlessly caught up in the polemics of the participants themselves." In short, Wood understands impartiality as neutrality between the claims of different historical actors but rejects the possibility of impartiality through objectivity—that is, an analysis that provides

such a strong account of one side in a historical debate that it discounts the other side. The quote is from Wood, "Rhetoric and Reality," 16.

90. More often, historians side with one group of historical participants against another, and revisionism results when historians move from the perspectives and judgments of one group to another or when they discover a neglected or forgotten perspective. Most recently, this has been true in debates about the culpability of the Founders on the question of slavery. Here, in particular, revisionist views of the Jeffersonians have been generated by historians who resurrected the criticisms lodged against the Jeffersonians by their Federalist Party opponents, not by achieving a transcendent, impartial position. See, for example, Garry Wills, *"Negro President": Jefferson and the Slave Power* (Boston: Houghton Mifflin, 2003), and the commentary on this new revisionism by Sean Wilentz, "American Historians versus American Founders: The Details of Greatness," *New Republic,* March 29, 2004, 27–35.

91. Wood, *Creation of the American Republic,* especially 519–524.

92. See "Ideology and the Origins of Liberal America," 631–632, where Wood chides Ralph Ketcham and Pauline Maier for adopting the arguments of the Federalists in criticizing his interpretation of the Constitution as an aristocratic document.

93. Ibid., 632.

94. Skinner, "Meaning and Understanding," 50.

95. Ibid., 65 (emphasis added).

96. Jean-Jacques Rousseau, *On the Social Contract with Geneva Manuscript and Political Economy,* ed. Roger D. Masters (New York: St. Martin's Press, 1978), 46–52.

97. Dennis Dalton, ed., *Mahatma Gandhi: Selected Political Writings* (Indianapolis: Hackett, 1996), 12.

98. Skinner, "Meaning and Understanding," 48. Paul Rahe's pithy comment that "the only doctrine that historicists are inclined to exempt from historicity is historicism itself" is illuminating on this issue. What Rahe means is that historicists often fail to see how current their own assumptions about the past are, including important questions about whether there are perennial questions or whether it is possible to learn from the past. Many past historical agents simply took for granted what the linguistic contextualists deny. Skinner and Pocock in particular make ahistorical assumptions about the capabilities and assumptions of the individuals they are interpreting, with remarkable disregard for their own admonitions about disregarding the categories of analysis available to historical actors and the necessity of producing an account that they would have found acceptable. Rahe, *Republics: Ancient and Modern,* 235.

99. Ronald Dworkin, *A Matter of Principle* (Cambridge, Mass.: Harvard University Press, 1985), 48–50.

100. For a study that traces precisely this kind of evolution of the idea of separation of powers, see William B. Gwyn, *The Meaning of the Separation of Powers: An Analysis of the Doctrine from Its Origin to the Adoption of the United States Constitution* (New Orleans: Tulane University, 1965).

101. Tarcov, "Skinner's Method and Machiavelli's *Prince,*" 203.

102. Skinner, "Meaning and Understanding," 66.

103. Even if Skinner is correct here, one wonders why anyone would engage (for very long, at least) in the study of the history of political thought. After beginning its

study, we would be led to conclude with Skinner that the past teaches us only that our moral assumptions are conventional and that our institutions are peculiar and contingent. We might want to perfect or occasionally renew our respect for these insights by engaging in further historical studies. We might also want to show, for political purposes, the contingency of a particular historical arrangement that is said to be natural (although we could not suggest that a path not taken was somehow now viable). Nevertheless, after learning these lessons, the rest of what we could learn would be of mere antiquarian interest. We would spend our scholarly lives expanding our cosmopolitan understanding of the past as an avenue for reinforcing our already firmly held beliefs in the peculiarity and conventionality of our moral assumptions and the contingency of our practices and institutions.

Finally, it is impossible to resist the observation that for all the linguistic contextualists' strictures about taking an agenda to the study of the history of political thought, there is clearly a political agenda behind this methodology. Historical cosmopolitanism and emphatic understanding are valued for their role in teaching us the peculiarity and contingency of our moral values and institutional arrangements. These are hardly uncontroversial or apolitical beliefs.

104. As Michael Zuckert has written: "To argue or to suspect that a work contains 'timeless elements,' or truths about politics does not imply in any way that one should or must ignore the context in attempting to understand that work. All thought finds expression or is communicated in some context; *an appreciation of the context may be requisite to understanding the thought expressed*, but that fact of itself says nothing whatever about whether the thought is true or 'relevant.' To have relation to a particular context is not necessarily to be bound exclusively to that context" (Zuckert, "Appropriation and Understanding," 406 [emphasis added]). To slightly rephrase Zuckert's point in order to reinforce it, context helps to establish *what* thought is expressed. It helps the interpreter avoid attributing the wrong thought (most likely the thought of some future thinker) to an author. Engaging in contextual analysis should therefore help establish the interpreter's claim not to be manipulating the past. See also Tarcov, "Skinner's Method and Machiavelli's *Prince*," 195.

105. Bailyn, *Ideological Origins*, 323.

106. Indeed, taken seriously, Wood's and Skinner's approach would seemingly preclude analogical thinking about the past altogether. To say the X from the past is like Y in the present would, by definition, be ahistorical. Contrary to Wood's and Skinner's claims, however, historians who trace out only the radical differentness between the past and the present are not engaged in an impartial and objective investigation. The past flows into the present with points of continuity and discontinuity. A mode of analysis that focuses only on the points of discontinuity—on the radical differentness—is necessarily partial and not objective. This form of analysis makes differentness and discontinuity prior in importance to sameness and continuity. Historians cannot reasonably object that the past is totally different from the present. If this were true, it would be impossible to interpret it at all. It would be like a message sent from another planet that we had no possibility of decoding. Also, such an argument runs into the problem of establishing when the past becomes radically different (when it becomes "the past") and thus when it becomes legitimate to look at the past only for its differentness. Should

proper historical analysis of an event that happened ten days ago look only at the differentness of that time from our own? What about ten years ago? What about two hundred years ago?

Wood's understanding of objective historical scholarship runs into yet another problem—namely, it is not clear that the positivists' assumptions behind Wood's goal of objective historical scholarship can be made congruent with the postmodern assumptions behind his understanding of the function of ideology. Specifically, Wood's analysis of the proper role of the historian ultimately rests on a positivist understanding of the reality of the past. The past, according to Wood, contains real facts that the historian impartially documents and describes. In this process, the historian need not ultimately be bound to values, theories, or social processes and conventions but can instead describe facts and provide accounts about how the past "really was." But Wood's understanding of how ideology functions relies heavily on what he calls the philosophy of the "post-psychological age," which, as Wood notes, denies the positivists' division of ideas and social reality. Ideology understood as a matrix of social conventions is responsible in this account for the mediation and construction of "reality." Reality, in other words, does not exist apart from the social conventions used to construct it—it is not, like the reality of the past, capable of simply being grasped as a set of facts. Most important, these conflicting accounts of the nature of reality raise questions that Wood does not address: How do historians achieve the impartial stance toward the facts of the past that others are denied in understanding even present reality? Why is their understanding of the reality of the past not mediated by social processes and conventions? Compare Wood, "Writing History: An Exchange," 59; Wood, "Intellectual History and the Social Sciences," 27–41; Wood, "Ideology and the Origins of Liberal America," 628–634.

107. Zuckert, "Appropriation and Understanding," 409.

108. Stanley Elkins and Eric McKitrick, *The Age of Federalism: The Early American Republic, 1788–1800* (New York: Oxford University Press, 1993), 37, 5.

109. *The Oxford English Dictionary,* prepared by J. A. Simpson and E. S. C. Weiner (Oxford: Clarendon Press, 1989), 4:752–753.

110. Wood, "Interests and Disinterestedness in the Making of the Constitution," especially 81–91.

111. Pocock, "The History of Political Thought," 186.

112. Bailyn, *Ideological Origins,* vi.

113. The comments in this paragraph are indebted to the discussions in Lerner, "Constitution of the Thinking Revolutionary," 38–68; and Thomas Pangle, *The Spirit of Modern Republicanism: The Moral Vision of the American Founders and the Philosophy of Locke* (Chicago: University of Chicago Press, 1988), 1–4.

114. Zuckert, "Appropriation and Understanding," 420–421.

115. Wood, *Creation of the American Republic,* xvi.

116. Lance Banning, *Jefferson and Madison: Three Conversations from the Founding* (Madison, Wis.: Madison House, 1995), xi.

117. Lance Banning, *The Sacred Fire of Liberty: James Madison and the Founding of the Federal Republic* (Ithaca, N.Y.: Cornell University Press, 1995), 367.

Chapter 4: Ancients, Moderns, and Americans

1. Antipathy for the republicanism-liberalism debate grew throughout the 1990s. Daniel Rodgers's important article "Republicanism: The Career of a Concept," *Journal of American History* 79 (June 1992): 11–39, reads like an obituary for the concept of republicanism and the republicanism-liberalism debate. See also the comments by Drew McCoy in the introduction to *The Republican Synthesis Revisited: Essays in Honor of George Athan Billias*, ed. Milton M. Klein, Richard D. Brown, and John B. Hench (Worcester, Mass.: American Antiquarian Society, 1992), 12, and Rogan Kersh, "The Founding: Liberalism Redux: Review of *The Foundations of American Citizenship: Liberalism, the Constitution, and Civic Virtue*, by Richard Sinopoli," *Review of Politics* 55 (Fall 1993): 729.

2. Kersh, "The Founding: Liberalism Redux," 729.

3. Over the past ten years, this point has become increasingly popular, and the list of scholars who ascribe to this thesis is now impressive. In addition to the scholars and works cited later in this chapter, see Saul Cornell, "Liberal Republicans or Republican Liberals? The Political Thought of the Founders Reconsidered," *Reviews in American History* 21 (March 1993): 29–30; Steven Dworetz, *The Unvarnished Doctrine: Locke, Liberalism, and the American Revolution* (Durham, N.C.: Duke University Press, 1990), 37–38, 191; Morton Horwitz, "Republicanism and Liberalism in American Constitutional Thought," *William and Mary Law Review* 29 (Fall 1987): 57–74, especially 64; Isaac Kramnick, "The 'Great National Discussion': The Discourse of Politics in 1787," *William and Mary Quarterly* 45 (January 1988): 3–32; Kramnick, *Republicanism and Bourgeois Radicalism: Political Ideology in Late 18th Century England and America* (Ithaca, N.Y.: Cornell University Press, 1990); Kramnick, "Communications," *William and Mary Quarterly* 45 (October 1988): 818; Forrest McDonald, *Novus Ordo Seclorum: The Intellectual Origins of the Constitution* (Lawrence: University Press of Kansas, 1985); McDonald, "The Intellectual World of the Founding Fathers" in *Requiem: Variations on Eighteenth-Century Themes*, ed. Forrest McDonald and Ellen Shapiro McDonald (Lawrence: University Press of Kansas, 1988), 9; John Murrin, "Fundamental Values, the Founding Fathers, and the Constitution," in *To Form a More Perfect Union: The Critical Ideas of the Constitution*, ed. Herman Belz, Ronald Hoffman, and Peter J. Albert (Charlottesville: University of Virginia Press, 1992), 11–25; J. G. A. Pocock, "Communications," *William and Mary Quarterly* 45 (October 1988): 817; Cass Sunstein, "Beyond the Republican Revival," *Yale Law Journal* 97 (July 1988): 1539–1590; Mark Tushnet, *Red, White, and Blue: A Critical Analysis of Constitutional Law* (Cambridge, Mass.: Harvard University Press, 1988), 4–5; Gordon S. Wood, "Afterword," in Klein, Brown, and Hench, *The Republican Synthesis Revisited*, 143–151. For discussions of the movement toward paradigmatic pluralism, see Peter Onuf, "Reflections on the Founding: Constitutional Historiography in Bicentennial Perspective," *William and Mary Quarterly* 46 (April 1989): 341–375; Rodgers, "Republicanism: The Career of a Concept," 35–37.

4. Michael Zuckert, *The Natural Rights Republic: Studies in the Foundation of the American Political Tradition* (Notre Dame, Ind.: University of Notre Dame Press, 1996), 209. Lance Banning's "Jeffersonian Ideology Revisited: Liberal and Classical Ideas in the New American Republic," *William and Mary Quarterly* 42 (July 1987): 11–19, was central in catapulting the debate over the intellectual origins of the American Republic out of the "either republicanism or liberalism" phase and into its current configuration, which has

scholars trying to determine how liberalism, republicanism, and perhaps other intellectual traditions are related to one another. See also Banning, "Quid Transit? Paradigms and Process in the Transformation of Republican Ideas," *Reviews in American History* 17 (June 1989): 199–204, and "The Republican Interpretation: Retrospect and Prospect," in Klein, Brown, and Hench, *The Republican Synthesis Revisited*, 91–117.

5. James T. Kloppenberg, "The Virtues of Liberalism: Christianity, Republicanism, and Ethics in Early American Political Discourse," *Journal of American History* 74 (June 1987): 11. Interpretations that ignore the diversity of intellectual traditions in the American Founding are often deterministic and question-begging and have been presented by scholars on both sides of this debate. J. G. A. Pocock, for example, has argued that to understand the eighteenth century fully, we must trace the persistence of civic humanism, and he has largely ignored documents that would undermine this thesis. In *The Machiavellian Moment: Florentine Political Thought and the Atlantic Republican Tradition* (Princeton, N.J.: Princeton University Press, 1975), he does not explicate central documents, such as the Declaration of Independence, that illustrate the importance of the natural rights–social contract tradition in American political thought. Indeed, Pocock's most famous work contains almost no analysis of primary documents from the American Founding at all.

In a letter dated August 10, 2000, Pocock challenged the charge I made in an earlier version of this chapter published as an essay in *History of Political Thought*. There, I said that he had "cast out of vision" and "simply ignored" the Declaration of Independence. In his defense, Pocock pointed to three writings where he had provided a "good deal" of discussion of the Declaration. In each of these brief analyses, Pocock interprets the Declaration as a statement of the separation of one people from another and as "a document performed in the language of *jus gentium* [law of nations] rather than *jus civile* [civil law]." See J. G. A. Pocock, "Political Thought in the English-Speaking Atlantic: I. The Imperial Crisis," in *The Varieties of British Political Thought, 1500–1800*, ed. J. G. A. Pocock (Cambridge: Cambridge University Press, 1995), 281; Pocock, "States, Republics, and Empires: The American Founding in Early Modern Perspective," in *Conceptual Change and the Constitution*, ed. Terence Ball and J. G. A. Pocock (Lawrence: University Press of Kansas, 1988), 57–61; Pocock, "Empire, State and Confederation: The War of American Independence as a Crisis in Multiple Monarchy," in *A Union for Empire: Political Thought and the Union of 1707*, ed. John Robertson (Cambridge: Cambridge University Press, 1995), 342–345.

Strictly speaking, then, my earlier statement that Pocock has totally ignored the Declaration of Independence is incorrect. Pocock's brief analyses of the Declaration, however, fail to provide an account of the clear statement of the natural rights–social contract, liberal tradition in the second paragraph of the Declaration and also fail to explain the ubiquity of similar statements in numerous other "declarations of independence" written in 1776. In short, although Pocock provides an interpretation of the Declaration, he does so in a way that ignores its status as a statement of the principles of liberalism. My basic point, then, remains unchanged, despite Pocock's protests: Pocock has ignored the liberal dimensions of political thought in the Founders' writings that would challenge his thesis about the ubiquity of republicanism. See Pauline Maier, *American Scripture: Making the Declaration of Independence* (New York: Alfred A. Knopf, 1997), especially 47–96, for the natural rights tradition in other declarations of independence.

Moreover, as Joyce Appleby has most persistently charged, the republican revisionists have been guilty of determinism, in particular by fastening onto a mode of interpretation that is unable to take into account the numerous changes in social practice and ideology that were taking place in the eighteenth century. In the initial stages of this debate, at least, the republican revisionists were too quick to say that the Founders were locked into a conceptual world of classical republican language that precluded the development and use of other political languages. Similarly, Thomas Pangle, Paul Rahe, and before them Martin Diamond have interpreted the Founders' political thought as a species of the "new science of politics" of Machiavelli, Hobbes, and Locke. They have ignored or presented perverse interpretations of important dimensions of the Founders' political thought that challenge this reading, especially Jeffersonian political economy.

For the republican revisionists' tendency to ignore the Declaration of Independence and the natural rights tradition, see Scott Gerber, "What Ever Happened to the Declaration? A Commentary on the Republican Revisionism in the Political Thought of the American Revolution," *Polity* 26 (Winter 1993): 207–231, and Gerber, *To Secure These Rights: The Declaration of Independence and Constitutional Interpretation* (New York: New York University Press, 1995), especially 19–56. For the deterministic tendencies of the republican revisionists' methodology, see Joyce Appleby, "Republicanism in Old and New Contexts," *William and Mary Quarterly* 43 (January 1986): 26–31. See Eugene Miller, "What Publius Says about Interest," *Political Science Reviewer* 19 (Spring 1990): 20–21, for warnings about how interpreting the political thought of the Founders through the lens of the "new science of politics" can lead to interpretations that take for granted what they are designed to prove. The reductionism of Rahe's, Pangle's, and Diamond's interpretations of Jeffersonian political economy can be grasped by comparing Martin Diamond, "Democracy and *The Federalist*: A Reconsideration of the Framers' Intent" and "Ethics and Politics," in *As Far as Republican Principles Will Admit: Essays by Martin Diamond,* ed. William A. Schambra (Washington, D.C.: American Enterprise Institute, 1992), especially 31–35, 337–368; Diamond, *The Founding of the Democratic Republic* (Itasca, Ill.: F. E. Peacock, 1981), 71–78; Thomas Pangle, *The Spirit of Modern Republicanism: The Moral Vision of the American Founders and the Philosophy of Locke* (Chicago: University of Chicago Press, 1988), 98–104; and Paul Rahe, *Republics: Ancient and Modern: Classical Republicanism and the American Revolution* (Chapel Hill: University of North Carolina Press, 1992), 726–747, with Drew McCoy, *The Elusive Republic: Political Economy in Jeffersonian America* (Chapel Hill: University of North Carolina Press, 1980), 120–135. See also Alan Gibson, "The Commercial Republic and the Pluralist Critique of Marxism: An Analysis of Martin Diamond's Interpretation of *Federalist* 10," *Polity* 25 (Summer 1993): 521–528. For the way paradigms of interpretation change because scholars identify new sets of problems as central, not necessarily because new paradigms envelop old ones and provide a more comprehensive interpretation of the facts, see Rodgers, "Republicanism: The Career of a Concept," 11–12.

6. Gordon Wood, "Ideology and the Origins of Liberal America," *William and Mary Quarterly* 44 (July 1987): 634.

7. See, for example, Banning, "Jeffersonian Ideology Revisited," 12; Banning, "Quid Transit?" 201; Banning, "Republican Interpretation: Retrospect and Prospect," 92–93, 111–113; Robert Shalhope, *The Roots of Democracy: American Thought and Culture, 1760–1800*

(Boston: Twayne, 1990), xii; Zuckert, *The Natural Rights Republic*, 209–210; Ralph Ketcham, "Review of *If Men Were Angels: James Madison and the Heartless Empire of Reason* by Richard K. Matthews," *William and Mary Quarterly* 52 (October 1995): 697–702.

8. For a particularly clear and forceful statement of this position, see Zuckert, *The Natural Rights Republic*, 7–8, 95–96, 209–210.

9. Not all scholars have come to this conclusion. Many continue to interpret the Founders' political thought as a species of liberalism. In addition to the works of Gerber and Pangle cited earlier, see John Patrick Diggins, *The Lost Soul of American Politics: Virtue, Self-Interest, and the Foundations of Liberalism* (New York: Basic Books, 1984); Jennifer Nedelsky, *Private Property and the Limits of American Constitutionalism: The Madisonian Framework and Its Legacy* (Chicago: University of Chicago Press, 1990); Richard Matthews, *If Men Were Angels: James Madison and the Heartless Empire of Reason* (Lawrence: University Press of Kansas, 1995); Asher Horowitz and Richard K. Matthews, "Narcissism of the Minor Differences: What Is at Issue and What Is at Stake in the Civic Humanism Question," *Polity* 30 (Fall 1997): 1–27.

10. Kramnick, "The 'Great National Discussion,'" 4.

11. Banning, "Jeffersonian Ideology Revisited," 19.

12. I borrow the phrase "multiple traditions approach" from Rogers Smith, "Beyond Tocqueville, Myrdal, and Hartz: The Multiple Traditions in America," *American Political Science Review* 87 (September 1993): 549–566.

13. In addition to the works analyzed in the text, Jeffery Isaac and Alan Craig Houston have published studies that do not directly interpret the American Founding but have important implications for its study and should be read in conjunction with the works discussed here. Both Isaac and Houston argue that the political thought of the "Commonwealthmen" or "radical Whigs" of seventeenth- and eighteenth-century England was a synthesis composed centrally of liberalism but also containing important strains of republicanism. They then hypothesize—although it is not their goal to prove—that this synthesis was also characteristic of the American Founders. See Jeffrey Isaac, "Republicanism vs. Liberalism?" *History of Political Thought* 9 (Summer 1988): 349–377, and Alan Craig Houston, *Algernon Sidney and the Republican Heritage in England and America* (Princeton, N.J.: Princeton University Press, 1991).

Moreover, James Kloppenberg's oft-cited essay "The Virtues of Liberalism," his book by the same name, and excellent studies by Jerome Huyler, Richard Sinopoli, Joshua Foa Dienstag, and James P. Young also present modified consensualist interpretations that suggest that the Founders incorporated diverse strains of political thought within a capacious and peculiarly eighteenth-century conception of Lockean liberalism. See Kloppenberg, "The Virtues of Liberalism," 9–33; Kloppenberg, *The Virtues of Liberalism* (New York: Oxford University Press, 1998); Jerome Huyler, *Locke in America: The Moral Philosophy of the Founding Era* (Lawrence: University Press of Kansas, 1995); Richard Sinopoli, *The Foundations of American Citizenship: Liberalism, the Constitution, and Civic Virtue* (New York: Oxford University Press, 1992); Joshua Foa Dienstag, "Serving God and Mammon: The Lockean Sympathy in Early American Political Thought," *American Political Science Review* 90 (September 1996): 497–511; James P. Young, *Reconsidering American Liberalism: The Troubled Odyssey of the Liberal Idea* (Boulder, Colo.: Westview Press, 1996).

14. J. David Greenstone, *The Lincoln Persuasion: Remaking American Liberalism* (Princeton, N.J.: Princeton University Press, 1993), 51.

15. J. David Greenstone, "Against Simplicity: The Cultural Dimensions of the Constitution," *University of Chicago Law Review* 40 (Spring 1988): 438–442 (the quote is on 439); Greenstone, "Political Culture and American Political Development: Liberty, Union, and the Liberal Bipolarity," *Studies in American Political Development: An Annual* 1 (1986): 5–6; Greenstone, *The Lincoln Persuasion*, 51–53. This interpretation is also explored by one of Greenstone's students; see David Ericson, *The Shaping of American Liberalism: The Debates over Ratification, Nullification, and Slavery* (Chicago: University of Chicago Press, 1993).

16. Greenstone, "Against Simplicity," 51.

17. Michael Zuckert, *Natural Rights and the New Republicanism* (Princeton, N.J.: Princeton University Press, 1994), 167–168.

18. Ibid., 299.

19. Ibid.

20. Ibid., 305, 308.

21. Zuckert, *The Natural Rights Republic*, 2, 16, 106.

22. Ibid., 31, 7, 240, 241, 95.

23. I also interpret this as one of the central purposes of Huyler's excellent work, *Locke in America.*

24. Nathan Tarcov, "A 'Non-Lockean' Locke and the Character of Liberalism," in *Liberalism Reconsidered,* ed. Douglas MacLean and Claudia Mills (Totowa, N.J.: Rowman and Allanheld, 1983), 130–140. Such reappraisals of Locke's political thought parallel the efforts of a number of scholars, including William Galston, Michael Walzer, Stephen Macedo, Amy Gutman, and James Kloppenberg, to provide a more sympathetic understanding of liberalism by arguing that it is more capacious than its critics charge. See William Galston, "Defending Liberalism," *American Political Science Review* 76 (September 1982): 621–629; Galston, *Liberal Purposes: Goods, Virtues, and Diversity in the Liberal State* (New York: Cambridge University Press, 1991); Michael Walzer, *Spheres of Justice: A Defense of Pluralism and Equality* (New York: Basic Books, 1983); Stephen Macedo, *Liberal Virtues: Citizenship, Virtue, and Community in Liberal Constitutionalism* (Oxford: Clarendon Press, 1990); Amy Gutman, "Communitarian Critics of Liberalism," *Philosophy and Public Affairs* 14 (Summer 1985): 308–322; Kloppenberg, *The Virtues of Liberalism.*

25. Tarcov, "A 'Non-Lockean' Locke," 131.

26. Ibid., 130.

27. Banning, "Republican Interpretation: Retrospect and Prospect," 99, 113.

28. Ibid., 93.

29. Banning, "Quid Transit?" 201.

30. Pocock often makes this same suggestion. Republicanism, he further contends, was never displaced by liberalism but rather has "survived to furnish liberalism with one of its modes of self-criticism and self-doubt." See J. G. A. Pocock, "Between Gog and Magog: The Republican Thesis and the *Ideologia Americana*," *Journal of the History of Ideas* 48 (April–June 1987): 341.

31. Michael Lienesch's narrative of the transformation of the Founders' political thought also suggests both its duality and its ambiguous legacy. See Lienesch, *The New*

Order of the Ages: Time, the Constitution, and the Making of Modern American Political Thought (Princeton, N.J.: Princeton University Press, 1988).

32. Ralph Ketcham, *Framed for Posterity: The Enduring Philosophy of the Constitution* (Lawrence: University Press of Kansas, 1993), 38–45, 165–172; the quotes are on 169 and 166. For a similar understanding of the Framers' conception of "liberty," see also Banning, "Jeffersonian Ideology Revisited," 17–19.

33. See, for example, the study of Robert Shalhope, who treats republicanism in the early American Republic as a "familiar ideology permeating all walks of life" but liberalism as more of an "unarticulated behavioral pattern." The rise of liberalism in his account is partly a story of how liberal practices eventually became ascendant and demanded intellectual justifications. Shalhope, *The Roots of Democracy,* 50. It is in this sense that the works of Joyce Appleby are relevant, and she can also be considered a scholar who accepts the multiple traditions approach. Although she argues for an exclusively liberal interpretation of the Jeffersonians, Appleby believes that members of the Federalist Party accepted the precepts of opposition ideology. She thus sees the eighteenth century as a period of transition in which liberalism and republicanism vied for ascendancy. Even more than Shalhope, she contends that liberalism emerged as an intellectual justification for the liberal practices that accompanied the English financial revolution and became commonplace during the eighteenth century. See especially Appleby, "Republicanism in Old and New Contexts"; *Liberalism and Republicanism in the Historical Imagination* (Cambridge, Mass.: Harvard University Press, 1992); and *Capitalism and the New Social Order: The Republican Vision of the 1790s* (New York: New York University Press, 1984).

34. McCoy, *The Elusive Republic,* 134.

35. Several additional works have traced the synthetic quality of the political thought of individual Founders. See, for example, Steven Conrad, "Polite Foundation: Citizenship and Common Sense in James Wilson's Republican Theory," *1984: Supreme Court Review* (1985): 359–388, especially 383–385; Lance Banning, *The Sacred Fire of Liberty: James Madison and the Founding of the Federal Republic* (Ithaca, N.Y.: Cornell University Press, 1995). For broader studies that analyze the synthetic thought of the Founders considered collectively, see Banning, "Jeffersonian Ideology Revisited," 11–19; Sunstein, "Beyond the Republican Revival," 1539–1590; Jean Yarbrough, "Republicanism Reconsidered: Some Thoughts on the Foundation and Preservation of the American Republic," *Review of Politics* 41 (January 1979): 61–95.

36. Garrett Ward Sheldon, *The Political Philosophy of Thomas Jefferson* (Baltimore: Johns Hopkins University Press, 1991), 169, 93, 94. See also Sheldon, *The Political Philosophy of James Madison* (Baltimore: Johns Hopkins University Press, 2001), for a similar multiple traditions interpretation.

37. Ketcham, "Publius: Sustaining the Republican Principle,"579.

38. Rogers Smith, *Civic Ideals: Conflicting Visions of Citizenship in U.S. History* (New Haven, Conn.: Yale University Press, 1997). This study was preceded by a number of essays in which Smith outlined dimensions of his complex argument. See "The 'American Creed' and American Identity: The Limits of Liberal Citizenship in the United States," *Western Political Quarterly* 41 (1988): 225–251; "'One United People': Second-Class Female Citizenship and the American Quest for Community," *Yale Journal of Law and Humanities* 1 (1989): 229–293; "Beyond Tocqueville," 549–566; "Unfinished Liberalism," *Social Re-*

search 61 (Fall 1994): 631–670. See also the exchanges between Smith and his critics: Jacqueline Stevens, "Beyond Tocqueville, Please!" and Rogers Smith, "Response to Jacqueline Stevens," *American Political Science Review* 89 (December 1995): 987–995; and Karen Orren, "Structure, Sequence, and Subordination in American Political Culture: What's Traditions Got to Do with It?" and Rogers Smith, "Response to Karen Orren," *Journal of Policy History* 8 (1996): 470–490.

Similar interpretations that emphasize the cultural dissensus and ideological confrontations in American political thought can be found in Richard J. Ellis, *American Political Cultures* (New York: Oxford University Press, 1993), and James A. Morone, "The Struggle for American Culture," *PS: Political Science and Politics* 29 (September 1996): 425–430.

39. Smith, "Beyond Tocqueville," 555.

40. Ibid., 549.

41. Smith, "One United People," 229.

42. Coverture was a feudal doctrine that became embedded in common law; it held that upon marriage, the legal identity of a married woman (a *feme covert*) was "absolutely subsumed" to that of her husband. This doctrine, according to Smith, was enforced in colonial and Revolutionary America, with single women (*feme soles*) being accorded only slightly greater legal rights. In documenting the importance of the concept of "republican motherhood" in early America, Smith follows the scholarship of Linda Kerber. Republican motherhood is the belief that although women are citizens and the moral equals of men, their peculiar, apolitical function is to raise children to be virtuous republican citizens. In general, Smith documents that custom, common-law doctrine, Protestant ideology, and republicanism all converged in early America to support what he refers to as "domestic sphere" ideology—the belief that "women had no proper place in the public realm and only a subordinate one in the home." See Smith, "One United People," 241–250 (the quote is on 241); Smith, *Civic Ideals*, 67–69.

43. Smith, *Civic Ideals*, 9.

44. Smith, "Response to Stevens," 991; Smith, "One United People," 233; Smith, "Beyond Tocqueville," 554 (emphasis added).

45. Smith, *Civic Ideals*, 6.

46. Smith, "Beyond Tocqueville," 555.

47. Smith, *Civic Ideals*, 6, 29 (emphasis added).

48. Stevens, "Beyond Tocqueville, Please!" 987. A group of scholars including Stevens, Uday Mehta, Carole Pateman, Carol Horton, and Ira Katznelson has adopted a Hartzian framework and resisted or overtly criticized Smith's effort to establish the conceptual identity of inegalitarian and ascriptive ideologies as rival idioms of liberalism. Although there are important differences among these scholars' claims, their basic theme is that racial hierarchies and sexism are endemic to liberalism. Liberalism, they argue, makes abstract and universalistic claims about who is eligible to exercise basic rights but then establishes concrete criteria that exclude women and different racial groups from political participation because they do not meet minimum requirements of rationality. Mehta, for example, argues that exclusion is a projection from the theoretical core of liberalism, not simply a historical aberration and betrayal of the universalistic claims of liberalism. Mehta supports this argument by identifying a distinction

within liberal theory between the universalistic principles from which it purports to derive political identity and "a thicker set of social credentials that *constitute the real bases of political inclusion.*" Locke, for example, contends that, by birth, individuals are free, equal, and rational, but he does not presuppose that everyone is capable of exercising reason. Instead, as his *Thoughts Concerning Education* illustrates, Locke believes that the ability to reason and thus to be included in political society is contingent on education, cultivation, and breeding. Locke, according to Mehta, intends for these social credentials for political inclusion to serve as a barrier that only a select few can hurdle. Thus, far from imagining a world in which all individuals are governed by their consent because of their natural equality, Locke believes that political inclusion depends on rational capacity, which in turn depends on proper training. In general, these scholars want to prevent liberalism from being exonerated for its historical links to racism and sexism. See Uday Mehta, "Liberal Strategies of Exclusion," *Politics and Society* 18 (December 1990): 427–454. For similar criticisms of Smith, see Carol Horton, "Liberal Equality and the Civic Subject: Identity and Citizenship in Reconstruction America," in *The Liberal Tradition in American Politics: Reassessing the Legacy of American Liberalism,* ed. David Ericson and Louisa Bertch Green (New York: Routledge, 1999), 115–136; Horton, *Race and the Making of American Liberalism* (Oxford: Oxford University Press, 2005); Carol Pateman, *The Sexual Contract* (Stanford, Calif.: Stanford University Press, 1988); Ira Katznelson, *City Trenches* (Chicago: University of Chicago Press, 1981).

Smith agrees that there is an association between the practices of liberal democratic regimes and illiberal ideas, and that this association is not simply a historical accident. Nevertheless, he prefers to characterize the linkages between liberalism and inegalitarian and ascriptive ideologies as social and psychological rather than to view illiberal ideologies as endemic to liberalism. Illiberal ideologies, he notes, have often been allied with liberalism by historical actors attempting to meet immediate and long-term political imperatives, especially those arising from state building. Nevertheless, he insists that there is no reason that liberalism has to be allied with inegalitarian ideologies and that such an alliance can be achieved only if the rational capabilities of nonwhites and women are ignored. Smith also insists on recognizing the contradictions between liberalism and illiberal ideologies, because that contradiction has served as "the staple of effective protest rhetoric by disempowered groups in America." Finally, unlike some of his critics, Smith argues that there are no compelling reasons to suggest that the openings liberalism provides to illiberal ideologies have been the key to liberalism's success. Instead, he prefers to define and view liberalism and illiberal ideologies as discrete, rival components of a complex American political thought. See Smith, *Civic Ideals,* 27–30; "Reply to Stevens," 991; and "Liberalism and Racism: The Problem of Analyzing Traditions," in Ericson and Green, *The Liberal Tradition in American Politics,* 20–22.

49. Smith, *Civic Ideals,* 28; see also "Response to Stevens," 991.

50. Smith, *Civic Ideals,* 140, 138.

51. Ibid., 28, 122.

52. The common ground that has emerged within this debate is the product of movement by scholars on both sides. Scholars have argued, learned, and made concessions (often silently), and we are now closer in our interpretations of the Founders than we suspect. Specifically, the "republican revolution" in scholarship led to the identifica-

tion of a constellation of concepts and a language of political thought that had either been ignored or lost by previous generations of scholars. Scholars began to recognize the importance of concepts such as public virtue, liberty (understood as freedom to participate in public affairs), and the public good (understood as something more than an aggregation of the individual interests of the citizenry). But almost from the beginning, the choice to call this strain of eighteenth-century English opposition ideology "*classical* republicanism" and to interpret it as an alternative to Lockean liberalism met with strong opposition from numerous scholars. These scholars therefore conducted a counterrevolution that subjected virtually every aspect of the republican interpretation to intense scrutiny and simultaneously reemphasized the importance of liberalism in the American Founding. Neo-Lockean scholars have argued that because the republican revisionists were saddled to a deterministic approach to the study of political thought, it was impossible for them to recognize and account for the numerous changes that took place during the eighteenth century. Republican revisionists have also been charged with providing inaccurate definitions of republicanism that, in the words of one scholar, have "been plagued by language too weak to rule out anything and, hence, to mean anything" (Sinopoli, *Foundations of American Citizenship*, 10). Scholars have also challenged the republican revisionists' interpretations of Greek and Roman republicanism, Machiavelli, James Harrington, the neo-Harringtonians, and the influence of republicanism in America. On the various criticisms lodged against the republican synthesis, see Zuckert, *The Natural Rights Republic*, 207–208.

Nevertheless, the response of many of the principal proponents of the republican interpretation to this counterrevolution was *not* to redouble their efforts and argue for the exclusivity of republicanism in the American Founding. Instead, many of these scholars hastily retreated from some of their strongest claims, maintained that they had never meant to suggest that republicanism and liberalism were rival and mutually exclusive traditions of political thought, and thus made considerable room for liberalism within their interpretations of the Founding. But the strategic retreat of the republican revisionists is only half of this story—and, unfortunately, it seems to be the only half told in most accounts of this debate. The liberal interpretation of the American Founding has also been transformed in response to the challenge posed by republican revisionists. However exaggerated some of their claims were, the republican revisionists convincingly documented the presence of English opposition ideology (rightly understood) in the Founders' political thought; focused attention on a rich vocabulary of discourse, including concepts such as virtue and the public good, which had previously been neglected by scholars; and thereby mounted a successful challenge to the possessive-individualist interpretation of eighteenth-century political thought in general and the American Founding in particular. In other words, just as criticisms from the neo-Lockean scholars forced concessions and a reorientation from the republican revisionists, criticisms of the possessive-individualist interpretation forced neo-Lockean scholars to formulate a more complex and subtle interpretation.

The new liberal interpretation that has emerged from this dialectic is significantly different from the interpretations of Louis Hartz, Robert Dahl, Richard Hofstadter, Martin Diamond, and C. B. MacPherson. Whereas this earlier generation of scholars argued that the Founders considered men to be atoms of self-interest, hoped to exacerbate selfishness in the belief that an invisible hand would render private vice into public good, and sought to establish a mechanistic government or a "machine that would run of itself," neo-Lockean or liberal interpretations of the American Founding now contend that liberalism has a need for virtue, community, and the common good. A "kinder, gentler liberalism," in other words, has replaced the possessive-individualist and pluralist interpretations of an earlier generation of scholars.

53. This is true even for the leading proponents of the republican synthesis, who have recently argued that they never meant to suggest otherwise. Banning, for example, has recently stated: "I do not now, nor did I ever, think of the republican tradition as a rival or alternative to a Lockean or liberal conception of the origins and limits of political society. Indeed, I do not think that any of the major architects of the republican interpretation ever claimed that revolutionary thinking could be fully understood without regard to Locke and other early modern theories of natural rights and social compacts." Banning, "Republican Interpretation: Retrospect and Prospect," 98–99.

54. Two different kinds of arguments have been made by scholars to suggest that the Founders, like classical republicans, constructed a political system that would engage in the formation of opinion and the development of a common character among the citizenry. The first, I contend, fails; the second is yet unproved. Several West Coast Straussians have pointed to the Founders' goal of refining or filtering public opinion, especially through representation, and equated it with the classical republican goal of educating and molding public opinion and thus forming a common character among the citizenry. Madison and his colleagues, of course, did hope to refine public opinion and believed that representatives should represent the reason, not the passions, of the public. Still, the Founders' conception of "opinion" was modern and Humean, not classical. They argued that governments "rest on opinion" and thus sought to secure an affective bond between the people and their government and elected respresentatives in order to create stability. Furthermore, Madison and many of his colleagues conceived of public opinion in a remarkably modern manner as a product of the society independent of the government, and they believed that when public opinion had crystallized, it was sovereign. In other words, whereas the West Coast Straussians have emphasized the degree to which the Framers hoped to influence or even consciously mold public opinion toward fundamental values, Madison and his colleagues saw their role and the role of government in general as the much more limited one of refining existing public opinion in areas where it was not already set. The opinion of the citizenry, most of them believed, would be formed through religion, education, and participation in voluntary organizations, not by government. In general, then, the Founders' goal of refining public opinion was far different from the classical goal of promoting *homonoia* (political oneness) through the use of sumptuary laws and laws that establish religious belief.

For examples of the West Coast Straussians' efforts to interpret the American regime as designed to achieve classical ends, see the essays in Charles Kesler, ed., *Saving the Revolution: The Federalist Papers and the American Founding* (New York: Free Press, 1987); Kesler, "The Founders and the Classics," in *The Revival of Constitutionalism*, ed. James W. Muller (Lincoln: University of Nebraska Press, 1988), 57–90; Colleen Sheehan, "Madison's Party Press Essays," *Interpretation: A Journal of Political Philosophy* 17 (Spring 1990): 355–377; Sheehan, "The Politics of Public Opinion: James Madison's 'Notes on Government,'" *William and Mary Quarterly* 44 (October 1992): 609–627. For a judicious evaluation of this interpretation, see Harvey Flaumenhaft, "Review of *Saving the Revolution: The Federalist Papers and the American Founding," Constitutional Commentary* 5 (Summer 1988): 460–476. See also the exchange between Sheehan and me on the issue of whether Madison hoped that the government would promote civic education: Alan Gibson, "Veneration and Vigilance: James Madison and Public Opinion, 1785–1800," *Review of Politics* 67 (Winter 2005), 5–35, 69–76; Colleen Sheehan, "Public Opinion and the Formation of Civic Character in Madison's Republican Theory," *Review of Politics* 67 (Winter 2005): 37–48. For Madison's understanding of the relationship of government to public opinion, see *Federalist* No. 49, in Alexander Hamilton, James Madison, and John Jay, *The Federalist Papers,* ed. Jacob E. Cooke (1961; reprint, Middletown, Conn.: Wesleyan University Press, 1989), 314–315 (all subsequent references are to this volume), and the essays "Public Opinion" and "Charters," in *The Papers of James Madison,* 17 vols., ed. William T. Hutchinson et al. (Chicago: University of Chicago Press; Charlottesville: University of Virginia Press, 1962–), 14:170, 191.

Another case for the thesis that the Framers did not abandon concern for the development of character can perhaps be built by emphasizing the federal nature of the Constitution. This argument suggests that although the Constitution did not explicitly provide for the education of statesmen and citizens, public support of religion, and institutions that would foster political participation, the Framers simply assumed that these concerns would be addressed by the state governments. See Jean Yarbrough, "The Constitution and Character: The Missing Critical Principle?" in Belz, Hoffman, and Albert, *To Form a More Perfect Union,* 220–221, 237–248. This argument, however, depends on documentation that state laws actually addressed such concerns and that the Framers knew this and consciously made the decision that state governments were the proper arena for fostering education, religion, and political participation. As far as I know, no study has proved this to be the case, and Peter Onuf has challenged this argument, suggesting that few of the Founders "put much faith in state-supported churches or even in public education" to inculcate the virtue necessary to sustain republican governments. See Peter Onuf, "State Politics and Republican Virtue: Religion, Education, and Morality in Early American Federalism," in *Toward a Usable Past: Liberty under State Constitutions,* ed. Paul Finkelman and Stephen E. Gottlieb (Athens: University of Georgia Press, 1991), 91–116.

55. Rigorous definitions and conceptual clarity, however, are what this debate has lacked. As a result, much of the disagreement between scholars who espouse a republican interpretation and their neo-Lockean opponents has really been a submerged debate over the meaning of classical republicanism itself, not simply the content of the Founders' political thought. These scholars, in other words, have often argued past each other because they are using different standards to determine what constitutes classical republicanism.

For their part, the republican revisionists have implied or set forth a series of definitions in their works. Indeed, as Zuckert has pointed out, a retrospective rereading of the masterworks of the republican interpretation challenges whether these scholars ever achieved a common characterization of republicanism and thus whether this interpretation merits its appellation as a synthesis. As initially formulated by Bernard Bailyn in

The Ideological Origins of the American Revolution (1967; reprint, Cambridge, Mass.: Belknap Press of Harvard University Press, 1992), English opposition ideology (he did not call it classical republicanism) is characterized as a set of concepts, anxieties, and hopes and calls for specific institutional arrangements and reforms that were pervasive in seventeenth- and eighteenth-century English radical thought and became especially important in America during the Revolution. Specifically, Bailyn argues that this ideology was grounded in then common political concepts such as natural rights, the contractual basis of government, and praise for England's mixed constitution. But its peculiarity came from the emphasis placed on the fragility of republics; the encroaching nature of power, and the threat to liberty by rulers wielding it; fear of ministerial corruption by placemen; the necessity of vigilance against government; concern for the moral qualities required to preserve liberty, including an independent, uncorrupted, landholding citizenry; and appeals for a range of institutional reforms from adult male suffrage to binding instructions on representatives.

Bailyn then interprets this universe of concepts and apprehensions as a form of libertarianism, or a "peculiar strain of anti-authoritarianism" rooted in "extreme solicitude for the individual and an equal hostility to government." This ideology, he contends, carried into modernity "the traditional anti-statist convictions of seventeenth-century liberalism." Bailyn thus does not contrast Anglo-American republicanism with the natural right–social contract tradition or charge it with many of the connotations it would later be given. Bailyn, *Ideological Origins*, xii, 48; Bailyn, "The Central Themes of the American Revolution: An Interpretation," in *Essays on the American Revolution*, ed. Stephen G. Kurtz and James H. Hutson (Chapel Hill: University of North Carolina Press, 1973), 9.

In different ways, Gordon Wood's *The Creation of the American Republic, 1776–1787* (1969; reprint, Chapel Hill: University of North Carolina Press, 1998) and Pocock's *The Machiavellian Moment* transformed this understanding of Anglo-American republicanism. Wood links English opposition ideology to an organic conception of the public good and argues that the American Revolutionaries believed that the sole purpose of government was to promote the public good. Meanwhile, Pocock maintains that English opposition ideology was a restatement of the classical republican or, as he called it, civic humanism conception of political liberty. For Zuckert's analysis of the different variations of republicanism present in the republican synthesis and the evolution of this interpretation, see *Natural Rights and the New Republicanism*, 151–164.

During the 1980s, as the interpretations of the republican synthesis became more influential and began to be used by a variety of scholars for contemporary political purposes, classical republicanism seemingly came to be identified with the hopes, anxieties, concepts, and institutional arrangements identified by Bailyn from radical Whig ideology and with the three political concepts identified in the writings of Pocock and Wood: political liberty (understood as the necessity of participating in ruling and being ruled in a political community), virtue (understood as requiring self-sacrifice for the public good), and the public good or common interest (understood as an entity that transcends the aggregate interests of the community and is not simply a residue of self-interested competition among special-interest groups). In contrast to these understandings of classical republicanism, the Aristotelian characterization of classical republicanism that I use as a standard is drawn from Rahe's *Republics: Ancient and Modern*. Rahe brings an extraordinarily deep understanding of ancient republicanism to this debate and provides a rigorous, undiluted, and—I believe—accurate characterization of it. Whereas scholars of the republican synthesis have been interested in tracing the continuity of classical republican concepts through a series of transmutations in Renaissance Italy, seventeenth-century England, and then eighteenth-century America, Rahe provides an extensive interpretation of the meaning of classical republicanism among the ancients themselves. He thus provides a stable and surefooted standard for determining whether the political thought of the American Founding is truly classical.

56. *The Politics of Aristotle,* ed. Ernest Barker (London: Oxford University Press, 1958), book I, especially chs. 1 and 2, pp. 1–8; the quote is on 7. See also Rahe, *Republics: Ancient and Modern,* 28–54.

57. Rahe, *Republics: Ancient and Modern,* 31.

58. *Federalist* No. 10, 61.

59. Rahe, *Republics: Ancient and Modern,* especially 29–31.

60. Ibid., 31. Jean Bethke Elshtain has also emphasized this difference between classical and modern republics. "The classical view," she observes, "is that the city-state should have complete control of human bodies for the purposes of labor, procreation, and war." Elshtain, "'In Common Together': Unity, Diversity, and Civic Virtue," in *"The Constitution of the People": Reflections on Citizens and Civil Society,* ed. Robert E. Calvert (Lawrence: University Press of Kansas, 1991), especially 69–72; the quote is on 70.

61. On this point, see the famous quote by Benjamin Constant in Rahe, *Republics: Ancient and Modern,* 15.

62. Banning acknowledges this when he writes: "'Classical Republicanism' it now appears, has proved a deeply troubling term for the collection of ideas whose influence on the Revolution scholars have been emphasizing since the publication of Wood's *Creation of the American Republic.* Over time, that term, which was originally employed for sensible and solid reasons, has encouraged an impression that the thinking of the early Revolution was considerably less modern than it was—less modern, at a minimum, than 'modern' ordinarily implies for scholars trained in political theory." Banning, *The Sacred Fire of Liberty,* 215.

63. See Hamilton, *Federalist* No. 15, 110–111; James Madison, "Vices of the Political System of the United States," in *Papers of James Madison,* 9:356.

64. Indeed, classical democracy and the conception of political liberty that went with it were never options for the Founders in the first place. Representation was accepted within Anglo-American republicanism long before the American Founding, and none of the Founders envisioned anything but a representative republic. Furthermore, at the time of the adoption of the Constitution, the state governments were designed on the principle of representation, not collective deliberation, and were, as Hamilton pointed out, already much larger than ancient republics. See Banning, *The Sacred Fire of Liberty,* 216–217; Hamilton, *Federalist* No. 9, 73–74.

65. The Founders believed that promotion of the public good or common interest was still one of the primary purposes of government. Thus, on the surface at least, they shared this understanding of the function of government with classical republicanism. Nevertheless, the Founders' understanding of the common interest was profoundly different from the classical conception of the public good. In classical political thought, the

public good implied a full-blown defense of a specific conception of the good life. In the Founders' conception of a common interest, this concept took on a much more economic meaning—a meaning that does not involve the promotion of a single conception of the good life and thus does not challenge the characterization of their political system as a species of deontological liberalism. In other words, the Founders' conception of a common interest was compatible with individual autonomy and a high degree of skepticism about what constitutes the good life, along with an unwillingness to have the government foster it.

66. Greenstone, *The Lincoln Persuasion*, 51.

67. Zuckert makes this point with characteristic clarity: "The distance of the republican conception from the theory of the Declaration should be apparent from even this brief sketch. According to the republican thesis, human beings are intensely political (Pocock) and/or communal (Wood); according to the Declaration, human beings are not originally or naturally political—the origin is a state of nature understood as an apolitical condition. Although polity is essential, it is not natural; it is made by human beings. Politics, according to the Declaration, is for the sake of natural rights, and natural rights are emphatically pre-political. The Declaration nowhere intimates that in political participation lies human fulfillment; in place of human fulfillment is the right to the pursuit of happiness." Zuckert, *The Natural Rights Republic*, 206.

68. Bailyn, *Ideological Origins*, 43; Bernard Bailyn, *The Origin of American Politics* (New York: Alfred A. Knopf, 1968), 53.

69. The significance of *Cato's Letters* is stressed by Huyler, *Locke in America*, 211–230; Zuckert, *Natural Rights and the New Republicanism*, xix–xx, 305–319; and Shalhope, *The Roots of Democracy*, 41–42.

70. Bailyn, *Ideological Origins*, 351–379; *Federalist* Nos. 24 and 26, 157–162, 168–174.

71. Lance Banning, *The Jeffersonian Persuasion: Evolution of a Party Ideology* (Ithaca, N.Y.: Cornell University Press, 1978); Banning, "Republican Ideology and the Triumph of the Constitution, 1789 to 1793," *William and Mary Quarterly* 31 (April 1974): 178–179; John Murrin, "The Great Inversion, or Court versus Country: A Comparison of the Revolutionary Settlements in England (1688–1721) and America (1776–1816)," in *Three British Revolutions: 1641, 1688, 1776*, ed. J. G. A. Pocock (Princeton, N.J.: Princeton University Press, 1980), 368–453; McCoy, *The Elusive Republic*; Stanley Elkins and Eric McKitrick, *The Age of Federalism: The Early American Republic, 1788–1800* (New York: Oxford University Press, 1993).

72. Elkins and McKitrick, *The Age of Federalism*, 23.

73. See Lance Banning, "Some Second Thoughts on Virtue and the Course of Revolutionary Thinking," in Ball and Pocock, *Conceptual Change and the Constitution*, 194–212; Banning, "Republican Interpretation: Retrospect and Prospect," 106–117; Banning, *Jefferson and Madison: Three Conversations from the Founding* (Madison, Wis.: Madison House, 1995), 57–99. Bailyn, *Ideological Origins*, 368–379; Richard Vetterli and Gary Bryner, *In Search of the Republic: Public Virtue and the Roots of American Government* (Lanham, Md.: Rowman and Littlefield, 1996); John Ashworth, "The Jeffersonians: Classical Republicans or Liberal Capitalists?" *Journal of American Studies* 18 (December 1984): 428–430; Kloppenberg, "The Virtues of Liberalism," 9–33; Sinopoli, *Foundations of American Citizenship*; Richard Sinopoli, "Liberalism, Republicanism and the Constitution," *Polity* 19

(Spring 1984): 331–352. Most scholars seem to have concluded that this understanding of virtue was further modified during the late eighteenth and early nineteenth centuries and increasingly became equated with "benevolence," "bourgeois propriety," and "feminine purity." See Kloppenberg, "The Virtues of Liberalism," 29; Gordon Wood, *The Radicalism of the American Revolution* (New York: Vintage Books, 1991), 213–225, 356–357.

74. Vetterli and Bryner, *In Search of the Republic*, 6 (emphasis in original).

75. See the classic expressions of this view in David Truman, *The Governmental Process: Political Interests and Public Opinion* (New York: Alfred A. Knopf, 1951), 50–51, and Arthur Bentley, *The Process of Government: A Study of Social Pressures* (Chicago: University of Chicago Press, 1908).

76. See *Federalist* No. 49, 317.

77. *Federalist* No. 51, 322.

78. This phrase is from Micheal Kammen, *A Machine that Would Go of Itself: The Constitution in American Culture* (New York: Alfred A. Knopf, 1986).

79. Richard Hofstadter, *The American Political Tradition and the Men Who Made It* (1948; reprint, New York: Vintage Books, 1974), 10.

80. Benjamin Barber, "The Compromised Republic: Public Purposelessness in America," in *The Moral Foundations of the American Republic,* ed. Robert H. Horwitz (Charlottesville: University of Virginia Press, 1979), 19.

81. George Will, *Statecraft as Soulcraft: What Government Does* (New York: Simon and Schuster, 1983), 31, 38. Examples of this thesis can be found in Barber, "The Compromised Republic," especially 20–30; Robert Dahl, *A Preface to Democratic Theory* (Chicago: University of Chicago Press, 1956), 1–33; Martin Diamond, "Democracy and *The Federalist*: A Reconsideration of the Framers' Intent," "*The Federalist*, 1787–1788," and "Ethics and Politics: The American Way," in *As Far as Republican Principles Will Admit*, 17–36, 37–57, 337–368; Hofstadter, *The American Political Tradition*, 3–21; Isaac Kramnick, "Editor's Introduction," in *The Federalist Papers*, ed. Isaac Kramnick (London: Penguin Press, 1987), 73–74; Arthur Lovejoy, "The Theory of Human Nature in the American Constitution and the Method of Counterpoise," in *Reflections on Human Nature* (Baltimore: Johns Hopkins Press, 1961), 37–65; Sheldon Wolin, *Politics and Vision: Continuity and Innovation in Western Political Thought* (Boston: Little Brown, 1960), 388–393. Even Wood's *The Creation of the American Republic* can be read as setting forth a pluralist interpretation; consider his analysis on 605–606.

82. Ralph Lerner, "Commerce and Character," in *The Thinking Revolutionary: Principle and Practice in the New Republic* (Ithaca, N.Y.: Cornell University Press, 1979), 195–221; Hiram Caton, *The Politics of Progress: The Origins and Development of the Commercial Republic, 1600–1835* (Gainesville: University of Florida Press, 1988), 459–478; Martin Diamond, "Ethics and Politics: The American Way," in *As Far as Republican Principles Will Admit*, 337–368; John R. Nelson, *Liberty and Property: Political Economy and Policymaking in the New Nation, 1789–1812* (Baltimore: Johns Hopkins Press, 1987). See also Albert Hirshman, *The Passions and the Interests: Political Arguments for Capitalism before Its Triumph* (Princeton, N.J.: Princeton University Press, 1977).

83. Alan Gibson, "Impartial Representation and the Extended Republic: Towards a Comprehensive and Balanced Interpretation of the Tenth *Federalist*," *History of Political Thought* 12 (Summer 1991): 276–279.

84. Rahe, *Republics: Ancient and Modern*, 601.

85. Joseph M. Bessette, "Deliberative Democracy: The Majority Principle in Republican Government," in *How Democratic Is the Constitution?* ed. Robert A. Goldwin and William A. Schambra (Washington, D.C.: American Enterprise Institute, 1980), 102–116.

86. McCoy, *The Elusive Republic*, 120–135; see also Elkins and McKitrick, *The Age of Federalism*, 79–92, 195–208; Lienesch, *New Order of the Ages*, 83–96; Lance Banning, "Political Economy and the Creation of the Federal Republic," in *Devising Liberty: Preserving and Creating Freedom in the New American Republic*, ed. David Thomas Konig (Stanford, Calif.: Stanford University Press, 1995), 11–49.

87. Pangle, *The Spirit of Modern Republicanism*, 98–104; Rahe, *Republics: Ancient and Modern*, 726–747.

88. This is the essential truth in Joyce Appleby's characterization of Jeffersonian political economy. See especially Appleby, "Commercial Farming and the 'Agrarian Myth' in the Early Republic," *Journal of American History* 68 (March 1982): 833–849.

89. Madison, "Republican Distribution of Citizens," in *Papers of James Madison*, 14:245.

90. McCoy, *The Elusive Republic*, 120–135. See also Ashworth, "The Jeffersonians," 425–435; Lienesch, *New Order of the Ages*, 82–115.

91. Banning, "Jeffersonian Ideology," 14.

92. Banning, *Jefferson and Madison*, 57–99.

93. Jean Bethke Elshtain seemingly speaks for many scholars when she writes: "Curiously, the framers of the American Constitution paid little explicit attention to such institutions, including the family. Perhaps they did not do so because they simply assumed that these associations of civil society were vital and would be long-lasting." Elshtain, *Democracy on Trial* (New York: Basic Books, 1995), 6. So far, little scholarship has been devoted to exploring this question; however, for two exceptions, see the essays in Calvert, *"The Constitution of the People,"* and Onuf, "State Politics and Republican Virtue," 91–116.

94. The belief that the Founders saw themselves as participants in a battle between the ancients and the moderns seems to be an almost universally accepted point in this debate. As a result of the scholarship of the late Martin Diamond, many Straussians begin from this point. See Diamond's *As Far as Republican Principles Will Admit;* Pangle's *The Spirit of Modern Republicanism* and *The Ennobling of Democracy: The Challenge of the Postmodern Era* (Baltimore: Johns Hopkins University Press, 1992), 93–102; and especially Rahe, *Republics: Ancient and Modern*. The proponents of the republican synthesis seem to hold this same view in a modified form. The Pocock-Banning St. Louis version of the republican interpretation traces the continuity of classical republican concepts (especially positive liberty) into the American Founding and then throughout American history. In contrast, the Bailyn-Wood Harvard republican interpretation suggests that the American Founding should be viewed as resting on the pivot between the exhaustion of classical political concepts and the emergence of modern ones. Both these interpretations, however, suggest that the Founders held a dualistic view of the history of political thought and viewed themselves somewhere on a continuum between liberal and classical political thought.

95. In a short but highly provocative appreciation of the scholarship of Martin Diamond, Diamond's friend Marvin Meyers eloquently makes several points that have in-

fluenced the interpretation presented here. The Founders, Meyers writes, "simply did not cast themselves in a universal war between the Moderns and the Ancients." We should, he continues, "try faithfully to look through their eyes and texts, acknowledge provisionally their chosen masters, friends, and adversaries. In short, we might do well to borrow their map to the great political and moral campaign of history before superimposing our own." According to Meyers, such an approach will teach us that the Framers did indeed engage in a "great campaign," but not against classical Athens or Rome. Instead, Meyers insists, "their evil Old Regime was rather a model of Early Modern polity that blended remnants of the canon and the feudal law, loosely conceived (by John Adams, for example) as general forms of clerical and aristocratic oppression, with a new kind of enlightened despotism, concentrating and rationalizing and enlarging the power of the state through its monarchical head." This model of the early modern polity was evident to the Founders most immediately in the corrupt British monarchy of George III, but it was also evident in numerous other regimes led by ambitious princes. Finally, Meyers notes that when this view of the Founders' project is accepted, it becomes clear that they did not view themselves as lowering the ends of politics, but rather as elevating America to the "full dignity of human nature." See Marvin Meyers, "The Least Imperfect Government: On Martin Diamond's 'Ethics and Politics,'" *Interpretation: A Journal of Political Philosophy* 8 (May 1980): 5–15, 11–13.

96. *Federalist* No. 10, 81. See also *Federalist* No. 9, 71–72; *Federalist* No. 10, 77.

97. *Federalist* No. 18, 128.

98. *Federalist* No. 20, 138.

99. Madison's "Notes on Ancient and Modern Confederacies," in *Papers of James Madison*, 9:3–24; *Federalist* Nos. 18–20, 122–138.

100. In contrast, the anti-Federalists and many of the Jeffersonians remained closely fastened to the synthesis of opposition ideology and natural rights philosophy that had accompanied the Revolution. In particular, their undiluted attachment to the fears and anxieties of opposition ideology led them to interpret the experiences of the 1780s profoundly differently from the way the Framers of the Constitution did. Unlike the Framers, the anti-Federalists continued to believe that the central threat to liberty was unaccountable rulers (not majority factions); therefore, they could not accept the institutional innovations the Framers offered. Direct forms of representation, a scheme of separation of powers designed to prevent independent acts of tyranny by rulers, a small republic, and a revitalized confederation in which the lion's share of power remained in the states, according to the anti-Federalists, would be necessary if liberty was to be preserved.

101. McCoy, *The Elusive Republic*, 19–23. See also Lienesch, *New Order of the Ages*, 83–85.

102. When the synergism between natural rights philosophy and opposition ideology is recognized, it becomes possible to understand how many of the Founders not only could have viewed the American Revolution as a response to the loss of virtue in Britain but also could have believed that this loss of virtue threatened the natural rights of mankind, violated the terms of the original contract, and justified rebellion.

103. Smith, *Civic Ideals*, 2.

104. Zuckert, *The Natural Rights Republic*, 2.

105. Stevens, "Beyond Tocqueville, Please!" 987.

106. Zuckert, *The Natural Rights Republic*, 241–243; the quote is on 241.

107. Smith, "Beyond Tocqueville," 563, and "Response to Stevens," 992.

108. Smith, *Civic Ideals*, 4–5, 9.

Chapter 5. How Could They Have Done That?

1. Cindy Peng, "School Mulls Moral Dilemma in Deciding Whether to Change Name," *Daily Californian*, May 5, 2005, http://www.dailycal.org/sharticle.php?id=18617.

2. Marguerite Talley-Hughes, "Thomas Jefferson: A Man of His Time?" *Berkeley Daily Planet*, March 9, 2004, http://www.berkeleydailyplanet.com/issue/2004-03-09/article/18442.

3. J. Douglas Allen Taylor, "Board Vetoes Jefferson School Name Change," *Berkeley Daily Planet*, June 24, 2005, http://www.berkeleydailyplanet.com/issue/2005-06-24/article/21673?headline=Board-Vetoes-Jefferson-School-Name-Change-By-J.-DOUGLAS-ALLEN-TAYLOR. For verification that opponents of the name change were labeled racists, see also Elliot Cohen, "Commentary: Berkeley Strays from Democratic Path," *Berkeley Daily Planet*, July 12, 2005, http://www.berkeleydailyplanet.com/issue/2005-07-12/article/21832?headline=Commentary-Berkeley-Strays-From-Democratic-Path-By-ELLIOT-COHEN.

4. Allen-Taylor, "Board Vetoes Jefferson Name Change."

5. For some of the conservative bloggers' commentary, see Kristin Bender, "In Berkeley School Vote, Jefferson Out (Sequoia In)," *Free Republic*, June 2, 2005, http://www.freerepublic.com/focus/f-news/1415149/posts. Blogger responses follow the reprinting of this news article by Kristin Bender; "Wordsmith from Nantucket" and "The Little Known History of Slavery, Part Three," February 24, 2007, http://hammeringsparksfromtheanvil.blogspot.com/2007/02/little-known-history-of-slavery-part_24.html. See also the particularly intelligent and informed commentary by Rob Browning, a local Berkeley resident and former editor of Berkeley's Mark Twain papers. Rob Browning, "Commentary: Jefferson School: What's the Rush?" *Berkeley Daily Planet*, June 14, 2005, http://www.berkeleydailyplanet.com/article.cfm?archiveDate=06-14-05&storyID=21617. For verification that Bishop Berkeley owned slaves, see "The First Scholarship Fund," http://www.yaleslavery.org/Endowments/e2schol.html.

6. Additional blogger comments can be found at "Berkeley School Wants to Change Name from Jefferson," *Free Republic*, March 22, 2005, http://www.freerepublic.com/focus/f-news/1368449/posts; Bender, "In Berkeley School Vote, Jefferson Out (Sequoia In)." Blogger comments follow the publication of local newspaper stories on the name change. Titles above are to these news stories.

7. Matthew Artz, "Renaming Vote Stirs School," *Berkeley Daily Planet*, February 3, 2004, http://www.berkeleydailyplanet.com/issue/2004-02-03/article/18197?headline=Renaming-Vote-Stirs-School.

8. Cindy Peng, "Community Votes to Drop Jefferson, Rename School," *Daily Californian*, June 2, 2005, http://www.dailycal.org/article/18791/community_votes_to_drop_jefferson_rename_school; Patrick Hoge, "Berkeley School to Vote on Renaming Jefferson Elementary, President's Slave Holdings Perturb Families, Teachers," *SF Gate*,

March 22, 2005, http://www.sfgate.com/cgi-bin/article.cgi?f=/c/a/2005/03/22/BAGI IBSTMA1.DTL; Kristin Bender, "Jefferson Stays as Name for School," *Oakland Tribune,* June 24, 2005, http://findarticles.com/p/articles/mi_qn4176/is_20050624/ai_n15838645/.

9. Taylor, "Board Vetoes Jefferson School Name Change."

10. The News Hour reports that there are about 450 schools named after George Washington and hundreds more named after other American presidents and Founders who owned slaves. Perhaps the most dramatic effort to rename schools has come in New Orleans. In 1992, the Orleans Parish School Board adopted a specific policy calling for the renaming of all schools named after former slaveholders. Since the adoption of that policy, twenty-two schools have been renamed. "Re-assessing Civic Symbols," November 25, 1997, http://www.pbs.org/newshour/bb/race_relations/july-dec97/schools_11-25.html.

11. I have struggled in the multiple drafts of this chapter to develop adequate categories to group scholars on the question of moral responsibility. The categories above represent my best effort to characterize the terrain of this debate and capture its dynamics, but they are admittedly imperfect in at least three ways that should be explicitly acknowledged. First, unlike most of the other categories or labels used in this book, they are not ones that scholars have themselves adopted. Although some scholars call themselves historicists, none call themselves prosecutors, and only one speaks explicitly of vindicating the Founders. All scholars believe that they are presenting historically accurate interpretations and are engaged in a good-faith effort to praise or blame the Founders as they deserve it. Those scholars that I included among prosecutors and vindicators are thus especially likely to resent and resist my designation of their place in this debate. Second, the account above gives the impression that scholars neatly distribute themselves into three camps, when in fact these categories are much more slippery and are best understood as describing tendencies rather than as rigid groupings. Historicists present a particularly difficult problem because although they see their first goal as recreating the moral universe of the Founders, they often end up giving quite explicit and pronounced moral judgments. Thus, there are historicists who criticize and others who defend the Founders. The problem here is that these categories are based on different criteria—or, put more specifically, they conflate and thus risk confusing issues of judgment with those of approach or methodology. Prosecutors are differentiated from vindicators on the basis of the ultimate judgment that they make about the Founders, but historicists are distinguished from both by their deeply contextualized approach. For the purposes of this chapter, the most important differentiating principle between prosecutors and vindicators on the one hand and historicists on the other is that the former readily enter into a debate in which the Founders are put on trial. Historicists, however, see their role as first returning the Founders to the foreign world they inhabited. Ostensibly at least, the judgments that historicists make follow from the moral universe that they have discovered. Third, while I argue that most prosecutors and vindicators commit interpretive errors because they set out with a lawyer's mind-set, we cannot rule out the possibilities of either a balanced, philosophical apologia for the Founders that admits their shortcomings but nevertheless defends them against their critics. We also cannot rule out the possibility of decisive criticism. Ultimately concluding that the Founders have been unjustly criticized or unduly celebrated, then, may be a conclusion

that follows from mature reflection on the evidence and is not necessarily endemic to the very goal of either prosecuting or vindicating the Founders.

12. In addition to the works of Finkelman and O'Brien analyzed and cited below, other works that represent the approach of prosecutors include Thurgood Marshall, "The Constitution: A Living Document," *Howard Law Journal* 30 (1987): 915–920; John Hope Franklin, "The Moral Legacy of the Founding Fathers," in *Race and History: Selected Essays, 1938–1988* (Baton Rouge: Louisiana State University Press, 1989), 153–162; Staughton Lynd, *Class Conflict, Slavery, and the United States Constitution: Ten Essays* (Indianapolis: Bobbs-Merrill, 1967); Michael Zuckerman, "The Power of Blackness: Thomas Jefferson and the Revolution in St. Domingue," in *Almost Chosen People: Oblique Biographies in the American Grain* (Berkeley: University of California Press, 1993): 175–218; Lawrence Goldstone, *Dark Bargain: Slavery, Profits, and the Struggle for the Constitution* (New York: Walker, 2005). Gary B. Nash, *The Unknown American Revolution: The Unruly Birth of Democracy and the Struggle to Create America* (New York: Viking, 2005); See also the essays in *The United States Constitution: 200 Years of Anti-Federalist, Abolitionist, Feminist, Muckraking, Progressive, and Especially Socialist Criticism,* ed. Bertell Ollman and Jonathan Birnbaum (New York: New York University Press, 1990).

13. The central works of vindicators are also cited below. Additional works not cited include Jean Yarbrough and Richard E. Morgan, "Why the Founding is Back in Fashion," *City Journal,* Autumn 1999, http://www.city-journal.org/html/9_4_urbanities-why_the_foundin.html; Herbert Storing, "Slavery and the Moral Foundations of the American Republic," in *The Moral Foundations of the American Republic,* ed. Robert H. Horwitz (Charlottesville: University of Virginia Press, 1979), 313–332.

14. For a quintessential statement of the historicist sensibility, see Gordon S. Wood, *The Purpose of the Past: Reflections on the Uses of History* (New York: Penguin Press, 2008), 1–18.

15. Peter S. Onuf, *The Mind of Thomas Jefferson* (Charlottesville: University of Virginia Press, 2007), 8.

16. Paul Finkelman, *Slavery and the Founders: Race and Liberty in the Age of Jefferson,* 2nd ed. (Armonk, N.Y.: M. E. Sharpe, 2001). Quote is from page 130. Paul Finkelman, "The Murky Proslavery Origins of the Electoral College," http://jurist.law.pitt.edu/election/electionfink.htm; Paul Finkelman, "Garrison's Constitution: The Covenant with Death and How It Was Made," *Prologue Magazine* 32 (Winter 2000), http://www.archives.gov/publications/prologue/2000/winter/garrisons-constitution-1.html. In addition to Finkelman's neo-Garrisonian interpretation, see also William M. Wiecek, "The Witch at the Christening: Slavery and the Constitution's Origins," in *The Framing and Ratification of the Constitution,* ed. Leonard W. Levy and Dennis J. Mahoney (New York: MacMillan, 1987), 167–184; Akhil Reed Amar, *America's Constitution: A Biography* (New York: Random House, 2005), 20–21, 87–98, 119–120, 156–158, 256–270, 274–275, 291; David Waldstreicher, *Slavery's Constitution: From Revolution to Ratification* (New York: Hill and Wang, 2009).

17. The most sophisticated versions of this argument are found in Don E. Fehrenbacher with Ward M. McAfee, *The Slaveholding Republic: An Account of the United States Government's Relations to Slavery* (New York: Oxford University Press, 2001), 10, 36, 41, 44; Don E. Fehrenbacher, *The Dred Scott Case: Its Significance in American Law and Poli-*

tics (New York: Oxford University Press, 1978), 27; Don E. Fehrenbacher, "Slavery, the Framers, and the Living Constitution," in *Slavery and Its Consequences: The Constitution, Equality, and Race,* ed. Robert A. Goldman and Art Kaufman (Washington, D.C.: American Enterprise Institute, 1988), 5, 10–11; Michael Zuckert, "Legality and Legitimacy in *Dred Scott:* The Crisis of the Incomplete Constitution," *Chicago-Kent Law Review* 82 (2007): 294–295.

18. Finkelman, *Slavery and the Founders,* 6, 34. Quote is from page 6. Slaves were referred to as "other persons," "such persons," and as a "person held to service or labor" in Article I, Section 2; Article I, Section 9; and Article IV, Section 2, respectively, in the United States Constitution.

19. Finkelman points to four provisions in the Constitution that supplemented the five main pro-slavery clauses. These included provisions that (1) prevented either the states or the national government from taxing exports (and thus taxing the products of slave labor); (2) guaranteed federal force for suppressing "insurrections" (especially slave rebellions); (3) provided slave states with greater weight in the election of the president because the number of electors assigned to each state in the Electoral College was based on their number of representatives, which in turn was based on the added weight given by the three-fifths clause; and (4) required three-quarters of the states to ratify amendments to the Constitution and thus effectively gave the slave states a veto power over the amendment process. He also points to four provisions that did not inherently promote slavery but were, according to Finkelman, easily interpreted in this direction: the naturalization clause that allowed Congress to prohibit naturalization of nonwhites, the diversity jurisdiction clause that allowed judges to deny slaves and free blacks access to federal courts, the full faith and credit clause that was interpreted to require free states to recognize laws creating and protecting slavery, and a provision that allowed Congress the power to regulate territories but was interpreted in *Dred Scott v. Sanford* not to allow Congress to forbid slavery in any territory.

20. Finkelman, *Slavery and the Founders,* 7.

21. Ibid., 7.

22. Ibid., 12.

23. Ibid., 13.

24. Ibid., 26.

25. See "Interview with Paul Finkelman," http://www.pbs.org/jefferson/archives/interviews/Finkelman.htm.

26. Finkelman, *Slavery and the Founders,* 32. My emphasis.

27. Finkelman, *Slavery and the Founders,* x.

28. Ibid., 139. Finkelman and other contemporary scholars who criticize Jefferson's positions on race and slavery build on the pioneering studies of William Cohen and Winthrop Jordan and the later and more comprehensive study of Thomas Jefferson and slavery by John Chester Miller. See William Cohen, "Thomas Jefferson and the Problem of Slavery," *Journal of American History* 56 (December 1969): 503–526; Winthrop Jordan, *White over Black: American Attitudes toward the Negro, 1550–1812* (Chapel Hill: University of North Carolina Press, 1968), xii, 321–322, 381, 386, 429–481, 489–490, 546–547, 552, 563–564, 568. John Chester Miller, *The Wolf by the Ears: Thomas Jefferson and Slavery* (Charlottesville: University Press of Virginia, 1991).

29. Finkelman, *Slavery and the Founders*, 137.

30. Ibid., 129.

31. Ibid., 131–132.

32. Ibid., 131.

33. Ibid., 141.

34. Jefferson's wife was Martha Wayles Skelton. Her father was John Wayles. Sally Hemings was, according to Merrill Peterson and most other Jefferson authorities, the offspring of John Wayles and Elizabeth Hemings. Thus, Jefferson was, Finkelman observes, "related through marriage, and probably through blood, to the Hemings family, even if he fathered no children with Sally." Ibid., 169.

35. Ibid., 169.

36. Ibid., 134. Finkelman has made the even more remarkable statement that "in some ways, Thomas Jefferson invented racism in America." Finkelman's only compliments for Jefferson include his felicity with language and his role as a champion of religious freedom and separation of church and state. For these statements, see "Interview with Paul Finkelman," http://www.pbs.org/jefferson/archives/interviews/Finkelman.htm.

37. Finkelman, *Slavery and the Founders*, 135.

38. Ibid., 130, 232, note 4.

39. Ibid., 134, 130.

40. Ibid., 150–151.

41. Conor Cruise O'Brien, *The Long Affair: Thomas Jefferson and the French Revolution, 1785–1800* (Chicago: University of Chicago Press, 1996); O'Brien, "Thomas Jefferson: Radical and Racist," http://www.theatlantic.com/issues/96oct/obrien/obrien.htm.

42. O'Brien, *Long Affair*. Quotes are on 308, 322.

43. Ibid., xii. O'Brien suggests that Jefferson's enthusiasm for the French Revolution only cooled when the revolution inspired the triumphant slave revolt in St. Domingue, not because Jefferson became repulsed by the violence it had unleashed. Before the summer of 1793, according to O'Brien, Jefferson was gripped by a religious-like faith in the French Revolution and viewed it as a polar star of the holy cause of liberty. That faith, according to O'Brien, went unshaken by events until the slave revolt in St. Domingue. Ibid., 148–151.

44. Jefferson to William Smith, November 13, 1787, in *Thomas Jefferson: Writings: Autobiography/Notes on the State of Virginia/Public and Private Papers/Addresses/Letters*, ed. Merrill Peterson (New York: Literary Classics of the United States, 1984), 911.

45. Jefferson to William Short, January 3, 1793, in *Jefferson: Writings*, 1004.

46. O'Brien, *Long Affair*, xii, 309.

47. Ibid., 309.

48. Ibid., xii, 310, 150.

49. Ibid., 315.

50. Ibid., 316.

51. Ibid., 319.

52. Ibid., 315.

53. Ibid., 317.

54. Ibid., 316.

55. Ibid., 317.

56. Ibid., 324, 325.

57. Fehrenbacher, *Slaveholding Republic,* especially 15–47; Fehrenbacher, Dred Scott, 19–27; Fehrenbacher, "Slavery," 1–22.

Michael Zuckert provides a similar—but more qualified, and ultimately more defensible—counter to the Garrisonians than Fehrenbacher based on a foundational distinction between the legality of slavery and its legitimacy in the Constitution and the constitutional order. The Founders, Zuckert emphasizes, established a federal regime that did not give the national government unqualified sovereignty, but rather recognized the internal autonomy of the states. Within this system, slavery was recognized as an institution of the member states and was legal within them. The creation of a federation, as opposed to a political system that reached into the member states, according to Zuckert, made it nearly inevitable that the Constitution would fail to say or do anything about slavery in the states.

The Constitution, however, did extend the legality of slavery to a degree in areas such as the return of fugitive slaves, the slave trade, and the three-fifths clause where slavery impinged on the union. In these areas where "national account" was taken of slavery, Zuckert acknowledges that the Constitution gave some protection and aid to slavery. The Framers, he maintains, "willingly gave such aid and did so without much of a fight." Even more significantly, although several Framers gave impassioned speeches at the Convention expressing the repugnance of slavery, none suggested that the Constitution prohibit slavery or that Congress be empowered to prohibit slavery in the states. Neo-Lincolnians have thus exaggerated the degree to which constitutional provisions came about as a result of duress and the commitment of the Framers to its imminent extinction.

Nevertheless, more broadly, according to Zuckert, the Founders believed that slavery was fundamentally opposed to the theory of political right or legitimacy—set forth in the Declaration of Independence—that was nearly universally recognized as the moral core of the American constitutional order. They were thus careful not to endorse the institution of slavery or accord it legitimacy in the Constitution. This was vividly evident in their unwillingness to use the word *slavery* in the Constitution. Overall, then, the Constitution was incomplete in the sense that the principle of legitimacy on which it was founded was incompletely realized in it. The Constitution was hardly anti-slavery. It did not "declare war on slavery or commit to ending the practice"—which is the direction where the principle of political legitimacy pointed. Still, contrary to "neo-Garrisonian" scholars, the Constitution was not permanently built on the institution of slavery, but rather was compatible with the hope that the institution would pass away. See Zuckert, "Legality and Legitimacy in *Dred Scott,*" 291–299. Quotes from page 299 and 295. Zuckert, "What Really Happened in the *Dred Scott* Case," unpublished paper. For another account similar to that of Fehrenbacher and Zuckert, see Earl Maltz, "The Idea of the Pro-Slavery Constitution," *Journal of the Early Republic* 17 (Spring 1997): 37–59; Earl Maltz, *The Presidency, the Electoral College, and the Three-Fifths Clause* (February 24, 2009), http://ssrn.com/abstract=1348676; Earl Maltz, *Dred Scott and the Politics of Slavery* (Lawrence: University Press of Kansas, 2007).

58. Fehrenbacher, *Slaveholding Republic,* 28.

59. Fehrenbacher, "Slavery," 16.

60. Fehrenbacher, *Slaveholding Republic*, 10, 36.

61. Fehrenbacher, "Slavery," 16; Fehrenbacher, *Slaveholding Republic*, 10, 41.

62. Fehrenbacher, *Dred Scott*, 27.

63. Fehrenbacher, *Slaveholding Republic*, 36.

64. Ibid., 40. Akhil Reed Amar has recently responded to this point by arguing that "as a matter of basic political theory circa 1787, one perspective surely *was* instrinsically sounder." The difference between representing women, children, and slaves is that women and children could plausibly be said to be virtually represented in 1787 by the men who were elected. It is hard to see how representatives could be said to virtually represent the interests of slaves in 1789. So the real reason for counting three-fifths of the slaves for purposes of representation must be that they were recognized as property in Article I. Amar writes: "The candid 1787 argument for counting slaves was not that masters sincerely represented them but that masters, rightly or wrongly, owned them. They were property, and property, many openly argued deserved representation alongside population. On this account, however, the interests to be represented were not the slaves, but the masters." Thus, according to Amar, the three-fifths clause "was neither neutral nor democratic. As antislavery men repeated time and again at Philadelphia and throughout the ratification debates, Article I treated slavery as *preferred* property. Animal chattel didn't count, securities didn't count, specie didn't count—only slave property could count." Amar, *America's Constitution*, 92–93. At the Constitutional Convention during discussions of the three-fifths clause, Gouverneur Morris made this same point when he admonished his colleagues: "Upon what principle is it that the slaves shall be computed in the representation? Are they men? Then make them citizens and let them vote. Are they property? Why then is no other property included?" Gouverneur Morris, speech of August 8, in *Notes of Debates in the Federal Convention of 1787 Reported by James Madison*, ed. Adrienne Koch (New York: W. W. Norton, 1987), 411.

65. Fehrenbacher, *Slaveholding Republic*, 43, 42.

66. Ibid., 43.

67. Ibid., 42.

68. Ibid., 43.

69. Ibid. My emphasis.

70. Ibid., 42.

71. Ibid., 35–36, 44, 207–209, for Fehrenbacher's discussion of the creation and original understanding of the fugitive slave clause. Quote is from 44.

72. Ibid., 36.

73. Ibid., 44.

74. Fehrenbacher, *Slaveholding Republic*, 207–208.

75. Fehrenbacher, *Slaveholding Republic*, 44, 207–209. Quotes are on 208, 209; Fehrenbacher, *Dred Scott*, 25; see also Fehrenbacher, "Slavery," 12, where Fehrenbacher calls the fugitive slave clause a "declaratory limitation on state authority."

76. Fehrenbacher, *Dred Scott*, 27.

77. Ibid., 29.

78. Ibid., 27.

79. Thomas G. West, *Vindicating the Founders: Race, Sex, Class, and Justice in the Origins of America* (Lanham, Md.: Rowman & Littlefield, 1997).

80. Ibid., 7.

81. Ibid., 8.

82. Ibid., 10.

83. Ibid., 6.

84. Ibid., 14.

85. Ibid., 20.

86. Ibid.

87. Ibid.

88. Ibid.

89. Ibid., 27, 28. West's emphasis.

90. Ibid., 30. My emphasis. West surely does not mean to say that emancipation would not have been a "real" victory for liberty as compared to union and the Constitution. He seems to mean that the victories of liberty in the Constitution and the creation of the union were already *realized* but were tenuous and that they would have been risked with abolition.

91. Ibid., 29–30.

92. Ibid., 15.

93. Ibid., 14.

94. Ibid., 16.

95. Ibid., 17.

96. Ibid.

97. I have included Malone's biography in this section rather than in the section on historicists, even though Malone was a historian's historian and accepted much of the sensibility and ethic of the historicists, because his biography is essentially an apologia for Jefferson. See *Thomas Jefferson and His Time*, 6 vols. (Boston: Little, Brown, 1948–1981), vol. 1, *Jefferson the Virginian*, 121–122, 141, 187, 228, 264–269, 414–416; vol. 2, *Jefferson and the Rights of Man*, 95–96; vol. 3, *Jefferson and the Ordeal of Liberty*, 207–212; vol. 4, *Jefferson the President: First Term, 1801–1805*, 58, 360; vol. 5, *Jefferson the President: Second Term, 1805–1809*, 541–547; and vol. 6, *The Sage of Monticello*, 316–327. Hereafter each volume in this biography is cited as *Jefferson and His Time* with volume number used to indicate the specific title.

Malone's anti-slavery Jefferson draws on and contributes to an interpretive tradition with its own rich and complex history. Several early abolitionists evoked Jefferson's name. These men emphasized the anti-slavery implications of the Declaration of Independence, pointed to Jefferson's public record as a proponent of emancipation, and repeated his stirring statements from *Notes on the State of Virginia* about the divine wrath that awaited Americans because of slavery and the corrupting effects of slavery on both master and slave. Many abolitionists, however, also acknowledged the limitations of Jefferson's opposition to slavery, which, they concluded, was more theoretical than practical. Jefferson, they observed, advocated the delusion of colonization, helped to establish "slave power," and fostered the myth of Negro inferiority. The most famous proponent of the anti-slavery interpretation of Jefferson—Abraham Lincoln—was unambiguous in his praise of the Virginian and the Declaration of Independence, which he saw as the embodiment of the moral propositions animating American democracy: liberty and political equality. See Merrill Peterson, *The Jefferson Image in the American Mind* (New York: Oxford University Press, 1960), especially 46–51, 162–189, 220–222. For Lincoln's use of

Jefferson, see Harry Jaffa, *The Crisis of the House Divided: An Interpretation of the Issues in the Lincoln–Douglas Debates* (1959; reprint, Chicago: University of Chicago Press, 1982), especially 308–329; Harry Jaffa, *A New Birth of Freedom: Abraham Lincoln and the Coming of the Civil War* (Lanham, Md.: Rowman & Littlefield, 2000).

98. Gordon Wood, "The Disappointments of Jefferson," *New York Review of Books,* August 13, 1981, http://www.nybooks.com/articles/6931.

99. Malone, *Jefferson and His Time,* 6:323.

100. Malone, *Jefferson and His Time,* 1:414. See also William G. Merkel, "Jefferson's Failed Anti-Slavery Proviso of 1784 and the Nascence of Free Soil Constitutionalism," http://works.bepress.com/cgi/viewcontent.cgi?article=1000&context=william_merkel (accessed May 24, 2010).

101. Ibid., 6:317.

102. Ibid., 1:266.

103. Ibid., 3:209, 207.

104. Ibid., 3:207.

105. Ibid., 6:324.

106. Ibid., 3:208.

107. Ibid., 1:266.

108. Ibid., 1:267.

109. Ibid., 5:542; 6:323.

110. Ibid., 5:543.

111. Ibid., 5:542.

112. Ibid., 6:319.

113. Historicists defend a "deeply contextualist approach to history—an immersion in the detailed circumstance of a distant era and an effort to understand the world not as it anticipated the future but as it was experienced by those who lived it." Bernard Bailyn, *The Ideological Origins of the American Revolution,* enlarged edition (1967; reprint, Cambridge, Mass.: Belknap Press of Harvard University Press, 1992), 323.

114. See in particular Bernard Bailyn, "The Central Themes of the American Revolution: An Interpretation," in *Essays on the American Revolution,* ed. Stephen G. Kurtz and James H. Hutson (Chapel Hill: University of North Carolina Press, 1973), 28–31; Gordon Wood, "Reading the Founders' Minds," *New York Review of Books* 54 (June 28, 2007), http://www.nybooks.com/articles/20342; Wood, "Equality and Social Conflict in the American Revolution," *William and Mary Quarterly* 51 (October 1991): 703–716, especially 705–707; Wood, *The Radicalism of the American Revolution* (New York: Alfred A. Knopf, 1992).

115. Quote is from Wood, "Reading the Founders' Minds."

116. Wood, "Equality and Social Conflict," 707.

117. Bailyn, "Central Themes," 222.

118. Ibid., 223.

119. Wood, *Radicalism,* 7.

120. Wood, *Purpose of the Past,* 11.

121. E-mail from Gordon Wood, February 12, 2010.

122. Douglas Wilson, "Thomas Jefferson and the Character Issue," *Atlantic Monthly* 270 (November 1992): 57–74.

123. Ibid., 62.

124. Ibid., 66.

125. Ibid., 69.

126. Ibid., 74.

127. See Eric Foner, "Looking Again at Slavery's Sins," *New York Times*, August 25, 2001, http://www.nytimes.com/2001/08/25/opinion/l-looking-again-at-slavery-s-sins-869503.html.

128. Henry Wiencek, *An Imperfect God: George Washington, His Slaves, and the Creation of America* (New York: Farrar, Straus, and Giroux, 2003).

129. Ibid., 111, 125–126, 131–133.

130. Ibid., 123–125, 349–350. Quote on page 123.

131. Ibid., 178–182.

132. Ibid., 185, 188.

133. Ibid., 191, 220.

134. Ibid., 190–191, 204–205.

135. Ibid., 205–214, 218–220, 259–264.

136. Ibid., especially 4–6, 353–357.

137. E-mail from Henry Wiencek, January 21, 2010.

138. Wiencek, *Imperfect God*, 135.

139. Ibid., 174.

140. E-mail from Henry Wiencek, January 21, 2010.

141. Wiencek, "Yale and the Price of Slavery," *New York Times*, August 18, 2001, http://www.nytimes.com/2001/08/18/opinion/yale-and-the-price-of-slavery.html.

142. Onuf, *Mind of Thomas Jefferson*, 4 for quote. For Onuf's approach to questions of moral responsibility, particularly on questions of race and slavery, see Peter Onuf, *Jefferson's Empire: The Language of American Nationhood* (Charlottesville: University of Virginia Press, 2000), especially 147–188; Onuf, *Mind of Thomas Jefferson*, especially 205–270; Peter Onuf, "Thomas Jefferson and American Democracy" in *Seeing Jefferson Anew: In His Time and Ours*, eds. John B. Boles and Randal L. Hall (Charlottesville: University Press of Virginia, forthcoming); Peter Onuf, review of *Jefferson and the Indians: The Tragic Fate of the First Americans*, by Anthony F. C. Wallace, H-Law, H-Net Reviews, May 2000, http://www.h-net.org/reviews/showrev.cgi?path=24409959285535.

143. Onuf, *Mind of Thomas Jefferson*, 4.

144. Ibid., 5.

145. Ibid., 12.

146. Onuf, *Jefferson's Empire*, 4.

147. Onuf, *Mind of Thomas Jefferson*, 2.

148. Ibid., 14.

149. Ibid., 3.

150. Merrill D. Peterson, *Thomas Jefferson and the New Nation: A Biography* (New York: Oxford University Press, 1970), viii; Joseph J. Ellis, *American Sphinx: The Character of Thomas Jefferson* (New York: Alfred A. Knopf, 1997), xvii.

151. Onuf, *Mind of Thomas Jefferson*, 3.

152. Ibid., 23.

153. Ibid., 8.

154. Ibid., 7.

155. Ibid., 34.

156. Ibid., 7.

157. Ibid., 249.

158. Ibid., 210, 217, 220.

159. Ibid., 220, 218. "Boisterous passions" is from Query XVIII, *Notes on the State of Virginia* in *Thomas Jefferson: Writings*, 288.

160. Onuf, *Mind of Thomas Jefferson*, 250.

161. Ibid., 250.

162. Ibid., 214, 208.

163. Ibid., 237.

164. Ibid., 250.

165. Fehrenbacher, *Slaveholding Republic*, 46.

166. Fehrenbacher, "Slavery," 1–22.

167. Vindicators nevertheless often still charge prosecutors with "presentism" and suggest that they inappropriately judge the Founders on the basis of contemporary standards of race and gender. This charge is true, however, only of a few prosecutors, including John Hope Franklin, Thurgood Marshall, and Conor Cruise O'Brien.

168. Fehrenbacher, "Slavery," 5. See also Fehrenbacher, *Slaveholding Republic*, 39.

169. "Interview with Paul Finkelman," http://www.pbs.org/jefferson/archives/interviews/Finkelman.htm.

170. Gary Nash has recently provided a particularly forceful statement of this argument. The opportunity to abolish slavery during the Founding, Nash argues, arose from the widespread recognition in the early republic that slavery was fundamentally unjust, the need of the lower South for union, the widespread belief that blacks were degraded not because of natural inferiority but because of subjection, the ability of the Founders to use the land of the trans-Appalachian West as a fund for compensating slaveholders, and the fact that, as the French example of the emancipation of half a million slaves in 1794 illustrated, the Western world was "trembling with the prospect of reversing the sordid, three-century history of European-sponsored Atlantic slavery." To be sure, Nash has conceded, the abolition of slavery in the United States during the earliest days of the republic faced huge obstacles, including the fragility of the nation, the threat of secession by Georgia and South Carolina, and "the reluctance of northern states to be a part of a national remedy for a national problem." Still, slavery was left intact in the United States, according to Nash, not because it could not have been eradicated, but because the nation's most important leaders—including Washington and Jefferson—failed to exercise moral and political leadership.

Nash concludes "If Washington had carried through with his pledge in 1783 to join Lafayette in 'the grand experiment,' if Jefferson, Madison, and a few other luminous Virginians who professed to hate slavery had stepped forward to support the Methodists' appeal to the Virginia legislature in 1785 for a gradual emancipation plan, if Northern leaders such as John Adams and Benjamin Franklin had drawn on their vast respect to support such a plan, the course of history might have been changed at that moment.

Eighty years later, more than 600,000 American lives were lost accomplishing the goal of emancipation, roughly one for each of the slaves in the new United States as of 1785." Nash, *Unknown American Revolution*, 429–435. Quotes are from 431, 435.

171. Similar criticisms can be made of O'Brien's interpretation of Jefferson. Although he accuses Jefferson's defenders of partial use of quotes and acontextual interpretations, O'Brien, as Douglas Wilson has judiciously shown, commits these same errors. Neither Jefferson's "Tree of Liberty" letter nor his "Adam and Eve" letter say quite what O'Brien says they do. Far from being approving of anarchy or revolutionary violence, or setting forth a doctrine that justified any act in which the participants sincerely believed that they were furthering liberty as they understood it, Jefferson's tree of liberty letter defends protest and is extremely guarded. Jefferson defends Shays's rebels because he believed that they acted out of ignorance, not wickedness; because their grievances were real and their conduct honorable; and because protest is necessary to prevent the death of public liberty. See Wilson, "Counter Points: Jefferson scholar Douglas L. Wilson Responds to Conor Cruise O'Brien," *Atlantic Online*, October 1996, http://www.theatlantic.com/past/docs/issues/96oct/obrien/response.htm.

172. Finkelman, *Slavery and the Founders*, ix, x.

173. Ibid., 138.

174. Thomas Jefferson to Henri Gregoire, February 25, 1809, in *Jefferson: Writings*, 1202.

175. The conclusions of the scientific findings of DNA investigations are stated succinctly in an introductory essay provided on the Web site Monticello.org: "The results of the study established that an individual carrying the male Jefferson Y chromosome fathered Eston Hemings (born 1808), the last known child born to Sally Hemings. There were approximately 25 adult male Jeffersons who carried this chromosome living in Virginia at that time, and a few of them are known to have visited Monticello. The study's authors, however, said 'the simplest and most probable' conclusion was that Thomas Jefferson had fathered Eston Hemings." See "Thomas Jefferson and Sally Hemings: A Brief Account," http://www.monticello.org/plantation/hemingscontro/hemings-jefferson_contro.html.

176. See Alan Gibson, *Interpreting the Founding: Guide to the Enduring Debates over the Origins and Foundations of the American Republic* (Lawrence: University Press of Kansas, 2006), 83–85.

177. Finkelman, *Slavery and the Founders*, 138.

178. Ibid., 139.

179. Ibid., 137. For Jefferson's account of this incident, see Jefferson to Edward Coles, August 25, 1814, in *Jefferson: Writings*, 1344, and "Autobiography" in *Jefferson: Writings*, 5.

180. Finkelman, *Slavery and the Founders*, 138.

181. Ibid., 151.

182. E-mail from Nic Wood to Alan Gibson, November 1, 2008.

183. Jefferson consistently acknowledged the humanitarian aspect of banning the slave trade. In 1787, he congratulated Edward Rutledge for his role in the passage of a state law banning (temporarily it turns out) the slave trade in South Carolina: "I congratulate you, my dear friend, on the law of your State, for suspending the importation of slaves, and for the glory you have justly acquired by endeavoring to prevent it forever. This abomination must have an end. And there is a superior bench reserved in heaven

for those who hasten it." Jefferson to Edward Rutledge, July 14, 1787, in *The Works of Thomas Jefferson*, 12 vols., ed. Paul Leicester Ford (New York: G. P. Putnam's Sons, 1904–1905), 5:305.

184. The bill provided enormously high fines of up to $20,000 and prison terms of up to ten years for individuals caught participating in the slave trade or building ships for that purpose. It allowed for enforcement of this act by the United States navy and rewarded citizens and the crews of naval ships that seized illegal traders with money raised from the sale of confiscated vessels. Unfortunately, it also stipulated that illegally imported Africans be sold as slaves rather than be freed by the government. See "The Act of 1807" in "The Abolition of the Slave Trade," Schomburg Center for Research in Black Culture, http://abolition.nypl.org/essays/us_constitution/5.

185. William Freehling, "The Founding Fathers, Conditional Anti-Slavery, and the Nonradicalism of the American Revolution," in *The Reintegration of American History: Slavery and the Civil War* (New York: Oxford University Press, 1994), 27–28.

186. Ibid., 27.

187. On the influence of the Declaration of Independence in the world, see David Armitage, *The Declaration of Independence: A Global History* (Cambridge, Mass.: Harvard University Press, 2007), especially 103–138.

188. Jefferson was of course appropriated by both pro-slavery forces and abolitionists, most of whom understood the limitations of appeals to his ideas and actions. See Peterson, *Jefferson Image*, especially 46–51, 162–189.

189. Sean Wilentz, "The Details of Greatness: American Historians versus American Founders," *New Republic*, March 29, 2004, 27–35. Quote on page 31.

190. Ibid., 31.

191. Ibid.

192. Even this claim, however, is not true if by "Founders" we mean any of the Revolutionary leaders. South Carolina and Georgia Revolutionary leaders invoked many of the arguments later used to defend slavery as a positive good, including biblical and paternal arguments. See Joseph C. Burke, "The Pro-Slavery Argument in the First Congress," *Duquesne Review* 16 (1969): 3–15.

193. Rogers Smith, *Civic Ideals: Conflicting Visions of Citizenship in U.S. History* (New Haven, Conn.: Yale University Press, 1997), 105. See also Jordan, *White over Black*, 429. See also xii, 441–444.

194. West, *Vindicating the Founders*, 8.

195. In addition to his statements in *Notes on the State of Virginia* about his "great diffidence" in concluding that blacks were naturally inferior and his refusal to hazard this conclusion as more than a "suspicion," see Jefferson's correspondence with Benjamin Banneker and Henri Grégoire (a French Roman Catholic priest and advocate of racial equality). In 1791, Banneker, the African American mathematician, astronomer, and clockmaker, provided Jefferson with an almanac that Banneker had written as evidence of the intelligence of blacks. Jefferson wrote back, "No body wishes more than I do, to see such proofs as you exhibit, that nature has given to our black brethren talents equal to those of the other colors of men; and that the appearance of the want of them, is owing merely to the degraded condition of their existence, both in Africa and America. I can add with truth, that no body wishes more ardently to see a good system commenced, for raising

the condition, both of their body and mind, to what it ought to be, as far as the imbecility of their present existence, and other circumstances, which cannot be neglected, will admit." See Jefferson to Benjamin Banneker, August 30, 1791, in *Thomas Jefferson: Writings*, 982; see also Jefferson to Henri Grégoire, February 25, 1809, ibid., 1202.

196. Compare West's account with other scholars who conclude that Jefferson believed in the innate or natural inferiority of blacks or point to the inconsistency of Jefferson's position. See Jordan, *Black over White*, 429–445; Onuf, *Mind of Thomas Jefferson*, 206–208, 211, 217, 219; Onuf, *Jefferson's Empire*, 167–169, 181; Miller, *Wolf by the Ears*, 46–59; Jean Yarbrough, "Race and the Moral Foundation of the American Republic: Another Look at the Declaration and the Notes on Virginia," *Journal of Politics* 53 (February 1991): 90–105. Yarbrough—no proponent of the political views of the leftist cultural elite— observes that Jefferson never ruled out the possibility that blacks were "a separate and inferior species" (99).

197. These quotes are drawn from Jefferson's comparisons between blacks and whites in Query 14 from *Notes on the State of Virginia* in *Jefferson: Writings*, 264–270. Quotes on 270, 264, 267, 268. Jefferson's opinion that blacks were naturally inferior to whites does not seem to have changed during his lifetime. In his autobiography, he wrote: "Nothing is more certainly written in the book of fate than that these people [blacks] are to be free. Nor is it less certain that the two races, equally free, cannot live in the same government. *Nature*, habit, opinion has drawn indelible lines of distinction between them." Thomas Jefferson, "Autobiography," in *Jefferson: Writings*, 44. And in 1807, Jefferson apparently told Augustus John Foster, a British diplomat in the United States, that blacks were "as inferior to the rest of mankind as the mule is to the horse, and as made to carry burthens." As an oral account recorded by a British diplomat, this quote is more suspect than Jefferson's writings, but it is consistent with Jefferson's other statements and revealing in its suggestion that Jefferson believed that, like mules and horses, blacks and whites were a different species. Miller, *Wolf by the Ears*, 57.

198. Query 14, *Notes on the State of Virginia*, in *Jefferson: Writings*, 264–270.

199. Ibid.

200. The most comprehensive study of white prejudices toward blacks is Jordan, *White over Black*.

201. These qualifications and corrections of West's case are drawn primarily from William W. Freehling's important article, "The Founding Fathers, Conditional Anti-Slavery, and the Nonradicalism of the American Revolution," 12–33. This essay resulted from Freehling's "regret" for his "overemphasis on anti-slavery accomplishment" in his earlier and more frequently cited essay, "The Founding Fathers and Slavery," *American Historical Review* 77 (February 1972): 81–93. Freehling's second article, which establishes his interpretation of the "conditional" anti-slavery character of the American Founding, is one of the most judicious and balanced overviews of the Founders' accomplishments and failures regarding slavery in print and represents an essential starting place for those considering this question.

202. West, *Vindicating the Founders*, 10. My emphasis.

203. Peter Kolchin, *American Slavery, 1619–1877* (New York: Hill and Wang, 1993, 2003), 79. See also Freehling, "Conditional Anti-Slavery," 27.

204. West, *Vindicating the Founders*, 11.

205. Freehling, "Conditional Anti-Slavery," 16–18.

206. In addition to the problems indicated above, a more general confusion permeates West's treatment of this issue. Containment was not synonymous with opposition to slavery in the Founding era, especially beginning in the early nineteenth century. By the 1820s, many anti-slavery leaders (including Jefferson and many Virginians) abandoned the idea of containing slavery in favor of "diffusion." These anti-slavery leaders concluded that whites would never free blacks in areas where blacks were heavily concentrated. Thus, it made sense to diffuse them across greater territory. Ibid., 23–24.

207. West, *Vindicating the Founders*, 14, 12 for quotes.

208. Freehling, "Conditional Anti-Slavery," 22–23; for Finkelman's strikingly different account of the motives behind the Northwest Ordinance and its effects, including a discussion of the persistence of slavery in Indiana and Illinois, see Finkelman, *Slavery and the Founders*, 37–80.

209. Quoted in Freehling, "Conditional Anti-Slavery," 21.

210. Ibid., 30; West, *Vindicating the Founders*, 14 for the quote.

211. West, *Vindicating the Founders*, 11–14. Quotes are from page 14.

212. Ibid., 11.

213. Freehling, "Conditional Anti-Slavery," 19–20.

214. West, *Vindicating the Founders*, 6. The Southern historian William Cooper writes: "From 1776 to 1860 the white southern celebration of liberty always included the freedom to preserve black slavery." William Cooper, *Liberty and Slavery: Southern Politics to 1860* (1983; reprint, Columbia: University of South Carolina Press, 2000), 28–39. Quote is on 39. See also Michael Zuckerman, "Thermidor in America: The Aftermath of Independence in the South," *Prospectus* 8 (1983): 349–368.

215. More generally, American leadership was guarded about the presence of blacks in either the Continental forces or militias. Initially, blacks were banned altogether from service in the Continental army. In October 1775, a council of war composed of Washington and seven of his generals made a decision to reject the services of both free blacks and slaves, and in November 1775, Washington issued a general order to this effect. This policy, however, does not seem to have been strictly enforced (blacks served in both militias and the Continental forces) and it was reversed in stages. In December 1775, Washington issued an order authorizing the enlistment of free blacks. In January 1778, he then supported a Rhode Island plan for emancipation to raise a black regiment. Passage of this plan resulted in the formation of the famous Rhode Island Regiment. Washington deployed these troops in an important maneuver at Yorktown. See Wiencek, *Imperfect God*, 200–205, 218.

216. See Betty Wood, "Betty Wood on Controlling Slaves after Dunmore's Proclamation," *Africans in America*, http://www.pbs.org/wgbh/aia/part2/2i1619.html.

217. West evokes an emancipation plan for South Carolina blacks to become patriot soldiers as evidence of the anti-slavery impulse of the American Revolution. West, *Vindicating the Founders*, 12. He seems to be referring here to John and Henry Lauren's combined efforts to get an emancipation plan passed to recruit black soldiers in South Carolina that Hamilton enthusiastically supported, helped design, and lobbied for, and that George Washington initially endorsed but then backed away from. At John Lauren's prompting, this plan eventually gained the endorsement of the Continental Congress,

which in March 1779 sent out a resolution encouraging Georgia and South Carolina to pursue such a scheme. The plan, however, was voted down in South Carolina in May 1779. What West does not tell his readers is that many Southern slaveholders were horrified at the prospect of arming their slaves, and that such proposals gained support only during desperate times of low troop levels or British occupation. American leaders, including Washington, worried that such schemes would create discontent among blacks who remained slaves. See Wiencek, *Imperfect God*, 220–236.

218. Cooper, *Liberty and Slavery*, 37, 35.

219. Richard S. Dunn, "Black Society in the Chesapeake," in *Slavery and Freedom in the Age of the American Revolution*, ed. Ira Berlin and Ronald Hoffman (Urbana: Published for the United States Capitol Historical Society by the University of Illinois Press, 1983), 52.

220. Fehrenbacher, *Slaveholding Republic*, 25.

221. West, *Vindicating the Founders*, 20–21.

222. Ibid., 21.

223. See Jefferson to Edward Coles, August 25, 1814, in *Jefferson: Writings*, 1343–1346. The issue of private manumission points to another problem in West's account. West accepts the Founders' fears that a race war and disunion would result from emancipation. He also contends that the conclusions reached by several Founders and some contemporary blacks that slaves were not yet ready for self-government were based on observations and experience and thus were sound or at least should not be second-guessed. Nevertheless, he celebrates private manumissions as one of the Founders' accomplishments and suggests that most scholars do not appreciate how extensive they were. The obvious unaddressed problem here is that West does not explain how private manumissions were any less threatening or imprudent than immediate administrative manumission. Didn't private manumissions also pose the same risks of racial violence and the destruction of free institutions, especially if a large number of slaveholders released their slaves? This consideration is why Jefferson always coupled emancipation with expatriation of slaves and considered private manumissions a dangerous indulgence.

224. For Madison's support of colonization, see Drew McCoy, *The Last of the Fathers: James Madison and the Republican Legacy* (New York: Cambridge University Press, 1989), 5–6, 252, 265–266, 276–286, 295–298, 301–303, 306–308; for Adams, see John R. Howe, "John Adam's Views of Slavery," *Journal of Negro History* 49 (July 1964): 204–205.

225. In 1790, three weeks before his death, Franklin wrote a "hoax" against slavery meant to ridicule the arguments used to challenge the immediate abolition of slave trade and the manumission of slaves. In this hoax, Franklin assumed the persona of a fictitious Muslim statesman, Sidi Mehemet Ibrahim, answering a petition to halt the practice of enslaving Christians. As Edmund Morgan observes, with this response, Franklin "turned the tables on every argument offered then or later against the immediate abolition of slavery." See Edmund Morgan, *Benjamin Franklin* (New Haven, Conn.: Yale University Press, 2002), 38–39. The text of Franklin's letter can be found at http://www.jmu.edu/madison/center/main_pages/madison_archives/era/african/elite/trade.htm.

226. The height of West's willingness to defend any proposal set forth by the Founders comes in his defense of colonization of slaves. To consider colonization just means that we defend the forcible expulsion of a million slaves who had been forcibly brought to the United States in the first place and who had created much of the wealth

and prosperity of the young nation. As Freehling notes, "To coerce a million enslaved humans to leave a republic as a condition for ending coercive slavery could also seem to be a dubious step toward government by consent." Colonization would also have been a logistical nightmare. Again, it would have involved the forcible exile of a million slaves. Most plans for colonization—including Jefferson's—contained provisions for the payment of slaveowners for their slaves. It thus would have been profoundly expensive. It would have involved splitting up many families and sending them to some other nation. By colonizing only willing slaves, the American colonization society rarely resettled more than a thousand blacks a year, and only resettled ten thousand in its forty-five-year history. Freehling, "Conditional Anti-Slavery," 15, 25.

227. Freehling, "Conditional Anti-Slavery," 16.

228. Foner, "Looking Again at Slavery's Sins."

229. Wood, "Reading the Founders' Minds."

230. Foner, "Looking Again at Slavery's Sins"; Nash, *Unknown American Revolution;* Wiencek, *Imperfect God,* 135, 174.

231. Richard Hofstadter, *The Progressive Historians: Turner, Beard, and Parrington* (New York: Alfred A. Knopf, 1968), 248.

232. Quote is from Wilson, "Thomas Jefferson and the Character Issue," 62.

233. Wood, "Reading the Founders' Minds."

234. For an introduction to the question of the conditions of blameworthiness and moral responsibility, see Joel Feinberg, *Doing and Deserving: Essays in the Theory of Responsibility* (Princeton: Princeton University Press, 1970); H. L. A. Hart, *Punishment and Responsibility: Essays in the Philosophy of Law* (New York: Oxford University Press, 1968); David H. Jones, *Moral Responsibility in the Holocaust: A Study in the Ethics of Character* (Lanham, Md.: Rowman & Littlefield, 1999), 1–96; J. R. Lucas, *Responsibility* (New York: Oxford University Press, 1993); Gabriel Moran, *A Grammar of Responsibility* (New York: Crossroad, 1996); Eugene Schlossberger, *Moral Responsibility and Persons* (Philadelphia: Temple University Press, 1992); Winston Davis, ed., *Taking Responsibility: Comparative Perspectives* (Charlottesville: University Press of Virginia, 2001); Michael J. Zimmerman, *An Essay on Moral Responsibility* (Totowa, N.J.: Rowman & Littlefield, 1988); Michael J. Zimmerman, "Responsibility," in *Encyclopedia of Ethics,* 3 vols., ed. Lawrence C. Becker III (New York: Routledge, 2001) 3:1486–1492.

235. Fehrenbacher, "Slavery," 9–11, 16.

236. The only scholar that I can find who argues that the Founders had to choose between the preservation of the union and a firmer stand against slavery, but then concludes that the Founders were morally culpable for choosing union is Henry Wiencek. Wiencek writes: "If the founders had such misgivings over slavery, how is it that they allowed slavery to continue? The answer is not that they didn't know any better, but that they kept slavery so the Southern states would join the union. It was a transaction, a deal, just like the deal that put the national capital on the Potomac in exchange for the federal assumption of states' debts. . . . With their eyes open, the founders traded away the rights of African-Americans, many of whom had fought bravely in the Revolution, so that the national enterprise could go forward. . . . This country was founded upon a bargain for which we continue to pay the price. We compound the mistake by draping a veil of innocence over the transaction." Wiencek, "Yale and the Price of Slavery."

237. Allan Megill, *Historical Knowledge, Historical Error: A Contemporary Guide to Practice* (Chicago: University of Chicago Press, 2007), 151–156. See also Niall Ferguson, ed., *Virtual History: Alternatives and Counterfactuals* (New York: Perseus Books, 1997); Andrew Roberts, ed., *What Might Have Been: Leading Historians on Twelve "What Ifs" of History* (London: Weidenfeld & Nicolson, 2004).

238. Garry Wills, *"Negro President": Jefferson and the Slave Power* (Boston: Houghton Mifflin, 2003), xiv.

239. Present controversies may provide constructive heuristics for these questions—with of course reservations about the uniqueness of slavery. Such present controversies as steroid use in sports in the "age of steroids," the proper stance of incumbents toward the existing system of campaign finance, the willingness of lawyers to zealously defend guilty clients and guard their secrets within an adversarial system, and even the ethics of eating meat in a context in which animals are fattened and slaughtered in horrific conditions raise many of the same issues as moral culpability within a slave system. In each of these examples, moral responsibility is considered within the context of a broader system that historical actors often find reprehensible and would not themselves re-create, but that contains incentives to act in ways that reinforce the system and inhibit efforts to reform it.

240. Wiencek, *Imperfect God,* 115.

Chapter 6. Taking Historiography Seriously

1. Thus admonitions such as Gordon Wood's recent ones against scholars for misusing historical concepts such as republicanism are unlikely to be heeded. See Gordon Wood, "Preface to the 1998 Edition," in *The Creation of the American Republic, 1776–1787* (1969; reprint, Chapel Hill: University of North Carolina Press, 1998), v–xiii.

2. Jean Bethke Elshtain, "In Common Together: Unity, Diversity, and Civic Virtue," in *The Constitution of the People: Reflections on Citizens and Civil Society,* ed. Robert E. Calvert (Lawrence: University Press of Kansas, 1991), 65.

3. In addition to the specific citations, the discussion below is based on an exchange between Michael Zuckert and Rogers Smith at California State University, Chico, on April 9, 2003, entitled "Living Up to the Declaration of Independence: Liberalism and the American Experience," as well as discussions and e-mails between the author and Zuckert and Smith.

4. Michael Zuckert, "Living Up to the Declaration of Independence: Multiple Versions of the Multiple Traditions Thesis," paper presented at California State University, Chico, April 9, 2003, 7–8. See also Zuckert, *Launching Liberalism: On Lockean Political Philosophy* (Lawrence: University Press of Kansas, 2003), 274–293, for Zuckert's discussion of the way in which the American Revolutionaries fused British constitutionalism and natural rights liberalism into an American amalgam.

5. Zuckert, *The Natural Rights Republic: Studies in the Foundation of the American Political Tradition* (Notre Dame, Ind.: University of Notre Dame Press, 1996), 240.

6. Ibid., 118–201.

7. Ibid., 7–8.

8. Rogers Smith, *Civic Ideals: Conflicting Visions of Citizenship in U.S. History* (New Haven, Conn.: Yale University Press, 1997), 16.

9. On how Smith's commitment to liberalism informs his interpretation, see Barry Shain, "Multiple Citizenships," review of *Civic Ideals: Conflicting Visions of Citizenship in U.S. History,* by Rogers Smith, *Review of Politics* 61 (Spring 1999): 350–354.

10. Zuckert, *Natural Rights Republic,* 2, 241.

11. Smith makes a distinction between implicit and explicit traditions on the basis of whether the "ism" being analyzed is a heuristic construct created by scholars to aid the analysis of a problem or a set of ideas that existed as social phenomena and were espoused explicitly by the historical actors. This distinction, Smith further suggests, is "best conceived as two ends of a spectrum rather than as wholly distinct entities." Thus, any given tradition is to be found along a continuum between implicit and explicit. Interestingly enough, Smith considers racism an explicit tradition but liberalism more along the lines of an implicit tradition, because few Americans before the twentieth century identified themselves as liberals or meant anything by it like what scholars mean today. Rogers Smith, "Liberalism and Racism: The Problem of Analyzing Traditions," in *The Liberal Tradition in American Politics: Reassessing the Legacy of American Liberalism,* ed. David Ericson and Louisa Bertch Green (New York: Routledge, 1999), 11–14.

12. Thomas Jefferson, *Notes on the State of Virginia,* ed. Thomas P. Abernethy (New York: Harper and Row, 1964), 132–139. Smith calls Jefferson's description of African Americans a "cornerstone statement of American scientific racism." Smith, *Civic Ideals,* 105; James Wilson, *The Works of James Wilson,* ed. Robert G. McCloskey (Cambridge, Mass.: Belknap Press of Harvard University Press, 1967), 85–88. Smith, *Civic Ideals,* 105.

13. Smith, *Civic Ideals,* 75.

14. Ibid., 59.

15. Zuckert, "Multiple Versions," 6.

16. See Louis Hartz, *The Liberal Tradition in America: An Interpretation of American Political Thought since the Revolution* (San Diego: Harcourt Jovanovich, 1955); Seymour Martin Lipset, *The First New Nation: The United States in Historical and Comparative Perspective* (New York: Basic Books, 1963); Seymour Martin Lipset, *American Exceptionalism: A Double-Edged Sword* (New York: W. W. Norton, 1996); Deborah L. Madsen, *American Exceptionalism* (Jackson: University Press of Mississippi, 1998).

17. See Paul Carrese, "The Complexity, and Principles, of the American Founding: A Response to Alan Gibson," *History of Political Thought* 21 (Winter 2000): 711–717.

18. James W. Ceaser, *Nature and History in American Political Development: A Debate* (Cambridge, Mass.: Harvard University Press, 2006), 11–12. In addition to Ceaser's book, this summary and analysis of his approach has been aided by a taped public presentation available on the Web. See James Ceaser, "Foundational Ideas in American Political Thought," audio recording of a presentation given on October 13, 2006, Ashbrook Center for Public Affairs at Ashland University, http://www.ashbrook.org/events/colloqui/2006/ceaser.html.

19. Ceaser, *Nature and History,* 12.

20. Ibid., 13.

21. Ibid., 5.

22. Ibid., 9–10.

23. Ibid., 6.

24. Ibid.

25. Ibid., 10.

26. Ibid., 6, 82.

27. Ibid., 83.

28. Quentin Skinner, "Meaning and Understanding in the History of Ideas," in *Meaning and Context: Quentin Skinner and his Critics,* ed. James Tully (Princeton, N.J.: Princeton University Press, 1988), 29–67; J. G. A. Pocock, "Languages and Their Implications: The Transformation of the Study of Political Thought," in *Politics, Language, and Time: Essays on Political Thought and History* (New York: Atheneum, 1971), 3–41.

29. Rogers Smith, "What If God Was One of Us? The Challenges of Studying Foundational Concepts," in Ceaser, *Nature and History,* 147.

30. Ceaser, *Nature and History,* 191.

31. Ibid., 6.

32. See my full analysis of this interpretation paradigm in Alan Gibson, *Interpreting the Founding: Guide to the Enduring Debates over the Origins and Foundations of the American Republic,* 2nd ed. (Lawrence: University Press of Kansas, 2010), 86–122.

33. For the assumptions underlying this methodology, see Terence Ball, *Transforming Political Discourse: Political Theory and Critical Conceptual History* (Oxford: Basil Blackwell, 1988); Terrence Ball and J. G. A. Pocock, eds., *Conceptual Change and the Constitution* (Lawrence: University Press of Kansas, 1988); Terence Ball, James Farr, and Russell Hanson, eds., *Political Innovation and Conceptual Change* (Cambridge: Cambridge University Press, 1989).

34. Peter S. Onuf, *The Mind of Thomas Jefferson* (Charlottesville: University Press of Virginia, 2007), 72.

35. David Hendrickson, *Peace Pact: The Lost World of the American Founding* (Lawrence: University Press of Kansas, 2003), 24.

36. See Jack P. Greene, *Negotiated Authorities: Essays in Colonial Political and Constitutional History* (Charlottesville: University Press of Virginia, 1994); Jack P. Greene, *Peripheries and Center: Constitutional Development in the Extended Polities of the British Empire and the United States, 1607–1788* (Athens: University of Georgia Press, 1986); Jack P. Greene, "The American Revolution," *American Historical Review* 105 (February 2000): 93–102.

37. John Phillip Reid, *Constitutional History of the American Revolution,* abridged ed. (Madison: University of Wisconsin Press, 1995).

38. David Armitage, *The Declaration of Independence: A Global History* (Cambridge, Mass.: Harvard University Press, 2007); David Armitage, "The Declaration of Independence and International Law," *William and Mary Quarterly* 59 (January 2002): 39–64.

39. Hendrickson, *Peace Pact;* Max Edling, *A Revolution in Favor of Government: Origins of the U.S. Constitution and the Making of the American State* (New York: Oxford University Press, 2003); Cathy D. Matson and Peter S. Onuf, *A Union of Interests: Political and Economic Thought in Revolutionary America* (Lawrence: University Press of Kansas, 1990).

40. Peter Onuf, *Jefferson's Empire: The Language of American Nationhood* (Charlottesville: University Press of Virginia, 2000); Karl-Friedrich Walling, *Republican Empire:*

Alexander Hamilton on War and Free Government (Lawrence: University Press of Kansas, 1999); Lance Banning, *The Sacred Fire of Liberty: James Madison and the Founding of the Federal Republic* (Ithaca, N.Y.: Cornell University Press, 1995).

41. Peter McNamara, "Unionist Paradigm," review of *Peace Pact: The Lost World of the American Founding*, by David Hendrickson, *Review of Politics* 66 (Spring 2004): 313.

42. For an insightful but much different effort to defend the Founding, see Ralph Lerner, "Facing Up to the Founding," in *To Form a More Perfect Union: The Critical Ideas of the Constitution*, ed. Herman Belz, Ronald Hoffman, and Peter J. Albert (Charlottesville: University Press of Virginia, 1992), 250–271, and Ralph Lerner, *Revolutions Revisited: Two Faces of the Politics of Enlightenment* (Chapel Hill: University of North Carolina Press, 1994).

43. See Richard Sinopoli, *The Foundations of American Citizenship: Liberalism, the Constitution, and Civic Virtue* (New York: Oxford University Press, 1992).

44. For classic expressions of this interpretation, see Irving Kristol, "The American Revolution as a Successful Revolution," and Martin Diamond, "The Revolution of Sober Expectations," both in *The American Revolution: Three Views* (New York: American Brands, 1795), 20–52 and 54–85, respectively; Hannah Arendt, *On Revolution* (New York: Viking Press, 1970).

45. Peter Onuf, "The Scholars' Jefferson," *William and Mary Quarterly* 50 (October 1993): 696.

46. Alexander Hamilton, James Madison, and John Jay, *The Federalist*, ed. Jacob Cooke (Middletown, Conn.: Wesleyan University Press, 1961), No. 10, 58. All subsequent citations are to this edition of *The Federalist*.

47. Elshtain, "In Common Together," 70.

48. *Federalist* No. 10, 58. For a discussion of an interesting critique by Madison of the eighteenth-century socialist Robert Owen, see Drew McCoy, *The Last of the Fathers: James Madison and The Republican Legacy* (Cambridge: Cambridge University Press, 1989), 204–207.

49. James Madison to Thomas Jefferson, October 17, 1788, in *The Papers of James Madison*, ed. William T. Hutchinson et al. (Chicago and Charlottesville: University of Chicago Press and University Press of Virginia, 1962–), 11:299 and 298, respectively, for quotes.

50. See in particular James Read, *Power versus Liberty: Madison, Hamilton, Wilson, and Jefferson* (Charlottesville: University Press of Virginia, 2000); Bernard Bailyn, *To Begin the World Anew: The Genius and Ambiguities of the American Founders* (New York: Alfred A. Knopf, 2003), especially 105–125.

51. See Michael P. Zuckert, "Federalism and the Founding: Toward a Reinterpretation of the Constitutional Convention," *Review of Politics* 48 (1986): 166–210; Michael Zuckert, "A System without a Precedent: Federalism in the American Constitution," in *The Framing and Ratification of the Constitution*, ed. Leonard W. Levy and Dennis J. Mahoney (New York: Macmillan, 1987), 132–150.

52. Zuckert, "System without a Precedent," 141, 149.

53. *Federalist* No. 72, 488. See also Douglass Adair, *Fame and the Founding: Essays by Douglass Adair*, ed. Trevor Colbourn (New York: W. W. Norton, 1974), 3–26; John A. Schultz and Douglass Adair, eds., *The Spur of Fame: Dialogues of John Adams and Benjamin*

Rush, 1805–1813 (San Marino, Calif.: Huntington Library University Press, 1966); Gerald Stourzh, *Alexander Hamilton and the Idea of Republican Government* (Stanford, Calif.: Stanford University Press, 1970), 95–106.

54. *Federalist* No. 10, 63.

55. *Federalist* No. 57, 384–390.

56. *Federalist* No. 51, 349.

57. This phrase and many close to it are used frequently in Madison's writings. See, for example, James Madison to Thomas Jefferson, October 17, 1787, in *Papers of James Madison*, 11:299.

58. Quote is from Gordon Wood, "Heroics," review of *Explaining America: "The Federalist,"* by Garry Wills, in *New York Review of Books*, April 2, 1981, 17. The interpretation that the Framers' primary goal was to ensure disinterested and virtuous leadership is set forth most boldly by Garry Wills in *Explaining America: The Federalist* (Garden City, N.Y.: Doubleday, 1981). See also Gordon Wood, "Interests and Disinterestedness in the Making of the Constitution," in *Beyond Confederation: Origins of the Constitution and American National Identity*, ed. Richard Beeman, Stephen Botein, and Edward C. Carter (Chapel Hill: University of North Carolina Press, 1987), 91–93; Wood, "Heroics," 16–18. Examples of the contrary thesis—that the Framers relied on institutional structure to remedy the absence of virtue—can be found in Benjamin Barber, "The Compromised Republic: Public Purposelessness in America," in *The Moral Foundations of the American Republic*, ed. Robert H. Horwitz (Charlottesville: University Press of Virginia, 1979), esp. 20–30; Robert Dahl, *A Preface to Democratic Theory* (Chicago: University of Chicago Press, 1956), 1–33; Richard Hofstadter, *The American Political Tradition and the Men Who Made It* (New York: Vintage Books, 1974), 3–21. A more subtle and refined version of this interpretation also runs through the works of Martin Diamond. See Martin Diamond, *As Far as Republican Principles Will Admit*, ed. William A. Schambra (Washington, D.C.: AEI Press, 1992).

59. Most interpretations of the Founders' political thought do not take into account this distinction but rather are informed by a simplistic conception of self-interest. They assume that any behavior that is begun because of a self-regarding *motive* is necessarily a self-interested *action*. Obviously, however, this is true in only a limited sense. A person may be motivated to feed the poor by a desire to be known as a generous person, or he may be motivated to join the army and endanger his life by a desire to receive money for a college education. Even if we suppose that the motive for these actions is narrowly self-regarding, the behavior they produce benefits many people. The point in the discussion above is that the Founders—especially the authors of *The Federalist*—realized this and hoped to produce public-spirited behavior even if that behavior sprang from self-interested motives. The Founders did not, however, lose any of their antipathy for narrowly self-regarding behavior. They continued to disapprove of public officials who sought office in order to increase their own wealth, or who used their position to serve the particular interests of their constituents at the expense of the public good. They were willing to put self-regarding motives in the service of public actions, but they did not assume that self-regarding actions would inadvertently serve the public good.

60. Wood, *Creation of the American Republic*, 615.

61. Hendrickson, *Peace Pact*, 28.

62. Ibid., 28, 15, for quotes. More recently, Hendrickson has written, "Nearly all

works in the history of internationalism, which trace the rise and fall of the peace plans and the modalities of international cooperation from the seventeenth to the early twentieth century, focus exclusively on European developments. The present work is informed by the assumption that American thought concerning international relations is just as important to the course of world history and just as rich in its capacity to inform speculation into the enduring problems of international cooperation as European thought over the same 150-year period." David Hendrickson, *Union, Nation, or Empire: The American Debate over International Relations, 1789–1941* (Lawrence: University Press of Kansas, 2009), xiv.

63. Hendrickson, *Peace Pact,* 260. See also David Hendrickson, "The Renovation of American Foreign Policy," *Foreign Affairs* 71 (Spring 1992): 48–63, for Hendrickson's understanding of the enduring value of the Founders' writings within the unionist paradigm.

64. Jennifer Nedelsky, *Private Property and the Limits of American Constitutionalism: The Madisonian Framework and Its Legacy* (Chicago: University of Chicago Press, 1990). The conclusions of this work are crystallized in Jennifer Nedelsky, "The Protection of Property in the Origins and Development of the American Constitution," in *To Form a More Perfect Union: The Critical Ideas of the Constitution,* ed. Herman Belz, Ronald Hoffman, and Peter J. Albert (Charlottesville: University Press of Virginia, 1992), 38–72.

65. Nedelsky, *Private Property,* 11.

66. Ibid., 148.

67. Ibid., 7.

68. Ibid., 3.

69. Ibid., 2, 1, 15.

70. Robert Dahl, *How Democratic Is the American Constitution?* (New Haven, Conn.: Yale University Press, 2001).

71. Ibid., 49.

72. Ibid., 88–89.

73. Ibid., 31.

74. Ibid., 117.

75. Jean Yarbrough, "Republicanism Reconsidered: Some Thoughts on the Foundation and Preservation of the American Republic," *Review of Politics* 41 (January 1979): 86.

76. Here, however, it should be noted that it was not Federalists such as Madison, Wilson, and Hamilton who were responsible for this unjust feature of the original institutional design, but rather the defenders of state autonomy and state influence at the convention and the anti-Federalists. Indeed, as Dahl points out, Madison, Wilson, and Hamilton offered a still unanswered case against equal representation of all states. Dahl, *How Democratic Is the American Constitution?* 13–15, 46–54.

77. Frances E. Lee and Bruce I. Oppenheimer, *Sizing Up the Senate: The Unequal Consequences of Equal Representation* (Chicago: University of Chicago Press, 1999), 20–23. On this point, see also William N. Eskridge Jr., "The One Senator, One Vote Clause" and Suzanna Sherry, "Our Unconstitutional Senate," both in "Constitutional Stupidities: A Symposium," *Constitutional Commentary* 12 (Summer 1995): 159–162 and 213–215, respectively. Richard N. Rosenfeld, "What Democracy? The Case for Abolishing the United States Senate," *Harpers Magazine,* May 2004, 35–44.

78. Lee and Oppenheimer, 20–23, 83–234.

79. Nedelsky, *Private Property,* 144. My emphasis.

80. Ibid., 2.

81. Dahl, *How Democratic Is the American Constitution?* 91–92 for quotes.

82. Nedelsky, *Private Property,* 205.

83. Jack Rakove, "The Liberal Prince on the Democratic Seesaw," *Reviews in American History* 23 (1995): 586.

84. For recent work on freedom of the press, political parties, and public opinion during the 1790s, see Robert W. T. Martin, *The Free and Open Press: The Founding of American Democratic Press Liberty, 1640–1800* (New York: New York University Press, 2001); Colleen Sheehan, "The Politics of Public Opinion: James Madison's Notes on Government," *William and Mary Quarterly* 44 (1992): 609–627; Colleen Sheehan, "Madison and the French Enlightenment: The Authority of Public Opinion," *William and Mary Quarterly* 59 (2002): 925–956; Colleen Sheehan, "Madison v. Hamilton: The Battle over Republicanism and the Role of Public Opinion," *American Political Science Review* 98 (August 2004): 405–424; Alan Gibson, "Veneration and Vigilance: James Madison and Public Opinion, 1785–1800," *Review of Politics* 67 (Winter 2005): 5–35; Todd Estes, "Shaping the Politics of Public Opinion: Federalists and the Jay Treaty Debate," *Journal of the Early Republic* 20 (Fall 2000): 393–422; Estes, *The Jay Treaty Debate, Public Opinion, and the Evolution of Early American Political Culture* (Amherst: University of Massachusetts Press, 2006). See also Jeffrey L. Pasley, "The Cheese and the Words: Popular Political Culture and Participatory Democracy in the Early American Republic," in *Beyond the Founders: New Approaches to the Political History of the Early American Republic,* eds. David Waldstreicher, Jeffrey L. Pasley, and Andrew W. Robertson (Chapel Hill: University of North Carolina Press, 2004), 31–56, for an innovative exploration of new forms of democratic participation that were arising in the early republic.

85. M. Margaret Conway, *Political Participation in the United States* (Washington, D.C.: QC Press, 2000), 108–111; Robert J. Dinkin, *Before Equal Suffrage: Women in Partisan Politics from Colonial Times to 1920* (Westport, Conn.: Greenwood Press, 1995); Alexander Keyssar, *The Right to Vote: The Contested History of Democracy in the United States* (New York: Basic Books, 2000), 8–25, 54, 172–221.

86. Keyssar, *The Right to Vote,* 26.

87. Lance Banning, *The Sacred Fire of Liberty: James Madison and the Founding of the Federal Republic* (Ithaca, N.Y.: Cornell University Press, 1995), 367.

88. David Hackett Fischer, *Historians' Fallacies: Toward a Logic of Historical Thought* (New York: Harper and Row, 1970), 298.

89. See Cass Sunstein, "Interest Groups in American Public Law," *Stanford Law Review* 38 (November 1985): 29–87; Cass Sunstein, "Beyond the Republican Revival," *Yale Law Journal* 97 (July 1988): 1539–1590; Cass Sunstein, *The Partial Constitution* (Cambridge, Mass.: Harvard University Press, 1993), 17–39.

90. *Federalist* No. 51, 353.

91. Lani Guinier, *The Tyranny of the Majority: Fundamental Fairness in Representative Democracy* (New York: Free Press, 1994), especially 3–5. For the Federalists' view of actual representation as "visionary," see *Federalist* No. 35, 214–217.

92. This is most vividly illustrated in Conor Cruise O'Brien's analysis of Jefferson,

which is intended to establish that Jefferson's views on race and slavery disqualify him from a place within the American civil religion. Conor Cruise O'Brien, *The Long Affair: Thomas Jefferson and the French Revolution, 1785–1800* (Chicago: University of Chicago Press, 1996).

93. I draw this line of reasoning from a presentation that Peter Onuf gave at the First Annual Gainesville Jefferson Symposium, February 10–12, 2006, University of Florida, Gainesville, Orthopedic and Sports Medicine Institute. This symposium was directed by Tom Dowd and Peter Onuf.

94. Lewis, quoted in Anne Matthews, "Leading Men: Authorities on the Revolutionary Era Say How the Founding Fathers Became Cultural Heroes," *American Scholar* 74 (Spring 2005), 127.

Bibliography

"The Act of 1807." In "The Abolition of the Slave Trade." Schomburg Center for Research in Black Culture, http://a/bolition.nypl.org/essays/us_constitution/5 (accessed January 6, 2010).

Adair, Douglass. *Fame and the Founding Fathers: Essays by Douglass Adair,* edited by Trevor Colbourn. New York: W. W. Norton, 1974.

Adams, William Howard. *Gouverneur Morris: An Independent Life.* New Haven, Conn.: Yale University Press, 2003.

Adams, Willi Paul. *The First American Constitutions: Republican Ideology and the Making of the States' Constitutions in the Revolutionary Era,* translated by Rita Kimber and Robert Kimber. Chapel Hill: University of North Carolina Press, 1980.

Allen-Taylor, J. Douglas. "Board Vetoes Jefferson School Name Change." *Berkeley Daily Planet,* June 24, 2005, http://www.berkeleydailyplanet.com/issue/2005-06-24/article/21673?headline=Board-Vetoes-Jefferson-School-Name-Change-By-J.-DOUGLAS-ALLEN-TAYLOR (accessed January 6, 2010).

Allgor, Catherine. *Parlor Politics: In Which the Ladies of Washington Help Build a City and a Government.* Charlottesville: University Press of Virginia, 2000.

Amar, Akhil Reed. *America's Constitution: A Biography.* New York: Random House, 2005.

Anderson, Frank Maloy, ed. *The Constitutions and Other Select Documents Illustrative of the History of France, 1789–1907,* 2nd ed. New York: Russell and Russell, 1908.

Appleby, Joyce. "Commercial Farming and the 'Agrarian Myth' in the Early Republic." *Journal of American History* 68 (March 1982): 833–849.

———. *Capitalism and the New Social Order: The Republican Vision of the 1790s.* New York: New York University Press, 1984.

———. "Republicanism and Ideology." *American Quarterly* 37 (Fall 1985): 461–473.

———. "Republicanism in Old and New Contexts." *William and Mary Quarterly* 43 (January 1986): 20–34.

———. *Liberalism and Republicanism in the Historical Imagination.* Cambridge, Mass.: Harvard University Press, 1992.

———. "Having It All; Two New Books Reckon with a President's Complicated Legacy." Review of *"Negro President": Jefferson and the Slave Power* by Garry Wills and *Jefferson's Demons: Portrait of a Restless Mind,* by Michael Knox Beran. *Washington Post,* November 16, 2003, T05.

Arendt, Hannah. *On Revolution*. New York: Viking Press, 1970.

Aristotle's Posterior Analytics, translated by Hippocrates G. Apostle. Grinnell, Iowa: Peripatetic Press, 1981.

Armitage, David. "The Declaration of Independence and International Law." *William and Mary Quarterly* 59 (January 2002): 39–64.

———. *The Declaration of Independence: A Global History*. Cambridge, Mass.: Harvard University Press, 2007.

Artz, Matthew. "Renaming Vote Stirs School." *Berkeley Daily Planet*, February 3, 2004, http://www.berkeleydailyplanet.com/issue/2004-02-03/article/18197?headline= Renaming-Vote-Stirs-School (accessed January 6, 2010).

Ashworth, John. "The Jeffersonians: Classical Republicans or Liberal Capitalists?" *Journal of American Studies* 18 (December 1984): 428–430.

Austin, J. L. *How to Do Things with Words*. New York: Oxford University Press, 1965.

Avalon Project at Yale Law School. http://yale.edu/lawweb/avalon/18th.htm (accessed January 6, 2010).

Bailyn, Bernard. "Political Experience and Enlightenment Ideas in Eighteenth-Century America." *American Historical Review* 67 (1961–1962): 339–351.

———. *The Ideological Origins of the American Revolution*. 1967. Reprint, Cambridge, Mass.: Belknap Press of Harvard University Press, 1992.

———. *The Origin of American Politics*. New York: Alfred A. Knopf, 1968.

———. "The Central Themes of the American Revolution: An Interpretation." In *Essays on the American Revolution*, edited by Stephen G. Kurtz and James H. Hutson, 3–31. Chapel Hill: University of North Carolina Press, 1973.

———. "Notes on State Constitutions, 1776–1790." In *The Debate on the Constitution*, 2 vols., edited by Bernard Bailyn, 1:1117–1122. New York: Library of America, 1993.

———. *To Begin the World Anew: The Genius and Ambiguities of the American Founders*. New York: Alfred A. Knopf, 2003.

Ball, Terence. *Transforming Political Discourse: Political Theory and Critical Conceptual History*. Oxford: Basil Blackwell, 1988.

Ball, Terence, and J. G. A. Pocock, eds. *Conceptual Change and the Constitution*. Lawrence: University Press of Kansas, 1988.

Ball, Terence, James Farr, and Russell L. Hanson, eds. *Political Innovation and Conceptual Change*. Cambridge: Cambridge University Press, 1989.

Banning, Lance. "Republican Ideology and the Triumph of the Constitution, 1789 to 1793." *William and Mary Quarterly* 31 (April 1974): 167–188.

———. *The Jeffersonian Persuasion: Evolution of a Party Ideology*. Ithaca, N.Y.: Cornell University Press, 1978.

———. "James Madison and the Nationalists, 1780–1783." *William and Mary Quarterly* 40 (1983): 237–255.

———. "James Madison and the Dynamics of the Constitutional Convention." *Political Science Reviewer* 16 (1987): 5–48.

———. "Jeffersonian Ideology Revisited: Liberal and Classical Ideas in the New American Republic." *William and Mary Quarterly* 42 (July 1987): 3–19.

———. "Some Second Thoughts on Virtue and the Course of Revolutionary Thinking."

In *Conceptual Change and the Constitution*, edited by Terence Ball and J. G. A. Pocock, 194–212. Lawrence: University Press of Kansas, 1988.

———. "Quid Transit? Paradigms and Process in the Transformation of Republican Ideas." *Reviews in American History* 17 (June 1989): 199–204.

———. "The Republican Interpretation: Retrospect and Prospect." In *The Republican Synthesis Revisited: Essays in Honor of George Athan Billias*, edited by Milton M. Klein, Richard D. Brown, and John B. Hench, 91–117. Worcester, Mass.: American Antiquarian Society, 1992.

———. *Jefferson and Madison: Three Conversations from the Founding.* Madison, Wis.: Madison House, 1995.

———. "Political Economy and the Creation of the Federal Republic." In *Devising Liberty: Preserving and Creating Freedom in the New American Republic*, edited by David Thomas Konig, 11–49. Stanford, Calif.: Stanford University Press, 1995.

———. *The Sacred Fire of Liberty: James Madison and the Founding of the Federal Republic.* Ithaca, N.Y.: Cornell University Press, 1995.

———. "Three-Fifths Historian." Review of *"Negro President": Jefferson and the Slave Power,* by Garry Wills. Claremont Institute for the Study of Statesmanship and Political Philosophy, http://www.claremont.org/writings/crb/fall2004/banning.html (accessed January 6, 2010).

Barber, Benjamin. "The Compromised Republic: Public Purposelessness in America." In *The Moral Foundations of the American Republic*, edited by Robert H. Horwitz, 19–38. Charlottesville: University Press of Virginia, 1979.

Barker, Ernest, ed. *The Politics of Aristotle.* London: Oxford University Press, 1958.

Barrow, Clyde. *More Than a Historian: The Political and Economic Thought of Charles A. Beard.* New Brunswick, N.J.: Transaction, 2000.

Barry, Norman. *An Introduction to Modern Political Theory.* New York: St. Martin's Press, 1989.

Beard, Charles A. *An Economic Interpretation of the Constitution of the United States.* 1913. Reprint, New York: Free Press, 1986.

———. *Economic Origins of Jeffersonian Democracy.* New York: Macmillan, 1915.

———. *The Supreme Court and the Constitution.* New York: Macmillan, 1926.

Beeman, Richard, Stephen Botein, and Edward C. Carter II, eds. *Beyond Confederation: Origins of the Constitution and American National Identity.* Chapel Hill: University of North Carolina Press, 1987.

Beers, William. *An Address to Legislature and People of the State of Connecticut, on the Subject of Dividing the State into Districts for the Election of Representatives in Congress.* New Haven, Conn.: Printed by T & S Green, 1791.

Belz, Herman. "Liberty and Equality for Whom? How to Think Inclusively about the Constitution and the Bill of Rights." *History Teacher* 25 (May 1992): 263–277.

Bender, Kristin. "In Berkeley School Vote, Jefferson Out (Sequoia In)." *Oakland Tribune,* June 2, 2005, reprinted at *Free Republic,* http://www.freerepublic.com/focus/f-news/1415149/posts (accessed January 6, 2010).

———. "Jefferson Stays as Name for School." *Oakland Tribune,* June 24, 2005, at BNET, http://findarticles.com/p/articles/mi_qn4176/is_20050624/ai_n15838645/ (accessed January 6, 2010).

Benson, Lee. *Turner and Beard: American Historical Writing Reconsidered.* Glencoe, Ill.: Free Press, 1960.

Bentley, Arthur. *The Process of Government: A Study of Social Pressures.* Chicago: University of Chicago Press, 1908.

Berger, Peter L., and Thomas Luckman. *The Social Construction of Reality: A Treatise in the Sociology of Knowledge.* Garden City, N.Y.: Doubleday, 1967.

"Berkeley School Wants to Change Name from Jefferson." *Free Republic,* March 22, 2005, http://www.freerepublic.com/focus/f-news/1368449/posts (accessed January 6, 2010).

Berns, Walter. "Does the Constitution 'Secure These Rights'?" In *How Democratic Is the Constitution?* edited by Robert A. Goldwin and William A. Schambra, 59–78. Washington, D.C.: American Enterprise Institute, 1980.

Bessette, Joseph. "Deliberative Democracy: The Majority Principle in Republican Government." In *How Democratic Is the Constitution?* edited by Robert A. Goldwin and William A. Schambra, 102–116. Washington, D.C.: American Enterprise Institute, 1980.

Best, Judith A. "Legislative Tyranny and the Liberation of the Executive: A View from the Founding." *Presidential Studies Quarterly* 17 (Fall 1987): 697–709.

Bevir, Mark. "Mind and Method in the History of Ideas." *History and Theory* 36 (May 1997): 167–189.

Boyd, William K. Review of *An Economic Interpretation of the Constitution of the United States,* by Charles A. Beard. *South Atlantic Quarterly* 12 (July 1913): 269–273.

Brogan, D. W. "The Quarrel over Charles Austin Beard and the American Constitution." *Economic History Review* 18 (August 1965): 199–223.

Brookheiser, Richard. "The Founding Yokels." Review of *To Begin the World Anew: The Genius and Ambiguities of the American Founders,* by Bernard Bailyn. *New York Times Book Review,* February 16, 2003, 11.

———. *Gentleman Revolutionary: Gouverneur Morris, the Rake Who Wrote the Constitution.* New York: Free Press, 2003.

Brown, Richard D. "The Founding Fathers of 1776 and 1787: A Collective View." *William and Mary Quarterly* 33 (1976): 465–480.

Brown, Robert E. "Economic Democracy before the Constitution." *American Quarterly* 7 (1955): 257–274.

———. *Middle-Class Democracy and the Revolution in Massachusetts, 1691–1780.* Ithaca, N.Y.: Cornell University Press, 1955.

———. *Charles Beard and the Constitution: A Critical Analysis of "An Economic Interpretation of the Constitution."* Princeton, N.J.: Princeton University Press, 1956.

———. *Reinterpretation of the Formation of the American Constitution.* Boston: Boston University Press, 1963.

———. *Virginia, 1705–1786: Democracy or Aristocracy?* East Lansing: Michigan State University Press, 1964.

Browning, Rob. "Commentary: Jefferson School: What's the Rush?" *Berkeley Daily Planet,* June 14, 2005, http://www.berkeleydailyplanet.com/article.cfm?archiveDate=06-14-05&storyID=21617 (accessed January 6, 2010).

Bruchey, Stuart. "The Forces behind the Constitution: A Critical Review of the Framework of E. James Ferguson's *The Power of the Purse.*" *William and Mary Quarterly* 19 (July 1962): 429–434.

Buchanan, James, and Gordon Tullock. *The Calculus of Consent: Logical Foundations of Constitutional Democracy.* Ann Arbor: University of Michigan Press, 1962.

Buckley, Thomas E. *Church and State in Revolutionary Virginia, 1776–1787.* Charlottesville: University Press of Virginia, 1977.

Burke, Joseph C. "The Pro-Slavery Argument in the First Congress." *Duquesne Review* 16 (1969): 3–15.

Butterfield, L. H., ed. *Adams Family Correspondence.* Cambridge, Mass.: Belknap Press of Harvard University Press, 1963.

Cain, William E., ed. *William Lloyd Garrison and the Fight against Slavery: Selections from "The Liberator."* Boston: Bedford Books, 1995.

Calhoun, John C. "Southern Address," http://sciway3.net/2001/john-c-calhoun/SAddress.htm (accessed January 6, 2010).

Calhoun, John C. "Oregon Bill Speech," http://www.teachingamericanhistory.org/library/index.asp?document=944 (accessed January 6, 2010).

Calvert, Robert E., ed. *"The Constitution of the People": Reflections on Citizens and Civil Society.* Lawrence: University Press of Kansas, 1991.

Carey, George. "Separation of Powers and the Madisonian Model: A Reply to the Critics." *American Political Science Review* 22 (March 1978): 151–164.

———. *The Federalist: Design for a Constitutional Republic.* Urbana: University of Illinois Press, 1989.

———. *In Defense of the Constitution.* Indianapolis: Liberty Fund, 1995.

Carrese, Paul. "The Complexity, and Principles, of the American Founding: A Response to Alan Gibson." *History of Political Thought* 21 (Winter 2000): 711–717.

Caton, Hiram. *The Politics of Progress: The Origins and Development of the Commercial Republic, 1600–1835.* Gainesville: University of Florida Press, 1988.

Ceaser, James W. *Nature and History in American Political Development: A Debate.* Foreword by Theda R. Scocpol and responses by Jack N. Rakove, Nancy L. Rosenblum, and Rogers M. Smith. Cambridge, Mass.: Harvard University Press, 2006.

———. "Foundational Ideas in American Political Thought." Audio recording of a presentation given on October 13, 2006. Ashbrook Center for Public Affairs at Ashland University, http://www.ashbrook.org/events/colloqui/2006/ceaser.html (accessed January 6, 2010).

Chase, Salmon P. *Reclamation of Fugitives from Services: An Argument for the Defendant, Submitted to the Supreme Court of the United States, at the December Term, 1846, in the Case of Wharton Jones vs. John Vangandt.* Cincinnati: R. P. Donogh, 1847.

Coates, Eyler Robert, ed. *The Jefferson–Hemings Myth: An American Travesty.* Charlottesville, Va.: Jefferson Editions, 2001.

Cohen, Elliot. "Commentary: Berkeley Strays from Democratic Path." *Berkeley Daily Planet,* July 12, 2005, http://www.berkeleydailyplanet.com/issue/2005-07-12/article/21832?headline=Commentary-Berkeley-Strays-From-Democratic-Path-By-ELLIOT-COHEN (accessed January 6, 2010).

Cohen, William. "Thomas Jefferson and the Problem of Slavery." *Journal of American History* 56 (December 1969): 503–526.

Collier, Christopher. *All Politics Is Local: Family, Friends, and Provincial Interests in the Creation of the Constitution.* Hanover, N.H.: University Press of New England, 2003.

Conrad, Steven. "Polite Foundation: Citizenship and Common Sense in James Wilson's Republican Theory." *1984: Supreme Court Review* (1985): 359–388.

Conway, M. Margaret. *Political Participation in the United States.* Washington, D.C.: QC Press, 2000.

Cooper, William. *Liberty and Slavery: Southern Politics to 1860.* 1983. Reprint, Columbia: University of South Carolina Press, 2000.

Cornell, Saul. "Liberal Republicans or Republican Liberals? The Political Thought of the Founders Reconsidered." *Reviews in American History* 21 (March 1993): 26–30.

———. *The Other Founders: Anti-Federalism and the Dissenting Tradition in America, 1788–1828.* Chapel Hill: University of North Carolina Press, 1999.

Corwin, Edward S. Review of *An Economic Interpretation of the Constitution of the United States,* by Charles A. Beard. *History Teachers Magazine* 5 (February 1914): 65–66.

———. "The Progress of Constitutional Theory between the Declaration of Independence and the Meeting of the Philadelphia Convention." *American Historical Review* 30 (1925): 511–536.

———. *The President, Offices and Powers: History and Analysis of Practice and Opinion.* New York: New York University Press, 1941.

Crane, Elaine Forman. "Political Dialogue and the Spring of Abigail's Discontent." *William and Mary Quarterly* 56 (October 1999): 745–774.

Crowl, Philip A. "Anti-Federalism in Maryland, 1787–1788." *William and Mary Quarterly* 4 (October 1947): 446–469.

Dahl, Robert. *A Preface to Democratic Theory.* Chicago: University of Chicago Press, 1956.

———. *How Democratic Is the American Constitution?* New Haven, Conn.: Yale University Press, 2001.

Dalton, Dennis, ed. *Mahatma Gandhi: Selected Political Writings.* Indianapolis: Hackett, 1996.

Davis, David Brion. *The Problem of Slavery in Western Culture.* Ithaca, N.Y.: Cornell University Press, 1966.

———. "Slavery and the American Revolution." In *Slavery and Freedom in the Age of the American Revolution,* edited by Ira Berlin and Ronald Hoffman, 262–280. Charlottesville: University Press of Virginia, 1983.

———. *The Problem of Slavery in the Age of Revolution, 1770–1823.* New York: Oxford University Press, 1999.

———. *Inhuman Bondage: The Rise and Fall of Slavery in the New World.* New York: Oxford University Press, 2006.

Davis, Winston, ed. *Taking Responsibility: Comparative Perspectives.* Charlottesville: University Press of Virginia, 2001.

Diamond, Ann Stuart. "The Zenith of Separation of Powers Theory: The Federal Convention of 1787." *Publius* 8 (Summer 1978): 45–70.

———. "Decent, Even though Democratic." In *How Democratic Is the Constitution?* edited by Robert A. Goldwin and William A. Schambra, 18–38. Washington, D.C.: American Enterprise Institute, 1980.

Diamond, Martin. "Democracy and *The Federalist.*" *American Political Science Review* 53 (March 1959): 52–68.

———. "The Revolution of Sober Expectations." In *The American Revolution: Three Views*, 54–85. New York: American Brands, 1975.

———. "The American Idea of Equality: The View from the Founding." *Review of Politics* 37 (July 1976): 313–331.

———. *The Founding of the Democratic Republic.* Itasca, Ill.: F. E. Peacock, 1981.

———. "What the Framers Meant by Federalism." In *As Far as Republican Principles Will Admit: Essays by Martin Diamond,* edited by William A. Schambra, 93–107. Washington, D.C.: American Enterprise Institute Press, 1992.

Dienstag, Joshua Foa. "Serving God and Mammon: The Lockean Sympathy in Early American Political Thought." *American Political Science Review* 90 (September 1996): 497–511.

Diggins, John Patrick. "Power and Authority in American History: The Case of Charles A. Beard and His Critics." *American Historical Review* 86 (October 1981): 701–730.

———. *The Lost Soul of American Politics: Virtue, Self-Interest, and the Foundations of Liberalism.* New York: Basic Books, 1984.

———. "The Oyster and the Pearl: The Problem of Contextualism in Intellectual History." *History and Theory* 23 (May 1984): 151–169.

Dinkin, Robert J. *Before Equal Suffrage: Women in Partisan Politics from Colonial Times to 1920.* Westport, Conn.: Greenwood Press, 1995.

Douglass, Elisha P. *Rebels and Democrats: The Struggle for Equal Political Rights and Majority Rule during the American Revolution.* Chapel Hill: University of North Carolina Press, 1955.

Dreisbach, Daniel L. "The Constitution's Forgotten Religion Clause: Reflections on the Article VI Religious Test Ban." *Journal of Church and State* 38 (1996): 261–295.

Dunn, Richard S. "Black Society in the Chesapeake." In *Slavery and Freedom in the Age of the American Revolution,* edited by Ira Berlin and Ronald Hoffman, 49–82. Urbana: Published for the United States Capitol Historical Society by the University of Illinois Press, 1983.

Dworetz, Steven. *The Unvarnished Doctrine: Locke, Liberalism, and the American Revolution.* Durham, N.C.: Duke University Press, 1990.

Dworkin, Ronald. *A Matter of Principle.* Cambridge, Mass.: Harvard University Press, 1985.

———. *Freedom's Law: The Moral Reading of the American Constitution.* Cambridge, Mass.: Harvard University Press, 1996.

Edling, Max. *A Revolution in Favor of Government: Origins of the U.S. Constitution and the Making of the American State.* New York: Oxford University Press, 2003.

Elkins, Stanley, and Eric McKitrick. *The Age of Federalism: The Early American Republic, 1788–1800.* New York: Oxford University Press, 1993.

Ellis, Joseph. *American Sphinx: The Character of Thomas Jefferson.* New York: Alfred A. Knopf, 1997.

———. *His Excellency George Washington.* New York: Alfred A. Knopf, 2004.

Ellis, Richard. *American Political Cultures.* New York: Oxford University Press, 1993.

Elshtain, Jean Bethke. "'In Common Together': Unity, Diversity, and Civic Virtue." In *"The Constitution of the People": Reflections on Citizens and Civil Society,* edited by Robert E. Calvert, 64–84. Lawrence: University Press of Kansas, 1991.

———. *Democracy on Trial.* New York: Basic Books, 1995.

Elster, Jon, ed. *Rational Choice.* Washington Square: New York University Press, 1986.

Epstein, David F. *The Political Theory of* The Federalist. Chicago: University of Chicago Press, 1984.

Ericson, David. *The Shaping of American Liberalism: The Debates over Ratification, Nullification, and Slavery.* Chicago: University of Chicago Press, 1993.

———. *The Debate over Slavery: Antislavery and Proslavery Liberalism in Antebellum America.* New York: New York University Press, 2000.

Eskridge, William N., Jr. "The One Senator, One Vote Clause." In *Constitutional Stupidities: Constitutional Tragedies,* edited by William N. Eskridge Jr. and Sanford Levinson, 35–39. New York: New York University Press, 1998.

Estes, Todd. "Shaping the Politics of Public Opinion: Federalists and the Jay Treaty Debate." *Journal of the Early Republic* 20 (Fall 2000): 393–422.

———. *The Jay Treaty Debate, Public Opinion, and the Evolution of Early American Political Culture.* Amherst: University of Massachusetts Press, 2006.

Farrand, Max, ed. *The Records of the Federal Convention of 1787.* 1911. Revised, New Haven, Conn.: Yale University Press, 1937.

Fehrenbacher, Don E. *The Dred Scott Case: Its Significance in American Law and Politics.* New York: Oxford University Press, 1978.

———. "Slavery, the Framers, and the Living Constitution." In *Slavery and Its Consequences: The Constitution, Equality, and Race,* edited by Robert A. Goldman and Art Kaufman, 1–22. Washington, D.C.: American Enterprise Institute, 1988.

———. *The Slaveholding Republic: An Account of the United States Government's Relations to Slavery,* completed and edited by Ward M. McAfee. New York: Oxford University Press, 2001.

Feinberg, Joel. *Doing and Deserving: Essays in the Theory of Responsibility.* Princeton, N.J.: Princeton University Press, 1970.

Ferguson, E. James. "Currency Finance: An Interpretation of Colonial Monetary Practices." *William and Mary Quarterly* 10 (April 1953): 153–180.

———. *The Power of the Purse: A History of American Public Finance, 1776–1790.* Chapel Hill: University of North Carolina Press, 1961.

———. "E. James Ferguson's Rebuttal." *William and Mary Quarterly* 19 (July 1962): 434–438.

———. "The Nationalists of 1781–1783 and the Economic Interpretation of the Constitution." *William and Mary Quarterly* 56 (September 1969): 241–261.

———. "Political Economy, Public Liberty, and the Formation of the Constitution." *William and Mary Quarterly* 40 (April 1983): 389–412.

Ferguson, Niall. *Virtual History: Alternatives and Counterfactuals.* New York: Perseus Books, 1997.

Finkelman, Paul. "Slavery and the Constitutional Convention: Making a Covenant with Death." In *Beyond Confederation: Origins of the Constitution and National Identity,* edited by Richard Beeman, Stephen Botein, and Edward C. Carter II, 188–225. Chapel Hill: University of North Carolina Press, 1987.

———. "Garrison's Constitution: The Covenant with Death and How It Was Made." *Prologue Magazine* 32 (Winter 2000), http://www.archives.gov/publications/prologue/2000/winter/garrisons-constitution-1.html (accessed January 6, 2010).

———. "The Murky Proslavery Origins of the Electoral College." *Jurist Legal Intelligence,* November 30, 2000, http://jurist.law.pitt.edu/election/electionfink.htm (accessed January 6, 2010).

———. *Slavery and the Founders: Race and Liberty in the Age of Jefferson,* 2nd ed. Armonk, N.Y.: M. E. Sharpe, 2001.

———. "The Proslavery Origins of the Electoral College." *Cardozo Law Review* 23 (2001–2002): 1145–1157.

"The First Scholarship Fund." Yale, Slavery, and Abolition, http://www.yaleslavery.org/ Endowments/e2schol.html (accessed January 6, 2010).

Fischer, David Hackett. *Historians' Fallacies: Toward a Logic of Historical Thought.* New York: Harper and Row, 1970.

Fisher, Louis. "The Efficiency Side of Separated Powers." *Journal of American Studies* 5 (August 1971): 113–131.

Flaumenhaft, Harvey. Review of *Saving the Revolution: The Federalist Papers and the American Founding,* edited by Charles Kesler. *Constitutional Commentary* 5 (Summer 1988): 460–476.

Foner, Eric. "Looking Again at Slavery's Sins." *New York Times,* August 25, 2001, http:// www.nytimes.com/2001/08/25/opinion/l-looking-again-at-slavery-s-sins-869503 .html (accessed January 6, 2010).

"Forum: Thomas Jefferson and Sally Hemings Redux." *William and Mary Quarterly* 57 (January 2000): 121–210.

Franklin, John Hope. "The Moral Legacy of the Founding Father." In *Race and History: Selected Essays, 1938–1988,* 153–162. Baton Rouge: Louisiana State University Press, 1989.

Freehling, William W. "The Founding Fathers and Slavery." *American Historical Review* 77 (February 1972): 81–93.

———. "The Founding Fathers, Conditional Anti-Slavery, and the Nonradicalism of the American Revolution." In *The Reintegration of American History: Slavery and the Civil War,* 12–33. New York: Oxford University Press, 1994.

Galston, William. "Defending Liberalism." *American Political Science Review* 76 (September 1982): 621–629.

———. *Liberal Purposes: Goods, Virtues, and Diversity in the Liberal State.* New York: Cambridge University Press, 1991.

Geertz, Clifford. *The Interpretation of Cultures.* New York: Basic Books, 1973.

Geospatial Statistical Data Center at the University of Virginia Library. "The Reintegration of American History: Slavery and the Civil War." http://fisher.lib.virginia .edu/ (accessed January 6, 2010).

Gerber, Scott. "What Ever Happened to the Declaration? A Commentary on the Republican Revisionism in the Political Thought of the American Revolution." *Polity* 26 (Winter 1993): 207–231.

———. *To Secure These Rights: The Declaration of Independence and Constitutional Interpretation.* New York: New York University Press, 1995.

Gibson, Alan. "Impartial Representation and the Extended Republic: Towards a Comprehensive and Balanced Interpretation of the Tenth *Federalist.*" *History of Political Thought* 12 (Summer 1991): 263–304.

———. "The Commercial Republic and the Pluralist Critique of Marxism: An Analysis of Martin Diamond's Interpretation of *Federalist 10.*" *Polity* 25 (Summer 1993): 497–528.

———. "Ancients, Moderns, and Americans: The Republicanism-Liberalism Debate Revisited." *History of Political Thought* 21 (Summer 2000): 261–307.

———. "Searching for the Soul of the American Amalgam: A Reply to Paul Carrese." *History of Political Thought* 22 (Spring 2001): 166–173.

———. "Veneration and Vigilance: James Madison and Public Opinion, 1785–1800." *Review of Politics* 67 (Winter 2005): 5–35.

———. "The American Founding and the Culture Wars (In Celebration of Constitution Day)." An Alpheus T. Mason Lecture in Constitutional Law and Political Thought: The Quest for Freedom. James Madison Program in American Ideals and Institutions, Audio recording of presentation on September 18, 2007, http://web.princeton.edu/sites/jmadison/calendar/archives/0708.html (accessed January 6, 2010).

———. "Beyond Ancients, Moderns, Heroes, and Villains: Thinking about the Founding with Richard Zinman." *Interpretation: A Journal of Political Philosophy* 36 (Summer 2009): 273–303.

———. *Interpreting the Founding: Guide to the Enduring Debates over the Origins and Foundations of the American Republic,* 2nd ed. Lawrence: University Press of Kansas, 2010.

Goldstone, Lawrence. *Dark Bargain: Slavery, Profits, and the Struggle for the Constitution.* New York: Walker, 2005.

Goldwin, Robert A. *Why Blacks, Women, and Jews Are Not Mentioned in the Constitution, and Other Unorthodox Views.* Washington, D.C.: American Enterprise Press, 1990.

Goldwin, Robert A., and William A. Schambra, eds. *How Democratic Is the Constitution?* Washington, D.C.: American Enterprise Institute, 1980.

Gordon, Charles. "Who Can Be President of the United States: The Unresolved Enigma." *Maryland Law Review* 28 (1968): 1–32.

Gordon-Reed, Annette. *Thomas Jefferson and Sally Hemings: An American Controversy.* 1997. Reprint, Charlottesville: University Press of Virginia, 1999.

Green, Donald P., and Ian Shapiro. *Pathologies of Rational Choice Theory: A Critique of Applications in Political Science.* New Haven, Conn.: Yale University Press, 1994.

Greene, Jack P. *Peripheries and Center: Constitutional Development in the Extended Polities of the British Empire and the United States, 1607–1788.* Athens: University of Georgia Press, 1986.

———. *Negotiated Authorities: Essays in Colonial Political and Constitutional History.* Charlottesville: University Press of Virginia, 1994.

———. "The American Revolution." *American Historical Review* 105 (February 2000): 93–102.

Greenstone, J. David. "Political Culture and American Political Development: Liberty, Union, and Liberal Bipolarity." *Studies in American Political Development* 1 (1986): 4–49.

———. "Against Simplicity: The Cultural Dimension of the Constitution." *University of Chicago Law Review* 40 (Spring 1988): 428–449.

———. *The Lincoln Persuasion: Remaking American Liberalism.* Princeton, N.J.: Princeton University Press, 1993.

Guinier, Lani. *The Tyranny of the Majority: Fundamental Fairness in Representative Democracy.* New York: Free Press, 1994.

Gunnell, John. *Political Theory: Tradition and Interpretation*. Cambridge, Mass.: Winthrop, 1979.

———. "Method, Methodology, and the Search for Traditions in the History of Political Theory: A Reply to Pocock's Salute." *Annals of Scholarship* 1 (1980): 26–56.

Gutman, Amy. "Communitarian Critics of Liberalism." *Philosophy and Public Affairs* 14 (Summer 1985): 308–322.

Gwyn, William B. *The Meaning of the Separation of Powers: An Analysis of the Doctrine from Its Origins to the Adoption of the United States Constitution*. New Orleans: Tulane University, 1965.

Hall, Mark David. *The Political and Legal Philosophy of James Wilson, 1742–1798*. Columbia: University of Missouri Press, 1997.

Hall, Van Beck. *Politics without Parties: Massachusetts, 1780–1781*. Pittsburgh: University of Pittsburgh Press, 1972.

Hamburger, Phillip. *Separation of Church and State*. Cambridge, Mass.: Harvard University Press, 2002.

Hamilton, Alexander, James Madison, and John Jay. *The Federalist Papers*, edited by Clinton Rossiter. New York: Penguin Books, 1961.

———. *The Federalist Papers*, edited by Jacob E. Cooke. 1961. Reprint, Middletown, Conn.: Wesleyan University Press, 1989.

Hammond, Scott J., Kevin R. Hardwick, and Howard L. Lubert, eds. *Classics of American Political and Constitutional Thought*, 2 vols. Indianapolis: Hackett, 2007.

Hamowy, Ronald. "Jefferson and the Scottish Enlightenment: A Critique of Garry Wills's *Inventing America: Jefferson's Declaration of Independence*." *William and Mary Quarterly* 36 (October 1979): 503–523.

Hart, H. L. A. *Punishment and Responsibility: Essays in the Philosophy of Law*. New York: Oxford University Press, 1968.

Hartz, Louis. *The Liberal Tradition in America: An Interpretation of American Political Thought since the Revolution*. San Diego: Harcourt Brace Jovanovich, 1955.

Hendrickson, David. "The Renovation of American Foreign Policy." *Foreign Affairs* 71 (Spring 1992): 48–63.

———. *Peace Pact: The Lost World of the American Founding*. Lawrence: University Press of Kansas, 2003.

———. *Union, Nation, or Empire: The American Debate over International Relations, 1789–1941*. Lawrence: University Press of Kansas, 2009.

Hirshman, Albert. *The Passions and the Interests: Political Arguments for Capitalism before Its Triumph*. Princeton, N.J.: Princeton University Press, 1977.

Hoff, Joan. *Law, Gender, and Injustice: A Legal History of U.S. Women*. New York: New York University Press, 1991.

Hofstadter, Richard. *The American Political Tradition and the Men Who Made It*. 1948. Reprint, New York: Vintage Books, 1974.

———. *The Progressive Historians: Turner, Beard, Parrington*. New York: Alfred A. Knopf, 1968.

———. *The Idea of a Party System: The Rise of Legitimate Opposition in the United States, 1780–1840*. Berkeley: University of California Press, 1969.

Hoge, Patrick. "Berkeley School to Vote on Renaming Jefferson Elementary, President's

Slave Holdings Perturb Families, Teachers." *SF Gate,* March 22, 2005, http://www
.sfgate.com/cgi-bin/article.cgi?f =/c/a/2005/03/22/BAGIIBSTMA1.DTL (accessed
January 6, 2010).

Hollinger, David. "T. S. Kuhn's Theory of Science and Its Implications for History." *American Historical Review* 78 (April 1973): 370–393.

Holton, Woody. "'Divide et Impera': *Federalist 10* in a Wider Sphere." *William and Mary Quarterly* 62 (April 2005): 175–212.

Horowitz, Asher, and Richard Matthews. "Narcissism of the Minor Differences: What Is at Issue and What Is at Stake in the Civic Humanism Question." *Polity* 30 (Fall 1997): 1–27.

Horton, Carol. "Liberal Equality and the Civic Subject: Identity and Citizenship in Reconstruction America." In *The Liberal Tradition in American Politics: Reassessing the Legacy of American Liberalism,* edited by David Ericson and Louisa Bertch Green, 115–136. New York: Routledge, 1999.

———. *Race and the Making of American Liberalism.* Oxford: Oxford University Press, 2005.

Horwitz, Morton. "Republicanism and Liberalism in American Constitutional Thought." *William and Mary Law Review* 29 (Fall 1987): 57–74.

Houston, Alan Craig. *Algernon Sidney and the Republican Heritage in England and America.* Princeton, N.J.: Princeton University Press, 1991.

Howe, John R. "John Adam's Views of Slavery." *Journal of Negro History* 49 (July 1964): 201–206.

Hutchinson, William T., et al., eds. *The Papers of James Madison.* Vols. 1–10, Chicago: University of Chicago Press, 1962–1977. Vols. 11–17, Charlottesville: University Press of Virginia, 1977–1991,

Hutson, James H. "The Constitution: An Economic Document?" In *The Framing and Ratification of the Constitution,* edited by Leonard Levy and Dennis Mahoney, 259–270. New York: Macmillan, 1987.

Huyler, Jerome. *Locke in America: The Moral Philosophy of the Founding Era.* Lawrence: University Press of Kansas, 1995.

"In Berkeley School Vote, Jefferson Out (Sequoia In)." *Free Republic,* June 2, 2005, http://
www.freerepublic.com/focus/f-news/1415149/posts (accessed January 6, 2010).

Ireland, Owen S. *Religion, Ethnicity, and Politics: Ratifying the Constitution in Pennsylvania.* University Park: Pennsylvania State University Press, 1995.

Isaac, Jeffrey. "Republicanism vs. Liberalism?" *History of Political Thought* 9 (Summer 1988): 349–377.

Jackson, Jonathan. *Thoughts upon the Political Situation of the United States of America.* Worcester, Mass.: Printed by Isaiah Thomas, 1788.

Jaffa, Harry. *The Crisis of the House Divided: An Interpretation of the Issues in the Lincoln-Douglas Debates.* Chicago: University of Chicago Press, 1959, 1982.

———. *A New Birth of Freedom: Abraham Lincoln and the Coming of the Civil War.* Lanham, Md.: Rowman & Littlefield, 2000.

"Jefferson-Hemings Scholars Commission Report on the Jefferson-Hemings Matter." Thomas Jefferson Heritage Society, April 12, 2001, http://www.tjheritage.org/
scholars.html (accessed January 6, 2010).

Jefferson, Thomas. *The Works of Thomas Jefferson*, 12 vols., edited by Paul Leicester Ford. New York: G. P. Putnam's Sons, 1904–1905.

———. *Notes on the State of Virginia*, edited by Thomas P. Abernethy. New York: Harper and Row, 1964.

Jensen, Merrill. *The Articles of Confederation: An Interpretation of the Social-Constitutional History of the American Revolution, 1774–1781.* Madison: University of Wisconsin Press, 1940, 1948.

Jillson, Calvin. *Constitution Making: Conflict and Consensus in the Federal Convention of 1787.* New York: Agathon Press, 1988.

Jones, David H. *Moral Responsibility in the Holocaust: A Study in the Ethics of Character.* Lanham, Md.: Rowman & Littlefield, 1999.

Jordon, Winthrop. *White over Black: American Attitudes toward the Negro, 1550–1812.* Chapel Hill: University of North Carolina Press, 1968.

Kalman, Laura. *The Strange Career of Legal Liberalism.* New Haven, Conn.: Yale University Press, 1996.

Kaminski, John P., and Richard Leffler, eds. *Federalists and Antifederalists: The Debate over the Ratification of the Constitution.* 1989. Reprint, Lanham, Md.: Madison House, 1998.

Kammen, Michael. *A Machine that Would Go of Itself: The Constitution in American Culture.* New York: Alfred A. Knopf, 1986.

Katznelson, Ira. *City Trenches.* Chicago: University of Chicago Press, 1981.

Kennedy, Randall. "A Natural Aristocracy?" In *Constitutional Stupidities, Constitutional Tragedies,* edited by William N. Eskridge Jr. and Sanford Levinson, 54–56. New York: New York University Press, 1998.

Kennedy, Roger. *Mr. Jefferson's Lost Cause: Land, Farmers, Slavery, and the Louisiana Purchase.* New York: Oxford University Press, 2003.

Kenyon, Cecelia. "Men of Little Faith: The Anti-Federalists on the Nature of Representative Government." *William and Mary Quarterly* 12 (January 1955): 3–43.

———. "'An Economic Interpretation of the Constitution' after Fifty Years." *Centennial Review of Arts and Science* 7 (1963): 327–352.

Kerber, Linda. "The Republican Mother: Women and the Enlightenment—An American Perspective." *American Quarterly* 28 (Summer 1976): 187–205.

———. *Women of the Republic: Intellect and Ideology in Revolutionary America.* Chapel Hill: University of North Carolina Press, 1980.

———. "The Meanings of Citizenship." *Journal of American History* 84 (December 1997): 833–854.

Kernell, Samuel. "'The True Principles of Republican Government': Reassessing James Madison's Political Science." In *James Madison: The Theory and Practice of Republican Government,* 92–125. Stanford, Calif.: Stanford University Press, 2005.

Kersh, Rogan. "The Founding: Liberalism Redux." Review of *The Foundations of American Citizenship: Liberalism, the Constitution, and the Civic Virtue,* by Richard Sinopoli. *Review of Politics* 55 (Fall 1993): 729–731.

Kesler, Charles. "*Federalist* 10 and American Republicanism." In *Saving the Revolution: The Federalist Papers and the American Founding,* 13–39. New York: Free Press, 1987.

———, ed. *Saving the Revolution: The Federalist Papers and the American Founding.* New York: Free Press, 1987.

———. "The Founders and the Classics." In *The Revival of Constitutionalism,* edited by James W. Muller, 57–90. Lincoln: University of Nebraska Press, 1988.

Ketcham, Ralph. "Publius: Sustaining the Republican Principle." *William and Mary Quarterly* 54 (July 1987): 576–582.

———. *Framed for Posterity: The Enduring Philosophy of the Constitution.* Lawrence: University Press of Kansas, 1993.

———. Review of *If Men Were Angels: James Madison and the Heartless Empire of Reason,* by Richard K. Matthews. *William and Mary Quarterly* 52 (October 1995): 697–702.

Keyssar, Alexander. *The Right to Vote: The Contested History of Democracy in the United States.* New York: Basic Books, 2000.

Kirkpatrick, Jeane. "Martin Diamond and the American Idea of Democracy." *Publius* 8 (Summer 1978): 7–31.

Kirschke, James J. *Gouverneur Morris: Author, Statesman, and Man of the World.* New York: Thomas Dunne Books, 2005.

Klein, Milton, Richard Brown, and John Hench, eds. *The Republican Synthesis Revisited: Essays in Honor of George Athan Billias.* Worcester, Mass.: American Antiquarian Society, 1992.

Klinghoffer, Judith Apter, and Lois Elkins. "'The Petticoat Electors': Women's Suffrage in New Jersey, 1776–1807." *Journal of the Early Republic* 12 (Summer 1992): 159–193.

Kloppenberg, James T. "The Virtues of Liberalism: Christianity, Republicanism, and Ethics in Early American Political Discourse." *Journal of American History* 74 (June 1987): 9–33.

———. *The Virtues of Liberalism.* New York: Oxford University Press, 1998.

Koch, Adrienne, ed. *Notes of Debates in the Federal Convention of 1787 Reported by James Madison.* New York: W. W. Norton, 1987.

Kolchin, Peter. *American Slavery, 1619–1877.* 1993. Reprint, New York: Hill and Wang, 2003.

Kramnick, Isaac. "Republicanism Revisionism Revisited." *American Historical Review* 87 (June 1982): 629–664.

———. "Editor's Introduction." In *The Federalist Papers,* 11–81. London: Penguin Press, 1987.

———. "The 'Great National Discussion': The Discourse of Politics in 1787." *William and Mary Quarterly* 45 (January 1988): 3–32.

———. "Communications." *William and Mary Quarterly* 45 (October 1988): 818.

———. *Republicanism and Bourgeois Radicalism: Political Ideology in Late 18th Century England and America.* Ithaca, N.Y.: Cornell University Press, 1990.

Kristol, Irving. "The American Revolution as a Successful Revolution." In *The American Revolution: Three Views,* 20–52. New York: American Brands, 1975.

Kristol, William. "The Problem of Separation of Powers: *Federalist* 47–51." In *Saving the Revolution: The Federalist Papers and the American Founding,* edited by Charles Kesler, 100–130. New York: Free Press, 1987.

Kruman, Marc W. *Between Authority and Liberty: State Constitution Making in Revolutionary America.* Chapel Hill: University of North Carolina Press, 1997.

Kuhn, Thomas. *The Structure of Scientific Revolutions,* 2nd ed. Chicago: University of Chicago Press, 1970.

Kurland, Phillip B., and Ralph Lerner, eds. *The Founders' Constitution*, 5 vols. Indianapolis: Liberty Fund Press, 1987.

Kyvig, David. *Explicit and Authentic Acts: Amending the U.S. Constitution, 1776–1995*. Lawrence: University Press of Kansas, 1996.

Laman, David, Joe Oppenheimer, and Piotr Swistak. "Formal Rational Choice Theory: A Cumulative Science of Politics." In *Political Science: The State of the Discipline II*, edited by Ada W. Finifter, 77–104. Washington, D.C.: American Political Science Association, 1993.

Latane, John H. Review of *An Economic Interpretation of the Constitution of the United States*, by Charles A. Beard. *American Political Science Review* 7 (November 1913): 697–700.

Lazare, Daniel. *The Frozen Republic: How the Constitution Is Paralyzing Democracy*. New York: Harcourt Brace, 1996.

Lee, Frances E., and Bruce I. Oppenheimer. *Sizing Up the Senate: The Unequal Consequences of Equal Representation*. Chicago: University of Chicago Press, 1999.

Lerner, Max. "Economic Interpretation of the Constitution." In *Books that Changed Our Minds*. New York: Doubleday, Doran, 1939.

———. "The Political Theory of Charles A. Beard." *American Quarterly* 2 (Winter 1950): 303–332.

Lerner, Ralph. "Commerce and Character." In *The Thinking Revolutionary: Principle and Practice in the New Republic*, 195–221. Ithaca, N.Y.: Cornell University Press, 1979.

———. "The Constitution of the Thinking Revolutionary." In *Beyond Confederation: Origins of the Constitution and American National Identity*, edited by Richard Beeman, Stephen Botein, and Edward C. Carter II, 38–68. Chapel Hill: University of North Carolina Press, 1987.

———. "Facing Up to the Founding." In *To Form a More Perfect Union: The Critical Ideas of the Constitution*, edited by Herman Belz, Ronald Hoffman, and Peter J. Albert, 250–271. Charlottesville: University Press of Virginia, 1992.

———. *Revolutions Revisited: Two Faces of the Politics of Enlightenment*. Chapel Hill: University of North Carolina Press, 1994.

Leslie, Margaret. "In Defense of Anachronism." *Political Studies* 18 (1970): 433–447.

Lewis, Jan. "'Of Every Age Sex and Condition': Representation of Women in the Constitution." In *What Did the Constitution Mean to Early Americans*, edited by Edward Countryman, 115–140. New York: Bedford/St. Martin's Press, 1999.

———. "The Three-Fifths Clause and the Origins of Sectionalism." In *Congress and the Emergence of Sectionalism: From the Missouri Compromise to the Age of Jackson*, edited by Paul Finkelman and Donald R. Kennon, 19–46. Athens: Ohio State University Press, 2008.

Lewis, Jan Ellen, and Peter Onuf. *Sally Hemings and Thomas Jefferson: History, Memory, and Civic Culture*. Charlottesville: University Press of Virginia, 1999.

Libby, Orin Grant. *The Geographical Distribution of the Vote of the Thirteen States on the Federal Constitution*. Madison: University of Wisconsin, 1894.

———. Review of *An Economic Interpretation of the Constitution of the United States* by Charles A. Beard. *Mississippi Valley Historical Review* 1 (June 1914): 113–117.

———. Review of *Economic Origins of Jeffersonian Democracy*, by Charles A. Beard. *Mississippi Valley Historical Review* 3 (June 1916): 99–102.

Lienesch, Michael. *The New Order of the Ages: Time, the Constitution, and the Making of Modern American Political Thought.* Princeton, N.J.: Princeton University Press, 1988.

Lind, Michael. *The Next American Nation.* New York: Free Press, 1995.

Lipset, Seymour Martin. *The First New Nation: The United States in Historical and Comparative Perspective.* New York: Basic Books, 1963.

———. *American Exceptionalism: A Double-Edged Sword.* New York: W. W. Norton, 1996.

"The Little Known History of Slavery, Part Three," February 24, 2007, http://hammeringsparksfromtheanvil.blogspot.com/2007/02/little-known-history-of-slavery-part_24.html (accessed January 6, 2010).

Litwack, Leon. *North of Slavery: The Negro in the Free States, 1790–1860.* Chicago: University of Chicago Press, 1961.

Lovejoy, Arthur. "The Theory of Human Nature in the American Constitution and the Method of Counterpoise." In *Reflections on Human Nature,* 37–65. Baltimore: Johns Hopkins University Press, 1961.

Lucas, J. R. *Responsibility.* New York: Oxford University Press, 1993.

Lutz, Donald. "The Theory of Consent in the Early State Constitutions." *Publius* 9 (Spring 1979): 11–42.

———. *Popular Consent and Popular Control: Whig Political Theory in the Early State Constitutions.* Baton Rouge: Louisiana State University Press, 1980.

———. "The First State Constitutions." In *The Framing and Ratification of the Constitution,* edited by Leonard Levy and Dennis J. Mahoney, 69–81. New York: Macmillan, 1987.

———. "Political Participation in Eighteenth-Century America." *Albany Law Review* 53 (Winter 1989): 327–355.

Lutz, Donald, Philip Abbott, Barbara Allen, and Russell Hanson. "The Electoral College in Historical and Philosophical Perspective." In *Choosing a President: The Electoral College and Beyond,* edited by Paul D. Schumaker and Burdett A. Loomis, 31–52. New York: Chatman House, 2002.

Lynch, Jack, ed. *Samuel Johnson's Dictionary: Selections from the 1755 Work that Defined the English Language.* Delray Beach, Fla.: Levenger Press, 2002.

Lynd, Staughton. *Anti-Federalism in Dutchess County, New York: A Study of Democracy and Class Conflict in the Revolutionary Era.* Chicago: Loyola University Press, 1962.

———. *Class Conflict, Slavery, and the United States Constitution.* Indianapolis: Bobbs-Merrill, 1967.

Macedo, Stephen. *Liberal Virtues: Citizenship, Virtue, and Community in Liberal Constitutionalism.* Oxford: Clarendon Press, 1990.

Madsen, Deborah L. *American Exceptionalism.* Jackson: University Press of Mississippi, 1998.

Maier, Pauline. *American Scripture: Making the Declaration of Independence.* New York: Alfred A. Knopf, 1997.

Main, Jackson Turner. "Charles A. Beard and the Constitution: A Critical Review of Forrest McDonald's *We the People.*" *William and Mary Quarterly* 17 (January 1960): 86–110.

———. *The Social Structure of Revolutionary America.* Princeton, N.J.: Princeton University Press, 1965.

———. "Government by the People: The American Revolution and Democratization of the Legislatures." *William and Mary Quarterly* 17 (July 1966): 391–407.

———. *The Upper House in Revolutionary America, 1763–1788*. Madison: University of Wisconsin Press, 1967.

———. *Political Parties before the Constitution*. Chapel Hill: University of North Carolina Press, 1973.

———. *The Antifederalists: Critics of the Constitution, 1781–1788*. New York: W. W. Norton, 1974.

———. "An Agenda for Research on the Origins and Nature of the Constitution of 1787–1788." *William and Mary Quarterly* 44 (July 1987): 591–596.

Malone, Dumas. *Thomas Jefferson and His Time,* 6 vols. Boston: Little, Brown, 1948–1981.

Maltz, Earl M. "The Idea of the Proslavery Constitution." *Journal of the Early Republic* 17 (Spring 1997): 37–59.

———. *Dred Scott and the Politics of Slavery*. Lawrence: University Press of Kansas, 2007.

———. The Presidency, the Electoral College, and the Three-Fifths Clause. February 24, 2009, http://ssrn.com/abstract=1348676 (accessed January 6, 2010).

Mansbridge, Jane. *Beyond Self-Interest*. Chicago: University of Chicago Press, 1990.

Marshall, Thurgood. "The Constitution: A Living Document." *Howard Law Journal* 30 (1987): 915–920.

———. "A Bicentennial View from the Supreme Court." In *The United States Constitution: 200 Years of Anti-Federalist, Abolitionist, Feminist, Muckraking, Progressive, and Especially Socialist Criticism,* edited by Bertell Ollman and Jonathan Birnbaum, 300–305. New York: New York University Press, 1990.

Marston, Jerrilyn Greene. *King and Congress: The Transfer of Political Legitimacy, 1774–1776*. Princeton, N.J.: Princeton University Press, 1987.

Martin, Robert W. T. *The Free and Open Press: The Founding of American Democratic Press Liberty, 1640–1800*. New York: New York University Press, 2001.

Martis, Kenneth C. *The Historical Atlas of United States Congressional Districts, 1789–1983*. New York: Free Press, 1982.

Massachusetts Constitution of 1780. National Humanities Institute. http://www.nhinet .org/ccs/docs/ma-1780.htm (accessed January 6, 2010).

Matson, Cathy D., and Peter S. Onuf. *A Union of Interests: Political and Economic Thought in Revolutionary America*. Lawrence: University Press of Kansas, 1990.

Matthews, Anne. "Leading Men: Authorities on the Revolutionary Era Say How the Founding Fathers Became Cultural Heroes." *American Scholar* 74 (Spring 2005): 126–130.

Matthews, Richard. *If Men Were Angels: James Madison and the Heartless Empire of Reason*. Lawrence: University Press of Kansas, 1995.

McCloskey, Robert G., ed. *The Works of James Wilson,* 2 vols. Cambridge, Mass.: Belknap Press of Harvard University Press, 1967.

McCorkle, Pope. "The Historian as Intellectual: Charles Beard and the Constitution Reconsidered." *American Journal of Legal History* 28 (1984): 314–363.

McCoy, Drew. *The Elusive Republic: Political Economy in Jeffersonian America*. Chapel Hill: University of North Carolina Press, 1980.

———. *The Last of the Fathers: James Madison and the Republican Legacy*. Cambridge: Cambridge University Press, 1989.

———. "Introduction." In *The Republican Synthesis Revisited: Essays in Honor of George*

Athan Billias, edited by Milton M. Klein, Richard D. Brown, and John B. Hench, 11–17. Worcester, Mass.: American Antiquarian Society, 1992.

McDonald, Forrest. *We the People: The Economic Origins of the Constitution.* Chicago: University of Chicago Press, 1958.

———. "Charles A. Beard and the Constitution: Forrest McDonald's Rebuttal." *William and Mary Quarterly* 17 (January 1960): 102–110.

———. "The Anti-Federalists." *Wisconsin Magazine of History* 46 (Spring 1963): 206–214.

———. *E Pluribus Unum: The Formation of the American Republic, 1776–1790.* Boston: Houghton Mifflin, 1965.

———. *Novus Ordo Seclorum: The Intellectual Origins of the Constitution.* Lawrence: University Press of Kansas, 1985.

———. "A New Introduction." In *An Economic Interpretation of the Constitution of the United States,* by Charles A. Beard, vii–xl. New York: Free Press, 1986.

———. "The Intellectual World of the Founding Fathers." In *Requiem: Variations on Eighteenth-Century Themes,* edited by Forrest McDonald and Ellen Shapiro McDonald, 1–22. Lawrence: University Press of Kansas, 1988.

McGiffert, Michael, ed. "Forum: How Revolutionary Was the Revolution? A Discussion of Gordon S. Wood's *The Radicalism of the American Revolution.*" *William and Mary Quarterly* 51 (October 1994): 677–716.

McGuire, Robert. "Constitution Making: A Rational Choice Model of the Federal Convention of 1787." *American Journal of Political Science* 32 (1988): 483–522.

———. "Economic Interests and the Adoption of the United States Constitution." In *EH.Net Encyclopedia,* edited by Robert Whaples, http://www.eh.net/encyclopedia/article/mcguire.constitution.us.economic.interests (accessed August 15, 2001).

———. *To Form a More Perfect Union: A New Economic Interpretation of the United States Constitution.* New York: Oxford University Press, 2003.

McGuire, Robert, and Robert Ohsfeldt. "Economic Interests and the American Constitution: A Quantitative Rehabilitation of Charles A. Beard." *Journal of Economic History* 44 (1984): 509–519.

———. "An Economic Model of Voting Behavior over Specific Issues at the Constitutional Convention of 1787." *Journal of Economic History* 46 (1986): 79–111.

———. "Public Choice Analysis and the Ratification of the Constitution." In *The Federalist Papers and the New Institutionalism,* edited by Bernard Grofman and Donald Wittman, 175–204. New York: Agathon Press, 1989.

———. "Self-Interest, Agency Theory, and Political Voting Behavior: The Ratification of the United States Constitution." *American Economic Review* 79 (1989): 219–234.

McNamara, Peter. "Unionist Paradigm." Review of *Peace Pact: The Lost World of the American Founding,* by David Hendrickson. *Review of Politics* 66 (Spring 2004): 313–315.

Megill, Allan. *Historical Knowledge, Historical Error: A Contemporary Guide to Practice.* Chicago: University of Chicago Press, 2007.

Mehta, Uday. "Liberal Strategies of Exclusion." *Politics and Society* 18 (December 1990): 427–454.

Merkel, William G. "Jefferson's Failed Anti-Slavery Proviso of 1784 and the Nascence of Free Soil Constitutionalism." http://works.bepress.com/cgi/viewcontent.cgi?article=1000&context=william_merkel (accessed May 27, 2010).

Meyers, Marvin. "The Least Imperfect Government: On Martin Diamond's 'Ethics and Politics.'" *Interpretation: A Journal of Political Philosophy* 8 (May 1980): 5–15.

Michael, Matthew D. "The Presidential Age Requirement and Public Policy." In *Constitutional Stupidities, Constitutional Tragedies,* edited by William N. Eskridge Jr. and Sanford Levinson, 67–70. New York: New York University Press, 1998.

Miller, Eugene. "What Publius Says about Interest." *Political Science Reviewer* 19 (Spring 1990): 11–48.

Miller, John Chester. *The Wolf by the Ears: Thomas Jefferson and Slavery.* Charlottesville: University Press of Virginia, 1991.

Miller, Joshua. "The Ghostly Body Politic: *The Federalist Papers* and Popular Sovereignty." *Political Theory* 16 (February 1988): 99–119.

Miller, Perry. *The New England Mind: The Seventeenth Century.* New York: Macmillan, 1939.

———. *Errand into the Wilderness.* Cambridge, Mass.: Belknap Press of Harvard University Press, 1956.

Miller, William Lee. *Arguing about Slavery: The Great Battle in the United States Congress.* New York: Alfred A. Knopf, 1996.

Monroe, Kristen Renwick. "The Theory of Rational Action: What Is It? How Useful Is It for Political Science?" In *Political Science: Looking to the Future,* 1:77–98. Evanston, Ill.: Northwestern University Press, 1991.

Montesquieu, Baron Charles Secondat. *On the Spirit of the Laws (1748),* edited and translated by Anne M. Cohler, Basia Carolyn Miller, and Harold Samuel Stone. Cambridge: Cambridge University Press, 1989.

Moran, Gabriel. *A Grammar of Responsibility.* New York: Crossroad, 1996.

Morgan, Edmund. *Inventing the People: The Rise of Popular Sovereignty in England and America.* New York: W. W. Norton, 1988.

———. *Benjamin Franklin.* New Haven, Conn.: Yale University Press, 2002.

Morgan, Edmund S., and Helen M. Morgan. *The Stamp Act Crisis: Prologue to Revolution.* Chapel Hill: University of North Carolina Press, 1953.

Morgan, Kenneth. "George Washington and the Problem of Slavery." *Journal of American Studies* 34 (2000): 279–301.

Morone, James A. "The Struggle for American Culture." *PS: Political Science and Politics* 29 (September 1996): 425–430.

Murrin, John. "The Great Inversion, or Court versus Country: A Comparison of the Revolutionary Settlements in England (1688–1721) and America (1776–1816)." In *Three British Revolutions: 1641, 1688, 1776,* edited by J. G. A. Pocock, 368–453. Princeton, N.J.: Princeton University Press, 1980.

———. "Fundamental Values, the Founding Fathers, and the Constitution." In *To Form a More Perfect Union: The Critical Ideas of the Constitution,* edited by Herman Belz, Ronald Hoffman, and Peter J. Albert, 11–25. Charlottesville: University Press of Virginia, 1992.

Nash, Gary B. *The Unknown American Revolution: The Unruly Birth of Democracy and the Struggle to Create America.* New York: Viking, 2005.

Nedelsky, Jennifer. *Private Property and the Limits of American Constitutionalism: The Madisonian Framework and Its Legacy.* Chicago: University of Chicago Press, 1990.

———. "The Protection of Property in the Origins and Development of the American

Constitution." In *To Form a More Perfect Union: The Critical Ideas of the Constitution,* edited by Herman Belz, Ronald Hoffman, and Peter J. Albert, 38–72. Charlottesville: University Press of Virginia, 1992.

Nelson, John R. *Liberty and Property: Political Economy and Policymaking in the New Nation, 1789–1812.* Baltimore: Johns Hopkins University Press, 1987.

Nevins, Allan. *The American States during and after the Revolution, 1775–1789.* New York: Macmillan, 1924.

Nicomachean Ethics. Translated by Martin Ostwald. Indianapolis: Bobbs-Merrill, 1962.

Nore, Ellen. *Charles A. Beard: An Intellectual Biography.* Carbondale: Southern Illinois University Press, 1983.

O'Brien, Conor Cruise. *The Long Affair: Thomas Jefferson and the French Revolution, 1785–1800.* Chicago: University of Chicago Press, 1996.

———. "Thomas Jefferson: Radical and Racist." *Atlantic Monthly* 278 (October 1996): 53–74.

Ohline, Howard A. "Republicanism and Slavery: Origins of the Three-fifths Clause in the United States Constitution." *William and Mary Quarterly* 28 (October 1971): 563–584.

Ollman, Bertell, and Jonathan Birnbaum, eds. *The United States Constitution: 200 Years of Anti-Federalist, Abolitionist, Feminist, Muckraking, Progressive, and Especially Socialist Criticism.* New York: New York University Press, 1990.

Onuf, Peter. "The First Federal Constitution: The Articles of Confederation." In *The Framing and Ratification of the Constitution,* edited by Leonard Levy and Dennis J. Mahoney, 82–97. New York: Macmillan, 1987.

———. "Reflections on the Founding: Constitutional Historiography in Bicentennial Perspective." *William and Mary Quarterly* 46 (April 1989): 341–375.

———. "State Politics and Republican Virtue: Religion, Education, and Morality in Early American Federalism." In *Toward a Usable Past: Liberty under State Constitutions,* edited by Paul Finkelman and Stephen E. Gottlieb, 91–116. Athens: University of Georgia Press, 1991.

———. "The Scholars' Jefferson." *William and Mary Quarterly* 50 (October 1993): 671–699.

———. "The Origins and Early Development of State Legislatures." In *Encyclopedia of the American Legislative System: Studies of the Principal Structures, Processes, and Policies of Congress and the State Legislatures since the Colonial Era,* 3 vols., edited by Joel H. Silbey, 1:175–194. New York: Charles Scribner's Sons, 1994.

———. *Jefferson's Empire: The Language of American Nationhood.* Charlottesville: University Press of Virginia, 2000.

———. Review of Anthony F. C. Wallace, *Jefferson and the Indians: The Tragic Fate of the First Americans.* H-Law, H-Net Reviews. May 2000, http://www.h-net.org/reviews/showrev.php?id=4129 (accessed January 6, 2010).

———. *The Mind of Thomas Jefferson.* Charlottesville: University Press of Virginia, 2007.

———. "Thomas Jefferson and American Democracy." In *Seeing Jefferson Anew: In His Time and Ours,* edited by John B. Boles and Randal L. Hall. Charlottesville: University Press of Virginia, forthcoming.

Orren, Karen. "Structure, Sequence, and Subordination in American Political Culture: What's Traditions Got to Do with It?" *Journal of Policy History* 8 (1996): 470–478.

Palmer, Robert R. "Notes on the Use of the Word 'Democracy,' 1789–1799." *Political Science Quarterly* 68 (June 1953): 203–226.

———. *The Age of the Democratic Revolution: A Political History of Europe and America, 1760–1800,* 2 vols. Princeton, N.J.: Princeton University Press, 1959, 1964.

Pangle, Thomas. *The Spirit of Modern Republicanism: The Moral Vision of the American Founders and the Philosophy of Locke.* Chicago: University of Chicago Press, 1988.

———. *The Ennobling of Democracy: The Challenge of the Postmodern Era.* Baltimore: Johns Hopkins University Press, 1992.

The Papers of Benjamin Franklin. Sponsored by the American Philosophical Society and Yale University. Digital Edition by The Packard Humanities Institute, http://franklinpapers.org/franklin/framedVolumes.jsp (accessed January 6, 2010).

Parekh, Bhikhu, and R. N. Berki. "The History of Political Ideas: A Critique of Quentin Skinner's Methodology." *Journal of the History of Ideas* 34 (1973): 163–184.

Parenti, Michael. "The Constitution as an Elitist Document." In *How Democratic Is the Constitution?* edited by Robert A. Goldwin and William A. Schambra, 39–58. Washington, D.C.: American Enterprise Institute, 1980.

Pasley, Jeffrey L. "The Cheese and the Words: Popular Political Culture and Participatory Democracy in the Early American Republic." In *Beyond the Founders: New Approaches to the Political History of the Early American Republic,* edited by David Waldstreicher, Jeffrey L. Pasley, and Andrew W. Robertson, 31–56. Chapel Hill: University of North Carolina Press, 2004.

Pateman, Carole. *The Sexual Contract.* Stanford, Calif.: Stanford University Press, 1988.

———. "Paul Finkelman/Historian," http://www.pbs.org/jefferson/archives/interviews/Finkelman.htm (accessed January 6, 2010).

Peng, Cindy. "School Mulls Moral Dilemma in Deciding Whether to Change Name." *Daily Californian,* May 5, 2005, http://www.dailycal.org/sharticle.php?id=18617 (accessed January 6, 2010).

———. "Community Votes to Drop 'Jefferson,' Rename School." *Daily Californian,* June 2, 2005, http://www.dailycal.org/article/18791/community_votes_to_drop_jefferson_rename_school (accessed January 6, 2010).

Peterson, Merrill. *The Jefferson Image in the American Mind.* New York: Oxford University Press, 1960.

———. *Thomas Jefferson and the New Nation: A Biography.* New York: Oxford University Press, 1970.

———, ed. *Thomas Jefferson: Writings: Autobiography/Notes on the State of Virginia/Public and Private Papers/Addresses/Letters.* New York: Literary Classics of the United States, 1984.

Peterson, Merrill, et al., eds. *The Documentary History of the Ratification of the Constitution.* 23 vols. Madison: State Historical Society of Wisconsin, 1976–.

Phillips, Wendell. *The Constitution A Pro-Slavery Compact: Selections from "The Madison Papers," &c.* 1844. Reprint, New York: Negro Universities Press, 1969.

Pocock, J. G. A. "The History of Political Thought: A Methodological Enquiry." In *Philosophy, Politics, and Society,* edited by Peter Laslett and W. G. Runciman, 183–202. Oxford: Basil Blackwell, 1962.

———. "Languages and Their Implications: The Transformation of the Study of Political Thought." In *Politics, Language, and Time: Essays on Political Thought and History*, 3–41. New York: Atheneum, 1971.

———. "Virtue and Commerce in the Eighteenth Century." *Journal of Interdisciplinary History* 3 (Summer 1972): 119–134.

———. *The Machiavellian Moment: Florentine Political Thought and the Atlantic Republican Tradition*. Princeton, N.J.: Princeton University Press, 1975.

———. "Intention, Tradition, and Methods: Some Sounds on a Fog-horn." *Annals of Scholarship* 1 (1980): 57–62.

———. "Political Theory, History, and Myth: A Salute to John Gunnell." *Annals of Scholarship* 1 (1980): 3–25.

———. "*The Machiavellian Moment* Revisited: A Study in History and Ideology." *Journal of Modern History* 53 (March 1981): 49–72.

———. "Virtues, Rights, and Manners: A Model for Historians of Political Thought." *Political Theory* 9 (July 1981): 353–368.

———. "Introduction: The State of the Art." In *Virtue, Commerce, and History: Essays on Political Thought and History, Chiefly in the Eighteenth Century*, 1–34. Cambridge: Cambridge University Press, 1985.

———. "Between Gog and Magog: The Republican Thesis and the *Ideologia Americana*." *Journal of the History of Ideas* 48 (April–June 1987): 325–346.

———. "The Concept of a Language and the *Metier d' historien*: Some Considerations on Practice." In *The Languages of Political Theory in Early-Modern Europe*, edited by Anthony Pagden, 19–38. Cambridge: Cambridge University Press, 1987.

———. "Communications." *William and Mary Quarterly* 45 (October 1988): 817.

———. "States, Republics, and Empires: The American Founding in Early Modern Perspective." In *Conceptual Change and the Constitution*, edited by Terence Ball and J. G. A. Pocock, 55–77. Lawrence: University Press of Kansas, 1988.

———. "Empire, State and Confederation: The War of American Independence as a Crisis in Multiple Monarchy." In *A Union for Empire: Political Thought and the Union of 1707*, edited by John Robertson, 318–348. Cambridge: Cambridge University Press, 1995.

———. "Political Thought in the English–Speaking Atlantic. I. The Imperial Crisis." In *The Varieties of British Political Thought, 1500–1800*, edited by J. G. A. Pocock, 246–282. Cambridge: Cambridge University Press, 1995.

———. "Machiavellian Moments." *New York Review of Books*, October 19, 2000, 68.

Pole, J. R. "Historians and the Problem of Early American Democracy." *American Historical Review* 67 (April 1962): 626–646.

Polybius. *The Histories of Polybius*. Translated from the text of F. Hultsch by Evelyn S. Shuckburgh. Bloomington: Indiana University Press, 1962.

Pool, William C. "An Economic Interpretation of the Ratification of the Federal Constitution in North Carolina." *North Carolina Historical Review* 27 (April, July, October 1950): 119–141, 289–313, 437–461.

Pryor, Jill A. "The Natural-Born Citizen Clause and Presidential Eligibility: An Approach for Resolving Two Hundred Years of Uncertainty." *Yale Law Journal* 97 (1998): 881–899.

Rahe, Paul. *Republics: Ancient and Modern: Classical Republicanism and the American Revolution*. Chapel Hill: University of North Carolina Press, 1992.

Rakove, Jack. *The Beginnings of National Politics: An Interpretive History of the Continental Congress*. New York: Alfred A. Knopf, 1979.

———. "The Structure of Politics at the Accession of George Washington." In *Beyond Confederation: Origins of the Constitution and American National Identity*, edited by Richard Beeman, Stephen Botein, and Edward C. Carter II, 261–294. Chapel Hill: University of North Carolina Press, 1987.

———. "The Liberal Prince on the Democratic Seesaw." *Reviews in American History* 23 (1995): 582–587.

———. *Original Meanings: Politics and Ideas in the Making of the Constitution*. New York: Alfred A. Knopf, 1996.

Read, James. *Power versus Liberty: Madison, Hamilton, Wilson, and Jefferson*. Charlottesville: University Press of Virginia, 2000.

"Re-assessing Civic Symbols," Online News Hour, November 25, 1997, http://www.pbs.org/newshour/bb/race_relations/july-dec97/schools_11-25.html (accessed January 6, 2010).

Reid, John Phillip. *Constitutional History of the American Revolution*, abridged ed. Madison: University of Wisconsin Press, 1995.

"Report of the Research Committee on Thomas Jefferson and Sally Hemings." Thomas Jefferson's Monticello, January 2000, http://www.monticello.org/plantation/hemingscontro/hemings_report.html (accessed January 6, 2010).

Richards, Leonard. *The Slave Power: The Free North and Southern Domination, 1780–1800*. Baton Rouge: Louisiana State University Press, 2000.

Riker, William. "The Lessons of 1787." *Public Choice* 55 (1987): 9–21.

Roberts, Andrew. *What Might Have Been: Leading Historians on Twelve "What Ifs" of History*. London: Weidenfeld & Nicolson, 2004.

Robinson, Donald. *Slavery in the Structure of American Politics, 1765–1820*. New York: W. W. Norton, 1979.

Roche, John P. "The Founding Fathers: A Reform Caucus in Action." *American Political Science Review* 55 (December 1961): 799–816.

Rodgers, Daniel. "Republicanism: The Career of a Concept." *Journal of American History* 79 (June 1992): 11–38.

Rosenfeld, Richard N. "What Democracy? The Case for Abolishing the United States Senate." *Harpers Magazine*, May 2004, 35–44.

Rossiter, Clinton. *1787: The Grand Convention*. New York: Macmillan, 1966.

Rousseau, Jean-Jacques. *On the Social Contract with Geneva Manuscript and Political Economy*, edited by Roger D. Masters. New York: St. Martin's Press, 1978.

Sartori, Giovanni. *The Theory of Democracy Revisited*. Chatham, N.J.: Chatham House, 1987.

Schlossberger, Eugene. *Moral Responsibility and Persons*. Philadelphia: Temple University Press, 1992.

Schochet, Gordon. "Quentin Skinner's Method." *Political Theory* 2 (August 1974): 261–276.

Schultz, John A., and Douglass Adair, eds. *The Spur of Fame: Dialogues of John Adams and Benjamin Rush, 1805–1813*. San Marino, Calif.: Huntington Library University Press, 1966.

Schuyler, Robert Livingston. "Forrest McDonald's Critique of Beard's Thesis." *Journal of Southern History* 27 (1961): 73–80.

Scott, Jack, ed. *An Annotated Edition of Lectures on Moral Philosophy by John Witherspoon.* Newark: University of Delaware Press, 1982.

Shain, Barry. "Multiple Citizenships." Review of *Civic Ideals: Conflicting Visions of Citizenship in U.S. History* by Rogers Smith. *Review of Politics* 61 (Spring 1999): 350–354.

Shalhope, Robert. "Toward a Republican Synthesis: The Emergence of an Understanding of Republicanism in American Historiography." *William and Mary Quarterly* 29 (1972): 49–80.

———. "Republicanism and Early American Historiography." *William and Mary Quarterly* 39 (1982): 334–356.

———. *The Roots of Democracy: American Thought and Culture, 1760–1800.* Boston: Twayne, 1990.

Sheehan, Colleen. "Madison's Party Press Essays." *Interpretation: A Journal of Political Philosophy* 17 (Spring 1990): 355–377.

———. "The Politics of Public Opinion: James Madison's 'Notes on Government.'" *William and Mary Quarterly* 44 (October 1992): 609–627.

———. "Madison and the French Enlightenment: The Authority of Public Opinion." *William and Mary Quarterly* 59 (2002): 925–956.

———. "Madison v. Hamilton: The Battle over Republicanism and the Role of Public Opinion." *American Political Science Review* 98 (August 2004): 405–424.

———. "Public Opinion and the Formation of Civic Character in Madison's Republican Theory." *Review of Politics* 67 (Winter 2005): 37–48.

Sheldon, Garrett Ward. *The Political Philosophy of Thomas Jefferson.* Baltimore: Johns Hopkins University Press, 1991.

———. *The Political Philosophy of James Madison.* Baltimore: Johns Hopkins University Press, 2001.

Sherry, Suzanna. "Our Unconstitutional Senate." In *Constitutional Stupidities: Constitutional Tragedies,* edited by William N. Eskridge Jr. and Sanford Levinson, 95–97. New York: New York University Press, 1998.

Siemers, David. *Ratifying the Republic: Antifederalists and Federalists in Constitutional Time.* Stanford, Calif.: Stanford University Press, 2002.

———. *The Antifederalists: Men of Great Faith and Forbearance.* Lanham, Md.: Rowman & Littlefield, 2003.

Simpson, J. A., and E. S. C. Weiner, eds. *The Oxford English Dictionary.* Oxford: Clarendon Press, 1989.

Sinopoli, Richard. "Liberalism, Republicanism and the Constitution." *Polity* 19 (Spring 1984): 331–352.

———. *The Foundations of American Citizenship: Liberalism, the Constitution, and Civic Virtue.* New York: Oxford University Press, 1992.

Skinner, Quentin. "Conventions and the Understanding of Speech Acts." *Philosophical Quarterly* 20 (1970): 118–138.

———. "Motives, Intentions, and the Interpretation of Texts." *New Literary History* 3 (1972): 393–408.

———. "Some Problems in the Analysis of Political Thought and Action." *Political Theory* 2 (August 1974): 277–303.

———. "Hermeneutics and the Role of History." *New Literary History* 7 (1975–1976): 209–232.

———. *The Foundations of Modern Political Thought,* 2 vols. Cambridge: Cambridge University Press, 1978.

———. "Meaning and Understanding in the History of Ideas." In *Meaning and Context: Quentin Skinner and His Critics,* edited by James Tully, 29–67. Princeton, N.J.: Princeton University Press, 1988.

Slonim, Shlomo. "Beard's Historiography and the Constitutional Convention." *Perspectives in American History* 3 (1986): 173–206.

Smith, J. Allen. *The Spirit of American Government.* 1907. Reprint, Cambridge, Mass.: Harvard University Press, 1965.

Smith, Rogers. "The 'American Creed' and American Identity: The Limits of Liberal Citizenship in the United States." *Western Political Quarterly* 41 (1988): 225–251.

———. "'One United People': Second-Class Female Citizenship and the American Quest for Community." *Yale Journal of Law and Humanities* 1 (1989): 229–293.

———. "Beyond Tocqueville, Myrdal, and Hartz: The Multiple Traditions in America." *American Political Science Review* 87 (September 1993): 549–566.

———. "Unfinished Liberalism." *Social Research* 61 (Fall 1994): 631–670.

———. "Response to Jacqueline Stevens." *American Political Science Review* 89 (December 1995): 987–995.

———. "Response to Karen Orren." *Journal of Policy History* 8 (1996): 478–490.

———. *Civic Ideals: Conflicting Visions of Citizenship in U.S. History.* New Haven, Conn.: Yale University Press, 1997.

———. "Liberalism and Racism: The Problem of Analyzing Traditions." In *The Liberal Tradition in American Politics: Reassessing the Legacy of American Liberalism,* edited by David Ericson and Louisa Bertch Green, 9–27. New York: Routledge, 1999.

Stephenson, Carl, and Frederick George Marcham, eds. and trans. *Sources of English History: A Selection of Documents from A.D. 600 to the Present.* New York: Harper and Brothers, 1937.

Stevens, Jacqueline. "Beyond Tocqueville, Please!" *American Political Science Review* 89 (December 1995): 987–995.

Storing, Herbert. "The Constitutional Convention: Toward a More Perfect Union." In *American Political Thought: The Philosophic Dimension of American Statesmanship,* edited by Morton J. Frisch and Richard G. Stevens, 51–68. New York: Scribner, 1971.

———. "Slavery and the Moral Foundations of the American Republic." In *The Moral Foundations of the American Republic,* edited by Robert H. Horwitz, 313–332. Charlottesville: University Press of Virginia, 1979.

Stourzh, Gerald. *Alexander Hamilton and the Idea of Republican Government.* Stanford, Calif.: Stanford University Press, 1970.

Strout, Cushing. *The Pragmatic Revolt in American History: Carl Becker and Charles Beard.* New Haven, Conn.: Yale University Press, 1958.

Sunstein, Cass. "Interest Groups in American Public Law." *Stanford Law Review* 38 (November 1985): 29–87.

———. "Beyond the Republican Revival." *Yale Law Journal* 97 (July 1988): 1539–1590.

———. *The Partial Constitution.* Cambridge, Mass.: Harvard University Press, 1993.

Swindler, William F., ed. *Sources and Documents of United States Constitutions.* Dobbs Ferry, N.Y.: Oceana Publications, 1976.

Talley-Hughes, Marguerite. "Thomas Jefferson: A Man of His Time?" *Berkeley Daily Planet,* March 9, 2004, http://www.berkeleydailyplanet.com/issue/2004-03-09/article/18442 (accessed January 6, 2010).

Tarcov, Nathan. "A 'Non-Lockean' Locke and the Character of Liberalism." In *Liberalism Reconsidered,* edited by Douglas MacLean and Claudia Mills, 130–140. Totowa, N.J.: Rowman & Allanheld, 1983.

———. "Quentin Skinner's Method and Machiavelli's *Prince.*" In *Meaning and Context: Quentin Skinner and His Critics,* edited by James Tully, 194–203. Princeton, N.J.: Princeton University Press, 1988.

———. "On a Certain Critique of 'Straussian.'" *Review of Politics* 53 (Winter 1991): 3–18.

Tarlton, Charles D. "Historicity, Meaning, and Revisionism in the Study of Political Thought." *History and Theory* 12 (1973): 307–328.

Tarr, G. Allan. *Understanding State Constitutions.* Princeton, N.J.: Princeton University Press, 1998.

Taylor, Robert, et al., eds. *Papers of John Adams.* Cambridge, Mass.: Belknap Press of Harvard University Press, 1979.

"Thomas Jefferson and Sally Hemings: A Brief Account." Thomas Jefferson's Monticello, http://www.monticello.org/plantation/hemingscontro/hemings-jefferson_contro.html (accessed January 6, 2010).

Thomas, Robert. "The Virginia Convention of 1788: A Criticism of Charles Beard's *An Economic Interpretation of the Constitution.*" *Journal of Southern History* 19 (February 1953): 63–72.

Truman, David. *The Governmental Process: Political Interests and Public Opinion.* New York: Alfred A. Knopf, 1951.

Tucker, St. George. *View of the Constitution of the United States with Selected Writings.* Foreword by Clyde N. Wilson. Indianapolis: Liberty Fund, 1999.

Turner, Robert F. "The Truth about Jefferson." *Wall Street Journal,* July 3, 2001, A14.

Tushnet, Mark. *Red, White, and Blue: A Critical Analysis of Constitutional Law.* Cambridge, Mass.: Harvard University Press, 1988.

Vetterli, Richard, and Gary Bryner. *In Search of the Republic: Public Virtue and the Roots of American Government.* Lanham, Md.: Rowman & Littlefield, 1996.

Waldstreicher, David. *Slavery's Constitution: From Revolution to Ratification.* New York: Hill and Wang, 2009.

Wallace, Anthony F. C. *Jefferson and the Indians: The Tragic Fate of the First Americans.* Cambridge, Mass.: Belknap Press of Harvard University Press, 1999.

Wallenborn, White McKenzie (Ken). "Thomas Jefferson Foundation DNA Study Committee Minority Report." Thomas Jefferson's Monticello, April 12, 1999, http://www.monticello.org/plantation/hemingscontro/minority_report.html (accessed January 6, 2010).

Walling, Karl-Friedrich. *Republican Empire: Alexander Hamilton on War and Free Government.* Lawrence: University Press of Kansas, 1999.

Walters, Ronald. "Signs of the Times: Clifford Geertz and Historians." *Social Research* 47 (1980): 537–556.

Walzer, Michael. *Spheres of Justice: A Defense of Pluralism and Equality.* New York: Basic Books, 1983.

Webster, Noah. Review of *Thoughts upon the Political Situation of the United States of America, etc.,* by Jonathan Jackson. *American Magazine,* October 1788, 804–807.

West, Thomas. *Vindicating the Founders: Race, Sex, Class, and Justice in the Origins of America.* Lanham, Md.: Rowman & Littlefield, 1997.

White, Morton. *Social Thought in America: The Revolt against Formalism.* London: Oxford University Press, 1976.

Whittington, Keith. "The Separation of Powers at the Founding." In *The Separation of Powers: Documents and Commentary,* edited by Katy J. Harriger, 1–14. Washington, D.C.: Congressional Quarterly Press, 2003.

Wiecek, William M. "The Witch at the Christening: Slavery and the Constitution's Origins." In *The Framing and Ratification of the Constitution,* edited by Leonard W. Levy and Dennis J. Mahoney, 167–184. New York: Macmillan, 1987.

Wiencek, Henry. "Yale and the Price of Slavery." *New York Times,* August 18, 2001, http://www.nytimes.com/2001/08/18/opinion/yale-and-the-price-of-slavery.html (accessed January 6, 2010).

———. *An Imperfect God: George Washington, His Slaves, and the Creation of the American Republic.* New York: Farrar, Straus, and Giroux, 2003.

Wilentz, Sean. "The Details of Greatness: American Historians versus American Founders." *New Republic,* March 29, 2004, 27–35.

Will, George. *Statecraft as Soulcraft: What Government Does.* New York: Simon and Schuster, 1983.

———. *Restoration: Congress, Term Limits and the Recovery of Deliberative Democracy.* New York: Free Press, 1992.

Williamson, Chilton. *American Suffrage: From Property to Democracy, 1760–1860.* Princeton, N.J.: Princeton University Press, 1960.

Wills, Garry. *Inventing America: Jefferson's Declaration of Independence.* Garden City, N.Y.: Doubleday, 1978.

———. *Explaining America: The Federalist.* Garden City, N.Y.: Doubleday, 1981.

———. "James Wilson's New Meaning for Sovereignty." In *Conceptual Change and the Constitution,* edited by Terence Ball and J. G. A. Pocock, 99–106. Lawrence: University Press of Kansas, 1988.

———. "Undemocratic Vistas." *New York Review of Books,* November 19, 1992, 28–34, http://www.nybooks.com/articles/2756 (accessed January 6, 2010).

———. "Storm over Jefferson." *New York Review of Books* 47 (March 9, 2000), http://www.nybooks.com/articles/197 (accessed January 6, 2010).

———. *"Negro President": Jefferson and the Slave Power.* Boston: Houghton Mifflin, 2003.

Wilson, Douglas. "Thomas Jefferson and the Character Issue." *Atlantic Monthly* 270 (November 1992): 57–74.

———. "Counter Points: Jefferson Scholar Douglas L. Wilson Responds to Conor Cruise O'Brien." *Atlantic Online,* October 1996, http://www.theatlantic.com/past/docs/issues/96oct/obrien/response.htm (accessed March 9, 2010).

Wilson, James. *An Introductory Lecture to a Course of Law Lectures.* Philadelphia: Press of T. Dobson, 1791.

Wittgenstein, Ludwig. *Philosophical Investigations.* Oxford: Basil Blackwell, 1984.

Wolfley, Jeanette. "Jim Crow, Indian Style: The Disenfranchisement of Native Americans." *American Indian Law Review* 16 (1991): 167–202.

Wolin, Sheldon. *Politics and Vision: Continuity and Innovation in Western Political Thought.* Boston: Little, Brown, 1960.

Wood, Betty. "Betty Wood on Controlling Slaves after Dunmore's Proclamation." *Africans in America,* http://www.pbs.org/wgbh/aia/part2/2i1619.html (accessed January 6, 2010).

Wood, Gordon. "Rhetoric and Reality in the American Revolution." *William and Mary Quarterly* 23 (October 1966): 3–32.

———. *The Creation of the American Republic, 1776–1787.* 1969. Reprint, Chapel Hill: University of North Carolina Press, 1998.

———. "Intellectual History and the Social Sciences." In *New Directions in Intellectual History,* edited by Paul Conkin and John Higham, 27–41. Baltimore: Johns Hopkins University Press, 1979.

———. "Democracy and the Constitution." In *How Democratic Is the Constitution?* edited by Robert A. Goldwin and William A. Schambra, 1–17. Washington, D.C.: American Enterprise Institute, 1980.

———. "Heroics." Review of *Explaining America: "The Federalist,"* by Garry Wills. *New York Review of Books,* April 2, 1981, 16–18.

———. "The Disappointments of Jefferson." *New York Review of Books* 28 (August 13, 1981), http://www.nybooks.com/articles/6931 (accessed January 6, 2010).

———. "Conspiracy and the Paranoid Style: Causality and Deceit in the Eighteenth Century." *William and Mary Quarterly* 39 (July 1982): 401–441.

———. "Writing History: An Exchange." *New York Review of Books,* December 16, 1982, 58–59.

———. "Ideology and the Origins of Liberal America." *William and Mary Quarterly* 44 (July 1987): 628–634.

———. "Interests and Disinterestedness in the Making of the Constitution." In *Beyond Confederation: Origins of the Constitution and American National Identity,* edited by Richard Beeman, Stephen Botein, and Edward C. Carter II, 69–109. Chapel Hill: University of North Carolina Press, 1987.

———. "The Fundamentalists and the Constitution." *New York Review of Books,* February 18, 1988, 33–40.

———. "The Political Ideology of the Founders." In *Towards a More Perfect Union: Six Essays on the Constitution,* edited by Neil York, 7–27. Provo, Utah: Brigham Young University Press, 1988.

———. "The Significance of the Early Republic." *Journal of the Early Republic* 8 (1988): 1–20.

———. *The Radicalism of the American Revolution: How a Revolution Transformed a Monarchical Society into a Democratic One Unlike Any that Had Ever Existed.* New York: Vintage Books, 1991.

———. "Equality and Social Conflict in the American Revolution." *William and Mary Quarterly* 51 (October 1991): 703–716.

———. Afterword to *The Republican Synthesis Revisited: Essays in Honor of George Athan*

Billias, edited by Milton M. Klein, Richard D. Brown, and John B. Hench, 143–151. Worcester, Mass.: American Antiquarian Society, 1992.

———. "The Founding Realist." *New York Review of Books,* October 19, 1995, 58–61.

———. "An Exchange on James Madison." *New York Review of Books,* May 23, 1996, 53.

———. "The Greatest Generation." *New York Review of Politics,* March 29, 2001, 17–22.

———. "Rambunctious American Democracy," *New York Review of Books,* May 9, 2002, 20–21.

———. "Slaves in the Family." *New York Times Book Review,* December 14, 2003, 10.

———. "How Democratic Is the Constitution." *New York Review of Books,* February 23, 2006, http://www.nybooks.com/articles/18717 (accessed January 6, 2010).

———. *Revolutionary Characters: What Made the Founders Different.* New York: Penguin Press, 2006.

———. "Reading the Founders' Minds." *New York Review of Books* 54 (June 28, 2007), http://www.nybooks.com/articles/20342 (accessed January 6, 2010).

———. *The Purpose of the Past: Reflections on the Uses of History.* New York: Penguin Press, 2008.

"The Wordsmith from Nantucket," February 24, 2007, http://hammeringsparks fromtheanvil.blogspot.com/2007/02/little-known-history-of-slavery-part_24.html (accessed January 6, 2010).

Yarbrough, Jean. "Representation and Republicanism: Two Views." *Publius* 9 (1979): 77–98.

———. "Republicanism Reconsidered: Some Thoughts on the Foundation and Preservation of the American Republic." *Review of Politics* 41 (January 1979): 61–95.

———. "Race and the Moral Foundation of the American Republic: Another Look at the Declaration and the Notes on Virginia." *Journal of Politics* 53 (February 1991): 90–105.

———. "The Constitution and Character: The Missing Critical Principle?" In *To Form a More Perfect Union: The Critical Ideas of the Constitution,* edited by Herman Belz, Ronald Hoffman, and Peter J. Albert, 217–249. Charlottesville: University Press of Virginia, 1992.

Yarbrough, Jean, and Richard E. Morgan. "Why the Founding is Back In Fashion." *City Journal,* Autumn 1999, http://www.city-journal.org/html/9_4_urbanities-why_the_foundin.html (accessed January 6, 2010).

Young, Alfred. "Conservatives, the Constitution, and the 'Spirit of Accommodation.'" In *How Democratic Is the Constitution?* edited by Robert A. Goldwin and William A. Schambra, 117–147. Washington, D.C.: American Enterprise Institute, 1980.

Young, James P. *Reconsidering American Liberalism: The Troubled Odyssey of the Liberal Idea.* Boulder, Colo.: Westview Press, 1996.

Zimmerman, Michael J. *An Essay on Moral Responsibility.* Totowa, N.J.: Rowman & Littlefield, 1988.

———. "Responsibility." In *Encyclopedia of Ethics,* 3 vols., edited by Lawrence C. Becker III, 1486–1492. New York: Routledge, 2001.

Zuckerman, Michael. "Thermidor in America: The Aftermath of Independence in the South." *Prospectus* 8 (1983): 349–368.

———. "The Power of Blackness: Thomas Jefferson and the Revolution in St. Domingue." In *Almost Chosen People: Oblique Biographies in the American Grain,* 175–218. Berkeley: University of California Press, 1993.

Zuckert, Michael. "Appropriation and Understanding in the History of Political Philosophy: On Quentin Skinner's Method." *Interpretation* 13 (1985): 403–423.

———. "Federalism and the Founding: Toward a Reinterpretation of the Constitutional Convention." *Review of Politics* 48 (Spring 1986): 166–210.

———. "A System without a Precedent: Federalism in the American Constitution." In *The Framing and Ratification of the Constitution,* edited by Leonard W. Levy and Dennis J. Mahoney, 132–150. New York: Macmillan, 1987.

———. *Natural Rights and the New Republicanism.* Princeton, N.J.: Princeton University Press, 1994.

———. *The Natural Rights Republic: Studies in the Foundation of the American Political Tradition.* Notre Dame, Ind.: University of Notre Dame Press, 1996.

———. *Launching Liberalism: On Lockean Political Philosophy.* Lawrence: University Press of Kansas, 2003.

———. "Living Up to the Declaration of Independence: Multiple Versions of the Multiple Traditions Thesis." Paper presented at California State University, Chico, April 9, 2003.

———. "The Political Science of James Madison." In *History of American Political Thought,* edited by Bryan-Paul Frost and Jeffrey Sikkenga, 149–166. Lanham, Md.: Lexington Press, 2003.

———. "Legality and Legitimacy in *Dred Scott*: The Crisis of the Incomplete Constitution." *Chicago-Kent Law Review* 82 (2007): 291–328.

———. "What Really Happened in the *Dred Scott* Case." Unpublished paper.

Index

anti-Federalists
  and behavioralists, 100, 102
  debate between Federalists and, 35–38,
    46–48, 65–67, 132, 288n112
  on Constitution as undemocratic, 50,
    78–79
  and electoral districts, 70, 308n81
  economic interests of, 5, 45–46, 284n58,
    328n87
  ideology of, 289–290n7
  opposition ideology and, 153, 348n100
  as ratification delegates, 45–46, 47,
    288n111
  and small-state advantage, 371n76
  See also Federalists
Appleby, Joyce, 116, 325n58, 325n68,
    333–334n5, 337n33, 347n88
appropriation of ideas, 97
  and application, 132–133
  boundaries of, 268–270
  historicists and, 271–272, 321n1
  opposition to, 10, 96, 103, 116, 120–128,
    272, 274
Aristotle, 8, 106, 150, 234, 292n21
Armitage, David, 244–245, 246
Articles of Confederation, 1, 8
  ancient confederacies compared to,
    128, 163–164
  Constitution compared to, 78–80
  decentralized government under, 22,
    23, 70, 78–80, 88–89, 93, 251–252
  delegates to Confederation Congress
    under, 308n81
  office holding under, 287n95, 302n53,
    316n133
  Revolutionary War and, 251–252
  "short-leash republicanism embodied
    in," 77, 78–79, 309n91
  and slavery under Constitution, 175,
    178, 183, 214–215
ascriptive hierarchy. See inegalitarian as-
    criptive ideologies
Austin, J. L., 96, 107, 109

Bailyn, Bernard, 10, 104, 108, 109, 130,
    323n19
  on appropriation of ideas, 126
  on Articles of Confederation, 79
  on ideas and ideology, 116, 118

methodological writings, 96, 98, 112–113
  and moral responsibility, 190–193, 202,
    204, 221
  and opposition ideology, 97–100, 102,
    153, 249, 342–343n55
  See also linguistic contextualists
Baker v. Carr, 89
Ball, Terence, 116
Banneker, Benjamin, 361n195
Banning, Lance
  on American democratic development,
    267
  on classical republicanism, 344n62
  defense of Madison by, 294n23
  and Hamilton, 154
  on Jeffersonians, 159
  and multiple traditions approach, 13,
    136
  and republican hypothesis, 141–145,
    341n53, 344n62
  and unionist paradigm, 244–245
Barrow, Clyde, 26, 281n5
Barry, Norman, 55–56
Beard, Charles
  challenges to thesis of, 24–33, 281n6,
    282n18, 283n49
  and competing interpretations, 33–38
  and economic interpretation rebirth,
    38–42
  historiography and, 17–18, 19–20, 21,
    42–49, 95, 233
  influence of, 4, 19, 275n3
  Progressives and, 101, 118–119, 233,
    280–281n5
  and property qualifications, 58, 298n40
  and ratification process, 288n110
  thesis of, 4–6, 19, 21–24, 280–281n5
  See also economic interpretations of
    Constitution
Beers, William, 309n86
behavioralists, 97–102, 113, 116–117, 118,
    327n85, 327n86, 327n87
Belz, Herman, 298n46, 299–300n47
Benson, Lee, 24, 26, 27, 43, 46, 288n111
Berkeley school vote, 169–172
Berlin, Isaiah, 142–143
Berns, Walter, 293n22
Bevir, Mark, 321n1
Bill of Rights, 60, 142–143, 312n105

Constitution, federal (*continued*)

citizenship in, 62–63, 143, 262, 302n53, 304–305n62

class-based character of, 46, 258–259, 261–263

democratic interpretation of, 52, 79, 91–93, 293n22, 295n29

gender-specific language in, 301–302n52

multicultural critics of, 7, 14, 17, 51–53, 57, 61, 91, 173

naturalization clause in, 62–63, 352n19

neo-Lincolnian defense of, 182–185, 354n57

office holding qualifications in, 61–63, 64, 65, 68–69, 262, 302–303n56

and political equality, 7, 56–57, 72–74, 84–90

political systems compared to, 64–65

and race and gender, 52, 58–62, 90, 301–302n52

and slavery, 175–177, 183, 185, 188, 205, 227–228, 352n19, 354n57

and voting rights, 58, 60–61

See also Constitutional Convention; economic interpretations of Constitution; state constitutions; state ratifying conventions; three-fifths clause

Constitutional Convention

apportionment debate at, 83, 308–309n83, 317–318n148

and democracy, 50, 52, 60–63, 91–93

economic interests of delegates to, 29–33, 36–37, 39–40, 286n94, 287n100, 304n62

and freehold requirement, 296–297n37

and national identity, 274

and slavery, 174–177, 183, 205–206, 227–228, 279n23, 352n19, 354n57, 355n64

and suffrage, 296–297n37, 317–318n148

and three-fifths clause, 84–86, 89, 188

See also Constitution, federal

contextualists. *See* linguistic contextualists

Continental Army, 34, 363n215, 363–364n217

Continental Congress, 177, 214–215, 314n123, 316n133, 363–364n217

Cooper, William, 363n214

Cornell, Saul, 288n108

Corwin, Edward S., 30–31, 302n53

coverture, 146, 299n46, 338n42. *See also* common law

Crowl, Philip A., 24, 33

"currency" system of finance, 35–36, 49

Dahl, Robert, 257, 259–261, 264, 267–268, 293n22, 341–342n52

Dallymar, Fred, 320–321n1

Davis, David Brion, 277n20

debtors, 4, 21, 22, 26–27, 29, 33, 36–37, 62, 302–303n56. *See also* "realty" interests

Declaration of Independence

inegalitarian ascriptive ideologies in, 238

liberalism in, 139–140, 148–149

and national identity, 273

natural rights principle in, 139–140, 148–149, 188, 193, 242, 333–334n5, 345n67

reinterpretations of, 245, 246

and slavery, 14, 177, 208–210, 217, 277–278n20, 354n57, 356n97

Declaration of Rights, states,' 81

"deliberative" democracy, 71, 73–74, 77, 269, 294n23

democracy

American development of, 2–2, 16

accountability and responsiveness in, 69–83

Constitution's relationship to, 7, 45, 50–51, 56–57, 60–63, 72–74, 289n3, 293n22, 294n24

definitions of, 7–8, 54, 55–57, 292n21, 294–295n29

"deliberative," 71, 73–74, 77, 269, 294n23

electoral districts and, 68–69, 307n74

Federalists and, 69, 73–79, 82–83

normative concept of, 7–8, 55–56, 129, 292n21

and political equality, 7, 8, 52, 53, 56–57, 69, 84–85, 88, 89–90, 91, 92–93, 259–260, 320n164

and political participation, 8, 51–52, 56–57, 58–69, 84, 90–91, 94, 124–125, 259, 261, 264, 292n21, 300–301n47

pure, 75, 78, 151, 292

and responsiveness to public prefer-

ences, 8, 55, 56, 69, 73–74, 80, 84, 94,
292n21
standards of, 54–56, 88, 90, 91, 92–93
and ward republicanism, 77, 82–83, 144,
265
democratic interpretation of Constitution,
50–55, 60–63, 91–93, 290–291n12,
291–292n20
democratic nationalism, 8, 56, 77, 82–83, 93,
290–291n12, 317n140
deontological liberalism, 151–152, 157, 161,
344–345n65
Diamond, Martin, 7, 51, 54, 291–292n20,
293–294n23, 334n5, 347n94
Dickinson, John, 50, 296–297n37
Dienstag, Joshua Foa, 335n13
direct elections, 69, 79–80, 167
disenfranchisement
of free blacks, 61, 295–296n32
of Washington, D.C., residents, 300n49
of white men, 7, 23, 26–27, 50–51,
297n37, 297n39
of women, 60–61, 238, 266, 298–299n46
"domestic sphere" ideology, 146, 238, 239,
298–299n46, 338n42. *See also* women
Douglass, Frederick, 184, 210, 277–278
Dred Scott v. Sanford, 352n19
Dunn, Richard S., 217
Dworkin, Ronald, 122

economic determinism, 25
economic interests. *See* economic interpretations of Constitution; "personalty" interests; "realty" interests
economic interpretations of Constitution
ambiguity in, 20–21, 95
competing, 33–38
debates on, 4–6, 21–23, 27, 34, 95
and democracy, 6, 45
and ratification, 46–49, 95–96, 288n110,
288–289n115
and "rational choice" theory, 38–42
rebirth of, 38–42
See also Beard, Charles; "personalty" interests; "realty" interests
Edling, Max, 244, 249
elections
age requirements, 303–304n59
in Britain, 313n113

direct, 69, 79–80, 167
and electoral districts, 65–69, 69–70,
262–263, 307n74, 309n86, 320n164
equal representation and, 52–53,
317n141, 320n165
in France, 301n50
indirect, 69, 79, 82, 258, 263, 290n12
presidential, 52–53, 85, 86, 304n59,
310n94
staggered, 23, 51, 69, 70, 71, 316n133
under state constitutions, 313n120,
315n128, 315–316n131
See also Electoral College; state constitutions; suffrage; three-fifths
clause
Electoral College, 54–55, 71–72, 82, 175,
259–260, 261, 310n94
and presidential elections, 317n143
purpose of, 310n94
and slave-states, 85, 352n19
and small-state advantage, 52–53, 86–87,
291n14
electoral districts, 81–82, 84–90, 93,
308–309n83, 317–318n148, 320n164,
320n165
electoral districts, expanded, 55, 65–69, 82,
258, 262–266, 270, 294n27, 307n74,
308–309n83. *See also* Federalists
Ellis, Joseph, 279n23
Elshtain, Jean Bethke, 233, 344n60,
347n93
emancipation
historiography and, 187–188, 204,
214–218, 229, 356n90, 359n170,
363n217, 363n223
Jefferson and, 177–179, 189, 207, 209,
356n97, 364n223
Washington and, 179, 194–197, 209–210,
218, 227, 229–230
See also slavery
England. *See* Great Britain
equality. *See* political equality
exceptionalism. *See* American exceptionalism
extended republic, 23, 35, 51, 72, 77–83, 151,
254–255, 265

federal interpretation. *See* unionist paradigm

Jefferson, Thomas (*continued*)
    See also Jeffersonians
Jeffersonians, 143–144, 147–148, 154, 159,
    164–165, 265, 329n90, 337n33, 348n100
Jensen, Merrill, 79, 88
Jillson, Calvin, 20, 39–40, 43–44, 287n100
Jordan, Winthrop, 352n28
judicial review, 51, 74, 81, 258, 310n99
judiciary, 23, 78, 80–82, 156, 314n126,
    316n132, 316n136

Katznelson, Ira, 338n48
Kenyon, Cecelia, 27, 289–290n7
Kerber, Linda, 299n46
Ketcham, Ralph, 141, 142–143, 144–145, 154
Keyssar, Alexander, 266–267, 298n39
King, Martin Luther, Jr., 210
Kloppenberg, James, 135, 335n13, 336n24
Kolchin, Peter, 213
Kruman, Marc W., 306n69
Kuhn, Thomas, 96, 109–111
Kyvig, David E., 73

landowners. *See* "realty" interests
language paradigms, concept of, 96,
    109–110, 111–113, 117
Laurens, John and Henry, 179, 363–364n217
Lee, Frances E., 86, 261
Lenin, Vladimir, 124–126
Lerner, Max, 280n5
Lewis, Jan, 60, 273, 298n45
liberalism
    deontological, 151–152, 157, 161,
        344–345n65
    and illiberal ideologies, 129, 136,
        145–148, 165–167, 236–239, 338–339n48
    and neo-Lockean synthesis, 137–141, 163
    and opposition ideology, 152–154, 161
    republicanism debate with, 11–13, 53–54,
        134–136, 151–155, 160–162, 233, 250,
        337n33, 339–340n52, 342n54
    and republican synthesis, 10–11, 13,
        134–135, 141–147, 165–166, 236–239
    See also Lockean liberalism; multiple
        traditions approach
liberal-pluralist interpretation, 157–159
libertarianism, 153, 168, 182, 251, 343n55
Lienesch, Michael, 336–337n31
Lincoln, Abraham, 182–183, 193, 210, 356n97

linguistic contextualists
    approach of, 96–98, 100–104, 129, 130,
        243, 320–321n1, 330n103
    contributions of, 10, 112–115
    inadequacies of, 115–128
    See also Bailyn, Bernard; Pocock,
        J. G. A.; Skinner, Quentin; Wood,
        Gordon S.
Litwack, Leon, 295–296n32
Locke, John, 104, 117, 135–136, 140–141, 149,
    235, 326n83, 336n24, 338–n48. *See also*
    Lockean liberalism
Lockean liberalism, 10
    and Founders' political thought, 134,
        138–141, 163–165, 335n13, 341n53
    and illiberal ideologies, 238–239
    and Jefferson, 144
    natural rights philosophy of, 234–236
    and neo-Lockean interpretation, 11, 136,
        137–141, 340–341n52, 342n55
    See also Locke, John
"long-leash" republicanism, 82, 91, 309n91
Lutz, Donald, 63, 289n115, 297–298n39,
    300n50, 306n67, 316n135
Lynd, Staughton, 20, 35, 36–37, 38, 45–46,
    47, 280n5, 288n113

Macedo, Stephen, 336n24
Machiavelli, 107, 256, 324n46, 340n52
MacPherson, C. B., 340–341n52
Madison, James, 88, 180, 260, 307n79,
    311n99, 313n120
    and ancient confederacies, 128, 150,
        311n103
    at Constitutional Convention, 30, 45,
        63, 77, 296–297n37, 308n81, 317n148
    Constitution and, 58, 62–63, 82,
        312–312n112, 313–314n120
    and democracy, 265, 269–270,
        293–294n23
    and electoral districts, 263, 270,
        308–309n83, 310n94
    in Federalist Papers, 70, 75–76, 254,
        300n49, 311n103, 313–314n120
    and Founders' political thought, 130,
        144
    on freehold requirement, 296–297n37
    "long-leash" republicanism of, 309n91
    and majority factions, 269–270, 311n99

three-fifths clause as violation of, 7, 52, 53, 89–90

political inequality. *See* inegalitarian ascriptive ideologies

political participation

and Declaration of Independence, 345n67

and democracy, 94, 259, 261, 264, 292n21

in France, 300n50

inclusiveness in, 8, 51–52, 56–57, 58–69, 84, 90–91, 124–125, 300–301n47

liberalism and, 338–339n48

republicanism and, 147–148, 150–151, 165

state governments and, 342n54

political parties, 36–37, 57, 165, 167, 242, 265, 294–295n29

Pol Pot, 181

Polybius, 77–78

Pool, William C., 24, 33

popular sovereignty, 54–55, 75–76, 311n103, 312n105

"positive" liberty, 131, 139, 143, 347n94

possessive-individualist interpretation, 156, 157–158, 341–342n52

"presentism," 192, 196, 220–223, 272, 359n167

presidency

creation of, 203

elections for, 52–53, 85, 86, 310n94

qualifications for, 61–62, 63, 90, 302n53, 303–304n59, 304–305n62

terms of, 80, 314n120

and veto power, 74, 310n99

See also Electoral College

Progressives

and American Revolution, 98–99, 249

behavioralists and, 327n86

and Charles Beard, 5, 6, 19, 95, 101, 118–119, 233, 280–281n5

versus democratic interpretation, 50–55, 91, 290n12, 291–292n20

and linguistic contextualists, 95–97, 113

and Progressive interpretation, 7, 13–14, 17, 47–51, 57, 78–79, 248–249, 258, 289n7

and republican-liberalism debate, 134

property. *See* "personalty" interests; property rights; "realty" interests

property rights, 25, 59, 72, 156, 157, 180–181, 257–258, 296–297n37

proportional representation, 70–71, 79, 82, 84–89, 93, 183, 269, 290n12, 320n12. *See also* electoral districts; electoral districts, expanded; three-fifths clause

prosecutors and vindicators. *See* moral responsibility, interpretive frameworks of

Protestantism, 140, 144, 234–235, 237, 240, 306n69, 338n42

proto-capitalists, 159, 161–162

Pryor, Jill A., 304–305n62

"public choice" theory. *See* "rational choice" theory

public opinion, 57, 69, 208, 267, 341–342n54

public securities, 22–23, 25, 28–33, 36, 42, 286n94

Puritans, 101, 235

race and gender, contemporary standards of, 204, 222, 225–226, 271–272, 359n167

race and racism. *See* African Americans; emancipation; inegalitarian ascriptive ideologies; slavery

race war, fear of, 178, 187, 190, 199, 201, 202, 217–218, 219, 364n223

Rahe, Paul, 149–151, 326n74, 329n98, 334n5, 343–344n55

Rakove, Jack, 59, 265, 309n86

Randolph, Edmund, 63

Randolph, John, 179

Ranke, Leopold Von, 109

ratification. *See* state ratifying conventions

"rational choice" theory, 20, 38–42

"realty" interests, 4, 6, 21–23, 26–29, 32–34, 38, 42, 49. *See also* "personalty" interests

Reid, John Phillip, 246

religion

church-state relationship, 132, 235, 239, 342n54, 353n36

and office holding among clergy, 64, 306n69

Protestantism, 140, 144, 234–235, 237, 240, 306n69, 338n42

and test oaths, 63, 64

republicanism
  in Articles of Confederation, 77–79,
    309n91
  of Jefferson, 137–138, 144
  and liberalism debate, 10–12, 13, 134–135,
    141–147, 151–155, 165–166, 236–239,
    250, 337n33, 342n54
  "long-leash" v. "short leash," 77–79,
    81–82, 91, 309n91, 314–315n126
  of Madison, 75–79, 81–82, 149, 309n91,
    312n108, 314–315n126
  natural rights philosophy and, 129,
    161–162, 251
  and political participation, 147–148,
    150–151, 165
  and revisionism, 138–139, 152, 325n58,
    333n5, 336n30, 342n55, 343n55, 345n67
"republican motherhood," 146, 238, 338n42
republican revisionism, 138–139, 152, 325n58,
    333n5, 336n30, 342n55, 343n55, 345n67
Revolutionary War. See American Revolu-
    tion
Rhode Island Regiment, 363n215
Richards, Leonard, 85
rights. See civil rights; natural rights, prin-
    ciple of; property rights; suffrage
Rodgers, Daniel, 113, 332n1
Rorty, Richard, 241
Rossiter, Clinton, 287n98, 287n99
Rousseau, Jean-Jacques, 121

Santa Clara County v. Southern Pacific Rail-
    road, 263
Schuyler, Robert, 284n58
securities holdings. See "personalty" inter-
    ests; public securities
separation of powers, 310–311n99. See also
    checks and balances, system of
Sequoia, 171
sexism. See inegalitarian ascriptive ideolo-
    gies; women
Shalhope, Robert, 276n10, 337n33
Shays's Rebellion, 180–181, 255, 360n171
Sheldon, Garrett Ward, 141, 144
"short-leash" republicanism, 77, 78–79, 81,
    309n91, 314–315n126
Siemers, David, 282n34, 288n108
Sinopoli, Richard, 335n13
Skelton, Martha Wayles, 353n34

Skinner, Quentin
  and appropriation of ideas, 126–128,
    330n106
  and challenge to great-books approach,
    104–108, 117, 123–124, 324n34, 324n46,
    326–327n84
  and ideology, 118, 327n85
  and linguistic contextualists, 9–10, 96,
    97–98, 112–116, 320–321n1, 325n65,
    329n98
  methodological errors of, 117, 120–126
  See also linguistic contextualists
slavery
  and colonization, 218
  and Constitution, 85, 175–176, 183–185,
    188, 205, 209, 227–228, 352n18,
    352n19, 354n57
  and "containment," 363n206
  in Northwest Ordinance, 59, 214
  and political power of slave states, 85,
    352n19
  "presentism" defense of, 192, 196,
    220–223, 272, 359n167
  and public opinion, 208
  and state sovereignty, 175–177
  See also African Americans; emancipa-
    tion; moral responsibility, interpre-
    tive frameworks of; three-fifths
    clause
slave trade provision, Constitution's, 85,
    175–176, 183–185, 188, 205, 209, 227,
    228, 354n57
Slonim, Shlomo, 280n5, 314n126
small-state advantage, 52–53, 86–87,
    291n14
Smith, Adam, 143
Smith, Melancton, 66
Smith, Rogers
  on the Constitution, 58–59, 63, 304n62
  on implicit v. explicit traditions, 243,
    367n11
  on inegalitarian ideologies, 13, 145–148,
    165–167, 236–240, 338n42, 338–339n48,
    339n48
  on Jefferson, 211, 367n12
  and multiple traditions approach,
    277n17
sovereignty. See popular sovereignty; state
    sovereignty

West, Thomas (*continued*)
   as "vindicator," 173, 185–186, 193, 204,
      206, 211, 299–300n47
Whig ideology, 97–98, 99–100, 102, 138–139,
      224–225, 239, 289n115, 335n13
Wiencek, Henry, 173, 191, 193, 194–197, 221,
      227, 229–230, 365n236
Wilentz, Sean, 209–210
Wills, Garry, 104, 117, 229, 231, 326n83
Wilson, Douglas, 191, 192, 360n171
Wilson, James
   democratic nationalism of, 8, 56, 77,
      82–83, 93, 290–291n12, 317n140
   and disenfranchisement of women, 60,
      238, 298–299n46
   and Electoral College, 310n94, 317n143
   and linguistic contextualists, 130
   on majority rule, 88, 317n141
   and representative apportionment,
      70–71
   security holdings of, 30
Winthrop, John, 235
Wittgenstein, Ludwig, 96, 107, 113
women
   in ancient republics, 150–151
   and apportionment of representatives,
      84, 298n45, 318n149
   and the Constitution, 7, 55, 58–59, 61,
      65, 90, 91, 260, 266–267, 301–302n52
   and coverture, 146, 299n46, 338n42
   and exclusion from political process,
      51–52, 238, 302n52, 302n53
   in French constitutions, 65
   and inalienable rights, 185–186
   and inegalitarian ascriptive ideologies,
      13–14, 60, 146–148, 166, 238–239,
      298–299n46, 338n42
   liberalism and, 338–339n48
   and moral responsibility, 172
   as officeholders, 301–302n52, 302n53
   in "parlor politics," 57

and suffrage, 58–61, 90, 93, 266–267,
      295–296n32
   See also Nineteenth Amendment; suf-
      frage
Wood, Gordon S.
   on Beard's economic interpretation, 35,
      275n3
   on democracy and the Constitution,
      289n3, 293n22, 294n24
   on expanded electoral districts, 65,
      294n27, 307n74
   and Founders' political thought,
      255–256, 271
   and historiography of republicanism,
      342–343n55, 366n1
   and linguistic contextualism, 10, 96,
      97–98, 100–104
   and moral judgment, 173, 189, 190–192,
      193, 224, 226
   and republicanism-liberalism debate,
      135, 138
   and suffrage requirements, 297–298n39
   See also linguistic contextualists

Yarbrough, Jean, 362n196
Young, James P., 335n13

Zuckert, Michael
   and American political development,
      234–238, 239, 240
   and liberal republicanism, 13, 83, 128,
      135, 138–140, 141, 144
   and linguistic contextualism, 108,
      326–327n84, 330n104
   and "long-leash" republicanism, 309n91
   on Madison's republicanism, 312n108
   and natural rights philosophy, 148,
      152–153, 166
   and republican revisionism, 342n55,
      345n67
   on slavery, 354n57